Dear Student:

You have chosen to begin a career as a business professional by majoring in a business discipline. If your experience is anything like mine, you will not regret your choice. Working in business leads to fulfilling and enjoyable experiences and relationships with interesting, quality people. Working in a company you admire that sells products or services in which you believe will enable you to feel positive about yourself, your contributions, and your professional life.

MIS is an important class; in fact, Chapter 1 claims that MIS is the most important class in the business curriculum. That claim rests on two observations: First, because today the cost of data communications and data storage is essentially zero, every business is confronted with significant, new opportunities for using information technology. Any business that does not take advantage of those new opportunities will fall woefully behind its competition. A typical example is the way that many leading businesses have incorporated Facebook and Twitter in their marketing efforts. You will learn many more possibilities in this course.

Because of these opportunities, it is essential for you to have the MIS background needed to assess technology-based possibilities. Of course, to be a leader in the early years of your career, you need more. You must be able not only to assess but also to envision innovative applications of technology, and even to lead teams of people to develop those innovative applications.

The second reason this course is the most important in the business curriculum is that it will teach you, better than any other course, essential skills you need early in your career. Robert Reich, former U.S. Secretary of Labor, states that business professionals in the twenty-first century must excel at four abilities: the ability to think abstractly, the ability to think in terms of systems, the ability to collaborate, and the ability to successfully experiment. As explained in Chapter 1, all four of these behaviors are keys to success in this course and you will have ample opportunity to practice them here.

To help you learn information systems, we will study the application of concepts of this course to problems and opportunities at two example businesses. In Chapters 1 through 6, we will apply MIS to the needs of FlexTime, a highly successful workout studio, and in Chapters 7 through 12 we will apply it to Majestic River Ventures, a successful, but struggling, company that offers river-rafting trips. These two example businesses are based on real companies, but have been adapted to make their needs (and opportunities) understandable in the time frame you have available. Both businesses are large enough to have interesting and complex problems, yet small enough so that you can understand them, even with little business experience.

Additionally, each chapter has three thought-provoking, two-page discussions and activities called *Guides*. These guides address practical business problems based on experiences in my own career. Perhaps you have formed the habit of ignoring boxes in textbooks. Do not ignore them here; in many ways, they contain the most important material for your future success.

Like all worthwhile endeavors, this course is work. That's just the way it is. No one succeeds in business without sustained focus, attention, desire, motivation, and hard work. It won't always be easy, and it won't always be fun. However, you will learn concepts, skills, and behaviors that will prepare you for an enjoyable and successful business career in the twenty-first century.

I wish you, as an emerging business professional, the very best success!

Sincerely,

David Kroenke

Seattle, Washington

Why This Third Edition?

The use of MIS in business, commerce, and government changes rapidly and, to stay current, this text must be frequently revised. In the two years since the 2nd edition was published, we have seen many important changes. One of the most obvious has been the rise of social networking in business, including businesses' use of social networking sites like Facebook and microblogging tools such as Twitter.

Figure 1 lists the major changes in this edition of this text. As you will learn in Chapter 1, the rapid utilization of emerging technologies has made, in my opinion, the MIS course into the most important class in the business school. Most prominently, two new cases (with videos) introduce the chapters in this text. Chapters 1–6 are introduced by the needs, problems, and opportunities for MIS at a popular workout studio named FlexTime. Chapters 7–12 are introduced by another case, Majestic River Ventures (MRV). MRV, unfortunately, does not know how to use or manage information systems, and you will learn about several serious consequences to them that result.

New Features in the Third Edition of *Using MIS*

Figure 1

FEATURE	CHAPTER
MIS described as the most important class in the b-school	Chapter 1
FlexTime case introduces Chapters 1–6	Chapters 1–6
Majestic River Ventures case introduces Chapters 7–12	Chapters 7–12
2020? feature	All Chapters
Data aggregators and related privacy concerns	Chapter 5
Updated discussion of WAN technology	Chapter 6
Business Process Management Notation (BPMN)	Chapter 7
Updated and expanded discussion of service-oriented architecture (SOA)	Chapter 7
Business use of social networking	Chapter 8
Business use of microblogging	Chapter 8
Facebook and Twitter in business	Chapter 8
User-Generated Content (UGC)	Chapter 8
Systems development project management	Chapter 10
Green computing	Chapter 11

MIS is a fast-changing, incredibly dynamic discipline. That characteristic is one of its major charms to those who love to learn and apply new technology in innovative ways. That characteristic does mean, however, that it is important for you to learn the latest technology, systems, and trends.

THE GUIDES

Each chapter includes three unique **guides** that focus on current issues in information systems. In each chapter, one of the guides focuses on an ethical issue in business. The other two guides focus on the application of the chapter's contents to other business aspects. The content of each guide is designed to stimulate thought, discussion, and active participation to help YOU develop your problem-solving skills and become a better business professional.

Learning Aids for Students

We have structured this book so you can maximize the benefit from the time you spend reading it. As shown in the following table, each chapter includes various learning aids to help you succeed in this course.

RESOURCE	DESCRIPTION	BENEFIT	EXAMPLE
Guides	Each chapter includes three guides that focus on current issues in information systems. One of the three in each chapter addresses ethics.	Stimulate thought and discussion. Address ethics once per chapter. Help develop your problem-solving skills.	Dialing for Dollars, p. 250
Chapter-introduction Business Example	Each chapter begins with a description of a business situation that motivates the need for the chapter's contents. Two businesses are used: FlexTime, a workout studio, and Majestic River Ventures, a river-rafting company.	Understand the relevance of the chapter's content by applying it to a business situation.	Chapter 1, "Fired," p. 2; Chapter 7, "But I paid for," p. 232
Query-based Chapter Format	Each chapter starts with a list of questions; each major heading is a question; the Active Review contains tasks for you to perform to demonstrate you are able to answer the questions.	Use the questions to manage your time, guide your study, and review for exams.	Chapter 2, starting on p. 32 with "Q1 What Is Collaboration?"
2020?	Each chapter concludes with a discussion of how the concepts, technology, and systems described in that chapter might change by 2020.	Learn to anticipate changes in technology and recognize how those changes may impact the future business environment.	Chapter 5, Data Aggregators, p. 160; Chapter 7, SOA, p. 259
Active Review	Provides a set of activities for you to perform to demonstrate you are able to answer the primary questions addressed by the chapter.	After reading the chapter, use the Active Review to check your comprehension. Use for class and exam preparation.	Chapter 2, Active Review, p. 58
Using Your Knowledge	These exercises ask you to take your new knowledge one step further and apply it to a practice problem.	Tests your critical-thinking skills.	Questions 1–6, pp. 87–88
Collaboration Exercises	These exercises and cases ask you to collaborate with a group of fellow students, using collaboration tools introduced in Chapter 2.	Gives you practice in working with colleagues toward a stated goal.	pp. 168–170

RESOURCE	DESCRIPTION	BENEFIT	EXAMPLE
Application Exercises	These exercises ask you to solve situations using spreadsheet (Excel) or database (Access) applications.	Helps develop your computer skills.	Exercise 1, p. 270; Exercise 2, p. 270
Case Studies	Each chapter includes a case study at the end of the chapter. Also, one additional case study appears at the end of each part.	Requires you to apply newly acquired knowledge to real-world situations.	Case Study 2, Intermountain Healthcare, p. 61; Case Study 7, Process Cast in Stone, p. 271
International Dimension	Each part (a sequence of three chapters) includes a discussion of the international aspects of the topics addressed in the part.	Understand the international implications and applications of the chapters' content.	International Dimension, Part 3, p. 358.
LearningMIS.com	A Web site developed by the author for use by students of this text. This site has five lessons that accompany five chapters of this book.	Reviews content of chapter in an entertaining and pedagogically sound fashion. Enhances understanding of the corresponding chapter.	*www.LearningMIS.com*
Videos	(1) All chapter-opening scenarios are depicted in a series of short dramatizations that emphasize the importance of the chapter content. (2) Author Video Tutorials, in which David Kroenke further explains selected concepts from the chapters.	(1) Videos increase interest and relevance of introductory cases. (2) Expands and relates chapter material and helps you develop deeper conceptual understanding of the chapter.	An icon in the margin of the book (e.g., see p. 8) indicates related video clips of the author.
MyMISLab	A student and instructor portal that contains an Online Microsoft Office 2007 tutorial, SharePoint collaboration tools and assignments, a class-testing program tied to AACSB standards, and classroom and tutorial videos.	Expands the classroom experience with valuable hands-on activities and tools.	*www.mymislab.com*

Using MIS

third edition

Using MIS

David M. Kroenke

Prentice Hall
Boston   Columbus   Indianapolis   New York   San Francisco   Upper Saddle River
Amsterdam   Cape Town   Dubai   London   Madrid   Milan   Munich   Paris   Montreal   Toronto
Delhi   Mexico City   Sao Paulo   Sydney   Hong Kong   Seoul   Singapore   Taipei   Tokyo

Editorial Director: Sally Yagan
Editor in Chief: Eric Svendsen
Executive Editor: Bob Horan
Director of Development: Steve Deitmer
Development Editor: Laura Town
Editorial Project Manager: Kelly Loftus
Editorial Assistant: Jason Calcano
Director of Marketing: Patrice Jones
Senior Marketing Manager: Anne Fahlgren
Marketing Assistant: Melinda Jensen
Senior Managing Editor: Judy Leale
Senior Operations Supervisor: Arnold Vila
Creative Director: Christy Mahon
Senior Art Director: Janet Slowik
Interior and Cover Designer: Liz Harasymczuk
Interior Illustrations and Cover Icons: Simon Alicea

Cover Phone Illustration: Christophe Testi/ Shutterstock
Manager, Visual Research: Beth Brenzel
Manager, Rights and Permissions: Zina Arabia
Image Permission Coordinator: Richard Rodrigues
Manager, Cover Visual Research & Permissions: Karen Sanatar
Media Project Manager: Lisa Rinaldi
Media Assistant Editor: Denise Vaughn
Full-Service Project Management: Jen Welsch/ BookMasters, Inc.
Composition: Integra Inc.
Printer/Binder: Courier/Kendallville
Cover Printer: Lehigh-Phoenix Color/Hagerstown
Text Font: 10/12 Utopia

Credits and acknowledgments borrowed from other sources and reproduced, with permission, in this textbook appear on appropriate page within text.

Microsoft® and Windows® are registered trademarks of the Microsoft Corporation in the U.S.A. and other countries. Screen shots and icons reprinted with permission from the Microsoft Corporation. This book is not sponsored or endorsed by or affiliated with the Microsoft Corporation.

Library of Congress Cataloging-in-Publication Data

Kroenke, David.
    Using MIS / David M. Kroenke.—3rd ed.
        p. cm.
    Includes bibliographical references and index.
    ISBN 978-0-13-610075-1 (pbk. : alk. paper)
1. Management information systems.   I. Title.
    HD30.213.K76 2011
    658.4'038011—dc22
                            2009040537

10 9 8 7 6 5 4 3 2 1

Prentice Hall
is an imprint of

www.pearsonhighered.com

ISBN 10:   0-13-610075-9
ISBN 13: 978-0-13-610075-1

Dedicated to CJ, Carter, and Charlotte

Brief Contents

Defines MIS, describes how MIS relates to students as future business professionals, and explains what students should learn in the course.

Explains the nature of collaboration, describes the use of collaboration tools, and explains how collaboration pertains to decision making and problem solving.

Describes reasons why organizations create and use information systems: to gain competitive advantage, to solve problems, and to support decisions.

Three chapters focus on key components of IT.

This chapter appendix discusses another type of network—internets—and explains how the Internet works.

Discusses IS within organizations, including functional and cross-functional systems.

Discusses IS among organizations, including e-commerce, Web 2.0, social networking, microblogging, and more.

Describes business intelligence and knowledge management, including reporting systems, data mining, and knowledge management systems.

Describes the processes for developing information systems.

Describes the role, structure, and function of the IS department; the role of the CIO and CTO; outsourcing; and related topics.

Describes organizational response to information security: security threats, policy, and safeguards.

Contents

2 Collaboration Information Systems   30

3 Information Systems for Competitive Advantage   64

5 Database Processing   134

6 Data Communication   174

8 E-Commerce and Web 2.0   272

9 Business Intelligence Systems   318

About the Author

David Kroenke has many years of teaching experience at Colorado State University, Seattle University, and the University of Washington. He has led dozens of seminars for college professors on the teaching of information systems and technology; in 1991 the International Association of Information Systems named him Computer Educator of the Year. In 2009, David was named Educator of the Year by the Association of Information Technology Professionals-Education Special Interest Group (AITP-EDSIG).

David worked for the U.S. Air Force and Boeing Computer Services. He was a principal in the startup of three companies. He also was vice president of product marketing and development for the Microrim Corporation and was chief of technologies for the database division of Wall Data, Inc. He is the father of the semantic object data model. David's consulting clients have included IBM, Microsoft, and Computer Sciences Corporations, as well as numerous smaller companies. Recently, David has focused on using information systems for teaching collaboration.

His text *Database Processing* was first published in 1977 and is now in its 11th edition. He has published many other textbooks, including *Database Concepts,* 4th ed. (2010), *Experiencing MIS,* 2nd ed. (2010), and *MIS Essentials* (2010). David lives in Seattle. He is married and has two children and three grandchildren.

Why MIS?

FlexTime is a hip, urban, sophisticated workout studio located in downtown Indianapolis. Kelly Summers started FlexTime 20 years ago after teaching aerobics at another firm. She began modestly, teaching a few classes a week at a small facility in the back of a downtown Indianapolis office building. Over time, she hired other instructors to help. Within a few months, she realized she could expand her business if she focused on finding new clients and hired other, "star" instructors to teach most of the classes. She paid those instructors a percent of the class revenue and worked hard to make their lives easier and to make them feel appreciated, and they, in turn, took care of the clients.

The formula worked. Over the years, FlexTime expanded from the small backroom to a full floor, then two floors, and, by 2005, FlexTime occupied all four stories of its building. Today, FlexTime clients make more than 15,000 visits a month. During prime time, the building is packed, the tempo is fast-paced, and the atmosphere is intense; loud music and well-dressed urban professionals flow through the hallways.

About the time that Kelly started FlexTime, Neil West was ranked as the number one amateur surfer in Southern California. Neil finished college at San Diego State and took a job in telemarketing sales for a small software company. He excelled at his job, and within a few years was selling large enterprise solutions for Siebel Systems, then a leading vendor of customer relationships management software (discussed in Chapter 7). Neil sold software through the heyday of the dot-com explosion and by 2005 was in a financial position to retire. His last major client was located in Indianapolis, where he enrolled in a kickboxing class taught by Kelly.

At that point, FlexTime was a screaming success in every aspect save one—the back office was a disorganized mess. Kelly and her staff were running the business out of several file cabinets with temporary record storage in an orange crate. Neil experienced numerous delays when attempting to pay for goods and services at the front desk, and he noticed the inefficiency of FlexTime's business processes. When Neil mentioned that he was about to leave Siebel, Kelly asked if he'd be willing to help her organize FlexTime's office records.

Up to that point, Neil had planned on returning to California, but he agreed to help Kelly redesign FlexTime's accounting, customer management, operations, and related processes in what he thought would be a 6-month consulting job. He led several projects to install information systems, convert FlexTime from manual to electronic records, and train personnel on the use of the new systems. As he got into the project, he saw great potential for FlexTime and bought out Kelly's financial partners to become a co-owner and partner of FlexTime. In 2008, they were married.

With Kelly running the client/trainer side of the business and Neil managing the back-office system, today FlexTime is an unqualified success. However, that does not mean that it does not have problems and challenges, as you are about to learn.

The Importance of MIS

"Fired? You're firing me?"

"Well, *fired* is a harsh word, but . . . well, FlexTime has no further need for your services."

"But, Kelly, I don't get it. I really don't. I worked hard, and I did everything you told me to do."

"Jennifer, that's just it. You did everything *I* told you to do."

"I put in so many hours. How could you fire me????"

"Your job was to find ways we can generate additional revenue from our existing club members."

"Right! And I did that."

"No, you didn't. You followed up on ideas *that I gave you*. But we don't need someone who can follow up on my plans. We need someone who can figure out what we need to do, create her own plans, and bring them back to me. . . . And others."

"How could you expect me to do that? I've only been here 4 months!!!"

"It's called teamwork. Sure, you're just learning our business, but I made sure all of our senior staff would be available to you . . ."

"I didn't want to bother them."

" But today, they're not enough. "

"Well, you succeeded. I asked Jason what he thought of the plans you're working on. 'Who's Jennifer?' he asked."

"But, doesn't he work at night?"

"Right. He's the night staff manager . . . and 37 percent of our weekday business occurs after 7 P.M. Probably worth talking to him."

"I'll go do that!"

"Jennifer, do you see what just happened? I gave you an idea and you said you'll do it. That's not what I need. I need you to find solutions on your own."

"I worked really hard. I put in a lot of hours. I've got all these reports written."

"Has anyone seen them?"

"I talked to you about some of them. But, I was waiting until I was satisfied with them."

"Right. That's not how we do things here. We develop ideas and then kick them around with each other. Nobody has all the smarts. Our plans get better when we comment and rework them . . . I think I told you that."

"Maybe you did. But I'm just not comfortable with that."

"Well, it's a key skill here."

"I know I can do this job."

"Jennifer, you've been here almost 4 months; you have a degree in business. Several weeks ago, I asked you for your first idea about how to upsell our customers. Do you remember what you said?"

"Yes, I wasn't sure how to proceed. I didn't want to just throw something out that might not work."

"But how would you find out if it would work?"

"I don't want to waste money . . . "

"No, you don't. So, when you didn't get very far with that task, I backed up and asked you to send me a diagram of the life cycle for one of our clients . . . how we get them in the door, how we enroll them in their first classes, how we continue to sell to them . . . "

"Yes, I sent you that diagram."

"Jennifer, it made no sense. Your diagram had people talking to Neil in accounts receivable before they were even customers."

"I know that process, I just couldn't put it down on paper. But, I'll try again!"

"Well, I appreciate that attitude, but times are tight. We don't have room for trainees. When the economy was strong, I'd have been able to look for a spot for you, see if we can bring you along. But, we can't afford to do that now."

"What about my references?"

"I'll be happy to tell anyone that you're reliable, that you work 40 to 45 hours a week, and that you're honest and have integrity."

"Those are important!"

"Yes, they are. But today, they're not enough." ∎

>> STUDY QUESTIONS

Q1 Why is Introduction to MIS the most important class in the business school?

Q2 What is MIS?

Q3 How can you use the five-component model?

Q4 What is information?

Q5 What makes some information better than other information?

Q6 Why is the difference between information technology and information systems important?

Q7 2020?

CHAPTER PREVIEW

"But today, they're not enough."

Do you find that statement sobering? And if timely, hard work isn't enough, what is? We'll begin this book by discussing the key skills that Jennifer (and you) need and explain why this course is the single best course in all of the business school for teaching you those key skills.

You may find that last statement surprising. If you are like most students, you have no clear idea of what your MIS class will be about. If someone were to ask you, "What do you study in that class?" you might respond that the class has something to do with computers and maybe computer programming. Beyond that, you might be hard-pressed to say more. You might add, "Well, it has something to do with computers in business," or maybe, "We are going to learn to solve business problems with computers using spreadsheets and other programs." So, how could this course be the most important one in the business school?

We begin with that question. After you understand how important this class will be to your career, we will discuss fundamental concepts. We'll wrap up with some practice on one of the key skills you need to learn.

Q1 Why Is Introduction to MIS the Most Important Class in the Business School?

Introduction to MIS is the most important class in the business school. That statement was not true in 2005, and it may not be true in 2020. But it is true in 2010.

Why?

The ultimate reason lies in a principle known as **Moore's Law**. In 1965, Gordon Moore, cofounder of Intel Corporation, stated that because of technology improvements in electronic chip design and manufacturing, "The number of transistors per square inch on an integrated chip doubles every 18 months." His statement has been commonly misunderstood to be, "The speed of a computer doubles every 18 months," which is incorrect, but captures the sense of his principle.

Because of Moore's Law, the ratio of price to performance of computers has fallen from something like $4,000 dollars for a standard computing device to something around a penny for that same computing device.[1] See Figure 1-1.

As a future business professional, however, you needn't care how fast a computer your company can buy for $100. That's not the point. Here's the point:

> **Because of Moore's Law, the cost of data communications and data storage is essentially zero.**

Think about that statement before you hurry to the next paragraph. What happens when those costs are essentially zero? Here are some consequences:

- YouTube
- iPhone
- Facebook
- Second Life
- HuLu
- Twitter
- LinkedIn

None of these was prominent in 2005, and, in fact, most didn't exist in 2005.

---

[1]These figures represent the cost of 100,000 transistors, which can roughly be translated into a unit of a computing device. For our purposes, the details don't matter. If you doubt any of this, just look at your $199 iPhone and realize that you pay $40 a month to use it.

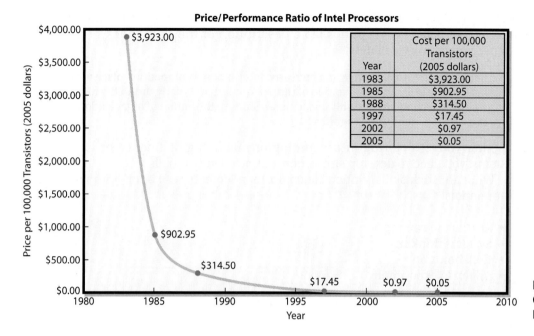

Figure 1-1
Computer Price/Performance
Ratio Decreases

Are There Cost-Effective Business Applications of Facebook and Twitter?

Of course. FlexTime is profitably using them today. Fitness instructors post announcements via Twitter. FlexTime studio collects those tweets and posts them on its Facebook page. Total cost to FlexTime studio? Zero.

But ask another question: Are there wasteful, harmful, useless business applications of Facebook and Twitter? Of course. Do I care to follow the tweets of the mechanic who changes the oil in my car? I don't think so.

But there's the point. Maybe I'm not being creative enough. Maybe there are great reasons for the mechanic to tweet customers and I'm just not able to think of them. Which leads us to the first reason Introduction to MIS is the most important course in the business school today:

> **Future business professionals need to be able to assess, evaluate, and apply emerging information technology to business.**

Keep up to date!

You need the knowledge of this course to attain that skill.

How Can I Attain Job Security?

Many years ago I had a wise and experienced mentor. One day I asked him about job security, and he told me that the only job security that exists is "a marketable skill and the courage to use it." He continued, "There is no security in our company, there is no security in any government program, there is no security in your investments, and there is no security in Social Security." Alas, how right he turned out to be.

So what is a marketable skill? It used to be that one could name particular skills, such as computer programming, tax accounting, or marketing. But today, because of Moore's Law, because the cost of data storage and data communications is essentially zero, any routine skill can and will be outsourced to the lowest bidder. And if you live in the United States, Canada, Australia, Europe, and so on, that is unlikely to be you. Numerous organizations and experts have studied the question of what skills will be marketable during your career. Consider two of them. First, the RAND Corporation, a think tank located in Santa Monica, California, has published innovative and groundbreaking ideas for more than 60 years, including the initial design for the Internet. In 2004, RAND published a description of the skills that workers in the twenty-first century will need:

Always Be learning ✦

> Rapid technological change and increased international competition place the spotlight on the skills and preparation of the workforce, particularly the ability to adapt to changing technology and shifting demand. Shifts in the nature of organizations . . . favor strong nonroutine cognitive skills.[2]

Whether you're majoring in accounting or marketing or finance or information systems, you need to develop strong nonroutine cognitive skills.

What are such skills? Robert Reich, former Secretary of Labor, enumerates four components:[3]

- Abstract reasoning
- Systems thinking
- Collaboration
- Ability to experiment

Figure 1-2 shows an example of each. Reread the FlexTime studio case that started this chapter, and you'll see that Jennifer lost her job because of her inability to practice these skills.

How Can Intro to MIS Help You Learn Nonroutine Skills?

Introduction to MIS is the best course in the business school for learning these four key skills, because every topic will require you to apply and practice them. Here's how.

Abstract Reasoning

Abstract reasoning is the ability to make and manipulate models. You will work with one or more models in every course topic and book chapter. For example, later in this chapter you will learn about a *model* of the five components of an information system.

Skill	Example	Jennifer's Problem
Abstraction	Construct a model or representation.	Inability to model the customer life cycle.
Systems thinking	Model system components and show how components' inputs and outputs relate to one another.	Confusion about how customers contact accounts payable.
Collaboration	Develop ideas and plans with others. Provide and receive critical feedback.	Unwilling to work with others with work-in-progress.
Experimentation	Create and test promising new alternatives, consistent with available resources.	Fear of failure prohibited discussion of new ideas.

Figure 1-2
Examples of Critical Skills for Nonroutine Cognition

---

[2]Lynn A. Kaoly and Constantijn W. A. Panis, *The 21st Century at Work* (Santa Monica, CA: RAND Corporation, 2004), p. xiv.
[3]Robert B. Reich, *The Work of Nations* (New York: Alfred A. Knopf, 1991), p. 229.

This chapter will describe how to use this model to assess the scope of any new information system project; other chapters will build upon this model.

In this course, you will not just manipulate models that your instructor or I have developed, you will also be asked to construct models of your own. In Chapter 5, for example, you'll learn how to create data models and in Chapter 7 you'll learn to make process models.

Systems Thinking

Can you go down to a grocery store, look at a can of green beans, and connect that can to U.S. immigration policy? Can you watch tractors dig up a forest of pulp wood trees and connect that woody trash to Moore's Law? Do you know why one of the major beneficiaries of YouTube is Cisco Systems?

Answers to all of these questions require **systems thinking**. They require you to model the components of the system and to connect the inputs and outputs among those components into a sensible whole, one that explains the phenomenon observed.

As you are about to learn, this class is about information *systems*. We will discuss and illustrate systems; you will be asked to critique systems; you will be asked to compare alternative systems; you will be asked to apply different systems to different situations. All of those tasks will prepare you for systems thinking as a professional.

Collaboration

Chapter 2 will teach you collaboration skills and illustrate several sample collaboration information systems. Every chapter of this book includes collaboration exercises that you may be assigned in class or as homework.

Here's a fact that surprises many students: Effective collaboration isn't about being nice. In fact, surveys indicate the single most important skill for effective collaboration is to give and receive critical feedback. Advance a proposal in business that challenges the cherished program of the VP of marketing, and you'll quickly learn that effective collaboration skills differ from party manners at the neighborhood barbeque. So, how do you advance your idea in the face of the VP's resistance? And without losing your job? In this course, you can learn both skills and information systems for such collaboration. Even better, you will have many opportunities to practice them.

Ability to Experiment

"I've never done this before."
"I don't know how to do it."
"But will it work?"
"Is it too weird for the market?"

Fear of failure: the fear that paralyzes so many good people and so many good ideas. In the days when business was stable, when new ideas were just different verses of the same song, professionals could allow themselves to be limited by fear of failure.

But think again about the application of social networking to the oil change business. Is there a legitimate application of social networking there? If so, has anyone ever done it? Is there anyone in the world who can tell you what to do? How to proceed? No. As Reich says, professionals in the twenty-first century need to be able to experiment.

Successful **experimentation** is not throwing buckets of money at every crazy idea that enters your head. It does mean, however, making a careful and reasoned analysis of an opportunity, envisioning potential products or solutions or applications of technology, and then developing those ideas that seem to have the most promise, consistent with the resources you have.

In this course, you will be asked to use products with which you have no familiarity. Those products might be Microsoft Excel or Access, or they might be features and functions of Blackboard that you've not used. Or, you may be asked to collaborate using Microsoft SharePoint or Google Docs & Spreadsheets. Will your instructor explain and show every feature of those products that you'll need? You should hope not. You should hope your instructor will leave it up to you to experiment, to envision new possibilities on your own, and experiment with those possibilities, consistent with the time you have available.

The bottom line? This course is the most important course in the business school because

1. **It will give you the background you need to assess, evaluate, and apply emerging information systems technology to business.**
2. **It can give you the ultimate in job security—marketable skills—by helping you learn abstraction, systems thinking, collaboration, and experimentation.**

With that introduction, let's get started! Welcome aboard.

Q2 What Is MIS?

We've used the term *MIS* several times, and you may be wondering exactly what it is. **MIS** stands for **management information systems**, which we define as *the development and use of information systems that help businesses achieve their goals and objectives.* This definition has three key elements: *development and use, information systems,* and *business goals and objectives.* Let's consider each, starting first with information systems and their components.

Components of an Information System

A **system** is a group of components that interact to achieve some purpose. As you might guess, an **information system (IS)** is a group of components that interact to produce information. That sentence, although true, raises another question: What are these components that interact to produce information?

Figure 1-3 shows the **five-component framework**—a model of the components of an information system: **computer hardware, software,**[4] **data, procedures,** and **people**. These five components are present in every information system, from the simplest to the most complex. For example, when you use a computer to write a class report, you are using hardware (the computer, storage disk, keyboard, and monitor), software (Word, WordPerfect, or some other word-processing program), data (the words, sentences, and paragraphs in your report), procedures (the methods you use

Figure 1-3
Five Components of an
Information System

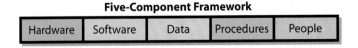

Five-Component Framework

Hardware	Software	Data	Procedures	People

---

[4]In the past, the term *software* was used to refer to computer components that were not hardware (e.g., programs, procedures, user manuals, etc.). Today, the term *software* is used more specifically to refer only to programs, and that is how we use the term throughout this book.

to start the program, enter your report, print it, and save and back up your file), and people (you).

Consider a more complex example, say an airline reservation system. It, too, consists of these five components, even though each one is far more complicated. The hardware consists of dozens or more computers linked together by telecommunications hardware. Further, hundreds of different programs coordinate communications among the computers, and still other programs perform the reservations and related services. Additionally, the system must store millions upon millions of characters of data about flights, customers, reservations, and other facts. Hundreds of different procedures are followed by airline personnel, travel agents, and customers. Finally, the information system includes people, not only the users of the system, but also those who operate and service the computers, those who maintain the data, and those who support the networks of computers.

The important point here is that the five components in Figure 1-3 are common to all information systems, from the smallest to the largest. As you think about any information system, including a new one like social networking by mechanics, learn to look for these five components. Realize, too, that an information system is not just a computer and a program, but rather an assembly of computers, programs, data, procedures, and people.

As we will discuss later in this chapter, these five components also mean that many different skills are required besides those of hardware technicians or computer programmers when building or using an information system. People are needed who can design the databases that hold the data and who can develop procedures for people to follow. Managers are needed to train and staff the personnel for using and operating the system. We will return to this five-component framework later in this chapter, as well as many other times throughout this book.

Before we move forward, note that we have defined an information system to include a computer. Some people would say that such a system is a **computer-based information system**. They would note that there are information systems that do not include computers, such as a calendar hanging on the wall outside of a conference room that is used to schedule the room's use. Such systems have been used by businesses for centuries. Although this point is true, in this book we focus on computer-based information systems. To simplify and shorten the book, we will use the term *information system* as a synonym for *computer-based information system*.

Development and Use of Information Systems

The next element in our definition of MIS is the *development and use* of information systems. This course in particular, and MIS in general, are concerned with development because information systems do not pop up like mushrooms after a hard rain; they must be constructed. You may be saying, "Wait a minute, I'm a finance (or accounting or management) major, not an information systems major. I don't need to know how to build information systems."

If you are saying that, you are like a lamb headed for fleecing. Throughout your career, in whatever field you choose, information systems will be built for your use, and sometimes under your direction. To create an information system that meets your needs, you need to take an *active role* in that system's development. Even if you are not a programmer or a database designer or some other IS professional, you must take an active role in specifying the system's requirements and in helping manage the development project. Without active involvement on your part, it will only be good luck that causes the new system to meet your needs.

As a business professional, you are the person who understands the business needs and requirements. If you want to apply social networking to your products, you are the one who knows how best to obtain customer response. The technical people who build networks, the database designers who create the database, the IT people who configure the computers—none of these people know what is needed and whether the system you have is sufficient. You do!

In addition to development tasks, you will also have important roles to play in the *use* of information systems. Of course, you will need to learn how to employ the system to accomplish your goals. But you will also have important ancillary functions as well. For example, when using an information system, you will have responsibilities for protecting the security of the system and its data. You may also have tasks for backing up data. When the system fails (most do, at some point), you will have tasks to perform while the system is down as well as tasks to accomplish to help recover the system correctly and quickly.

Some chapters in this book will include guides that will detail security issues related to the material in the chapter. For the first of these, see the Guide on pages 22–23 about password protection of information.

Achieving Business Goals and Objectives

The last part of the definition of MIS is that information systems exist to help businesses achieve their *goals and objectives*. First, realize that this statement hides an important fact: Businesses themselves do not "do" anything. A business is not alive, and it cannot act. It is the people within a business who sell, buy, design, produce, finance, market, account, and manage. So, information systems exist to help people who work in a business to achieve the goals and objectives of that business.

Information systems are not created for the sheer joy of exploring technology. They are not created so that the company can be "modern" or so that the company can show it has a social networking presence on the Web. They are not created because the information systems department thinks it needs to be created or because the company is "falling behind the technology curve."

This point may seem so obvious that you might wonder why we mention it. Every day, however, some business somewhere is developing an information system for the wrong reasons. Right now, somewhere in the world, a company is deciding to create a Facebook presence for the sole reason that "every other business has one." This company is not asking questions such as:

- "What is the purpose of our Facebook page?"
- "What is it going to do for us?"
- "Is Facebook the best choice?"
- "Should we be using Microsoft Vine instead of Facebook?"
- "Are the costs of maintaining the page sufficiently offset by the benefits?"

But that company should ask those questions!

Again, MIS is the development and use of information systems that help businesses achieve their goals and objectives. Already you should be realizing that there is much more to this class than buying a computer, working with a spreadsheet, or creating a Web page.

Q3 How Can You Use the Five-Component Model?

The five-component model in Figure 1-3 can help guide your learning and thinking about IS, both now and in the future. To understand this framework better, first note in Figure 1-4 that these five components are symmetrical. The outermost components, hardware and people, are both actors; they can take actions. The software and procedure components are both sets of instructions: Software is instruction for hardware, and procedures are instructions for people. Finally, data is the bridge between the computer side on the left and the human side on the right.

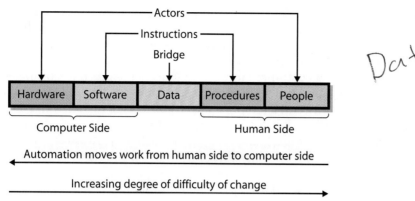

Data is a Bridge

Figure 1-4
Characteristics of the Five
Components

Now, when we automate a business process, we take work that people are doing by following procedures and move it so that computers will do that work, following instructions in the software. Thus, the process of automation is a process of moving work from the right side of Figure 1-4 to the left.

The Most Important Component—YOU

You are part of every information system that you use. When you consider the five components of an information system, the last component, *people*, includes you. Your mind and your thinking are not merely *a* component of the information systems you use, they are *the most important* component.

Consider an example. Suppose you have the perfect information system, one that can predict the future. No such information system exists, but assume for this example that it does. Now suppose that on December 14, 1966, your perfect information system tells you that the next day, Walt Disney will die. Say you have $50,000 to invest; you can either buy Disney stock or you can short it (an investment technique that will net you a positive return if the stock value decreases). Given your perfect information system, how do you invest?

Before you read on, think about this question. If Walt Disney is going to die the next day, will the stock go up or down? Most students assume that the stock will go down, so they short it, on the theory that the loss of the founder will mean a dramatic drop in the share price.

In fact, the next day, the value of Disney stock increased substantially. Why? The market viewed Walt Disney as an artist; once he died, he would no longer be able to create more art. Thus, the value of the existing art would increase because of scarcity, and the value of the corporation that owned that art would increase as well.

Here's the point: Even if you have the perfect information system, if you do not know what to do with the information that it produces, you are wasting your time and money. The *quality of your thinking* is a large part of the quality of the information system. Substantial cognitive research has shown that although you cannot increase your basic IQ, you can dramatically increase the quality of your thinking. You cannot change the computer in your brain, so to speak, but you can change the way you have programmed your brain to work.

video ►

We discuss thinking skills in an MIS book, because improving your thinking improves the quality of every information system that you use. The Guide on pages 20–21 presents ideas from cognitive science and applies them to business situations.

High-Tech Versus Low-Tech Information Systems

Information systems differ in the amount of work that is moved from the human side (people and procedures) to the computer side (hardware and programs). For example, consider two different versions of a customer support information system: A system that consists only of a file of email addresses and an email program is a very low-tech system. Only a small amount of work has been moved from the human side to the computer side. Considerable human work is required to determine when to send which emails to which customers.

In contrast, a customer support system that keeps track of the equipment that customers have and the maintenance schedules for that equipment and then automatically generates email reminders to customers is a higher-tech system. This simply means that more work has been moved from the human side to the computer side. The computer is providing more services on behalf of the humans.

Often, when considering different information systems alternatives, it will be helpful to consider the low-tech versus high-tech alternatives in light of the amount of work that is being moved from people to computers.

Understanding the Scope of New Information Systems

The Ethics Guide in each chapter of this book considers the ethics of information systems use. These guides challenge you to think deeply about ethical standards, and they provide for some interesting discussions with classmates. The Ethics Guide on pages 14–15 considers the ethics of using information that is not intended for you.

The five-component framework can also be used when assessing the scope of new systems. When in the future some vendor pitches the need for a new technology to you, use the five components to assess how big of an investment that new technology represents. What new hardware will you need? What programs will you need to license? What databases and other data must you create? What procedures will need to be developed for both use and administration of the information system? And, finally, what will be the impact of the new technology on people? Which jobs will change? Who will need training? How will the new technology affect morale? Will you need to hire new people? Will you need to reorganize?

Components Ordered by Difficulty and Disruption

Finally, as you consider the five components keep in mind that Figure 1-4 shows them in order of ease of change and the amount of organizational disruption. It is usually a simple matter to order new hardware and install it. Obtaining or developing new programs is more difficult. Creating new databases or changing the structure of existing databases is still more difficult. Changing procedures, requiring people to work in new ways, is even more difficult. Finally, changing personnel responsibilities and reporting relationships and hiring and terminating employees are both very difficult and very disruptive to the organization.

Q4 What Is Information?

Using the discussions in the last two sections, we can now define an information system as an assembly of hardware, software, data, procedures, and people that interact to produce information. The only term left undefined in that definition is *information*, and we turn to it next.

Definitions Vary

Information is one of those fundamental terms that we use every day but that turns out to be surprisingly difficult to define. Defining information is like defining words such as *alive* and *truth*. We know what those words mean, we use them with each other without confusion, but nonetheless, they are difficult to define.

In this text, we will avoid the technical issues of defining information and will use common, intuitive definitions instead. Probably the most common definition is that **information** is knowledge derived from data, whereas *data* is defined as recorded facts or figures. Thus, the facts that employee James Smith earns $17.50 per hour and that Mary Jones earns $25.00 per hour are *data*. The statement that the average hourly wage of all the aerobics instructors is $22.37 per hour is *information*. Average wage is knowledge that is derived from the data of individual wages.

Another common definition is that *information is data presented in a meaningful context*. The fact that Jeff Parks earns $10.00 per hour is data.[5] The statement that Jeff Parks earns less than half the average hourly wage of the aerobics instructors, however, is information. It is data presented in a meaningful context.

Another definition of information that you will hear is that *information is processed data*, or sometimes, *information is data processed by summing, ordering, averaging, grouping, comparing, or other similar operations*. The fundamental idea of this definition is that we do something to data to produce information.

There is yet a fourth definition of information, which is presented in the Guide on page 20. There, information is defined as *a difference that makes a difference*.

For the purposes of this text, any of these definitions of information will do. Choose the definition of information that makes sense to you. The important point is that you discriminate between data and information. You also may find that different definitions work better in different situations.

Information Is Subjective

Consider the definition that information is data presented in a meaningful context. What exactly is a *meaningful context*? Clearly, context varies from person to person. If I manage the aerobics instructors and you are the managing partner, our contexts differ. To me, the average hourly wage of the aerobics instructors is information. To you, it is a data point—the average hourly wage of employees in one of your departments. To you, as overall manager, information would be the average hourly wage of all employees in all departments, a list of all departmental averages presented in ascending order, or some other arrangement of the average wages in the context of the entire company.

Sometimes you will hear this same idea expressed as, "One person's information is another person's data." This statement simply means that information in one person's context is just a data point in another person's context. All of us have experienced this phenomenon one time or another when we excitedly report something to another person, only to have them suppress a yawn and say, "Yeah, so what's your point?"

Context changes occur in information systems when the output of one system feeds a second system—a process illustrated in Figure 1-5. For example, suppose an

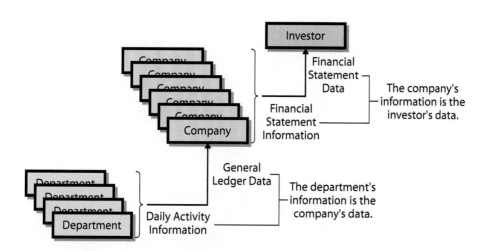

Figure 1-5
One User's Information
Is Another User's Data

---

[5]Actually the word *data* is plural; to be correct we should use the singular form *datum* and say "The fact that Jeff Parks earns $10 per hour is a datum." The word *datum* however, sounds pedantic and fussy, and we will avoid it in this text.

Ethics

Ethics of Misdirected Information Use

Consider the following situations:

Situation A: Suppose you are buying a condo and you know that at least one other party is bidding against you. While agonizing over your best strategy, you stop at a local Starbucks. As you sip your latte, you overhear a conversation at the table next to yours. Three people are talking loudly enough that it is difficult to ignore them, and you soon realize that they are the real estate agent and the couple who is competing for the condo you want. They are preparing their offer. Should you listen to their conversation? If you do, do you use the information you hear to your advantage?

Situation B: Consider the same situation from a different perspective—instead of overhearing the conversation, suppose you receive that same information in an email. Perhaps an administrative assistant at the agent's office confuses you and the other customer and mistakenly sends you the terms of the other party's offer. Do you read that email? If so, do you use the information that you read to your advantage?

Situation C: Suppose that you sell computer software. In the midst of a sensitive price negotiation, your customer accidentally sends you an internal email that contains the maximum amount that the customer can pay for your software. Do you read that email? Do you use that information to guide your negotiating strategy? If your customer discovers that the email may have reached you and asks, "Did you read my email?" how do you answer?

Situation D: In this scenario, a friend mistakenly sends you an email that contains sensitive personal medical data. Further, suppose you read the email before you know what you're reading and you're embarrassed to learn something very personal that truly is none of your business. Your friend asks you, "Did you read that email?" How do you respond?

Situation E: Finally, suppose that you work as a network administrator and your position allows you unrestricted access to the mailing lists for your company. Assume that you have the skill to insert your email address into any company mailing list without anyone knowing about it. You insert your address into several lists and, consequently, begin to receive confidential emails that no one intended for you to see. One of those emails indicates that your best friend's department is about to be eliminated and all of its personnel fired. Do you forewarn your friend? ∎

Discussion Questions

1. Answer the questions in situations A and B. Do your answers differ? Does the medium by which the information is obtained make a difference? Is it easier to avoid reading an email than it is to avoid hearing a conversation? If so, does that difference matter?

2. Answer the questions in situations B and C. Do your answers differ? In situation B, the information is for your personal gain; in C, the information is for both your personal and your organization's gain. Does this difference matter? How do you respond when asked if you have read the email?

3. Answer the questions in situations C and D. Do your answers differ? Would you lie in one case and not in the other? Why or why not?

4. Answer the question in situation E. What is the essential difference between situations A through D and situation E? Suppose you had to justify your behavior in situation E. How would you argue? Do you believe your own argument?

5. In situations A through D, if you access the information you have done nothing illegal. You were the passive recipient. Even for item E, although you undoubtedly violated your company's employment policies, you most likely did not violate the law. So, for this discussion, assume that all of these actions are legal.

   a. What is the difference between legal and ethical? Look up each term in a dictionary and explain how they differ.

   b. Make the argument that business is competitive, and that if something is legal then it is acceptable if it helps to further your goals.

   c. Make the argument that it is never appropriate to do something unethical.

6. Summarize your beliefs about proper conduct when you receive misdirected information.

information system in the manufacturing department produces a summary of the day's activity as its information. That summary is input to the general ledger system in the accounting department, where the summary is just another data point. The general ledger system takes inputs from manufacturing, sales, accounts receivable, accounts payable, and so forth and transforms those data into the information that it produces, such as the monthly balance sheet and income statement. Those financial statements go to investors, where they become data points in the portfolios of the investors.

The bottom line is that information is always understood in a context, and that context varies from one user to another. Therefore, information is always subjective.

Q5 What Makes Some Information Better Than Other Information?

All information is not equal: Some information is better than other information. Figure 1-6 lists the characteristics of good information.

Accurate

First, good information is **accurate**. Good information is based on correct and complete data, and it has been processed correctly as expected. Accuracy is crucial; managers must be able to rely on the results of their information systems. The IS function can develop a bad reputation in the organization if a system is known to produce inaccurate information. In such a case, the information system becomes a waste of time and money as users develop work-arounds to avoid the inaccurate data.

A corollary to this discussion is that you, a future user of information systems, ought not to rely on information just because it appears in the context of a Web page, a well-formatted report, or a fancy query. It is sometimes hard to be skeptical of information delivered with beautiful, active graphics. Do not be misled. When you begin to use a new information system, be skeptical. Cross-check the information you are receiving. After weeks or months of using a system, you may relax. Begin, however, with skepticism.

Timely

Good information is **timely**—produced in time for its intended use. A monthly report that arrives 6 weeks late is most likely useless. The information arrives long after the decisions have been made that needed that information. An information system that

> - **Accurate**
> - **Timely**
> - **Relevant**
>   - To context
>   - To subject
> - **Just sufficient**
> - **Worth its cost**

Figure 1-6
Characteristics of Good Information

tells you not to extend credit to a customer after you have shipped the goods is unhelpful and frustrating. Notice that timeliness can be measured against a calendar (6 weeks late) or against events (before we ship).

When you participate in the development of an IS, timeliness will be part of the requirements you will ask for. You need to give appropriate and realistic timeliness needs. In some cases, developing systems that provide information in near real time is much more difficult and expensive than producing information a few hours later. If you can get by with information that is a few hours old, say so during the requirements specification phase.

Consider an example. Suppose you work in marketing and you need to be able to assess the effectiveness of new online ad programs. You want an information system that not only will deliver ads over the Web, but that also will enable you to determine how frequently customers click on those ads. Determining click ratios in near real time will be very expensive; saving the data in a batch and processing it some hours later will be much easier and cheaper. If you can live with information that is a day or two old, the system will be easier and cheaper to implement.

Relevant

Information should be **relevant** both to the context and to the subject. Considering context, you, the CEO, need information that is summarized to an appropriate level for your job. A list of the hourly wage of every employee in the company is unlikely to be useful. More likely, you need average wage information by department or division. A list of all employee wages is irrelevant in your context.

Information should also be relevant to the subject at hand. If you want information about short-term interest rates for a possible line of credit, then a report that shows 15-year mortgage interest rates is irrelevant. Similarly, a report that buries the information you need in pages and pages of results is also irrelevant to your purposes.

Just Barely Sufficient

Information needs to be **sufficient** for the purpose for which it is generated, but **just barely so**. We live in an information age; one of the critical decisions that each of us has to make each day is what information to ignore. The higher you rise into management, the more information you will be given, and, because there is only so much time, the more information you will need to ignore. So, information should be sufficient, but just barely.

Worth Its Cost

Information is not free. There are costs for developing an information system, costs of operating and maintaining that system, and costs of your time and salary for reading and processing the information the system produces. For information to be **worth its cost**, an appropriate relationship must exist between the cost of information and its value.

Consider an example. What is the value of a daily report of the names of the occupants of a full graveyard? Zero, unless grave robbery is a problem for the cemetery. The report is not worth the time required to read it. It is easy to see the importance of information economics for this silly example. It will be more difficult, however, when someone proposes new technology to you. You need to be ready to ask, "What's the value of the information?" "What is the cost?" "Is there an appropriate relationship between value and cost?" Information systems should be subject to the same financial analyses to which other assets are subjected.

Q6 Why Is the Difference Between Information Technology and Information Systems Important?

Information technology and information systems are two closely related terms, but they are different. **Information technology (IT)** refers to the products, methods, inventions, and standards that are used for the purpose of producing information. IT pertains to the hardware, software, and data components. As stated in the previous section, an *information system (IS)* is an assembly of hardware, software, data, procedures, and people that produces information.

Information technology drives the development of new information systems. Advances in information technology have taken the computer industry from the days of punched cards to the Internet, and such advances will continue to take the industry to the next stages and beyond.

Why does this difference matter to you? Knowing the difference between IT and IS can help you avoid a common mistake: You cannot buy an IS.

You can buy IT; you can buy or lease hardware, you can license programs and databases, and you can even obtain predesigned procedures. Ultimately, however, it is *your* people who execute those procedures to employ that new IT.

For any new system, you will always have training tasks (and costs), you will always have the need to overcome employees' resistance to change, and you will always need to manage the employees as they utilize the new system. Hence, you can buy IT, but you cannot buy IS.

Consider a simple example. Suppose your organization decides to develop a Facebook page. Facebook provides the hardware and programs, the database structures, and standard procedures. You, however, provide the data to fill your portion of their database, and you must extend their standard procedures with your own procedures for keeping that data current. Those procedures need to provide, for example, a means to review your page's content regularly and a means to remove content that is judged inappropriate. Furthermore, you need to train employees on how to follow those procedures and manage those employees to ensure that they do.

Managing your own Facebook page is as simple an IS as exists. Larger, more comprehensive IS that involve many, even dozens, of departments and thousands of employees require considerable work. Again, you can buy IT, but you can never buy an IS!

Q7 2020?

In Q1, we said that future businesspeople need to be able to assess, evaluate, and apply emerging technology. What technology might that be? And how might it pertain to future business?

Let's take a guess at technology in the year 2020. Of course, we won't have 20/20 vision, and, in fact, these guesses will probably seem ludicrous to the person who finds this book for sale for a dollar at a Goodwill Store in 2020. But, let's exercise our minds in that direction.

One reasonable guess is that most computers won't look like computers. The current Amazon Kindle (which as of this writing displays graphics poorly and black-and-white text only) will probably display decent graphics and color by the time you read this. Regardless, what happens when you turn on that Kindle? You are connected, magically as it were, to the Amazon store. You can buy books and magazine subscriptions, and so on, with a single click.

The Kindle, which is advertised as a reading device, is a computer. It just doesn't look like one. We can expect that televisions and autos and parking meters will all be computers or at least have a computer inside. We can further imagine some middle-aged, overweight man sitting at a Pizza Hut when the 911 staff arrives to carry him away.

"Why are you here?" he'll say, "I'm fine."

"Oh, no you're not. Your pacemaker called us because you're having a heart attack."

So it seems reasonable to assume that between now and 2020 you should be on the lookout for opportunities to include networked computers into whatever products you're making, marketing, or selling.

But let's apply systems thinking to a larger view. What will all of these **computers-in-a-product** mean to industry in general? Who will be the winners and who will be the losers? The U.S. Postal Service will continue to lose, but who else? What about Dell? If Dell continues to define itself as a maker of computers, then by 2020 Dell will be a shadow of its present self. Who else will be affected? Microsoft? Microsoft may be a loser, depending on how it responds to this change.

Who will be the big winners? Students. Publishers will sell innovative content over the Kindles-to-be. If they do so in a way that eliminates used books, students will pay $40 instead of $140 for a textbook. Book resellers will lose.

And what about classrooms? Why go to class if you have a classroom in a box? Let's phrase this differently, because the traditional classroom does have value, especially to those students who learn from comments and questions asked by more able students.[6] Put it this way: Suppose you can go to a traditional classroom for $25,000 a year or go to the classroom in a box for $3,500 per year. Either way, you earn a degree; maybe the box's degree is not as prestigious, but it is an accredited degree. Which would you choose?

We'll take a 2020 look at the end of each chapter. For now, think about it: Who are the winners and the losers in the computers-in-products era?

---

[6]Louise Nemanich, Michael Banks, and Dusya Vera, "Enhancing Knowledge Transfer in Classroom Versus OnLine Settings: The Interplay Among Instructor, Student, and Context," *Decision Sciences Journal of Innovative Education* 7, no. 1 (2009): 140.

Understanding Perspectives and Points of View

Every human being speaks and acts from the perspective of a personal point of view. Everything we say or do is based on—or equivalently, is biased by—that point of view. Thus, everything you read in any textbook, including this one, is biased by the author's point of view. The author may think that he is writing an unbiased account of neutral subject material. But no one can write an unbiased account of anything, because we all write from a perspective.

Similarly, your professors speak to you from their points of view. They have experience, goals, objectives, hopes, and fears, and, like all of us, those elements provide a framework from which they think and speak.

The statement in Q1 that this course is the single most important course in the business school is clearly an opinion. Other professors in other departments may disagree. Is one of us right and the other wrong? I think so, but do you?

Other opinions are less apparently opinions. Consider the following definition of information: "Information is a difference that makes a difference." By this definition, there are many differences, but only those that make a difference qualify as information.

This definition is not obviously an opinion, but it nevertheless was written from a biased perspective. The perspective is just less evident because the statement appears as a definition, not an opinion. But, in fact, it is the definition of information in the opinion of the well-known psychologist Gregory Bateson.

I find his definition informative and useful. It is imprecise, but it is a good guideline, and I have used it to advantage when designing reports and queries for end users. I ask myself, "Does this report show someone a difference that makes a difference to them?" So, I find it a useful and helpful definition.

My colleagues who specialize in quantitative methods, however, find Bateson's definition vapid and useless. They ask, "What does it say?" "How could I possibly use that definition to formalize anything?" or "A difference that makes a difference to what or whom?" Or they say, "I couldn't quantify anything about that definition; it's a waste of time."

And they are right, but so am I, and so was Gregory Bateson. The difference is a matter of perspective, and, surprisingly, conflicting perspectives can all be true at the same time.

One last point: Whether it is apparent or not, authors write and professors teach not only from personal perspectives, but also with personal goals. I write this textbook in the hope that you will find the

material useful and important and tell your professor that it is a great book so that he will use it again. Whether you (or I) are aware of that fact, it and my other hopes and goals bias every sentence in this book.

Similarly, your professors have hopes and goals that influence what and how they teach. Your professors may want to see light bulbs of recognition on your face, they may want to win the Professor of the Year award, or they may want to gain tenure status in order to be able to do some advanced research in the field. Whatever the case, they, too, have hopes and goals that bias everything they say.

So, as you read this book and as you listen to your professor, ask yourself, "What is her perspective?" and "What are her goals?" Then compare those perspectives and goals to yours. Learn to do this not just with your textbooks and your professors, but with your colleagues as well. When you enter the business world, being able to discern and adapt to the perspectives and goals of those with whom you work will make you much more effective. ∎

Discussion Questions

1. Consider the following statement: "The quality of your thinking is the most important component of an information system." Do you agree with this statement? Do you think it is even possible to say that one component is the most important one?

2. This text claims that although it is not possible to increase your IQ, it is possible to improve the quality of your thinking. Do you agree? Whether or not you agree, give three examples that illustrate differences in quality of thinking. They can be all from one person or they can be examples from three different people.

3. Though it does not appear to be so, the statement, "There are five components of an information system: hardware, software, data, procedures, and people" is an opinion based on a perspective. Suppose you stated this opinion to a computer engineer who said, "Rubbish. That's not true at all. The only components that count are hardware and maybe software." Contrast the perspective of the engineer with that of your MIS professor. How do those perspectives influence their opinions about the five-component framework? Which is correct?

4. Consider Bateson's definition, "Information is a difference that makes a difference." How can this definition be used to advantage when designing a Web page? Explain why someone who specializes in quantitative methods might consider this definition to be useless. How can the same definition be both useful and useless?

5. Some students hate open-ended questions. They want questions that have one correct answer, like 7.3 miles per hour. When given a question like that in question 4, a question that has multiple, equally valid answers, some students get angry or frustrated. They want the book or the professor to give them the answer. How do you feel about this matter?

6. Questions like those in the 2020 section obviously have no correct answer. Or, they have a correct answer, but that answer won't be known until 2020. Because this is true, are such questions worthless? Are you wasting your time thinking about them? Why or why not? Because the answer cannot be known on a timely basis, is any answer as good as any other? Why or why not?

7. Do you think someone can improve the quality of his or her thinking by learning to hold multiple, contradictory ideas in mind at the same time? Or, do you think that doing so just leads to indecisive and ineffective thinking? Discuss this question with some of your friends. What do they think? What are their perspectives?

Passwords and Password Etiquette

All forms of computer security involve passwords. Most likely, you have a university account that you access with a user name and password. When you set up that account, you were probably advised to use a **"strong password."** That's good advice, but what is a strong password? Probably not "sesame," but what then? Microsoft, a company that has many reasons to promote effective security, provides a definition that is commonly used. Microsoft defines a strong password as one with the following characteristics:

- Has seven or more characters
- Does not contain your user name, real name, or company name
- Does not contain a complete dictionary word, in any language
- Is different from previous passwords you have used
- Contains both upper- and lowercase letters, numbers, and special characters (such as ~ ! @; # $ % ^ &; * ( ) _ +; - =; { } | [ ] \ : " ; ' < ; > ; ? , . /)

Examples of good passwords are:

- Qw37^T1bb?at
- 3B47qq<3>5!7b

The problem with such passwords is that they are nearly impossible to remember. And the

Enter Username:

DonaldT

Enter Password:

✶✶✶✶✶✶✶✶

LOG IN

last thing you want to do is write your password on a piece of paper and keep it near the workstation where you use it. Never do that!

One technique for creating memorable, strong passwords is to base them on the first letter of the words in a phrase. The phrase could be the title of a song or the first line of a poem or one based on some fact about your life. For example, you might take the phrase, "I was born in Rome, New York, before 1990." Using the first letters from that phrase and substituting the character < for the word *before*, you create the password IwbiR,NY<1990.

That's an acceptable password, but it would be better if all of the numbers were not placed on the end. So, you might try the phrase, "I was born at 3:00 A.M. in Rome, New York." That phrase yields the password Iwba3:00AMiR,NY which is a strong password that is easily remembered.

Once you have created a strong password, you need to protect it with proper behavior. Proper password etiquette is one of the marks of a business professional. Never write down your password, and do not share it with others. Never ask someone else for his

password, and never give your password to some-one else.

But, what if you need someone else's password? Suppose, for example, you ask someone to help you with a problem on your computer. You sign on to an information system, and for some reason, you need to enter that other person's password. In this case, say to the other person, "We need your password," and then get out of your chair, offer your keyboard to the other person, and look away while she enters the password. Among professionals working in organizations that take security seriously, this little "do-si-do" move—one person getting out of the way so that another person can enter her password—is common and accepted.

If someone asks for your password, do not give it out. Instead, get up, go over to that person's machine, and enter your own password, yourself. Stay present while your password is in use, and ensure that your account is logged out at the end of the activity. No one should mind or be offended in any way when you do this. It is the mark of a professional. ■

Discussion Questions

1. Here are the first two lines of a famous poem by T. S. Eliot, "Let us go then, you and I, When the evening is spread out against the sky." Explain how to use these lines to create a password. How could you add numbers and special characters to the password in a way that you will be able to remember?

2. List two different phrases that you can use to create a strong password. Show the password created by each.

3. One of the problems of life in the cyber-world is that we all are required to have multiple passwords—one for work or school, one for bank accounts, another for eBay or other auction sites, and so forth. Of course, it is better to use different passwords for each. But in that case you have to remember three or four different passwords. Think of different phrases you can use to create a memorable, strong password for each of these different accounts. Relate the phrase to the purpose of the account. Show the passwords for each.

4. Explain proper behavior when you are using your computer and you need to enter, for some valid reason, another person's password.

5. Explain proper behavior when someone else is using her computer and that person needs to enter, for some valid reason, your password.

ACTIVE REVIEW

Use the chapter's questions to manage your study time. Read (or reread) the material in the chapter until you can answer each question. Use the tasks in this Active Review to verify that your answers are complete and sufficient.

Q1 Why is Introduction to MIS the most important class in the business school?

Define *Moore's Law* and explain why its consequences are important to business professionals today. State how business professionals should relate to emerging information technology. Give the text's definition of *job security* and use Reich's enumeration to explain how this course will help you attain that security.

Q2 What is MIS?

Identify the three important phrases in the definition of *MIS*. Name the five components of an information system. Explain why end users need to be involved in the development of information systems. Explain why it is a misconception to say that organizations do something.

Q3 How can you use the five-component model?

Name and define each of the five components. Explain the symmetry in the five-component model. Show how automation moves work from one side of the five-component structure to the other. Explain how the components are ordered according to difficulty of change and disruption. Name the most important component and state why it is the most important. Use the five-component model to describe the differences between high-tech and low-tech information systems. Explain how you can use the five components when considering new information systems.

Q4 What is information?

State four different definitions of information. Identify the one that is your favorite and explain why. Explain how information is subjective; use the example in Figure 1-5 in your answer.

Q5 What makes some information better than other information?

Create a mnemonic device for remembering the characteristics of good information. Explain why good information must fit each of the characteristics.

Q6 Why is the difference between information technology and information systems important?

Using the five-component model, explain the difference between IT and IS. Explain why you can buy IT, but you can never buy IS. What does that mean to you, as a potential future business manager?

Q7 2020?

Explain the term *computers-in-a-product*. Explain how Dell might be a loser in this new era. What must Dell do to respond to this movement? Under which circumstances will Microsoft lose in this environment? What must Microsoft do? What should I, as an author, be doing to respond to this change? Why is your college or university challenged by computers-in-a-box? Is it seriously challenged or is this just a passing fad? If your school is publicly funded, is it more at risk? Summarize how answering these questions contributes to your skill as a nonroutine thinker.

KEY TERMS AND CONCEPTS

Abstract reasoning 6
Accurate (information) 16
Computer hardware 8
Computer-based information system 9
Computers-in-a-product 19

Data 8
Experimentation 7
Five-component framework 8
Information 12
Information system (IS) 8
Information technology (IT) 18

Just-barely-sufficient (information) 17
Management information systems (MIS) 8
Moore's Law 4
People 8

USING YOUR KNOWLEDGE

1. One of life's greatest gifts is to be employed doing work that you love. Reflect for a moment on a job that you would find so exciting that you could hardly wait to get to sleep on Sunday night so that you could wake up and go to work on Monday.

   a. Describe that job. Name the industry, the type of company or organization for whom you'd like to work, the products and services they produce, and your specific job duties.

   b. Explain what it is about that job that you find so compelling.

   c. In what ways will the skills of abstraction, systems thinking, collaboration, and experimentation facilitate your success in that job?

   d. Given your answers to parts a through c, define three to five personal goals for this class. None of these goals should include anything about your GPA. Be as specific as possible. Assume that you are going to evaluate yourself on these goals at the end of the quarter or semester. The more specific you make these goals, the easier it will be to perform the evaluation. Use Figure 1-2 for guidance.

2. Consider costs of a system in light of the five components: costs to buy and maintain the hardware; costs to develop or acquire licenses to the software programs and costs to maintain them; costs to design databases and fill them with data; costs of developing procedures and keeping them current; and finally, human costs both to develop and use the system.

   a. Over the lifetime of a system, many experts believe that the single most expensive component is people. Does this belief seem logical to you? Explain why you agree or disagree.

   b. Consider a poorly developed system that does not meet its defined requirements. The needs of the business do not go away, but they do not conform themselves to the characteristics of the poorly built system. Therefore, something must give. Which component picks up the slack when the hardware and software programs do not work correctly? What does this say about the cost of a poorly designed system? Consider both direct money costs as well as intangible personnel costs.

   c. What implications do you, as a future business manager, take from parts a and b? What does this say about the need for your involvement in requirements and other aspects of systems development? Who eventually will pay the costs of a poorly developed system? Against which budget will those costs accrue?

3. Consider the four definitions of information presented in this chapter. The problem with the first definition, "knowledge derived from data," is that it merely substitutes one word we don't know the meaning of (*information*) for a second word we don't know the meaning of (*knowledge*). The problem with the second definition, "data presented in a meaningful context," is that it is too subjective. Whose context? What makes a context meaningful? The third definition, "data processed by summing, ordering, averaging, etc.," is too mechanical. It tells us what to do, but it doesn't tell us what information is. The fourth definition, "a difference that makes a difference," is vague and unhelpful.

   Also, none of these definitions helps us to quantify the amount of information we receive. What is the information content of the statement that every human being has a navel? Zero—you already know that. In contrast, the statement that someone has just deposited $50,000 into your checking account is chock-full of information. So, good information has an element of surprise.

   Considering all of these points, answer the following questions:

   a. What is information made of?

   b. If you have more information, do you weigh more? Why or why not?

   c. If you give a copy of your transcript to a prospective employer, is that information? If you show that same transcript to your dog, is it still information? Where is the information?

   d. Give your own best definition of information.

e. Explain how you think it is possible that we have an industry called the *information technology industry,* but we have great difficulty defining the word *information.*

4. The text states that information should be worth its cost. Both cost and value can be broken into tangible and intangible factors. *Tangible* factors can be directly measured; *intangible* ones arise indirectly and are difficult to measure. For example, a tangible cost is the cost of a computer monitor; an intangible cost is the lost productivity of a poorly trained employee.

Give five important tangible and five important intangible costs of an information system. Give five important tangible and five important intangible measures of the value of an information system. If it helps to focus your thinking, use the example of the class scheduling system at your university or some other university information system. When determining whether an information system is worth its cost, how do you think the tangible and intangible factors should be considered?

COLLABORATION EXERCISE

Collaborate with a group of fellow students to answer the following questions. For this exercise do not meet face to face. Coordinate all of your work using email and email attachments, only. Your answers should reflect the thinking of the entire group, and not just one or two individuals.

1. Abstract reasoning.

   a. Define *abstract reasoning,* and explain why it is an important skill for business professionals.
   b. Explain how a list of items in inventory and their quantity on hand is an abstraction of a physical inventory.
   c. Give three other examples of abstractions commonly used in business.
   d. Explain how Jennifer failed to demonstrate effective abstract-reasoning skills.
   e. Can people increase their abstract-reasoning skills? If so, how? If not, why not?

2. Systems thinking.

   a. Define *systems thinking,* and explain why it is an important skill for business professionals.
   b. Explain how you would use systems thinking to explain why Moore's Law caused a farmer to dig up a field of pulp wood trees. Name each of the elements in the system, and explain their relationships to each other.
   c. Give three other examples of the use of system thinking with regard to consequences of Moore's Law.
   d. Explain how Jennifer failed to demonstrate effective systems thinking skills.
   e. Can people improve their system thinking skills? If so, how? If not, why not?

3. Collaboration.

   a. Define *collaboration,* and explain why it is an important skill for business professionals.
   b. Explain how you are using collaboration to answer these questions. Describe what is working with regards to your group's process and what is not working.
   c. Is the work product of your team better than any one of you could have done separately? If not, your collaboration is ineffective. If that is the case, explain why.
   d. Does the fact that you cannot meet face to face hamper your ability to collaborate? If so, how?
   e. Explain how Jennifer failed to demonstrate effective collaboration skills.
   f. Can people increase their collaboration skills? If so, how? If not, why not?

4. Experimentation.

   a. Define *experimentation,* and explain why it is an important skill for business professionals.
   b. Explain several creative ways you could use experimentation to answer this question.
   c. How does the fear of failure influence your willingness to engage in any of the ideas you identified in part b.
   d. Explain how Jennifer failed to demonstrate effective experimentation skills.
   e. Can people increase their willingness to take risks? If so, how? If not, why not?

5. Job security.

   a. State the text's definition of *job security.*
   b. Evaluate the text's definition of job security. Is it effective? If you think not, offer a better definition of job security.

c. As a team, do you agree that improving your skills on the four dimensions in Collaboration Exercises 1–4 will increase your job security?

d. Do you think technical skills (accounting proficiency, financial analysis proficiency, etc.) provide job security? Why or why not. Do you think you would have answered this question differently in 1980? Why or why not?

APPLICATION EXERCISES

1. The spreadsheet in Microsoft Excel file **Ch1Ex1** contains records of employee activity on special projects. Open this workbook and examine the data that you find in the three spreadsheets it contains. Assess the accuracy, relevancy, and sufficiency of this data to the following people and problems.

   a. You manage the Denver plant, and you want to know how much time your employees are spending on special projects.

   b. You manage the Reno plant, and you want to know how much time your employees are spending on special projects.

   c. You manage the Quota Computation project in Chicago, and you want to know how much time your employees have spent on that project.

   d. You manage the Quota Computation project for all three plants, and you want to know the total time employees have spent on your project.

   e. You manage the Quota Computation project for all three plants, and you want to know the total labor cost for all employees on your project.

   f. You manage the Quota Computation project for all three plants, and you want to know how the labor-hour total for your project compares to the labor-hour totals for the other special projects.

   g. What conclusions can you make from this exercise?

2. The database in the Microsoft Access file **Ch1Ex2** contains the same records of employee activity on special projects as in Application Exercise 1. Before proceeding, open that database and view the records in the Employee Hours table.

   a. Seven queries have been created that process this data in different ways. Using the criteria of accuracy, relevancy, and sufficiency, select the single query that is most appropriate for the information requirements in Application Exercise 1, parts a–f. If no query meets the need, explain why.

   b. What conclusions can you make from this exercise?

   c. Comparing your experiences on these two projects, what are the advantages and disadvantages of spreadsheets and databases?

CASE STUDY 1 video

Requirements Creep at the IRS

The United States Internal Revenue Service (IRS) serves more people in the United States than any other public or private institution. Each year it processes over 200 million tax returns from more than 180 million individuals and more than 45 million businesses. The IRS itself employs more than 100,000 people in over 1,000 different sites. In a typical year, it adapts to more than 200 tax law changes and services more than 23 million telephone calls.

Amazingly, the IRS accomplishes this work using information systems that were designed and developed in the 1960s. In fact, some of the computer programs that process tax returns were first written in 1962. In the mid-1990s, the IRS set out on a Business System Modernization (BSM) project that would replace this antiquated system with modern technology and capabilities. However, by 2003 it was clear that this project was a disaster. Billions of dollars had been spent on the project, and all major components of the new system were months or years behind schedule.

In 2003, newly appointed IRS commissioner Mark W. Everson called for an independent review of all BSM projects. Systems development experts from the Software Engineering Institute at Carnegie Mellon University and the Mitre Corporation and managers from the IRS examined the project and made a list of factors that contributed to the failure and recommendations for solutions. In their report, the first two causes of failure cited were:

- "There was inadequate business unit ownership and sponsorship of projects. This resulted in unrealistic business cases and continuous project scope 'creep' (gradual expansion of the original scope of the project)."
- "The much desired environment of trust, confidence, and teamwork between the IRS business units, the BSM organization [the team of IRS employees established to manage the BSM project], the Information Technology Services (ITS) [the internal IRS organization that operates and maintains the current information systems], and the Prime [the prime contractor, Computer Sciences Corporation] did not exist. In fact, the opposite was true, resulting in an inefficient working environment and, at times, finger pointing when problems arose."

The BSM team developed the new system in a vacuum. The team did not have the acceptance, understanding, or support for the new system from either the existing IRS business units (the future users of the system) or from the existing ITS staff. Consequently, the BSM team poorly understood the system needs, and that misunderstanding resulted in continual changes in project requirements, changes that occurred after systems components had been designed and developed. Such requirements creep is a sure sign of a mismanaged project and always results in schedule delays and wasted money. In this case, the delays were measured in years and the waste in billions of dollars.

In response to the problems that it identified, the IRS Oversight Board recommended the following two actions:[7]

- "The IRS business units must take direct leadership and ownership of the Modernization program and each of its projects. In particular, this must include defining the scope of each project, preparing realistic and attainable business cases, and controlling scope changes throughout each project's life cycle. . . ."
- "Create an environment of trust, confidence, and teamwork between the business units, the BSM and ITS organizations, and the Prime. . . ."

In 2004, the IRS hired Richard Spires to take over and manage the BSM project. Spires, who had been president of the consulting firm Mantas Inc., facilitated a turnaround in the BSM project and was subsequently appointed Chief Information Officer, the senior IT person at the IRS. Spires left the IRS in 2008 to pursue other interests. In his departure email he stated, "Through March 7, 2008, CADE (a key component of the BSM project) processed 15.1 million individual tax returns out of the more than 59 million received."

Unfortunately, it is not publicly known what specific steps Spires took to affect this turnaround. What is known, however, is that because of the initial mistake of not involving users in the specification of requirements and the feasibility of potential solutions, the IRS endured a 10-year delay and billions of dollars of cost overruns.

Sources: IRS Oversight Board, 2003, *www.treas.gov/irsob/index.html*; "For the IRS, There's No EZ Fix," *CIO Magazine,* April 1, 2004; "Spires to Leave IRS," *nextgov,* July 22, 2008, *http://techinsider.nextgov.com/2008/07/spires_to_leave_irs.php.*

Questions
1. Why did the Oversight Board place leadership and ownership of the Modernization program on the business units? Why did it not place these responsibilities on the ITS organization?
2. Why did the Oversight Board place the responsibility for controlling scope changes on the business units? Why was this responsibility not given to the BSM? To ITS? To Computer Sciences Corporation?
3. The second recommendation is a difficult assignment, especially considering the size of the IRS and the complexity of the project. How does one go about creating "an environment of trust, confidence, and teamwork"?

To make this recommendation more comprehensible, translate it to your local university. Suppose, for example, that your College of Business embarked on a program to modernize its computing facilities, including computer labs, and the computer network facilities used for teaching, including Internet-based distance learning. Suppose that the Business School dean created a committee like the BSM that hired a vendor to create the new computing facilities for the college. Suppose, further, that the committee proceeded without any involvement of the faculty, staff, students, or the existing computer support

---

[7]The report identified more than two problems and made more than two recommendations. See the "Independent Analysis of IRS Business Systems Modernization Special Report" at *www.itsoversightboard.treas.gov.*

department. Finally, suppose that the project was 1 year late, had spent $400,000, was not nearly finished, and that the vendor complained that the requirements kept changing. Now, assume that you have been given the responsibility of creating "an environment of trust, confidence, and teamwork" among the faculty, staff, other users, the computer support department, and the vendor. How would you proceed?

4. The problem in question 3 involves at most a few hundred people and a few sites. The IRS problem involves 100,000 people and over 1,000 sites. How would you modify your answer to question 3 for a project as large as the IRS's?

5. If the existing system works (which apparently it does), why is the BSM needed? Why fix a system that works?

Collaboration Information Systems

"No, Felix! Not again! Over, and over, and over! We decide something one meeting and then go over it again the next meeting and again the next. What a waste!"

"What do you mean, Tara? I think it's important we get this right."

"Well, Felix, if that's the case, why don't you come to the meetings?"

"I just missed a couple."

"Right. Last week we met here for, oh, 2, maybe 3, hours and we decided to look for ways to save costs without changing who we are as a studio."

"But Tara, if we could raise revenue, we wouldn't have to save costs. I think I have a couple of good ideas on how to do that."

"Felix! Last week we discussed that and decided it was too risky . . . we wouldn't see results in time. Plus, that's not what Kelly asked us to do."

"Look, Tara, Kelly just wants the studio to be profitable. Sales are down and costs aren't. All we need to do is raise sales."

"Right. But how do you do it? And what's the cost of raising sales? Come on, Felix, you're driving me nuts. We discussed this *ad nausea* last week. Let's make some progress. Why don't some of you other guys help me! Jan, what do you think?"

"Felix, Tara is right. We did have a long discussion on what we're doing—and we did agree to focus on saving money."

"Well, Jan, I think it's a mistake. Why didn't anyone tell me? I put a lot of time into developing my sales plan."

"Did you read the email?" Jan asks tentatively.

"What email?"

"The meeting summary email that Jan sends out each week."

"I got the email but I couldn't download the attachment. Something weird about a virus checker couldn't access a gizmo or something like that . . . "

Tara can't stand that excuse, "Here, Felix, take a look at mine. I'll underline the part where we concluded that we'd focus on sales so you can be sure to see it."

"Tara, there's no reason to get snippy about this. I thought I had a good idea."

"OK, so we're agreed—*again this week*—that we're going to look for ways of reducing costs. Now, we've wasted enough time covering old ground. Let's get some new thinking going."

Felix slumps back into his chair and looks down at his cell phone.

"Oh, no, I missed a call from Mapplethorpe. Ahhhh."

"Felix, what are you talking about?"

"Mapplethorpe, my best client. Wants to change his PT appointment this afternoon. I'm sorry, but I've got to call him. I'll be back in a few minutes."

Felix leaves the room.

Tara looks at the three team members who are left.

"Now what?" she asks. "If we go forward we'll have to rediscuss everything we do when Felix comes back. Maybe we should just take a break?"

Jan shakes her head. "Tara, let's not. It's tough for me to get to these meetings. I don't have a class until tonight, so I drove down here just for this. I've got to pick up Simone from day care. We haven't done anything yet. Let's just ignore Felix."

"OK, Jan, but it isn't easy to ignore Felix."

The door opens and Kelly, FlexTime's co-owner, walks in.

"Hi everyone! How's it going? OK if I sit in on your meeting?" ∎

>> STUDY QUESTIONS

Q1 What is collaboration?

Q2 What are the components of a collaboration information system?

Q3 How can you use collaboration systems to improve team communication?

Q4 How can you use collaboration systems to manage content?

Q5 How can you use collaboration systems to control workflow?

Q6 How do businesses use collaboration systems?

Q7 2020?

CHAPTER PREVIEW

Does that FlexTime meeting sound like meetings you have with fellow students? It doesn't have to be that way. One of the best ways of improving team meetings is to use collaboration information systems, as you'll learn in this chapter.

We begin by defining and describing *collaboration*. Given that definition, we'll then look at the five components of a collaboration system and consider the procedure and people components in particular. Then, we'll examine how three different types of collaboration system can be used to facilitate communication, manage the team's work product, and control team workflow. We'll then consider collaboration in the business context. We'll examine how information systems improve collaboration for problem solving, project management, and decision making.

As you read this chapter, keep in mind (from Chapter 1) that collaboration is one of the four critical skills that Robert Reich identified for twenty-first-century workers. As you'll see, the ability to use collaboration systems is a key part of modern collaboration skills.

Q1 What Is Collaboration?

Collaboration occurs when two or more people work together to achieve a common goal, result, or work product. When collaboration is effective, the results of the group are greater than could be produced by any of the individuals working alone. Collaboration involves coordination and communication, but it is greater than either of those alone.

Consider an example of a student team that is assigned a term project. Suppose the team meets and divides the work into sections and then team members work independently on their individual pieces. An hour before the project is due the team members meet again to assemble their independent pieces into a whole. Such a team evidences both communication and coordination, but it is not collaborative.

The Importance of Feedback and Iteration

Collaborative work involves feedback and iteration. In a collaborative environment, team members review each others' work product and revise that product as a result. The effort proceeds in a series of steps, or iterations, in which one person produces something, others comment on what was produced, a revised version is produced, and so forth. Further, in the process of reviewing others' work, team members learn from each other and change the way they work and what they produce. The feedback and iteration enable the group to produce something greater than any single person could accomplish working independently.

Kelly, the co-owner of FlexTime, gave the team an important assignment: how to reduce costs without losing what makes FlexTime the popular studio that it is, or, expressed in terms you'll learn in Chapter 3, without compromising FlexTime's competitive strategy. No single employee or contractor on that team has the best solution. That solution should evolve from feedback and iteration among team members.

Critical Collaboration Drivers

The effectiveness of a collaborative effort is driven by three critical factors:

- Communication
- Content management
- Workflow control

Communication has two key elements. The first is the communication skills and abilities of the group members. The ability to give and receive critical feedback is particularly important. Work product can improve only when group members can criticize each other's work without creating rancor and resentment and can improve their contributions based on criticism received.

The second key communication element is the availability of effective communication systems. Today, few collaborative meetings are conducted face-to-face. Group members may be geographically distributed, or they may be unable to meet at the same time, or both. In such cases, the availability of email and more sophisticated and effective communications systems is crucial.

The second driver of collaboration effectiveness is **content management**. When multiple users are contributing and changing documents, schedules, task lists, assignments, and so forth, one user's work might interfere with another's. Users need to manage content so that such conflict does not occur. Also, it is important to know who made what changes, when, and why. Content-management systems track and report such data. Finally, in some collaborations members have different rights and privileges. Some team members have full **permissions** to create, edit, and delete content, others are restricted to edit, and still others are restricted to a read-only status. Information systems play a key role in enforcing such restrictions.

Workflow control is the third key driver of collaboration effectiveness. A **workflow** is a process or procedure by which content is created, edited, used, and disposed. For a team that supports a Web site, for example, a workflow design may specify that certain members create Web pages, others review those pages, and still others post the reviewed and approved pages to the Web site. The workflow specifies particular ordering of tasks and includes processes for handling rejected changes as well as for dealing with exceptions.

The three collaboration drivers are not equally important for all collaborations. For one-time, *ad hoc* workgroups, it is seldom worthwhile to create and formalize workflows. For such groups, communication is the most important driver. In contrast, formally defined workflow for a team of engineers designing a new airplane is crucial.

Q2 What Are the Components of a Collaboration Information System?

Collaboration information systems have the five information systems components that you learned in Chapter 1: hardware, software, data, procedures, and people. Consider each.

Hardware

Two types of hardware are used in collaboration information systems: client hardware and server hardware. **Client hardware** consists of the computers and other communication devices (iPhones, BlackBerries) that users employ to participate in collaboration activities. **Server hardware** consists of computers that are installed and operated by IT professionals that support the collaboration system. For example, Google Docs & Spreadsheets runs server hardware to store, process, and share the documents and spreadsheets it manages. You will learn more about servers in Chapter 4 and again in Chapter 8. For now, just understand that there are server computers "somewhere out there" that support your collaboration.

Software

Many different collaboration computer programs exist. In this chapter, we will consider the three programs shown in Figure 2-1. Google Docs & Spreadsheets is free and requires users only to have a browser such as Internet Explorer or Firefox on their

Hardware	Software	Data	Procedures	People
Client computers Server computers	Examples: • Google Docs & Spreadsheets • Microsoft Groove • Microsoft SharePoint	Examples: • Documents • Discussion lists • Task lists • Wikis • Blogs	Procedures for: • Using the software • Team collaboration	Communication & collaboration skills

Figure 2-1
Components of a Collaboration
Information System

client computers. Google maintains a complex array of computer programs on its servers to support this application, but users need know nothing about them to use Google Docs & Spreadsheets.

Microsoft Groove is the second collaboration application we consider. Business users pay a fee to use Groove; however, students who are enrolled in universities that participate in the Microsoft Academic program can obtain Groove for free. Groove must be installed on the client computers of all the users who are participating in a Groove collaboration session. Groove can optionally be installed on a server computer as well.

Microsoft SharePoint is the third collaboration application that we will consider in this chapter. SharePoint must be installed on a server computer. Business users pay fees to use SharePoint on their servers, and that fee can be large. Pearson, this textbook's publisher, has contracted with a third-party company to host SharePoint free of charge for purchasers of this text. Your instructor can contact Pearson to set up that arrangement.

Once SharePoint is set up on a server computer, users need only a browser to use it. Either Internet Explorer or Firefox will work, but users have a better experience if they use Internet Explorer. SharePoint is integrated with Microsoft Office. So, if you are using Microsoft Word, Excel, PowerPoint, or another Office application, you can readily integrate documents in those applications with SharePoint.

Data

Collaboration data consists of documents, discussions, tasks lists, and other types of team data. The particular types of data allowed depend on the collaboration software used. Google Docs & Spreadsheets will store and manage Word and Excel documents, as you would expect from its name. Groove allows users to store almost any kind of computer file, including Word, Excel, PowerPoint, Acrobat, pictures, drawings, and other document types. As you'll see, you can do multiparty text chat with Groove, and you can store a log of a chat session as part of your collaboration data.

SharePoint allows a much broader range of data to be stored. In addition to documents and other files, SharePoint can store discussion lists, task lists, announcements, calendars, and more. SharePoint also support team Wikis and team member blogs.

We will illustrate examples of most of this data in sections that follow.

Procedures

Two types of procedures are important for collaboration: procedures for using the collaboration software and procedures for conducting the collaborative project. Considering the former, both Google Docs & Spreadsheets and Microsoft Groove are quite easy to learn and use.

Phase	Decisions and Procedures
Starting	What is the team's authority? What is the purpose of the team? Who is on the team? What is expected from team members? What are team members' roles and authorities?
Planning	What tasks need to be accomplished? How are the tasks related to one another? Who is responsible for each task? When will tasks be completed?
Doing	Executing project tasks Task status reporting Managing exceptions
Wrapping-up	Are we done? Documenting team results Documenting team learnings for future teams Closing down the project

Figure 2-2
Decisions and Procedures
for Project Phases

Learning to use SharePoint can be more difficult, depending on which SharePoint features you use. It is quite easy to perform basic tasks such as creating announcements, reading and storing documents, adding items to lists, responding to surveys, and so forth. Some of the more advanced features, such as workflow control, require more time and effort to learn.

The second type of collaboration procedures concerns how the team will perform its collaborative work. Figure 2-2 presents a summary of decisions and procedures needed for team management at various stages of a project. An in-depth discussion of the items in this list is beyond the scope of this text. However, you can use this list to guide your activities in collaboration exercises in this and other classes. Hackman's *Leading Teams*[1] is an excellent source if you want to learn more. For now, consider the following brief descriptions of collaboration procedures.

Starting Phase

The fundamental purpose of the starting phase is to set the ground rules for the collaboration. In industry, teams need to consider what authority they have; in most student collaborations, team authority will be set by the instructor. Generally, student teams do not have the authority to define the project, but they do have the authority to determine how that project will be accomplished.

The key item for most student collaborations is to set expectations for team members. What role will each team member play, and what authority will he or she have? Procedures for conducting team meetings are also often developed.

Planning Phase

The purpose of the planning phase is to determine "who will do what and by when." As you'll learn when we discuss project management in Chapter 10, tasks often depend on one other. For example, you cannot evaluate alternatives until you have created a list of alternatives to evaluate. In this case, we say there is a *task dependency* between the task *evaluate alternatives* and the task *create a list of alternatives*. The *evaluate alternatives* task cannot begin until the completion of the *create alternative list* task.

---

[1] J. Richard Hackman, *Leading Teams* (Boston: Harvard Business School Press, 2002).

For most student assignments, task dependencies are simple and readily understood. The key for student groups is to make clear assignments of tasks to team members and to ensure that team members know by when they will accomplish those tasks.

Doing

Tasks are accomplished during the doing phase. The key management challenge here is to ensure that tasks are accomplished on time, and, if not, to identify schedule problems as early as possible. As work progresses, it is often necessary to add or delete tasks, change task assignments, add or remove task labor, and so forth.

Wrapping-Up

Are we done? This question is an important and sometimes difficult one to answer. If work is not finished, the team needs to define more tasks and continue the doing phase. If the answer is yes, then the team needs to document its results, document information for future teams, close down the project, and disband the team.

Use Figure 2-2 as a simple checklist for the collaboration projects that you do in this and other classes.

Iteration and Feedback

Before moving on, notice that iteration and feedback are part of every phase of a project. Each question in Figure 2-2 has multiple answers, and team members may disagree with one another. Such disagreement is normal and appropriate; team members answer questions, provide feedback on those answers, produce revised answers, and so forth. That loop is the nature and power of collaboration.

People

Chapter 1 stated that the most important component in an information system is people. That statement is especially true for collaboration systems. Good communication skills are important, but what other traits lead to effective collaboration?

Researchers Ditkoff, Allen, Moore, and Pollard surveyed 108 business professionals on the qualities, attitudes, and skills that make a good collaborator.[2] Figure 2-3 lists the most and least important characteristics reported in the survey. Most students are surprised to learn that 5 of the top 12 characteristics involve disagreement (highlighted in red in Figure 2-3). Most students believe that "we should all get along" and more or less have the same idea and opinions about team matters. Although it is important for the team to be social enough to work together, this research indicates that it is also important for team members to have different ideas and opinions and to express them to each other.

When we think about collaboration as an iterative process in which team members give and receive feedback, these results are not surprising. During collaboration, team members learn from each other, and it will be difficult to learn if no one is willing to express different or even unpopular ideas. The respondents also seem to be saying, "You can be negative, as long as you care about what we're doing." These collaboration skills do not come naturally to people who have been taught to "play well with others," but that may be why they were so highly ranked in the survey.

---

[2]Dave Pollard, "The Ideal Collaborative Team." Available at: *http://blogs.salon.com/0002007/stories/ 2005/11/18/theIdealCollaborativeTeamAndAConversationOnTheCollaborativeProcess.html* (accessed May 2009).

Twelve Most Important Characteristics for an Effective Collaborator

1. Is enthusiastic about the subject of our collaboration.

2. Is open-minded and curious.

3. Speaks their mind even if it's an unpopular viewpoint.

4. Gets back to me and others in a timely way.

5. Is willing to enter into difficult conversations.

6. Is a perceptive listener.

7. Is skillful at giving/receiving negative feedback.

8. Is willing to put forward unpopular ideas.

9. Is self-managing and requires "low maintenance."

10. Is known for following through on commitments.

11. Is willing to dig into the topic with zeal.

12. Thinks differently than I do/brings different perspectives.

Nine Least Important Characteristics for an Effective Collaborator

1. Is well organized.

2. Is someone I immediately liked. The chemistry is good.

3. Has already earned my trust.

4. Has experience as a collaborator.

5. Is a skilled and persuasive presenter.

6. Is gregarious and dynamic.

7. Is someone I knew beforehand.

8. Has an established reputation in field of our collaboration.

9. Is an experienced businessperson.

Figure 2-3
Important and Not-Important Characteristics of a Collaborator

Source: Based on Dave Pollard, "The Ideal Collaborative Team." *http://blogs.salon.com/ 0002007/ stories/2005/11/18/theIdeal CollaborativeTeamAndAConversationOn TheCollaborativeProcess.html* (accessed May, 2009).

The characteristics rated *not relevant* are also revealing. Experience as a collaborator or in business does not seem to matter. Being popular also is not important. A big surprise, however, is that being well organized was rated 31st out of 39 characteristics. Perhaps collaboration itself is not a very well-organized process?

Q3 How Can You Use Collaboration Systems to Improve Team Communication?

If you truly are going to *collaborate* on your team projects, if you are going to create work products (such as documents), encourage others to criticize those products, and revise those products in accordance with the criticism, then you will need to communicate. Similarly, if you are going to review others' work, make critical comments, and help them improve their product, then you will also need to communicate. So, improving communication capabilities is key to collaboration success.

Synchronous		Asynchronous
Shared calendars Invitation and attendance		
Single location	Multiple locations	Single or multiple locations
Office applications such as Word and PowerPoint	Conference calls Webinars Multiparty text chat Microsoft Groove Videoconferencing	Email Discussion forums Team surveys

Virtual meetings

Figure 2-4
Information Technology for
Communication

The Ethics Guide on pages 48–49 addresses some of the ethical challenges that arise when teams hold virtual meetings.

Figure 2-4 summarizes technology available to facilitate communication. **Synchronous communication** occurs when all team members meet at the same time, such as with conference calls or face-to-face meetings. **Asynchronous communication** occurs when team members do not meet at the same time. Employees who work different shifts at the same location, or team members who work in different time zones around the world, must meet asynchronously.

Most student teams attempt to meet face-to-face, at least at first. Arranging such meetings is always difficult, however, because student schedules and responsibilities differ. If you are going to arrange such meetings, consider creating an online group calendar in which team members post their availability, week by week. Also, use the meeting facilities in Microsoft Outlook to issue invitations and gather RSVPs. If you don't have Outlook, use an Internet site such as Evite (*www.evite.com*) for this purpose. For face-to-face meetings, you will need little other technology beyond standard Office applications such as Word and PowerPoint.

Given today's communication technology, most students should forgo face-to-face meetings. They are too difficult to arrange and seldom worth the trouble. Instead, learn to use **virtual meetings** in which participants do not meet in the same place, and possibly not at the same time.

If your virtual meeting is synchronous (all meet at the same time), you can use **conference calls, webinars,** or **multiparty text chat**. A webinar is a virtual meeting in which attendees view one of the attendees' computer screens. **WebEx** (*www.webex.com*) is a popular commercial webinar application used in virtual sales presentations. **SharedView** is a Microsoft product for sharing a computer screen that you can download for free at *www.connect.microsoft.com/site/sitehome.aspx?SiteID=94.*

Some students find it weird to use text chat for school projects, but why not? You can attend meetings wherever you are, silently. In the next section, we will describe Microsoft Groove, a tool you should consider because it has easy-to-use multiparty text chat, along with several other useful features.

If everyone on your team has a camera on his or her computer, you can also do **videoconferencing** like that shown in Figure 2-5. Microsoft NetMeeting is one such product, but you can find others on the Internet. Videoconferencing is more intrusive than text chat; you have to comb your hair, but it does have a more personal touch. Sometime during your student career you should use it to see what you think.

In some classes and situations, synchronous meetings, even virtual ones, are impossible to arrange. You just cannot get everyone together at the same time. In this circumstance, when the team must meet asynchronously, most students try to communicate via **email**. The problem with email is that there is too much freedom. Not everyone will participate, because it is easy to hide from email. (Did Felix, in the opening scenario, really not get the attachment?) Discussion threads become disorganized and disconnected. After the fact, it is difficult to find particular emails, comments, or attachments.

Figure 2-5
User Participating
in NetMeeting

Source: Courtesy of Zigy Kaluzny, Getty
Image/Getty Images, Inc.

Discussion forums are an alternative. Here, one group member posts an entry, perhaps an idea, a comment, or a question, and other group members respond. Figure 2-6 shows an example. Such forums are better than email because it is harder for the discussion to get off track. Still, however, it remains easy for some team members not to participate.

Team surveys are another form of communication technology. With these, one team member creates a list of questions and other team members respond. Surveys are an effective way to obtain team opinions; they are generally easy to complete, so most team members will participate. Also, it is easy to determine who has not

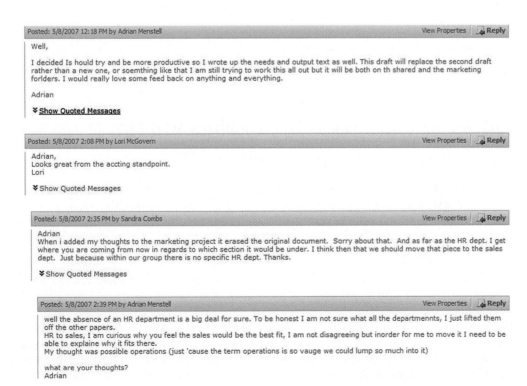

Figure 2-6
Example of Discussion Forum

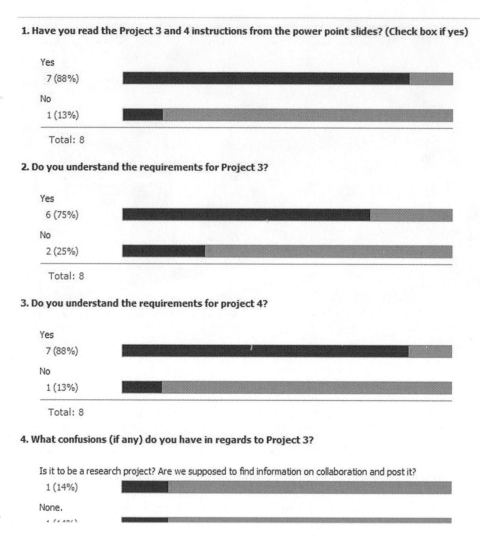

1. Have you read the Project 3 and 4 instructions from the power point slides? (Check box if yes)

Yes
7 (88%)

No
1 (13%)

Total: 8

2. Do you understand the requirements for Project 3?

Yes
6 (75%)

No
2 (25%)

Total: 8

3. Do you understand the requirements for project 4?

Yes
7 (88%)

No
1 (13%)

Total: 8

4. What confusions (if any) do you have in regards to Project 3?

Is it to be a research project? Are we supposed to find information on collaboration and post it?
1 (14%)

None.

Figure 2-7
Portion of Sample Team Survey

yet responded. Figure 2-7 shows the results of one team survey. SurveyMonkey (*www.surveymonkey.com*) is one common survey application program. You can find others on the Internet. Microsoft SharePoint has a built-in survey capability, as will be discussed later.

Q4 How Can You Use Collaboration Systems to Manage Content?

The second driver of collaboration performance is content management. You and your teammates will need to share documents, illustrations, spreadsheets, and other data. The information systems you use for sharing content depend on the degree of control that you want. Figure 2-8 lists three categories of content-management control: no control, version management, and version control. Consider each.

Shared Content with No Control

The most primitive way to share content is via email attachments. It is easy to share content this way, but email attachments have numerous problems. For one, there is always the danger that someone does not receive an email, does not notice it in his or her inbox, or does not bother to save the attachments. Then, too, if three users obtain

Alternatives for Sharing Content		
No Control	Version Management	Version Control
Email with attachments Shared files on a server	Wikis Google Docs & Spreadsheets Microsoft Groove	Microsoft SharePoint

Increasing degree of content control

Figure 2-8
Information Technology
for Sharing Content

the same document as an email attachment, each changes it, and each sends back the changed document via email, different, incompatible versions of that document will be floating around. So, although email is simple, easy, and readily available, it will not suffice for collaborations in which there are many document versions or for which there is a desire for content control.

Another way to share content is to place it on a shared **file server**, which is simply a computer that stores files . . . just like the disk in your local computer. If your team has access to a file server, you can put documents on the server and others can download them, make changes, and upload them back onto the server. Often a technology called **FTP** is used to get and put documents (discussed in Chapter 6).

Storing documents on servers is better than using email attachments because documents have a single storage location. They are not scattered in different team members' email boxes. Team members have a known location for finding documents.

However, without any additional control it is possible for team members to interfere with one another's work. For example, suppose team members A and B download a document and edit it, but without knowing about the other's edits. Person A stores his version back on the server and then person B stores her version back on the server. In this scenario, person A's changes will be lost.

Furthermore, without any version management it will be impossible to know who changed the document and when. Neither person A nor person B will know whose version of the document is on the server. To avoid such problems, some form of version management is recommended.

Shared Content with Version Management

Systems that provide **version management** track changes to documents and provide features and functions to accommodate concurrent work. The means by which this is done depends on the particular system used. In this section, we consider three systems that you should consider for your team's work: wikis, Google Docs & Spreadsheets, and Microsoft Groove.

Wikis

The simplest version-management systems are wikis. A **wiki** (pronounced *we-key*) is a shared knowledge base in which the content is contributed and managed by the wiki's users. The most famous wiki is Wikipedia, a general encyclopedia available to the public (see Figure 2-9).

Collaborative teams can use wiki technology to create and maintain private wikis that serve as a repository of team knowledge. When a user contributes a wiki entry, the system tracks who created the entry and the date of creation. As others modify the entry, the wiki software tracks the identity of the modifier, the date, and possibly other data. Some users are given permission to delete wiki entries.

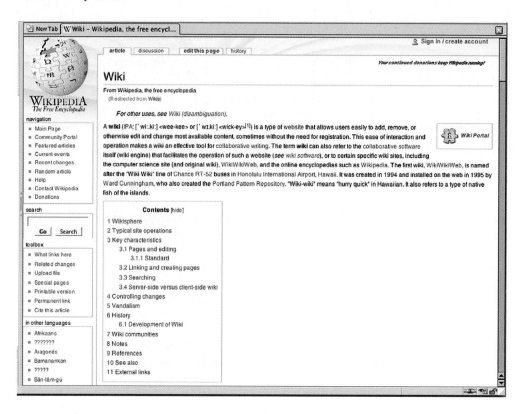

Figure 2-9
Wikipedia

Google Docs & Spreadsheets

As stated earlier, **Google Docs & Spreadsheets** is a collaboration application for sharing documents and spreadsheet data. (This application is rapidly evolving; by the time you read this, Google may have added additional file types or changed the system from what is described here. Google the name *Google Docs & Spreadsheets* to obtain the latest information about the application.)

With Google Docs & Spreadsheets, anyone who edits a document must have a Google account. (A Google account is not the same as a Gmail account.) You can establish a Google account using a Hotmail, a university, or any other email account. Your Google account will be affiliated with whatever email account you provide.

To create a Google document, go to *http://docs.google.com* (note there is no *www* in this address). Sign into (or create) your Google account. From that point on, you can upload documents and spreadsheets, share them with others, and download them to common file formats.

You can then make the document available to others by entering their email addresses (which need not be Google accounts). Those users are notified that the document exists and are given a link by which they can access it. If they have (or create) a Google account, they can edit the document as well.

With Google Docs & Spreadsheets, documents are stored on a Google server. Users can access the documents from Google and simultaneously see and edit documents. In the background, Google merges the users' activities into a single document. You are notified that another user is editing a document at the same time as you are, and you can refresh the document to see their latest changes. Google tracks document revisions, with brief summaries of changes made. Figure 2-10 shows a sample revision for a sample document that has been shared among three users.

Google Docs & Spreadsheets is free, and all documents must be processed by Google programs on its servers. A Microsoft Word or Excel document can be uploaded to a Google Docs & Spreadsheets server, but the document must be edited by Google programs. Documents can be saved in Word, Excel, or other common file formats.

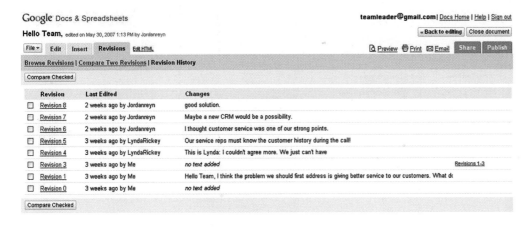

Figure 2-10
Sample Google Docs &
Spreadsheet Document
Versions

Source: GOOGLE Docs & Spreadsheets™.
GOOGLE is a trademark of Google Inc.

As of this writing, some common files, such as PowerPoint, cannot be shared. Again, that may change in the future, however.

Microsoft Office Groove

Microsoft Office Groove is a collaboration product that includes version management and other useful tools. Using Groove, a user creates a **workspace**, which is a collection of tools, documents, and users. The creator of the workspace invites others to join by sending them an email. The invitee accepts or declines the invitation. If the invitee accepts, he or she joins the workspace and can view all of the workspace content, including documents, schedules, drawings, announcements of meetings, and so forth.

Collaboration tools provide useful capabilities, but also some potential security risks. The Guide on pages 54–55 discusses these risks—and how to avoid them.

When a user changes a document, Groove automatically propagates that change to workspaces on other users' computers. If two users attempt to change the same document at the same time, Groove disallows one of them until the other is finished. Groove provides a wide number of tools, including document repositories, discussion forums, to-do lists, meeting agendas, drawing spaces, calendars, and other features. Whenever a team member makes changes to the workspace—say, adding a calendar or a file of drawings or setting up a sequence of meetings—Groove propagates those changes to all team members' computers.

Groove can be used synchronously or asynchronously. For the former, Groove supports multiuser text chat. It also uses **Voice over IP (VoIP)** (discussed in Chapter 6) to enable meeting participants to conduct telephone conversations using the Internet connection. No separate phone line is necessary.

Team members can use Groove asynchronously. Working alone, they can modify documents, leave messages for one another, create new tasks, and so forth. As other team members rejoin the workspace, Groove will show them all work that was done while they were away. Groove can be hosted on any personal computer, and it can also be hosted on a server. If on a server, then the workspace is always available. If on a personal computer, then the workspace is available only when that computer is connected to the Internet.

Figure 2-11 shows a sample Groove workspace. Shared files are listed in the middle column. The users in the workspace are listed in the pane in the upper right-hand corner, a chat session appears in the middle pane on the right-hand side, and a list of tasks appears in the lower right-hand corner.

The downside to Groove is that to participate all users must have purchased a license for Groove and have it installed on their computers. However, as stated earlier, if your university participates in the Microsoft Academic Alliance (and this is likely), you can obtain a license-free version of Groove through that program. Ask your instructor for more information.

Both Google Docs & Spreadsheets and Microsoft Groove are easy to set up and learn. Both are incredibly useful products that can make your collaborative work easier and result in higher-quality output. Take a look at them!

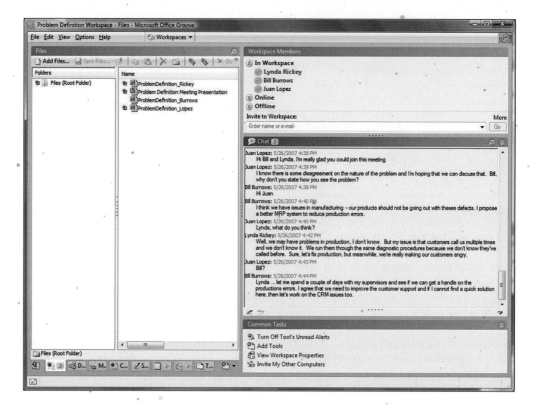

Figure 2-11
Example Groove Workspace

Source: Microsoft Office Groove Workspace.
Reprinted with permission from Microsoft
Corporation.

Shared Content with Version Control

Version-management systems improve the tracking of shared content and potentially eliminate problems caused by concurrent document access. They do not, however, provide **version control**. They do not limit the actions that can be taken by any particular user, and they do not give control over the changes to documents to particular users.

With version-control systems, each team member is given an account with a set of permissions. Shared documents are placed into shared directories, sometimes called **libraries**. For example, on a shared site with four libraries, a particular user might be given read-only permission for library 1; read and edit permission for library 2; read, edit, and delete permission for library 3; and no permission even to see library 4.

Furthermore, document directories can be set up so that users are required to check out documents before they can modify them. When a document is checked out, no other user can obtain it for the purpose of editing it. Once the document has been checked in, other users can obtain it for editing. Figure 2-12 shows a user (Lori McGovern—see the welcome message in the top banner of the screen) checking out a document named Problem_Definition_Rickey. Of course, for the system to allow the checkout the user must have permission to edit that document.

Numerous version-control applications exist. **Microsoft SharePoint** is the most popular for general business use. Other document-control systems include MasterControl (*www.mastercontrol.com*) and Document Locator (*www.documentlocator.com*). Software development teams use applications such as CVS (*www. nongnu.org/cvs/*) or Subversion (*subversion.tigris.org*) to control versions of software code, test plans, and product documentation.

By the way, SharePoint includes many collaboration features and functions besides document check-in/checkout. In addition to support for document libraries and lists, it has features for creating and managing the following team work products: surveys, discussion forums, wikis, member blogs, member Web sites, and workflow (see next section).

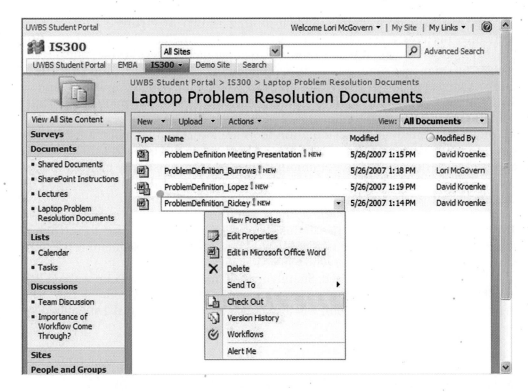

Figure 2-12
Example of Document
Checkout

Source: Microsoft Office SharePoint Designer
2007. Reprinted with permission from Microsoft
Corporation.

For any but the most trivial team project, SharePoint is exceedingly useful. Unfortunately, installing SharePoint requires a publicly accessible server and more skill, experience, and knowledge than most college students are likely to have. If you are interested in using SharePoint, talk to your instructor. He or she can arrange for Pearson (publisher of this text) to pay for free SharePoint hosting for your class, as mentioned in Q2.

Q5 How Can You Use Collaboration Systems to Control Workflow?

So far you have learned how information systems can be used to facilitate team communication and manage content. It is possible to gain even more control by using information systems to manage workflow.

Figure 2-13 shows a simple workflow example. This workflow is called a **sequential workflow** because activities occur in sequence. First, Burrows reviews the document, then McGovern, and finally Reynolds, one after the other in sequence. In a **parallel workflow**, the reviews would occur simultaneously. There are numerous other types of workflow that we will not consider here.[3]

Figure 2-13
Sample Sequential Workflow

---

[3]For more information about workflows and the Windows Workflow Foundation, see David Mann, *Workflow in the 2007 Microsoft Office System* (New York: Apress, 2007).

You *can* manage a workflow such as that shown in Figure 2-13 manually. Someone, perhaps the group's manager, sends an email to Burrows requesting the review, possibly with the document as an attachment. After Burrows finishes the review, the manager sends the reviewed document to McGovern, and so forth. If Burrows forgets to do the review, the manager would send a follow-up email, and so forth. As you can imagine, manual enforcement of workflows any more complicated than this one becomes an administrative nightmare.

However, a number of collaboration tools are available that will manage workflows for you. Microsoft SharePoint is one. Look again at Figure 2-12. The user is about to click the *Check Out* command. However, from this same menu, the user could also click *Workflows* (two commands below *Check Out*) to define a workflow on this document.

If the user were to click *Workflow,* the screen shown in Figure 2-14 would appear. The user would fill out the entries in this form and in the one in Figure 2-15 to define the workflow. Note in Figure 2-15 that the workflow is defined as sequential; the form is also used to identify the users who will review the document.

Once this workflow is defined, SharePoint will manage it. SharePoint will send an email to Burrows requesting the review and a copy of that email to the person who defined this workflow. SharePoint will also create a task in a new task list defined for

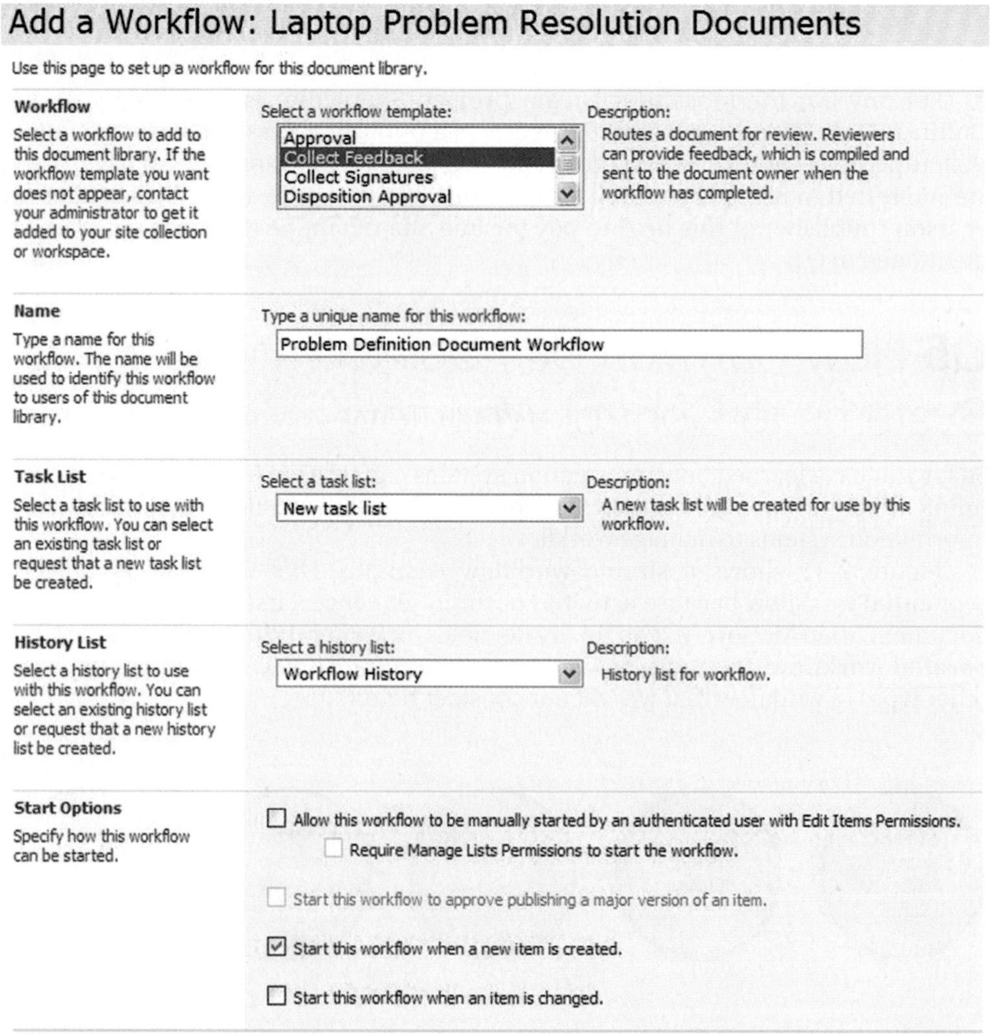

Figure 2-14
Defining a SharePoint
Workflow, Part 1

Source: Microsoft Office SharePoint Designer 2007. Reprinted with permission from Microsoft Corporation.

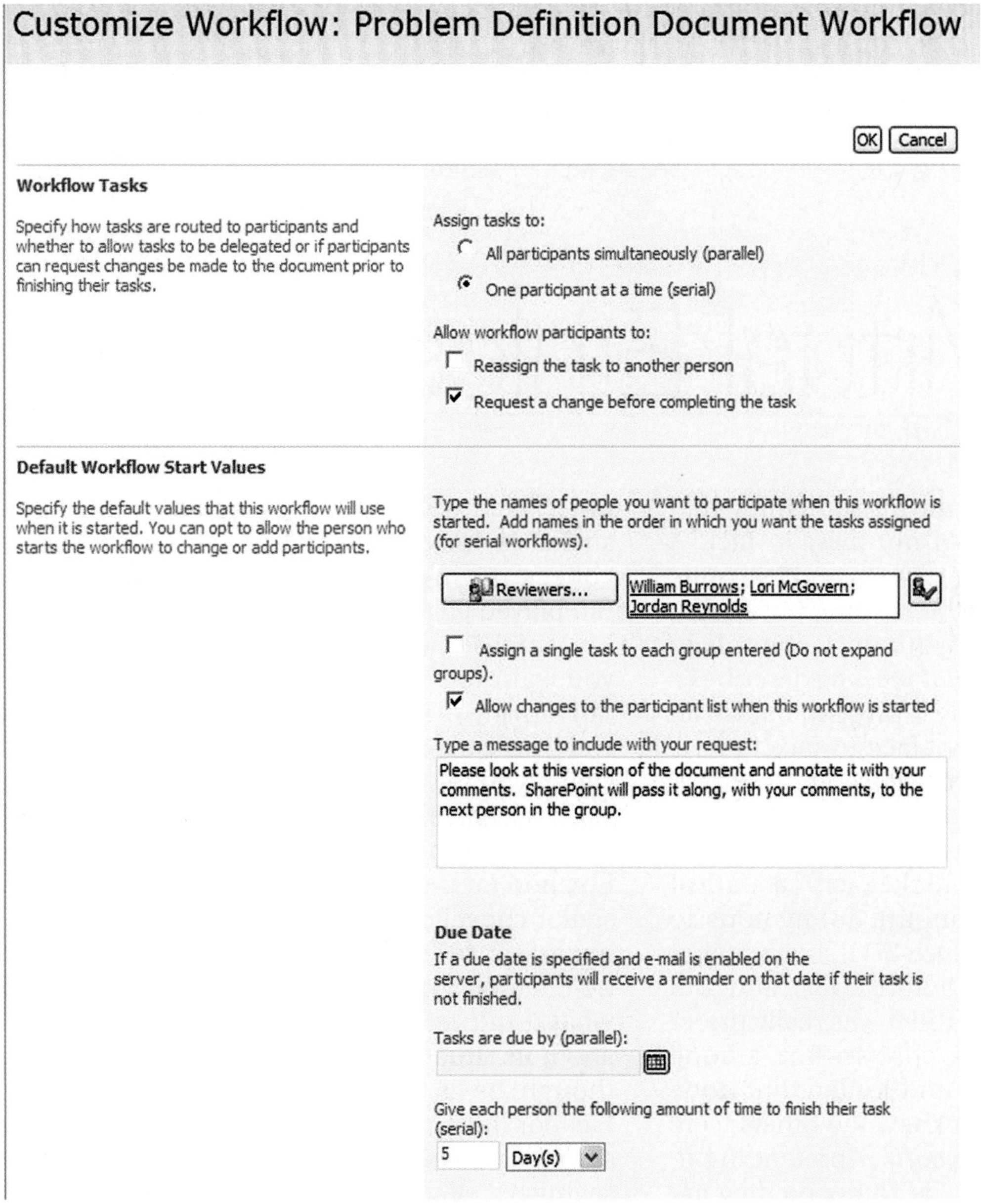

Customize Workflow: Problem Definition Document Workflow

[OK] [Cancel]

Workflow Tasks

Specify how tasks are routed to participants and whether to allow tasks to be delegated or if participants can request changes be made to the document prior to finishing their tasks.

Assign tasks to:
○ All participants simultaneously (parallel)
◉ One participant at a time (serial)

Allow workflow participants to:
☐ Reassign the task to another person
☑ Request a change before completing the task

Default Workflow Start Values

Specify the default values that this workflow will use when it is started. You can opt to allow the person who starts the workflow to change or add participants.

Type the names of people you want to participate when this workflow is started. Add names in the order in which you want the tasks assigned (for serial workflows).

[Reviewers...] [William Burrows; Lori McGovern; Jordan Reynolds]

☐ Assign a single task to each group entered (Do not expand groups).
☑ Allow changes to the participant list when this workflow is started

Type a message to include with your request:

Please look at this version of the document and annotate it with your comments. SharePoint will pass it along, with your comments, to the next person in the group.

Due Date

If a due date is specified and e-mail is enabled on the server, participants will receive a reminder on that date if their task is not finished.

Tasks are due by (parallel):
[_____] 📅

Give each person the following amount of time to finish their task (serial):
[5] [Day(s) ▾]

Figure 2-15
Defining a SharePoint Workflow, Part 2

Source: Microsoft Office SharePoint Designer 2007. Reprinted with permission from Microsoft Corporation.

this workflow. When Burrows completes his review, he will check the document back in, and SharePoint will mark the task as complete and send an email to McGovern, requesting her review. Copies of these emails will be sent to the workflow creator. If Burrows does not complete the task within 5 days (see the bottom of the form in Figure 2-15), SharePoint will send him a reminder as well as an advisory email to the creator of the workflow.

If you create a **SharePoint site**, you can define workflows just like this for your group. You can use this capability to ensure that all of your teammates perform the work they are requested to do.

By the way, SharePoint has several other default workflows that you can use. With some time and patience, you can also learn how to define custom workflows using Windows Office SharePoint Designer. And, if you are a programmer, you can use Visual Studio to create custom workflows that are limited only by your knowledge and programming skill.

Ethics

Virtual Ethics?

The term *virtual* means something that appears to exist but does not exist in fact. A *virtual private network (VPN)* is an electronic network that appears to be private, but in fact operates on a public network (more on this in Chapter 6). The term *virtual meeting* describes a meeting in which everyone is present, but via an information system and not face-to-face.

However, and it is a big *however*, "Is everyone present?" Is the person who signed on as Lynda Rickey truly Lynda Rickey? Or is it someone else? Or is it Lynda Rickey with a staff of seven people, all of whom are anonymous to the rest of the group? Figure 2-11 shows a chat session among Lynda, Juan Lopez, and Bill Burrows. What if none of them was really there? What if, in fact, it was a chat session among Ashley, Haley, and Jordan, but none of them knew the others were *spoofing* (pretending to be someone they are

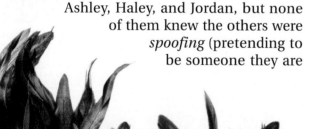

not)? What if Jordan was actually Bill's son sitting in his organizational behavior class at college, giving noncommittal answers, while Bill played golf?

Suppose you run a consulting company and you want to send less experienced consultants out on jobs. During an initial meeting (held electronically, using text chat) with a potential client, you tell the client that he is meeting with Drew Suenas, a new and inexperienced employee. But, the meeting actually includes Drew and Eleanor Jackson, your most experienced and senior consultant. During the meeting, all of the remarks attributed to Drew were actually made by Eleanor. The client is most impressed with what it thinks are Drew's perceptive comments about its situation and agrees to hire Drew, even though he is inexperienced. You keep using Eleanor this way, spoofing several of your young associates to get jobs for them. You justify this by saying, "Well, if they get into trouble, we'll send Eleanor out to fix the problem."

Consider another possibility. For the Groove meeting in Figure 2-11, suppose you disagree strongly with Bill Burrows' position. If you are setting up the meeting, what if you decide not to send Bill an invite? He does not know the meeting is scheduled, so he does not appear. Much to your joy, issues on which you disagree with him go unaddressed. During the meeting, you remain silent when people ask, "I wonder why Bill isn't here?"

Or, suppose you have an archrival, Ashley. You and Ashley compete for a future promotion, and you just cannot stand the idea of her moving ahead of you. So you set up a sequence of virtual meetings, but you never invite Ashley. Then, just before a crucial meeting, one that involves senior members of your organization, you invite Ashley to be your silent helper. You tell her you do not have the authority to invite her, but you want her to have a chance to express her thoughts. So you attend the meeting and you incorporate Ashley's thinking into your chat comments. People think you are the sole author of those ideas and are impressed. Ashley's work is never attributed to her.

Or, let's bring it closer to home. Suppose you take online tests as part of your class. What keeps you from taking the test with your brother, who happens to work for Google as a product manager for Google Docs & Spreadsheets? Suppose you take the test by yourself, but you believe others are taking their tests with silent helpers. Given that belief, are you justified in finding your own helper?

What do you think? Are your ethics virtual? ■

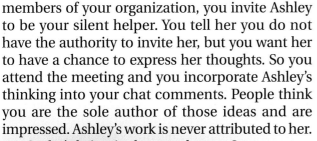

Discussion Questions

1. Is it *illegal* to spoof someone? Does it matter whether you have that person's permission to spoof them?

2. Is it *ethical* to spoof someone? Does it matter whether you have that person's permission?

3. Under what circumstances do you believe it is ethical to spoof someone?

4. Consider the meeting in which everyone was spoofing and no one knew it. What are the consequences to the organization of such a meeting? What happens when Bill meets Lynda in the hallway and Lynda asks, "What did you think of our meeting?" Who has the knowledge of the meeting? Who knows that they have that knowledge?

5. Considering Eleanor's spoofing of young associates, what is different between text chat and a speaker phone? Haven't we always had these problems, except Eleanor was passing notes and making comments while the phone was muted? What behavior should you follow when talking with someone who is on a speaker phone?

6. Is it ethical not to invite Bill to the meeting? Assume no one has asked you if you sent the invitation to him.

7. Is it cheating to have a helper on an online test? Are you justified if everyone else is doing it? What control is possible for online tests? Should such tests be used at all?

Q6 How Do Businesses Use Collaboration Systems?

So far we've focused on using collaboration systems to manage team projects in school. This is interesting and useful to you, but such tools were not developed solely to benefit students. They were developed to help collaborative groups in businesses accomplish their goals and objectives. The balance of this chapter discusses how businesses use collaboration systems for problem solving, project management, and decision making.

Using Collaboration Systems for Problem Solving

A **problem** is a perceived difference between what is and what ought to be. As a perception, it is a view held by an individual or a group. Because it is a perception, different users and groups can have different definitions of a problem. Often the most difficult part of solving a problem isn't finding a solution; it's getting everyone to agree on a common definition.

See the Guide on pages 56–57 to learn one technique that business professionals use to obtain a common definition of a problem. That technique requires effective communication, and any of the tools that you learned in Q3 can be used to that effect. Document libraries and Wikis can be used to record problem definitions, once they are agreed upon.

Consider the FlexTime meeting that started this chapter. Tara would likely define the problem as Felix doesn't regularly come to meetings. Felix would define the problem as the team is focused on cost savings when it should be focused on revenue. Other team members might have other definitions.

Using Collaboration Systems for Project Management

Businesses use collaboration tools for project management in the same ways that you will use them. The basic tasks shown in Figure 2-2 pertain to business projects just as much as they pertain to your projects. Consider Figure 2-16, which shows collaboration tools used in business for the tasks identified in Figure 2-2.

If you examine this list, you can see that email, file servers, and Google Docs & Spreadsheets provide just a portion of these capabilities. That fact is one of the

Figure 2-16
Procedures and Decisions for Project Phases

Phase	Tasks to Accomplish	Possible Collaboration Tools
Starting	What is the team's authority? What is the purpose of the team? Who is on the team? What is expected from team members? What are team members' roles and authorities?	Surveys Discussion lists Document libraries Webinar Text chat sessions
Planning	What tasks need to be accomplished? How are the tasks related to one another? Who is responsible for each task? When will tasks be completed?	Tasks lists Document libraries Webinar Text chat sessions
Doing	Executing project tasks Task status reporting Managing exceptions	Task lists (updated) Document libraries Discussion lists Wikis
Wrapping-up	Are we done? Documenting team results Documenting team learnings for future teams Closing down the project	Survey Discussion lists Webinar Wikis Document libraries

reasons that Microsoft SharePoint has had the fastest revenue growth of any product in Microsoft's history. In April 2009, SharePoint had more than 600 million users, worldwide. Consequently, it is a tool that every business professional should learn to use.

Using Collaboration Systems for Decision Making

Collaboration systems are used for certain types of decision making, but not all. So, to understand the role for collaboration we must first begin with an analysis of decision making. As Figure 2-17 shows, decisions occur at three levels in organizations: *operational, managerial,* and *strategic.* The types of decisions vary, depending on the level.

Operational decisions concern day-to-day activities. Typical operational decisions are: How many widgets should we order from vendor A? Should we extend credit to vendor B? Which invoices should we pay today? Information systems that support operational decision making are called **transaction processing systems (TPS).** In most cases, operational decisions require little in the way of collaboration.

Managerial decisions concern the allocation and utilization of resources. Typical managerial decisions are: How much should we budget for computer hardware and programs for department A next year? How many engineers should we assign to project B? How many square feet of warehouse space do we need for the coming year?

If a managerial decision requires consideration of different perspectives, then it necessitates team feedback and iteration, and will benefit from collaboration. Consider the decision of how much to increase employee pay in the coming year. No single individual has the answer. The decision depends on an analysis of inflation, industry trends, the organization's profitability, the influence of unions, and other factors. Senior managers, accountants, human resources personnel, labor relationships managers, and others will each bring a different perspective to the decision. They will produce work product, evaluate that product, and make revisions in an iterative fashion—the essence of collaboration.

Strategic decisions concern broader-scope, organizational issues. Typical decisions at the strategic level are: Should we start a new product line? Should we open a centralized warehouse in Tennessee? Should we acquire company A?

Strategic decisions are almost always collaborative. Consider a decision about whether to move manufacturing operations to China. This decision affects every employee in the organization, the organization's suppliers, its customers, and its shareholders. Many factors and many perspectives on each of those factors must be considered. Feedback and iteration will be crucial to this decision.

The Decision Process

Figure 2-18 also shows levels of information systems with two decision processes: *structured* and *unstructured.* These terms refer to the method or process by which the decision is to be made, not to the nature of the underlying problem. A **structured decision** process is one for which there is an understood and accepted method for

- **Decision Level**
  - Operational
  - Managerial
  - Strategic
- **Decision Process**
  - Structured
  - Unstructured

Figure 2-17
Decision-Making Dimensions

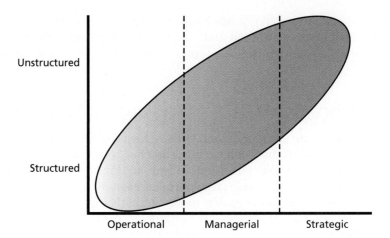

Figure 2-18
Decision Process
and Decision Type

making the decision. A formula for computing the reorder quantity of an item in inventory is an example of a structured decision process. A standard method for allocating furniture and equipment to employees is another structured decision process. Structured decisions seldom require collaboration.

An **unstructured decision** process is one for which there is no agreed-on decision-making method. Predicting the future direction of the economy or the stock market is a classic example. The prediction method varies from person to person; it is neither standardized nor broadly accepted. Another example of an unstructured decision process is assessing how well-suited an employee is for performing a particular job. Managers vary in the manner in which they make such assessments. Unstructured decisions are often collaborative.

The Relationship Between Decision Type and Decision Process

The decision type and decision process are loosely related. As Figure 2-18 shows, decisions at the operational level tend to be structured, and decisions at the strategic level tend to be unstructured. Managerial decisions tend to be both structured and unstructured.

We use the words *tend to be*, because there are exceptions to the relationship illustrated in Figure 2-18. Some operational decisions are unstructured (e.g., "How many taxicab drivers do we need on the night before the homecoming game?"), and some strategic decisions can be structured (e.g., "How should we assign sales quotas for a new product?"). In general, however, the relationship shown in Figure 2-18 holds.

Decision Making and Collaboration Systems

As stated, few structured decisions involve collaboration. Deciding, for example, how much of product A to order from vendor B does not require the feedback and iteration among members that typify collaboration. Although the process of generating the order might require the coordinated work of people in purchasing, accounting, and manufacturing, there is seldom a need for one person to comment on someone else's work. In fact, involving collaboration in routine, structured decisions is expensive, wasteful, and frustrating. "Do we have to have a meeting about everything?" is a common lament.

The situation is different for unstructured decisions, because feedback and iteration are crucial. Members bring different ideas and perspectives about what is to be decided, how the decision will be reached, what criteria are important, and how decision alternatives score against those criteria. The group may make tentative

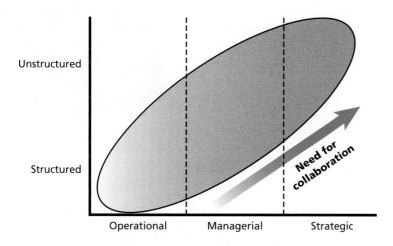

Figure 2-19
Collaboration Needs
for Decision Types

conclusions, discuss potential outcomes of those conclusions, and members will often revise their positions. Figure 2-19 illustrates the change in the need for collaboration as decision processes become less structured.

Q7 2020?

So, how will we collaborate in 2020? Where will the current trends take us? Clearly, free data communications and data storage will make collaboration systems cheaper and easier to use. One consequence is that by 2020 **face-to-face (F2F) meetings** will be rare.

F2F meetings require everyone to be in the same place at the same time, and both of those *sames* can be problematic. When employees work in different locations, bringing them together is expensive in travel cost and time. Employees standing in line in airport security or waiting in their cars in traffic are hardly productive. And, bringing everyone together is unfriendly to the environment.

Even when employees work at the same location, they may have schedule conflicts, or, like the employees at FlexTime at the start of this chapter, they may not work at that location at the same time. And, unless employees are providing an in-person service, such as physical training, or surgery, or construction, why do they need to work in the same location?

Furthermore, what happens when you finally do get employees together? Say you bring the top managers into the home office for training? They no sooner sit down then their cell phones ring, and off they go to the lobby to handle some raging problem. Twenty minutes later, they're back for another 5 minutes before their phones ring again. Meanwhile, a good portion of the managers who stayed in the meeting are texting their offices throughout the training.

In 2020, employees whose services need not be provided in person will work at home, if not full time, then at least several days a week. Nearly all corporate training will be online. Most will be asynchronous.

Business travel will be a shadow of its former self. The travel industry will reorganize for near-exclusive recreational travel. Even conventions will become, well, virtual.

Because of these trends, now is a great time for you to learn online, asynchronous, collaboration skills. And, when you are buying commercial real estate, buy that hotel in Hawaii, not the one in Paramus, New Jersey (unless, of course, it has a water slide for kids, a spa, a nearby golf course, and a casino)!

Securing Collaboration

The collaboration tools described in this chapter do indeed facilitate collaboration: They help groups improve the quality of their work, while reducing travel and other logistical expenses, and they can enable people to participate in meetings asynchronously. However, they also pose security risks—possibly serious ones.

Consider Google Docs & Spreadsheets. All documents are stored on Google computers, which are located, well, who knows where. Does Google protect those computers appropriately? If those computers are located in, say, San Francisco, will they survive an earthquake? Google is a responsible, rich, and knowledgeable company that understands the need for disaster preparedness. But, as outsiders, we do not know how they protect their sites. Natural disasters are not the only threat; computer crime, the actions of disgruntled employees, and computer **viruses** (computer programs that replicate themselves) must be considered as well.

But, chances are—even that phrase is revealing, do you really want to gamble with your data?— Google knows what it is doing, and your data is more than reasonably protected. However, how does the data get to a Google site? As you will learn in Chapter 6, most wireless traffic, including Google Docs & Spreadsheets, is unprotected from wireless snoopers. Are you processing that data at a local coffee shop? Do you care that anyone in that shop can copy your data?

Wireless snooping is not possible with Groove. All communications between your computer and the other Groove sites are automatically protected using up-to-date encryption technology (again, more to come in Chapter 6). No snooper can obtain your data. But Groove poses substantial security risks of a different kind.

Suppose you are the manager of a product line and you observe an odd pattern in sales for your products. That pattern might be related to differences in advertising among geographic regions, or it might have something to do with changes in consumer-purchasing behavior. You decide to have a Groove meeting with some of your staff, employees of your advertising agency, and a marketing guru who specializes in contemporary consumer behavior.

To prepare for the meeting, you access your corporate computer systems and obtain all of the sales for your products over the past 12 months. That data is highly confidential and is protected by your IS department in many ways. You can access it only because you have access authority as an employee. But, without thinking about security, you post that data in a Groove workspace so that both your advertising agency and the marketing guru can view it. You have just violated corporate security. That confidential data is now available to the agency and the consultant. Either party can copy it, and you have no way of knowing that the copy was made or what was done with it.

Suppose the marketing guru makes a copy and uses it to improve her knowledge of consumer behavior. Unknown to you, she also consults for your chief rival. She has used your data to improve her knowledge and is now using that knowledge to benefit your competitor. (This sets aside the even uglier possibility that she gives or sells your data to that competitor.)

SharePoint has extensive security features, and as long as the administrator of your SharePoint site has implemented a proper security plan it should be well protected. But, of course, SharePoint makes it easy to download data, and if you share that data with others via Google Docs & Spreadsheets or Groove . . . well, you get the picture.

Collaboration tools have many benefits, but they do open the door to loss of critical assets. Let the collaborator beware! ∎

Discussion Questions

1. Any email or instant message that you send over a wireless device is open. Anyone with some free software and a bit of knowledge can snoop on your communications. In class, your professor could read all of your email and instant messages, as could anyone else in the class. Does this knowledge change your behavior in class? Why or why not?

2. Unless you are so foolish as to reveal personal data, such as credit card numbers, Social Security number, or a driver's license number in an email or instant message, the loss of privacy to you as an individual is small. Someone might learn that you were gossiping about someone else and it might be embarrassing, but that loss is not critical. How does that situation change for business communications? Describe losses, other than those in this Guide, that could occur when using email or Google Docs & Spreadsheets.

3. In addition to Google Docs & Spreadsheets, Google offers Gmail, a free email service with an easy-to-use interface and that famous Google search capability. Using Gmail, searching through past emails is very easy, fast, and accurate. In addition, because mail is stored on Google computers, it is easy to access one's email, contacts, and other data from any computer at any location. Many employees prefer using Gmail to their corporate email system. What are the consequences to the organization of some employees doing most of their email via Gmail? What are the risks?

4. Summarize the risks of using Groove in a business setting. How can organizations protect themselves from such risks? Is there any new risk here? After all, organizations have been sharing data in other formats with their business partners for years. Is this much ado about nothing? Why or why not?

5. Do you think the risks of using Groove can be so large that it makes sense for organizations to disallow its use? Why or why not? What are the costs of disallowing such use? How would the organization prevent an employee from purchasing a license for Groove and installing it on his own laptop computer at home? If the employee said that he needs it for work that does not involve corporate data, how should the organization respond?

Egocentric Versus Empathetic Thinking

As stated earlier, a problem is a perceived difference between what is and what ought to be. When developing information systems, it is critical for the development team to have a common definition and understanding of the problem. This common understanding can be difficult to achieve, however.

Cognitive scientists distinguish between egocentric and empathetic thinking. Egocentric thinking centers on the self; someone who engages in egocentric thinking considers his or her view as "the real view" or "what really is." In contrast, those who engage in empathetic thinking consider their view as one possible interpretation of the situation and actively work to learn what other people are thinking.

Different experts recommend empathetic thinking for different reasons. Religious leaders say that such thinking is morally superior; psychologists say that empathetic thinking leads to richer, more fulfilling relationships. In business, empathetic thinking is recommended because it is smart. Business is a social endeavor, and those who can understand others' points of view are always more effective. Even if you do not agree with others' perspectives, you will be much better able to work with them if you understand their views.

Consider an example. Suppose you say to your MIS professor, "Professor Jones, I couldn't come to class last Monday. Did we do anything important?" Such a statement is a prime example of egocentric thinking. It takes no account of your professor's point of view and implies that your professor talked about nothing important. As a professor, it is tempting to say, "No, when I noticed you weren't there, I took out all the important material."

To engage in empathetic thinking, consider this situation from the professor's point of view. Students who do not come to class cause extra work for their professors. It does not matter how valid your reason for not attending class; you may actually have been contagious with a fever of 102. But, no matter what, your not coming to class is more work for your professor. He

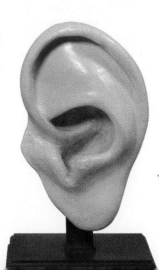

or she must do something extra to help you recover from the lost class time.

Using empathetic thinking, you would do all you can to minimize the impact of your absence on your professor. For example, you could say, "I couldn't come to class, but I got the class notes from Mary. I read through them, and I have a question about establishing alliances as competitive advantage.... Oh, by the way, I'm sorry to trouble you with my problem."

Before we go on, let's consider a corollary to this scenario: Never, ever, send an email to your boss that says, "I couldn't come to the staff meeting on Wednesday. Did we do anything important?" Avoid this for the same reasons as those for missing class. Instead, find a way to minimize the impact of your absence on your boss.

Now, what does all of this have to do with MIS? Consider the FlexTime team at the start of this chapter. What is the problem? Tara thinks it's Felix's not coming to meetings. Felix thinks the team is focused on costs and should focus on increasing sales. We're not sure how Jan sees the problem. Kelly, once she understands what is going on, is likely to be focused on wasted employee time.

Now imagine yourself in that meeting. If everyone engages in egocentric thinking, what will happen? The meeting will be argumentative and acrimonious and likely will end with nothing accomplished.

Suppose, instead, that the attendees think empathetically. In this case, Tara may make an effort to find out why Felix is missing meetings. Felix would make an effort to understand why his behavior is a problem to the team. The team would make a concerted effort to address the different points of view, and the outcome will be much more positive—possibly a recognition that the team should be meeting virtually and asynchronously. Either way, the attendees have the same information; the difference in outcomes results from the thinking style of the attendees.

Empathetic thinking is an important skill in all business activities. Skilled negotiators always know what the other side wants; effective

salespeople understand their customers' needs. Buyers who understand the problems of their vendors get better service. And students who understand the perspective of their professors get better . . . ■

Discussion Questions

1. In your own words, explain how egocentric and empathetic thinking differ.

2. Suppose you miss a staff meeting. Using empathetic thinking, explain how you can get needed information about what took place in the meeting.

3. How does empathetic thinking relate to problem definition?

4. Suppose you and another person differ substantially on a problem definition. Suppose she says to you, "No, the real problem is that . . ." followed by her definition of the problem. How do you respond?

5. Again, suppose you and another person differ substantially on a problem definition. Assume you understand his definition. How can you make that fact clear?

6. Explain the following statement: "In business, empathetic thinking is smart." Do you agree?

ACTIVE REVIEW

Use this Active Review to verify that you understand the ideas and concepts that answer the chapter's study questions.

Q1 What is collaboration?

Define *collaboration*. Explain how collaboration, communication, and coordination differ. Describe the role that feedback and iteration play in collaboration. Describe a team project that is cooperative but not collaborative. Name the three drivers of collaboration effectiveness and explain each.

Q2 What are the components of a collaboration information system?

Name the five components of an information system. Name two types of hardware and explain the role for each. Name the three collaboration programs discussed in this text and summarize their basic functionality. Describe five different types of collaboration data. Explain how iteration and feedback plays a role in the tasks for each of the four project phases in Figure 2-2. Name five of the most important characteristics of a good collaborator. Explain why it makes sense that 5 of the top 12 involve disagreement.

Q3 How can you use collaboration systems to improve team communication?

Explain why communication is important to student collaborations. Define *synchronous* and *asynchronous* communication, and explain when each is used. Name two collaboration tools that can be used to help set up synchronous meetings. Describe collaboration tools that can be used for face-to-face meetings. Describe tools that can be used for virtual, synchronous meetings. Describe tools that can be used for virtual, asynchronous meetings. Compare and contrast the advantages of email, discussion forums, and team surveys.

Q4 How can you use collaboration systems to manage content?

Describe two ways that content is shared with no control, and explain the problems that can occur. Explain how control is provided by the following collaboration tools: wikis, Google Docs & Spreadsheets, and Microsoft Groove. Define *workspace*, and explain how Groove uses workspaces. Explain the difference between version management and version control. Describe how user accounts, passwords, and libraries are used to control user activity. Explain how check-in/checkout works. Identify major features in Microsoft SharePoint.

Q5 How can you use collaboration systems to control workflow?

Explain the difference between content management and workflow control. Give an example of a sequential workflow. Describe why manual enforcement of workflow is an administrative nightmare. Explain how Microsoft SharePoint can be used to enforce sequential workflow.

Q6 How do businesses use collaboration systems?

Define *problem*. Explain the importance of the fact that a problem is a perception; use the example of the FlexTime meeting in your answer. Describe the ways that collaboration systems can be used for problem solving. Explain one use for each of the collaboration tools listed in Figure 2-16. Name three levels of decision making, and give an example of each. Describe the difference between structured and unstructured decision making, and give an example of each. Explain how the need for collaboration changes among decision levels and decision processes.

Q7 2020?

Describe the impact that free data storage and data communications have on collaboration systems. Describe the consequences for F2F meetings. Explain why F2F meetings are expensive in both cost and time. Explain why meetings such as F2F training sessions can be ineffective. Describe consequences of all this to the travel industry. If you disagree with any of the conclusions in this 2020, explain how and why.

KEY TERMS AND CONCEPTS

USING YOUR KNOWLEDGE

1. Reread about 2020 in Q7. Do you agree with the conclusions? Why or why not? If F2F meetings become rare, what additional impacts do you see on the travel industry? In light of this change, describe travel industry investments that make sense and those that do not. What are promising investments in training? What are promising investments in other industries?

2. This exercise requires you to experiment with Google Docs & Spreadsheets. You will need two Google accounts to complete this exercise. If you have two different email addresses, then set up two Google accounts using those addresses. Otherwise, use your school email address and set up a Google Gmail account. A Gmail account will automatically give you a Google account.

   a. Using Microsoft Word, write a memo to yourself. In the memo, explain the nature of the communication-collaboration driver. Go to *http://docs.google. com* and sign in with one of your Google accounts. Upload your memo using Google Docs & Spreadsheets. Save your uploaded document, and share your document with the email in your second Google account. Sign out of your first Google account.

      (If you have access to two computers situated close to each other, use both of them for this exercise. You will see more of the Google Docs & Spreadsheets functionality by using two computers. If you have two computers, do not sign out of your Google account. Perform step b and all actions for the second account on that second computer. If you are using two computers, ignore the instructions to sign out of the Google accounts in the following steps.)

   b. Open a new window in your browser. Access *http://docs.google.com* from that second window and sign in using your second Google account. Open the document that you shared in step a.

   c. Change the memo by adding a brief description of the content-management driver. Save the document from your second account. If you are using just one computer, sign out from your second account.

   d. Sign in on your first account. Open the most recent version of the memo and add a description of the workflow-control communication driver. Save the document. (If you are using two computers, notice how Google warns you that another user is editing the document at the same time. Click *Refresh* to see what happens.) If you are using just one computer, sign out from your first account.

   e. Sign in on your second account. Re-open the shared document. From the File menu, save the document as a Word document.

   f. Describe how Google processed the changes to your document.

3. This exercise requires you to experiment with Microsoft Office Groove. To perform it, you need to work with a classmate. Both you and your classmate must install a copy of Microsoft Office Groove. Check with your instructor to learn how to download a license-free version using the MSDN Academic Alliance. In the following steps, one of you should take the role of user A and the other should take the role of user B.

   a. User A should open the Groove launch bar and create a new workspace. Select *Standard*. In the lower right-hand section of the new workspace, invite user B to join the workspace by entering user B's email address. While you are waiting for user B to respond, use Word to write a memo briefly summarizing the need for version management. Save the memo using the file name *VersionManagement* and add it to the workspace by clicking *Add Files*.

   b. User B will receive an invitation to join the workspace. All user B needs to do is to click the link provided. The workspace will open. User B should write a memo summarizing the need for version control. Save that memo with the name *Version Control* and add it to the workspace.

c. User A should then open the chat window in the lower right-hand corner and enter a chat message asking user B to read *VersionManagement* and make comments.

d. User B should respond to user A's chat and send a chat message to user A asking for a review of *VersionControl*. Make a few changes and save the document.

e. User A should open and review *VersionManagement*. User B should open and review *VersionControl*. Make a few changes and save the document.

f. Using chat, coordinate your efforts so that both users attempt to open the same document at the same time. Note what happens.

g. Add a sketchpad tool to the workspace by clicking the icon (in the lower right-of-center section of the

workspace) that shows a document and a green plus sign and selecting *Sketchpad*.

h. Using chat, coordinate your efforts to modify the sketch at the same time. Note what happens.

i. Using chat, describe your experiences. Both users should comment on what they have seen.

j. Save your chat transcript as a file. Right-click in the chat window and select *Chat/Print transcript*. In the print window, select *print to file*. Submit your chat transcript as your answer to this exercise.

4. If your instructor has enabled a Microsoft SharePoint site for your class, you can perform exercises using SharePoint. Go to *www.pearsonhighered.com/kroenke* and find the file *Chapter 2 SharePoint Exercises*. Perform the exercises shown there.

COLLABORATION EXERCISE

With a team of your fellow students, develop an answer to the following four questions. Use Google Docs & Spreadsheets, Groove, SharePoint, or some other collaboration system to conduct your meetings.

a. What is collaboration? Reread Q1 in this chapter, but do not confine yourselves to that discussion. Consider your own experience working in collaborative teams, and search the Web to identify other ideas about collaboration. Dave Pollard, one of the authors of the survey that Figure 2-3 is based on, is a font of ideas on collaboration.

b. What characteristics make for an effective team member? Review the survey of effective collaboration skills in Figure 2-3 and discuss them as a group. Do you agree with them? What conclusions can you, as a team, take from this survey? Would

you change the rankings? Are important characteristics missing?

c. What would you do with an ineffective team member? Define an *ineffective team member*. Specify five or so characteristics of an ineffective team member. If your group has such a member, what action do you, as a group, believe should be taken?

d. How do you know if you are collaborating well? When working with a group, how do you know whether you are working well or poorly? Specify five or so characteristics that indicate collaborative success. How can you measure those characteristics?

Deliver your answers to these four questions to your instructor in the format required—on paper, as a Groove workspace, as a SharePoint site, or some other innovative format.

APPLICATION EXERCISES

1. Suppose that you have been asked to assist in the managerial decision about how much to increase pay in the next year. Assume you are given a list of the departments in your company, along with the average salary for employees in that department for major companies in your industry. Additionally, you are given the names and salaries of 10 people in each of three departments in your company.

Assume you have been asked to create a spreadsheet that shows the names of the 10 employees in each department, their current salary, the difference between their current salary and the industry average salary for their department, and the percent their salary would need to be increased to meet the industry

average. Your spreadsheet should also compute the average increase needed to meet the industry average for each department and the average increase, company-wide, to meet industry averages.

a. Use the data in the file **Ch2Ex1.doc** and create the spreadsheet.

b. How can you use this analysis to contribute to the employee salary decision? Based on this data, what conclusions can you make?

c. Suppose other team members want to use your spreadsheet. Name three ways you can share it with them and describe the advantages and disadvantages of each.

2. **A** Suppose that you have been asked to assist in the managerial decision about how much to increase pay in the next year. Specifically, you are tasked to determine if there are significant salary differences among departments in your company.

You are given an Access database with a table of employee data with the following structure:

EMPLOYEE (Name, Department, Specialty, Salary)

where *Name* is the name of an employee who works in a department, *Department* is the department name, *Specialty* is the name of the employee's primary skill, and *Salary* is the employee's current salary. Assume that no two employees have the same name. You have been asked to answer the following queries:

(1) List the names, department, and salary of all employees earning more than $100,000.

(2) List the names and specialties of all employees in the Marketing department.

(3) Compute the average, maximum, and minimum salary of employees in your company.

(4) Compute the average, minimum, and maximum salary of employees in the Marketing department.

(5) Compute the average, minimum, and maximum salary of employees in the Information Systems department.

(6) *Extra credit:* Compute the average salary for employees in every department. Use *Group By.*

a. Design and run Access queries to obtain the answers to these questions, using the data in the file **Ch2Ex2.mdb**.

b. Explain how the data in your answer contributes to the salary increase decision.

c. Suppose other team members want to use your Access application. Name three ways you can share it with them, and describe the advantages and disadvantages of each.

CASE STUDY 2

Microsoft SharePoint at Intermountain Healthcare

Intermountain Healthcare (*www.IntermountainHealthcare.org*) provides healthcare services to patients in Utah and southeastern Idaho. Intermountain operates a network of 21 hospitals with over 2,300 staffed hospital beds. In 2008, Intermountain admitted 130,000 patients and delivered 33,000 babies. In addition to hospitals, Intermountain operates more than 150 clinics. The non-profit organization employs more than 30,000 people.

Intermountain has developed numerous innovative information systems. A few examples are shown in Figure 2-20. Intermountain provides free private Web pages that patients or family members can create to communicate patient care and health matters to one another. It also provides a facility by which family and friends can send emails to patients that are received by volunteer staff members, printed, and delivered to patients in their rooms Additionally, the Intermountain site includes a Web-based portal that patients use to view test results, make appointments, view medical records, and conduct other healthcare matters. Although not shown in this figure, Intermountain also provides a Web nursery that features photos of babies recently born in the hospital.

In 2008, Intermountain converted its existing content management system to Microsoft SharePoint for both its public and employee sites. It uses SharePoint to publish traditional business documents such as announcements, policies, forms, pay schedules, and the like. It also has consolidated business reports under a SharePoint umbrella so that employees have one place to go to find and produce reports that they want. The result is reduced costs and better information for employees.

As you'll learn in Chapter 7, these are standard information system applications. Using SharePoint to deliver them saves Intermountain money and it helps employees find documents and other information resources more quickly. But these uses are not particularly innovative.

What is innovative is the way that Intermountain uses SharePoint to enable employees to self-publish within the organization. Employees who have developed new procedures or techniques or new ways of solving problems can describe them on SharePoint sites. They had been attempting to facilitate such publication prior to SharePoint, but according to Ryan Smith, Assistant Vice-President of eBusiness at Intermountain:

The content contribution process was really cumbersome. What should have taken 1 or 2 mouse-clicks took 15 to 20. It often took up to 30 minutes to post a simple piece of content. If users weren't frequent contributors, they got lost in the process, and the Internal eBusiness team had to get involved, which constituted a support burden.

Because of the difficulty of submitting content, only about 200 of Intermountain's 28,000 employees were active contributors.

ONLINE SERVICES

CarePages

CarePages are free, private web pages patients and families can create to communicate with family and friends about the care a patient is receiving.

Donate Online

Charitable efforts help make necessary resources available for medical clinics for underserved populations, educational programs, important community services and medical equipment. Donations even help to pay for the hospital care of those with no other means of payment and provide assistance to hospice patients.

Email a Patient

Send a message of love and support to your friends and loved ones. The messages hand-delivered to patients by our staff of volunteers during normal business hours at no charge to sender or recipient.

My Health

Registered patients can view test results, request appointments, renew prescriptions, view sections of their medical records, and communicate with their physician securely and privately online.

Figure 2-20
Sample of Online Services

Source: http://intermountainhealthcare.org/ onlineservices/Pages/home.aspx.

Intermountain wanted to use SharePoint to enable many more employees to contribute content. Accordingly, as stated by Jeff Johnson, Director of Internal eBusiness, "We made it easy for users to create Team Spaces where teams could collaborate on documents, share calendars, and perform other collaboration functions. Users really gravitated to these Team Spaces, which they could auto-provision without IT assistance."

In a short time, Intermountain had more than a thousand team spaces, all supported by a single part-time employee. Figure 2-21 shows the introductory team space page.

Johnson states that Intermountain did not hold any formal user training to help users create and use Team Spaces. Instead, it created a short video that walked the users through the process. As a result, nurses, administrative assistants, and other staff can create a Team Space in minutes. Johnson summed up the benefits of easy content contribution as follows: "Because it's so much easier to post content in SharePoint, thousands of employees can contribute. The more people that contribute, the smarter we become as an organization."

Sources: Intermountain Healthcare, http://intermountainhealthcare.org (accessed May 2009), www.microsoft.com/casestudies/casestudy. aspx? casestudyid=40000041499, and http://www.microsoft.com/casestudies/ Case_Study_Detail.aspx?casestudyid=4000004149.

Questions

1. Consider the applications illustrated in Figure 2-20. For each, explain:

   a. Whether you think the application will likely result in cost savings. Explain why or why not.

   b. Describe the benefits provided by the application. Consider benefits both to the patient and his or her family as well as benefits to Intermountain.

   c. An important political goal in the United States today is to "reduce health care costs." Explain how you think the Intermountain systems illustrated in Figure 2-20 contribute to that goal.

2. The case indicates that using the prior system, it would take up to 30 minutes to post a single piece of content. Suppose the new system reduced that to 10 minutes, a 20-minute saving. If each of the 200 contributors posted one item per day, what is the total annual cost savings provided by the new system? Make and justify assumptions about the number of days employees work as well as their likely cost, including salary and benefits. What would have been the savings if 1,000 employees had been contributing content?

3. When analysts compute the cost of an information system, they seldom include the costs of the employee

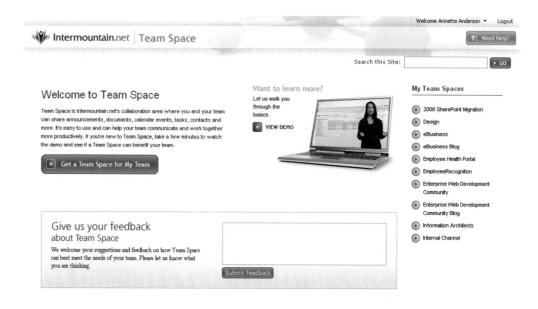

Figure 2-21
Team Space Page

labor for using that system. What does your answer to question 2 tell you about the hidden labor costs of a poorly designed information system?

4. According to the case, SharePoint made it vastly easier for users to contribute content, to the extent that more than a thousand Team Spaces were created in a few months. The case implies that this development is quite positive. Do you agree? Why or why not? Summarize the advantages and disadvantages of having so many employees involved in creating content. What, if anything, can Intermountain do to increase the advantages or decrease the disadvantages?

5. Reflect on Johnson's statement, "The more people that can contribute, the smarter we become as an organization." State in your own words what you think he means. What does it mean for an organization to be smarter? Is it possible for an organization to be overwhelmed with employee contributions? What factors limit employee contributions to those that are actually useful? On balance do you agree with his statement? Why or why not?

3) Information Systems for Competitive Advantage

"Look, I'm here . . . and early!" Felix remarks, sitting at the table as Tara, Jan, Kelly, and Neil enter the room.

Tara, offering peace with Felix, exclaims, "Yes, Felix, you are!"

"I could come to a lot more 'meetings' once we stopped trying to meet in person and all at once. It was just such a drag to get everyone together at the same time."

"I'll say. Kelly, this is the first time we've met in person in a month, and we're doing it now just so we can show you and Neil what we've got so far." As Jan makes this statement, she's thinking about the time and money she saved not having to arrange for child care for multiple meetings.

"Great. What have you got?" Kelly asks, excited to hear what the team has developed.

"Well," Tara says, clearly struggling with her words, "well, we found that we really didn't know who we are . . . No, that's not right. I mean, we know who we are, but we had trouble expressing it in words."

Felix jumps in, "Kelly, it's like this. We think we succeed because we offer the best work-out in the city. But, what does *best* really mean? It isn't because of our great juice bar, even though it is great. We decided we're best because of our *intensity*. People come here, it's all business, we get to it and provide a fast-paced, to-the-max cardio workout. People leave here pumped and upbeat!"

> *"I can look at that data and see how many classes might be affected."*

"OK, that makes sense to me. Go on."

"So, in an effort to reduce costs, we can't lose that." Felix says, wistfully.

Tara jumps back into the conversation. "So, in our discussion board, we wrote about ways to reduce costs. We had a long thread going and we weren't getting very far until Jan pointed out that the size of the class doesn't seem to impact intensity . . . in fact, packing her spinning classes actually adds to the intensity."

"Yeah, I did," admits Jan. "But I'm not crazy about where this goes. Because, if we pack our classes more, well, we'll save FlexTime money, but . . . well, I may as well say it, fewer classes means less money to us. If we're not teaching we're not getting paid . . . "

An awkward pause fills the room.

Felix jumps in, "We love FlexTime and we're willing to take a hit in the short run. But, how much of a hit will it be? And for how long? We don't know. And we're worried, too."

"Maybe I can help there." Neil speaks for the first time. Everyone turns to listen. "I've got a couple of thoughts. But, first, thanks for taking this so seriously and for bringing this issue to light. As you know, we record all of our class registration data into our database. We've got records going back several years. I can look at that data and see how many classes might be affected. We can look for classes that have lower enrollments, but also at the differences between average class size and maximum class size."

"And then what?" Kelly looks at Neil . . . wondering where he's going with this.

"That will tell us how many classes we might want to cancel, what the benefit would be. And, if there is substantial cost savings to be had, it will help to answer Felix's question about how much of a hit we'll have to take."

Later, Kelly and Neil are talking alone in Neil's office.

"This is risky, Neil. If we start cancelling classes, it will look like we're in trouble. We don't want the staff to start communicating that to our customers."

"Yeah, you're right. And we might lose some staff. But, we haven't decided anything yet. I need to look at the data and see the impact. It's not worth doing if it doesn't help our bottom line, and I'm not sure it will."

"Neil, isn't it great that they get what makes FlexTime special? I was really proud of them for coming up with this idea. These jobs mean a lot to them."

"If we do make classes larger, maybe I can come up with some bonus program . . . maybe we take the average maximum number of students for each class in each time slot and then provide a bonus for each student they enroll over that number . . . or . . . " Neil looks over Kelly's shoulder, deep in thought.

"I don't mean to be negative, but this sounds complicated. Anyway, I've got a class to teach."

"OK, Kelly, I'll get back to you with what I find out." ∎

>> STUDY QUESTIONS

Q1 How does organizational strategy determine information systems structure?

Q2 What five forces determine industry structure?

Q3 How does analysis of industry structure determine competitive strategy?

Q4 How does competitive strategy determine value chain structure?

Q5 How do business processes generate value?

Q6 How does competitive strategy determine business processes and the structure of information systems?

Q7 How do information systems provide competitive advantages?

Q8 2020?

CHAPTER PREVIEW

Recall from Chapter 1 that MIS is the development and use of information systems that enable organizations to achieve their goals and objectives. In Chapter 2, you learned how information systems can help people collaborate. This chapter focuses on how information systems support competitive strategy and how IS can create competitive advantages. As you will learn in your organizational behavior classes, a body of knowledge exists to help organizations analyze their industry, select a competitive strategy, and develop business processes. In the first part of this chapter, we will survey that knowledge and show how to use it, via several steps, to structure information systems. Then, in the last section, we will discuss how companies use information systems to gain a competitive advantage.

Q1 How Does Organizational Strategy Determine Information Systems Structure?

According to the definition of MIS, information systems exist to help organizations achieve their goals and objectives. As you will learn in your business strategy class, an organization's goals and objectives are determined by its *competitive strategy*. Thus, ultimately, competitive strategy determines the structure, features, and functions of every information system.

Figure 3-1 summarizes this situation. In short, organizations examine the structure of their industry and determine a competitive strategy. That strategy determines value chains, which, in turn, determine business processes. The structure of business processes determines the design of supporting information systems.

Michael Porter, one of the key researchers and thinkers in competitive analysis, developed three different models that can help you understand the elements of Figure 3-1. We begin with his five forces model.

Q2 What Five Forces Determine Industry Structure?

Organizational strategy begins with an assessment of the fundamental characteristics and structure of an industry. One model used to assess an industry structure is Porter's **five forces model**,[1] summarized in Figure 3-2. According to this model,

Figure 3-1
Organizational Strategy Determines Information Systems

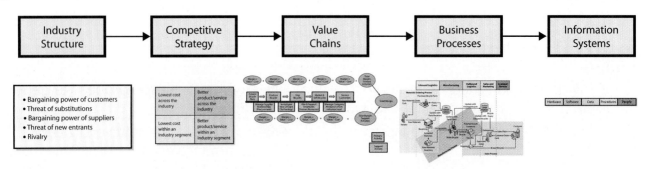

---

[1]Michael Porter, *Competitive Strategy: Techniques for Analyzing Industries and Competitors* (New York: Free Press, 1980).

Figure 3-2
Porter's Five Forces Model
of Industry Structure

Source: Based on Michael E. Porter,
*Competitive Advantage: Creating and
Sustaining Superior Performance* (The Free
Press, a Division of Simon & Schuster Adult
Publishing Group). Copyright © 1985, 1998
by Michael E. Porter.

- Bargaining power of customers
- Threat of substitutions
- Bargaining power of suppliers
- Threat of new entrants
- Rivalry

Force	Example of Strong Force	Example of Weak Force
Bargaining power of customers	Toyota's purchase of auto paint	Your power over the procedures and policies of your university
Threat of substitutions	Frequent-traveler's choice of auto rental	Patients using the only drug effective for their type of cancer
Bargaining power of suppliers	Students purchasing gasoline	Grain farmers in a surplus year
Threat of new entrants	Corner latte stand	Professional football team
Rivalry	Used car dealers	Internal Revenue Service

Figure 3-3
Examples of Five Forces

five competitive forces determine industry profitability: bargaining power of customers, threat of substitutions, bargaining power of suppliers, threat of new entrants, and rivalry among existing firms. The intensity of each of the five forces determines the characteristics of the industry, how profitable it is, and how sustainable that profitability will be.

To understand this model, consider the strong and weak examples for each of the forces in Figure 3-3. A good check on your understanding is to see if you can think of different forces of each category in Figure 3-3. Also, take a particular industry—say, auto repair—and consider how these five forces determine the competitive landscape of that industry.

Figure 3-4 illustrates FlexTime's analysis of these five forces. The two most serious threats are from their landlord (their location is critical to their clientele and FlexTime

Force	FlexTime Example	Force Strength	FlexTime's Response
Bargaining power of customers	"I want to pay less for my trainer."	Weak	Explain value delivered
Threat of substitutions	"I think I'll join a softball league."	Medium	Emphasize importance of cardio health and fitness to lifestyle
Bargaining power of suppliers	"We're raising your rent."	High	Acquire its own building
Threat of new entrants	"There's a hot new club across the street."	Medium	Superior product
Rivalry	"I'm going to the club on 12th Street."	High	Superior product

Figure 3-4
Five Forces at FlexTime

is in year 4 of a 5-year lease) and from rivalry. Its response to the rivalry threat is superior product. As you will see, information systems cannot help FlexTime with the landlord problem, but they can provide considerable help in creating a superior product.

Like FlexTime, organizations examine these five forces and determine how they intend to respond to them. That examination leads to competitive strategy.

video ▶

See the Ethics Guide on pages 72–73 to learn how a change in management can greatly affect a company's competitive strategy.

Q3 How Does Analysis of Industry Structure Determine Competitive Strategy?

An organization responds to the structure of its industry by choosing a **competitive strategy**. Porter followed his five forces model with the model of four competitive strategies, shown in Figure 3-5.[2] According to Porter, firms engage in one of these four strategies. An organization can focus on being the cost leader, or it can focus on differentiating its products from those of the competition. Further, the organization can employ the cost or differentiation strategy across an industry, or it can focus its strategy on a particular industry segment.

Consider the car rental industry, for example. According to the first column of Figure 3-5, a car rental company can strive to provide the lowest-cost car rentals across the industry, or it can seek to provide the lowest-cost car rentals to an industry segment—say, U.S. domestic business travelers.

As shown in the second column, a car rental company can seek to differentiate its products from the competition. It can do so in various ways—for example, by providing a wide range of high-quality cars, by providing the best reservation system, by having the cleanest cars or the fastest check-in, or by some other means. The company can strive to provide product differentiation across the industry or within particular segments of the industry, such as U.S. domestic business travelers.

According to Porter, to be effective, the organization's goals, objectives, culture, and activities must be consistent with the organization's strategy. To those in the MIS field, this means that all information systems in the organization must reflect and facilitate the organization's competitive strategy.

FlexTime has chosen a focused differentiation strategy. Its focus is on downtown, urban, city workers. The environment is sophisticated and adults-only. As stated by FlexTime's staff at the start of this chapter, it differentiates by providing a superior product—an intense, to-the-max workout that leaves clients pumped and excited.

	Cost	Differentiation
Industry-wide	Lowest cost across the industry	Better product/service across the industry
Focus	Lowest cost within an industry segment	Better product/service within an industry segment

Figure 3-5
Porter's Four Competitive Strategies

[2]Based on Michael Porter, *Competitive Strategy* (New York: Free Press, 1985).

Q4 How Does Competitive Strategy Determine Value Chain Structure?

Organizations analyze the structure of their industry, and, using that analysis, they formulate a competitive strategy. They then need to organize and structure the organization to implement that strategy. If, for example, the competitive strategy is to be *cost leader*, then business activities need to be developed to provide essential functions at the lowest possible cost.

A business that selects a *differentiation* strategy would not necessarily structure itself around least-cost activities. Instead, such a business might choose to develop more costly systems, but it would do so only if those systems provided benefits that outweighed their risks. Porter defined **value** as the amount of money that a customer is willing to pay for a resource, product, or service. The difference between the value that an activity generates and the cost of the activity is called the **margin**. A business with a differentiation strategy will add cost to an activity only as long as the activity has a positive margin.

A **value chain** is a network of value-creating activities. That generic chain consists of five **primary activities** and four **support activities**.

Primary Activities in the Value Chain

To understand the essence of the value chain, consider a small manufacturer—say, a bicycle maker (see Figure 3-6). First, the manufacturer acquires raw materials using the inbound logistics activity. This activity concerns the receiving and handling of raw materials and other inputs. The accumulation of those materials adds value in the sense that even a pile of unassembled parts is worth something to some customer. A collection of the parts needed to build a bicycle is worth more than an empty space on a shelf. The value is not only the parts themselves, but also the time required to contact vendors for those parts, to maintain business relationships with those vendors, to order the parts, to receive the shipment, and so forth.

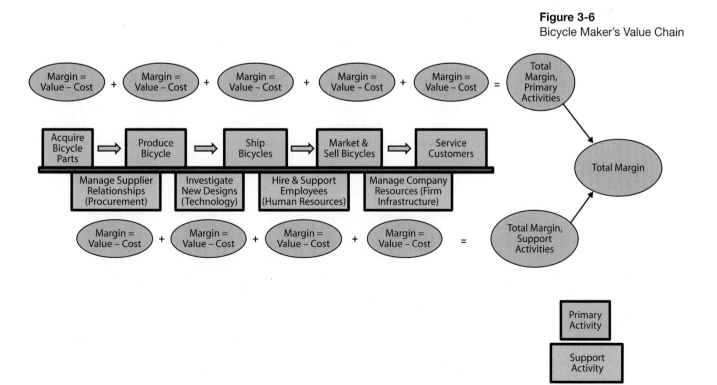

Figure 3-6
Bicycle Maker's Value Chain

Primary Activity	Description
Inbound logistics	Receiving, storing, and disseminating inputs to the product
Operations/Manufacturing	Transforming inputs into the final product
Outbound logistics	Collecting, storing, and physically distributing the product to buyers
Sales and Marketing	Inducing buyers to purchase the product and providing a means for them to do so
Customer Service	Assisting customer's use of the product and thus maintaining and enhancing the product's value

Figure 3-7
Task Descriptions for Primary
Activities of the Value Chain

Source: Based on Michael E. Porter,
*Competitive Advantage: Creating and
Sustaining Superior Performance* (The Free
Press, a Division of Simon & Schuster Adult
Publishing Group) Copyright © 1985, 1998
by Michael E. Porter.

In the operations activity, the bicycle maker transforms raw materials into a finished bicycle, a process that adds more value. Next, the company uses the outbound logistics activity to deliver the finished bicycle to a customer. Of course, there is no customer to send the bicycle to without the marketing and sales value activity. Finally, the service activity provides customer support to the bicycle users.

Each stage of this generic chain accumulates costs and adds value to the product. The net result is the total margin of the chain, which is the difference between the total value added and the total costs incurred. Figure 3-7 summarizes the primary activities of the value chain.

Support Activities in the Value Chain

The support activities in the generic value chain contribute indirectly to the production, sale, and service of the product. They include procurement, which consists of the processes of finding vendors, setting up contractual arrangements, and negotiating prices. (This differs from inbound logistics, which is concerned with ordering and receiving in accordance with agreements set up by procurement.)

Porter defined technology broadly. It includes research and development, but it also includes other activities within the firm for developing new techniques, methods, and procedures. He defined human resources as recruiting, compensation, evaluation, and training of full-time and part-time employees. Finally, firm infrastructure includes general management, finance, accounting, legal, and government affairs.

Supporting functions add value, albeit indirectly, and they also have costs. Hence, as shown in Figure 3-6, supporting activities contribute to a margin. In the case of supporting activities, it would be difficult to calculate the margin because the specific value added of, say, the manufacturer's lobbyists in Washington, D.C., is difficult to know. But there is a value added, there are costs, and there is a margin, even if it is only in concept.

Value Chain Linkages

Porter's model of business activities includes **linkages**, which are interactions across value activities. For example, manufacturing systems use linkages to reduce inventory costs. Such a system uses sales forecasts to plan production; it then uses the production plan to determine raw materials needs and then uses the material needs to schedule purchases. The end result is just-in-time inventory, which reduces inventory sizes and costs.

By describing value chains and their linkages, Porter started a movement to create integrated, cross-departmental business systems. Over time, Porter's work led to the creation of a new discipline called *business process design*. The central idea is that organizations should not automate or improve existing functional systems. Rather, they should create new, more efficient business processes that integrate the activities of all departments involved in a value chain. You will see an example of a linkage in the next section.

Value chain analysis has a direct application to manufacturing businesses like the bicycle manufacturer. However, value chains also exist in service-oriented companies like FlexTime. The difference is that most of the value in a service company is generated by the operations, marketing and sales, and service activities. Inbound and outbound logistics are not typically as important. You will have a chance to reflect on these differences in Using Your Knowledge Question 1, page 87.

Q5 How Do Business Processes Generate Value?

A **business process** is a network of activities that generate value by transforming inputs into outputs. The **cost** of the business process is the cost of the inputs plus the cost of the activities. The **margin** of the business process is the value of the outputs minus the cost.

A business process is a network of activities; each **activity** transforms **input resources** into **output resources**. Resources **flow** between or among activities. **Facilities** store resources; some facilities, such as inventories, store physical items. Other facilities, such as databases, hold data. You can think of facilities as resources at rest. The organization's bank accounts are the facility of cash at rest.[3]

Consider the three business processes for a bicycle manufacturer shown in Figure 3-8. The materials ordering process transforms cash[4] into a raw materials

Figure 3-8
Three Examples
of Business Processes

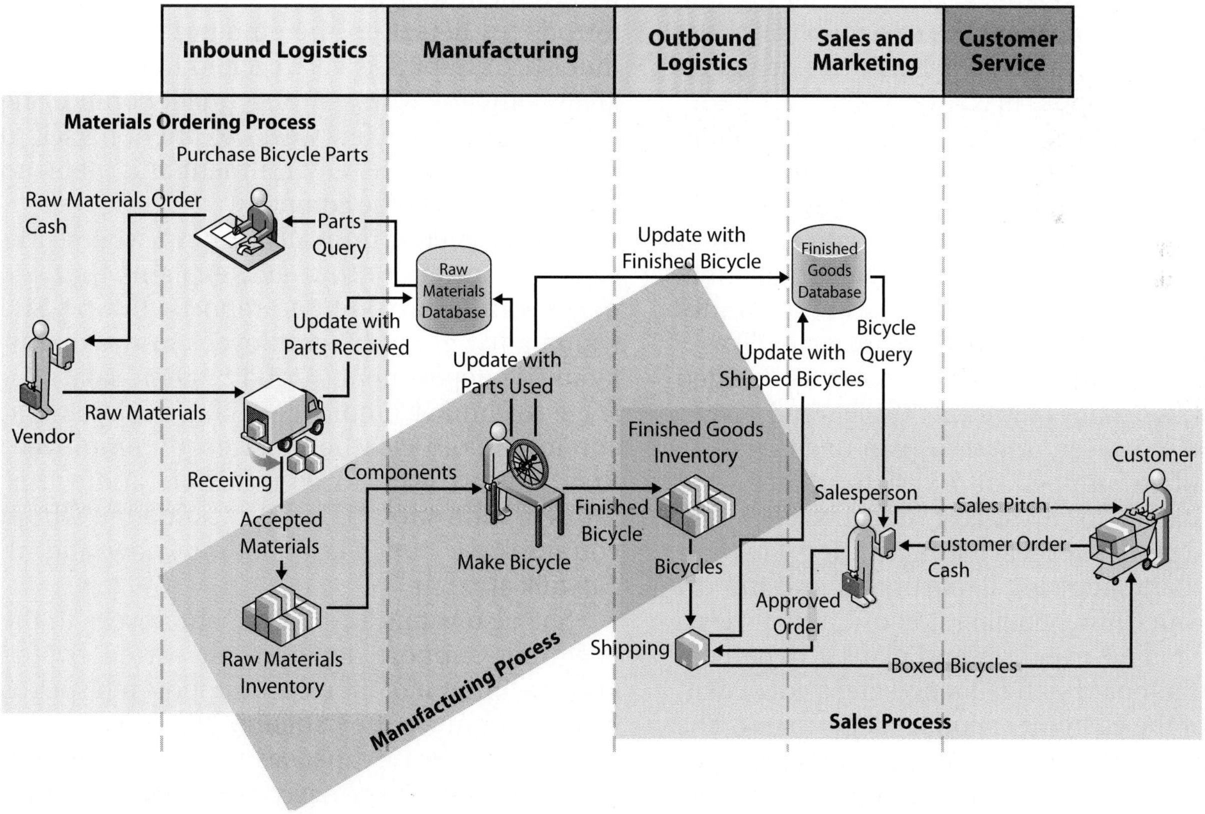

---

[3]OK, if you want to quibble, cash is earning interest, so it is not at rest. But that is another way of saying that we have not considered the interest-generating business process that transforms cash into more cash via investment activities.

[4]For simplicity, the flow of cash is abbreviated in this diagram. Business processes for authorizing, controlling, making payments, and receiving revenue are, of course, vital. You will learn more about such processes in Chapter 7.

Ethics

Yikes! Bikes

Suppose you are an operations manager for Yikes! Bikes, a manufacturer of high-end mountain bicycles with $20 million in annual sales. Yikes! has been in business over 25 years, and the founder and sole owner recently sold the business to an investment group, Major Capital. You know nothing about the sale until your boss introduces you to Andrea Parks, a partner at Major Capital, who is in charge of the acquisition. Parks explains to you that Yikes! has been sold to Major Capital and that she will be the temporary general manager. She explains that the new owners see great potential in you, and they want to enlist your cooperation during the transition. She hints that if your potential is what she thinks it is, you will be made general manager of Yikes!

Parks explains that the new owners decided there are too many players in the high-end mountain bike business, and they plan to change the competitive strategy of Yikes! from high-end differentiation to lowest-cost vendor. Accordingly, they will eliminate local manufacturing, fire most of the manufacturing department, and import bikes from China. Further, Major Capital sees a need to reduce expenses and plans a 10 percent across-the-board staff reduction and a cut of two-thirds of the customer support department. The new bikes will be of lesser quality than current Yikes! bikes, but the price will be substantially less. The new ownership group believes it will take a few years for the market to realize that Yikes! bikes are not the same quality as they were. Finally, Parks asks you to attend an all-employee meeting with the founder and her.

At the meeting, the founder explains that due to his age and personal situation, he decided to sell Yikes! to Major Capital and that starting today Andrea Parks is the general manager. He thanks the employees for their many years of service, wishes them well, and leaves the building. Parks introduces herself to the employees and states that Major Capital is very excited to own such a great company with a strong, quality brand. She says she will take a few weeks to orient herself to the business and its environment and plans no major changes to the company.

You are reeling from all this news when Parks calls you into her office and explains that she needs you to prepare two reports. In one, she wants a list of all the employees in the manufacturing department, sorted by their salary (or wage for hourly employees). She explains that she intends to cut the most costly employees first. "I don't want to be inflexible about this, though," she says. "If there is someone whom you think we should keep, let me know, and we can talk about it."

She also wants a list of the employees in the customer support department, sorted by the average amount of time each support rep spends with customers. She explains, "I'm not so concerned with payroll expense in customer support. It's not how much we're paying someone; it's how much time they're wasting with customers. We're going to have a bare-bones support department, and we want to get rid of the gabby chatters first."

You are, understandably, shocked and surprised . . . not only at the speed with which

the transition has occurred, but also because you wouldn't think the founder would do this to the employees. You call him at home and tell him what is going on.

"Look," he explains, "when I sold the company, I asked them to be sure to take care of the employees. They said they would. I'll call Andrea, but there's really nothing I can do at this point; they own the show."

In a black mood of depression, you realize you don't want to work for Yikes! anymore, but your wife is 6 months' pregnant with your first child. You need medical insurance for her at least until the baby is born. But what miserable tasks are you going to be asked to do before then? And you suspect that if you balk at any task, Parks won't hesitate to fire you, too.

As you leave that night you run into Lori, the most popular customer support representative and one of your favorite employees. "Hey," Lori asks you, "what did you think of that meeting? Do you believe Andrea? Do you think they'll let us continue to make great bikes?" ∎

Discussion Questions

1. In your opinion, did the new owners take any illegal action? Is there evidence of a crime in this scenario?

2. Was the statement that Parks made to all of the employees unethical? Why or why not? If you questioned her about the ethics of her statement, how do you think she would justify herself?

3. What do you think Parks will tell the founder if he calls as a result of your conversation with him? Does he have any legal recourse? Is Major Capital's behavior toward him unethical? Why or why not?

4. Parks is going to use information to perform staff cuts. What do you think about her rationale? Ethically, should she consider other factors, such as number of years of service, past employee reviews, or other criteria?

5. How do you respond to Lori? What are the consequences if you tell her what you know? What are the consequences of lying to her? What are the consequences of saying something noncommittal?

6. If you actually were in this situation, would you leave the company? Why or why not?

7. In business school, we talk of principles like competitive strategy as interesting academic topics. But, as you can see from the Yikes! case, competitive strategy decisions have human consequences. How do you plan to resolve conflicts between human needs and tough business decisions?

8. How do you define *job security*?

inventory. The manufacturing process transforms raw materials into finished goods. The sales process transforms finished goods into cash. Notice that the business processes span the value chain activities. The sales process involves sales and marketing as well as outbound logistics activities, as you would expect. Note, too, that while none of these three processes involve a customer-service activity, customer service plays a role in other business processes.

Also notice that activities get and put data resources from and to databases. For example, the purchase-bicycle-parts activity queries the raw materials database to determine the materials to order. The receiving activity updates the raw materials database to indicate the arrival of materials. The make-bicycle activity updates the raw materials database to indicate the consumption of materials. Similar actions are taken in the sales process against the finished goods database.

Business processes vary in cost and effectiveness. In fact, the streamlining of business processes to increase margin (add value, reduce costs, or both) is key to competitive advantage. You will learn about process design when we discuss **business process management** in Chapter 7. To get a flavor of process design, however, consider Figure 3-9, which shows an alternate process for the bicycle manufacturer. Here, the purchase-bicycle-parts activity not only queries the raw materials inventory database, it also queries the finished goods inventory database. Querying both databases allows the purchasing department to make decisions not just on raw materials quantities, but also on customer demand. By using this data, purchasing can reduce the size of raw materials inventory, reducing production costs and thus adding margin to the value chain. This is an example of using a linkage across business processes to improve process margin.

As you will learn, however, changing business processes is not easy to do. Most process design requires people to work in new ways, to follow different procedures,

Figure 3-9
Improved Material
Ordering Process

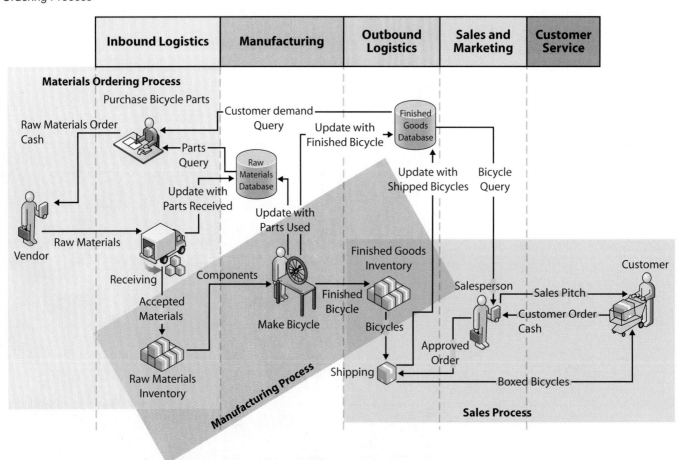

and employees often resist such change. In Figure 3-9, the employees who perform the purchase-bicycle-parts activity need to learn to adjust their ordering processes to use customer purchase patterns. Another complication is that data stored in the finished goods database likely will need to be redesigned to keep track of customer demand data. As you will learn in Chapter 7, that redesign effort will require that some application programs be changed as well.

Q6 How Does Competitive Strategy Determine Business Processes and the Structure of Information Systems?

Figure 3-10 shows a business process for renting bicycles. The value-generating activities are shown in the top of the table and the implementation of those activities for two companies with different competitive strategies is shown in the rows below.

Figure 3-10
Operations Value Chains
for Bicycle Rental Companies

	Value-Generating Activity	Greet Customer	Determine Needs	Rent Bike	Return Bike & Pay
Low-cost rental to students	Message that implements competitive strategy	"You wanna bike?"	"Bikes are over there. Help yourself."	"Fill out this form, and bring it to me over here when you're done."	"Show me the bike." "OK, you owe $23.50. Pay up."
	Supporting business process	None.	Physical controls and procedures to prevent bike theft.	Printed forms and a shoe box to store them in.	Shoebox with rental form. Minimal credit card and cash receipt system.
High-service rental to business executives at conference resort	Message that implements competitive strategy	"Hello, Ms. Henry. Wonderful to see you again. Would you like to rent the WonderBike 4.5 that you rented last time?"	"You know, I think the WonderBike Supreme would be a better choice for you. It has ..."	"Let me just scan the bike's number into our system, and then I'll adjust the seat for you."	"How was your ride?""Here, let me help you. I'll just scan the bike's tag again and have your paperwork in just a second." "Would you like a beverage?" "Would you like me to put this on your hotel bill, or would you prefer to pay now?"
	Supporting business process	Customer tracking and past sales activity system.	Employee training and information system to match customer and bikes, biased to "up-sell" customer.	Automated inventory system to check bike out of inventory.	Automated inventory system to place bike back in inventory. Prepare payment documents. Integrate with resort's billing system.

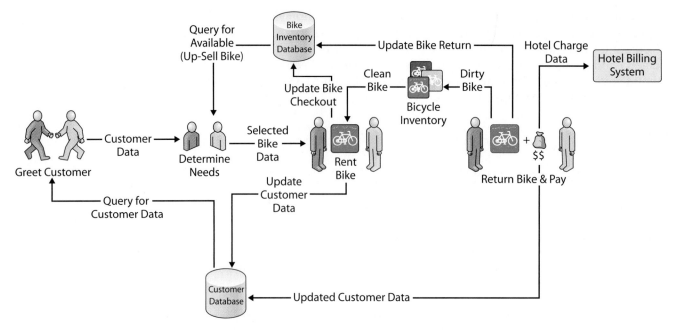

Figure 3-11
Business Process and
Information Systems for
High-Service Bike Rental

The first company has chosen a competitive strategy of low-cost rentals to students. Accordingly, this business implements business processes to minimize costs. The second company has chosen a differentiation strategy. It provides "best-of-breed" rentals to executives at a high-end conference resort. Notice that this business has designed its business processes to ensure superb service. To achieve a positive margin, it must ensure that the value added will exceed the costs of providing the service.

Now, consider the information systems required for these business processes. The student rental business uses a shoe box for its data facility. The only computer/software/data component in its business is the machine provided by its bank for processing credit card transactions.

The high-service business, however, makes extensive use of information systems, as shown in Figure 3-11. It has a CRM database that tracks past customer rental activity, and an inventory database that is used to select and up-sell bicycle rentals as well as to control bicycle inventory with a minimum of fuss to its high-end customers.

So the bottom line is this: Organizations analyze their industry and choose a competitive strategy. Given that strategy, they design business processes that span value-generating activities. Those processes determine the scope and requirements of each organization's information systems. Given this background, we will now examine how information systems generate a competitive advantage.

You can also apply these principles to your personal competitive advantage, as discussed in the Guide on pages 84–85.

Q7 How Do Information Systems Provide Competitive Advantages?

In your business strategy class, you will study the Porter models in greater detail than we have discussed here. When you do so, you will learn numerous ways that organizations respond to the five competitive forces. For our purposes, we can distill those ways into the list of principles shown in Figure 3-12. Keep in mind that we are applying these principles in the context of the organization's competitive strategy.

Some of these competitive techniques are created via products and services, and some are created via the development of business processes. Consider each.

Product Implementations
1. Create a new product or service
2. Enhance products or services
3. Differentiate products or services

Process Implementations
4. Lock in customers and buyers
5. Lock in suppliers
6. Raise barriers to market entry
7. Establish alliances
8. Reduce costs

Figure 3-12
Principles of Competitive Advantage

Competitive Advantage via Products

The first three principles in Figure 3-12 concern products or services. Organizations gain a competitive advantage by creating *new* products or services, by *enhancing* existing products or services, and by *differentiating* their products and services from those of their competitors. FlexTime differentiates on the basis of quality of workout.

Information systems create competitive advantages either as part of a product or by providing support to a product. Consider, for example, a car rental agency like Hertz or Avis. An information system that produces information about the car's location and provides driving instructions to destinations is part of the car rental and thus is part of the product itself (see Figure 3-13a). In contrast, an information system that schedules car maintenance is not part of the product, but instead supports the product (see Figure 3-13b). Either way, information systems can help achieve the first three principles in Figure 3-12.

The remaining five principles in Figure 3-12 concern competitive advantage created by the implementation of business processes.

Competitive Advantage via Business Processes

Organizations can *lock in customers* by making it difficult or expensive for customers to switch to another product. This strategy is sometimes called establishing

a. Information System as Part of a Car Rental Product

b. Information System That Supports a Car Rental Product

Daily Service Schedule — November 17, 2005

StationID   22
StationName   Lubrication

ServiceDate	ServiceTime	VehicleID	Make	Model	Mileage	ServiceDescription
11/17/2005	12:00 AM	155890	Ford	Explorer	2244	Std. Lube
11/17/2005	11:00 AM	12448	Toyota	Tacoma	7558	Std. Lube

StationID   26
StationName   Alignment

ServiceDate	ServiceTime	VehicleID	Make	Model	Mileage	ServiceDescription
11/17/2005	9:00 AM	12448	Toyota	Tacoma	7558	Front end alignment inspect

StationID   28
StationName   Transmission

ServiceDate	ServiceTime	VehicleID	Make	Model	Mileage	ServiceDescription
11/17/2005	11:00 AM	155890	Ford	Explorer	2244	Transmission oil change

Figure 3-13
Two Roles for Information Systems Regarding Products

high **switching costs**. Organizations can *lock in suppliers* by making it difficult to switch to another organization, or, stated positively, by making it easy to connect to and work with the organization. Finally, competitive advantage can be gained by *creating entry barriers* that make it difficult and expensive for new competition to enter the market.

Another means to gain competitive advantage is to *establish alliances* with other organizations. Such alliances establish standards, promote product awareness and needs, develop market size, reduce purchasing costs, and provide other benefits. Finally, organizations can gain competitive advantage by *reducing costs*. Such reductions enable the organization to reduce prices and/or to increase profitability. Increased profitability means not just greater shareholder value, but also more cash, which can fund further infrastructure development for even greater competitive advantage.

All of these principles of competitive advantage make sense, but the question you may be asking is, "How do information systems help to create competitive advantage?" To answer that question, consider a sample information system.

How Does an Actual Company Use IS to Create Competitive Advantages?

ABC, Inc.,[5] is a worldwide shipper with sales well in excess of $1 billion. From its inception, ABC invested heavily in information technology and led the shipping industry in the application of information systems for competitive advantage. Here we consider one example of an information system that illustrates how ABC successfully uses information technology to gain competitive advantage.

ABC maintains customer account data that include not only the customer's name, address, and billing information, but also data about the people, organizations, and locations to which the customer ships. Figure 3-14 shows a Web form that an ABC customer is using to schedule a shipment. When the ABC system creates the form, it fills the Company name drop-down list with the names of companies that the customer has shipped to in the past. Here, the user is selecting Prentice Hall.

When the user clicks the Company name, the underlying ABC information system reads the customer's contact data from a database. The data consist of names,

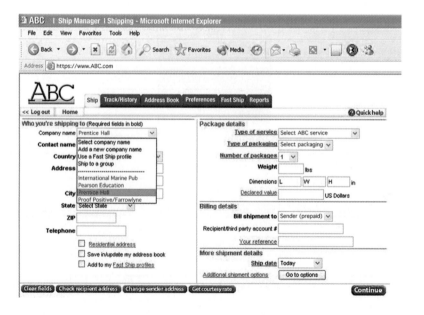

Figure 3-14
ABC, Inc., Web Page to Select a Recipient from the Customer's Records

---

[5]The information system described here is used by a major transportation company that did not want its name published in this textbook.

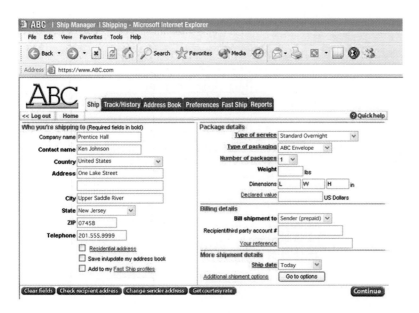

Figure 3-15
ABC, Inc., Web Page to Select a Contact from the Customer's Records

addresses, and phone numbers of recipients from past shipments. The user then selects a Contact name, and the system inserts that contact's address and other data into the form using data from the database, as shown in Figure 3-15. Thus, the system saves customers from having to reenter data for people to whom they have shipped in the past. Providing the data in this way also reduces data-entry errors.

Figure 3-16 shows another feature of this system. On the right-hand side of this form, the customer can request that ABC send email messages to the sender (the customer), the recipient, and others as well. The customer can choose for ABC to send an email when the shipment is created and when it has been delivered. In Figure 3-16, the user has provided three email addresses. The customer wants all three addresses to receive delivery notification, but only the sender will receive shipment notification. The customer can add a personal message as well. By adding this capability to the shipment scheduling system, ABC has extended its product from a package-delivery service to a package- *and* information-delivery service.

Figure 3-17 shows one other capability of this information system. It has generated a shipping label, complete with bar code, for the user to print. By doing this, the company not only reduces errors in the preparation of shipping labels, but it also

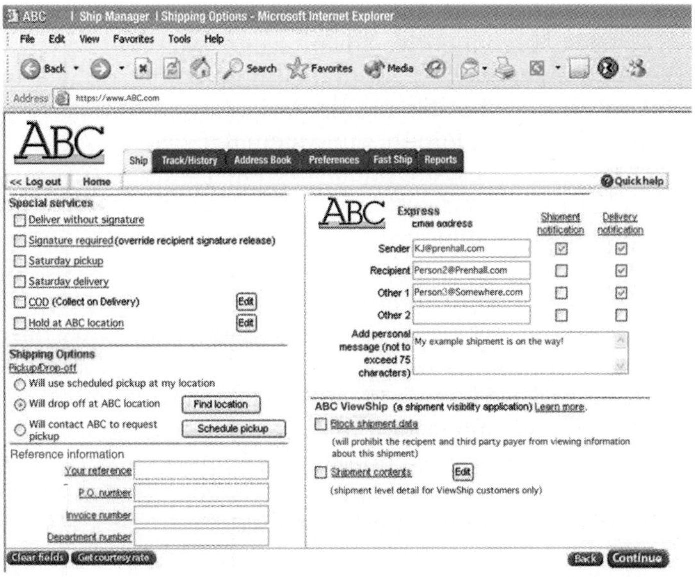

Figure 3-16
ABC, Inc., Web Page to Specify Email Notification

Figure 3-17
ABC, Inc., Web Page
to Print a Shipping Label

causes the customer to provide the paper and ink for document printing! Millions of such documents are printed every day, resulting in a considerable savings to the company.

How Does This System Create a Competitive Advantage?

Only customers who have access to the Internet can use this shipping system. Do organizations have an ethical obligation to provide equivalent services to those who do not have access? The Guide on pages 82–83 explores this question.

Now consider the ABC shipping information system in light of the competitive advantage factors in Figure 3-12. This information system *enhances* an existing service because it eases the effort of creating a shipment to the customer while reducing errors. The information system also helps to *differentiate* the ABC package delivery service from competitors that do not have a similar system. Further, the generation of email messages when ABC picks up and delivers a package could be considered to be a *new* service.

Because this information system captures and stores data about recipients, it reduces the amount of customer work when scheduling a shipment. Customers will be *locked in* by this system: If a customer wants to change to a different shipper, he or she will need to rekey recipient data for that new shipper. The disadvantage of rekeying data may well outweigh any advantage of switching to another shipper.

This system achieves a competitive advantage in two other ways as well: First, it raises the barriers to market entry. If another company wants to develop a shipping service, it will not only have to be able to ship packages, but it will also need to have a similar information system. In addition, the system reduces costs. It reduces errors in shipping documents, and it saves ABC paper, ink, and printing costs.

Of course, to determine if this system delivers a *net savings* in costs, the cost of developing and operating the information system will need to be offset against the gains in reduced errors and paper, ink, and printing costs. It may be that the system costs more than the savings. Even still, it may be a sound investment if the value of intangible benefits, such as locking in customers and raising entry barriers, exceeds the net cost.

Before continuing, review Figure 3-12. Make sure that you understand each of the principles of competitive advantage and how information systems can help achieve them. In fact, the list in Figure 3-12 probably is important enough to memorize, because you can also use it for non-IS applications. You can consider any business project or initiative in light of competitive advantage.

Q8 2020?

What does FlexTime look like in 2020? Put on your rose-colored glasses and assume that FlexTime overcomes the current downturn, revenue picks up, and FlexTime addresses the threat of its landlord by buying its own, four-story, ultra-hip building . . . a former warehouse that oozes urban charm. What kinds of communications facilities does it put into the new building? What data connectivity do clients want? It depends on what systems FlexTime decides to implement.

Assume that FlexTime keeps pace with emerging research on optimal workout schedules (see *www.angelfire.com/wa3/loserschallenge/cardio.html* and *www.sportsci.org/jour/0101/cf.htm*). Given this research and that developed between now and 2020, FlexTime could develop information systems that track client workouts and their intensity and relate that data to net cardiovascular benefits. It could also correlate workout data with dietary data and relate all of that to client weight loss or gain. Maybe FlexTime provides this data to medical insurers and helps its active clients to obtain reductions in their medical insurance premiums.

But notice the word *could.* Should it? Is it worthwhile for FlexTime to develop such systems? This chapter provides a framework for deciding. Would such capability increase FlexTime's ability to meet its competitive strategy? Or, perhaps in light of these technologies, FlexTime will reevaluate the five forces and adjust its competitive strategy and then assess whether such systems are needed in that new competitive environment.

Now put on your dark-colored glasses. Suppose the economic downturn proves too much for FlexTime and it is forced to reconfigure into a shadow of its former self. Maybe FlexTime is no longer a single business entity. Maybe it becomes a federation of trainers, workout spaces, dieticians, and recreational sports leagues. Maybe that federation uses free data storage, data communication, emerging collaboration tools and systems to appear as a virtual organization to clients, but one that is composed of independently owned and operated small business entities.

Who knows? But you can be the beneficiary of this story, regardless of how it turns out. You can, if you attain marketable skills that include the ability to access, evaluate, and integrate emerging technology into business as it dynamically unfolds.

Limiting Access to Those Who Have Access

An adage of investing is that it's easier for the rich to get richer. Someone who has $10 million invested at 5 percent earns $500,000 per year. Another investor with $10,000 invested at that same 5 percent earns $500 per year. Every year, the disparity increases as the first investor pulls farther and farther ahead of the second.

This same adage applies to intellectual wealth as well. It's easier for those with considerable knowledge and expertise to gain even more knowledge and expertise. Someone who knows how to search the Internet can learn more readily than someone who does not. And every year, the person with greater knowledge pulls farther and farther ahead. Intellectual capital grows in just the same way that financial capital grows.

Searching the Internet is not just a matter of knowledge, however. It's also a matter of access. The increasing reliance on the Web for information and commerce has created a **digital divide** between those who have Internet access and those who do not. This divide continues to deepen as those who are connected pull farther ahead of those who are not.

Various groups have addressed this problem by making Internet access available in public places, such as libraries, community centers, and retirement homes. As of 2007, The Bill and Melinda Gates Foundation has given more than $262 million to public libraries for the purchase of personal computers and Internet access. Total donations since then are not published, but their foundation continues to give more support to libraries, particularly with matching funds to support computer maintenance and faster Internet connectivity (see *www.gatesfoundation. org/topics/Pages/libraries.aspx#*).

Such gifts help, but not everyone can be served this way, and even with such access, there's a big convenience difference between going to the library and walking across your bedroom to access the Internet—and you don't have to stand in line.

The advantages accrue to everyone with access, every day. For the connected, it is the primary means of learning, well, anything. Directions to your friend's house? Movies at local theaters? Want to buy music, books, or tools? Want convenient access to your checking account? Want to decide whether to refinance your condo? Want to know what TCP/IP means? Use the Internet, if you have it.

All of this intellectual capital resides on the Internet because businesses benefit by putting it there. It's much cheaper to provide product support information over the Internet than on printed documents. The savings include not only the costs of printing, but also the costs of warehousing and mailing. Further, when product specifications change, the organization just changes the Web site. There is no obsolete material to dispose of and no costs for printing and distributing the revised material. Those who have Internet access gain current information faster than those who do not.

What happens to those who do not have Internet access? They fall farther and farther behind. The digital divide segregates the haves from the have-nots, creating new class structures. Such segregation is subtle, but it is segregation, nonetheless.

Discussion Questions

1. Do you see evidence of a digital divide on your campus? In your hometown? Among your relatives? Describe personal experiences you've had regarding the digital divide.

2. Do organizations have a legal responsibility to provide the same information for nonconnected customers that they do for connected customers? If not, should laws be passed requiring organizations to do so?

3. Even if there is no current legal requirement for organizations to provide equal information to nonconnected customers, do they have an ethical responsibility to do so?

4. Are your answers to questions 2 and 3 different for government agencies than they are for commercial organizations?

5. Because it may be impossible to provide equal information, another approach for reducing the digital divide is for the government to enable nonconnected citizens to acquire Internet access via subsidies and tax incentives. Do you favor such a program? Why or why not?

6. Suppose that nothing is done to reduce the digital divide and that it is allowed to grow wider and wider. What are the consequences? How will society change? Are these consequences acceptable?

Do organizations have a responsibility to address this matter? If 98 percent of a company's market segment has Internet access, does the company have a responsibility to provide non-Internet materials to that other 2 percent? On what basis does that responsibility lie? Does a government agency have a responsibility to provide equal information to those who have Internet access and those who do not? When those who are connected can obtain information nearly instantaneously, 24/7, is it even possible to provide equal information to the connected and the unconnected?

It's a worldwide problem. Connected societies and countries pull farther and farther ahead. How can any economy that relies on traditional mail compete with an Internet-based economy?

If you're taking MIS, you're already connected; you're already one of the haves, and you're already pulling ahead of the have-nots. The more you learn about information systems and their use in commerce, the faster you'll pull ahead. The digital divide increases. ■

Your Personal Competitive Advantage

Consider the following possibility: You work hard, earning your degree in business, and you graduate, only to discover that you cannot find a job in your area of study. You look for 6 weeks or so, but then you run out of money. In desperation, you take a job waiting tables at a local restaurant. Two years go by, the economy picks up, and the jobs you had been looking for become available. Unfortunately, your degree is now 2 years old; you are competing with students who have just graduated with fresh degrees (and fresh knowledge). Two years of waiting tables, good as you are at it, does not appear to be good experience for the job you want. You're stuck in a nightmare—one that will be hard to get out of, and one that you cannot allow to happen.

Examine Figure 3-12 again, but this time consider those elements of competitive advantage as they apply to you personally. As an employee, the skills and abilities you offer are your personal product. Examine the first three items in the list, and ask yourself, "How can I use my time in school—and in this MIS class, in particular—to create new skills, to enhance those I already have, and to differentiate my skills from the competition?" (By the way, you will enter a national/international market. Your competition is not just the students in your class; it's also students in classes in Ohio, California, British Columbia, Florida, New York, and every place else they're teaching MIS today.)

Suppose you are interested in a sales job. Perhaps you want to sell in the pharmaceutical industry. What skills can you learn from your MIS class that will make you more competitive as a future salesperson? Ask yourself, "How does the pharmaceutical industry use MIS to gain competitive advantage?" Get on the Internet and find examples of the use of information systems in the pharmaceutical industry. How does Parke-Davis, for example, use a customer information system to sell to doctors? How can your knowledge of such systems differentiate you from your competition for a job there? How does Parke-Davis use a knowledge management system? How does the firm keep track of drugs that have an adverse effect on each other?

The fourth and fifth items in Figure 3-12 concern locking in customers, buyers, and suppliers. How can you interpret those elements in terms of your personal competitive advantage? Well, to lock in, you first have to have a relationship to lock in. So do you have an internship? If not, can you get one? And once you have an internship, how can you use your knowledge of MIS to lock in your job so that you get a job offer? Does the company you are interning for have a CRM system (or any other information system that is important to the company)? If users are happy with the system, what characteristics make it worthwhile? Can you lock in a job by becoming an expert user of this system? Becoming an expert user not only locks you into your job, but it also raises barriers to entry for others who might be competing for the job. Also, can you suggest ways to improve the system, thus using your knowledge of the company and the system to lock in an extension of your job?

Human resources personnel say that networking is one of the most effective ways of finding a job. How can you use this class to establish alliances with other students? Is there an email list server for the students in your class? What about Facebook? LinkedIn? Twitter? How can you use those facilities to develop job-seeking alliances with other students? Who in your class already has a job or an internship? Can any of those people provide hints or opportunities for finding a job?

Don't restrict your job search to your local area. Are there regions of your country where jobs are more plentiful? How can you find out about student organizations in those regions? Search the Web for MIS classes in other cities, and make contact with students there. Find out what the hot opportunities are in other cities.

Finally, as you study MIS, think about how the knowledge you gain can help you save costs for your employers. Even more, see if you can build a case that an employer would actually save money by hiring you. The line of reasoning might be that because of your knowledge of IS you will be able to facilitate cost savings that more than compensate for your salary.

In truth, few of the ideas that you generate for a potential employer will be feasible or pragmatically useful. The fact that you are thinking creatively, however, will indicate to a potential employer that you have initiative and are grappling with the problems that real businesses have. As this course progresses, keep thinking about competitive advantage, and strive to understand how the topics you study can help you to accomplish, personally, one or more of the principles in Figure 3-12. ∎

Discussion Questions

1. Summarize the efforts you have taken thus far to build an employment record that will lead to job offers after graduation.

2. Considering the first three principles in Figure 3-12, describe one way in which you have a competitive advantage over your classmates. If you do not have such competitive advantage, describe actions you can take to obtain one.

3. In order to build your network, you can use your status as a student to approach business professionals. Namely, you can contact them for help with an assignment or for career guidance. For example, suppose you want to work in banking and you know that your local bank has a customer information system. You could call the manager of that bank and ask him or her how that system creates a competitive advantage for the bank. You also could ask to interview other employees and go armed with the list in Figure 3-12. Describe two specific ways in which you can use your status as a student and the list in Figure 3-12 to build your network in this way.

4. Describe two ways that you can use student alliances to obtain a job. How can you use information systems to build, maintain, and operate such alliances?

ACTIVE REVIEW

Use this Active Review to verify that you understand the ideas and concepts that answer the chapter's study questions.

Q1 How does organizational strategy determine information systems structure?

Diagram and explain the relationship of industry structure, competitive strategy, value chains, business systems, and information systems. Working from industry structure to IS, explain how the knowledge you've gained in these first three chapters pertains to that diagram.

Q2 What five forces determine industry structure?

Name and briefly describe the five forces. Give your own examples of both strong and weak forces of each type, similar to those in Figure 3-3.

Q3 How does analysis of industry structure determine competitive strategy?

Describe four different strategies as defined by Porter. Give an example of four different companies that have implemented each of the strategies.

Q4 How does competitive strategy determine value chain structure?

Define the terms *value*, *margin*, and *value chain*. Explain why organizations that choose a differentiation strategy can use value to determine a limit on the amount of extra cost to pay for differentiation. Name the primary and support activities in the value chain and explain the purpose of each. Explain the concept of linkages.

Q5 How do business processes generate value?

Define *business process, cost,* and *margin* as they pertain to business processes. Explain the purpose of an activity and describe three types of facilities. Define *activity, resource, flow,* and *facility* and explain the role of each in Figure 3-8. Explain the importance of business process redesign and describe the difference between the business processes in Figure 3-8 and those in Figure 3-9.

Q6 How does competitive strategy determine business processes and the structure of information systems?

In your own words, explain how competitive strategy determines the structure of business processes. Use the examples of a clothing store that caters to struggling students and a clothing store that caters to professional businesspeople in a high-end neighborhood. List the activities in the business process for the two companies and create a chart like that in Figure 3-9. Explain how the information systems requirements differ between the two stores.

Q7 How do information systems provide competitive advantages?

List and briefly describe eight principles of competitive advantage. Consider your college bookstore. List one application of each of the eight principles. Strive to include examples that involve information systems.

Q8 2020?

Assume that FlexTime overcomes the current revenue challenge and buys a new building. Describe the new information systems that FlexTime could create by 2020. Summarize how FlexTime should go about deciding which systems to implement. In contrast, describe what is likely to happen if FlexTime fails and becomes a shadow of its former self. Explain how technology could help its remnants merge with others to become a virtual company.

KEY TERMS AND CONCEPTS

Activity 71
Business process 71
Business process management 74
Competitive strategy 68
Cost [of a business process] 71
Digital divide 82
Facilities 71

Five forces model 66
Flow 71
Input resources 71
Linkages 70
Margin 69
Margin [of a business process] 71
Output resources 71

Primary activities 69
Support activities 69
Switching costs 78
Value 69
Value chain 69

USING YOUR KNOWLEDGE

1. Apply the value chain model to FlexTime. FlexTime does have some inventory, principally fruit and soft drinks, energy bars, and other health food that it sells at its juice bar. But, fundamentally, FlexTime is a service business. It provides facilities, equipment, and skilled personnel to teach classes and provide personal training to clients. It also provides towels, soap, shampoo, and showers for client's to use after working out.

   a. Describe how each of the primary value chain activities pertains to FlexTime. Rank the importance of that activity to FlexTime's success on a scale of 1 (low) to 5 (high). Justify your ranking.

   b. Describe how each support value chain activity pertains to FlexTime. Rank the importance of that activity to FlexTime's success on a scale of 1 (low) to 5 (high). Justify your ranking.

   c. Diagram two business processes that support the primary activities you identified as most important in part a. Use Figures 3-8 and 3-9 as a guide.

   d. Explain how each of the business processes in your answer to part c adds value to FlexTime. How does the business process need to be designed to support FlexTime's competitive strategy of a high-intensity workout? How would the value chain be different if FlexTime wanted to be the lowest-cost provider of healthcare services?

   e. Describe an information system that would support the business process you identified in your answer to part d. How would that information system differ for a company with FlexTime's competitive strategy, as compared to a company with a lowest-cost competitive strategy?

2. Apply the value chain model to a mail-order company such as L.L.Bean (*www.llbean.com*). What is its competitive strategy? Describe the tasks L.L.Bean must accomplish for each of the primary value chain activities. How does L.L.Bean's competitive strategy and the nature of its business influence the general characteristics of its information systems?

3. Suppose you decide to start a business that recruits students for summer jobs. You will match available students with available jobs. You need to learn what positions are available and what students are available for filling those positions. In starting your business, you know you will be competing with local newspapers, Craig's List (*www.craigslist.org*), and with your college. You will probably have other local competitors as well.

   a. Analyze the structure of this industry according to Porter's five forces model.

   b. Given your analysis in part a, recommend a competitive strategy.

   c. Describe the primary value chain activities as they apply to this business.

   d. Describe a business process for recruiting students.

   e. Describe information systems that could be used to support the business process in part d.

   f. Explain how the process you describe in part d and the system you describe in part e reflect your competitive strategy.

4. Consider the two different bike rental companies in Figure 3-10. Think about the bikes that they rent. Clearly, the student bikes will be just about anything that can be ridden out of the shop. The bikes for the business executives, however, must be new, shiny, clean, and in tip-top shape.

   a. Compare and contrast the operations value chains of these two businesses as they pertain to the management of bicycles.

   b. Describe a business process for maintaining bicycles for both businesses.

   c. Describe a business process for acquiring bicycles for both businesses.

   d. Describe a business process for disposing of bicycles for both businesses.

   e. What roles do you see for information systems in your answers to the earlier questions? The information systems can be those you develop within your company or they can be those developed by others, such as Craig's List.

5. Samantha Green owns and operates Twigs Tree Trimming Service. Samantha graduated from the forestry program of a nearby university and worked for a large landscape design firm, performing tree trimming and removal. After several years of experience, she bought her own truck, stump grinder, and other equipment and opened her own business in St. Louis, Missouri.

   Although many of her jobs are one-time operations to remove a tree or stump, others are recurring, such as trimming a tree or groups of trees every year or every other year. When business is slow, she calls former clients to remind them of her services and of the need to trim their trees on a regular basis.

   Samantha has never heard of Michael Porter or any of his theories. She operates her business "by the seat of her pants."

   a. Explain how an analysis of the five competitive forces could help Samantha.

   b. Do you think Samantha has a competitive strategy? What competitive strategy would seem to make sense for her?

c. How would knowledge of her competitive strategy help her sales and marketing efforts?

d. Describe, in general terms, the kind of information system that she needs to support sales and marketing efforts.

6. FiredUp, Inc., is a small business owned by Curt and Julie Robards. Based in Brisbane, Australia, FiredUp manufactures and sells a lightweight camping stove called the Fired Now. Curt, who previously worked as an aerospace engineer, invented and patented a burning nozzle that enables the stove to stay lit in very high winds—up to 90 miles per hour. Julie, an industrial designer by training, developed an elegant folding design that is small, lightweight, easy to set up, and very stable. Curt and Julie manufacture the stove in their garage, and they sell it directly to their customers over the Internet and via phone.

a. Explain how an analysis of the five competitive forces could help FiredUp.

b. What does FiredUp's competitive strategy seem to be?

c. Briefly summarize how the primary value chain activities pertain to FiredUp. How should the company design these value chains to conform to its competitive strategy?

d. Describe business processes that FiredUp needs in order to implement its marketing and sales and also its service value chain activities.

e. Describe, in general terms, information systems to support your answer to part d.

COLLABORATION EXERCISE

Singing Valley Resort is a top-end 50-unit resort located high in the Colorado mountains. Rooms rent for $400 to $4,500 per night, depending on the season and the type of accommodations. Singing Valley's clientele are well-to-do; many are famous entertainers, sports figures, and business executives. They are accustomed to, and demand, superior service.

Singing Valley resides in a gorgeous mountain valley and is situated a few hundred yards from a serene mountain lake. It prides itself on superior accommodations; tip-top service; delicious, healthful, organic meals; and exceptional wines. Because it has been so successful, Singing Valley is 90 percent occupied except during the "shoulder seasons" (November, after the leaves change and before the snow arrives, and late April, when winter sports are finished but the snow is still on the ground.)

Singing Valley's owners want to increase revenue, but because the resort is nearly always full and because its rates are already at the top of the scale it cannot do so via occupancy revenue. Thus, over the past several years it has focused on up-selling to its clientele activities such as fly-fishing, river rafting, cross-country skiing, snowshoeing, art lessons, yoga and other exercise classes, spa services, and the like.

To increase the sales of these optional activities, Singing Valley prepared in-room marketing materials to advertise their availability. Additionally, it trained all registration personnel on techniques of casually and appropriately suggesting such activities to guests on arrival.

The response to these promotions was only mediocre, so Singing Valley's management stepped up its promotions. The first step was to send email to its clientele advising them of the activities available during their stay. An automated system produced emails personalized with names and personal data.

Unfortunately, the automated email system backfired. Immediately upon its execution, Singing Valley management received numerous complaints. One long-term customer objected that she had been coming to Singing Valley for 7 years and asked if they had yet noticed that she was confined to a wheelchair. If they had noticed, she said, why did they send her a personalized invitation for a hiking trip? The agent of another famous client complained that the personalized email was sent to her client and her husband, when anyone who had turned on a TV in the past 6 months knew the two of them were involved in an exceedingly acrimonious divorce. Yet another customer complained that, indeed, he and his wife had vacationed at Singing Valley 3 years ago, but he had not been there since. To his knowledge, his wife had not been there, either, so he was puzzled as to why the email referred to their visit last winter. He wanted to know if, indeed, his wife had recently been to the resort, without him. Of course, Singing Valley had no way of knowing about customers it had insulted who never complained.

During the time the automated email system was operational sales of extra activities were up 15 percent. However, the strong customer complaints conflicted with its competitive strategy so, in spite of the extra revenue, Singing Valley stopped the automated email system, sacked the vendor who had developed it, and demoted the Singing Valley employee who had brokered the system. Singing Valley was left with the problem of how to increase its revenue.

Your team's task is to develop two innovative ideas for solving Singing Valley's problem. At the minimum, include the following in your response:

a. An analysis of the five forces of the Singing Valley market. Make and justify any necessary assumptions about their market.

b. A statement of Singing Valley's competitive strategy.

c. A statement of the problem. Recall from Chapter 2 that a problem is a perceived difference between what is and what ought to be. If the members of your group have different perceptions of the problem, all the better. Use a collaborative process to obtain the best possible problem description to which all can agree.

d. Document in a general way (like the top row of Figure 3-10), the process of up-selling an activity

e. Develop two innovative ideas for solving the Singing Valley problem. For each idea, provide:
  • A brief description of the idea
  • A process diagram (like Figure 3-11) of the idea. Figure 3-11 was produced using Microsoft Visio; if you have access to that product, you'll save time and have a better result if you also use it.
  • A description of the information system needed to implement the idea

f. Compare the advantages and disadvantages of your alternatives in part e and recommend one of them for implementation.

APPLICATION EXERCISES

1. Figure 3-18 shows an Excel spreadsheet that the resort bicycle rental business uses to value and analyze its bicycle inventory. Examine this figure to understand the meaning of the data. Now use Excel to create a similar spreadsheet. Note the following:

   • The top heading is in 20-point Calibri font. It is centered in the spreadsheet. Cells A1 through H1 have been merged.
   • The second heading, Bicycle Inventory Valuation, is in 18-point Calibri, italics. It is centered in Cells A2 through H2, which have been merged.
   • The column headings are set in 11-point Calibri, bold. They are centered in their cells, and the text wraps in the cells.

   a. Make the first two rows of your spreadsheet similar to that in Figure 3-18. Choose your own colors for background and type, however.

   b. Place the current date so that it is centered in cells C3, C4, and C5, which must be merged.

   c. Outline the cells as shown in the figure.

   d. Figure 3-18 uses the following formulas:

      Cost of Current Inventory = Bike Cost × Number on Hand

      Revenue per Bike = Total Rental Revenue/Number on Hand

      Revenue as a Percent of Cost of Inventory = Total Rental Revenue/Cost of Current Inventory

      Please use these formulas in your spreadsheet, as shown in Figure 3-18.

   e. Format the cells in the columns, as shown.

   f. Give three examples of decisions that management of the bike rental agency might make from this data.

   g. What other calculation could you make from this data that would be useful to the bike rental management? Create a second version of this spreadsheet in your worksheet document that has this calculation.

Make of Bike	Bike Cost	Number on Hand	Cost of Current Inventory	Number of Rentals	Total Rental Revenue	Revenue per Bike	Revenue as percent of Cost of Inventory
			Resort Bicycle Rental				
			Bicycle Inventory Valuation				
			Monday, October 29, 2007				
Wonder Bike	$325	12	$3,900	85	$6,375	$531	163.5%
Wonder Bike II	$385	4	$1,540	34	$4,570	$1,143	296.8%
Wonder Bike Supreme	$475	8	$3,800	44	$5,200	$650	136.8%
LiteLift Pro	$655	8	$5,240	25	$2,480	$310	47.3%
LiteLift Ladies	$655	4	$2,620	40	$6,710	$1,678	256.1%
LiteLift Racer	$795	3	$2,385	37	$5,900	$1,967	247.4%

Figure 3-18

2. In this exercise, you will learn how to create a query based on data that a user enters and how to use that query to create a data entry form.

   a. Download the Microsoft Access file **Ch03Ex02**. Open the file and familiarize yourself with the data in the Customer table.

   b. Click *Create* in the Access ribbon. On the far right, select *Query Design*. Select the Customer table as the basis for the query. Drag Customer Name, Customer Email, Date Of Last Rental, Bike Last Rented, Total Number Of Rentals, and Total Rental Revenue into the columns of the query results pane (the table at the bottom of the query design window).

   c. In the CustomerName column, in the row labeled Criteria, place the following text:

   [Enter Name of Customer:]

   Type this exactly as shown, including the square brackets. This notation tells Access to ask you for a customer name to query.

   d. In the ribbon, click the red exclamation mark labeled *Run*. Access will display a dialog box with the text "Enter Name of Customer:" (the text you entered in the query Criteria row). Enter the value *Scott, Rex* and click OK.

   e. Save your query with the name *Parameter Query*.

   f. Click the Home tab on the ribbon and click the Design View (upper left-hand button on the Home ribbon). Replace the text in the Criteria column of the CustomerName column with the following text. Type it exactly as shown:

   Like "*" & [Enter part of Customer Name to search by:] & "*"

   g. Run the query by clicking Run in the ribbon. Enter *Scott* when prompted *Enter part of Customer Name to search by*. Notice that the two customers who have the name Scott are displayed. If you have any problems, ensure that you have typed the phrase above *exactly* as shown into the Criteria row of the CustomerName column of your query.

   h. Save your query again under the name *Parameter Query*. Close the query window.

   i. Click *Create* in the Access ribbon. Under the Forms group, select the down arrow to the right of More Forms. Choose *Form Wizard*. In the dialog that opens, in the Tables/Queries box, click the down arrow. Select *Parameter Query*. Click the double chevron (>>) symbol and all of the columns in the query will move to the Selected Fields area.

   j. Click *Next* three times. In the box under *What title do you want for your form?* enter *Customer Query Form* and click *Finish*.

   k. Enter *Scott* in the dialog box that appears. Access will open a form with the values for Scott, Rex. At the bottom of the form, click the right-facing arrow and the data for Scott, Bryan will appear.

   l. Close the form. Select *Object Type* and *Forms* in the Access Navigation Pane. Double-click on Customer Query Form and enter the value *James*. Access will display data for all six customers having the value James in their name.

CASE STUDY 3   video

Bosu Balance Trainer

The Bosu balance trainer is a device for developing balance, strength, and aerobic conditioning. Invented in 1999, Bosu has become popular in leading health clubs, in athletic departments, and in homes. Bosu stands for "both sides up," because either side of the equipment can be used for training. Figure 3-19 shows a Bosu in use.

Bosu is not only a new training device, but it also reflects a new philosophy in athletic conditioning that focuses on balance. According to the Bosu inventor, David Weck, "The Bosu Balance Trainer was born of passion to improve my balance. In my lifelong pursuit of enhanced athleticism, I have come to understand that balance is the foundation on which all other performance components are built." In order to obtain broad market acceptance both for his philosophy as well as for the Bosu product, Weck licensed the sales and marketing of Bosu to FitnessQuest in 2001.

Bosu devices have been very successful and that success attracted copycat products. FitnessQuest successfully defeated such products using a number of techniques, but primarily by leveraging its alliances with professional trainers.

According to Dustin Schnabel, Bosu product manager,

"We have developed strong and effective relationships with more than 10,000 professional trainers. We do all we can to make sure those trainers succeed with Bosu and they in turn encourage their clients to purchase our product rather than some cheap imitation.

"It's all about quality. We build a quality product, we create quality relationships with the trainers, and we make sure those trainers have everything they need from us to provide a quality experience to their clients."

That strategy worked well. In the fall of 2004, Fitness Quest had a serious challenge to Bosu from a large sports equipment vendor who had preexisting alliances with major chains such as Target and Wal-Mart. The competitor

Figure 3-19

Figure 3-20

new, fun, and innovative group training medium, and Indo-Row offers a solution to that need.

You can learn more about Bosu devices at *www.bosu.com*, more about IndoRow at *www.IndoRow.com*, and more about FitnessQuest at *www.FitnessQuest.com*.

Sources: Bosu, *www.bosu.com* (accessed June 2009); IndoRow, *www.indorow.com* (accessed June 2009); and Conversation with Dustin Schnabel, July 2009.

Questions

1. Review the principles of competitive advantage in Figure 3-12. Which types of competitive advantage has Bosu used to defeat copycat products?

2. What role did information systems play in your answer to question 1?

3. What additional information systems could Fitness Quest develop to create barriers to entry to the competition and to lock in customers?

4. In 2004, FitnessQuest had alliances with trainers and their competitor had alliances with major retailers. Thus, both companies were competing on the basis of their alliances. Why do you think FitnessQuest won this competition? To what extent did their success leveraging relationships with trainers depend on information systems? On other factors?

5. The case does not state all of the uses that FitnessQuest makes of its trainer database. List five applications of that database that would increase FitnessQuest's competitive position.

6. Describe major differences between the Bosu product and the IndoRow product. Consider product use, product price, customer resistance, competition, competitive threats, and other factors related to market acceptance.

7. Describe information systems that FitnessQuest could use to strengthen its strategy for bringing IndoRow to market. Consider the factors you identified in your answer to question 6 in your response.

introduced a Bosu copycat at a slightly lower price. Within a few months, in an effort to gain sales, they reduced their price, eventually several times, until it was less than half the price of the Bosu. Today, that copycat product is not to be seen. According to Schnabel, "They couldn't give that product away. Why? Because customers were coming in the store to buy the Bosu product that their trainers recommended."

Fitness Quest maintains a database of trainer data. They use that database for email and postal correspondence, as well as for other marketing purposes. For example, after a marketing message has been sent, Schnabel and others watch the database for changes in trainer registration. Registrations increase after a well-received message and they fall off when messages are off-target.

Fitness Quest and Schnabel are in the process of introducing new cardio training class equipment called Indo-Row (shown in Figure 3-20), for which they intend to use the same marketing strategy. First, they will leverage their relationships with trainers to obtain trainer buy-in for the new concept. Then, when that buy-in occurs, they will use it to sell Indo-Row to individuals.

Go to *www.IndoRow.com* and watch the video. As you'll see, IndoRow competes directly with other equipment-based forms of group exercise like Spinning®. Schnabel states that many clubs and workout studios are looking for a

THE INTERNATIONAL DIMENSION

The Global Economy

Q1 Why Is the Global Economy Important Today?

Businesses compete today in a global market. International business has been sharply increasing since the middle of the twentieth century. After World War II, the Japanese and other Asian economies exploded when those countries began to manufacture and sell goods to the West. The rise of the Japanese auto industry and the semiconductor industry in Southeast Asia greatly expanded international trade. At the same time, the economies of North America and Europe became more closely integrated.

Since then, a number of other factors have caused international business to explode. The fall of the Soviet Union opened the economies of Russia and Eastern Europe to the world market. More important, the telecommunications boom during the dot-com heyday caused the world to be encircled many times over by optical fiber that can be used for data and voice communications.

After the dot-com bust, this fiber was largely underutilized and could be purchased for pennies on the dollar. Plentiful, cheap telecommunications enabled people worldwide to participate in the global economy. Prior to the advent of the Internet, for a young Indian professional to participate in the Western economy, he or she had to migrate to the West—a process that was politicized and limited. Today, that same young Indian professional can sell his or her goods or services over the Internet without leaving home. During this same period, the Chinese economy became more open to the world, and it, too, benefits from plentiful, cheap telecommunications.

Thomas Friedman estimates that from 1991 until now, some 3 billion people have been added to the world economy.[1] Not all of those people speak English, and not all are well enough educated (or equipped) to participate in the world economy. But even if just 10 percent are, then 300 million people have been added to the world economy in just the last 15 years!

Q2 How Does the Global Economy Change the Competitive Environment?

To understand the impact of globalization, consider each of the elements in Figure 3-1 (page 66), starting with industry structure. The changes have been so dramatic that the structure of seemingly every industry has changed. The enlarged and Internet-equipped world economy has altered every one of the five competitive forces. Suppliers have to reach a wider range of customers, and customers have to consider a wider range of vendors. As you will learn when we address e-commerce in Chapter 8, suppliers and customers benefit not just from the greater size of the economy, but also by the ease with which businesses can learn of each other using infrastructure like Google.

Because of the information available on the Internet, customers can more easily learn of substitutions. The Internet has made it easier for new market entrants, although not in all cases. Amazon.com, Yahoo!, and Google, for example, have garnered such a large market share that it would be difficult for any new entrant to challenge them. Still, in other industries, the global economy facilitates new entrants. Finally, the global economy has intensified rivalry by increasing product and vendor choices and by accelerating the flow of information about price, product, availability, and service.

Q3 How Does the Global Economy Change Competitive Strategy?

Today's global economy changes competitive strategies analysis in two major ways. First, the sheer size and complexity of the global economy means that any organization that chooses a strategy to compete industry-wide is taking a very big bite! Competing in many different countries, with products localized to the language and culture of those countries, is an enormous and expensive task.

For example, to promote its Windows monopoly, Microsoft must produce a version of Windows in dozens of different languages. Even in English, there are U.K. versions, U.S. versions, Australian versions, and so forth. The problem for Microsoft is even greater because different countries use different character sets. In some languages, one writes left to right. In other languages, one writes right to left. When Microsoft set out to sell Windows worldwide, it embarked on an enormous project.

The second major way today's world economy changes competitive strategies is that its size, combined with the Internet, enables unprecedented product differentiation. If

---

[1]Thomas L. Friedman, *The World Is Flat* [Updated and Expanded]: *A Brief History of the Twenty-First Century* (New York: Farrar, Strauss, and Giroux, 2006).

you choose to produce the world's highest quality and most exotic oatmeal—and if your production costs require you to sell that oatmeal for $350 a pound—your target market may contain only 200 people worldwide. The Internet allows you to find them—and them to find you.

Decisions involving global competitive strategies involve the consideration of these two changing factors.

Q4 How Does the Global Economy Change Value Chains and Business Processes?

The growth in the world economy has major impacts on all activities in the value chain model. An excellent example concerns the manufacture of the Boeing 787. Every primary activity for this airplane has an international component. Companies all over the world produce its parts and subassemblies. Major components of the airplane are constructed in worldwide locations and shipped for final assembly to Boeing's plant in Everett, Washington. *Outbound logistics* for Boeing refers not just to the delivery of an airplane, but also to the delivery of spare parts and supporting maintenance equipment. All of those items are produced at factories worldwide and delivered to customers worldwide. The global sales also change the marketing, sales, and service activities for the 787.

As you learned in Chapter 3, each value chain activity is supported by one or more business processes. Those processes span the globe and need to address differences in language, culture, and economic environments. A process for servicing 787 customers in Egypt will be very different from the same service process in China, the United States, or India. For example, a business process organized around a central leader with strong authority may be expected in one culture and resisted in another. Global companies must design their business processes with these differences in mind.

Q5 How Does the Global Economy Change Information Systems?

To understand the impact of internationalization on information systems, consider the five components. Computer hardware is sold worldwide, and most vendors provide documentation in at least the major languages, so internationalization has little impact on that component. The remaining components of an information system, however, are markedly affected.

To begin, consider the user interface for an international information system. Does it include a localized version of Windows? What about the software application itself? Does an inventory system used worldwide by Boeing suppose that each user speaks English? If so, at what level of proficiency? If not, what languages must the user interface support? Most computer programs are written in computer languages that have an English base, but not all. Can an information system use a localized programming language?

Next, consider the data component. Suppose that the inventory database has a table for parts data and that table contains a column named *Remarks*. Suppose Boeing needs to integrate parts data from three different vendors: one in China, one in India, and one in Canada. What language is to be used for recording remarks? Does someone need to translate all of the remarks into one language? Into three languages?

The human components—procedures and people—are obviously affected by language and culture. As with business processes, information systems procedures need to reflect local cultural values and norms. For systems users, job descriptions and reporting relationships must be appropriate for the setting in which the system is used. We will say more about this in Part 4, when we discuss the development and management of information systems.

ACTIVE REVIEW

Use this Active Review to verify that you understand the ideas and concepts that answer the study questions in the International Dimension.

Q1 Why is the global economy important today?

Describe how the global economy has changed since the mid-twentieth century. Explain how the dot-com bust influenced the global economy and changed the number of workers worldwide.

Q2 How does the global economy change the competitive environment?

Summarize the ways in which today's global economy influences the five competitive forces. Explain how the global economy changes the way organizations analyze industry structure.

Q3 How does the global economy change competitive strategy?

Explain how size and complexity change the costs of a competitive strategy. Describe what the size of the global economy means to differentiation.

Q4 How does the global economy change value chains and business processes?

Describe, in general terms, how international business impacts value chains and business processes. Use the example of the Boeing 787 in your answer.

Q5 How does the global economy change information systems?

Describe how international business impacts each of the five components of an information system. Identify the components that are most impacted by the need to support multiple cultures and languages.

CASE Getty Images Serves Up Profit and YouTube Grows Exponentially

Chapter 1 stated that near-free data communication and data storage have created unprecedented opportunities for highly profitable businesses. Here we will consider two: Getty Images and YouTube.

Getty Images was founded in 1995 with the goal of consolidating the fragmented photography market by acquiring many small companies, applying business discipline to the merged entity, and developing modern information systems. The advent of the Web drove the company to e-commerce and in the process enabled Getty to change the workflow and business practices of the professional visual-content industry. Getty Images had grown from a startup to become, by 2004, a global, $600 million plus, publicly traded, very profitable company. By 2007, Getty had increased its revenue to more than $880 million. More recent financial information is unavailable, because in July 2008 Getty was purchased by the private equity firm Hellman & Friedman, LLC for $2.4 billion.

Getty Images obtains its imagery (still, video, and audio) from photographers and other artists under contract, and it owns the world's largest private archive of imagery. Getty also employs staff photographers to shoot the world's news, sport, and entertainment events. In the case of photography and film that it does not own, it provides a share of the revenue generated to the content owner. Getty Images is both a producer and a distributor of imagery, and all of its products are sold via e-commerce on the Web.

Getty Images employs three licensing models: The first is *subscription*, by which customers contract to use as many images as they want as often as they want (this applies to the news, sport, and entertainment imagery). The second model is *royalty-free*. In this model, customers pay a fee based on the file size of the image and can use the image any way they want and as many times as they want. However, under this model, customers have no exclusivity or ability to prevent a competitor from using the same image at the same time.

The third model, *rights managed*, also licenses creative imagery. In this model, which is the largest in revenue terms, users pay fees according to the rights that they wish to use—size, industry, geography, prominence, frequency, exclusivity, and so forth.

According to its Web site:

Getty Images has been credited with the introduction of royalty-free photography and was the first company to license imagery via the Web, subsequently moving the entire industry online. The company was also the first to employ creative researchers to anticipate the visual content needs of the world's communicators (*http://corporate.gettyimages.com/ source/company.html,* accessed December 2007).

Because Getty Images licenses photos in digital format, its variable cost of production is essentially zero. Once the company has obtained a photo and placed it in the commerce server database, the cost of sending it to a customer

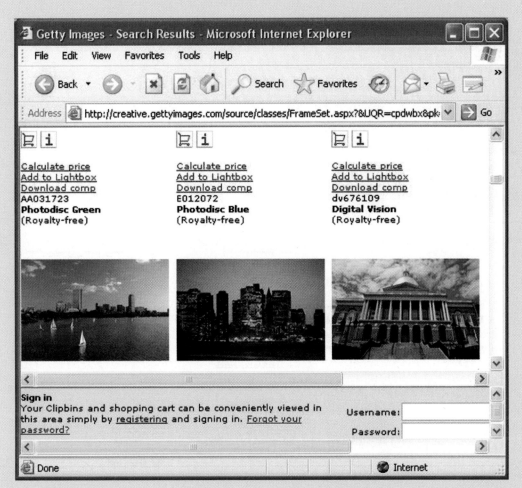

Figure 1
Getty Images' Search
Results

Source: Used with permission from Getty
Images, Inc. All Rights Reserved. © 2007 Getty
Images, Inc.

is zero. Getty Images does have the overhead costs of setting up and operating the e-commerce site, and it does pay some costs for its images—either the cost of employing the photographer or the cost of setting up and maintaining the relationship with out-of-house photographers. For some images, it also pays a royalty to the owner. Once these costs are paid, however, the cost of producing a photo is nil. This means that Getty Images' profitability increases substantially with increased volume.

Why did Hellman & Friedman purchase GettyImages? According to its Web site, Hellman & Friedman, "focuses on investing in businesses with strong, defensible franchises and predictable revenue and earnings growth and which generate high levels of free cash flow or attractive returns on the capital reinvested in the business." With a near zero cost of production, it is likely that Getty Images does indeed generated high levels of free cash flow!

At the same time that Getty Images was achieving its peak as a public company, another team of entrepreneurs found a different way to take advantage of near-free data communications and data storage. On February 15, 2005, Chad Hurley, Steve Chen, and Jawed Karim registered the domain "YouTube" and by April 23 had posted their first video. By November, YouTube had 200,000 registered users and was showing 2 million videos per day. In 9 months, YouTube had grown from nothing to 200,000 users.

By January 2006, YouTube was showing 25 million videos per day. By May 2006, YouTube was showing 43 percent of all videos viewed over the Internet. By July 2006, users were viewing 100 million videos and uploading 65,000 new videos per day. YouTube had a total of 30 employees. Think about that:

Figure 2
Price Calculation for an Image
of Boston

Source: Used with permission from Getty
Images, Inc. All Rights Reserved. © 2007 Getty
Images, Inc.

30 employees were serving 100 million videos per day. That's 3.33 million videos *per employee*, all accomplished in just over 1 year.

That phenomenal success was capped by Google's $1.65 billion acquisition of YouTube in October 2006. In just 20 months, YouTube's founders had turned nothing but an idea into $1.65 billion. That's a rate of $2,750,000 of equity per day.

What's the point of these examples? The opportunities were there in 1995, in 2005, and they are still there today. Although it is unlikely that you, too, will have such success, think about it: How can you use free data communications and data storage in your business? Or, in a job interview, how might you suggest that your prospective employer use such resources?

Sources: www.gettyimages.com (accessed December 2004, May 2007, June 2009); *www.hf.com* (accessed June 2009); and *www.youtube.com/watch?v=x2NQiVcdZRY* (accessed June 2009).

QUESTIONS

1. Visit *www.gettyimages.com*, and select "Images/Creative/Search royalty-free." Search for an image of a major city of interest to you. Select a photo and determine its default price. Follow the link on the photographer's name to find other images by that photographer.

2. Explain how Getty Images' business model takes advantage of the opportunities created by IT as described in Chapter 1.

3. Evaluate the photography market using Porter's five forces. Do you think Getty Images' marginal cost is sustainable? Are its prices sustainable? What is the key to its continued success?

4. What seems to be Getty Images' competitive strategy?

5. Explain how Getty Images' use of information systems contributed to the company's value when it was acquired.

6. How did the availability of near-free data communication and data storage facilitate YouTube's success? Would YouTube have been possible without them?

7. Even though the cost of data communication and data storage is very low, for the volume at which YouTube operates they are still substantial expenses. How did YouTube fund these expenses? (Search the Internet for "History of YouTube" to find information to answer this question.)

8. How does YouTube (now owned by Google) earn revenue?

Using the cases of Getty Images and YouTube as a guide, answer the following questions:

9. Choose a corporation located in the geographic vicinity of your college or university. In what ways is it already taking advantage of the low cost of data communication and data storage?

10. Using the corporation you identified in question 9, identify three innovative ways that the corporation could take advantage of the low cost of data communication and storage.

11. Create an outline of a statement about this importance of near-zero cost data storage and data communication that you could use in a job interview. Assume you wish to demonstrate that you have knowledge of the power of emerging technology as well as the capacity to think innovatively. Incorporate the example you used in your answer to questions 9 and 10 in your answer.

Information Technology

The next three chapters address the technology that underlies information systems. You may think that such technology is unimportant to you as a business professional. However, as you will see at FlexTime, today's managers and business professionals work with information technology all the time, as consumers, if not in a more involved way.

Chapter 4 discusses hardware and software and defines basic terms and fundamental computing concepts. You will see that Neil and Kelly have important decisions to make about the next version of software that they will use to run their business.

Chapter 5 addresses the data component of information technology by describing database processing. You will learn essential database terminology and be introduced to techniques for processing databases. We will also introduce data modeling, because you may be required to evaluate data models for databases that others develop for you. At FlexTime, Neil will use a database to analyze the cost-saving alternatives the team identified in Chapter 3.

Chapter 6 continues the discussion of computing devices begun in Chapter 4 and describes data communications and Internet technologies. FlexTime is responding to the threat of its landlord (a supplier) by buying its own building. FlexTime needs to save costs, but it also needs to wire the building for data communications in the next 10 years. What capabilities does FlexTime need?

The purpose of these three chapters is to teach you technology sufficient for you to be an effective IT consumer, like Neil at FlexTime. You will learn basic terms, fundamental concepts, and useful frameworks so that you will have the knowledge to ask good questions and make appropriate requests of the information systems professionals who will serve you. Those concepts and frameworks will be far more useful to you than the latest technology trend, which may be outdated by the time you graduate!

4 Hardware and Software

"Neil, I hate to interrupt our night out together, but I'm confused about the software problem at work. Why didn't you upgrade the program?"

"Let me back up, Kelly. Four years ago, we paid $35,000 for Version 2 of the Studio Management software."

"OK, I've got that."

"Since then, we've paid a support fee of $5,000 a year. That fee enables us to call their tech support when something goes wrong, like when we installed the three new printers last year. They help us in other ways, too."

"So, Neil, that means we've paid them $55,000 so far?"

"Right. Now, 2 years ago they came out with Version 3 of their software. I looked at it and didn't see any reason to upgrade, and they wanted another $25,000 license fee. So, I passed on it."

"OK, that seems logical. So what's the problem?"

"When I was at Siebel, we called it *strangle and cram*. Actually, I think the term came from IBM in the 1960s, but it doesn't matter. The idea is that you cut off support to an older version of the product (that's the *strangle*) and tell your customers that to get support, they have to upgrade to the new version (that's the *cram*)."

"Wow. Can we sue them or something?"

"Do we want to mess up our lives with a lawsuit?"

"No."

> *"When I was at Siebel, we called it strangle and cram."*

"Besides, the contracts say they can do this."

"So we upgrade?"

"Maybe, Kelly. The thing is, though, their architecture is old. Even with the new version they're still using thick clients and I just don't think we want to stay there."

"Neil, I have absolutely no idea what you're talking about. And I'm hungry. Let's order."

They order.

"Kelly, you know that computer that sits in the corner of my office? That's our server. It's a computer that receives requests from the other computers and processes them. All the other computers at FlexTime are client computers; they call the server to do things like store data in our database. But, to make that work, we had to install a special computer program on each client."

"So what are you telling me?"

"Thick clients are out; they're based on 1980s' technology. The new way is to use Internet technology and substitute a browser for the thick client. Lots of reasons to do that, but one is that nobody needs a special program installed on their computer to access our systems. They can do it from a browser. So, I don't have to keep installing and uninstalling software on our trainers' computers. People can also access the system from their iPhones, or whatever they're using. They just use their browsers."

"So this upgrade that they're cramming is based on older technology?"

"Right. I've been looking at other options. Problem is we'd have to train everyone to use the new system . . . and that would be ugly. . . and costly."

"Well, if we have to do it, we have to do it."

"Yeah. We could wait until we have the new building, but I hate to put that much change on everyone at once."

"OK, so what's holding you back?"

"Cost. They want $65,000 up front and 10 percent, $6,500, a year for support."

"Ouch."

"There's another option: open source. There's a group that's created a version that might do the job, and it's free."

"How can it be free?"

"Well, I should say license free. We won't have to pay the up-front cost but we would pay the company that supports it."

"But why no up-front cost?"

"Because the programmers who build it are unpaid volunteers."

"Neil, are you saying we're going to run our business on a program created by a bunch of amateurs?"

"No, not amateurs. Think Wikipedia. It's done by volunteers, and the quality of the information there is high. The Wikipedia community sees to that. It's the same for good open source software. Linux was built that way."

"Linux? Oh no, another term. That's enough. Let's eat."

"How do other small businesses do it? I mean you spent all those years selling software, you know the game. How does the average club owner make these decisions?"

"They waste a lot of money."

"And time." ∎

>> STUDY QUESTIONS

Q1 What do business professionals need to know about computer hardware?

Q2 What is the difference between a client and a server?

Q3 What do business professionals need to know about software?

Q4 Why are thin clients preferred to thick clients?

Q5 Is open source software a viable alternative?

Q6 How can you use this knowledge?

Q7 2020?

CHAPTER PREVIEW

Like Neil, you might go into the computer industry and then transition to some other business. If so, you'll know "how the game is played," as Kelly says. However, you might not. You might become a department manager, or own your own small business, or be appointed to your law firm's technology committee. Whatever direction your career takes, you don't want to be one of those professionals who "waste a lot of money . . . and time." The knowledge from this chapter can help.

You don't need to be an expert. You don't need to be a hardware engineer or a computer programmer. You do need to know enough, however, to be an effective consumer. You need the knowledge and skills to ask important, relevant questions and understand the answers. We begin with basic hardware and software concepts. Then we will discuss how you can use your knowledge to prepare a computer budget for your department and then we wrap up by forecasting trends in hardware and software in 2020.

Q1 What Do Business Professionals Need to Know About Computer Hardware?

As discussed in the five-component framework, **hardware** consists of electronic components and related gadgetry that input, process, output, and store data according to instructions encoded in computer programs or software. Figure 4-1 shows the components of a generic computer. Notice that the basic hardware categories are input, process, output, and storage.

Basic Components

As shown in Figure 4-1, typical **input hardware** devices are the keyboard, mouse, document scanners, and bar-code (Universal Product Code) scanners like those used in grocery stores. Microphones also are input devices; with tablet PCs, human handwriting can be input as well. Older input devices include magnetic ink readers (used for reading the ink on the bottom of checks) and scanners such as the Scantron test scanner shown in Figure 4-2.

Processing devices include the **central processing unit (CPU),** which is sometimes called "the brain" of the computer. Although the design of the CPU has nothing in common with the anatomy of animal brains, this description is helpful, because the CPU does have the "smarts" of the machine. The CPU selects instructions, processes

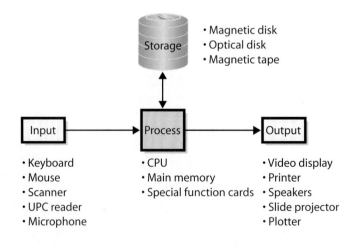

Figure 4-1
Input, Process, Output, and Storage Hardware

Figure 4-2
Scantron Scanner

Source: Courtesy of Harrison Public Relations Group, Scantron Corporation.

them, performs arithmetic and logical comparisons, and stores results of operations in memory. Some computers have two or more CPUs. A computer with two CPUs is called a **dual-processor** computer. **Quad-processor** computers have four CPUs. Some high-end computers have 16 or more CPUs.

CPUs vary in speed, function, and cost. Hardware vendors such as Intel, Advanced Micro Devices, and National Semiconductor continually improve CPU speed and capabilities while reducing CPU costs (as discussed under Moore's Law in Chapter 1). Whether you or your department needs the latest, greatest CPU depends on the nature of your work, as you will learn.

The CPU works in conjunction with **main memory**. The CPU reads data and instructions from memory, and it stores results of computations in main memory. We will describe the relationship between the CPU and main memory later in the chapter. Main memory is sometimes called **RAM**, for random access memory.

Finally, computers also can have **special function cards** (see Figure 4-3) that can be added to the computer to augment its basic capabilities. A common example is a card that provides enhanced clarity and refresh speed for the computer's video display.

Output hardware consists of video displays, printers, audio speakers, overhead projectors, and other special-purpose devices, such as large flatbed plotters.

Storage hardware saves data and programs. Magnetic disk is by far the most common storage device, although optical disks such as CDs and DVDs also are popular. In large corporate data centers, data is sometimes stored on magnetic tape.

Computer Data

Before we can further describe hardware, we need to define several important terms. We begin with binary digits.

Binary Digits

Computers represent data using **binary digits**, called **bits**. A bit is either a zero or a one. Bits are used for computer data because they are easy to represent electronically, as illustrated in Figure 4-4. A switch can be either closed or open. A computer can be

Figure 4-3
Special Function Card

Source: Photo courtesy of Creative Labs, Inc. Sound Blaster and Audigy are registered trademarks of Creative Technology Ltd. In the United States and other countries.

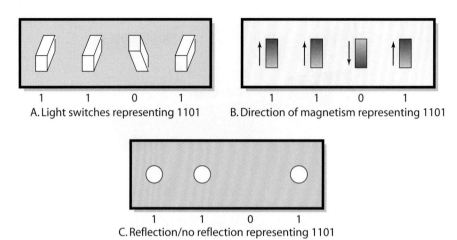

Figure 4-4
Bits Are Easy to Represent
Physically

designed so that an open switch represents zero and a closed switch represents one. Or the orientation of a magnetic field can represent a bit; magnetism in one direction represents a zero, magnetism in the opposite direction represents a one. Or, for optical media, small pits are burned onto the surface of the disk so that they will reflect light. In a given spot, a reflection means a one; no reflection means a zero.

Sizing Computer Data

All computer data are represented by bits. The data can be numbers, characters, currency amounts, photos, recordings, or whatever. All are simply a string of bits.

For reasons that interest many but are irrelevant for future managers, bits are grouped into 8-bit chunks called **bytes**. For character data, such as the letters in a person's name, one character will fit into one byte. Thus, when you read a specification that a computing device has 100 million bytes of memory, you know that the device can hold up to 100 million characters.

Bytes are used to measure sizes of noncharacter data as well. Someone might say, for example, that a given picture is 100,000 bytes in size. This statement means the length of the bit string that represents the picture is 100,000 bytes or 800,000 bits (because there are 8 bits per byte).

The specifications for the size of main memory, disk, and other computer devices are expressed in bytes. Figure 4-5 shows the set of abbreviations that are used to represent data-storage capacity. A **kilobyte**, abbreviated **K**, is a collection of 1,024 bytes. A **megabyte**, or **MB**, is 1,024 kilobytes. A **gigabyte**, or **GB**, is 1,024 megabytes, and a **terabyte**, or **TB**, is 1,024 gigabytes.

Sometimes you will see these definitions simplified as 1K equals 1,000 bytes and 1MB equals 1,000K. Such simplifications are incorrect, but they do ease the math. Also, disk and computer manufacturers have an incentive to propagate this

Figure 4-5
Important Storage-Capacity
Terminology

Term	Definition	Abbreviation
Byte	Number of bits to represent one character	
Kilobyte	1,024 bytes	K
Megabyte	1,024 K = 1,048,576 bytes	MB
Gigabyte	1,024 MB = 1,073,741,824 bytes	GB
Terabyte	1,024 GB = 1,099,511,627,776 bytes	TB

misconception. If a disk maker defines 1MB to be 1 million bytes—and not the correct 1,024K—the manufacturer can use its own definition of MB when specifying drive capacities. A buyer may think that a disk advertised as 100MB has space for $100 \times 1,024K$ bytes, but in truth the drive will have space for only $100 \times 1,000,000$ bytes. Normally, the distinction is not too important, but be aware of the two possible interpretations of these abbreviations.

In Fewer Than 300 Words, How Does a Computer Work?

Figure 4-6 shows a snapshot of a computer in use. The CPU is the major actor. To run a program or process data, the computer first transfers the program or data from disk to *main memory*. Then, to execute an instruction, it moves the instruction from main memory into the CPU via the **data channel** or **bus**. The CPU has a small amount of very fast memory called a **cache**. The CPU keeps frequently used instructions in the cache. Having a large cache makes the computer faster, but cache is expensive.

Main memory of the computer in Figure 4-6 contains program instructions for Microsoft Excel, Adobe Acrobat, and a browser (Microsoft Internet Explorer or Mozilla Firefox). It also contains a block of data and instructions for the **operating system (OS)**, which is a program that controls the computer's resources.

Main memory is too small to hold all of the programs and data that a user might want to process. For example, no personal computer has enough memory to hold all of the code in Microsoft Word, Excel, and Access. Consequently, the CPU loads programs into memory in chunks. In Figure 4-6, one portion of Excel was loaded into memory. When the user requested additional processing (say, to sort the spreadsheet), the CPU loaded another piece of Excel.

If the user opens another program (say, Word) or needs to load more data (say, a picture), the operating system will direct the CPU to attempt to place the new program or data into unused memory. If there is not enough memory, it will remove something, perhaps the block of memory labeled More Excel, and then it will place the just-requested program or data into the vacated space. This process is called **memory swapping**.

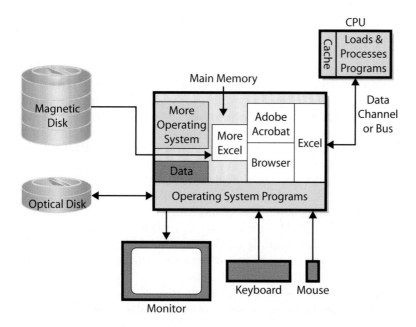

Figure 4-6
Computer Components, in Use

Why Does a Manager Care How a Computer Works?

You can order computers with varying sizes of main memory. An employee who runs only one program at a time and who processes small amounts of data requires very little memory—1GB will be adequate. However, an employee who processes many programs at the same time (say, Word, Excel, Firefox, Access, Acrobat, and other programs) or an employee who processes very large files (pictures, movies, or sound files) needs lots of main memory, perhaps 3GB or more. If that employee's computer has too little memory, then the computer will constantly be swapping memory, and it will be slow. (This means, by the way, that if your computer is slow and if you have many programs open, you likely can improve performance by closing one or more programs. Depending on your computer and the amount of memory it has, you might also improve performance by adding more memory.)

The Ethics Guide on pages 110–111 poses questions about computer hardware and software that offer more than most users need.

You can also order computers with CPUs of different speeds. CPU speed is expressed in cycles called *hertz*. In 2009, a slow personal computer has a speed of 1.5 Gigahertz. A fast personal computer has a speed of 3+ Gigahertz, with dual processing. As predicted by Moore's Law, CPU speeds continually increase.

Additionally, CPUs today are classified as **32-bit** or **64-bit**. Without delving into the particulars, a 32-bit is less capable and cheaper than a 64-bit CPU. The latter can address more main memory; you need a 64-bit processor to effectively utilize more than 4GB of memory. 64-bit processors have other advantages as well, but they are more expensive than 32-bit processors.

An employee who does only simple tasks such as word processing does not need a fast CPU; a 32-bit, 1.5 Gigahertz CPU will be fine. However, an employee who processes large, complicated spreadsheets or who manipulates large database files or edits large picture, sound, or movie files needs a fast computer like a 64-bit, dual processor with 3.5 Gigahertz or more.

One last comment: The cache and main memory are **volatile**, meaning their contents are lost when power is off. Magnetic and optical disks are **nonvolatile**, meaning their contents survive when power is off. If you suddenly lose power, the contents of unsaved memory—say, documents that have been altered—will be lost. Therefore, get into the habit of frequently (every few minutes or so) saving documents or files that you are changing. Save your documents before your roommate trips over the power cord.

Q2 What Is the Difference Between a Client and a Server?

Before we can discuss computer software, you need to understand the difference between a client and a server. Figure 4-7 shows the computing environment of the typical user. Users employ **client** computers for word processing, spreadsheets, database access, and so forth. Most client computers also have software that enables them to connect to a network. It could be a private network at their company or school, or it could be the Internet, which is a public network. (We will discuss networks and related topics in Chapter 6. Just wait!)

Servers, as their name implies, provide some service. Some servers process email; others process Web sites; others process large, shared databases; and some provide all of these functions or other, similar functions.

A server is just a computer, but as you might expect, server computers must be fast and they usually have multiple CPUs. They need lots of main memory, at least 4GB, and they require very large disks—often a terabyte or more. Because servers are almost always accessed from another computer via a network, they have limited video displays, or even no display at all. For the same reason, many have no keyboard.

For sites with large numbers of users (e.g., Amazon.com), servers are organized into a collection of servers called a **server farm** like the one shown in Figure 4-8.

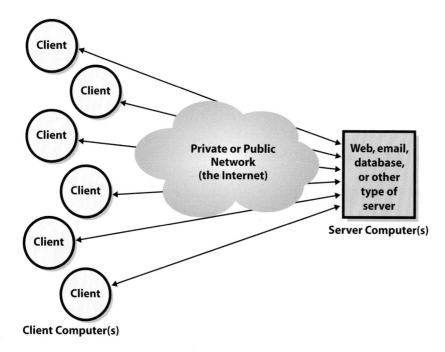

Figure 4-7
Client and Server Computers

Servers in a farm coordinate their activities in an incredibly sophisticated and fascinating technology dance. They receive and process hundreds, possibly thousands, of service requests per minute. For example, in December 2005 Amazon.com processed an average of 41 order items per second for 24 hours straight. In this dance, computers hand off partially processed requests to each other while keeping track of the current status of each request. They can pick up the pieces when a computer in the farm fails. All of this is done in the blink of an eye, with the user never knowing any part of the miracle underway. It is absolutely gorgeous engineering!

You may hear two new terms that have become popular with regard to server computers. A **grid** is a network of computers that operates as an integrated whole; the grid appears to be a single computer. The grid may operate to support a server farm, or it may support some other computing need. Organizations lease time on a grid

Figure 4-8
A Server Farm

Ethics

Churn and Burn

An anonymous source, whom we'll call Mark, made the following statements about computing devices:

"I never upgrade my system. At least, I try not to. Look, I don't do anything at work but write memos and access email. I use Microsoft Word, but I don't use any features that weren't available in Word 3.0, 20 years ago. This whole industry is based on 'churn and burn': They churn their products so we'll burn our cash.

"All this hype about 3.0GHz processors and 500GB disks—who needs them? I'm sure I don't. And if Microsoft hadn't put so much junk into Windows, we could all be happy on an Intel 486 processor like the one I had in 1993. We're suckers for falling into the 'you gotta have this' trap.

"Frankly, I think there's a conspiracy between hardware and software vendors. They both want to sell new products, so the hardware people come up with these incredibly fast and huge computers. Then, given all that power, the software types develop monster products bloated with features and functions that nobody uses. It would take me months to learn all of the features in Word, only to find out that I don't need those features.

"To see what I mean, open Microsoft Word, click on View, then select Toolbars. In my version of Word, there are 19 toolbars to select, plus one more to customize my own toolbar. Now what in the world do I need with 19 toolbars? I write all the time, and I have two selected: Standard and Formatting. Two out of 19! Could I pay Microsoft 2/19 of the price of Word, because that's all I want or use?

"Here's how they get you, though. Because we live in a connected world, they don't have to get all of us to use those 19 toolbars, just one of us. Take Bridgette, over in Legal, for example. Bridgette likes to use the redlining features, and she likes me to use them when I change draft contracts she sends me. So if I want to work on her documents, I have to turn on the Reviewing toolbar. You get the idea; just get someone to use a feature and, because it is a connected world, then all of us have to have that feature.

"Viruses are one of their best ploys. They say you better buy the latest and greatest in software—and then apply all the patches that follow so that you'll be protected from the latest zinger from the computer 'bad guys.' Think about that for a minute. If vendors had built the products correctly the first time, then there would be no holes for the baddies to find, would there? So they have a defect in their products that they turn to a sales advantage. You see, they get us to focus on the virus and not on the hole in their product. In truth, they should be saying, 'Buy our latest product to protect yourself from the defective junk we sold you last year.' But truth in advertising hasn't come that far.

"Besides that, users are their own worst enemies as far as viruses are concerned. If I'm down on 17th Street at 4 in the morning, half drunk and with a bundle of cash hanging out of my pocket, what's likely to happen to me? I'm gonna get mugged. So if I'm out in some weirdo chat room—you know, out where you get pictures of weird sex acts and whatnot—and download and run a file, then of course I'm gonna get a virus. Viruses are brought on by user stupidity, that's all.

"One of these days, users are going to rise up and say, 'That's enough. I don't need any more. I'll stay with what I have, thank you very much.' In fact, maybe that's happening right now. Maybe that's why software sales aren't growing like they were. Maybe people have finally said, 'No more toolbars!'" ■

Discussion Questions

1. Summarize Mark's view of the computer industry. Is there merit to his argument? Why or why not?

2. What holes do you see in the logic of his argument?

3. Someone could take the position that these statements are just empty rantings—that Mark can say all he wants, but the computer industry is going to keep on doing as it has been. Is there any point in Mark sharing his criticisms?

4. Comment on Mark's statement—"Viruses are brought on by user stupidity, that's all."

5. All software products ship with known problems. Microsoft, Adobe, and Apple all ship software that they know has failures. Is it unethical for them to do so? Do software vendors have an ethical responsibility to openly publish the problems in their software? How do these organizations protect themselves from lawsuits for damages caused by known problems in software?

6. Suppose a vendor licenses and ships a software product that has both known and unknown failures. As the vendor learns of the unknown failures, does it have an ethical responsibility to inform the users about them? Does the vendor have an ethical responsibility to fix the problems? Is it ethical for the vendor to require users to pay an upgrade fee for a new version of software that fixes problems in an existing version?

from other organizations that create, support, and manage that grid. For example, IBM leases time on a grid for applications that require intensive arithmetic computing. It also leases time on a special-purpose grid that is used to archive medical records (see *www-03.ibm.com/grid*).

A second new term is **cloud**. The cloud refers to the computing network on the Internet. When you access a video from a site like Facebook, you are accessing computing services in the cloud. You don't know which server is processing your Facebook requests or which server is playing the video. You just know that somewhere in the cloud one or more servers are causing the video to be downloaded to your computer. You'll learn more about servers, server virtualization, and clouds in Chapter 11.

Q3 What Do Business Professionals Need to Know About Software?

As a future manager or business professional, you need to know the essential terminology and software concepts that will enable you to be an intelligent software consumer. To begin, consider the basic categories of software shown in Figure 4-9.

Every computer has an *operating system,* which is a program that controls that computer's resources. Some of the functions of an operating system are to read and write data, allocate main memory, perform memory swapping, start and stop programs, respond to error conditions, and facilitate backup and recovery. In addition, the operating system creates and manages the user interface, including the display, keyboard, mouse, and other devices.

Although the operating system makes the computer usable, it does little application-specific work. If you want to write a document or query a customer database, you need *application programs* such as Microsoft Word or Oracle Customer Relationship Management (CRM). These programs must be licensed in addition to the operating system.

Both client and server computers need an operating system, though they need not be the same. Further, both clients and servers can process application programs. The application's design determines whether the client, the server, or both, process it.

You need to understand two important software constraints. First, a particular version of an operating system is written for a particular type of hardware. For example, Microsoft Windows works only on processors from Intel and companies that make processors that conform to the Intel **instruction set** (the commands that a CPU can process). Furthermore, the 32-bit version of Windows runs only on Intel computers with 32-bit CPUs and the 64-bit version of Windows runs only on Intel computers with 64-bit CPUs. In other cases, such as Linux, many versions exist for many different instruction sets and for both 32- and 64-bit computers.

Second, application programs are written to use a particular operating system. Microsoft Access, for example, will run only on the Windows operating system. Some applications come in multiple versions. There are, for example, Windows and Macintosh versions of Microsoft Word. But unless informed otherwise, assume that a particular application runs on just one operating system.

We will next consider the operating system and application program categories of software.

	Operating System	Application Programs
Client	Programs that control the client computer's resources	Applications that are processed on client computers
Server	Programs that control the server computer's resources	Applications that are processed on server computers

Figure 4-9
Categories of Computer Software

What Are the Four Major Operating Systems?

The four major operating systems are listed in Figure 4-10. Consider each.

Windows

For business users, the most important operating system is Microsoft **Windows**. Some version of Windows resides on more than 85 percent of the world's desktops, and, considering just business users, the figure is more than 95 percent. Many different versions of Windows are available: Windows 7, Windows Vista, and Windows XP run on user computers. Windows Server is a version of Windows designed for servers. As stated, Windows runs the Intel instruction set on both 32- and 64-bit computers.

Mac OS

Apple Computer, Inc., developed its own operating system for the Macintosh, **Mac OS**. The current version is Mac OS X. Macintosh computers are used primarily by graphic artists and workers in the arts community. Mac OS was designed originally to run the line of CPU processors from Motorola. In 1994, Mac OS switched to the PowerPC processor line from IBM. As of 2006, Macintosh computers are available for both PowerPC and Intel CPUs. A Macintosh with an Intel processor is able to run both Windows and the Mac OS.

Most people would agree that Apple has led the way in developing easy-to-use interfaces. Certainly, many innovative ideas have first appeared in a Macintosh and then later been added, in one form or another, to Windows.

Figure 4-10
What a Manager Needs to Know About Software

Category	Operating System (OS)	Instruction Set	Common Applications	Typical User
Client	Windows	Intel	Microsoft Office: Word, Excel, Access, PowerPoint, many other applications	Business. Home.
	Mac OS (pre–2006)	Power PC	Macintosh applications plus Word and Excel	Graphic artists. Arts community.
	Mac OS (post–2006)	Intel	Macintosh applications plus Word and Excel Can also run Windows on Macintosh hardware	Graphic artists. Arts community.
	Unix	Sun and others	Engineering, computer-assisted design, architecture	Difficult for the typical client, but popular with some engineers and computer scientists.
	Linux	Just about anything	Open Office (Microsoft Office look-alike)	Rare—used where budget is very limited.
Server	Windows Server	Intel	Windows server-type applications	Business with commitment to Microsoft.
	Unix	Sun and others	Unix server applications	Fading . . . Linux taking its market.
	Linux	Just about anything	Linux & Unix server applications	Very popular—promulgated by IBM.

Unix

Unix is an operating system that was developed at Bell Labs in the 1970s. It has been the workhorse of the scientific and engineering communities since then. Unix is generally regarded as being more difficult to use than either Windows or the Macintosh. Many Unix users know and employ an arcane language for manipulating files and data. However, once they surmount the rather steep learning curve most Unix users become fanatic supporters of the system. Sun Microsystems and other vendors of computers for scientific and engineering applications are the major proponents of Unix. In general, Unix is not for the business user.

Linux

Linux is a version of Unix that was developed by the **open source community** (see Q5, page 116). This community is a loosely coupled group of programmers who mostly volunteer their time to contribute code to develop and maintain Linux. The open source community owns Linux, and there is no fee to use it. Linux can run on client computers, but it is most frequently used for servers, particularly Web servers.

IBM is the primary proponent of Linux. Although IBM does not own Linux, IBM has developed many business systems solutions that use Linux. By using Linux, IBM does not have to pay a license fee to Microsoft or another OS vendor.

Own Versus License

When you buy a computer program, you are not actually buying that program. Instead, you are buying a **license** to use that program. For example, when you buy a Windows license, Microsoft is selling you the right to use Windows. Microsoft continues to own the Windows program. Large organizations do not buy a license for each computer user. Instead, they negotiate a **site license**, which is a flat fee that authorizes the company to install the product (operating system or application) on all of that company's computers or on all of the computers at a specific site.

In the case of Linux, no company can sell you a license to use it. It is owned by the open source community, which states that Linux has no license fee (with certain reasonable restrictions). Large companies such as IBM and smaller companies such as RedHat can make money by supporting Linux, but no company makes money selling Linux licenses.

What Types of Applications Exist, and How Do Organizations Obtain Them?

Application software performs a service or function. Some application programs are general purpose, such as Microsoft Excel or Word. Other application programs provide specific functions. QuickBooks, for example, is an application program that provides general ledger and other accounting functions. We begin by describing categories of application programs and then describe sources for them.

What Categories of Application Programs Exist?

Horizontal-market application software provides capabilities common across all organizations and industries. Word processors, graphics programs, spreadsheets, and presentation programs are all horizontal-market application software.

Examples of such software are Microsoft Word, Excel, and PowerPoint. Examples from other vendors are Adobe's Acrobat, Photoshop, and PageMaker and Jasc Corporation's Paint Shop Pro. These applications are used in a wide variety of businesses, across all industries. They are purchased off-the-shelf, and little customization of features is necessary (or possible).

Vertical-market application software serves the needs of a specific industry. Examples of such programs are those used by dental offices to schedule appointments and bill patients, those used by auto mechanics to keep track of customer data and customers' automobile repairs, and those used by parts warehouses to track inventory, purchases, and sales.

Vertical applications usually can be altered or customized. Typically, the company that sold the application software will provide such services or offer referrals to qualified consultants who can provide this service.

One-of-a-kind application software is developed for a specific, unique need. The IRS develops such software, for example, because it has needs that no other organization has.

How Do Organizations Acquire Application Software?

You can acquire application software in exactly the same ways that you can buy a new suit. The quickest and least risky option is to buy your suit off-the-rack. With this method, you get your suit immediately, and you know exactly what it will cost. You may not, however, get a good fit. Alternately, you can buy your suit off-the-rack and have it altered. This will take more time, it may cost more, and there's some possibility that the alteration will result in a poor fit. Most likely, however, an altered suit will fit better than an off-the-rack one.

Finally, you can hire a tailor to make a custom suit. In this case, you will have to describe what you want, be available for multiple fittings, and be willing to pay considerably more. Although there is an excellent chance of a great fit, there is also the possibility of a disaster. Still, if you want a yellow and orange polka-dot silk suit with a hissing rattlesnake on the back, tailor-made is the only way to go. You can buy computer software in exactly the same ways: **off-the-shelf software**, **off-the-shelf with alterations software**, or tailor-made. Tailor-made software is called **custom-developed software**.

Organizations develop custom application software themselves or hire a development vendor. Like buying the yellow and orange polka-dot suit, such development is done in situations in which the needs of the organization are so unique that no horizontal or vertical applications are available. By developing custom software, the organization can tailor its application to fit its requirements.

Custom development is difficult and risky. Staffing and managing teams of software developers is challenging. Managing software projects can be daunting. Many organizations have embarked on application development projects only to find that the projects take twice as long—or longer—to finish as planned. Cost overruns of 200 and 300 percent are not uncommon. We will discuss such risks further in Chapter 10.

In addition, every application program needs to be adapted to changing needs and changing technologies. The adaptation costs of horizontal and vertical software are amortized over all of the users of that software, perhaps thousands or millions of customers. For custom software developed in-house, however, the developing company must pay all of the adaptation costs itself. Over time, this cost burden is heavy.

Because of the risk and expense, in-house development is the last-choice alternative and is used only when there is no other option. Figure 4-11 summarizes software sources and types.

What Is Firmware?

Firmware is computer software that is installed into devices such as printers, print servers, and various types of communication devices. The software is coded just like other software, but it is installed into special, read-only memory of the printer or other device. In this way, the program becomes part of the device's memory; it is as if the program's logic is designed into the device's circuitry. Users do not need to load firmware into the device's memory.

Software Source

	Off-the-shelf	Off-the-shelf and then customized	Custom-developed
Software Type Horizontal applications	■■■		
Vertical applications	■■■	■■■	
One-of-a-kind applications			▓▓▓

Figure 4-11
Software Sources and Types

Firmware can be changed or upgraded, but this is normally a task for IS professionals. The task is easy, but it requires knowledge of special programs and techniques that most business users choose not to learn.

Q4 Why Are Thin Clients Preferred to Thick Clients?

When you use client applications such as Word, Excel, or Acrobat, those programs run only on your computer. You need not be connected to the Internet or any other network for them to run.

Other applications, called **client-server applications**, require code on both the client and the server. Email is a good example. When you send email, you run a client program such as Microsoft Outlook that has been installed on your computer. Outlook then connects over the Internet or a private network to mail server software on a server. Similarly, when you access a Web site, you run a browser (client software) on your computer that connects over a network to Web server software on a server.

A client-server application that requires nothing more than a browser is called a **thin client**. An application such as Microsoft Outlook that requires programs other than a browser on the user's computer is called a **thick client**. The terms *thin* and *thick* refer to the amount of code that must run on the client computer. All other things being equal, thin-client applications are preferred to thick-client applications because they require only a browser; no special client software needs to be installed. Additionally, for reasons that you will learn in Chapter 6, thin (browser-only) clients make it easier for people to access systems from remote locations and from special-purpose devices such as cell phones.

As stated, client and server computers can run different operating systems. Many organizations have standardized on Windows for their clients but use Windows Server or Linux for their servers. Figure 4-12 shows an example. Two thin clients are connecting via browsers to a Web server that is running Windows Server. Two thick clients are connecting via an email client to an email server that is running Linux. Those two clients are thick because they have client email software installed.

Q5 Is Open Source Software a Viable Alternative?

To answer this question, you first need to know a bit about the open source movement and process. Most computer historians would agree that Richard Matthew Stallman is the father of the movement. In 1983, he developed a set of tools called **GNU** (a self-referential acronym meaning *GNU Not Unix)* for creating a free Unix-like

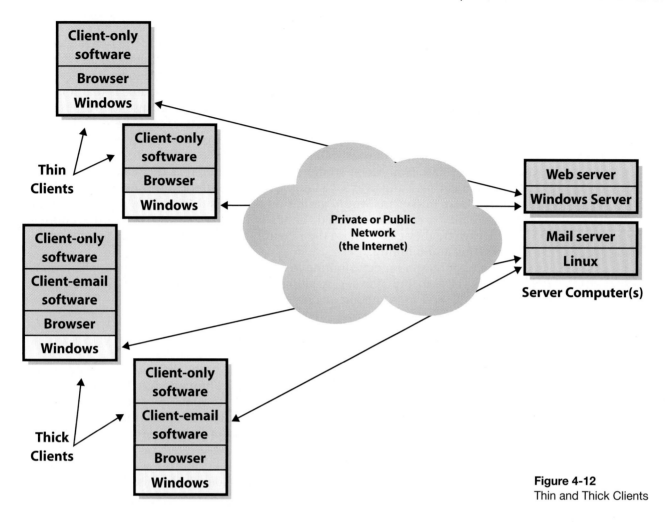

Figure 4-12
Thin and Thick Clients

operating system. Stallman made many other contributions to open source, including the **GNU general public license (GPL) agreement**, one of the standard license agreements for open source software. Stallman was unable to attract enough developers to finish the free Unix system, but continued making other contributions to the open source movement.

In 1991, Linus Torvalds, working in Helsinki, began work on another version of Unix, using some of Stallman's tools. That version eventually became Linux, the high-quality and very popular operating system discussed previously.

The Internet proved to be a great asset for open source, and many open source projects became successful, including:

- Open Office (a Microsoft Office look-alike)
- Firefox (a browser)
- MySQL (a DBMS, see Chapter 5)
- Apache (a Web server, see Chapter 8)
- Ubuntu (a Windows-like desktop operating system)
- Android (a mobile-device operating system)

Why Do Programmers Volunteer Their Services?

To anyone who has never enjoyed writing computer programs, it is difficult to understand why anyone would donate their time and skills to contribute to open source projects. Programming is, however, an intense combination of art and logic, and designing and writing a complicated computer program is exceedingly pleasurable (and addictive). Like many programmers, at times in my life I have gleefully devoted 16 hours a day to writing computer programs—day after day—and the days would fly by. If you have an artistic and logical mind, you ought to try it.

Anyway, the first reason that people contribute to open source is that it is great fun! Additionally, some people contribute to open source because it gives them the freedom to choose the projects upon which they work. They may have a programming day job that is not terribly interesting, say, writing a program to manage a computer printer. Their job pays the bills, but it's not fulfilling.

In the 1950s, Hollywood studio musicians suffered as they recorded the same style of music over and over for a long string of uninteresting movies. To keep their sanity, those musicians would gather on Sundays to play jazz, and a number of high-quality jazz clubs resulted. That's what open source is to programmers. A place where they can exercise their creativity while working on projects they find interesting and fulfilling.

Another reason for contributing to open source is to exhibit one's skill, both for pride as well as to find a job or consulting employment. A final reason is to start a business selling services to support an open source product.

How Does Open Source Work?

The term *open source* means that the source code of the program is available to the public. **Source code** is computer code as written by humans and that is understandable by humans. Figure 4-13 shows a portion of the computer code that I wrote for the Web site *www.LearningMIS.com*. Source code is compiled into **machine code** that is processed by a computer. Machine code is, in general, not understandable by humans and cannot be modified. When you access *www.LearningMIS.com*, the machine code version of the program in Figure 4-13 runs on your computer. We do not show machine code in a figure because it would look like this:

11010010100101111110011101111001000111000001111110111101111100111 . . .

In a **closed source** project, say Microsoft Office, the source code is highly protected and only available to trusted employees and carefully vetted contractors. The source code is protected like gold in a vault. Only those trusted programmers can make changes to a closed source project.

```
#region Dependency Properties

public static readonly DependencyProperty
    LessonIDProperty = DependencyProperty.Register(
        "LessonID",
        typeof(int),
        typeof(Lesson),
        new PropertyMetadata(new PropertyChangedCallback(Lesson.OnLessonDataChanged)));

public int LessonID
{
    get { return (int)GetValue(LessonIDProperty); }
    set { SetValue(LessonIDProperty, value); }
}

private static void OnLessonDataChanged(DependencyObject d, DependencyPropertyChangedEventArgs e)
{

    // reload the stage for the new TopicID property
    Lesson thisLesson = d as Lesson;

    lessonObject = thisLesson; // there is only one lesson object ... this is a static ref to it

    thisLesson.LoadLessonData(); // get data from xml file on server
    //call to thisLesson.CreateLessonForm(); must be done after load b/c of asynchronous read
}

#endregion
```

Figure 4-13
Source Code Sample

With open source, anyone can obtain the source code from the open source project's Web site. Programmers alter or add to this code depending on their interests and goals. In most cases, programmers can incorporate code they find into their own projects. They may be able to resell those projects depending on the type of license agreement the project uses.

Open source succeeds because of collaboration. A programmer examines the source code and identifies a need or project that seems interesting. He or she then creates a new feature, redesigns or reprograms an existing feature, or fixes a known problem. That code is then sent to others in the open source project who then evaluate the quality and merits of the work and add it to the product, if appropriate.

Typically, there is a lot of give and take. Or, as described in Chapter 2, there are many cycles of iteration and feedback. Because of this iteration, a well-managed project with strong peer reviews can result in very high-quality code, like that in Linux.

So, Is Open Source Viable?

The answer depends on to whom and for what. Open source has certainly become legitimate. According to *The Economist,* "It is now generally accepted that the future will involve a blend of both proprietary and open-source software."[1] During your career, open source will likely take a greater and greater role in software. However, whether open source works for a particular situation depends on the requirements and constraints of that situation. You will learn more about matching requirements and programs in Chapter 10.

By the way, Neil at FlexTime eventually decided not to use the open source software he had identified. You'll learn why in Chapter 7, Using Your Knowledge Question 6, page 267.

In some cases, companies choose open source software because it is "free." It turns out that this advantage may be less important than you'd think, because in many cases, support and operational costs swamp the initial licensing fee.

Q6 How Can You Use This Knowledge?

As a future business professional, you will need basic knowledge of hardware and software for two major reasons. First, you will need it to make some decisions about which products you use. Second, as a manager, you will be involved in creating or approving hardware budgets. Consider each.

What Buying Decisions Do You Make?

In general, most business professionals have some role in the specification of the client hardware and software they use. Business managers also play a role in the specification of client hardware and software for employees whom they manage. The particular role depends on the policy of the manager's organization. Large organizations will have an IS department that is likely to set standards for client hardware and software. You will learn more about such standards in Chapter 11.

In medium to small organizations, policies are often less formal, and managers will need to take an active role in setting the specifications for their own and their employees' computers. Figure 4-14 summarizes sources of costs and Figure 4-15 lists the major criteria for selecting both hardware and software. The goal, of course, is to select the hardware and software that will meet requirements at the minimum total system cost.

Except in rare circumstances, medium to small organizations will usually standardize on a single client operating system because the costs of supporting more than

Over the course of your career, application software, hardware, and firmware will change, sometimes rapidly. The Guide on pages 124–125 challenges you to choose a strategy for addressing this change.

---

[1]"Unlocking the Cloud," *The Economist,* May 28, 2009. Available at *www.economist.com/ opinion/displaystory.cfm?story_id=13740181* (accessed June 2009).

	Development	Operational
Hardware	Hardware purchases	Hardware maintenance fees
Software	Software licenses Project costs for custom software	Software maintenance and support fees and costs
Data	Data conversion costs	Data acquisition costs
Procedures	Design, development, and documentation	Procedure maintenance costs
People	Initial training costs	Labor costs of using system

Figure 4-14
Sources of System Costs

Category	Hardware	Software
Client	Specify: • CPU speed • Size of main memory • Size of magnetic disk • CD or DVD and type • Monitor type and size	Specify: • Windows, Mac, or Linux OS. May be dictated by organizational standard. • PC applications such as Microsoft Office, Adobe Acrobat, Photoshop, Paint Shop Pro. May be dictated by organizational standard. • Browser such as Internet Explorer, FireFox, or Netscape Navigator. • Requirements for the client side of client-server applications. • Need for thin or thick client.
Server	In most cases, a business manager has no role in the specification of server hardware (except possibly a budgetary one).	• Specify requirements for the server side of client-server applications. • Work with technical personnel to test and accept software.

Figure 4-15
A Business Manager's
Role in Hardware and
Software Specifications

one are unjustifiable. Most organizations choose Microsoft Windows clients. Some arts and design businesses standardize on the Macintosh, and some engineering firms standardize on Unix. Organizations that have limited budgets might choose to use Linux with Ubuntu and Open Office on the clients, but this is rare.

Managers and their employees might have a role in specifying horizontal application software, such as Microsoft Office, or other software appropriate for their operating systems. They will also have an important role in specifying requirements for vertical market or custom applications. We will say more about this role in Chapter 10.

Concerning the server, a business manager typically has no role in the specification of server hardware, other than possibly approving the budget. Instead, technical personnel make such decisions. A business manager and those who will be the clients of a client-server application specify the requirements for vertical and custom-server software. They will also work with technical personnel to test and accept that software.

What Process Should I Use to Establish a Computer Budget?

The steps for preparing a departmental hardware budget are summarized in Figure 4-16. You need first to determine the base requirements. This involves assessing the work your employees perform, creating job categories, and determining the computer workload requirements for each category.

Determine base requirements:
• The types of workload your employees perform
• The hardware requirements for each type
• The software requirements for each type

Forecast requirement changes during the budget period:
• Changes in the number of employees
• Changes in workload—new job tasks or information systems
• Mandatory changes in hardware or software

Prepare the budget:
• Using guidance from the IT department and accounting, price the hardware and software
• Determine if your department will be charged for networks, servers, communications, or other overhead expenses
• Add overhead charges as necessary

Assess results:
• Consider budget in context of competitive strategy
• If substantial increases in budget size, prepare justification
• Consider budget in context of prior year's budget
• Determine sources of significant difference and explain
• Modify budget as appropriate

Document results:
• Prepare for justification
• Save documents and notes for preparation of next year's IT budget

Figure 4-16
A Process for Preparing a Departmental IT Budget

In accounts payable, for example, you might determine that you have three categories of workers: administrators, accounts payable specialists, and managers. You further determine that the administrators need hardware and software to access the company's Web portal, to email, and to perform minimal word processing. The accounts payable specialists need the same capabilities as the administrators, but they also need access to the organization's accounts payable system. Finally, you and other managers need to be able to perform the same work as the specialists, plus you need to process large spreadsheets for preparing budgets. You also need to access the company's payroll and human resources systems.

Once you have identified the job categories and the computer workload requirements for each, you can apply the knowledge from this chapter to determine hardware and software requirements for each type. You can also use past departmental experience as a guide. If employees complain about computer performance with the equipment they have, you can determine if more is needed. If there are no bottlenecks or performance problems, you know the current equipment will do.

Given the base requirements, the next step is to forecast changes. Will you be adding or losing employees during the year? Will the workload change? Will your department be given new tasks that will necessitate additional hardware or software? Finally, during the year will your organization mandate changes in hardware or software? Will you be required to upgrade your operating system or applications software? If so, will your budget be charged for those upgrades?

Once you have the base requirements and your change forecasts, you can prepare the budget. The first task is to price the hardware and software. As you will learn in Chapter 11, your IT department will most likely have established standards for hardware and software from which you will select. They will probably have negotiated prices on your behalf. If not, the accounting department can probably help you estimate costs based on their prior experience. You can also learn from the past experience of your own department.

Establishing a computer budget involves knowing the right questions to ask. The Guide on pages 126–127 discusses the importance of improving your ability to ask intelligent questions.

Your organization may have a policy of charging the department's overhead fees for networks, servers, and communications. If so, you will need to add those charges to the budget as well.

When you have finished the preparation of the budget, you should assess it for feasibility and reasonableness. First, consider your organization's competitive strategy. If your organization is a cost leader, any increases in your budget will be carefully scrutinized, and you should be prepared with strong justifications. If your organization uses a differentiation strategy, then be certain that any increases in your budget relate directly to the ways in which your company differentiates. Before submitting your budget, prepare justifications for any such increases.

You can expect that your budget will be reviewed in the context of prior years' budgets. If you are proposing substantial changes to your budget, anticipate that you will be asked to justify them. Reasons that you may need more equipment include:

- Substantial change in your departmental head count
- Important new departmental functions or responsibilities
- Upgrading to major new versions of operating system or other software
- Implementation of new systems that require additional hardware
- Change in the way overhead expenses are allocated to your department

If you find it difficult to justify budgetary increases, you may need to review and revise your budget. Perhaps you can do with refurbished equipment, or maybe you can delay the upgrade of all of your computers to the new operating system, or maybe you can find ways of reallocating hardware among the employees in your department that will save costs. Even if none of these options are workable, you can document that you investigated them in your budget justification or mention them in any budgetary review meetings.

Finally, document your results. You can use such documentation not only to justify your budget this year but also to help you prepare next year's budget. Keep any spreadsheets (like the one in Figure 4-19 on page 131) as well as notes and documents used to prepare and justify your budget.

Q7 2020?

Because of Moore's Law, hardware and software will likely undergo major changes by 2020. As stated in Chapter 1, most computing devices will not look like computers. The components of what we consider to be a PC will be built into phones, other communication devices, TV consoles, automobiles, home appliances, medical devices, and even the kitchen mop (well, vacuum). User interfaces to these devices will change as well. Although keyboards and mice will still be in use, command by voice and touch will be popular. Devices that respond to the simultaneous touch of many people will become common (see, for example, *www.microsoft.com/surface*). Some devices will sense body presence and movement and respond to it, like the computer games now emerging.

All such changes can be loosely anticipated.

Less predictable is the impact of open source on the software industry. In 2008, Microsoft earned 82 percent of its revenue ($60 billion) via the sale of licenses for closed source Windows and Office products. Will it be able to maintain these sales in the face of license-free open source software?

Consider an example. Android, an open source operating system initiated by Google for mobile phones, has recently been expanded to the PC. Meanwhile, Google announced in June 2009 that it would expand its browser, named Chrome, into a full-blown PC operating system as well. Will Chrome or Android supplant Windows? And how will Microsoft respond if that appears likely?

As of 2009, Microsoft has $23.6 billion in cash in the bank; it could lose $2.36 billion a year and still be in business by 2020. And there is no danger they will lose that kind of money. So, we can bet that Microsoft will still be around. Still, if the threats to closed source revenue increase, Microsoft must respond. But how?

Maybe Microsoft can surround its closed source software with sufficient services that customers will judge the lifetime cost of its closed source software to be less than that for open source alternatives. In that case, organizations will continue to license Microsoft's closed source software. Or, perhaps Microsoft will bow to open source by releasing some product code to open source and hold back other code as closed. They've done exactly that with software development tools like Silverlight.

Or, Microsoft could become a service company; selling software on large servers as a service. In one form of this model, customers would pay a few pennies every time they use Word or Excel, etc.

Companies such as Amazon.com, Oracle, and Microsoft have in recent years developed large server farms on which they lease computing time and storage space. Such facilities become part of the computing cloud. Maybe Microsoft will move Windows and Office into its cloud and require organizations to license both the hardware and software from it.

Many other responses to the threat of open source are possible.

Although all of these changes, risks, and dangers are tough on Microsoft, Oracle, and even Google, they are good for you. They will create many opportunities for individuals versed in technology to guide their companies around the technology pitfalls and into legitimate opportunities. MIS is the most important course in the business school today. Keep reading!

Keeping Up to Speed

Have you ever been to a cafeteria where you put your lunch tray on a conveyor belt that carries the dirty dishes into the kitchen? That conveyor belt reminds me of technology. Like the conveyor, technology just moves along, and all of us run on top of the technology conveyor, trying to keep up. We hope to keep up with the relentless change of technology for an entire career without ending up in the techno-trash.

Technology change is a fact, and the only appropriate question is, "What am I going to do about it?" One strategy you can take is to bury your head in the sand: "Look, I'm not a technology person. I'll leave it to the pros. As long as I can send email and use the Internet, I'm happy. If I have a problem, I'll call someone to fix it."

That strategy is fine, as far as it goes, and many businesspeople use it. Following that strategy won't give you a competitive advantage over anyone, and it will give someone else a competitive advantage over you, but as long as you develop your advantage elsewhere, you'll be OK—at least for yourself.

What about your department, though? If an expert says, "Every computer needs a 500GB disk," are you going to nod your head and say, "Great. Sell 'em to me!" Or are you going to know enough to realize that's a big disk (by 2009 standards, anyway) and ask why everyone needs such a large amount of storage? Maybe then you'll be told, "Well, it's only another $150 per machine from the 120GB disk." At that point, you can make a decision, using your own decision-making skills, and not rely solely on the IS expert. Thus, the prudent business professional in the twenty-first century has a number of reasons not to bury his or her head in the technology sand.

At the other end of the spectrum are those who love technology. You'll find them everywhere—they may be accountants, marketing professionals, or production-line supervisors who not only know their field, but also enjoy information technology. Maybe they were IS majors or had double majors that combined IS with another area of expertise (e.g., IS with accounting). These people read CNET News and ZDNet most days, and they can tell you the latest on IPv6 addresses (Chapter 6—just wait!). Those people are sprinting along the technology conveyor belt; they will never end up in the techno-trash, and they will use their knowledge of IT to gain competitive advantage throughout their careers.

Many business professionals fall in between these extremes. They don't want to bury their heads, but they don't have the desire or interest to become technophiles (lovers of technology) either. What to do? There are a couple of strategies. For one, don't allow yourself to ignore technology. When you see a technology article in the *Wall Street Journal*, read it. Don't just skip it because it's about technology. Read the technology ads, too. Many vendors invest heavily in ads that instruct without seeming to. Another option is to take a seminar or pay attention to professional events that combine your specialty with technology. For example, when you go to the banker's convention, attend a session or two on "Technology Trends for Bankers." There are always sessions like that, and you might make a contact with similar problems and concerns in another company.

Probably the best option, if you have the time for it, is to get involved as a user representative in technology committees in your organization. If your company is doing a review of its CRM system, for instance, see if you can get on the review committee. When there's a need for a representative from your department to discuss needs for the next-generation help-line system, sign up. Or, later in your career, become a member of the business practice technology committee, or whatever they call it at your organization.

Just working with such groups will add to your knowledge of technology. Presentations made to such groups, discussions about uses of technology, and ideas about using IT for competitive advantage will all add to your IT knowledge. You'll gain important contacts and exposure to leaders in your organization as well.

It's up to you. You get to choose how you relate to technology. But be sure you choose; don't let your head fall into the sand without thinking about it. ∎

Discussion Questions

1. Do you agree that the change of technology is relentless? What do you think that means to most business professionals? To most organizations?
2. Think about the three postures toward technology presented here. Which camp will you join? Why?
3. Write a two-paragraph memo to yourself justifying your choice in question 2. If you chose to ignore technology, explain how you will compensate for the loss of competitive advantage. If you're going to join one of the other two groups, explain why, and describe how you're going to accomplish your goal.
4. Given your answer to question 2, assume that you're in a job interview and the interviewer asks about your knowledge of technology. Write a three-sentence response to the interviewer's question.

Questioning Your Questions

Many school experiences mislead you to believe that answering a question is the important part of learning. In fact, answering a question is the easy part. For most problems in the business world, the difficult and creative acts are generating the questions—and formulating a strategy for getting the answers. Once the questions and strategy are set, the rest is simply legwork.

As a future consumer of information technology and services, you will benefit from being able to ask good questions and effectively obtain answers to them. It is probably the single most important behavior you can learn. Because of the rapid change of technology, you will constantly be required to learn about new IS alternatives and how you can apply them in your business.

Perhaps you've heard that "there is no such thing as a bad question." This statement is nonsense. There are billions of bad questions, and you will be better off if you learn not to ask them.

Questions can be bad in three ways: They can be irrelevant, dead, or asked of the wrong source. Consider the first way. If you know the subject and if you're paying attention, you can avoid asking irrelevant questions. One of the goals of this text is to teach you about IT and IS so that you can avoid asking irrelevant technology questions.

A dead question is one that leads to nowhere—it provides no insight into the subject. Here's an example of a dead question: "Is the

material on How a Computer Works going to be on the test?" The answer will tell you whether you need to study that topic for the exam, but it won't tell you why. The answer will help you in school, but it won't help you use MIS on the job.

Instead, ask questions like, "What is the purpose of the section on how a computer works?" "Why are we studying it?" or "How will it help me use MIS in my career?" These are good questions because they go somewhere. Your professor may respond, "From that discussion you'll learn how to save money because you'll know whether to buy your staff more memory or a faster CPU." Possibly, you won't understand that answer; in that case, you can ask more questions that will lead you to understand how it pertains to your use of MIS.

Or, your professor may say, "Well, I think that section is a waste of time, and I told the author that in a recent email." From there, you can ask your professor why she thinks it's a waste of time, and you can wonder why the author would write something that is a waste of time. Maybe the author and your professor have different points of view. Such musings are excellent because they lead you to more learning.

The third way questions can be bad is that they are asked of the wrong source. Information technology questions fall into three types: "What is it?" "How can I use it?" and "Is it the best choice?" The

> It is not possible to become a good thinker and be a poor questioner. Thinking is not driven by answers, but rather, by questions.[2]

[2]Richard Paul and Linda Elder, *Critical Thinking* (Upper Saddle River, NJ: Prentice Hall, 2001), p. 113.

first type asks for a simple definition. You can easily Google or Bing the answers to such questions. Hence, you ought not to ask "What is it?" questions of valuable or expensive sources; you are wasting your money and their time if you do. And, when you ask such a question, you appear unprepared because you didn't take the time to find the easy answer.

The next type of question, "How can I use it?" is harder. Answering that question requires knowledge of both technology and your business. Although you can research that question over the Internet, you need knowledge to relate it to your present circumstance. In a few years, this is the sort of question that you will be expected to answer for your organization. It's also the type of question you might ask an expert.

Finally, the most difficult type of question is, "Is it the best choice for our company or situation?" Answering this type of question requires the ability to judge among alternatives according to appropriate criteria. These are the kinds of questions you probably do want to ask an expensive source.

Notice, too, that only "What is it?" questions have a verifiably correct answer. The next two types are questions of judgment. No answer can be shown to be correct, but some answers

are better than others. As you progress in your educational career, you should be learning how to discern the quality of judgment and evaluative answers. Learn to question your questions. ∎

Discussion Questions

Suppose you are interviewing an expert about how she thinks Microsoft will respond to the challenge of open source. Using that as an example, answer questions 1 through 7.

1. Using your own words, what is the difference between a good question and a bad one?

2. What types of questions waste time?

3. What types of questions are appropriate to ask your professor?

4. How do you know when you have a good answer to a question? Consider the three types of questions described here in your answer.

5. Under what circumstances would you ask a question to which you already know the answer?

6. Suppose you have 15 minutes with your boss's boss's boss. What kinds of questions are appropriate in such an interview? Even though you don't pay money to meet with this person, explain how this is an expensive source.

7. Evaluate the quality of questions 1 through 5. Which are the best questions? What makes one better than the other? If you can, think of better ways of asking these questions, or even better questions.

ACTIVE REVIEW

Use this Active Review to verify that you understand the ideas and concepts that answer the chapter's study questions.

Q1 What do business professionals need to know about computer hardware?

List categories of hardware and explain the purpose of each. Define *bit* and *byte*. Explain why bits are used to represent computer data. Define the units of bytes used to size memory. In general terms, explain how a computer works. Explain how a manager can use this knowledge. Explain why you should save your work from time to time while you are using your computer.

Q2 What is the difference between a client and a server?

Explain the functions of client and server computers. Describe how the hardware requirements vary between the two types. Define *server farm* and describe the technology dance that occurs on a server farm.

Q3 What do business professionals need to know about software?

Review Figure 4-10 and explain the meaning of each cell in this table. Explain the difference between software ownership and software licenses. Explain the differences among horizontal-market, vertical-market, and one-of-a-kind applications. Describe the three ways that organizations can acquire software.

Q4 Why are thin clients preferred to thick clients?

Define *client-server application* and differentiate it from, say, Microsoft Excel. Explain the difference between thin and thick clients. Describe two advantages of thin clients.

Q5 Is open source software a viable alternative?

Define *GNU* and *GPL*. Name three successful open source projects. Describe four reasons programmers contribute to open source projects. Define *open source, closed source, source code,* and *machine code*. In your own words, explain why open source is a legitimate alternative but may or may not be appropriate for a given application.

Q6 How can you use this knowledge?

Describe the two major reasons you need the knowledge of this chapter. Review Figure 4-15 and explain each cell of this table. Summarize the process you should use to develop a computer budget.

Q7 2020?

Summarize likely changes to hardware and user interfaces that will occur before 2020. Describe the threats of open source to Microsoft and other closed source software vendors. Explain two possible responses Microsoft could take. Describe how all of this change and uncertainty creates an opportunity for you.

KEY TERMS AND CONCEPTS

USING YOUR KNOWLEDGE

1. Suppose that your roommate, a political science major, asks you to help her purchase a new laptop computer. She wants to use the computer for email, Internet access, and for note-taking in class. She wants to spend less than $1,000.

   a. What CPU, memory, and disk specifications would you recommend?
   b. What software does she need?
   c. Shop *www.dell.com*, *www.hp.com*, and *www.lenovo.com* for the best computer deal.
   d. Which computer would you recommend, and why?

2. Suppose that your father asks you to help him purchase a new computer. He wants to use his computer for email, Internet access, downloading pictures from his digital camera, uploading those pictures to a shared photo service, and writing documents to members of his antique auto club.

   a. What CPU, memory, and disk specifications would you recommend?
   b. What software does he need?
   c. Shop *www.dell.com*, *www.hp.com*, and *www.lenovo.com* for the best computer deal.
   d. Which computer would you recommend, and why?

3. Microsoft offers free licenses of certain software products to students at colleges and universities that participate in the Microsoft Developer Network (MSDN) Academic Alliance (AA). If your college or university participates in this program, you have the opportunity to obtain hundreds of dollars of software, for free. Here is a partial list of the software you can obtain:

   - Microsoft Access 2007
   - OneNote
   - Expression Studio
   - Windows 2008 Server
   - Microsoft Project 2007
   - Visual Studio Developer
   - SQL Server 2008
   - Visio

   a. Search *www.microsoft.com*, *www.google.com*, or *www.bing.com* and determine the function of each of these software products.
   b. Which of these software products are operating systems and which are application programs?
   c. Which of these programs are DBMS products (the subject of the next chapter)?
   d. Which of these programs should you download and install tonight?
   e. Either (1) download and install the programs in your answer to part d, or (2) explain why you would not choose to do so.
   f. Does the MSDN AA provide an unfair advantage to Microsoft? Why or why not?

4. Suppose you work at FlexTime and Neil has asked you to help analyze the software situation. He wants to compute the total costs of three alternatives: (1) upgrading to Version 3 of the current software, (2) licensing the open source software, and (3) licensing another vendor's thin-client software. He has asked you to identify all of the costs that should be considered. Note that he is not asking you to determine those costs, nor even to know how to determine those costs. He simply wants a list of costs to consider.

   a. Using Figure 4-14 as a guide, identify potential costs for each component for development and operation of the new system.
   b. Using your intuition, do you think the list of costs that you identified in part a is likely to swamp the costs of the software license fee? Why or why not?

COLLABORATION EXERCISE

Collaborate with a group of students on the following exercise. Recall from Chapter 2 that collaboration is more than cooperation. Collaboration involves iteration and feedback. Post a document, a discussion item, a wiki item, or an idea and obtain feedback from your team members. Similarly, read the ideas of others and comment on them. Try to innovate in both the process by which you collaborate and the work product that you create. Avoid face-to-face meetings. Instead, use collaborative software such as Google Docs & Spreadsheets, Microsoft Groove, or Microsoft SharePoint to facilitate your ideas.

Suppose you manage the sales and marketing department at a company that generates $100 million in sales—say, a manufacturer of fireplace inserts and related equipment. Assume you just started the job and that at the end of your second day the corporate operations officer (COO) sticks her head into your office and announces, "I'm in a rush and have to go, but I wanted to let you know that I put $80,000 in the budget for computers for your department next year. Is that OK? Unfortunately, I've got to know by the day after tomorrow. Thanks."

How do you respond? You have 2 days to decide. If you agree to the $80,000 and it turns out to be insufficient, then sometime next year your department will lack computing resources and you'll have a management problem. If that happens, you may have to spend over your budget. You know that cost control is important to your new employer, so you dread overspending. However, if you ask for more than $80,000, you need to justify why you need it. You will need to document the computer equipment and software your department needs, explain why you need it, and estimate how much it will cost.

Given the short time frame, and given that as a new employee you probably have already scheduled the next 2 days full of meetings, you will need to delegate at least part of this problem to someone. You might delegate it to a computer salesperson, but that is akin to inviting the fox to babysit the chickens. Or, you could delegate it to some of your employees, but as a new employee you do not yet know who has the capability to answer this question. You could also ask the IS department at your organization to help you.

In any case, whether you find the time to answer this question yourself, assign it to your employees, or ask for help from the IS department, you will need knowledge of computer hardware and software capabilities and costs in order to assess the quality of the answer you have.

To respond to this request, assume you have been given the following list of data about the department and its information needs:

- You will upgrade all of your department's computers to Windows 7 and Office 2010 in the next year. Your company has negotiated a site license for these products, and the IS department allocates that license cost to each computer. For your department, you will pay $100 for each computer that uses Office 2010 and another $75 for each computer that uses Windows 7. You are not required nor allowed to buy any software for new computers. If the computer comes with software, that software will be destroyed by the IS department's standard installation process.
- You have identified three classes of computer users in your department. The main memory, RAM, and disk storage requirements for each class of user are shown in Figure 4-17. This figure shows the specifications of existing computers as well as the hardware requirements for each class after the upgrade.
- Figure 4-18 shows the job titles of employees in your department, the number of employees of each type, the class of computer they require, and whether they use a desktop or a laptop. (You are a new employee, do not yet have a computer, and can specify your own requirements.)

Class of Computer	Current Hardware Specification (Main Memory, Processor, Disk)	Hardware Required After Upgrade (Main Memory, Processor, Disk)
A	256MB, 0.5GHz, 30GB	1GB, 1GHz, 80GB
B	512MB, 1GHz, 80GB	2GB, 2GHz, 150GB
C	1GB, 2GHz, 2 x 125GB	4GB, 2GHz—dual, 2 x 250GB

Figure 4-17
Hardware Specifications for Three Classes of Computers

Job Title	Number of Employees	Computer System Required	Computer Type
Product manager	8	B	Laptop
Telesales	12	A	Desktop
Department administrator	2	A	Desktop
Marketing communications manager	4	B	Laptop
Marketing analyst	4	C (desktop) B (laptop)	Both, a desktop and laptop for each analyst
Marketing programs manager	6	B	Desktop
You	1	???	???

Figure 4-18
Department Employees and Computer Requirements

- A computer can be reassigned to other employees as long as the computer meets the minimum processing requirements. A laptop can substitute for a desktop if a display, keyboard, and mouse are purchased to go with it.
- The IS department assesses each computer an annual $1,200 fee for network, server, and other overhead costs.
- Assume that telesales personnel will grow by 10 percent in the next year but there will be no other changes in the number of personnel in your department.
- Ten of the existing class B computers have a maximum main memory of 1GB. The rest of the class B computers have a maximum main memory of

512MB. All of the existing class C computers have a maximum main memory of 4GB.

a. Given this data, is $80,000 enough? If not, how much money should be allocated in your department?
b. Explain how you will meet the computer needs of the employees in your department. Assume you are required to buy new computers and equipment from Dell, HP, or Lenova.
c. Describe how you will modify and reallocate existing computers (e.g., upgrading an existing class B computer and assigning it to an employee who next year needs a class A computer). You may wish to develop the spreadsheet in Application Exercise 1 below to facilitate your analysis.

APPLICATION EXERCISES

1. Read the Collaboration Exercise above. Create an Excel spreadsheet to compute the cost of new computers for the $80,000 problem. Use the spreadsheet in Figure 4-19 as an example.

   Construct your spreadsheet so that you can change prices, charges, and job title employee count and Excel will update the Total Cost for Category as well as Total Cost. As stated in the note in the spreadsheet, the costs shown here are only examples, as is the choice of computer for the manager (you).

2. Sometimes you will have data in one Office application and want to move it to another Office application without rekeying it. Often this

occurs when data was created for one purpose but then is used for a second purpose. For example, Figure 4-20 presents a portion of an Excel spreadsheet that shows the assignment of computers to employees.

Suppose that you want to use this data to help you assess how to upgrade computers. Let's say, for example, that you want to upgrade all of the computers' operating systems to Windows 7. Furthermore, you want to first upgrade the computers that most need upgrading, but suppose you have a limited budget. To address this situation, you would like to query the data in Figure 4-20, find all computers that do not

	A	B	C	D	E	F	G
2				New–Hardware Cost Calculator			
3							
4		Laptop	Desktop				
5	Price of Class A Computer	$1,500	$1,000		Note for teams answering the $80,000		
6	Price of Class B Computer	$2,000	$1,500		collaboration project: Prices shown are		
7	Price of Class C Computer	$2,500	$2,000		just examples. Actual prices will likely be		
8					different. Also, the choice of Laptop B for		
9	Vista Software Charge	$75	$75		the manager is only for example. Another		
10	Office 2007 Software Charge	$100	$100		choice may make more sense.		
11	Network and Server Charge	$1,200	$1,200				
12							
13							
14							
15	Job Title	Number of Employees	Computer System Required	Computer Type	Hardware and Software Cost	Total Cost for Category	
16	Product manager	8	B	Laptop	$3,375	$27,000	
17	Telesales	12	A	Desktop	$2,375	$28,500	
18	Department Admin	2	A	Desktop	$2,375	$4,750	
19	Marketing Communications Manager	4	B	Laptop	$3,375	$13,500	
20	Marketing Analyst	4	C (desktop)	Both, a desktop and	$3,375	$13,500	
21			B (laptop)	laptop for each analyst	$2,575	$10,300	
22	Marketing Programs Manager	6	B	Desktop	$1,375	$8,250	
23	Manager (You)	1	B	Laptop	$3,375	$3,375	
24							
25					Total Cost	$109,175	

Figure 4-19
New-Hardware Cost Calculator

Source: Microsoft product screenshot reprinted with permission from Microsoft Corporation.

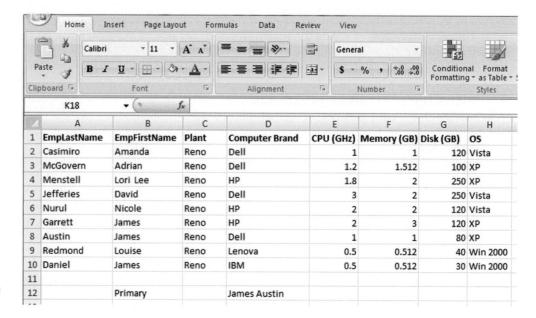

Figure 4-20
Sample Excel Data for Import

Source: Microsoft product screenshot reprinted
with permission from Microsoft Corporation.

have Windows 7, and then select those with slower CPUs or smaller memory as candidates for upgrading. To do this, you need to move the data from Excel and into Access.

Once you have analyzed the data and determined the computers to upgrade, you want to produce a report. In that case, you may want to move the data from Access and back to Excel, or perhaps into Word. In this exercise, you will learn how to perform these tasks.

a. To begin, download the Excel file **Ch04Ex02** from this text's Web site into one of your directories. We will import the data in this file into Access, but before we do so familiarize yourself with the data by opening it in Excel. Notice that there are three worksheets in this workbook. Close the Excel file.

b. Create a blank Access database. Name the database Ch04Ex02_Answer. Place it in some directory; it may be the same directory into which you have placed the Excel file, but it need not be. Close the default table that Access creates and delete it.

c. Now, we will import the data from the three worksheets in the Excel file **Ch04Ex02** into a single table in your Access database. In the ribbon, select *External Data* and *Import from Excel*. Start the import. For the first worksheet (Denver), you should select *Import the source data into a new table in the current database*. Be sure to click *First Row Contains Column Headings* when Access presents your data. You can use the default Field types and let Access add the primary key. Name your table *Employees* and click *Finish*. There is no need to save your import script.

For the second and third worksheets, again click *External Data, Import Excel*, but this time select *Append a copy of the records to the table Employees*. Import all data.

d. Open the *Employee* table and examine the data. Notice that Access has erroneously imported a blank line and the *Primary Contact* data into rows at the end of each data set. This data is not part of the employee records, and you should delete it (in three places—once for each worksheet). The *Employee* table should have a total of 40 records.

e. Now, create a parameterized query on this data. Place all of the columns except *ID* into the query. In the *OS* column, set the criteria to select rows for which the value is not *Windows 7*. In the *CPU* (GHz) column, enter the criterion: <=[Enter cutoff value for CPU] and in the *Memory* (GB) column, enter the criterion: <=[Enter cutoff value for Memory]. Test your query. For example, run your query and enter a value of *2* for both CPU and memory. Verify that the correct rows are produced.

f. Use your query to find values of CPU and memory that give you as close to a maximum of 15 computers to upgrade as possible.

g. When you have found values of CPU and memory that give you 15, or nearly 15, computers to upgrade, leave your query open. Now, click *External data, Word*, and create a Word document that contains the results of your query. Adjust the column widths of the created table so that it fits on the page. Write a memo around this table explaining that these are the computers that you believe should be upgraded.

CASE STUDY 4   video ▶

Dell Leverages the Internet, Directly, but for How Long?

When Michael Dell started Dell Computer in 1984, personal computers were sold only in retail stores. Manufacturers shipped to wholesalers, who shipped to retail stores, which sold to end users. Companies maintained expensive inventories at each stage of this supply chain. Dell thought that he could eliminate the retail channel by selling computers directly to consumers:

> I was inspired by how I saw computers being sold. It seemed to me that it was very expensive and it was inefficient. A computer cost at the time about $3,000 but there were only about $600 worth of parts inside the computer. And so I figured, hey, what if you sold the computer for $800? You don't need to sell it for $3,000. And so we changed the whole way computers were being sold by lowering the cost of distribution and sales and taking out this extra cost that was inefficient.
>
> Now, what I didn't know was that the Internet would come along and now people can go on the Internet and they can go to *Dell.com* and buy a computer and that makes it a lot easier.
>
> I'd say the most important thing we did was listen very carefully to our customers. We asked, what do they want, what do they need and how can we meet their needs and provide something that's really valuable to them? Because if we could take care of our customers, they'll want to buy more products from us, and they have.[3]

Eliminating retail stores not only reduced costs, but it also brought Dell closer to the customer, enabling it to listen better than the competition. It also eliminated sales channel inventories, which allowed Dell to rapidly bring new computers with new technology to the customer. This eliminates the need to recycle or sell off existing pipeline inventory whenever a new model is announced.

Additionally, Dell focused on its suppliers and now has one of the most efficient supply chains in the industry. Dell pays close attention to its suppliers and shares information with them on product quality, inventory, and related subjects via its secure Web site *http://valuechain.dell.com*. According to its Web site, the first two qualities Dell looks for in suppliers are (1) cost competitiveness and (2) an understanding of Dell's business.

In addition to computer hardware, Dell provides a variety of services. It provides basic technical support with every computer, and customers can upgrade this basic support by purchasing one of four higher levels of support. Additionally, Dell offers deployment services to organizations to configure and deploy Dell systems, both hardware and preinstalled software, into customers' user environments. Dell offers additional services to maintain and manage Dell systems once they have been deployed.

Dell enjoyed unprecedented success until the recent economic downturn. In May 2009, Dell reported that first-quarter earnings had fallen 63 percent compared to a year earlier, and sales had dropped 23 percent. This report was on top of the prior quarter in which earnings dropped 48 percent from the same quarter a year before.

The problem is not only Dell's however. Also in May 2009, HP said that it expected sales to decline 4 to 5 percent in 2009. The economy is responsible for some of this decline, and some of it is also due to the fact that customers were waiting to buy PCs after Windows 7 came out later in the year.

However, another financial result must be troubling to Dell. In that same month, Intel reported that sales were returning to "normal patterns," and Cisco (maker of routers and other communication devices) reported that sales seemed to have bottomed out. So, the components of PCs seem to be selling, but not PCs themselves. What might this mean?

Sources: © 2005 Dell Inc. All Rights Reserved. "Dell: No Relief in Sight," *BusinessWeek*, May 28, 2009. Available at *www.businessweek.com/technology/content/may2009/tc20090528_130058.htm* (accessed June 2009).

Questions

1. Explain how selling direct has given Dell a competitive advantage. Use the factors listed in Figure 3-12 (page 77) in your answer.

2. What information systems does Dell need to have to sell directly to the consumer? Visit *http://dell.com* for inspiration and ideas.

3. Besides selling direct, what other programs has Dell created that give it a competitive advantage?

4. Consider Dell's recent financial troubles.

   a. What are the implications of the company's tactics when revenue falls 63 percent but sales fall only 23 percent?

   b. Intel sells CPUs and memory, and its sales have stabilized. Dell and HP make computers, and their sales continue to decline. Assume the sales of other PC manufacturers are similar to those for Dell and HP. What do you conclude? Reread the 2020? sections in Chapter 1 (page 18) and in this chapter (page 122) before you finalize your answer.

---

[3]Michael Dell, speech before the Miami Springs Middle School, September 1, 2004. Retrieved from *www.dell.com*, under Michael/Speeches (accessed January 2005).

5 Database Processing

"Nope. It doesn't make any sense. I looked at the data and found we can't pack customers into classes. We don't have enough capacity."

"But, Neil, look at that Sunday night spinning class . . . it's half full. We could put another 25 people into that class."

"It's not what it seems. I queried the database, and at first glance you'd think we have plenty of opportunity to fill unoccupied seats. According to our database, we have a 9.7 percent vacancy rate in our classes."

"That's a lot."

"Yes, but looking more closely, I found that all of those empty seats occur in awkward time slots. The database shows that all of Monday–Saturday primetime class slots are full—99.8 percent occupancy."

"Wow."

"It's the Sunday and the mid-day classes that have the vacancies."

"Well, let's try to consolidate those classes."

"Not a good idea . . . for two reasons. One, we'd only be able to cancel two, maybe three classes, and that doesn't save us much. But, the stronger reason it won't

> *The database shows that all of Monday–Saturday primetime class slots are full—99.8 percent occupancy.*

work is that people are inflexible in the time slots they chose."

"How do you know that?"

"Felix I was amazed . . . but 93 percent of our customers always take a class on the same day and time. Even if they change classes, they always change to the same date and time."

"I guess that makes sense, Neil. They've got their lives set up to come here at a particular time on particular days and, well, they don't want to change that."

"That's true for more than 9 out of 10 customers."

"Hey, Neil, it's great that our software lets you query the data like that."

"Actually, it's not so flexible. I have about 25 standard queries that I can make against the database, selecting customers who've taken particular classes, etc. Those standard queries don't give me all the data I need. If I were a programmer type, I could write my own queries against the database, but I'm not."

"So what do you do?"

"Felix, I'm a whiz at Excel! I run a database query that's as close as possible to what I want and then bring the results into Excel. I move and sort and sum and average the data around in Excel until I get the information I want."

"That seems like a pain."

"Yeah, maybe, but it works."

"Neil, that leaves us where we started, doesn't it? If we can't save money by packing customers into classes, what are we going to do?"

"I'm looking at the juice bar right now. Seems like our inventory costs are too high and we may need to reduce its operating hours. But don't say anything to anyone about that. I haven't looked at the data yet."

"The trainers will be glad we aren't cancelling classes."

"Yes, why don't you tell them on your team site? And not cancelling classes saves us possible public relations problems with our customers. Anyway, we avoided a train wreck on this one. Hey, I'm gonna go for a run. Cheers!" ∎

>> STUDY QUESTIONS

Q1 What is the purpose of a database?

Q2 What is a database?

Q3 What are the components of a database application system?

Q4 How do database applications make databases more useful?

Q5 How are data models used for database development?

Q6 How is a data model transformed into a database design?

Q7 What is the users' role in the development of databases?

Q8 2020?

135

CHAPTER PREVIEW

You can find a free, supplemental study lesson for this chapter at:

www.LearningMIS.com

Businesses of every size organize data records into collections called *databases*. At one extreme, small businesses use databases to keep track of customers; at the other extreme, huge corporations such as Dell and Amazon.com use databases to support complex sales, marketing, and operations activities. In between, we have businesses like FlexTime that use databases as a crucial part of their operations, but they don't have a trained and experienced staff to manage and support the databases. To obtain answers to the one-of-a-kind queries he needs, Neil needs to be creative and adaptable in the way that he accesses and uses his database.

This chapter discusses the why, what, and how of database processing. We begin by describing the purpose of databases and then explain the important components of database systems. We then overview the process of creating a database system and summarize your role as a future user of such systems.

Users have a crucial role in the development of database applications. Specifically, the structure and content of the database depends entirely on how users view their business activity. To build the database, the developers will create a model of that view using a tool called the entity-relationship model. You need to understand how to interpret such models, because the development team might ask you to validate the correctness of such a model when building a system for your use. Finally, we describe the various database administration tasks.

This chapter focuses on database technology. Here we consider the basic components of a database and their functions. You will learn about the use of database reporting and data mining in Chapter 9.

Q1 What Is the Purpose of a Database?

The purpose of a database is to keep track of things. When most students learn that, they wonder why we need a special technology for such a simple task. Why not just use a list? If the list is long, put it into a spreadsheet.

In fact, many professionals do keep track of things using spreadsheets. If the structure of the list is simple enough, there is no need to use database technology. The list of student grades in Figure 5-1, for example, works perfectly well in a spreadsheet.

Suppose, however, that the professor wants to track more than just grades. Say that the professor wants to record email messages as well. Or, perhaps the professor wants to record both email messages and office visits. There is no place in Figure 5-1 to record that additional data. Of course, the professor could set up a separate spreadsheet for email messages and another one for office visits, but that awkward solution would be difficult to use because it does not provide all of the data in one place.

Instead, the professor wants a form like that in Figure 5-2. With it, the professor can record student grades, emails, and office visits all in one place. A form like the one in Figure 5-2 is difficult, if not impossible, to produce from a spreadsheet. Such a form is easily produced, however, from a database.

	A	B	C	D	E
1	**Student Name**	**Student Number**	**HW1**	**HW2**	**MidTerm**
2					
3	BAKER, ANDREA	1325	88	100	78
4	FISCHER, MAYAN	3007	95	100	74
5	LAU, SWEE	1644	75	90	90
6	NELSON, STUART	2881	100	90	98
7	ROGERS, SHELLY	8009	95	100	98
8	TAM, JEFFREY	3559		100	88
9	VALDEZ, MARIE	5265	80	90	85
10	VERBERRA, ADAM	4867	70	90	92

Figure 5-1
A List of Student Grades, Presented in a Spreadsheet

STUDENT

Student Name	BAKER, ANDREA
Student Number	1325
HW1	88
HW2	100
MidTerm	78

EMAIL

Date	Message
2/1/2007	For homework 1, do you want us to provide notes on our references?
3/15/2007	My group consists of Swee Lau and Stuart Nelson.
* 7/21/2007	

Record: ⏮ ◀ 2 of 2 ▶ ⏭ ▸* 🦅 No Filter   Search

OFFICE VISITS

Date	Notes
2/13/2007	Andrea had questions about using IS for raising barriers to entry.
*	

Record: ⏮ ◀ 1 of 8 ▶ ⏭ ▸* 🦅 No Filter   Search

Figure 5-2
Student Data Shown in a
Form, from a Database

The key distinction between Figures 5-1 and 5-2 is that the data in Figure 5-1 is about a single theme or concept. It is about student grades only. The data in Figure 5-2 has multiple themes; it shows student grades, student emails, and student office visits. We can make a general rule from these examples: Lists of data involving a single theme can be stored in a spreadsheet; lists that involve data with multiple themes require a database. We will say more about this general rule as this chapter proceeds.

To summarize, the purpose of a database is to keep track of things that involve more than one theme.

Q2 What Is a Database?

A **database** is a self-describing collection of integrated records. To understand this definition, you first need to understand the terms illustrated in Figure 5-3. As you learned in Chapter 4, a **byte** is a character of data. In databases, bytes are grouped into

As you will see, databases can be more difficult to develop than spreadsheets; this difficulty causes some people to prefer to work with spreadsheets—or at least pretend to—as described in the Guide on pages 162–163.

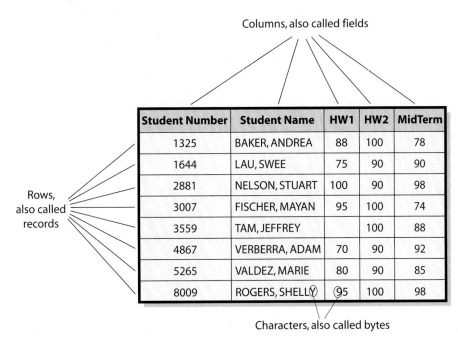

Columns, also called fields

Student Number	Student Name	HW1	HW2	MidTerm
1325	BAKER, ANDREA	88	100	78
1644	LAU, SWEE	75	90	90
2881	NELSON, STUART	100	90	98
3007	FISCHER, MAYAN	95	100	74
3559	TAM, JEFFREY		100	88
4867	VERBERRA, ADAM	70	90	92
5265	VALDEZ, MARIE	80	90	85
8009	ROGERS, SHELLY	95	100	98

Rows,
also called
records

Characters, also called bytes

Figure 5-3
Student Table (also called a file)

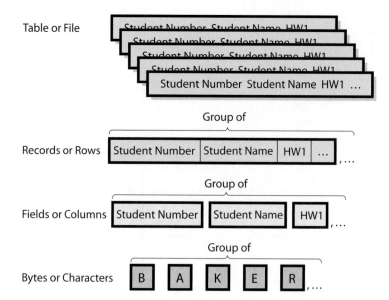

Figure 5-4
Hierarchy of Data Elements

columns, such as *Student Number* and *Student Name*. Columns are also called **fields**. Columns or fields, in turn, are grouped into **rows**, which are also called **records**. In Figure 5-3, the collection of data for all columns (*Student Number, Student Name, HW1, HW2,* and *MidTerm*) is called a *row* or a *record*. Finally, a group of similar rows or records is called a **table** or a **file**. From these definitions, you can see that there is a hierarchy of data elements, as shown in Figure 5-4.

It is tempting to continue this grouping process by saying that a database is a group of tables or files. This statement, although true, does not go far enough. As shown in Figure 5-5, a database is a collection of tables *plus* relationships among the rows in those tables, *plus* special data, called *metadata*, that describes the structure of the database. By the way, the cylindrical symbol 🛢 represents a computer disk drive. It is used in diagrams like that in Figure 5-5 because databases are normally stored on magnetic disks.

What Are Relationships Among Rows?

Consider the terms on the left-hand side of Figure 5-5. You know what tables are. To understand what is meant by *relationships among rows in tables,* examine Figure 5-6. It shows sample data from the three tables *Email, Student,* and *Office_Visit.* Notice the column named *Student Number* in the *Email* table. That column indicates the row in *Student* to which a row of *Email* is connected. In the first row of *Email,* the *Student Number* value is 1325. This indicates that this particular email was received from the student whose *Student Number* is 1325. If you examine the *Student* table, you will see that the row for Andrea Baker has this value. Thus, the first row of the *Email* table is related to Andrea Baker.

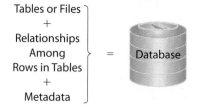

Figure 5-5
Components of a Database

Email Table

EmailNum	Date	Message	Student Number
1	2/1/2009	For homework 1, do you want us to provide notes on our references?	(1325)
2	3/15/2009	My group consists of Swee Lau and Stuart Nelson.	(1325)
3	3/15/2009	Could you please assign me to a group?	1644

Student Table

Student Number	Student Name	HW1	HW2	MidTerm
(1325)	BAKER, ANDREA	88	100	78
1644	LAU, SWEE	75	90	90
2881	NELSON, STUART	100	90	98
3007	FISCHER, MAYAN	95	100	74
3559	TAM, JEFFREY		100	88
(4867)	VERBERRA, ADAM	70	90	92
5265	VALDEZ, MARIE	80	90	85
8009	ROGERS, SHELLY	95	100	98

Office_Visit Table

VisitID	Date	Notes	Student Number
2	2/13/2009	Andrea had questions about using IS for raising barriers to entry.	1325
3	2/17/2009	Jeffrey is considering an IS major. Wanted to talk about career opportunities.	3559
4	2/17/2009	Will miss class Friday due to job conflict.	(4867)

Figure 5-6
Example of Relationships Among Rows

Now consider the last row of the *Office_Visit* table at the bottom of the figure. The value of *Student Number* in that row is 4867. This value indicates that the last row in *Office_Visit* belongs to Adam Verberra.

From these examples, you can see that values in one table relate rows of that table to rows in a second table. Several special terms are used to express these ideas. A **key** is a column or group of columns that identifies a unique row in a table. *Student Number* is the key of the *Student* table. Given a value of *Student Number*, you can determine one and only one row in *Student*. Only one student has the number 1325, for example.

Every table must have a key. The key of the *Email* table is *EmailNum*, and the key of the *Student_Visit* table is *VisitID*. Sometimes more than one column is needed to form a unique identifier. In a table called *City*, for example, the key would consist of the combination of columns (*City*, *State*), because a given city name can appear in more than one state.

Student Number is not the key of the *Email* or the *Office_Visit* tables. We know that about *Email* because there are two rows in *Email* that have the *Student Number* value 1325. The value 1325 does not identify a unique row, therefore *Student Number* cannot be the key of *Email*.

Nor is *Student Number* a key of *Office_Visit*, although you cannot tell that from the data in Figure 5-6. If you think about it, however, there is nothing to prevent a student from visiting a professor more than once. If that were to happen, there would be two rows in *Office_Visit* with the same value of *Student Number*. It just happens that no student has visited twice in the limited data in Figure 5-6.

Columns that fulfill a role like that of *Student Number* in the *Email* and *Office_Visit* tables are called **foreign keys**. This term is used because such columns are keys, but they are keys of a different (foreign) table than the one in which they reside.

Before we go on, databases that carry their data in the form of tables and that represent relationships using foreign keys are called **relational databases**. (The term *relational* is used because another, more formal name for a table is **relation**.) In the past, there were databases that were not relational in format, but such databases have nearly disappeared. Chances are you will never encounter one, and we will not consider them further.[1]

Metadata

Recall the definition of database: A database is a self-describing collection of integrated records. The records are integrated because, as you just learned, relationships among rows are represented in the database. But what does *self-describing* mean?

It means that a database contains, within itself, a description of its contents. Think of a library. A library is a self-describing collection of books and other materials. It is self-describing because the library contains a catalog that describes the library's contents. The same idea also pertains to a database. Databases are self-describing because they contain not only data, but also data about the data in the database.

Metadata are data that describe data. Figure 5-7 shows metadata for the *Email* table. The format of metadata depends on the software product that is processing the database. Figure 5-7 shows the metadata as they appear in Microsoft Access. Each row of the top part of this form describes a column of the *Email* table. The columns of these descriptions are *Field Name*, *Data Type*, and *Description*. *Field Name* contains the name of the column, *Data Type* shows the type of data the column may hold, and *Description* contains notes that explain the source or use of the column. As you can

Figure 5-7
Sample Metadata (in Access)

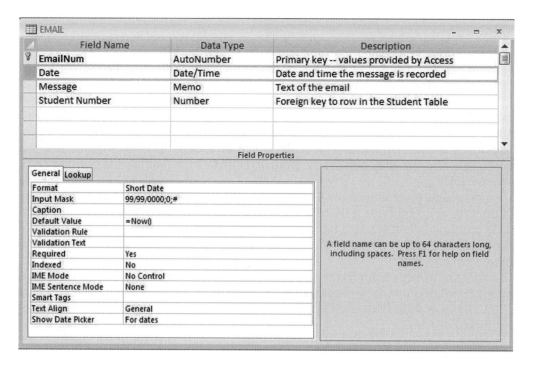

---

[1]Another type of database, the **object-relational database**, is rarely used in commercial applications. Search the Web if you are interested in learning more about object-relational databases. In this book, we will describe only relational databases.

see, there is one row of metadata for each of the four columns of the *Email* table: *EmailNum*, *Date*, *Message*, and *Student Number*.

The bottom part of this form provides more metadata, which Access calls *Field Properties*, for each column. In Figure 5-7, the focus is on the *Date* column (note the light rectangle drawn around the *Date* row). Because the focus is on *Date* in the top pane, the details in the bottom pane pertain to the *Date* column. The Field Properties describe formats, a default value for Access to supply when a new row is created, and the constraint that a value is required for this column. It is not important for you to remember these details. Instead, just understand that metadata are data about data and that such metadata are always a part of a database.

The presence of metadata makes databases much more useful. Because of metadata, no one needs to guess, remember, or even record what is in the database. To find out what a database contains, we just look at the metadata inside the database.

Metadata makes databases easy to use, for both authorized and unauthorized purposes, as described in the Ethics Guide on pages 142–143.

Q3 What Are the Components of a Database Application System?

A database, all by itself, is not very useful. The tables in Figure 5-6 have all of the data the professor wants, but the format is unwieldy. The professor wants to see the data in a form like that in Figure 5-2 and also as a formatted report. Pure database data are correct, but in raw form they are not pertinent or useful.

Figure 5-8 shows the components of a **database application system**. Such applications make database data more accessible and useful. Users employ a database application that consists of forms (like that in Figure 5-2), formatted reports, queries, and application programs. Each of these, in turn, calls on the database management system (DBMS) to process the database tables. We will first describe DBMSs and then discuss database application components.

What Is a Database Management System?

A **database management system (DBMS)** is a program used to create, process, and administer a database. As with operating systems, almost no organization develops its own DBMS. Instead, companies license DBMS products from vendors such as IBM, Microsoft, Oracle, and others. Popular DBMS products are **DB2** from IBM, **Access** and **SQL Server** from Microsoft, and **Oracle** from the Oracle Corporation. Another popular DBMS is **MySQL**, an open source DBMS product that is license-free for most applications.[2] Other DBMS products are available, but these five process the great bulk of databases today.

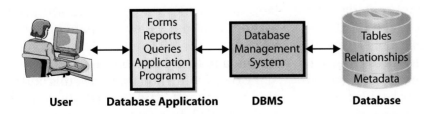

Figure 5-8
Components of a Database Application System

---

[2]MySQL was supported by the MySQL company. In 2008, that company was acquired by Sun Microsystems, which was, in turn, acquired by Oracle later that year. Because MySQL is open source, Oracle does not own the source code, however. As of 2009, a rumor was circulating the Web that one of the original MySQL developers was going to start another open source project based on the current code. What an industry!

Ethics

Nobody Said
I Shouldn't

"My name is Chris and I do systems support for our group. I configure the new computers, set up the network, make sure the servers are operating, and so forth. I also do all of the database backups. I've always liked computers. After high school, I worked odd jobs to make some money, then I got an associate degree in information technology from our local community college.

"Anyway, as I said, I make backup copies of our databases. One weekend, I didn't have much going on, so I copied one of the database backups to a DVD and took it home. I had taken a class on database processing as part of my associate degree, and we used SQL Server (our database management system) in my class. In fact, I suppose that's part of the reason I got the job. Anyway, it was easy to restore the database on my computer at home, and I did.

"Of course, as they'll tell you in your database class, one of the big advantages of database processing is that databases have metadata, or data that describe the content of the database. So, although I didn't know what tables were in our database, I did know how to access the SQL Server metadata. I just queried a table called *sysTables* to learn the names of our tables. From there it was easy to find out what columns each table had.

"I found tables with data about orders, customers, salespeople, and so forth, and, just to amuse myself, and to see how much of the query

language SQL that I could remember, I started playing around with the data. I was curious to know which order entry clerk was the best, so I started querying each clerk's order data, the total number of orders, total order amounts, things like that. It was easy to do and fun.

"I know one of the order entry clerks, Jason, pretty well, so I started looking at the data for his orders. I was just curious, and it was very simple SQL. I was just playing around with the data when I noticed something odd. All of his biggest orders were with one company, Valley Appliances, and even stranger, every one of its orders had a huge discount. I thought, well, maybe that's typical. Out of curiosity, I started looking at data for the other clerks, and very few of them had an order with Valley Appliances. But, when they did, Valley didn't get a big discount. Then I looked at the rest of Jason's orders, and none of them had much in the way of discounts, either.

"The next Friday, a bunch of us went out for a beer after work. I happened to see Jason, so I asked him about Valley Appliances and made a joke about the discounts. He asked me what I meant, and then I told him that I'd been looking at the data for fun and that I saw this odd pattern. He just laughed, said he just 'did his job,' and then changed the subject.

"Well, to make a long story short, when I got to work on Monday morning, my office was cleaned out. There was nothing there except a note telling me to go see my boss. The bottom line was, I was

fired. The company also threatened that if I didn't return all of its data, I'd be in court for the next 5 years . . . things like that. I was so mad I didn't even tell them about Jason. Now my problem is that I'm out of a job, and I can't exactly use my last company for a reference." ■

Discussion Questions

1. Where did Chris go wrong?
2. Do you think it was illegal, unethical, or neither for Chris to take the database home and query the data?
3. Does the company share culpability with Chris?
4. What do you think Chris should have done upon discovering the odd pattern in Jason's orders?
5. What should the company have done before firing Chris?
6. Is it possible that someone other than Jason is involved in the arrangement with Valley Appliances? What should Chris have done in light of that possibility?
7. What should Chris do now?
8. "Metadata make databases easy to use, for both authorized and unauthorized purposes." Explain what organizations should do in light of this fact.

Note that a DBMS and a database are two different things. For some reason, the trade press and even some books confuse the two. A DBMS is a software program; a database is a collection of tables, relationships, and metadata. The two are very different concepts.

Creating the Database and Its Structures

Database developers use the DBMS to create tables, relationships, and other structures in the database. The form in Figure 5-7 can be used to define a new table or to modify an existing one. To create a new table, the developer just fills the new table's metadata into the form.

To modify an existing table—say, to add a new column—the developer opens the metadata form for that table and adds a new row of metadata. For example, in Figure 5-9 the developer has added a new column called *Response?*. This new column has the data type *Yes/No*, which means that the column can contain only one value—*Yes* or *No*. The professor will use this column to indicate whether he has responded to the student's email. A column can be removed by deleting its row in this table, though doing so will lose any existing data.

Processing the Database

The second function of the DBMS is to process the database. Applications use the DBMS for four operations: to *read, insert, modify,* or *delete* data. The applications call upon the DBMS in different ways. From a form, when the user enters new or changed data, a computer program behind the form calls the DBMS to make the necessary database changes. From an application program, the program calls the DBMS directly to make the change.

Structured Query Language (SQL) is an international standard language for processing a database. All five of the DBMS products mentioned earlier accept and process SQL (pronounced "see-quell") statements. As an example, the following SQL statement inserts a new row into the *Student* table:

```
INSERT INTO Student
([Student Number], [Student Name], HW1, HW2, MidTerm)
VALUES
(1000, 'Franklin, Benjamin', 90, 95, 100);
```

As stated, statements like this one are issued "behind the scenes" by programs that process forms. Alternatively, they can be issued directly to the DBMS by an application program.

Figure 5-9
Adding a New Column
to a Table (in Access)

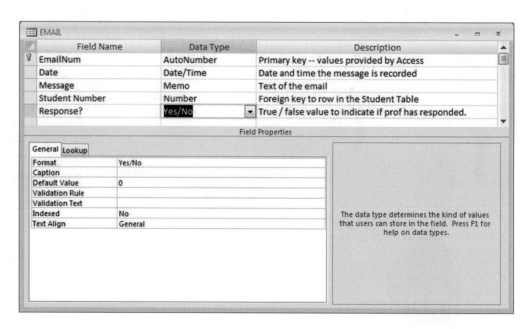

You do not need to understand or remember SQL language syntax. Instead, just realize that SQL is an international standard for processing a database. SQL can also be used to create databases and database structures. You will learn more about SQL if you take a database management class.

Administering the Database

A third DBMS function is to provide tools to assist in the administration of the database. Database administration involves a wide variety of activities. For example, the DBMS can be used to set up a security system involving user accounts, passwords, permissions, and limits for processing the database. To provide database security, a user must sign on using a valid user account before she can process the database.

Permissions can be limited in very specific ways. In the Student database example, it is possible to limit a particular user to reading only *Student Name* from the *Student* table. A different user could be given permission to read the entire *Student* table, but limited to update only the *HW1*, *HW2*, and *MidTerm* columns. Other users can be given still other permissions.

In addition to security, DBMS administrative functions include backing up database data, adding structures to improve the performance of database applications, removing data that are no longer wanted or needed, and similar tasks.

For important databases, most organizations dedicate one or more employees to the role of **database administration**. Figure 5-10 summarizes the major

Category	Database Administration Task	Description
Development	Create and staff DBA function	Size of DBA group depends on size and complexity of database. Groups range from one part-time person to small group.
	Form steering committee	Consists of representatives of all user groups. Forum for community-wide discussions and decisions.
	Specify requirements	Ensure that all appropriate user input is considered.
	Validate data model	Check data model for accuracy and completeness.
	Evaluate application design	Verify that all necessary forms, reports, queries, and applications are developed. Validate design and usability of application components.
Operation	Manage processing rights and responsibilities	Determine processing rights/restrictions on each table and column.
	Manage security	Add and delete users and user groups as necessary; ensure that security system works.
	Track problems and manage resolution	Develop system to record and manage resolution of problems.
	Monitor database performance	Provide expertise/solutions for performance improvements.
	Manage DBMS	Evaluate new features and functions.
Backup and Recovery	Monitor backup procedures	Verify that database backup procedures are followed.
	Conduct training	Ensure that users and operations personnel know and understand recovery procedures.
	Manage recovery	Manage recovery process.
Adaptation	Set up request tracking system	Develop system to record and prioritize requests for change.
	Manage configuration change	Manage impact of database structure changes on applications and users.

Figure 5-10
Summary of Database Administration Tasks

responsibilities for this function. You will learn more about this topic if you take a database management course.

Q4 How Do Database Applications Make Databases More Useful?

A **database application** is a collection of forms, reports, queries, and application programs that process a database. A database may have one or more applications, and each application may have one or more users. Figure 5-11 shows three applications used at FlexTime. The first one is used to bill and manage FlexTime memberships; the second schedules and bills scheduled classes; and the third tracks and supports personal training sessions. These applications have different purposes, features, and functions, but they all process the same FlexTime customer database.

What Are Forms, Reports, and Queries?

Figure 5-2 shows a typical database application data entry **form**, and Figure 5-12 shows a typical **report**. Data entry forms are used to read, insert, modify, and delete data. Reports show data in a structured context.

Recall from Chapter 1 that one of the definitions of information is "data presented in a meaningful context." The structure of this report creates information because it shows the student data in a context that will be meaningful to the professor. Some reports, like the one in Figure 5-12, also compute values as they present the data. An example is the computation of *Total weighted points* in Figure 5-12.

DBMS programs provide comprehensive and robust features for querying database data. For example, suppose the professor who uses the Student database remembers that one of the students referred to the topic *barriers to entry* in an office visit, but cannot remember which student or when. If there are hundreds of students and visits recorded in the database, it will take some effort and time for the professor to search through all office visit records to find that event. The DBMS,

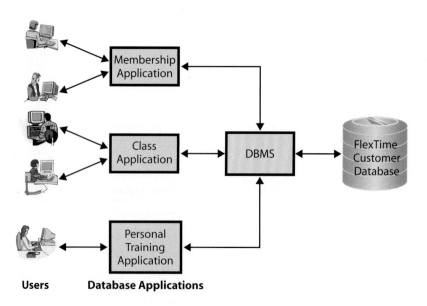

Figure 5-11
User of Multiple Database
Applications

Users   **Database Applications**

Student Report with Emails

Student Name	BAKER, ANDREA	HW1	88
		HW2	100
Student Number	1325	MidTerm	78 (= 3 homeworks)
		Total weighted points:	422

Emails Received

Date	Message
2/1/2009	For homework 1, do you want us to provide notes on our references?
3/15/2009	My group consists of Swee Lau and Stuart Nelson.

Student Name	LAU, SWEE	HW1	75
		HW2	90
		MidTerm	90 (= 3 homeworks)
Student Number	1644		
		Total weighted points:	435

Emails Received

Date	Message
3/15/2009	Could you please assign me to a group?

Figure 5-12
Example of a Student Report

however, can find any such record quickly. Figure 5-13(a) shows a **query** form in which the professor types in the keyword for which she is looking. Figure 5-13(b) shows the results of the query.

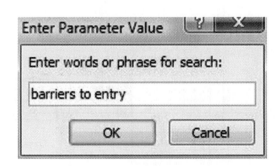

Figure 5-13a
Sample Query Form Used
to Enter Phrase for Search

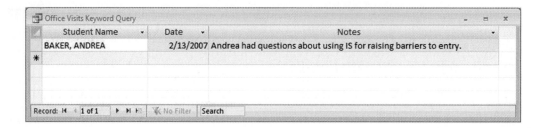

Figure 5-13b
Sample Query Results
of Query Operation

Why Are Database Application Programs Needed?

Forms, reports, and queries work well for standard functions. However, most applications have unique requirements that a simple form, report, or query cannot meet. For example, in an order-entry application what should be done if only a portion of a customer's request can be met? If someone wants 10 widgets and we only have 3 in stock, should a backorder for 7 more be generated automatically? Or, should some other action be taken?

Application programs process logic that is specific to a given business need. In the Student database, an example application is one that assigns grades at the end of the term. If the professor grades on a curve, the application reads the breakpoints for each grade from a form, and then processes each row in the *Student* table, allocating a grade based on the break points and the total number of points earned.

Another important use of application programs is to enable database processing over the Internet. For this use, the application program serves as an intermediary between the Web server and the database. The application program responds to events, such as when a user presses a submit button; it also reads, inserts, modifies, and deletes database data.

For example, Figure 5-14 shows four different database application programs running on a Web server computer. Users with browsers connect to the Web server via the Internet. The Web server directs user requests to the appropriate application program. Each program then processes the database as necessary. You will learn more about Web-enabled databases in the discussion of e-commerce in Chapter 8.

Multi-User Processing

Figures 5-11 and 5-14 show multiple users processing the database. Such **multi-user processing** is common, but it does pose unique problems that you, as a future manager, should know about. To understand the nature of those problems, consider the following scenario.

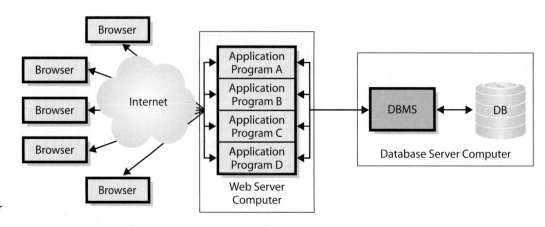

Figure 5-14
Four Application Programs
on a Web Server Computer

Two users, Andrea and Jeffrey, are FlexTime employees using the Class application in Figure 5-11. Andrea is on the phone with her customer, who wants to enroll in a particular spinning class. At the same time, Jeffrey is talking with his customer, who wants to enroll in that same class. Andrea reads the database to determine how many vacancies that class has. (She unknowingly invokes the Class application when she types in her data entry form.) The DBMS returns a row showing there is one slot left in that class.

Meanwhile, just after Andrea accesses the database, Jeffrey's customer says she wants in that class, and so he also reads the database (via the Class application program) to determine how many slots are available. The DBMS returns the same row to him, indicating that one slot is left.

Andrea's customer now says that he will enroll in the class, and Andrea records this fact in her form. The application rewrites that class row back to the database, indicating that there are no slots left.

Meanwhile, Jeffrey's customer says that she will take the class. Jeffrey records this fact in his form, and the application (which still is using the row it read indicating that a slot is available) rewrites that class row to the database, indicating there are no openings left. Jeffrey's application knows nothing about Andrea's work and hence does not know that her customer has already taken the last slot.

Clearly, there is a problem. Both customers have been assigned the same last slot in the class. When they attend the class, one of them will not have a bike to ride, which will be frustrating to the customers as well as the instructor.

This problem, known as the **lost-update problem**, exemplifies one of the special characteristics of multi-user database processing. To prevent this problem, some type of locking must be used to coordinate the activities of users who know nothing about one another. Locking brings its own set of problems, however, and those problems must be addressed as well. We will not delve further into this topic here, however.

Realize from this example that converting a single-user database to a multi-user database requires more than simply connecting another computer. The logic of the underlying application processing needs to be adjusted as well.

Be aware of possible data conflicts when you manage business activities that involve multi-user processing. If you find inaccurate results that seem not to have a cause, you may be experiencing multi-user data conflicts. Contact your IS department for assistance.

Enterprise DBMS Versus Personal DBMS

DBMS products fall into two broad categories. **Enterprise DBMS** products process large organizational and workgroup databases. These products support many, possibly thousands, of users and many different database applications. Such DBMS products support 24/7 operations and can manage databases that span dozens of different magnetic disks with hundreds of gigabytes or more of data. IBM's DB2, Microsoft's SQL Server, and Oracle's Oracle are examples of enterprise DBMS products.

Personal DBMS products are designed for smaller, simpler database applications. Such products are used for personal or small workgroup applications that involve fewer than 100 users, and normally fewer than 15. In fact, the great bulk of databases in this category have only a single user. The professor's Student database is an example of a database that is processed by a personal DBMS product.

In the past, there were many personal DBMS products—Paradox, dBase, R:base, and FoxPro. Microsoft put these products out of business when they developed Access and included it in the Microsoft Office suite. Today, about the only remaining personal DBMS is Microsoft Access.

To avoid one point of confusion for you in the future, the separation of application programs and the DBMS shown in Figure 5-11 is true only for enterprise DBMS products. Microsoft Access includes features and functions for application processing along with the DBMS itself. For example, Access has a form generator and a report generator. Thus, as shown in Figure 5-15, Access is both a DBMS *and* an application development product.

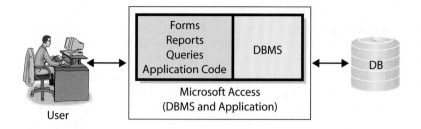

Figure 5-15
Personal Database System

Q5 How Are Data Models Used for Database Development?

In Chapter 10, we will describe the process for developing information systems in detail. However, business professionals have such a critical role in the development of database applications that we need to anticipate part of that discussion here by introducing two topics—data modeling and database design.

Because the design of the database depends entirely on how users view their business environment, user involvement is critical for database development. Think about the Student database. What data should it contain? Possibilities are: *Students, Classes, Grades, Emails, Office_Visits, Majors, Advisers, Student_Organizations*—the list could go on and on. Further, how much detail should be included in each? Should the database include campus addresses? Home addresses? Billing addresses?

In fact, there are dozens of possibilities, and the database developers do not and cannot know what to include. They do know, however, that a database must include all the data necessary for the users to perform their jobs. Ideally, it contains that amount of data and no more. So, during database development the developers must rely on the users to tell them what to include in the database.

Database structures can be complex, in some cases very complex. So, before building the database the developers construct a logical representation of database data called a **data model**. It describes the data and relationships that will be stored in the database. It is akin to a blueprint. Just as building architects create a blueprint before they start building, so, too, database developers create a data model before they start designing the database.

Figure 5-16 summarizes the database development process. Interviews with users lead to database requirements, which are summarized in a data model. Once the users have approved (validated) the data model, it is transformed into a database design. That design is then implemented into database structures. We will consider data modeling and database design briefly in the next two sections. Again, your goal should be to learn the process so that you can be an effective user representative for a development effort.

For a philopsophical perspective on data models, see the Guide on pages 164–165.

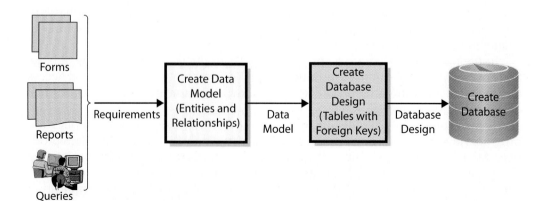

Figure 5-16
Database Development Process

What Is the Entity-Relationship Data Model?

The **entity-relationship (E-R) data model** is a tool for constructing data models. Developers use it to describe the content of a data model by defining the things (*entities*) that will be stored in the database and the *relationships* among those entities. A second, less popular, tool for data modeling is the **Unified Modeling Language (UML)**. We will not describe that tool here. However, if you learn how to interpret E-R models, with a bit of study you will be able to understand UML models as well.

Entities

An **entity** is some thing that the users want to track. Examples of entities are *Order*, *Customer*, *Salesperson*, and *Item*. Some entities represent a physical object, such as *Item* or *Salesperson*; others represent a logical construct or transaction, such as *Order* or *Contract*. For reasons beyond this discussion, entity names are always singular. We use *Order*, not *Orders*; *Salesperson*, not *Salespersons*.

Entities have **attributes** that describe characteristics of the entity. Example attributes of *Order* are *OrderNumber*, *OrderDate*, *SubTotal*, *Tax*, *Total*, and so forth. Example attributes of *Salesperson* are *SalespersonName*, *Email*, *Phone*, and so forth.

Entities have an **identifier**, which is an attribute (or group of attributes) whose value is associated with one and only one entity instance. For example, *OrderNumber* is an identifier of *Order*, because only one *Order* instance has a given value of *OrderNumber*. For the same reason, *CustomerNumber* is an identifier of *Customer*. If each member of the sales staff has a unique name, then *SalespersonName* is an identifier of *Salesperson*.

Before we continue, consider that last sentence. Is the salesperson's name unique among the sales staff? Both now and in the future? Who decides the answer to such a question? Only the users know whether this is true; the database developers cannot know. This example underlines why it is important for you to be able to interpret data models, because only users like you will know for sure.

Figure 5-17 shows examples of entities for the Student database. Each entity is shown in a rectangle. The name of the entity is just above the rectangle, and the identifier is shown in a section at the top of the entity. Entity attributes are shown in the remainder of the rectangle. In Figure 5-17, the *Adviser* entity has an identifier called *AdviserName* and the attributes *Phone*, *CampusAddress*, and *EmailAddress*.

Observe that the entities *Email* and *Office_Visit* do not have an identifier. Unlike *Student* or *Adviser*, the users do not have an attribute that identifies a particular email. We *could* make one up. For example, we could say that the identifier of *Email* is *EmailNumber*, but if we do so we are not modeling how the users view their world. Instead, we are forcing something onto the users. Be aware of this possibility when you review data models about your business. Do not allow the database developers to create something in the data model that is not part of your business world.

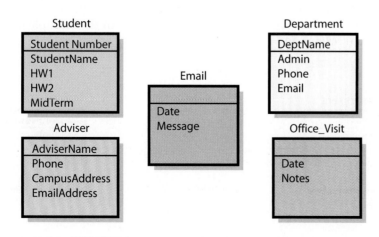

Figure 5-17
Student Data Model Entities

Figure 5-18
Example of Department,
Adviser, and Student Entities
and Relationships

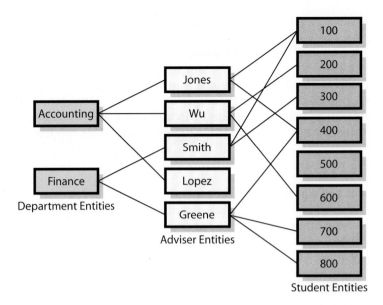

Relationships

Entities have **relationships** to each other. An *Order*, for example, has a relationship to a *Customer* entity and also to a *Salesperson* entity. In the Student database, a *Student* has a relationship to an *Adviser*, and an *Adviser* has a relationship to a *Department*.

Figure 5-18 shows sample *Department, Adviser,* and *Student* entities and their relationships. For simplicity, this figure shows just the identifier of the entities and not the other attributes. For this sample data, *Accounting* has three professors—Jones, Wu, and Lopez—and *Finance* has two professors—Smith and Greene.

The relationship between *Advisers* and *Students* is a bit more complicated, because in this example an adviser is allowed to advise many students, and a student is allowed to have many advisers. Perhaps this happens because students can have multiple majors. In any case, note that Professor Jones advises students 100 and 400 and that student 100 is advised by both Professors Jones and Smith.

Diagrams like the one in Figure 5-18 are too cumbersome for use in database design discussions. Instead, database designers use diagrams called **entity-relationship (E-R) diagrams**. Figure 5-19 shows an E-R diagram for the data in Figure 5-18. In this figure, all of the entities of one type are represented by a single rectangle. Thus, there are rectangles for the *Department, Adviser,* and *Student* entities. Attributes are shown as before in Figure 5-17.

Additionally, a line is used to represent a relationship between two entities. Notice the line between *Department* and *Adviser,* for example. The forked lines on the right side of that line signify that a department may have more than one adviser. The little lines, which are referred to as **crow's feet**, are shorthand for the multiple lines between *Department* and *Adviser* in Figure 5-18. Relationships like this one are called **1:N**, or

Figure 5-19
Sample Relationships
Version 1

one-to-many relationships, because one department can have many advisers, but an adviser has at most one department.

Now examine the line between *Adviser* and *Student*. Notice the short lines that appear at each end of the line. These lines are the crow's feet, and this notation signifies that an adviser can be related to many students and that a student can be related to many advisers, which is the situation in Figure 5-18. Relationships like this one are called **N:M**, or **many-to-many relationships**, because one adviser can have many students and one student can have many advisers.

Students sometimes find the notation N:M confusing. Interpret the *N* and *M* to mean that a variable number, greater than one, is allowed on each side of the relationship. Such a relationship is not written *N:N*, because that notation would imply that there are the same number of entities on each side of the relationship, which is not necessarily true. *N:M* means that more than one entity is allowed on each side of the relationship and that the number of entities on each side can be different.

Figure 5-20 shows the same entities with different assumptions. Here, advisers may advise in more than one department, but a student may have only one adviser, representing a policy that students may not have multiple majors.

Which, if either, of these versions is correct? Only the users know. These alternatives illustrate the kinds of questions you will need to answer when a database designer asks you to check a data model for correctness.

Figures 5-19 and 5-20 are typical examples of an entity-relationship diagram. Unfortunately, there are several different styles of entity-relationship diagrams. This one is called, not surprisingly, a **crow's-foot diagram** version. You may learn other versions if you take a database management class.

The crow's-foot notation shows the maximum number of entities that can be involved in a relationship. Accordingly, they are called the relationship's **maximum cardinality**. Common examples of maximum cardinality are 1:N, N:M, and 1:1 (not shown).

Another important question is, "What is the minimum number of entities required in the relationship?" Must an adviser have a student to advise, and must a student have an adviser? Constraints on minimum requirements are called **minimum cardinalities**.

Figure 5-21 presents a third version of this E-R diagram that shows both maximum and minimum cardinalities. The vertical bar on a line means that at least one entity of that type is required. The small oval means that the entity is optional; the relationship *need not* have an entity of that type.

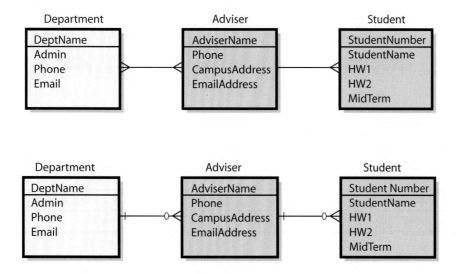

Figure 5-20
Sample Relationships
Version 2

Figure 5-21
Sample Relationships Showing
Both Maximum and Minimum
Cardinalities

Thus, in Figure 5-21 a department is not required to have a relationship to any adviser, but an adviser is required to belong to a department. Similarly, an adviser is not required to have a relationship to a student, but a student is required to have a relationship to an adviser. Note, also, that the maximum cardinalities in Figure 5-21 have been changed so that both are 1:N.

Is the model in Figure 5-21 a good one? It depends on the policy of the university. Again, only the users know for sure.

Q6 How Is a Data Model Transformed into a Database Design?

Database design is the process of converting a data model into tables, relationships, and data constraints. The database design team transforms entities into tables and expresses relationships by defining foreign keys. Database design is a complicated subject; as with data modeling, it occupies weeks in a database management class. In this section, however, we will introduce two important database design concepts: normalization and the representation of two kinds of relationships. The first concept is a foundation of database design, and the second will help you understand important design considerations.

Normalization

Normalization is the process of converting a poorly structured table into two or more well-structured tables. A table is such a simple construct that you may wonder how one could possibly be poorly structured. In truth, there are many ways that tables can be malformed—so many, in fact, that researchers have published hundreds of papers on this topic alone.

Consider the *Employee* table in Figure 5-22(a). It lists employee names, hire dates, email addresses, and the name and number of the department in which the employee

Employee

Name	HireDate	Email	DeptNo	DeptName
Jones	Feb 1, 2006	Jones@ourcompany.com	100	Accounting
Smith	Dec 3, 2008	Smith@ourcompany.com	200	Marketing
Chau	March 7, 2008	Chau@ourcompany.com	100	Accounting
Greene	July 17, 2007	Greene@ourcompany.com	100	Accounting

(a) Table Before Update

Employee

Name	HireDate	Email	DeptNo	DeptName
Jones	Feb 1, 2006	Jones@ourcompany.com	100	Accounting and Finance
Smith	Dec 3, 2008	Smith@ourcompany.com	200	Marketing
Chau	March 7, 2008	Chau@ourcompany.com	100	Accounting and Finance
Greene	July 17, 2007	Greene@ourcompany.com	100	Accounting

(b) Table with Incomplete Update

Figure 5-22
A Poorly Designed
Employee Table

works. This table seems innocent enough. But consider what happens when the Accounting department changes its name to Accounting and Finance. Because department names are duplicated in this table, every row that has a value of "Accounting" must be changed to "Accounting and Finance."

Data Integrity Problems

Suppose the Accounting name change is correctly made in two rows, but not in the third. The result is shown in Figure 5-22(b). This table has what is called a **data integrity problem**: Some rows indicate that the name of Department 100 is "Accounting and Finance," and another row indicates that the name of Department 100 is "Accounting."

This problem is easy to spot in this small table. But consider a table like the *Customer* table in the Amazon.com database or the eBay database. Those databases may have millions of rows. Once a table that large develops serious data integrity problems, months of labor will be required to remove them.

Data integrity problems are serious. A table that has data integrity problems will produce incorrect and inconsistent information. Users will lose confidence in the information, and the system will develop a poor reputation. Information systems with poor reputations become serious burdens to the organizations that use them.

Normalizing for Data Integrity

The data integrity problem can occur only if data are duplicated. Because of this, one easy way to eliminate the problem is to eliminate the duplicated data. We can do this by transforming the table in Figure 5-22 into two tables, as shown in Figure 5-23. Here, the name of the department is stored just once; therefore no data inconsistencies can occur.

Of course, to produce an employee report that includes the department name, the two tables in Figure 5-23 will need to be joined back together. Because such joining of tables is common, DBMS products have been programmed to perform it efficiently, but it still requires work. From this example, you can see a trade-off in database design: Normalized tables eliminate data duplication, but they can be slower to process. Dealing with such trade-offs is an important consideration in database design.

The general goal of normalization is to construct tables such that every table has a *single* topic or theme. In good writing, every paragraph should have a single theme.

Employee

Name	HireDate	Email	DeptNo
Jones	Feb 1, 2006	Jones@ourcompany.com	100
Smith	Dec 3, 2008	Smith@ourcompany.com	200
Chau	March 7, 2008	Chau@ourcompany.com	100
Greene	July 17, 2007	Greene@ourcompany.com	100

Department

DeptNo	DeptName
100	Accounting
200	Marketing
300	Information Systems

Figure 5-23
Two Normalized Tables

This is true of databases as well; every table should have a single theme. The problem with the table in Figure 5-22 is that it has two independent themes: employees and departments. The way to correct the problem is to split the table into two tables, each with its own theme. In this case, we create an *Employee* table and a *Department* table, as shown in Figure 5-23.

As mentioned, there are dozens of ways that tables can be poorly formed. Database practitioners classify tables into various **normal forms** according to the kinds of problems they have. Transforming a table into a normal form to remove duplicated data and other problems is called *normalizing* the table.[3] Thus, when you hear a database designer say, "Those tables are not normalized," she does not mean that the tables have irregular, not-normal data. Instead, she means that the tables have a format that could cause data integrity problems.

Summary of Normalization

As a future user of databases, you do not need to know the details of normalization. Instead, understand the general principle that every normalized (well-formed) table has one and only one theme. Further, tables that are not normalized are subject to data integrity problems.

Be aware, too, that normalization is just one criterion for evaluating database designs. Because normalized designs can be slower to process, database designers sometimes choose to accept non-normalized tables. The best design depends on the users' processing requirements.

Representing Relationships

Figure 5-24 shows the steps involved in transforming a data model into a relational database design. First, the database designer creates a table for each entity. The identifier of the entity becomes the key of the table. Each attribute of the entity becomes a column of the table. Next, the resulting tables are normalized so that each table has a single theme. Once that has been done, the next step is to represent relationship among those tables.

For example, consider the E-R diagram in Figure 5-25(a). The *Adviser* entity has a 1:N relationship to the *Student* entity. To create the database design, we construct a table for *Adviser* and a second table for *Student*, as shown in Figure 5-25(b). The key of the *Adviser* table is *AdviserName*, and the key of the *Student* table is *StudentNumber*.

> • Represent each entity with a table
>   – Entity identifier becomes table key
>   – Entity attributes become table columns
> • Normalize tables as necessary
> • Represent relationships
>   – Use foreign keys
>   – Add additional tables for N:M relationships

Figure 5-24
Transforming a Data Model into a Database Design

[3]See David Kroenke and David Auer, *Database Processing*, 11th ed. (Upper Saddle River, NJ: Prentice Hall, 2010) for more information.

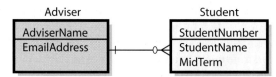

(a) 1:N Relationship Between Adviser and Student Entities

Adviser Table—Key is AdviserName

AdviserName	EmailAddress
Jones	Jones@myuniv.edu
Choi	Choi@myuniv.edu
Jackson	Jackson@myuniv.edu

Student Table—Key is StudentNumber

StudentNumber	StudentName	MidTerm
100	Lisa	90
200	Jennie	85
300	Jason	82
400	Terry	95

(b) Creating a Table for Each Entity

Adviser Table—Key is AdviserName

AdviserName	EmailAddress
Jones	Jones@myuniv.edu
Choi	Choi@myuniv.edu
Jackson	Jackson@myuniv.edu

Student—Key is StudentNumber

StudentNumber	StudentName	MidTerm	AdviserName
100	Lisa	90	Jackson
200	Jennie	85	Jackson
300	Jason	82	Choi
400	Terry	95	Jackson

Foreign Key Column Represents Relationship

(c) Using the *AdviserName* Foreign Key to Represent the 1:N Relationship

Figure 5-25
Representing a 1:N
Relationship

Further, the *EmailAddress* attribute of the *Adviser* entity becomes the *EmailAddress* column of the *Adviser* table, and the *StudentName* and *MidTerm* attributes of the *Student* entity become the *StudentName* and *MidTerm* columns of the *Student* table.

The next task is to represent the relationship. Because we are using the relational model, we know that we must add a foreign key to one of the two tables. The possibilities are: (1) place the foreign key *StudentNumber* in the *Adviser* table or (2) place the foreign key *AdviserName* in the *Student* table.

The correct choice is to place *AdviserName* in the *Student* table, as shown in Figure 5-25(c). To determine a student's adviser, we just look into the *AdviserName* column of that student's row. To determine the adviser's students, we search the *AdviserName* column in the *Student* table to determine which rows have that adviser's name. If a student changes advisers, we simply change the value in the *AdviserName* column. Changing *Jackson* to *Jones* in the first row, for example, will assign student 100 to Professor Jones.

For this data model, placing *StudentNumber* in *Adviser* would be incorrect. If we were to do that, we could assign only one student to an adviser. There is no place to assign a second adviser.

This strategy for placing foreign keys will not work for all relationships, however. Consider the data model in Figure 5-26(a); here advisers and students have a many-to-many relationship. An adviser may have many students, and a student may have multiple advisers (for multiple majors).

The foreign key strategy we used for the 1:N data model will not work here. To see why, examine Figure 5-26(b). If student 100 has more than one adviser, there is no place to record second or subsequent advisers.

To represent an N:M relationship, we need to create a third table, as shown in Figure 5-26(c). The third table has two columns, *AdviserName* and *StudentNumber*. Each row of the table means that the given adviser advises the student with the given number.

As you can imagine, there is a great deal more to database design than we have presented here. Still, this section should give you an idea of the tasks that need to be accomplished to create a database. You should also realize that the database design is a direct consequence of decisions made in the data model. If the data model is wrong, the database design will be wrong as well.

Q7 What Is the Users' Role in the Development of Databases?

As stated, a database is a model of how the users view their business world. This means that the users are the final judges as to what data the database should contain and how the records in that database should be related to one another.

The easiest time to change the database structure is during the data modeling stage. Changing a relationship from one-to-many to many-to-many in a data model is simply a matter of changing the 1:N notation to N:M. However, once the database has been constructed, loaded with data, and application forms, reports, queries, and application programs have been created, changing a one-to-many relationship to many-to-many means weeks of work.

You can glean some idea of why this might be true by contrasting Figure 5-25(c) with Figure 5-26(c). Suppose that instead of having just a few rows, each table has thousands of rows; in that case, transforming the database from one format to the other involves considerable work. Even worse, however, is that someone must change application components as well. For example, if students have at most one adviser, then a single text box can be used to enter *AdviserName*. If students can have multiple advisers, then a multiple-row table will need to be used to enter *AdviserName* and a program will need to be written to store the values of *AdviserName* into the *Adviser_Student_Intersection* table. There are dozens of other consequences, consequences that will translate into wasted labor and wasted expense.

Thus, *user review of the data model is crucial*. When a database is developed for your use, you must carefully review the data model. If you do not understand any aspect of it, you should ask for clarification until you do. *Entities must contain all of the data you and your employees need to do your jobs, and relationships must accurately reflect your view of the business.* If the data model is wrong, the database will be

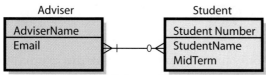

Adviser

AdviserName
Email

Student

Student Number
StudentName
MidTerm

(a) N:M Relationship Between Adviser and Student

Adviser—Key is AdviserName

AdviserName	Email
Jones	Jones@myuniv.edu
Choi	Choi@myuniv.edu
Jackson	Jackson@myuniv.edu

> No room to place second or third AdviserName

Student—Key is StudentNumber

StudentNumber	StudentName	MidTerm	AdviserName
100	Lisa	90	Jackson
200	Jennie	85	Jackson
300	Jason	82	Choi
400	Terry	95	Jackson

(b) Incorrect Representation of N:M Relationship

Adviser—Key is AdviserName

AdviserName	Email
Jones	Jones@myuniv.edu
Choi	Choi@myuniv.edu
Jackson	Jackson@myuniv.edu

Student—Key is StudentNumber

StudentNumber	StudentName	MidTerm
100	Lisa	90
200	Jennie	85
300	Jason	82
400	Terry	95

Adviser_Student_Intersection

AdviserName	StudentNumber
Jackson	100
Jackson	200
Choi	300
Jackson	400
Choi	100
Jones	100

> Student 100 has three advisers.

(c) Adviser_Student_Intersection Table Represents the N:M Relationship

Figure 5-26
Representing an N:M Relationship

designed incorrectly, and the applications will be difficult to use, if not worthless. Do not proceed unless the data model is accurate.

As a corollary, when asked to review a data model, take that review seriously. Devote the time necessary to perform a thorough review. Any mistakes you miss will come back to haunt you, and by then the cost of correction may be very high with regard to both time and expense. This brief introduction to data modeling shows why databases can be more difficult to develop than spreadsheets.

Q8 2020?

Investing $1,000 only makes sense if it generates more than $1,000 in value. But what if the cost is essentially zero, as with the cost of data storage and data communication? If the cost of an investment is near zero, you needn't have much value to justify the expense. One consequence of this is that by 2020 businesses will have generated and stored many more megabytes of data about you. Most of that data will find its way to data aggregators like Acxiom, which had $1.2 billion in sales in 2009 and has been described as the "biggest company you never heard of." See question 6 at the end of this chapter to delve further into Acxiom.

Data aggregators like Acxiom obtain data from public and private sources and store and process it in sophisticated ways. When you use your grocery store club card, that data is sold to a data aggregator. Credit card data, credit data, public tax records, insurance records, product warrantee card data, voter registration data, and hundreds of other types of data are sold to aggregators.

Not all of the data is identified in the same way (or, in terms of this chapter, not all of it has the same primary key). But, using a combination of phone number, address, email address, name, and other partially identifying data, such companies can integrate that disparate data into an integrated, coherent whole. They then query, report, and data mine (see Chapter 9) the integrated data to form detailed descriptions about companies, communities, zip codes, households, and individuals.

As you will learn in Chapter 12, laws limit the types of data that federal and other governmental agencies can acquire and store. There are also some legal safeguards on data maintained by credit bureaus and medical facilities. However, no such laws limit data storage by most companies (nor are there laws that prohibit governmental agencies from buying results from companies like Acxiom).

So how will this change by 2020? Absent any public outcry for legislation to limit such activity, aggregator data storage will continue to grow exponentially and companies will have even more data about you, the state of your health, your wealth, your purchase habits, your family, your travel, your driving record, and, well, anything you do. Query, reporting, and data mining technology will improve, and Moore's law will make computer operations that are too slow to be practical today feasible tomorrow. The picture of you will become more and more detailed.

Why do you care? Maybe you don't, at least as long as the data is not stolen and used for criminal activity against you or as long as the data that is maintained about you is accurate. But, aside from the government, credit bureaus, and certain medical facilities, no organization is required by law to tell you the data that it stores about you and what it does with it.

So, in 2020 you call technical support for assistance with your new home entertainment center. You call an 800 number, which enables the company you call to obtain your phone number, even if it is unlisted. Behind the scenes, before anyone answers the phone, that company accesses your records and determines your age, your income, your net worth, and your buying habits. The company then allocates support services based on your data. If you're over 65 and have limited net worth, your lifetime value to that company is low (soon you'll stop buying high-end entertainment equipment), so you're placed on hold for 40 minutes and eventually speak with a rude person having 2 days of training and limited English skills.

But suppose instead that you are an up-and-coming business professional with a high net worth. In that case, you have no wait at all. You speak with someone having years of training in tech support and with the equipment you purchased. She resolves your problem in 3 minutes. In neither scenario do you know what happened.

Or, maybe you enroll in a "healthy eaters" medical insurance program, similar to "safe drivers" auto insurance. Your premiums are lower because you eat well, except that the insurance company notes from last month's data that you bought four large packages of potato chips, and your health insurance premium is increased, automatically. You have no idea why.

By 2020, the data aggregators will have 10 more years of data about you, what you've eaten, the bottles of wine you've purchased, where you've traveled, the church you attend, the clothes you've purchased, what cars you own, the speeding tickets you've received, and probably what diseases you've had. And they won't forget about those three tattoos, either.

If you don't care, they do.

No, Thanks, I'll Use a Spreadsheet

"I'm not buying all this stuff about databases. I've tried them and they're a pain—way too complicated to set up, and most of the time, a spreadsheet works just as well. We had one project at the car dealership that seemed pretty simple to me: We wanted to keep track of customers and the models of used cars they were interested in. Then, when we got a car on the lot, we could query the database to see who wanted a car of that type and generate a letter to them.

"It took forever to build that system, and it never did work right. We hired three different consultants, and the last one finally did get it to work. But it was so complicated to produce the letters. You had to query the data in Access to generate some kind of file, then open Word, then go through some mumbo jumbo using mail/merge to cause Word to find the letter and put all the Access data in the right spot. I once printed over two hundred letters and had the name in the address spot and the address in the name spot and no date. And it took me over an hour to do even that. I just wanted to do the query and push a button to get my letters generated. I gave up.

Some of the salespeople are still trying to use it, but not me.

"No, unless you are getting billions in government bailouts, I wouldn't mess with a database. You have to have professional IS people to create it and keep it running. Besides, I don't really want to share my data with anyone. I work pretty hard to develop my client list. Why would I want to give it away?

"My motto is, 'Keep it simple.' I use an Excel spreadsheet with four columns: Name, Phone Number, Car Interests, and Notes. When I get a new customer, I enter the name and phone number, and then I put the make and model of cars they like in the Car Interests column. Anything else that I think is important I put in the Notes column—extra phone numbers, address data if I have it, email addresses, spouse names, last time I called them, etc. The system isn't fancy, but it works fine.

"When I want to find something, I use Excel's Data Filter. I can usually get what I need. Of course, I still can't send form letters, but it really doesn't matter. I get most of my sales using the phone, anyway." ■

Discussion Questions

1. To what extent do you agree with the opinions presented here? To what extent are the concerns expressed here justified? To what extent might they be due to other factors?

2. What problems do you see with the way that the car salesperson stores address data? What will he have to do if he ever does want to send a letter or an email to all of his customers?

3. From his comments, how many different themes are there in his data? What does this imply about his ability to keep his data in a spreadsheet?

4. Does the concern about not sharing data relate to whether or not he uses a database?

5. Apparently, management at the car dealership allows the salespeople to keep their contact data in whatever format they want. If you were management, how would you justify this policy? What disadvantages are there to this policy?

6. Suppose you manage the sales representatives, and you decide to require all of them to use a database to keep track of customers and customer car interest data. How would you sell your decision to this salesperson?

7. Given the limited information in this scenario, do you think a database or a spreadsheet is a better solution?

Immanuel Kant, Data Modeler

Only the users can say whether a data model accurately reflects their business environment. What happens when the users disagree among themselves? What if one user says orders have a single salesperson but another says that sales teams produce some orders? Who is correct?

It's tempting to say, "The correct model is the one that better represents the real world." The problem with this statement is that data models do not model "the real world." A data model is simply a model of what the data modeler perceives. This very important point can be difficult to understand; but if you do understand it, you will save many hours in data model validation meetings and be a much better data modeling team member.

The German philosopher Immanuel Kant reasoned that what we perceive as reality is based on our perceptive apparatus. That which we perceive he called phenomena. Our perceptions, such as of light and sound, are processed by our brains and made meaningful. But we do not and cannot know whether the images we create from the perceptions have anything to do with what might or might not really be.

Kant used the term *noumenal world* to refer to the essence of "things in themselves"—to whatever it is out there that gives rise to our perceptions and images. He used the term *phenomenal world* to refer to what we humans perceive and construct.

It is easy to confuse the noumenal world with the phenomenal world, because we share the phenomenal world with other humans. All of us have the same mental apparatus, and we all make the same constructions. If you ask your roommate to hand you the toothpaste, she hands you the toothpaste, not a hairbrush. But the fact that we share this mutual view does not mean that the mutual view describes in any way what is truly out there. Dogs construct a world based on smells, and orca whales construct a world based on sounds. What the "real world" is to a dog, a whale, and a human are completely different. All of this means that we cannot ever justify a data model as a "better representation of the real world." Nothing that humans can do represents the real, noumenal world. A data model, therefore, is a model of a human's model of what appears to be "out there." For example, a model of a salesperson is a model of the model that humans make of salespeople.

To return to the question that we started with, what do we do when people disagree about what should be in a data model? First, realize that anyone attempting to justify her data model as a better representation of the real world is saying, quite arrogantly, "The way I think of the world is the way that counts." Second, in times of disagreement we must ask the question, "How well does the data model fit the mental models of the people who are going to use the system?" The person who is constructing the data model may think the model under construction is a weird way of viewing the world, but that is not the point. The only valid point is whether it reflects how the users view their world. Will it enable the users to do their jobs? ∎

Discussion Questions

1. What does a data model represent?

2. Explain why it is easy for humans to confuse the phenomenal world with the noumenal world.

3. If someone were to say to you, "My model is a better model of the real world," how would you respond?

4. In your own words, how should you proceed when two people disagree on what is to be included in a data model?

ACTIVE REVIEW

Use this Active Review to verify that you understand the ideas and concepts that answer the chapter's study questions.

Q1 What is the purpose of a database?

State the purpose of a database. Explain the circumstances in which a database is preferred to a spreadsheet. Describe the key difference between Figures 5-1 and 5-2.

Q2 What is a database?

Define the term *database*. Explain the hierarchy of data and name three elements of a database. Define *metadata*. Using the example of *Student* and *Office_Visit* tables, show how relationships among rows are represented in a database. Define the terms *key, foreign key*, and *relational database*.

Q3 What are the components of a database application system?

Explain why a database, by itself, is not very useful to business users. Name the components of a database application system and sketch their relationship. Explain the acronym DBMS and name its functions. List five popular DBMS products. Explain the difference between a DBMS and a database. Summarize the functions of a DBMS. Define *SQL*. Describe the major functions of database administration.

Q4 How do database applications make databases more useful?

Name and describe the components of a database application. Explain the need for application programs. For multi-user processing, describe one way in which one user's work can interfere with another's. Explain why multi-user database processing involves more than just connecting another computer to the network. Define two broad categories of DBMS and explain their differences.

Q5 How are data models used for database development?

Explain why user involvement is critical during database development. Describe the function of a data model. Sketch the database development process. Define *e-r model, entity, relationship, attribute*, and *identifier*. Give an example, other than one in this text, of an e-r diagram. Define *maximum cardinality* and *minimum cardinality*. Give an example of three maximum cardinalities and two minimum cardinalities. Explain the notation in Figures 5-18 and 5-19.

Q6 How is a data model transformed into a database design?

Name the three components of a database design. Define *normalization* and explain why it is important. Define *data integrity problem* and describe its consequences. Give an example of a table with data integrity problems and show how it can be normalized into two or more tables that do not have such problems. Describe two steps in transforming a data model into a database design. Using an example not in this chapter, show how 1:N and N:M relationships are represented in a relational database.

Q7 What is the users' role in the development of databases?

Describe the users' role in the database development. Explain why it is easier and cheaper to change a data model than to change an existing database. Use the examples of Figures 5-25(c) and 5-26(c) in your answer. Describe two criteria for judging a data model. Explain why it is important to devote time to understanding a data model.

Q8 2020?

Explain why companies will store data about you. Describe a data aggregator and how data aggregators operate. Explain limits to the laws that govern data storage. Describe how the situation is likely to change by 2020. Illustrate two ways that data aggregator data might be used. Explain why you do or do not care about this issue.

KEY TERMS AND CONCEPTS

Access   141
Attributes   151
Byte   137
Columns   137
Crow's foot   153
Crow's-foot diagram   153
Data aggregators   160
Data integrity problem   155
Data model   150
Database   137
Database administration   145
Database application   145
Database application system   141
Database management system (DBMS)   141
DB2   141
Enterprise DBMS   149
Entity   151
Entity-relationship (E-R) data model   151
Entity-relationship (E-R) diagrams   152
Fields   137
File   137
Foreign keys   140
Form   145
Identifier   151

USING YOUR KNOWLEDGE

1. Draw an entity-relationship diagram that shows the relationships among a database, database applications, and users.

2. Consider the relationship between *Adviser* and *Student* in Figure 5-20. Explain what it means if the maximum cardinality of this relationship is:

   a. N:1

   b. 1:1

   c. 5:1

   d. 1:5

3. Identify two entities in the data entry form in Figure 5-27. What attributes are shown for each? What do you think are the identifiers?

4. Using your answer to question 3, draw an E-R diagram for the data entry form in Figure 5-27. Specify cardinalities. State your assumptions.

5. The partial E-R diagram in Figure 5-28 (next page) is for a sales order. Assume there is only one *Salesperson* per *SalesOrder*.

   a. Specify the maximum cardinalities for each relationship. State your assumptions, if necessary.

   b. Specify the minimum cardinalities for each relationship. State your assumptions, if necessary.

6. Visit *www.acxiom.com*. Navigate the site to answer the following questions.

   a. According to the Web site, what is Acxiom's privacy policy? Are you reassured by its policy? Why or why not?

   b. Navigate the Acxiom site and make a list of 10 different products that Acxiom provides.

   c. Describe Acxiom's top customers.

   d. Examine your answers in parts b and c and describe, in general terms, the kinds of data that Acxiom must be collecting to be able to provide those products to those customers.

   e. What is the function of InfoBase?

   f. What is the function of PersonicX?

   g. In what ways might companies like Acxiom need to limit their marketing so as to avoid a privacy outcry from the public?

   h. Should there be laws that govern companies like Acxiom? Why or why not?

   i. Should there be laws that govern the types of data services that governmental agencies can buy from companies like Acxiom? Why or why not?

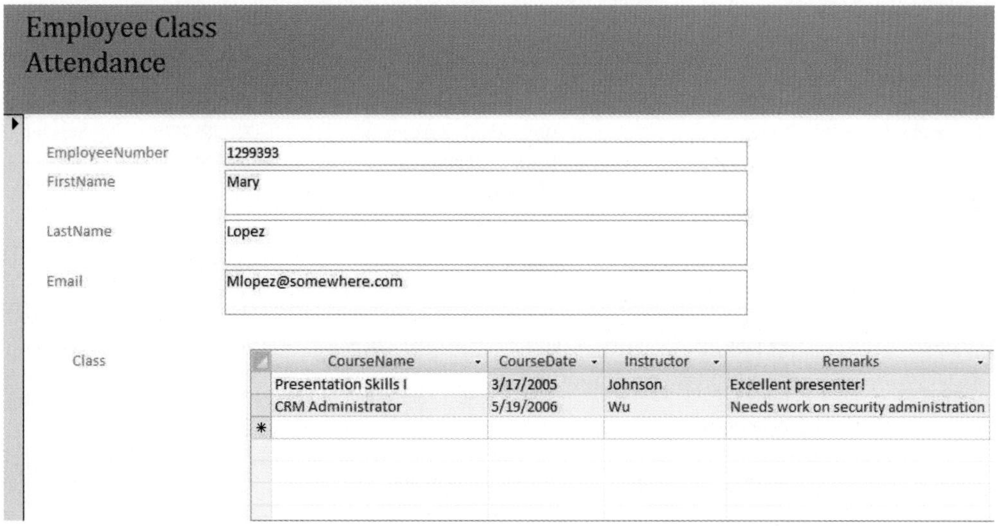

Figure 5-27
Sample Data Entry Form

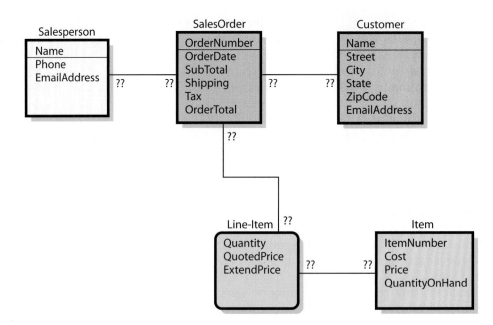

Figure 5-28
Partial E-R Diagram for
SalesOrder

COLLABORATION EXERCISE

Collaborate with a group of students on the following exercises. Recall from Chapter 2 that collaboration is more than cooperation because it involves iteration and feedback. Post a document, a discussion item, a wiki item, or an idea and obtain feedback from your team members. Similarly, read the ideas of others and comment on them. Try to innovate in both the process by which you collaborate and the work product that you create. Avoid face-to-face meetings. Instead, use collaborative software such as Google Docs & Spreadsheets, Microsoft Groove, or Microsoft SharePoint to facilitate your ideas.

Figure 5-29 shows a spreadsheet that is used to track the assignment of sheet music to a choir—it could be a church choir or school or community choir. The type of choir does not matter, because the problem is universal. Sheet music is expensive, choir members need to be able to take sheet music away for practice at home, and not all of the music

gets back to the inventory. (Sheet music can be purchased or rented, but either way, lost music is an expense.)

Look closely at this data and you will see some data integrity problems—or at least some possible data integrity problems. For one, do Sandra Corning and Linda Duong really have the same copy of music checked out? Second, did Mozart and J. S. Bach both write a Requiem, or in row 15 should J. S. Bach actually be Mozart? Also, there is a problem with Eleanor Dixon's phone number; several phone numbers are the same as well, which seems suspicious.

Additionally, this spreadsheet is confusing and hard to use. The column labeled *First Name* includes both people names and the names of choruses. *Email* has both email addresses and composer names, and *Phone* has both phone numbers and copy identifiers. Furthermore, to record a checkout of music the user must first add a new row and then reenter the name of the work, the composer's

Figure 5-29
Spreadsheet Used for
Assignment of Sheet Music

	A	B	C	D	E
1	**Last Name**	**First Name**	**Email**	**Phone**	**Part**
2	Ashley	Jane	JA@somewhere.com	703.555.1234	Soprano
3	Davidson	Kaye	KD@somewhere.com	703.555.2236	Soprano
4	Ching	Kam Hoong	KHC@overhere.com	703.555.2236	Soprano
5	Menstell	Lori Lee	LLM@somewhere.com	703.555.1237	Soprano
6	Corning	Sandra	SC2@overhere.com	703.555.1234	Soprano
7		B-minor mass	J.S. Bach	Soprano Copy 7	
8		Requiem	Mozart	Soprano Copy 17	
9		9th Symphony Chorus	Beethoven	Soprano Copy 9	
10	Wei	Guang	GW1@somewhere.com	703.555.9936	Soprano
11	Dixon	Eleanor	ED@thisplace.com	703.555.12379	Soprano
12		B-minor mass	J.S. Bach	Soprano Copy 11	
13	Duong	Linda	LD2@overhere.com	703.555.8736	Soprano
14		B-minor mass	J.S. Bach	Soprano Copy 7	
15		Requiem	J.S. Bach	Soprano Copy 19	
16	Lunden	Haley	HL@somewhere.com	703.555.0836	Soprano
17	Utran	Diem Thi	DTU@somewhere.com	703.555.1089	Soprano

name, and the copy to be checked out. Finally, consider what happens when the user wants to find all copies of a particular work: The user will have to examine the rows in each of four spreadsheets for the four voice parts.

In fact, a spreadsheet is ill-suited for this application. A database would be a far better tool, and situations like this are obvious candidates for innovation.

a. Analyze the spreadsheet shown in Figure 5-29 and list all of the problems that occur when trying to track the assignment of sheet music using this spreadsheet.

b. Figure 5-30(a) shows a two-entity data model for the sheet-music-tracking problem.

(1) Select identifiers for the *ChoirMember* and *Work* entities. Justify your selection.

(2) This design does not eliminate the potential for data integrity problems that occur in the spreadsheet. Explain why not.

(3) Design a database for this data model. Specify key and foreign key columns.

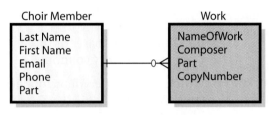

(a) Data-Model Alternative 1

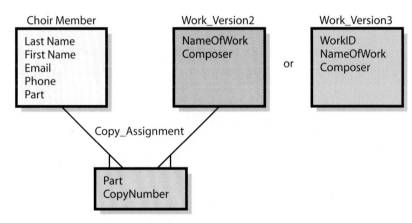

(b) Data-Model Alternative 2

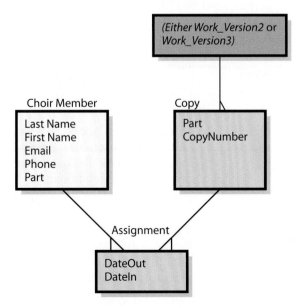

(c) Data-Model Alternative 3

Figure 5-30
Three Data-Model Alternatives

c. Figure 5-30(b) shows a second alternative data model for the sheet-music-tracking problem. This alternative shows two variations on the *Work* entity. In the second variation, an attribute named *WorkID* has been added to *Work_Version3*. This attribute is a unique identifier for the work; the DBMS will assign a unique value to *WorkID* when a new row is added to the *Work* table.

    (1) Select identifiers for *ChoirMember, Work_Version2, Work_Version3*, and *Copy_Assignment.* Justify your selection.

    (2) Does this design eliminate the potential for data integrity problems that occur in the spreadsheet? Why or why not?

    (3) Design a database for the data model that uses *Work_Version2.* Specify key and foreign key columns.

    (4) Design a database for the data models that uses *Work_Version3.* Specify key and foreign key columns.

    (5) Is the design with *Work_Version2* better than the design for *Work_Version3*? Why or why not?

d. Figure 5-30(c) shows a third alternative data model for the sheet-music-tracking problem. In this data model, use either *Work_Version2* or *Work_Version3*, whichever you think is better.

    (1) Select identifiers for each entity in your data model. Justify your selection.

    (2) Summarize the differences between this data model and that in Figure 5-30(b). Which data model is better? Why?

    (3) Design a database for this data model. Specify key and foreign key columns.

e. Which of the three data models is the best? Justify your answer.

APPLICATION EXERCISES

1.   Neil at Flextime used his database with Excel to obtain the data that he needs. A more common scenario is to use Microsoft Access with Excel: Users process relational data with Access, import some of the data into Excel, and use Excel's tools for creating professional looking charts and graphs. You will do exactly that in this exercise.

    Download the Access file **Ch05Ex01** from *www.pearsonhighered.com/kroenke*. Open the database, select *Database Tools/Relationships*. As you can see, there are three tables: *Product, VendorProductInventory,* and *Vendor.* Open each table individually to familiarize yourself with the data.

    For this problem, we will define *InventoryCost* as the product of *IndustryStandardCost* and *QuantityOnHand.* The query *InventoryCost* computes these values for every item in inventory for every vendor. Open that query and view the data to be certain you understand this computation. Open the other queries as well so that you understand the data they produce.

a. Sum this data by vendor and display it in a pie chart like that shown in Figure 5-31. Proceed as follows:

    (1) Open Excel and create a new spreadsheet.

    (2) Click *Data* on the ribbon and select *Access* in the *Get External Data* ribbon category.

    (3) Navigate to the location in which you have stored the Access file **Ch05Ex01**.

    (4) Select the query that contains the data you need for this pie chart.

    (5) Import the data into a table.

    (6) Format the appropriate data as currency.

    (7) Select the range that contains the data, press the function key, and proceed from there to create the pie chart. Name the data and pie chart worksheets appropriately.

b. Follow a similar procedure to create the bar chart shown in Figure 5-32. Place the data and the chart in separate worksheets and name them appropriately.

2.   Re-read the Guide on page 162. Suppose you are given the task of converting the salesperson's data into a database. Because his data is so poorly structured, it will be a challenge, as you will see.

a. Download the Excel file named **Ch05Ex02** from *www.pearsonhighered.com/kroenke*. This spreadsheet contains data that fits the salesperson's description in the Guide. Open the spreadsheet and view the data.

b. Download the Access file with the same name, **Ch05Ex02**. Open the database, select *Database Tools*, and click *Relationships*. Examine the four tables and their relationships.

c. Somehow, you have to transform the data in the spreadsheet into the table structure in the database. Because so little discipline was shown when creating the spreadsheet, this will be a labor-intensive task. To begin, import the spreadsheet data into a new table in the database; call that table *Sheet1* or some other name.

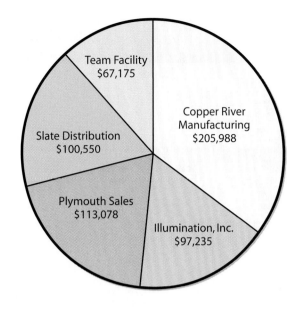

Figure 5-31
Data Displayed in Pie-Chart
Format

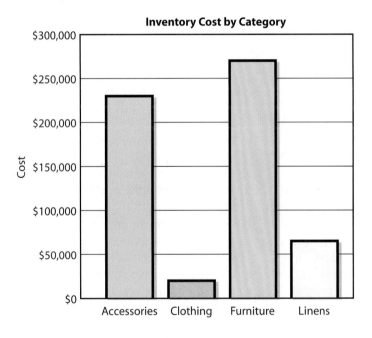

Figure 5-32
Data Displayed in Bar-Chart
Format

d. Copy the *Name* data in *Sheet1* onto the clipboard. Then, open the *Customer* table and paste the column of name data into that table.

e. Unfortunately, the task becomes messy at this point. You can copy the *Car Interests* column into *Make or Model of Auto*, but then you will need to straighten out the values by hand. Phone numbers will need to be copied one at a time.

f. Open the *Customer* form and manually add any remaining data from the spreadsheet into each customer record. Connect the customer to his or her auto interests.

g. The data in the finished database has much more structure than that in the spreadsheet. Explain why that is both an advantage and a disadvantage.

Under what circumstances is the database more appropriate? Less appropriate?

3. In this exercise, you will create a two-table database, define relationships, create a form and a report, and use them to enter data and view results.

a. Download the Excel file **Ch05Ex03** from *www. pearsonhighered.com/kroenke*. Open the spreadsheet and review the data in the *Employee* and *Computer* worksheets.

b. Create a new Access database with the name *Ch05Ex03_Solution*. Close the table that Access automatically creates and delete it.

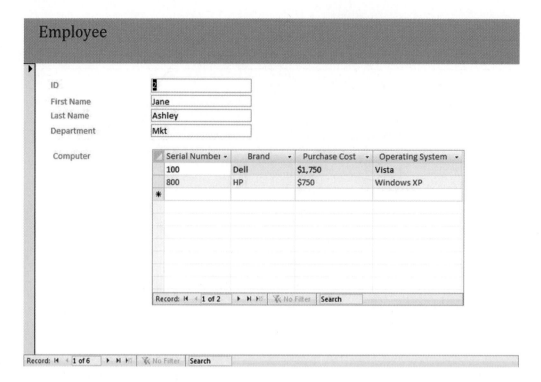

Figure 5-33
Employee Computer
Assignment Form

c. Import the data from the Excel spreadsheet into your database. Import the *Employee* worksheet into a table named *Employee*. Be sure to check *First Row Contains Column Headings*. Select *Choose my own primary key* and use the ID field as that key.

d. Import the *Computer* worksheet into a table named *Computer*. Check *First Row Contains Column Headings*, but let Access create the primary key.

e. Open the relationships window and add both *Employee* and *Computer* to the design space. Drag ID from *Employee* and drop it on *EmployeeID* in *Computer*. Check *Enforce Referential Integrity* and the two checkmarks below. Ensure you know what these actions mean.

f. Open the Form Wizard dialog box (under *Create, More Forms*) and add all of the columns for each of your tables to your form. Select *View your data by Customer*. Title your form *Employee* and your subform *Computer*.

g. Open the *Computer* subform and delete *EmployeeID* and *ComputerID*. These values are maintained by Access, and it is just a distraction to keep them. Your form should appear like the one shown in Figure 5-33.

h. Use your form to add two new computers to *Jane Ashley*. Both computers are Dells, and both use Vista; one costs $750, and the second costs $1,400.

i. Delete the Lenovo computer for Rex Scott.

j. Use the Report Wizard (under *Create*) to create a report having all data from both the *Employee* and *Computer* tables. Play with the report design until you find a design you like. Correct the label alignment if you need to.

CASE STUDY 5

Benchmarking, Bench Marketing, or Bench Baloney

Which DBMS product is the fastest? Which product yields the lowest price/performance ratio? What computer equipment works best for each DBMS product? These reasonable questions should be easy to answer. They are not.

In fact, the deeper you dig, the more problems you find. To begin with, which product is fastest at doing what?

To have a valid comparison, all compared products must do the same work. So, vendors and third parties have defined *benchmarks*, which are descriptions of work to be done along with the data to be processed. To compare performance, analysts run competing DBMS products on the same benchmark and measure the results. Typical measures are number of transactions processed per second, number of Web pages served per second, and average response time per user.

At first, DBMS vendors set up their own benchmark tests and published those results. Of course, when vendor A used its own benchmark to claim that its product was superior to all others, no one believed the results. Clearly, vendor A had an incentive to set up the benchmark to play to its product strengths. So, third parties defined standard benchmarks. Even that led to problems, however. According to *The Benchmark Handbook*[1] (at *www.benchmarkresources.com/handbook*, accessed August 2006):

> When comparative numbers were published by third parties or competitors, the losers generally cried foul and tried to discredit the benchmark. Such events often caused benchmark wars. Benchmark wars start if someone loses an important or visible benchmark evaluation. The loser reruns it using regional specialists and gets new and winning numbers. Then the opponent reruns it using his regional specialists, and of course gets even better numbers. The loser then reruns it using some one-star gurus. This progression can continue all the way to five-star gurus.

For example, in July 2002 *PC Magazine* ran a benchmark using a standard benchmark called the *Nile benchmark*. This particular test has a mixture of database tasks that are processed via Web pages. The faster the DBMS, the more pages that can be served. The test compared five DBMS products:

- DB2 (from IBM)
- MySQL (a free, open source DBMS)
- Oracle (from Oracle Corporation)
- SQL Server (from Microsoft)
- ASE (from Sybase Corporation)

SQL Server's performance was the worst. In the magazine review, the authors stated that they believed SQL Server scored poorly because the test used a new version of a non-Microsoft driver (a program that sends requests and returns results to and from the DBMS).

As you might imagine, no sooner was this test published than the phones and email server at *PC Magazine* were inundated by objections from Microsoft. *PC Magazine* reran the tests, replacing the suspect driver with a full panoply of Microsoft products. The article doesn't say, but one can imagine the five-star Microsoft gurus who chartered the next airplane to PC Labs, where the testing was done. (You can read about both phases of the benchmark at *www.eweek.com/article2/0,4149,293,00.asp.*)

Not surprisingly when the tests were rerun with Microsoft-supporting software, SQL Server performed better than all of the other products in the first test. But that second test compares apples and oranges. The first test used standard software, and the second test used Microsoft-specific software.

When the five-star gurus from Oracle or MySQL use *their* favorite supporting products and "tune" to this particular benchmark, their re-rerun results will be superior to those for SQL Server. And round and round it will go.

Questions

1. Suppose you manage a business activity that needs a new IS with a database. The development team is divided on which DBMS you should use. One faction wants to use Oracle, a second wants to use MySQL, and a third wants to use SQL Server. They cannot decide among themselves, and so they schedule a meeting with you. The team presents all of the benchmarks shown in the article at *www.eweek.com/article2/0,4149,293,00.asp*. How do you respond?

2. Performance is just one criterion for selecting a DBMS. Other criteria are the cost of the DBMS, hardware costs, staff knowledge, ease of use, ability to tune for extra performance, and backup and recovery capabilities. How does consideration of these other factors change your answer to question 1?

3. The Transaction Processing Council (TPC) is a nonprofit that defines transaction processing and database benchmarks and publishes vendor-neutral, verifiable performance data. Visit its Web site at *www.tpc.org*.

   a. What are TPC-C, TPC-R, and TPC-W?
   b. Suppose you work in the marketing department at Oracle. How would you use the TPC results in the TPC-C benchmark?
   c. What are the dangers to Oracle in your answer to part b?
   d. Suppose you work in the marketing department for DB2 at IBM. How would you use the TPC results in the TPC-C benchmark?
   e. Do the results for TPC-C change your answer to question 1?
   f. If you are a DBMS vendor, can you ignore benchmarks?

4. Reflect on your answers to questions 1 through 3. On balance, what good are benchmarks? Are they just footballs to be kicked around by vendors? Are advertisers and publishers the only true beneficiaries? Do DBMS customers benefit from the efforts of TPC and like groups? How should customers use benchmarks?

[1]Jim Gray (Ed.): The Benchmark Handbook for Database and Transaction Systems (2nd Edition). Morgan Kaufmann 1993

6 Data Communication

FlexTime's building lease is about to expire and the owner wants to increase the rent by 30 percent. The building's facilities need to be repaired and upgraded, and the new lease calls for FlexTime to pay for those improvements. In response, Neil and Kelly decided to buy their own building. They are walking through the door of the current building, discussing the difficult conversation they'd had with their banker.

"Neil, I don't want to put up the condo."

"Kelly, you were there. We heard him together: Our house valuation came in too low, and they want more collateral. It's either the condo or take another $150,000 out of the building infrastructure."

"If this economy doesn't improve and if FlexTime can't support the new mortgage, we could lose it all. The business, our house, everything. The condo would be all we have left."

"OK, Kelly, let's look again at the costs."
Neil opens his laptop computer on his desk. They look at it together.

"The land, the basic building construction, the parking lots . . . I don't see how we get those costs down, but I'll talk to the contractor again. What about the locker rooms? Can we do anything to bring the locker room costs down?"

"Neil, I've been thinking about that. Maybe we go to a warehouse look. Of course we have to have showers and toilets and sinks and mirrors . . . and the lockers, but what if we go radical industrial? We could save on tile and fixtures."

"OK, Kelly, that's a start. What else?"

"Hey, Neil, what's this $175,000 for network infrastructure? What do we need that for?"

"Hooking up all the computers."

"$175,000 to hook up a computer? Come on, Neil, get real."

"Kelly, it's not just one computer, it's all of our computers. Plus all the new gear."

"Speaking of new gear!" Felix sticks his head into Neil's office, "Check out my new shoes. They talk to my wristband and, if I have a wireless network nearby, the wristband talks to the network and stores my workout data on my workout Web site. Cool! This gonna work in the new building?"

Felix heads down the hall.

"See what I mean, Kelly? Plus all the new machines have network adapters—either wired or wireless. And this is just the tip of the iceberg. Everybody wants to have their workout data collected and stored and processed. We're going to have to store more and more personal workout data. And it's got to get from the spinning machine, or the shoes, or the whatever, to the network somehow."

"Neil, I can understand spending money on wires; they're made of something and they have to be installed. But wireless? How come the air costs $175,000?"

"That's not fair, Kelly. The $175,000 includes wires installed in the walls, but actually, that's not a big expense. The major expenses are equipment items like switches and routers and other equipment that can give us the performance we need."

"Neil, this stuff is expensive. Cisco router??? Why do we need four of them? Or, hey, what is a VPN/firewall appliance? Appliance? Like a toaster? Pricey little number. Can we get by without it? There must be some fat in here we can remove."

Neil grimaces.

"Neil, why don't we just use iPhones? They talk to shoes, too."

"You mean have our clients use an iPhone app?"

"Yeah. I tried one last week, Neil, and it was great. I was out running and it worked just like my cell phone. I didn't have a wireless network anywhere near me. When I got back here I used the app to download the data to our computer. Why don't our clients do that?"

"Kelly, where is FlexTime in that transaction?"

"FlexTime? Nowhere. It was just me and shoes and the iPhone and the app and, ah Neil, I get the picture. Why would they need us?"

"Plus we have to do all we can to support whatever devices are coming down the road in the next 10 years."

"Neil, I'm in over my head on this. I don't even know the difference between a LAN and a WAN. But, I'll talk to our architect and try to get the locker room costs down. Meanwhile, can you take a look at this $175,000? Do we need all of it? Do we need all of it now? Can we shave even $20,000 off?"

>> STUDY QUESTIONS

Q1 What is a computer network?

Q2 What are the components of a LAN?

Q3 What are the alternatives for a WAN?

Q4 Why do organizations use virtual private networks?

Q5 How does encryption work?

Q6 What is the purpose of a firewall?

Q7 2020?

CHAPTER PREVIEW

You can find a free, supplemental study lesson for this chapter at:

www.LearningMIS.com

If you go into business for yourself, there's an excellent chance you'll have a problem just like Neil's. How much do you really have to pay toward a network infrastructure? You'll need the knowledge of this chapter to understand the conversations you'll have to make that assessment. Of course, you can just rely on outside experts, but that probably doesn't work in the 21st century. Many of your competitors will be able to ask and understand those questions—and use the money their knowledge saves them for other facilities they need, like locker rooms and parking lots.

Or, what if you work in product management for a large company? Does your product "talk" to some network? If not, could it? Should it? Does it require a LAN or a WAN?

As stated mega-times already, data communication is nearly free today, generating exciting opportunities. This trend makes basic knowledge of this free resource even more important.

To help you be prepared, we will discuss the overarching concepts of computer networks and related technology. We will greatly simplify the discussion, but, even still, this topic involves the interaction of dozens of equipment types, methods, and standards and a sea of terms and acronyms. To help you deal with this complexity, we divide this topic into a conceptually oriented chapter and a supplemental appendix with more details.

In particular, this chapter defines three types of computer networks and discusses the components and alternatives for two of those types: local area networks (LANs) and wide area networks (WANs). It then explains, at a high level, how computer encryption works and finally describes firewalls, which are devices for protecting networks from unauthorized access and use.

The chapter appendix discusses the third type of network, internets, and explains in particular how one such network—the Internet—works. Using the example of email from a hotel in Hawaii to a company in Ohio, the appendix explains the nature of layered protocols and describes how the Internet uses the TCP/IP—OSI protocol architecture. The appendix also explains how the Internet transforms URLs such as *pearsonhighered.com* into globally unique logical addresses.

You may be tempted to skip the appendix, and, if time is short, you may need to. However, the Internet is the foundation of 21st-century commerce, and knowing Internet components and their interactions is part of a business professional's literacy. Just as you need to know terms like LIFO and FIFO and understand what it means when marginal revenue equals marginal cost, so, too, you need to know what TCP/IP and related protocols are and how they are used.

Q1 What Is a Computer Network?

A computer **network** is a collection of computers that communicate with one another over transmission lines or wireless. As shown in Figure 6-1, the three basic types of networks are local area networks, wide area networks, and internets.

A **local area network (LAN)** connects computers that reside in a single geographic location on the premises of the company that operates the LAN. The number of

Type	Characteristic
Local area network (LAN)	Computers connected at a single physical site
Wide area network (WAN)	Computers connected between two or more separated sites
The Internet and internets	Networks of networks

Figure 6-1
Major Network Types

connected computers can range from two to several hundred. The distinguishing characteristic of a LAN is *a single location*. **Wide area networks (WANs)** connect computers at different geographic locations. The computers in two separated company sites must be connected using a WAN. To illustrate, the computers for a College of Business located on a single campus can be connected via a LAN. The computers for a College of Business located on multiple campuses must be connected via a WAN.

The single- versus multiple-site distinction is important. With a LAN, an organization can place communications lines wherever it wants, because all lines reside on its premises. The same is not true for a WAN. A company with offices in Chicago and Atlanta cannot run a wire down the freeway to connect computers in the two cities. Instead, the company contracts with a communications vendor that is licensed by the government and that already has lines or has the authority to run new lines between the two cities.

An **internet** is a network of networks. Internets connect LANs, WANs, and other internets. The most famous internet is **"the Internet"** (with an uppercase letter *I*), the collection of networks that you use when you send email or access a Web site. In addition to the Internet, private networks of networks, called *internets*, also exist.

The networks that comprise an internet use a large variety of communication methods and conventions, and data must flow seamlessly across them. To provide seamless flow, an elaborate scheme called a *layered protocol* is used. You can learn more about the various protocols in the appendix that follows this chapter. For now, understand that a **protocol** is a set of rules that two communicating devices follow. There are many different protocols; some are used for LANs, some are used for WANs, some are used for internets and the Internet, and some are used for all of these. The important point is that for two programs to communicate, they must both use the same protocol.

Many employees use computers for personal business at work. Email, Facebook, Twitter, all are used by people at work. Are such actions ethical? We consider that question in the guide on pages 178–179.

Social networking online is a new phenomena created by the Internet. For information on social network theory and how it can benefit you, see the Guide on pages 196–197. Social networking is also covered in Chapter 8.

Q2 What Are the Components of a LAN?

A LAN is a group of computers connected together on a single company site. Usually the computers are located within a half mile or so of each other. The key distinction, however, is that all of the computers are located on property controlled by the company that operates the LAN. This means that the company can run cables wherever needed to connect the computers.

Consider the LAN in Figure 6-2. Here, five computers and two printers connect via a **switch**, which is a special-purpose computer that receives and transmits messages on the LAN. In Figure 6-2, when computer 1 accesses printer 1, it does so by sending the print job to the switch, which then redirects that data to printer 1.

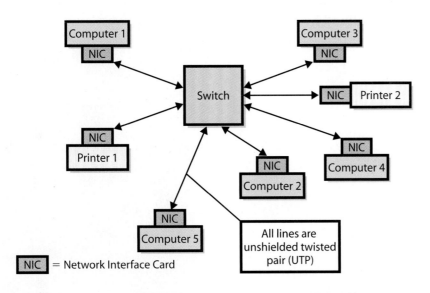

Figure 6-2
Local Area Network (LAN)

Personal Email at Work?

The Internet example used in the appendix to this chapter has you sending a personal email to a friend at his job at OhioCompany. Your email does not concern your friend's work or his company's business. It is not an emergency email, nor is it even a request for a ride to your house from the airport. Your email concerns your surfing skills! (We assume your friend's company is not involved in the surfing industry.) Even worse, your email is not just a few sentences that would consume a little file space. Rather, your email contains a picture, and, without noticing it, you sent a very high-quality picture that was 6.2 megabytes in size.

"Come on," you're saying, "give me a break! What's the matter with an email and a picture? It's me surfing, it's not some weird pornographic material."

Maybe you're right; maybe it's not a big deal. But consider the resources you've consumed by sending that email: Your message, all 6-plus megabytes of it, traveled over the Internet to OhioCompany's ISP. The packets of the email and picture were then transmitted to Ohio-Company's router and from that router to OhioCompany's email server. It consumed processing cycles on the router and on the email server computer. A copy of your picture was then stored on that email server until your friend deleted it, perhaps weeks later. Additionally, your friend will use his computer and the OhioCompany LAN to download the picture to his desktop computer, where it will also be stored. In fact, the entire computing infrastructure, from the ISP to your friend's desk, is owned, operated, and paid for by OhioCompany. Finally, if your friend reads his email during his working hours, he will be consuming company resources—his time and attention, which the company has paid for while he is at work. ∎

Discussion Questions

1. Is it ethical for you to send the email and picture to your friend at work?

2. Does your answer to question 1 change depending on the size of the picture?

3. Does your answer to question 1 change if your email concerns an injury to yourself? If it concerns your need for a ride from the airport?

4. Does your answer change if you send 10 pictures? If you send 100 pictures? If you send 1,000 pictures? If your answer does change, where do you draw the line?

5. Is it more ethical for you to send one picture to 100 friends in 100 different companies or 100 pictures to one friend in one company? Explain your answer.

6. Once the picture is stored on OhioCompany's email server, who owns the picture? Who controls the picture? Does OhioCompany have the right to inspect the contents of its employees' mailboxes? If so, what should managers do when they find your picture that has absolutely nothing to do with the company's business?

7. What company resources will be involved if your friend downloads your email from his private account at work? Is it more ethical to send your picture to your friend's private Yahoo! email account?

8. What do you think is the greater cost to OhioCompany: the cost of the infrastructure to transmit and store the email or the cost of the time your friend takes at work to read and view your picture? Does this consideration change any of your answers above?

9. Describe a reasonable policy for computer use at work. Consider email, Facebook, and Twitter.

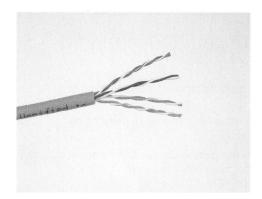

Figure 6-3
Unshielded Twisted Pair (UTP)
Cable

Source: Belkin Components. Courtesy
of Belkin Corporation.

Each device on a LAN (computer, printer, etc.) has a hardware component called a **network interface card (NIC)** that connects the device's circuitry to the cable. The NIC works with programs in each device to implement the protocols necessary for communication. On older machines, the NIC is a card that fits into an expansion slot. Almost every new computer today, however, has an **onboard NIC**, which is an NIC built into the computer's circuitry. Each NIC has a worldwide, unique identifier, which is called the **MAC (media access control) address**.

The computers, printers, switches, and other devices on a LAN are connected using one of two media. Most connections are made using **unshielded twisted pair (UTP) cable**. Figure 6-3 shows a section of UTP cable that contains four pairs of twisted wire. A device called an RJ-45 connector is used to connect the UTP cable into NIC devices on the LAN.

By the way, wires are twisted for reasons beyond aesthetics and style. Twisting the wires substantially reduces the cross-wire signal interference that occurs when wires run parallel for long distances.

Some LANs, usually those larger than the one in Figure 6-2, use more than one switch. Typically, in a building with several floors a switch is placed on each floor, and the computers on that floor are connected to the switch with UTP cable. As shown in Figure 6-4, the switches on each floor are connected together by a main switch, which is often located in the basement.

The connections between switches can use UTP cable, but if they carry a lot of traffic or are far apart UTP cable may be replaced by **optical fiber cables**. (See the left-hand photo in Figure 6-5.) The signals on such cables are light rays, and they are reflected inside the glass core of the optical fiber cable. The core is surrounded by a *cladding* to contain the light signals, and the cladding, in turn, is wrapped with an outer layer to protect it. In Figure 6-4, the switches are connected using optical fiber because there is a lot of traffic among them.

Optical fiber cable uses special connectors called ST and SC connectors, which are shown as the blue plugs in Figure 6-5. The meaning of the abbreviations ST and SC are unimportant; they are just the two most common optical connectors.

The IEEE 802.3, or Ethernet, Protocol

For a LAN to work, all devices on the LAN must use the same protocol. The Institute for Electrical and Electronics Engineers (IEEE, pronounced "I triple E") sponsors committees that create and publish protocols and other standards. The committee that addresses LAN standards is called the *IEEE 802 Committee*. Thus, IEEE LAN protocols always start with the numbers 802.

Today, the world's most popular protocol for LANs is the **IEEE 802.3 protocol**. This protocol standard, also called **Ethernet**, specifies hardware characteristics, such as

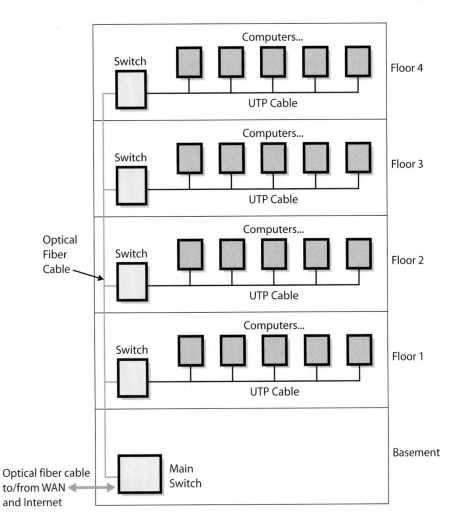

Figure 6-4
Typical Arrangement of
Switches in a Multistory
Building

Figure 6-5
Optical Fiber Cable

Source: Getty Images, Inc.–Photodisc
and Michael Smith, Getty Images, Inc.

which wire carries which signals. It also describes how messages are to be packaged and processed for transmission over the LAN.

Most personal computers today are equipped with an onboard NIC that supports what is called **10/100/1000 Ethernet**. These products conform to the 802.3 specification and allow for transmission at a rate of 10, 100, or 1,000 Mbps (megabits per second). Switches detect the speed that a given device can handle and communicate with it at that speed. If you check computer listings at Dell, HP, Lenovo, and other manufacturers, you will see PCs advertised as having 10/100/1000 Ethernet.

By the way, the abbreviations used for communications speeds differ from those used for computer memory. For communications equipment, k stands for 1,000, not 1,024 as it does for memory. Similarly, M stands for 1,000,000, not $1,024 \times 1,024$; G stands for 1,000,000,000, not $1,024 \times 1,024 \times 1,024$. Thus, 100 Mbps is 100,000,000 bits per second. Also, communications speeds are expressed in *bits*, whereas memory sizes are expressed in *bytes*.

IEEE 802.11 Wireless Protocol

In recent years, wireless connections have become popular for LANs. Figure 6-6 shows a LAN in which two of the computers and one printer have wireless connections. Notice that in the wireless devices the NIC has been replaced by a **wireless NIC (WNIC)**. Today, almost all personal computers have an onboard WNIC.

The technology that enables wireless connections is the **IEEE 802.11 protocol**. Several versions of 802.11 exist. As of 2009 the most popular is IEEE 802.11g. The differences among the variations are beyond the scope of this discussion. Just note that the current standard, 802.11g, allows speeds of up to 54 Mbps.

Observe that the LAN in Figure 6-6 uses both the 802.3 and 802.11 protocols. The NICs operate according to the 802.3 protocol and connect directly to the switch,

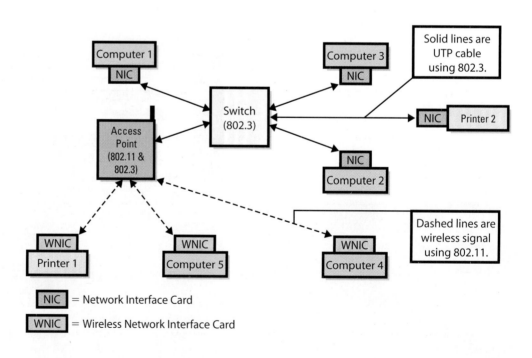

Figure 6-6
LAN with Wireless

which also operates on the 802.3 standard. The WNICs operate according to the 802.11 protocol and connect to an **access point (AP)**. The AP must be able to process messages according to both the 802.3 and 802.11 standards, because it sends and receives wireless traffic using the 802.11 protocol and then communicates with the switch using the 802.3 protocol. Characteristics of LANs are summarized in the top part of Figure 6-7.

Bluetooth is another common wireless protocol. It is designed for transmitting data over short distances, replacing cables. Some devices, such as wireless mice and keyboards, use Bluetooth to connect to the computer. Cell phones use Bluetooth to connect to automobile entertainment systems.

FlexTime has a LAN that connects computer workstations together and to the server. That network also makes Internet connections using a DSL modem (defined on page 185). Fixed, desktop computers and some of the stationary workout

Figure 6-7
Summary of LAN and WAN Networks

Type	Topology	Transmission Line	Transmission Speed	Equipment Used	Protocol Commonly Used	Remarks
Local area network	Local area network	UTP or optical fiber	10, 100, or 1,000 Mbps	Switch NIC UTP or optical	IEEE 802.3 (Ethernet)	Switches connect devices, multiple switches on all but small LANs.
	Local area network with wireless	UTP or optical for non-wireless connections	Up to 54 Mbps	Wireless access point Wireless NIC	IEEE 802.11g	Access point transforms wired LAN (802.3) to wireless LAN (802.11).
Wide area network	DSL modem to ISP	DSL telephone	Personal: Upstream to 256 kbps, downstream to 1.544 Mbps	DSL modem DSL-capable telephone line	DSL	Can have computer and phone use simultaneously. Always connected.
	Cable modem to ISP	Cable TV lines to optical cable	Upstream to 256 kbps Downstream 300–600 kbps (10 Mbps in theory)	Cable modem Cable TV cable	Cable	Capacity is shared with other sites; performance varies depending on others' use.
	WAN wireless	Wireless connection to WAN	500 kbps to 1 Mbps	Wireless WAN modem	EVDO, HSDPA, WiMax	Sophisticated protocol enables several devices to use the same wireless frequency.
	Point to point lines	Network of leased lines	T1–1.5 Mbps T3– 44.7 Mbps OC48–2.5 Gbps OC768–40 Gbps	Access devices Optical cable Satellite	PPP	Span geographically distributed sites using lines provided by licensed communications vendors. Expensive to set up and manage.
	PSDN	Lease usage of private network	56 Kbps–40 Mbps+	Leased line to PSDN POP	Frame relay ATM 10 Gbps and 40 Gbps Ethernet	Lease time on a public switched data network–operated by independent party. Ineffective for intercompany communication.

equipment use wires and Ethernet. Laptops and some of the other workout equipment are wireless and use a version of IEEE 802.11. Some of the devices used by clients at FlexTime, like shoes talking to sport bands, also use Bluetooth.

Q3 What Are the Alternatives for a WAN?

A WAN connects computers located at physically separated sites. A company with offices in Detroit and Atlanta must use a WAN to connect the computers together. Because the sites are physically separated, the company cannot string wire from one site to another. Rather, it must obtain connection capabilities from another company (or companies) licensed by the government to provide communications. Figure 6-7 shows five WAN alternatives, the first three concern Internet service providers.

Although you may not have realized it, when you connect your personal computer, or iPhone, or Kindle to the Internet, you are using a WAN. You are connecting to computers owned and operated by an **Internet service provider (ISP)** that are not located physically at your site.

An ISP has three important functions. First, it provides you with a legitimate Internet address. Second, it serves as your gateway to the Internet. The ISP receives the communications from your computer and passes them on to the Internet, and it receives communications from the Internet and passes them on to you. Finally, ISPs pay for the Internet. They collect money from their customers and pay access fees and other charges on your behalf.

We begin our discussion of WANs by considering modem connections to ISPs.

Connecting the Personal Computer to an ISP: Modems

Home computers and those of small businesses are commonly connected to an ISP in one of three ways: a special telephone line called a DSL line, a cable TV line, or a wireless satellite connection.

All three of these alternatives require that the *digital data* in the computer be converted to a wavy, or **analog signal**. A device called a **modem**, or modulator/demodulator, performs this conversion. Figure 6-8 shows one way of converting the digital byte 01000001 to an analog signal.

As shown in Figure 6-9, once the modem converts your computer's digital data to analog, that analog signal is then sent over the telephone line, TV cable, or air. If sent

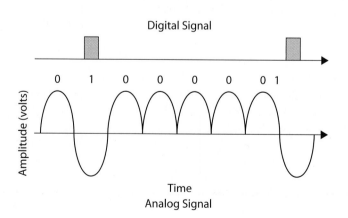

Figure 6-8
Analog Versus Digital Signals

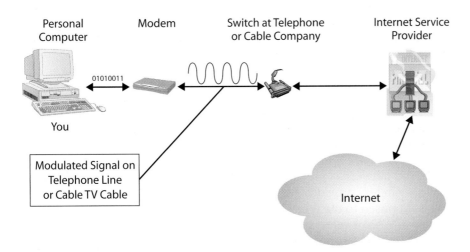

Personal Computer   Modem   Switch at Telephone or Cable Company   Internet Service Provider

01010011

You

Modulated Signal on Telephone Line or Cable TV Cable

Internet

Figure 6-9
Personal Computer (PC)
Internet Access

by telephone line, the first telephone switch that your signal reaches converts the signal into the form used by the international telephone system.

DSL Modems

A **DSL modem** is the first modem type. DSL stands for **digital subscriber line**. DSL modems operate on the same lines as voice telephones, but they operate so that their signals do not interfere with voice telephone service. Because DSL signals do not interfere with telephone signals, DSL data transmission and telephone conversations can occur simultaneously. A device at the telephone company separates the phone signals from the computer signals and sends the latter signal to the ISP. DSL modems use their own protocols for data transmission.

There are gradations of DSL service and speed. Most home DSL lines can download data at speeds ranging from 256 kbps to 1.544 Mbps and can upload data at slower speeds—for example, 256 kbps. DSL lines that have different upload and download speeds are called **asymmetric digital subscriber lines (ADSL)**. Most homes and small businesses can use ADSL because they receive more data than they transmit (e.g., pictures in news stories), and hence they do not need to transmit as fast as they receive.

Some users and larger businesses, however, need DSL lines that have the same receiving and transmitting speeds. They also need performance-level guarantees. **Symmetrical digital subscriber lines (SDSL)** meet this need by offering the same fast speed in both directions.

Cable Modems

A **cable modem** is a second modem type. Cable modems provide high-speed data transmission using cable television lines. The cable company installs a fast, high-capacity optical fiber cable to a distribution center in each neighborhood that it serves. At the distribution center, the optical fiber cable connects to regular cable-television cables that run to subscribers' homes or businesses. Cable modems modulate in such a way that their signals do not interfere with TV signals.

Because up to 500 user sites can share these facilities, performance varies depending on how many other users are sending and receiving data. At the maximum, users can download data up to 10 Mbps and can upload data at 256 kbps. Typically, performance is much lower than this. In most cases, the speed of cable modems and DSL modems is about the same. Cable modems use their own protocols. Figure 6-7 (page 183) summarizes these alternatives.

WAN Wireless Connection

A third way that you can connect your computer, iPhone, Kindle, or other communicating device is via a **WAN wireless** connection. Amazon's Kindle, for example, uses a Sprint wireless network to provide wireless data connections. The iPhone uses a LAN-based wireless network if one is available and a WAN wireless network if one is not. The LAN-based network is preferred because performance is considerably higher. As of 2009, WAN wireless provides average performance of 500 kbps, with peaks of up to 1.7 Mbps, as opposed to the typical 50 Mbps for LAN wireless.

A variety of WAN wireless protocols exist. Sprint and Verizon use a protocol called **EVDO**; AT&T, which supports the iPhone, and T-Mobile use one called **HSDPA**. Another protocol, **WiMax**, has been implemented by Clearwire and is available on Sprint's XOHM network (see Case 6 on page 201). The meaning of these acronyms and their particulars are unimportant to us; just realize that a marketing and technology battle is underway for WAN wireless. WiMax has the greatest potential for speed, but it is currently the least available.

When Kelly's shoes were communicating with her iPhone and the iPhone application was transferring data to a Web site, her shoes were using the Bluetooth wireless protocol and the iPhone was using a wireless WAN. Had she been inside the FlexTime building, to increase performance, the iPhone would have used the FlexTime wireless LAN rather than the wireless WAN.

You will sometimes hear the terms *narrowband* and *broadband* with regard to communications speeds. **Narrowband** lines typically have transmission speeds less than 56 kbps. **Broadband** lines have speeds in excess of 256 kbps. Today, all popular communication technologies provide broadband capability, and so these terms are likely to fade from use.

One day, we will have appliances that communicate with each other; or will we? See the Guide on pages 194–195 for a discussion of the interpretation of exponential phenomena.

Networks of Leased Lines

The fourth WAN alternative shown in Figure 6-7 is to create a **network of leased lines** between company sites. Figure 6-10 shows a WAN that connects computers located at three geographically distributed company sites. The lines that connect these sites are leased from telecommunications companies that are licensed to provide them.

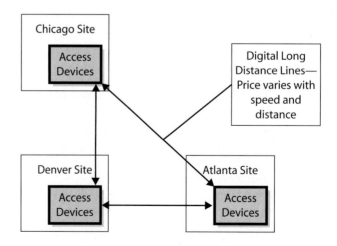

Figure 6-10
WAN Using Leased Lines

A variety of **access devices** connect each site to the transmission lines. These devices are typically special-purpose computers; the particular devices required depend on the line used and other factors. Sometimes switches are used; in other cases a device called a *router* is used. A **router** is a special-purpose computer that moves network traffic from one node on a network to another. See the appendix (page 202) for more information.

Several leased-line alternatives exist. As shown in Figure 6-11, lines are classified by their use and speed. A T1 line can support up to 1.544 Mbps; a T3 line can support up to 44.736 Mbps. Using optical fiber cable, even faster lines are possible; an OC-768 line supports 40 Gbps. Except for T1 speeds, faster lines require either optical fiber cable or satellite communication. T1 speeds can be supported by regular telephone wires, as well as by optical fiber cable and satellite communication.

Setting up a point-to-point line, once it has been leased, requires considerable work by highly trained, expensive specialists. Connecting the company's LANs and other facilities is a challenging task, and maintaining those connections is expensive. In some cases, organizations contract with third parties to set up and support the lines they have leased.

Notice, too, that with point-to-point lines, as the number of sites increases, the number of lines required increases dramatically. If another site is added to the network in Figure 6-10, up to three new leased lines will be needed. In general, if a network has n sites, as many as n additional lines need to be leased, set up, and supported to connect a new site to all the other sites.

Furthermore, only predefined sites can use the leased lines. It is not possible for an employee working at a temporary, remote location, such as a hotel, to use this network. Similarly, customers or vendors cannot use such a network, either.

However, if an organization has substantial traffic between fixed sites, leased lines can provide a low cost per bit transmitted. A company such as Boeing, for example, with major facilities in Seattle, St. Louis, and Los Angeles, could benefit by using leased lines to connect these sites. The operations of such a company require transmitting huge amounts of data between those fixed sites. Further, such a company knows how to hire and manage the technical personnel required to support this infrastructure.

Line Type	Use	Maximum Speed
Telephone line (twisted pair copper lines)	DSL modem	1.544 Mbps
	WAN—T1—using a pair of telephone lines	1.544 Mbps
Coaxial cable	Cable modem	Upstream to 256 kbps Downstream to 10 Mbps (usually much less, however)
Unshielded twisted pair (UTP)	LAN	100 Mbps
Optical fiber cable	LAN and WAN—T3, OC-768, etc.	40 Gbps or more
Satellite	WAN—OC-768, etc.	40 Gbps or more

Figure 6-11
Transmission Line Types, Uses, and Speeds

Public Switched Data Network

Yet another WAN alternative is a **public switched data network (PSDN)**, a network of computers and leased lines that is developed and maintained by a vendor that leases time on the network to other organizations. A PSDN is a utility that supplies a network for other companies to lease. Figure 6-12 shows the PSDN as a cloud of capability. What happens within that cloud is of no concern to the lessees. As long as they get the availability and speed they expect, the PSDN could consist of strings of spaghetti connected by meatballs. (This is not likely to be the case, however.)

When using a PSDN, each site must lease a line to connect to the PSDN network. The location at which this occurs is called a **point of presence (POP)**; it is the access point into the PSDN. Think of the POP as the phone number that one dials to connect to the PSDN. Once a site has connected to the PSDN POP, the site obtains access to all other sites connected to the PSDN.

PSDNs save the setup and maintenance activities required when using leased lines. They also save costs, because a company does not have to pay for the entire network; the company can pay just for the traffic that it sends. Further, using a PSDN requires much less management involvement than using leased lines. Another advantage of PSDNs is that only one line is required to connect a new site to all other sites.

Three protocols are used with PSDNs: Frame Relay, ATM (asynchronous transfer mode), and Ethernet. **Frame Relay** can process traffic in the range of 56 kbps to 40 Mbps. **Asynchronous transfer mode (ATM)** can process speeds from 1 to 156 Mbps. Frame Relay, although slower, is simpler and easier to support than ATM, and PSDNs can offer it at lower cost than ATM. However, some organizations need ATM's faster speed. Also, ATM can support both voice and data communications.

Often, PSDNs offer both Frame Relay and ATM on their network. Customers can choose whichever technique better fits their needs. Some companies use a PSDN network in lieu of a long-distance telephone carrier.

Ethernet, the protocol developed for LANs, also is used as a PSDN protocol. Newer versions of Ethernet can operate at speeds of 10 and 40 Gbps.

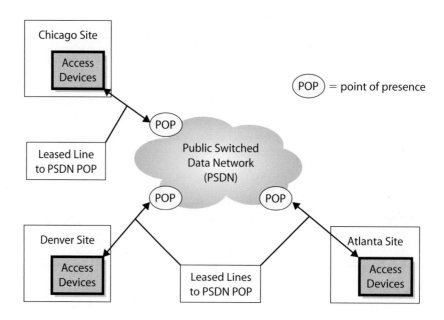

Figure 6-12
WAN Using PSDN

Q4 Why Do Organizations Use Virtual Private Networks?

A **virtual private network (VPN)** uses the Internet to create the appearance of private point-to-point connections. In the IT world, the term *virtual* means something that appears to exist that does not in fact exist. Here, a VPN uses the public Internet to create the appearance of a private connection.

A Typical VPN

Figure 6-13 shows one way to create a VPN to connect a remote computer, perhaps an employee working at a hotel in Miami, to a LAN at a Chicago site. The remote user is the VPN client. That client first establishes a connection to the Internet. The connection can be obtained by accessing a local ISP, as shown in the figure; or, in some hotels, the hotel itself provides a direct Internet connection.

In either case, once the Internet connection is made, VPN software on the remote user's computer establishes a connection with the VPN server in Chicago. The VPN client and VPN server then have a point-to-point connection. That connection, called a **tunnel**, is a virtual, private pathway over a public or shared network from the VPN client to the VPN server. Figure 6-14 illustrates the connection as it appears to the remote user.

VPN communications are secure, even though they are transmitted over the public Internet. To ensure security, VPN client software *encrypts*, or codes (see the Q5 discussion, page 190), the original message so that its contents are protected from snooping. Then the

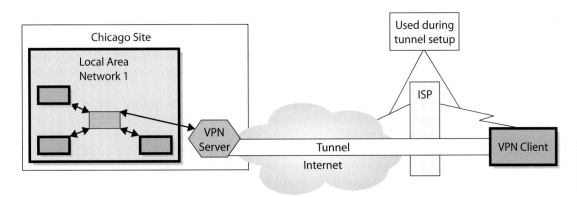

Figure 6-13
Remote Access Using VPN: Actual Connections

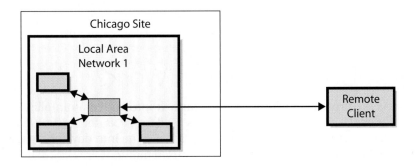

Figure 6-14
Remote Access Using VPN: Apparent Connection

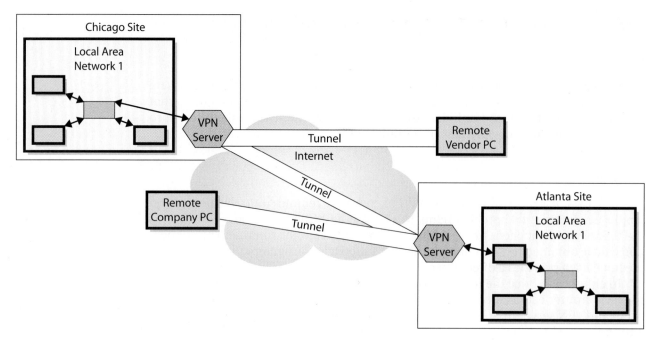

Figure 6-15
WAN Using VPN

VPN client appends the Internet address of the VPN server to the message and sends that package over the Internet to the VPN server. When the VPN server receives the message, it strips its address off the front of the message, *decrypts* the coded message, and sends the plain text message to the original address on the LAN. In this way, secure private messages are delivered over the public Internet.

VPNs offer the benefit of point-to-point leased lines, and they enable remote access, both by employees and by any others who have been registered with the VPN server. For example, if customers or vendors are registered with the VPN server, they can use the VPN from their own sites. Figure 6-15 shows three tunnels: one supports a point-to-point connection between the Atlanta and Chicago sites and the other two support remote connections.

Microsoft has fostered the popularity of VPNs by including VPN support in Windows. All versions of Microsoft Windows have the capability of working as VPN clients. Computers running Windows Server can operate as VPN servers.

FlexTime uses a VPN. Currently, Version 2 of its software can only be accessed via a LAN. But Kelly, Neil, and key employees need to be able to access that software from home or from another remote location. Accordingly, FlexTime has set up a VPN. Remote users sign on to the VPN and then they can work as if they were using a computer that is directly connected to the FlexTime LAN.

FlexTime could continue using the VPN in this way and not move to a thin-client application. However, it would still have the burden of installing and maintaining thick clients on user computers, and Neil wants to eliminate that burden. Furthermore, if it moved to a thin-client, customers could access the FlexTime system using their browsers.

Q5 How Does Encryption Work?

Encryption is the process of transforming clear text into coded, unintelligible text for secure storage or communication. Encryption is used for VPNs, for secure Web sites, and for other purposes as well. Considerable research has gone into developing **encryption algorithms** that are difficult to break. Commonly used methods are DES, 3DES, and AES; search the Internet for these terms if you want to know more about them.

A **key** is a number used to encrypt the data. The encryption algorithm applies the key to the original message to produce the coded message. Decoding (decrypting) a message is similar; a key is applied to the coded message to recover the original text. In **symmetric encryption**, the same key is used to encode and to decode. With **asymmetric encryption**, different keys are used; one key encodes the message, and the other key decodes the message. Symmetric encryption is simpler and much faster than asymmetric encryption.

A special version of asymmetric encryption, **public key/private key**, is popular on the Internet. With this method, each site has a public key for encoding messages and a private key for decoding them. (For now, suppose we have two generic computers, A and B.) To exchange secure messages, A and B send each other their public keys as plain, or uncoded, text. Thus, A receives B's public key and B receives A's public key, all as plain text. Now, when A sends a message to B, it encrypts the message using B's public key and sends the encrypted message to B. Computer B receives the encrypted message from A and decodes it using its private key. Similarly, when B wants to send an encrypted message to A, it encodes its message with A's public key and sends the encrypted message to A. Computer A then decodes B's message with its own private key. The private keys are never communicated.

Most secure communication over the Internet uses a protocol called **HTTPS**. With HTTPS, data are encrypted using a protocol called the **Secure Socket Layer (SSL)**, also known as **Transport Layer Security (TLS)**. SSL/TLS uses a combination of public key/private key and symmetric encryption. It works as follows: First, your computer obtains the public key of the Web server to which it will connect. Your computer then generates a key for symmetric encryption and encodes that key using the Web site's public key. It sends the encrypted symmetric key to the Web site. The Web site then decodes the symmetric key using its private key.

From that point forward, your computer and the Web site communicate using symmetric encryption. At the end of the session, your computer and the secure site discard the keys. Using this strategy, the bulk of the secure communication occurs using the faster symmetric encryption. Also, because keys are used for short intervals, there is less likelihood they can be discovered.

Use of SSL/TLS makes it safe to send sensitive data such as credit card numbers and bank balances. Just be certain that you see *https//:* in your browser and not just *http://*. You will learn more about SSL/TLS, HTTPS, and public/private keys in Chapter 12, Information Security Management.

Warning: Under normal circumstances, neither email nor instant messaging (IM) uses encryption. It would be quite easy for one of your classmates or your professor to read any email or IM that you send over a wireless network in your classroom, in the student lounge, at a coffee shop, or in any other wireless setting. Let the sender beware!

Q6 What Is the Purpose of a Firewall?

A **firewall** is a computing device that prevents unauthorized network access. A firewall can be a special-purpose computer, or it can be a program on a general-purpose computer or on a router.

Organizations normally use multiple firewalls. A **perimeter firewall** sits outside the organizational network; it is the first device that Internet traffic encounters. In addition to perimeter firewalls, some organizations employ **internal firewalls** inside the organizational network. Figure 6-16 shows the use of a perimeter firewall that protects all of an organization's computers and a second internal firewall that protects a LAN.

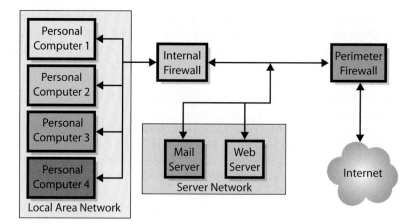

Figure 6-16
Use of Multiple Firewalls

A **packet-filtering firewall** examines each part of a message and determines whether to let that part pass. To make this decision, it examines the source address, the destination address(es), and other data.

Packet-filtering firewalls can prohibit outsiders from starting a session with any user behind the firewall. They can also disallow traffic from particular sites, such as known hacker addresses. They also can prohibit traffic from legitimate, but unwanted, addresses, such as competitors' computers. Firewalls can filter outbound traffic as well. They can keep employees from accessing specific sites, such as competitors' sites, sites with pornographic material, or popular news sites.

A firewall has an **access control list (ACL)**, which encodes the rules stating which addresses are to be allowed and which are to be prohibited. As a future manager, if you have particular sites with which you do not want your employees to communicate, you can ask your IS department to enforce that limit via the ACL in one or more routers. Most likely, your IS organization has a procedure for making such requests.

Packet-filtering firewalls are the simplest type of firewall. Other firewalls filter on a more sophisticated basis. If you take a data communications class, you will learn about them. For now, just understand that firewalls help to protect organizational computers from unauthorized network access.

No computer should connect to the Internet without firewall protection. Many ISPs provide firewalls for their customers. By nature, these firewalls are generic. Large organizations supplement such generic firewalls with their own. Most home routers include firewalls, and Windows XP, Vista, and Windows 7 have built-in firewalls as well. Third parties such as Norton and Symantec also license firewall products.

Q7 2020?

It can't last. Today's Internet access, that is. Right now you pay a fixed amount, say $35 to your ISP for Internet access. You can read just three emails a month, or you can download 1,000 movies a month; either way, you pay the same $35. But, that charging scheme just can't last; it's just too juicy a target. By 2020, ISPs will have figured out some way to charge based on the number of bits you transfer. So, enjoy it while you can.

State governments will find a way to get in on the Internet, too. Right now, in most states, businesses and individuals are legally required to pay taxes on goods they buy from out-of-state, over the Internet. But few do. States would like to require the sellers to collect the tax, but a 1992 U.S. Supreme Court ruling prohibits states from forcing a business to collect sales tax unless the business has a physical presence in that state. So, as long as you pick vendors that don't have facilities in your state, you can get away with paying no state sales tax on the online purchase.

Like flat-rate Internet access, this just can't last. In fact, as of 2009, 22 states have enacted legislation to conform to a state-developed program called the Streamlined Sales Tax Project. This project requires vendors to collect taxes on behalf of the state in which the purchaser resides. In addition to the 22 core states, another 20 or so states have laws that provide some degree of compliance with this project. So, by 2020 it's a safe bet you'll be paying state taxes on Internet purchases.

On the technology front, by 2020 everything will be connected to everything, everywhere, and everything will be interconnected. Today, most companies have a phone system that is separate from their computer networks. Employees get email and IM on their computers and telephone messages over the phone.

Products such as Microsoft Office Communicator plan to change that. Such products integrate phone, email, texting, video, and any other medium. By 2020, you'll receive your email via phone (a voice will read it to you) and phone calls via email (a voice-recognition system will type it for you). All messages, of whatever medium, will be stored in one location, like today's email inbox. Systems will also provide **presence**, a term that means you'll know who is on the system, who is available to the system, and who cannot currently be reached by the system.

And, finally, by 2020 communications will be ubiquitous. Devices will just take care of it. Today, the iPhone finds a LAN wireless connection if it can and a WAN wireless connection if it cannot. That philosophy will pervade communicating devices. They'll figure it out on their own.

Thinking Exponentially Is Not Possible, but...

Nathan Myhrvold, the chief scientist at Microsoft Corporation during the 1990s, once said that humans are incapable of thinking exponentially. Instead, when something changes exponentially, we think of the fastest linear change we can imagine and extrapolate from there, as illustrated in the figure on the next page. Myhrvold was writing about the exponential growth of magnetic storage. His point was that no one could then imagine how much growth there would be in magnetic storage and what we would do with it.

This limitation pertains equally well to the growth of computer network phenomena. We have witnessed exponential growth in a number of areas: the number of Internet connections, the number of Web pages, and the amount of data accessible on the Internet. And, all signs are that this exponential growth isn't over.

What, you might ask, does this have to do with me? Well, suppose you are a product manager for home appliances. When most homes have a wireless network, it will be cheap and easy for appliances to talk to one another. When that day arrives, what happens to your existing product line? Will the competition's talking appliances take away your market share? However, talking appliances may not satisfy a real need. If a toaster and a coffee pot have nothing to say to each other, you'll be wasting money to create them.

Every business, every organization, needs to be thinking about the ubiquitous and cheap connectivity that is growing exponentially. What are the new opportunities? What are the new threats? How will our competition react? How should we position ourselves? How should we respond? As you consider these questions, keep in mind that because humans cannot think exponentially, we're all just guessing.

So what can we do to better anticipate changes brought by exponential phenomena? For one, understand that technology does not drive people to do things they've never done before, no matter how much the technologists suggest it might. (Just because we *can do* something does not mean anyone will *want to do* that something.)

Social progress occurs in small, evolutionary, adaptive steps. Right now, for example, if you want to watch a movie with someone, you both need to be in the same room. It needn't be that way. Using data communications, several people can watch the same movie, at the same time, together, but not in the same location. They can have an open audio line to make comments to each other during the movie or even have a Web cam so they can see each other watching the same movie. That sounds like something people might want to do—it's an outgrowth of what people are already doing.

However, emerging network technology enables my dry cleaner to notify me the minute my clothes are ready. Do I want to know? How much do I care to know that my clothes are ready Monday at 1:45 rather than sometime after 4:00

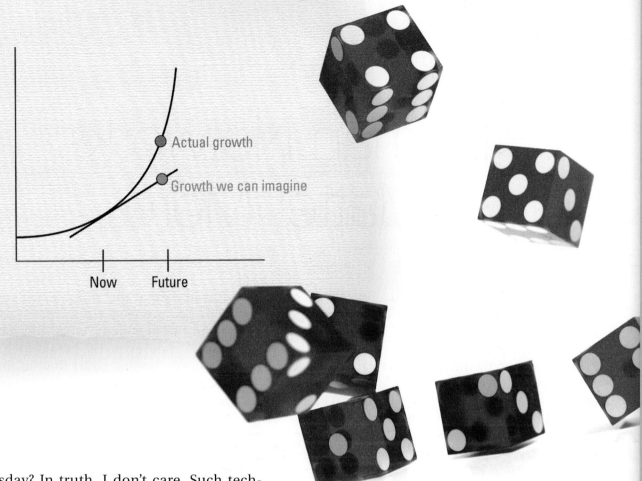

Actual growth

Growth we can imagine

Now   Future

on Tuesday? In truth, I don't care. Such technology does not solve a problem that I have.

So, even if technology enables a capability, that possibility doesn't mean anyone wants that capability. People want to do what they're already doing, but more easily; they want to solve problems that they already have.

Another response to exponential growth is to hedge your bets. If you can't know the outcome of an exponential phenomenon, don't commit to one direction. Position yourself to move as soon as the direction is clear. Develop a few talking appliances, position your organization to develop more, but wait for a clear sign of market acceptance before going all out.

Finally, notice in the exponential curve that the larger the distance between Now and the Future, the larger the error. In fact, the error increases exponentially with the length of the prediction. So, if you hear that the market for talking kitchen appliances will reach $1 billion in 1 year, assign that statement a certain level of doubt. However, if you hear that it will reach $1 billion in 5 years, assign that statement an exponentially greater level of doubt. ■

Discussion Questions

1. In your own words, explain the meaning of the claim that no one can think exponentially. Do you agree with this claim?

2. Describe a phenomenon besides connectivity or magnetic memory that you believe is increasing exponentially. Explain why it is difficult to predict the consequences of this phenomenon in 3 years.

3. To what extent do you think technology is responsible for the growth in the number of news sources? On balance, do you think having many news sources of varying quality is better than having a few with high quality control?

4. List three products or services, such as group movie viewing, that could dramatically change because of increased connectivity. Do not include movie viewing.

5. Rate your answers to question 4 in terms of how closely they fit with problems that people have today.

Human Networks Matter More

In case you missed it, *Six Degrees of Separation* is a play by John Guare that was made into a movie starring Stockard Channing and Donald Sutherland. The title is related to the idea, originated by the Hungarian writer Frigyes Karinthy, that everyone on earth is connected to everyone else by five (Karinthy) or six (Guare) people.* For example, according to the theory, you are connected to Eminem by no more than five or six people, because you know someone who knows someone, who knows someone, etc. By the same theory, you are also connected to a Siberian seal hunter. Today, in fact, with the Internet, the number may be closer to three people than to five or six, but in any case, the theory points out the importance of human networks.

Suppose you want to meet your university's president. The president has a secretary who acts as a gatekeeper. If you walk up to that secretary and say, "I'd like a half an hour with President Jones," you're likely to be palmed off to some other university administrator. What else can you do?

If you are connected to everyone on the planet by no more than six degrees, then surely you are connected to your president in fewer steps. Perhaps you play on the tennis team, and you know that the president plays tennis. In that case, it is likely that the tennis coach knows the president. So, arrange a tennis match with your coach and the president. Voilà! You have your meeting. It may even be better to have the meeting on the tennis court than in the president's office.

The problem with the six-degree theory, as Stockard Channing said so eloquently, is that even though those six people do exist, we don't know who they are. Even worse, we often don't know who the person is with whom we want to connect. For example, there is someone, right now who knows someone who has a job for which you are perfectly suited. Unfortunately, you don't know the name of that person.

It doesn't stop when you get your job, either. When you have a problem at work, like the need to understand the basics of TCP/IP, there is someone who knows exactly how to help you. You, however, don't know who that is.

Accordingly, most successful professionals consistently build personal human networks. They use Facebook and LinkedIn to build and maintain their networks because they know that somewhere there is someone whom they need to know or will need to know. They also meet people at professional and social situations, collect and pass out cards, and engage in pleasant conversation (all part of a social protocol) to expand their networks.

You are undoubtedly using Facebook right now. You may even be using LinkedIn. But you

---

*See "The Third Link" in Albert Laszlo Barabasi's book *Linked* (New York: Perseus Publishing, 2002) for background on this theory.

can use these applications more effectively if you think about the power of weak ties. To understand weak ties, consider the network diagram on page 196. Assume that each line represents a relationship between two people. Notice that the people in your department tend to know each other, and the people in the accounting department also tend to know each other. That's typical.

Now suppose you are at the weekly employee after-hours party and you have an opportunity to introduce yourself either to Linda or Eileen. Setting aside personal considerations, thinking just about network building, which person should you meet?

If you introduce yourself to Linda, you shorten your pathway to her from two steps to one and your pathway to Shawna from three to two. You do not open up any new channels because you already have them to the people in your floor.

However, if you introduce yourself to Eileen, you open up an entirely new network of acquaintances. So, considering just network building, you use your time better by meeting Eileen and other people who are not part of your current circle. It opens up many more possibilities.

The connection from you to Eileen is called a weak tie in social network theory,** and such links are crucial in connecting you to everyone in six degrees. *In general, the people you know the least contribute the most to your network.* This phenomenon is true whether your network is face-to-face or virtual, like LinkedIn.

This concept is simple, but you'd be surprised by how few people pay attention to it. At most company events, everyone talks with the people they know, and, if the purpose of

the function is to have fun, then that behavior makes sense. In truth, however, no business social function exists for having fun, regardless of what people say. Business functions exist for business reasons, and you can use them to create and expand networks. Given that time is always limited, you may as well use such functions efficiently. ∎

Discussion Questions

1. Determine the shortest path from you to your university's president. How many links does it have?

2. Give an example of a network to which you belong that is like your department in the figure on the preceding page. Sketch a diagram of who knows whom for six or so members of that group.

3. Recall a recent social situation and identify two people, one of whom could have played the role of Linda (someone in your group whom you do not know) and one of whom could have played the role of Eileen (someone in a different group whom you do not know). How could you have introduced yourself to either person?

4. Does it seem too contrived and calculating to think about your social relationships in this way? Even if you do not approach relationships like this, are you surprised to think that others do? Under what circumstances does this kind of analysis seem appropriate, and when does it seem inappropriate?

5. Consider the phrase, "It's not what you know, it's whom you know that matters." Relate this phrase to the diagram. Under what circumstances is this likely to be true? When is it false?

6. Describe how you can apply the principle "The people you know the least contribute the most to your network" to your use of Facebook or LinkedIn during a search for a job.

_____

**See Terry Granovetter, "The Strength of Weak Ties," *American Journal of Sociology*, May 1973.

ACTIVE REVIEW

Use this Active Review to verify that you understand the ideas and concepts that answer the chapter's study questions.

Q1 What is a computer network?

Define *computer network*. Explain the differences among LANs, WANs, internets, and the Internet. Describe the purpose of a protocol.

Q2 What are the components of a LAN?

Explain the key distinction of a LAN. Describe the purpose of each component in Figure 6-2. Define *MAC* and *UTP*. Describe the placement of switches in a multistory building. Explain when optical fiber cables are used for a LAN. Explain Ethernet. Describe the purpose of each of the wireless components in Figure 6-6.

Q3 What are the alternatives for a WAN?

Explain why your connection to an ISP is a WAN and not a LAN. Name three functions of an ISP. Describe the purpose of a modem. Explain three ways you can connect to the Internet. Describe the differences among DSL, cable, and WAN wireless alternatives. Explain the advantages and disadvantages of leased lines. Explain each cell of Figures 6-7 and 6-11.

Q4 Why do organizations use virtual private networks?

Describe the problem that a VPN solves. Use Figure 6-15 to explain one way that a VPN is set up and used. Define *tunnel*. Describe how encryption is used in a VPN. Explain why a Windows user does not need to license or install other software to use a VPN.

Q5 How does encryption work?

Define the terms *encryption* and *key*. Explain the difference between an encryption key and a key of a database table (Chapter 5). Explain the difference between symmetric and asymmetric encryption. Describe the advantages of each. Explain how public key/private key encryption works. Explain why SSL/TLS is important. Explain why you should be careful with what you write in emails and instant messages.

Q6 What is the purpose of a firewall?

Define *firewall*. Explain the role for each firewall in Figure 6-16. Describe how a manager might ask to shut off access to or from a particular site.

Q7 2020?

Explain how ISP charges may change by 2020. Explain how payments for state taxes will change. Describe ways that business communications today are not integrated. Explain how products such as Office Communicator may change that. Explain the meaning and implications of the statement "Devices will just take care of it."

KEY TERMS AND CONCEPTS

10/100/1000 Ethernet   182
Access control list (ACL)   192
Access devices   187
Access point (AP)   183
Analog signal   184
Asymmetric digital subscriber
   lines (ADSL)   185
Asymmetric encryption   191
Asynchronous transfer
   mode (ATM)   188
Bluetooth   183
Broadband   186
Cable modem   185
Digital subscriber line   185
DSL modem   185

Encryption   190
Encryption algorithms   190
Ethernet   182
EVDO   186
Firewall   191
Frame Relay   188
HSDPA   186
HTTPS   191
IEEE 802.3 protocol   182
IEEE 802.11 protocol   182
IEEE 802.16 protocol   201
Internal firewalls   191
internet   177
Internet service provider (ISP)   184
Key   191

Local area network (LAN)   176
MAC (media access control)
   address   180
Modem   184
Narrowband   186
Network   176
Network interface card (NIC)   180
Network of leased lines   186
Onboard NIC   180
Optical fiber cables   180
Packet-filtering firewall   192
Perimeter firewall   191
Point of presence (POP)   188
Presence   193
Problem of the last mile   201

USING YOUR KNOWLEDGE

1. Suppose you manage a group of seven employees in a small business. Each of your employees wants to be connected to the Internet. Consider two alternatives:

   - Alternative A: Each employee has his or her own modem and connects individually to the Internet
   - Alternative B: The employees' computers are connected using a LAN, and the network uses a single modem to connect.

   a. Sketch the equipment and lines required for each alternative.

   b. Explain the actions you need to take to create each alternative.

   c. Compare the alternatives using the criteria in Figure 6-16.

   d. Which of these two alternatives do you recommend?

2. Consider the situation of a company that has two offices at physically separated sites. Suppose each office has a group of 15 computers.

   a. If the two offices are retail art galleries, what is likely to be the most common type of interoffice communication? Given your answer, what type of WAN do you think is most appropriate?

   b. Suppose the two offices are manufacturing sites that communicate via email and that regularly exchange large drawings and plans. What are the advantages and disadvantages of each of the four WAN types for these offices? Under what circumstances would you recommend a leased-line WAN?

   c. Suppose the two offices are the same as described in part b, but that in addition each has salespeople on the road who need to connect to the office computers. How would your answer to part b change?

   d. Would you change your answer to part c if both offices are located in the same building? Why or why not?

   e. What additional factors would you need to consider if one of the offices in part c was in Los Angeles and the other was located in Singapore?

3. Suppose that you have a consulting practice implementing local area networks for fraternities and sororities on you campus.

   a. Consider a fraternity house. Explain how a LAN could be used to connect all of the computers in the house. Would you recommend an Ethernet LAN, an 802.11 LAN, or a combination? Justify your answer.

   b. This chapter did not provide enough information for you to determine how many switches the fraternity house might need. However, in general terms, describe how the fraternity could use a multiple-switch system.

   c. Considering the connection to the Internet, would you recommend that the fraternity house use a DSL, cable modem, or WAN wireless? Although you can rule out at least one of these alternatives with the knowledge you already have, what additional information do you need in order to make a specific recommendation?

   d. Should you develop a standard package solution for each of your customers? What advantages accrue from a standard solution? What are the disadvantages?

4. Consider Neil's problem at FlexTime. He wants to carefully review the $175,000 network infrastructure proposal and eliminate any equipment or services that he can. At the same time, while the building is being remodeled the walls will be open, and this will be the best possible time to add cabling and any other equipment that FlexTime may eventually need.

   Assume you have Neil's task. How would you proceed? We don't have enough information to analyze that proposal in detail. Instead, answer the following questions that concern how Neil might go about making this analysis.

   a. Describe FlexTime equipment that is likely to have a wired connection to a LAN.

   b. Describe FlexTime equipment that is likely to have a wireless connection to a LAN.

   c. Describe customer equipment that is likely to have a wireless connection to a FlexTime LAN.

d. Neil (and you) need to plan for the future. How are your answers to parts a–c likely to change in the next 5 years? In the next 10 years?

e. Describe a process for determining the total wireless demand for a room that contains 50 spinning bicycles.

f. Suppose the new FlexTime building has four floors and each floor has multiple workout rooms with wireless capability and several desktop computers that use wired capability. Also, assume there is a "computer room" that has two servers and a high-speed connection to the Internet. Using Figure 6-4 as a guide, describe how the new building is likely to be wired.

g. Using the knowledge you have gained from this chapter, list all of the equipment and cabling that FlexTime will need for their new building. Just list equipment categories; you do not have sufficient information to specify particular brands or models of equipment.

h. Suppose Neil receives three different bids for the network infrastructure. Does he necessarily choose the lowest cost one? Why or why not? What process should Neil use to analyze the three proposals?

COLLABORATION EXERCISE

Collaborate with a group of students on the following exercises. Recall from Chapter 2 that collaboration is more than cooperation because it involves iteration and feedback. Post a document, a discussion item, a wiki item, or an idea and obtain feedback from your team members. Similarly, read the ideas of others and comment on them. Try to innovate in both the process by which you collaborate and the work product that you create. Avoid face-to-face meetings. Instead, use collaborative software such as Google Docs & Spreadsheets, Microsoft Groove, or Microsoft SharePoint to facilitate your ideas.

Consider the information technology skills and needs of your parents, relatives, family friends, and others in the Baby Boomer generation. Though you may not know it, you possess many skills that generation wants but does not have. You know how to text chat, how to download music from iTunes, how to buy and sell items on eBay, how to use Craigslist, and how to use a PDA, an iPhone, and so forth. You probably can even run the navigation system in your parents' car.

a. Thinking about Baby Boomers whom you know, brainstorm with your team the skills that you possess that they do not. Consider all of the items just described and others that come to mind. Make a common team list of all those skills.

b. Interview, survey, or informally discuss the items on your list in part a with your parents and other Baby Boomers. As a team, determine the five most frustrating and important skills that these people do not possess.

c. The Baby Boomer market has both money and time, but not as much information technology capability as they need, and they do not like it.

With your team, brainstorm products that you could sell to this market that would address the Baby Boomers' techno-ignorance. For example, you might create a video of necessary skills, or you might provide a consulting service setting up Microsoft Home Server computers. Consider other ideas and describe them as specifically as you can. You should consider at least five different product concepts.

d. Develop sales material that describes your services, the benefits they provide, and why your target market should buy those products. Try your sales pitch on friends and family.

e. How viable is your concept? Do you think you can make money with these products? If so, summarize an implementation plan. If not, explain why not.

APPLICATION EXERCISES

1. Numerous Web sites are available that will test your Internet data communications speed. You can find one good at *www.speakeasy.net/speedtest/*. (If that site is no longer active, Google "What is my Internet speed?" to find another speed-testing site. Use it.)

   a. While connected to your university's network, go to Speakeasy and test your speed against servers in Seattle, New York City, and Atlanta. Compute your average upload and download speeds. Compare your speed to the speeds listed in Figure 6-11.

   b. Go home, or to a public wireless site, and run the Speakeasy test again. Compute your average upload and download speeds. Compare your speed to those listed in Figure 6-11. If you are performing this test at home, are you getting the performance you are paying for?

   c. Contact a friend or relative in another state. Ask him or her to run the Speakeasy test against those same three cities.

   d. Compare the results in parts a, b, and c. What conclusion, if any, can you make from these tests?

2. Suppose you work for a company that installs computer networks. Assume that you have been given the task of creating spreadsheets to generate cost estimates.

a. Create a spreadsheet to estimate hardware costs. Assume that the user of the spreadsheet will enter the number of pieces of equipment and the standard cost for each type of equipment. Assume that the networks can include the following components: NIC cards; WNIC cards; wireless access points; switches of two types, one faster, one slower, at two different prices; and routers. Also assume that the company will use both UTP and optical fiber cable and that prices for cable are stated as per foot. Use the network in Figure 6-6 as an example.

b. Modify your spreadsheet to include labor costs. Assume there is a fixed cost for the installation of each type of equipment and a per foot cost for the installation of cable.

c. Give an example of how you might use this spreadsheet for planning network installations. Explain how you could adapt this spreadsheet for project tracking and billing purposes.

CASE STUDY 6

Keeping Up with Wireless

Data communications technology is one of the fastest-changing technologies, if not *the* fastest changing, in all of IT. Substantial portions of the knowledge you gain from this chapter will be obsolete within the first 5 years of your career. Unfortunately, we do not know which portions that will be.

Consider the example of WAN wireless technology. Three protocol standards are in competition: EVDO, HSDPA, and WiMax. Because WiMax has the greatest potential performance, we will consider it further in this case.

Craig McCaw built one of the world's first cellular networks in the early 1980s and brought cells phones to the masses. In the 1990s, he sold his company to AT&T for $11.5 billion. In 2003, McCaw started a new venture, Clearwire, by buying rights to technology based on WiMax, to address what is called the "problem of the last mile." Will WiMax defeat the other WAN wireless technologies? We do not know. But, when someone with McCaw's knowledge, experience, and wealth starts a new venture based on that new technology, we should pay attention.

To begin, what is the **problem of the last mile**? The bottleneck on data communications into homes, and into smaller businesses, is the last mile. Fast optical-fiber transmission lines lie in the street in front of your apartment or office; the problem is getting that capacity into the building and to your computer or TV. Digging up the street and backyard of every residence and small business to install optical fiber is not an affordable proposition. Even if that could be done, such infrastructure cannot be used by mobile devices. You cannot watch a downloaded movie on a commuter train using an optical fiber line.

The WiMax standard, **IEEE 802.16** could be implemented by many companies, but only if those companies own wireless frequencies for data transmission. Hence the interest by people like McCaw and other cellular players such as Sprint. The WiMax standard includes two usage models: *fixed* and *mobile*. The former is akin to LAN wireless in existence today; mobile access allows users to move around, as they do with cell phones, staying connected.

On December 1, 2008, Clearwire merged with Sprint Nextel and received a $3.2 billion outside investment. In the process, Clearwire gained access to Sprint Nextel's spectrum holdings (authority to use certain frequencies for cellular signals). The merged company is called Clearwire and the products are marketed as Sprint Xohm.

Clearwire already provides fixed use in many cities. As of June 2009, mobile WiMax services were available only in Las Vegas, Atlanta, and Portland, Oregon. It is slated to offer mobile services in Baltimore, Chicago, Philadelphia, and Dallas/Fort Worth later in 2009.

Questions

1. Read the "Thinking Exponentially" Guide on pages 194–195. Keeping the principles of that guide in mind, list five possible commercial applications for mobile WiMax. Consider applications that necessitate mobility.

2. Evaluate each of the possible applications in your answer to question 1. Select the three most promising applications and justify your selection.

3. Clearwire went public in March 2007 at an initial price of $27.25. As of June 2009, the price was $4.50. Go online and research the company to find out what happened to its share price. Explain why its share price has dropped.

4. AT&T and T-Mobile have endorsed HSDPA, but it does not have the same potential maximum transmission rates. Rather than jump on the WiMax bandwagon, those companies plan to deploy a different technology called Long Term Evolution (LTE). Search the Web for LTE versus WiMax comparisons and compare and contrast these two technologies.

5. Where will this end? On which of these technologies would you be willing to invest $100 million? Why?

How the Internet Works

>> STUDY QUESTIONS

Q1 How does email travel?

Q2 What is a communications protocol?

Q3 What are the functions of the five TCP/IP—OSI layers?

Q4 How does the Internet work?

Q5 How does *www.pearsonhighered.com* become 165.193.123.253?

When you send something as simple as an email with an attachment, a true techno-miracle occurs. You are about to learn how. In the process, you will learn important terms such as *router, IP address*, and *TCP/IP*, and you will see how they relate to make the Internet work.

Q1 How Does Email Travel?

Suppose you are on vacation in Hawaii and you want to send a photo of your amazing surfing skills to a friend in snowbound Cincinnati, Ohio. You plug your laptop into the hotel's network, fire up your email program, write the email, attach the photo, and press Send. That's it. In a matter of minutes, your friend will be admiring your surfing antics. Even though you may not know it, a techno-miracle occurred.

Figure 6A-1 shows the networks involved in sending your email message and picture. There is a LAN at your hotel, a LAN at your friend's company, and the Internet connects the two. Assume that you sent your message from computer 3 (C3) at the hotel and that your friend is sitting at computer 10 (C10) in the company in Ohio.

You know that your email and picture traveled over the Internet, which is a network of networks. But how? A host of problems had to be overcome: Your friend has an Apple computer, and you have a Dell. The two of you use different operating systems and two different email programs. As shown, both you and your friend are connected to LANs, but your hotel's LAN uses wires, and your friend's company's LAN is wireless. Thus, the LANs are of different types and process messages differently.

Furthermore, your message and picture were sent over an optical fiber cable underneath the sea and received by a computer in San Francisco. But, your picture was too big to send in one big chunk, so it was broken into pieces, and the pieces traveled separately. When the pieces (called *packets*) arrived in San Francisco, a device (called a *router*) determined that the best way to get them to your friend was to send them to a router in Los Angeles, which sent the pieces to a router in Denver, which sent them to a router in Cincinnati, which sent them to a company that contracts with your friend's employer to provide Internet access, which sent them to the email server at your friend's company. Meanwhile, your computer determined that one of the pieces got lost along the way, and it automatically resent that piece.

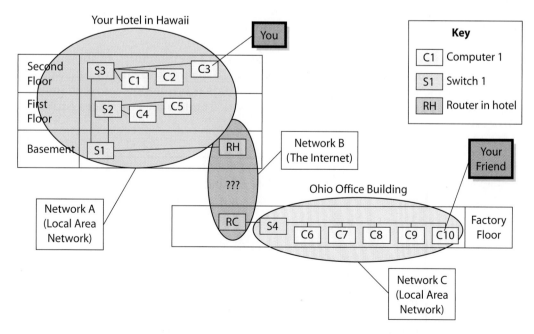

Figure 6A-1
Sample Networks

When all of the pieces have been assembled, your friend gets the "You've got mail" indicator on his computer. He looks at your picture and asks, "How does she do that?" What he should be asking is, "How does the Internet do that?"

The key concept is *divide and conquer*. All of the work is divided into categories, and the categories of work are arranged into layers. To understand this further, we must first explain communications protocols.

Q2 What Is a Communications Protocol?

As stated in Chapter 6, a **protocol** is a standardized means for coordinating an activity between two or more entities. Humans use social protocols. For example, a protocol exists for introducing two people to one another. Another human protocol, illustrated in Figure 6A-2, occurs at the grocery store. This protocol, like all protocols, proceeds through a sequence of ordered steps. If, in response to the clerk's query "Debit or credit," you enter your PIN, you are skipping steps and violating the protocol. The clerk will correct you and ask her question again. Notice, too, that the protocol has a decision branch. If you say, "credit," then the clerk will not ask the question about cash back or ask you to enter your PIN.

A **communications protocol** is a means for coordinating activity between two or more communicating computers. Two machines must agree on the protocol to use, and they must follow that protocol as they send messages back and forth. Because there is so much to do, communications protocols are broken up into levels or layers.

Q3 What Are the Functions of the Five TCP/IP—OSI Layers?

Several different **layered protocol** schemes, or **protocol architectures**, have been proposed. The **International Organization for Standardization (ISO)** developed the **Reference Model for Open Systems Interconnection (OSI)**, an architecture that has seven layers. Another group, the **Internet Engineering Task Force (IETF)**, developed a four-layer scheme called the **Transmission Control Program/Internet Protocol (TCP/IP) architecture**. For reasons that are beyond our discussion, the Internet uses a five-layer blend of these two architectures called the **TCP/IP—OSI architecture**. When people like Neil at FlexTime use the term *TCP/IP*, they mean TCP/IP—OSI architecture; that longer term, though correct, is seldom used.

Figure 6A-3 shows the five layers of this hybrid architecture. As shown in the right-most column, the bottom two layers concern the transmission of data within a single network. The next two layers are used for data transmission across an internet (a network of networks, including the Internet). The top layer provides protocols that enable applications to interact.

Figure 6A-2
Example of a Grocery
Store Protocol

Clerk:	Your total is $57.55.
You:	[You slide your credit/debit card through the machine.]
Clerk:	Debit or credit?
You:	Debit.
Clerk:	OK, any cash back?
You:	Yup, $50, please.
Clerk:	Enter your PIN.
You:	[You enter PIN.] OK?
Clerk:	OK, sign here.
You:	[You sign.]
Clerk:	Here's your $50.

Layer	Name	Specific Function	Broad Function
5	Application	The application layer governs how two applications work with each other, even if they are from different vendors.	Interoperability of application programs
4	Transport	Transport layer standards govern aspects of end-to-end communication between two end hosts that are not handled by the internet layer. These standards also allow hosts to work together even if the two computers are from different vendors and have different internal designs.	Transmission across an internet
3	Internet	Internet layer standards govern the transmission of packets across an internet—typically by sending them through several routers along the route. Internet layer standards also govern packet organization, timing constraints, and reliability.	
2	Data Link	Data link layer standards govern the transmission of frames across a single network—typically by sending them through several switches along the data link. Data link layer standards also govern frame organization, timing constraints, and reliability.	Transmission across a single network
1	Physical	Physical layer standards govern transmission between adjacent devices connected by a transmission medium.	

Figure 6A-3
TCP/IP—OSI Architecture

Source: Panko, Ray, *Business Data Networks and Telecommunications*, 5th, © 2005. Electronically reproduced by permission of Pearson Education, Inc.,Upper Saddle River, New Jersey.

Layer 5

Examine the networks in Figure 6A-1 between your hotel in Hawaii and your friend. Unknown to you or your friend, each of your computers contains programs that operate at all five layers of the TCP/IP—OSI architecture. Your email program operates at Layer 5. It generates and receives email (and attachments like your photo) according to one of the standard email protocols defined for Layer 5. Most likely, it uses a protocol called **Simple Mail Transfer Protocol (SMTP)**.

There are many other Layer-5 protocols. **Hypertext Transfer Protocol (HTTP)** is used for the processing of Web pages. When you type the address *www.ibm.com* into your browser, notice that your browser adds the notation *http://*. (Try this, if you've never noticed that it happens.) By filling in these characters, your browser is indicating that it will use the HTTP protocol to communicate with the IBM site.

By the way, the Web and the Internet are not the same thing. The Web, which is a subset of the Internet, consists of sites and users that process the HTTP protocol. The Internet is the communications structure that supports all application-layer protocols, including HTTP, SMTP, and other protocols.

File Transfer Protocol (FTP) is another application-layer protocol. You can use FTP to copy files from one computer to another. In Figure 6A-1, if computer 1 wants to copy a file from computer 9, it would use FTP.

Three important terms lurk in this discussion:

1. **Architecture**. An *architecture* is an arrangement of protocol layers in which each layer is given specific tasks to accomplish.
2. **Protocol**. At each layer of the architecture, there are one or more *protocols*. Each protocol is a set of rules that accomplish the tasks assigned to its layer.
3. **Program**. A *program* is a specific computer product that implements a protocol.

So, for example, the TCP/IP—OSI architecture has five layers. At the top level are numerous protocols, including HTTP, SMTP, and FTP. For each of those protocols, there are program products that implement the protocol. Some of the programs that implement the HTTP protocol of the TCP/IP—OSI architecture are called *browsers*. Two common browsers are Mozilla Firefox and Microsoft Internet Explorer. Thus, thin-client applications use HTTP at layer 5 of the TCP/IP–OSI architecture.

Layer 4

All of the protocols at layer 5 interact with another protocol, **Transmission Control Program (TCP)**, at Layer 4, the next layer down. For example, as shown in Figure 6A-4, your email program (which uses SMTP) interacts with programs that implement TCP. Note that we are using the acronym TCP in two ways: as the name of a Layer-4 *protocol* and as part of the name of the TCP/IP—OSI protocol architecture. In fact, the architecture gets its name because it usually includes the TCP protocol.

TCP performs many important tasks. Your Dell and your friend's Apple have different operating systems that represent data in different ways. Programs in those operating systems that implement the TCP protocol make conversions from one data representation to the other. Also, a TCP program examines your email and picture and breaks lengthy messages (like your picture) into pieces called **segments**. When it does this, it places identifying data at the front of each segment that are akin to the To and From addresses that you would put on a letter for the postal mail.

TCP programs also provide reliability. It was the TCP program on your computer that noticed that one of the pieces did not arrive at your friend's computer, and so it resent that piece.

Your friend's Apple computer also has a program that runs the TCP protocol. It receives the segments from your computer and sends acknowledgments back to your computer when it receives each segment. The TCP program also translates the segments from Windows (Dell) to Macintosh (Apple) format, reassembles the segments into a coherent whole, and makes that assembly available to your friend's email program.

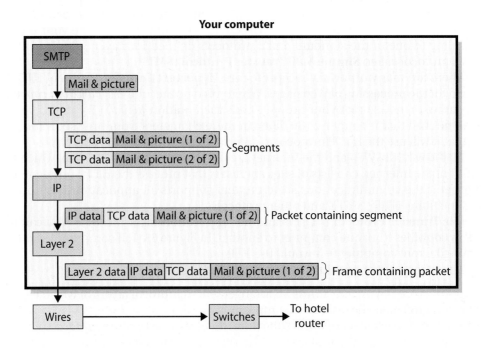

Figure 6A-4
TCP/IP—OSI Architecture
on Your Computer

Layer 3

TCP interacts with protocols that operate at Level 3, the next layer down. For the TCP/IP architecture, the Layer-3 protocol is the **Internet Protocol (IP)**. The chief purpose of IP is to route messages across an internet. In the case of your email, the IP program on your computer does not know how to reach your friend's computer, but it does know how to start. Namely, it knows to send all of the pieces of your email and picture to a device in your hotel's network called a *router*. In Figure 6A-1, that router is labeled RH. (This is not a brand of router, it is just the label we will put on the hotel's router in this figure.)

To send a segment to RH, the IP layer program on your computer first packages each segment into a **packet**. As shown in Figure 6A-4, it also places IP data in front of the packet, in front of the TCP data. This action is akin to wrapping a letter inside another envelope and placing additional To/From data in the header of the outer envelope.

Routers are special-purpose computers that implement the IP protocol. The router labeled RH examines the destination of your packets and uses the rules of the IP protocol to decide where to send them. RH does not know how to get them all the way to Ohio, but it does know how to get them started on their way. In this case, it decides to send them to another router located in San Francisco. Dozens of other routers on the Internet will eventually cause the packets containing your message and picture to arrive at a router at your friend's employer. We will explain more about this process later in this appendix.

Layers 1 and 2

As shown in Figure 6A-1, your hotel uses a LAN to connect the computers in its hotel rooms. (Lucky you—you're staying at such an exclusive hotel that it has just two floors and five rooms!) Basic computer connectivity is accomplished using Layers 1 and 2 of the TCP/IP—OSI architecture. As you learned in Chapter 6, computing devices called switches facilitate that data communication. (See Figure 6A-4.)

A program implementing a Layer-2 protocol will package each of your packets into **frames**, which are the containers used at Layers 1 and 2. (Segments go into packets, and packets go into frames.) Then, programs, switches, and other devices cause the pieces of your email and picture to pass from your computer to switch 3, from switch 3 to switch 1, and from switch 1 to router RH. (See Figure 6A-1.)

Q4 How Does the Internet Work?

Given this background, we can now explain how your email travels over the networks to reach your friend. This is the most complicated section in this textbook. To understand this material, we will break the discussion into four sections. First, we will consider the addressing of computers and other devices. As you will learn, each computer and device has two addresses, a physical address and a logical one. Next, we will consider how protocols at all five layers of the TCP/IP—OSI model operate to send a request to a Web server within a LAN. Third, we will consider how those same protocols work to send messages across the Internet. Finally, we will wrap up with some details about IP addresses and the domain name system. Be patient, and take your time; you may need to read this section more than once. We begin with addresses.

Network Addresses: MAC and IP

On most networks, and on every internet, two address schemes identify computers and other devices. Programs that implement Layer-2 protocols use *physical addresses,* or *MAC addresses.* Programs that implement Layer-3, -4, and -5 protocols use *logical addresses,* or *IP addresses.* We will consider each type.

Physical Addresses (MAC Addresses)

As stated in Chapter 6, every network device, including your computer, has a NIC for accessing the network. Each NIC is given an address at the factory. That address is the device's **physical address**, or **MAC address**. By agreement among computer manufacturers, such addresses are assigned so that no two NICs will ever have the same MAC address.

MAC addresses are used within networks at Layer 2 of the TCP/IP—OSI model. Physical addresses are only known, shared, and used within a particular network or network segment. For internets, including the Internet, another scheme of addresses must be used. That scheme turned out to be so useful that it is also used within LANs, in addition to MAC addressing.

Logical Addresses (IP Addresses)

Internets, including the Internet, and many private networks use **logical addresses**, which are also called **IP addresses**. You have probably seen IP addresses; they are written as a series of dotted decimals, for example, 192.168.2.28.[1]

IP addresses are not permanently associated with a given hardware device. They can be reassigned to another computer, router, or other device when necessary. To understand one advantage of logical addresses, consider what happens when an organization like IBM changes the device (a router) that receives requests when users type *www.ibm.com*. That name is associated with a particular IP address (as we will explain later in this appendix). If IP addresses were permanent, like MAC addresses, then when IBM upgrades its entry router, all of the users in the world would have to change the IP address associated with *http://www.ibm.com t*o the new address. Instead, with logical IP addresses, a network administrator need only reassign IBM's IP address to the new router.

Public Versus Private IP Addresses

In practice, two kinds of IP addresses exist. **Public IP addresses** are used on the Internet. Such IP addresses are assigned to major institutions in blocks by the **Internet Corporation for Assigned Names and Numbers (ICANN)**. (We'll talk more about ICANN later.) Each IP address is unique across all computers on the Internet. In contrast, **private IP addresses** are used within private networks and internets. They are controlled only by the company that operates the private network or internet.

Dynamic Host Configuration Protocol

Today, in most cases, when you plug your computer into a LAN (or sign on to a wireless LAN), a program in Windows or other operating system will search that network for a DHCP server, which is a computer or router that hosts a program called **Dynamic Host Configuration Protocol (DHCP)**. When the program finds such a device, your computer will request a temporary IP address from the DHCP server. That IP address is loaned to you while you are connected to the LAN. When you disconnect, that IP address becomes available, and the DHCP server will reuse it when needed.

Of course, within a private network, administrators can assign private IP addresses manually as well. Often, the strategy within a private network is to manually assign IP addresses to computers that operate Web servers or other shared devices for which it is desirable to have a fixed IP address. Today, most users, however, are assigned IP addresses using DHCP.

---

[1]Actually, there are two versions of IP addresses: **IPv4** and the newer **IPv6**. IPv4 addresses look like this one. IPv6 addresses are twice as long and are formatted differently. As of 2009, most routers and other communicating devices can process both versions.

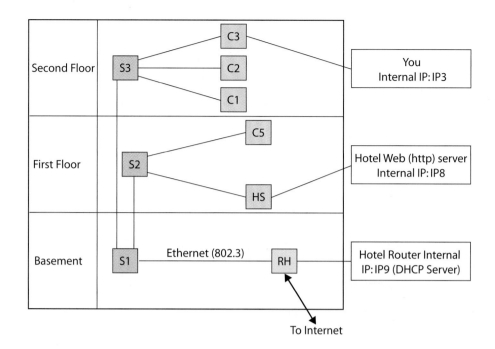

Figure 6A-5
Hotel LAN in Hawaii

Private IP Addresses at the Hawaii Hotel

To make sense of the discussion so far, consider Figure 6A-5, which shows the LAN operated by your hotel in Hawaii. Let's suppose that you occupy the penthouse suite (more good luck!) and that you plug your computer into the network as computer C3 in Figure 6A-5. When you do so, a program in your operating system searches the network for a DHCP server. It turns out that the router labeled RH is such a server. Your computer asks RH for an IP address, and RH assigns one. It will be a number like 192.168.2.28, but for simplicity let's denote your IP address by the symbol IP3.

Using TCP/IP—OSI Protocols Within the Hotel

Once you have an IP address, protocol programs on your computer at Layers 3, 4, and 5 can communicate with any other computer in your network. Suppose, for example, that the computer labeled HS is running a Web server that provides information to hotel guests. This Web server is private; the hotel wants only guests and others within the hotel to be able to access it. Hence, the server operates only within the LAN.

Suppose the IP address of the server has been assigned by a network administrator; let's denote that address as IP8. The router, RH in Figure 6A-5, also has an IP address. Denote that address as IP9. Now, let's see how all of these addresses are used within the hotel's LAN.

Communications Processing on Your Computer

The hotel provides a brochure in your room that tells you how to sign on to the local Web server by entering a name into your browser. When you follow those instructions, your browser constructs a request for the server and uses the HTTP protocol to send it to HS.

We can follow the action in Figure 6A-6 (next page). Your browser sends its service request for HS to a program that implements TCP. One function of TCP is to break requests into segments, when necessary. In this case, suppose it breaks the request into two segments. The TCP program adds additional data to the segments. Here we show a header with *IP3 To: IP8*, but other data, and possibly a trailer, are added as well. We will ignore the real headers and trailers to focus on basic concepts.

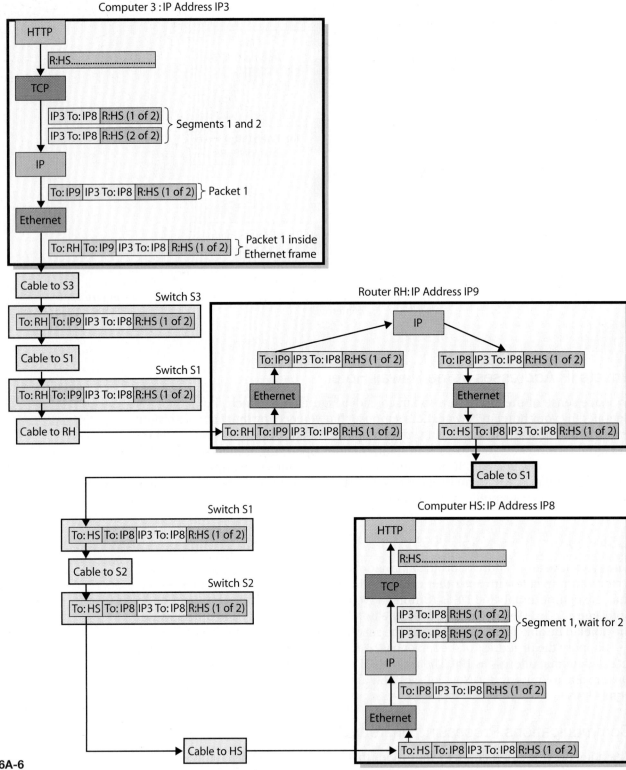

Figure 6A-6
Accessing the (Private)
Hotel Web Server

The TCP program hands the segment(s) to a program that implements IP. As stated, the major function of that IP program is routing. It determines that the only route to IP8 is through the router at RH, whose IP address is IP9. So, the IP program adds the IP9 header and passes the wrapped packet down to a program that implements Ethernet.

The Ethernet program translates the IP address into a MAC address. Ethernet determines that the device at IP9 has a particular MAC address, which will be a long number. Here, for simplicity, we denote that address as RH. Ethernet will wrap the packet into a frame that is addressed to device RH.

When you signed onto the LAN, your Ethernet program learned that the only way it can connect to other computers is via switch S3 (see Figure 6A-5). Accordingly, it sends the frame to S3.

Communications Processing on Your Computer

All switches have a table of data called a **switch table**. This table tells the switch where to send traffic to get it to its destination. The table on switch S3 has entries for every other device on the LAN. It knows, for example, that to get a frame to RH, it must send it to switch S1. Accordingly, it sends the frame to S1.

S1 also has a switch table. S1 consults that table and determines that it has a direct connection to RH. Therefore, it sends the frame to RH.

Communications Processing on the Router

When the frame arrives at RH, it has arrived at its destination, and so Ethernet unpacks the frame and sends the contained packet up to IP. IP examines the packet and determines that the packet's destination is IP8. RH, which is a router, has a **routing table** that tells it where to send traffic for IP8. This routing table indicates that IP8 is just one hop away. So, IP changes the destination of the packet to IP8 and passes it back down to Ethernet.

Ethernet determines that the device at IP8 has the MAC address HS. So, it packages the packet into a frame and gives that frame the address HS. It then sends the frame to its switch S1. S1 consults its switch table and sends the frame to S2; S2 sends the frame to HS.

Communications Processing on the Web Server

The Ethernet program at HS unpacks the frame and sends the contained packet to the IP program. IP8 is the destination for the packet, so the IP program strips off the IP header and sends the contained segment up to a program that implements TCP. That program examines the segment and determines that it is the first of two. TCP sends an acknowledgment back to your computer to indicate that it received the first segment. (Of course, the acknowledgment must be routed and switched as well.) TCP waits for the second segment to arrive.

Once both segments have arrived, the TCP program sends the complete request up to the Web server program that processes the HTTP protocol. (Whew!)

To summarize:

- *Switches* work with *frames* at *Layer 2.* They send frames from switch to switch until they arrive at their destination. They use *switch tables* and *MAC addresses*.
- *Routers* work with *packets* at *Layer 3.* They send packets from router to router until they arrive at their destination. They use *router tables* and *IP addresses*.

Using TCP/IP—OSI Protocols over the Internet

Finally, we are in position to describe how your email gets from you at the hotel in Hawaii to your friend in the company in Ohio. In fact, you need to know just one more topic to understand the techno-miracle that occurs: how private and public IP addresses are converted.

Network Address Translation

All of the IP addresses described in the prior section were private IP addresses. They are used within the LAN at your hotel. For Internet traffic, however, only public IP addresses can be used. These addresses are assigned in blocks to large companies and organizations such as ISPs.

Your hotel has an ISP that it uses to connect to the Internet. That ISP assigned one of its public IP addresses to the router in your hotel. We will denote that IP address as IPx. (Again, it will be a valid IP address like 192.168.2.28, but ignore that now.)

Therefore, as shown in Figure 6A-7, router RH has two IP addresses: a private one, *IP9*, and a public one, *IPx*. All Internet traffic aimed at any computer within the hotel LAN will be sent over the Internet using IP address IPx. The router will receive all packets for all computers at the hotel. When it receives a packet, it determines the internal IP address within the LAN for that computer. It then changes the address in the packet from IPx (the router's IP address) to the internal IP address of a computer in the hotel—the packet's true destination. Thus, if the router receives some traffic intended for you, it will change the packet's address from IPx to IP3 and send it to you.[2]

The process of changing public IP addresses into private IP addresses, and the reverse, is called **Network Address Translation (NAT)**. NAT uses a concept called ports. . . . But, let's stop there. We've had enough. If you take a data communications class, you can learn about NAT. Let's just move on and trust that NAT works.

Your Email(!)

Finally, we can describe how your email gets to your friend in Ohio. You start your email program, and you enter your friend's email address. Suppose that your friend's name is Carter, and his email address is CarterK@OhioCompany.com. Your email program works at the application layer, and it implements SMTP. According to this protocol, your email will be sent to a mail server at the Internet address *OhioCompany.com.*

Your email program will use the domain name system (described later) to obtain the public IP address for the mail server at *OhioCompany.com.* Let's denote that address as *IPz.*

The message to IPz is then sent to the router RH as follows: Your email program implements SMTP, which sends the message to TCP. There it is broken into segments, and each segment is sent to IP, where they are placed into packets and routed to RH. Then, each packet is sent to your Ethernet program, where it is placed in a frame and sent to switch S3, and then S1, and then the router.

When one of the packets from your email and picture arrives at the router, it implements NAT and replaces your private IP address, IP3, with its public IP address, IPx. Router RH consults its routing table and determines how best to get the packet to IPz. Suppose that it determines that it should send the packet to Internet router R2.

The processing of the packet over the Internet is just the same as that described for the hotel in Figure 6A-1. Packets are sent from router to router until they reach the router RC, the gateway router at your friend's company, which sends them to the mail server.

At that server, segments will be unpacked from packets and sent to a TCP program on the mail server that will send an acknowledgment back to your computer. Then TCP will wait for all of the segments in your mail (and picture) to arrive. TCP will then send the entire message and photo attachment to the program that implements

---

[2]Believe it or not, we are simplifying. This description is typical for a SOHO network (see page 219). A real hotel and company would use devices in addition to the router for DHCP and NAT.

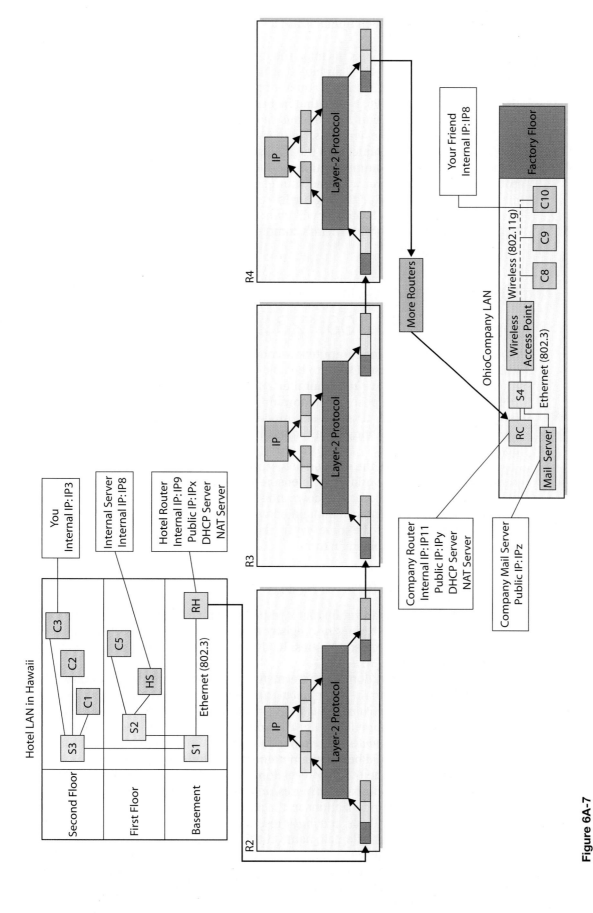

Figure 6A-7
Hawaii Hotel to OhioCompany
via Internet

213

SMTP. That program, which operates at Layer 5, will place the message and photo in the mailbox for CarterK.

When your friend checks his mail, the mail program on his computer will use all five layers of the TCP/IP—OSI architecture to send his mail check request to the mail server. His computer, which is also operating behind a router that provides NAT, has the internal IP address IP8. Notice that he has the same IP address as the server HS at your hotel. This duplication will not cause a problem, because these IP addresses are used only in local, private networks. Neither address is used on the public Internet.

Carter's computer connects to the mail server using a wireless protocol, 802.11g, but the essence of his communications to the mail server is the same as that on your hotel LAN. The mail server will send your email and picture to a TCP program on the mail server, from there to an IP program for routing to IP8, and from there to a program that processes Ethernet. Switch S4 will then convert the Ethernet frames into 802.11g frames and send them to your friend's computer.

That's how it works!

Q5 How Does *www.pearsonhighered.com* Become 165.193.123.253?

IP addresses are useful for computer-to-computer communication, but they are not well suited for human use. I want to be able to enter a name like *www.icann.org* into my browser and not have to remember and enter its public IP address, which is 208.77.188.103. The purpose of the **domain name system (DNS)** is to convert user-friendly names into their IP addresses. Any registered, valid name is called a **domain name**. The process of changing a name into its IP address is called *resolving the domain name*.

This process requires the solution of two problems. First, to be useful, every domain name must be unique, worldwide. To ensure that duplicates do not occur, an agency registers names and records the corresponding IP addresses in a global directory. Second, when the user enters a domain name into his or her browser or other Layer-5 application, there needs to be some way for the application to resolve the domain name. We will consider each problem in turn.

Domain Name Registration

ICANN is a nonprofit organization that is responsible for administering the registration of domain names. ICANN does not register domain names itself; instead, it licenses other organizations to register names. ICANN is also responsible for managing the *domain name resolution system.*

The last letters in any domain name are referred to as the **top-level domain (TLD)**. For example, in the domain name *www.icann.org*, the TLD is .*org*. Similarly, in the domain name *www.ibm.com.com* is the TLD. For non–U.S. domain names, the TLD is often a two-letter abbreviation for the country in which the service resides. For example, a name like *www.somewhere.cn* would be a domain name in China, and *www.somewhere.uk* would be a domain name in the United Kingdom.

Figure 6A-8 shows the U.S. top-level domains as of 2009. Some of these TLDs are restricted to particular industries, purposes, or organizations. The TLD .*aero*, for example, is restricted for use by organizations in the air transport industry. Similarly, .*name* is intended for use by individuals, and .*mil* is reserved for use by the U.S. military.

If you want to register a domain name, the first step is to determine the appropriate TLD. You must then visit *www.icann.org* and determine which agencies ICANN has licensed to register domains for that TLD. Finally, you need to follow the registration process required by one of those agencies. If the domain name you want is already in use, your registration will be disallowed, and you will need to select another domain name.

Top-Level Domain	Used by
.aero	Air-transport industry
.asia	Asia-Pacific region
.biz	Business
.com	Commercial
.coop	Cooperatives
.edu	Education
.gov	U.S. government
.info	Information
.int	International organizations
.jobs	Companies
.mil	U.S. military
.mobi	Mobile devices
.museum	Museums
.name	Individuals, by name
.net	Network
.org	Organization
.pro	Professions
.tel	Internet communication services
.travel	Travel and tourism

Figure 6A-8
Top-level U.S. Domains, 2009

Domain Name Resolution

A **uniform resource locator (URL)**, pronounced either by saying the three letters or as "Earl," is a document's address on the Web. URLs begin with a domain name and then are followed by optional data that locates a document within that domain. Thus, in the URL *www.pearsonhighered.com/kroenke,* the domain name is *www.pearsonhighered.com,* and */kroenke* is a directory within that domain.

Domain name resolution is the process of converting a domain name into a public IP address. The process starts from the TLD and works to the left across the URL. As of 2009, ICANN manages 13 special computers called **root servers** that are distributed around the world. Each root server maintains a list of IP addresses of servers that resolve each type of TLD.

For example, to resolve the address *www.somewhere.biz,* you would first go to a root server and obtain the IP address of a server that resolves *.biz* domain names. To resolve the address *www.somewhere.com,* you would go to a root server and obtain the IP address of a server that resolves *.com* domain names. In the first case, given the address of the server that resolves *.biz,* you would query that server to determine the IP address of the server that resolves the particular name *somewhere.biz.* Then you would go to that server to determine the IP address of the server that manages *www.somewhere.biz.*

In practice, domain name resolution proceeds more quickly because there are thousands of computers called **domain name resolvers** that store the correspondence of domain names and IP addresses. These resolvers reside at ISPs, at academic institutions, at large companies, at governmental organizations, and so forth. A domain name resolver may even be located on your campus. If so, whenever anyone on your campus resolves a domain name, that resolver will store, or **cache**, the domain name and IP address on a local file. Then, when someone else on campus needs to resolve that same domain name, there is no need to go through the entire resolution process. Instead, the resolver can supply the IP address from the local file.

Of course, domain names and their IP addresses can change. Therefore, from time to time, the domain name resolvers delete old addresses from their lists or refresh old addresses by checking their correctness.

By the way, if you're curious to know your current IP address, go to *www.WhatIs MyIPAddress.com*. That site will tell you not only your own address, but you can also obtain the IP address of any URL. Similarly, you can do a reverse lookup, enter an IP address, and it will give you the registered URL at that address, if any.

VoIP and IPTV

The TCP/IP—OSI architecture was originally designed to support text messages among computers on a network of networks. Nothing in this architecture required that it only carry text, however; as the email example shows, IP packets can carry photos or music just as well. In fact, packets can carry anything represented by bits.

Voice over IP (**VoIP**, pronounced "voyp") uses the TCP/IP—OSI architecture to carry telephone voice conversations. With VoIP, voice conversations are stored as bits, broken into IP packets, and routed over the Internet. No separate telephone line is required; the same connection that routes email, HTTP, and other data also carries the voice conversation. In Chapter 2, you learned that Microsoft Groove uses VoIP to transmit voice communications.

A problem occurs when a user who is connected to the Internet wants to dial someone who has only regular telephone access, or, equivalently, when someone who has a regular telephone wants to call someone who has a VoIP connection. Companies such as **Skype** (now owned by Yahoo!) have solved this problem and offer subscribers unrestricted telephone access using VoIP. Skype is particularly economical for those who make frequent international calls. Some users complain that the quality of transmission is not as high as for the regular telephone, but they use Skype anyway because the cost savings are worth it.

Internet Protocol Television (IPTV) uses TCP/IP—OSI to transmit television and other video signals. Because of the amount of data, a broadband connection is required. A device called a **set-top box** receives the IPTV signal and distributes it to multiple televisions or home entertainment centers. Some set-top devices provide VoIP, text chat, and other services as well. (For an example, perform a search for the *Tornado M10 Media Center*.)

You can expect to see increased use of both VoIP and IPTV in the years to come.

ACTIVE REVIEW

Use this Active Review to verify that you understand the ideas and concepts that answer the appendix's study questions.

Q1 How does email travel?

Identify the LANs and the Internet network in Figure 6A-1. Describe some of the problems that must be overcome in sending your email and picture to your friend. Explain why some of your message was broken into sections. Describe the route your message took. Explain what happened when one of the sections was lost.

Q2 What is a communications protocol?

Give an example of a social protocol other than paying at the grocery store. In your own words, describe what a protocol does. Define *communications protocol*.

Q3 What are the functions of the five TCP/IP—OSI layers?

Compare and contrast the terms *communications protocol architecture, communications protocol*, and *program*. Using the example of Firefox (a browser) processing a Web site on the Internet, give an example of each of these. Using Figure 6A-3 as a guide, explain the purpose of each layer of the TCP/IP architecture in layperson's terms. Name the layers used for an internet and the layers used for a LAN. Explain how Figure 6A-4 shows a message being wrapped in packages, packages within packages, and so forth.

Q4 How does the Internet work?

Define the terms *MAC address* and *IP address*. Define the terms *physical address* and *logical address*, and relate them to MAC and IP addresses. Explain which layers of the TCP/IP—OSI architecture use MAC addresses. Explain which use IP addresses. Explain the advantage of being able to transfer an IP address from one device or computer to another.

Compare and contrast a public IP address and a private IP address. State who assigns each type of address. Explain the meaning of the statement, "Most user computers obtain IP addresses from DHCP servers." Explain the process by which you were granted an IP address at your hotel. Identify the computer that provided that address to you.

Using the network structure in Figure 6A-5, explain the message processing shown in Figure 6A-6. Explain how switches use MAC addresses and switch tables, whereas the router and the Web server use IP addresses and routing tables. Ensure you understand the differences in each of the rectangles in Figure 6A-6.

Explain why the router in your hotel needs two IP addresses. Explain how it uses IP9 and how it uses IPx. Show an example value for either IP address. Explain why your internal, private IP address must be transformed. Explain why all traffic directed to you from outside of the hotel will be sent to address IPx. Identify the device that translates your IP address into IPx and the reverse. Explain, at a high level, the purpose of Network Address Translation.

Trace the flow of one email from you to your friend in Figure 6A-7. On each line that connects two devices, state whether a MAC or an IP address is used. If it is an IP address, state whether it is an internal or an external IP address. Explain why it is possible that your computer and the computer of your friend can have the same IP address. Compare and contrast segment, packet, and frame.

Q5 How does *www.pearsonhighered.com* become 165.193.123.253?

Explain the meaning of the phrase *resolving a domain name*. Define the term *top-level domain*, and indicate the top-level domains of *www.pearsonhighered.com*, *www.irs.gov*, and *www.myvalleyinn.uk*. Define *uniform resource locator*. Explain the role of ICANN with regard to domain registration. Summarize the process for registering the domain *www.mydogspot.info*. Explain ICANN's role with regard to domain name resolution, and describe the purpose of a root server. Summarize the process of resolving the URL *www.mydogspot.info*. Explain why it is likely that the first person to access *www.mydogspot.info* at a major university is likely to wait longer for a response than will subsequent people who access that same site. Describe the capabilities of VoIP and IPTV.

KEY TERMS AND CONCEPTS

Architecture   205
Cache   216
Communications protocol   204
Domain name   214
Domain name resolution   215
Domain name resolver   215
Domain name system (DNS)   214
Dynamic Host Configuration
   Protocol (DHCP)   208
File Transfer Protocol
   (FTP)   205
Frame   207
Hypertext Transfer Protocol
   (HTTP)   205
International Organization for
   Standardization (ISO)   204
Internet Corporation for Assigned
   Names and Numbers (ICANN)   208
Internet Engineering Task Force
   (IETF)   204

Internet Protocol
   (IP)   207
Internet Protocol television
   (IPTV)   216
IP address   208
IPv4   208
IPv6   208
Layered protocols   204
Logical address   208
MAC address   208
Network Address Translation
   (NAT)   212
Packet   207
Physical address   208
Private IP address   208
Program (that implements
   a protocol)   205
Protocol   204
Protocol architecture   204
Public IP address   208

Reference Model for Open Systems
   Interconnection (OSI)   204
Root server   215
Routing table   212
Segment   206
Set-top box   216
Simple Mail Transfer Protocol
   (SMTP)   205
Skype   216
Switch table   211
TCP/IP—OSI architecture   204
Top-level domain (TLD)   214
Transmission Control Program
   (TCP)   206
Transmission Control Program/
   Internet Protocol (TCP/IP)
   architecture   204
Uniform resource locator
   (URL)   215
Voice over IP (VoIP)   216

USING YOUR KNOWLEDGE

1. Assume you teach your MIS class and that a student comes to your office one day and asks, "Why do I have to learn how the Internet works? Give me three practical applications of this knowledge." How would you respond? Before you answer this question, read and think about the questions that follow.

2. How important do you think the existence of the TCP/IP—OSI protocols and architecture are to the success of the Internet? How did they contribute to the growth of the Internet? In what ways do protocols decrease competition? In what ways do they increase competition? In what ways do protocols stifle innovation? In what ways do they facilitate innovation? Explain how protocol architectures enable many different vendors to create interoperable products. In 2009 and beyond, what other industries might benefit from a similar standard?

3. Search the Internet for four companies that make products for one or more of the five layers of the TCP/IP—OSI architecture. Search for terms introduced in Chapter 6 and in this appendix, such as *802.3, 802.11, optical cable, VPN, firewall, switch, FTP,* and others. For each company, name one of their products, explain its function, and describe how that product relates to the TCP/IP—OSI architecture.

CASE STUDY 6A

A SOHO Network Administration

The photo in Figure 6A-9, below, shows LAN and Internet hardware used in a *SOHO (small office, home office)* company. This messy set of wires, devices, and office paraphernalia illustrates the use of many of the concepts in Chapter 6 and its appendix.

The small, flat, black box is a DSL modem that is connected to a telephone line. The DSL modem also connects to the silver, upright box with the small dark gray antenna. That silver box is a Microsoft Wireless Base Station. Wireless Base Station is a marketing term that Microsoft uses to soften the complexity of what's actually in that gray box. Amazingly, that little box contains an Ethernet LAN switch, an 802.11g wireless access point, and a router. Notice the several UTP cables that connect the Wireless Base Station to computers and other devices on the LAN. A generic term for Microsoft's Wireless Base Station is *device access router*, the term you should use when you go shopping for one.

In addition to the switch, access point, and router, the Wireless Base Station also contains a small special-purpose computer that has firmware programs installed. These programs provide DHCP service as well as NAT. The Wireless Base Station also has programs for administration and for setting up wireless security.

Notice the printer (behind the tape dispenser). The printer has a small black box with a gray UTP cable and a small black power line going into it. The black box is an NIC that connects the printer to the LAN. This NIC is called a *printer server*, and it, too, has a special-purpose computer with firmware that allows for setting up and

Figure 6A-9
A SOHO Network

Source: David M. Kroenke.

administering the printer server and printer. Using the printer server, the printer is not directly connected to any computer. Any of the users on the LAN can use the printer without turning on a computer to serve the printer.

Figure 6A-10 illustrates the structure of the SOHO network.

Both of these offices are in the same building. As shown, the base station includes an Ethernet switch, a wireless access point, a router, a DHCP server, and a NAT server. The base station, which is more generally called a *device access router*, has room for up to four physical connections from computers and servers.

Questions

1. Using the concepts from this chapter and its appendix, answer the following questions:

   a. What hardware is needed to add an additional computer to the LAN using Ethernet?

   b. Describe the advantages of using DHCP for the new computer.

   c. The line between the base station and the modem is not a telephone line. Which line(s) will be telephone line(s)?

   d. Which lines will be UTP cables?

   e. What hardware is needed to add another wireless computer?

   f. The computer user in office 2 must enter office 1 to access the printer. This is a problem to the occupants of both offices. What must be done to move the printer to a neutral location between the two offices?

   g. With regard to part f, suppose the users of this LAN decide to use a wireless printer server. Go to *http://cnet.com* or another site that lists computer hardware and determine the approximate cost of a wireless printer server. Under what conditions is it better to buy a wireless printer server? Under what conditions is it better to buy a second printer for office 2 instead of a printer server?

   h. The base station has room to connect only four Ethernet devices. If three computers and the printer are already connected using Ethernet, what options are available for adding yet another computer to the LAN?

   i. All of the computers in this LAN run Microsoft Windows. A user at computer 1 clicked the LAN icon at the bottom of his screen and the screen shown in Figure 6A-11 appeared.

      (1) Are the IP addresses in this screen internal or public IP addresses?

      (2) What computer is located at IP address 192.168.2.19?

      (3) What device is located at IP address 192.168.2.1?

2. The user did not know what device was located at IP address 192.168.2.28, so he opened his browser and typed: *http://192.168.2.28*. The screen shown in Figure 6A-12, on the next page, appeared.

   a. Which device on the SOHO LAN has been assigned this IP address?

   b. Which device created this display?

   c. What is the purpose of this display?

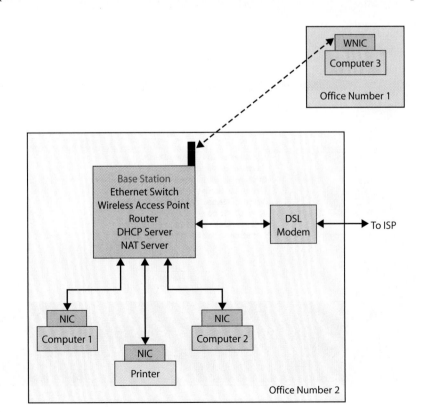

Figure 6A-10
Structure of a SOHO Network

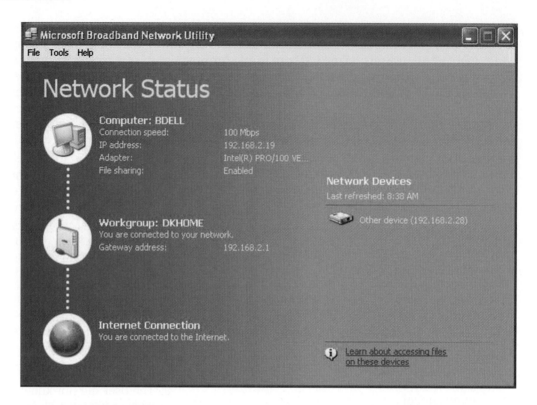

Figure 6A-11

Source: Microsoft product screenshot reprinted
with permission from Microsoft Corporation.

3. Out of curiosity, the user then entered *http://192.168.2.1*
into his browser. The display shown in Figure 6A-13
resulted. You have not learned what a *subnet mask* is.
However, you should be able to figure out the meanings
of the data in this display.

a. Which device produced this display?
b. What does "DHCP server: enabled" mean?
c. Explain the entries in the DHCP section.
d. The base station has two MAC addresses. What two
devices inside the base station do you think they refer to?

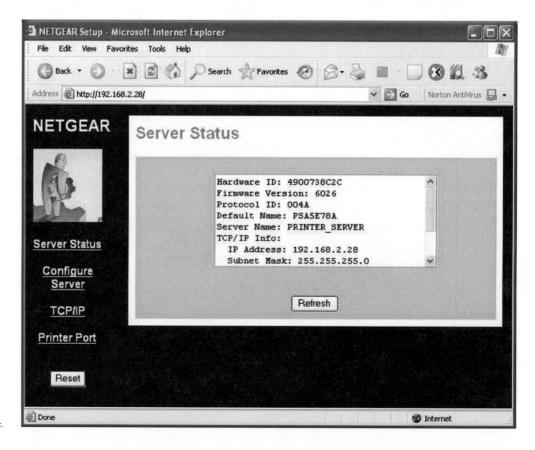

Figure 6A-12

Source: Used with permission of NETGEAR, Inc.

Local Area Network (LAN) Settings

This section displays a summary of settings for your LAN.

Local IP address: 192.168.2.1
Subnet mask: 255.255.255.0
DHCP server: Enabled
Firewall: Enabled

DHCP Client List

This section lists the computers and other devices that the base station detects on your network.

IP address	Host name	MAC address
192.168.2.28		0x00c002a5e78a
192.168.2.20		0x000e3589b565
192.168.2.19		0x000cf18e7a55

Base Station Information

Runtime code version: V1.11.017
Boot code version: V1.02
LAN MAC address: 00-50-F2-C7-B0-9A
MAC address: 00-01-03-21-AB-98
Serial number: A240054408

Figure 6A-13

e. What is the MAC address of the printer server? (Use data from the last two displays.)

f. The network administrator for this SOHO LAN can access a management utility within the base station. She did so and navigated to the display shown in Figure 6A-14.

(1) Do the data in this display pertain to the Ethernet switch or the router?

(2) This appendix showed the use of DHCP within a LAN. This screen allows the base station to use DHCP to obtain its own public IP address from the ISP. What benefits does the ISP accrue by using DHCP?

(3) When would the network administrator *not* use DHCP to connect to the ISP?

(4) Under what circumstances would someone use a base station and not connect it to the Internet?

Wide Area Network (WAN) Settings   Help

You can specify which type of Internet connection and the specific settings your Internet service provider (ISP) requires. To learn about the connection type and the settings you should use, refer to the information provided by your ISP.

Internet Connection Type
Select the type, and then specify your settings.

- Dynamic   Obtains an IP address dynamically from your ISP.
- Static   Uses a fixed IP address provided by your ISP.
- PPPoE   Uses Point-to-Point Protocol over Ethernet.
- Disabled   Do not connect the base station to the Internet.

Figure 6A-14

Q1 What Does It Mean to Localize Software?

The process of making a computer program work in a second language is called **localizing** that software. It turns out to be surprisingly hard to do. If you think about localizing a document or a Web page, all you need to do is hire a translator to convert your document or page from one language to another. The situation is more difficult for a computer program, however.

Suppose, for example, that your company has developed its own inventory-control database application and that your firm has just acquired a company in Mexico. You want to use that same inventory-control program for your Mexican operations. As a new manager, suppose you haven't even considered this matter during the acquisition process. After the acquisition is done, you ask your technical people to give you a time estimate for converting your inventory application into Spanish. Unless that program was designed from the beginning to be localized, you will be shocked at the effort and cost required. Why?

Consider a program you frequently use—say, Microsoft Word—and ask what would need to be done to translate it to a different language. The entire user interface will need to be translated. The menu bar and the commands on the menu bar will need to be translated. It is possible that some of the icons (the small graphics on a menu bar) will need to be changed because some graphic symbols that are harmless in one culture are confusing or offensive in another.

The inventory-control application is a database application, so it will have forms, reports, and queries. The labels on each of these will need to be translated. Of course, not all labels translate into words of the same length, and so the forms and reports may need to be redesigned. The questions and prompts for queries, such as "Enter part number for back order," must also be translated.

All of the documentation will need to be translated. That should be just a matter of hiring a translator, except that all of the illustrations in the documentation will need to be redrawn in the second language.

Think, too, about error messages. When someone attempts to order more items than there are in inventory, your

application produces an error message. All of those messages will need to be translated. There are other issues as well. Sorting order is one. Spanish uses accents on certain letters, and it turns out that an accented *ó* will sort after *z* when you use the computer's default sort ordering. Your programmers will have to deal with that issue as well.

Figure 1 presents a short list of issues that emerge when localizing a computer program.

Programming techniques can be used to simplify and reduce the cost of localization. However, those techniques must be used in the beginning. For example, suppose that when a certain condition occurs the program is to display the message, "Insufficient quantity in stock." If the programmer codes all such messages into the computer program, then, to localize that program, the programmer will have to find every such message in the code

- Translate the user interface, including menu bars and commands.
- Translate, and possibly redesign, labels in forms, reports, and query prompts.
- Translate all documentation and help text.
- Redraw and translate diagrams and examples in help text.
- Translate all error messages.
- Translate text in all message boxes.
- Adjust sorting order for different character set.
- Fix special problems in Asian character sets and in languages that read and write from right to left.

Figure 1
Issues to Address When Localizing a Computer Program

and then ask a translator to change that code. A preferred technique is to give every error message a number and to place the number and text of the error message into a separate file. Then, the code is written to display a particular error number from that file. During localization, translators simply translate the file of error messages into the second language.

The bottom line for you as a future manager is to understand two points: (1) Localizing computer programs is much more difficult, expensive, and time-consuming than translating documents. (2) If a computer program is likely to be localized, then plan for that localization from the beginning. In addition, when considering the acquisition of a company in a foreign country, be sure to budget time and expense for the localization of information systems.

Q2 What Are the Problems and Issues of Localizing and Distributing Databases Worldwide?

Consider the acquisition of the Mexican company just described. You have decided to localize your inventory-control application. The next question is, "Do you want to localize your inventory database?"

Assume that you have a centralized inventory database in the United States. Do you want the inventory-control programs that will run in Mexico to access that same database? With modern data communications, that is entirely possible.

However, your business requirements may dictate that you need to create a second database in Mexico. In that case, there are two issues. First, you will need to localize it. Second, you will need to determine the relationship between the two databases. Do the contents of those two databases refer to a single centralized inventory, or do they refer to two different inventories? If, for example, the two databases both indicate that there are 10 widgets in inventory, is that a single centralized inventory, or are there two separate inventories, one in the United States and one in Mexico, and do they both happen to have 10 widgets in stock?

Consider database localization first. In most cases, when companies localize databases they choose to translate the data, but not the metadata. Thus, the contents of the *Remarks* field or the *Description* files are translated. However, the names of tables, the names of fields, the description of the meaning of the fields, and other such metadata are left in English (or whatever the original language was). As stated in the previous section, forms, reports, queries, and database application programs will also need to be localized.

Now consider the relationship between the two databases. If they refer to two separate inventories, then there is no problem. Each database can be processed and administered as an independent entity. If the two databases refer to the *same* inventory, however, then they contain duplicated records. Such databases are said to be **replicated**. In this case, if it is possible to partition the workload so that the inventory application running on a server in Mexico updates different records than the inventory application running on a server in the United States, then the situation can be managed.

If, however, the two inventory applications running on the two servers can update the *same items at the same time*, serious problems occur.

Considerable time, expense, and sophisticated programming are necessary to develop and support such databases. Because of the expense, difficulty, and risk, most organizations define their business processes to avoid this situation.

This problem, by the way, is not strictly an international problem. The two separate servers could be running in the same country, and the problem will be the same. The situation arises more frequently, however, in international situations.

Q3 What Are the Consequences of Global Data Communication?

We discussed the impact of modern data communications on the development of the global economy in the previous part (page 92). In brief, data communications have tremendously expanded the size of the global economy and the global workforce.

In this section, consider the impact of data communications on less-developed countries. One of the most positive aspects of IT is that technology users can skip generations. People can benefit from the most modern technology without having to use the earlier technology. When Microsoft introduces a new version of Word, you can receive the benefit of that new version without having to learn Word 1.0, then Word 2.0, then Word 3.0, and so forth. Similarly, you can buy a cell phone and use it without ever having used a wired phone. You can do instant messaging with your friends without ever having sent an email.

What are the consequences of this? In many developing countries, cell or satellite phones are the first phones that most people use. Some parts of the world do not have telephone wires and never will. In some countries, the first weather forecast someone sees will be presented on a Web page that is delivered via a cell phone.

The economic, social, and political consequences of this phenomenon are staggering. A coffee farmer in Kenya, someone who has never sold his or her beans to anyone but a local trader, can suddenly sell them to Starbucks in Seattle. A basket weaver in Cameroon, who has sold her wares only at the local market, can suddenly sell her baskets to collectors in Tokyo. People whose world horizon has been restricted to rural villages or streets in their city suddenly find themselves connected to the rest of the world. Local laws and customs become outmoded, even irrelevant.

Furthermore, existing companies, organizations, and governments are seriously challenged. The public telephone utility in many countries has been a profitable monopoly and medium of control. Cell and satellite phones threaten this monopoly and reduce the power of individuals and cartels. In some countries, there has been a backlash and restriction of the spread of technology. Such measures only delay the inevitable. How can a country with serious penalties for using a copy machine for political purposes maintain control in the face of email, instant messaging, and the Web?

The uprisings in Iran after the disputed June 2009 election are a case in point. Demonstrators organized using Facebook and Twitter. When the government shut down the Internet, they continued to organize using Twitter and IM on their cell phones. Unlike demonstrations in the past, this popular uprising had no strong central organizer. Instead, crowds of citizens who were upset about the election emerged as a movement that was held together by communications technology. The impact was so strong that, during the crisis, Twitter was asked not to delay its planned shutdown for server maintenance.

During your career, all developing countries will see unprecedented change. This change will create many opportunities for interesting jobs, careers, and new businesses, worldwide.

ACTIVE REVIEW

Use this Active Review to verify that you understand the ideas and concepts that answer the study questions in the International Dimension.

Q1 What does it mean to localize software?

Explain why information systems, and software in particular, should be a consideration during the merger and acquisition process. Summarize the work required to localize a computer program. In your own words, explain why it is better to design a program to be localized rather than attempt to adapt an existing single-language program to a second language.

Q2 What are the problems and issues of localizing and distributing databases worldwide?

Explain what is required to localize a database. Explain possible relationships of two databases. Define *replicated*

databases. Explain the conditions under which replicated databases are not a problem. Explain the conditions under which replicated databases are a problem. How do most organizations deal with this problem?

Q3 What are the consequences of global data communication?

Explain the statement, "technology users can skip generations." Illustrate this principle with an example from your own life. Describe the economic consequences of this principle on developing countries. Describe the social and political consequences of this principle. Give an example of a job, career, or business opportunity that these changes will present. Describe the role that communications technology played in the June 2009 demonstrations in Iran.

KEY TERMS AND CONCEPTS

Localizing (software)   222
Replicated databases   224

The mission of the Aviation Safety Network (ASN) is to provide up-to-date, complete, and reliable information on airliner accidents and safety issues to those with a professional interest in aviation. ASN defines an *airliner* as an aircraft capable of carrying 14 or more passengers. ASN data include information on commercial, military, and corporate airplanes.

ASN gathers data from a variety of sources, including the International Civil Aviation Board, the National Transportation Safety Board, and the Civil Aviation Authority. Data are also taken from magazines, such as *Air Safety Week* and *Aviation Week and Space Technology*; from a variety of books; and from prominent individuals in the aviation safety industry.

ASN compiles the source data into a Microsoft Access database. The core table contains over 10,000 rows of data concerning incident and accident descriptions. This table is linked to several other tables that store data about airports, airlines, aircraft types, countries, and so forth. Periodically, the Access data are reformatted and exported to a MySQL database, which is used by programs that support queries on ASN's Web site (*http://aviation-safety. net/database*).

On that site, incident and accident data can be accessed by year, by airline, by aircraft, by nation, and in other ways. For example, Figure 1 shows a list of incidents and accidents that involved the Airbus 320. When the user clicks on a particular accident, such as the one on January 15, 2009, a summary of the incident is presented, as shown in Figure 2 on the next page.

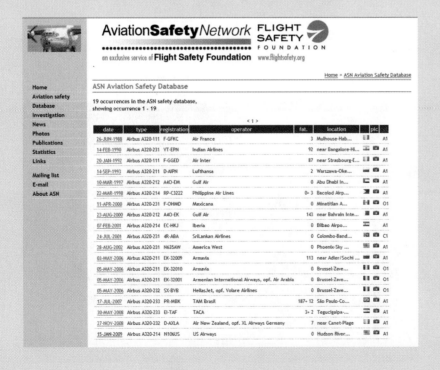

Figure 1

Incidents and Accidents Involving the Airbus 320 from the ASN Aviation Safety Database

Source: Reprinted by permission of Aviation Safety Network, © 2009 ASN. *www.aviation-safety.net.*

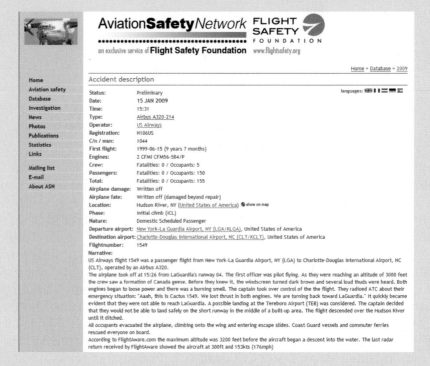

Figure 2
Incidents Description
Summary from the ASN
Aviation Safety Database

Source: Reprinted by permission
of Aviation Safety Network, © 2009 ASN.
www.aviation-safety.net.

In addition to descriptions of incidents and accidents, ASN also summarizes the data to help its users determine airliner accident trends. For example, Figure 3 shows the geographic locations of fatal accidents for 2007. Notice that there were almost no such accidents in Australia, Russia, or China. Either these countries are particularly vigilant about aircraft safety, were lucky, or not all accidents were reported.

Hugo Ranter of the Netherlands started the ASN Web site in 1995. Fabian I. Lujan of Argentina has maintained the site since 1998. ASN has nearly 10,000 email subscribers in 170 countries, and the site receives over 50,000 visits per week. For more information about this site, go to *http://aviation-saftey. net/about.*

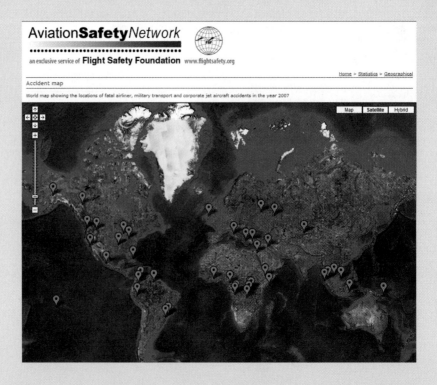

Figure 3
Fatal Accidents, Worldwide,
2007

Source: Reprinted by permission
of Aviation Safety Network, © 2009 ASN.
www.aviation-safety.net.

QUESTIONS

1. All of the data included in this database is available in public documents. Thus, what is the value of the Aviation Safety Network? Why don't users just consult the online version of the underlying references? In your answer, consider the difference between data and information.

2. What was the cause of the incident shown in Figure 2? That incident, in which no one was fatally injured, was caused by geese that stuck an Airbus 320 that was flown by US Airways out of La Guardia Airport in New York. It would be illogical to conclude from this one incident that it is dangerous to fly where there are geese or when flying Airbus 320s, US Airways, or out of La Guardia. Or, would it? Suppose that you wanted to determine whether there is a systematic pattern of flights downed by geese or with the Airbus 320, US Airways, or La Guardia. How would you proceed? How would you use the resources of *http://aviation-safety.net* to make this determination?

3. The ASN database and Web site were created and are maintained by two individuals. The database might be complete and accurate, or it might not be. To what extent should you rely on these data? What can you do to decide whether you should rely on the data at this site?

4. Consider the data in Figure 3. Describe indications you see that indicate this figure may not include all accident data. If you believe that not all data is included, what value does this figure have to you? What would be legitimate uses for this data, and what uses are likely to be erroneous?

5. Suppose you work in the marketing department for an airline. Can you use these data in your marketing efforts? If so, how? What are the dangers of basing a marketing campaign on safety?

6. Suppose you are a maintenance manager for a major airline. How can you use these data? Would it be wise to develop your own, similar database? Why or why not?

Using IS for Competitive Advantage

Majestic River Ventures (MRV)[1] provides river-rafting adventures in Oregon, Idaho, Arizona, and Alaska. The river-expedition industry is highly competitive—barriers to entry are low, and many adventure-oriented people choose river rafting as a way to make a living doing what they love.

Competitive strategies in this industry are near-perfect examples of the Porter model discussed in Chapter 3. Some companies compete on the basis of price on trips worldwide; others compete on price for certain rivers. Some companies differentiate on quality of food, type of boat, or other factor. Of the differentiation companies, some compete worldwide, and some compete on certain rivers.

Majestic River Ventures, a small company, uses a differentiation strategy within its region. Specifically, MRV's competitive strategy is to form quality relationships with quality people and to use those relationships to create repeat and word-of-mouth business.

MRV hires intelligent, experienced, interesting guides who enjoy their customers and their work. Many guides have advanced degrees in biology, history, and other topics relevant to river rafting and outdoor adventure. Although a few senior guides are part-time employees, most are independent contractors and are free to work for other rafting companies. Keeping guides satisfied is important to the successful implementation of the company's strategy.

MRV has two permanent facilities: a small office in Boise, Idaho, and an equipment warehouse in Baker, Oregon. Sue Yoholo, MRV's founder and owner, works year-round in the Boise office along with an office manager. Part-time employee guides also work in that office when planning trip logistics. All managerial and accounting functions are conducted at the Boise office.

The warehouse in Baker, Oregon, stores MRV's rafting equipment when it is not in use. Food is also stored in the warehouse for short periods of time, and during the off-season some equipment is repaired in the warehouse. The warehouse is managed by Harry Munsen, a management challenge: His knowledge of rafting logistics is superior, but work has a low priority in his life.

MRV hires independent contractors not only as guides, but also for transportation to the river's starting location, called the *put-in*, and transportation from the ending location, called the *take-out*.

Sue Yoholo grew up on an Indian reservation, attended Williams College on a reservation scholarship, and excelled as a student. During college, she was invited on a rafting trip and fell in love with the rhythm of rivers. After graduation, she managed businesses on the reservation, while working part-time as a river guide. After 10 years, she started MRV with money she had saved. She is quiet, exceedingly competent, and a quick study of her employees and customers. MRV is modestly profitable. Sue wants to take MRV to the next level, but has a few process problems to address, as you are about to learn.

---

[1]The MRV case is based on a real industry and company. However, to illustrate particular business problems, needs, and solutions, it was necessary to alter personnel and create fictitious events. For an example of an actual company that is similar to MRV, go to *www.sundogexpeditions.com*.

7

Business Process Management

"But I paid for a private tent!"

"I'm sure you did, Mr. Butterworth, but we don't have one."

"Then do something. I want what I paid for!"

"Well, what can I do? We're at the put-in. We've got 3 hours to set up the rafts, pack the gear, and get on the river. I don't have time to run back to the warehouse and pick up another tent. Besides, I doubt there's another one there."

"Don't tell me your problems. Tell me what I'm going to do!"

"Well, you can share a tent, or, as long as it isn't raining, sleep outside. I'll give you a boat cover for a ground cloth."

"But where will I change clothes? I mean, I want privacy."

"In the bushes, we do it all the time."

"Bushes? Are you joking? Aren't there snakes?"

"Sure, just be careful where you step. Hey, we could be on a river in Alaska. Up there, we have huge Alaskan brown bear, and a hungry brown bear would be a problem. Besides, it rains there all the time."

> *" In fact, MRV has a defective business process that, if not fixed, will cause similar problems in the future. "*

"I don't like this. Why don't you sleep outside and I'll take your tent."

"I often sleep outside. But this trip, Ringo, my wife, wouldn't like that."

MRV has a problem. A customer requested and paid for a private tent, but for some reason that tent was not delivered to the river and now it's too late to remedy the situation. The missing tent, however, is just a symptom. In fact, MRV has a defective business process that, if not fixed, will cause similar problems in the future. ■

>> STUDY QUESTIONS

Q1 Why is business process management important to organizations?

Q2 How do organizations solve business problems?

Q3 What role do information systems play in business processes?

Q4 What are the most common functional applications used today?

Q5 What are the problems with functional information systems?

Q6 What are the functions and characteristics of customer relationship management (CRM) information systems?

Q7 What are the functions and characteristics of enterprise resource planning (ERP) information systems?

Q8 2020?

CHAPTER PREVIEW

In this chapter, we will explore information systems within an organization. We will extend the business process discussion from Chapter 3 and work from the general to the specific. We begin with an overview of business process management, a systematic approach that modern businesses use to review and improve their business processes. Next we'll discuss the three ways of fixing business processes. Then, we'll examine the role information systems play in business processes and conclude the chapter with specific examples of information systems. We'll survey functional IS and discuss the two most important cross-functional IS: customer relationship management (CRM) and enterprise resource planning (ERP).

MRV has a process problem that has caused Mr. Butterworth to become "not a happy camper." We'll use that example to illustrate concepts in this chapter.

Q1 Why Is Business Process Management Important to Organizations?

If you are like most students, you've used computers for email or instant messaging (IM). You may be lucky enough to have an iPhone that you use for email and Web surfing. In school, you may use computer systems for word processing, or maybe you've completed Excel and Access exercises like those in the Part Review for Part 2. All of these uses are important, but they are limited to a single computer, or in the case of email and IM, two user computers (with some mysterious servers in the background). Given just that experience, you may not intuitively understand the difficulty and complexity that organizations face when they use information systems to support business processes. As you can see from the dialog in the introduction, MRV doesn't understand such complexity either.

The goal of this chapter is to enlarge the discussion of business processes that we began in Chapter 3 in order to demonstrate the role for information systems in supporting such processes and to introduce you to some of the important industry technology standards for business process management and information systems.

To gain perspective on the need for managing business processes, consider the processing of an order at a typical online retailer. Figure 7-1 shows a Web page for REI; you might find your way to this page if you were buying equipment for your own river-rafting trip. Undoubtedly you've used sites like this. You select products, put them into your shopping cart, and then proceed to checkout, where you provide a method of payment and shipping instructions.

Now, consider what has to happen at REI to process your transaction. As listed in Figure 7-2, the Web site has to be sufficiently rich to capture your intent. What items are you buying? What size? Color? Quantity? Then, how are you going to pay? Where do you want the goods to be sent? How fast do you want them delivered, and are there special terms, such as gift cards? Once you've provided that data, information systems then verify your credit, remove items from inventory, charge your credit card, cause your items to be packed and shipped, and record all of this for accounting, marketing, and service purposes. Also, information systems need to store sufficient data about this order so that REI can provide you customer support in case of a problem.

That's quite a bit of work, but there's more to it than you might imagine. For one, suppose that you do not provide all the necessary data, or that you provide inconsistent data, or that you make a keying mistake. Maybe you intend to order 10 pairs of shoes for you and your 9 best friends, but accidentally key 100. Should the Web site just accept that number? Or should the site be smart enough to realize that ordering 100 pairs of the same shoes is highly unusual and ask someone to verify your order?

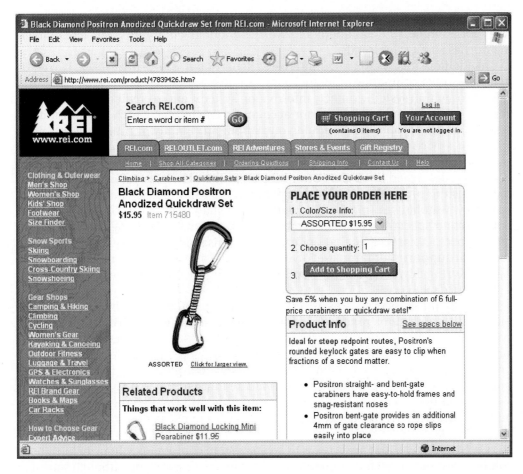

Figure 7-1
Sample E-Commerce Site

Source: Used with permission of REI & Black Diamond.

Further, what happens if the items you want are not available in inventory? Or what if only some of them are? Also, should the information system reorder to restock the inventory if the quantity left after your order falls below a certain level? In spring, the company may want to reorder summer shoes, but by fall it may not. How is all of that to be handled?

Notice that this information system crosses departmental boundaries. It involves all the primary value chain activities, as well as accounting. Each of those functions has

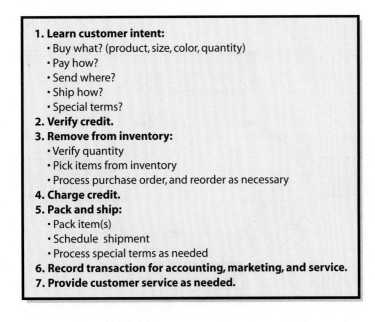

Figure 7-2
Tasks for Processing an Order

different goals and objectives. Accounting worries about complying with accounting rules, for example, whereas operations worries about inventory turnover, and marketing worries about sales trends.

In addition, this system not only crosses department boundaries at REI, it extends to include other companies. A financial institution handles the credit card operations: REI's information system contacts information systems at the credit card company to verify your credit and to charge your account. It also interacts with the information systems at the shipper to schedule your shipment. Finally, if there is a problem, customer service will need data about both REI processing and that of the credit card company and the shipper.

We've described considerable complexity, but there is another factor that redoubles the problems: *Nothing stays the same.* REI may buy another business, open new warehouses (maybe internationally), change its inventory-management policy, set up special accounts and credit cards, add more shipping choices, and so on. The business processes that underlie your transaction, and the information systems that support them, must evolve with the business. They must change while never shutting down. It's like performing heart surgery on someone who is running a 100-yard dash.

Because business processes are critical, complex, and dynamic in structure, well-managed organizations practice **business process management (BPM)**. BPM is the systematic process of creating, assessing, and altering business processes. It has four stages, as shown in Figure 7-3. The process begins by creating a model of the business process. The business users who have expertise and are involved in the particular process (this could be you!) adjust and evaluate that model. Usually teams build an **as-is model** that documents the current situation and then change that model to make adjustments necessary to solve process problems, as discussed later in this chapter in Q2.

Given the model, the next step is to create system components. In principle, those components include all five elements of every information system, although some are entirely automated (no people and procedures) and some are entirely manual (no hardware or software). The organizations involved then implement the business processes needed. We will investigate the role of IS for business processes in Q3.

Well-managed organizations don't stop there. Instead, they create policy, procedures, and committees to continually assess business process effectiveness. When a need for change arises, the company models a new, adjusted business process, and the cycle repeats. No business can avoid these activities. Every business needs business processes, and those processes will change, whether the organization wants them to or not. Thus, organizations can either plan to develop and modify business processes using BPM, or they can wait and let the need for change just happen to

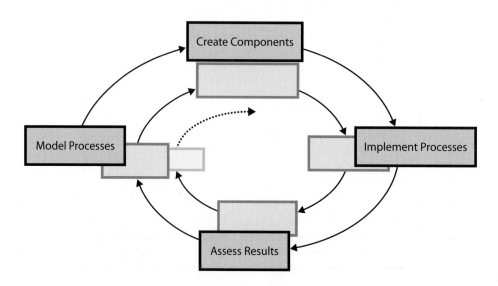

Figure 7-3
Stages of the BPM Cycle

Scope	Description	Example	BPM Role
Functional	Business process resides within a single business function.	Accounts payable	BPM authority belongs to a single departmental manager who has authority to resolve BPM issues.
Cross-functional	Business process crosses into multiple departments within a single company.	Customer relationship management (CRM); Enterprise resource management (ERP)	BPM authority shared across several or many departments. Problem resolution via committee and policy.
Interorganizational	Business process crosses into multiple companies.	Supply chain management (SCM)	BPM authority shared by multiple companies. Problem resolution via negotiation and contract.

Figure 7-4
Scope of Business Process Management

them. In the latter case, the business will continually be in crisis, dealing with one process failure after another. Majestic River Ventures is an example of such a company. As you might guess from the dialog at the beginning of the chapter, Majestic has never thought about business processes *per se*; it just let them evolve. The company has no program for assessing its business processes, and failures frequently occur. Mr. Butterworth's missing tent is one such failure.

The nature and difficulty of business process management varies with the scope of the business process. As summarized in Figure 7-4, some processes reside entirely within a single business function. Some cross departmental boundaries, and some cross organizational boundaries. Consider each.

Functional Processes

Functional processes involve activities within a single department or function. Examples are accounting, human resources, sales forecasting, and other processes that are contained in a single department. BPM is easier to accomplish with functional processes: A single department manager has authority over all of the activities and the resources assigned to them. If the department decides to change a business process, the change and attendant problems are localized within that manager's authority.

The problem with functional processes is their isolation. Functional processes lead to **islands of automation**, sometimes called **information silos**, because they work in isolation from one another. Unfortunately, independent, isolated processes cannot produce the productivity and efficiency necessary for many businesses. Purchasing influences inventory, which influences production, which influences customer satisfaction, which influences future sales. Decisions that are appropriate when considering only a single function like purchasing may create inefficiencies when the entire process is considered. We will consider these problems further in Q5.

Cross-Functional Processes

As the name implies, **cross-functional processes** involve activities among several, or even many, business departments. A classic example is customer relationship management (CRM), a process that integrates the activities of several departments, including sales, marketing, operations, accounting, and customer support. Cross-functional processes eliminate or at least drastically reduce the problems of isolated systems and data. For example, before an important sales call, salespeople can use a CRM system to learn if the customer has any outstanding issues or problems in customer support. Or, customer support can know which customers have high volume and thus justify high levels of support. Such integration is not possible with functional processes.

Process management is more difficult for cross-functional systems because no manager has authority over all of the activities and the resources assigned to them. (OK, the CEO or president has authority over all the activities, but it would be silly to tie up the CEO's time with most process management decisions. The CEO is likely to say, "That's what we pay you to do.") So, BPM for cross-functional processes is shared across several departments that most frequently need to resolve conflict via committee and policy. Q6 and Q7 address CRM and ERP, respectively; the two most common cross-functional IS.

Interorganizational Processes

Some business processes cross not only departmental boundaries, but organizational boundaries as well. The order-processing example at REI is an **interorganizational process**. It includes activities at REI of course, but it also includes activities at the company that processes your credit card transactions and activities at the shipper. Supply chain management (SCM) processes involve even greater organizational integration. In some cases, the SCM company will have information systems that directly access processes in your own company.

As you might imagine, BPM for interorganizational processes is much more difficult than for functional or cross-functional systems. Not only are different managers involved, but different owners are involved as well. Problem resolution occurs via negotiation, contracts, and (shudder) even litigation. Information systems that support interorganizational processes are discussed in Chapter 8.

By the way, do not assume that business process management applies only to commercial, profit-making organizations. Nonprofit and government organizations have all three types of processes, but most are service-oriented, rather than revenue-oriented. Your state's Department of Labor, for example, has a need to manage its processes, as does the Girl Scouts of America. BPM applies to all types of organizations.

Q2 How Do Organizations Solve Business Problems?

As stated in Chapter 2, a *problem* is a perceived difference between what is and what ought to be. Because it is a perception, different people can hold different concepts of what the problem is. Therefore, it is critical for a team to agree on both what is as well as what ought to be.

To attain that agreement, the team must be able to discuss the current and proposed processes, and to do that, they must have some notation for documenting processes. In this section, you will learn one common standard for creating process documentation. However, we will not use the example of the interorganizational process at REI; it is far too complex—we could devote this entire book to describing that business process. Instead, we will focus on the simpler, more easily understood example of Majestic River Ventures.

Need for a Business Process Notation Standard

In Chapter 3, you learned that a business process is a network of activities, resources, facilities, and data that interact to achieve a function or purpose. To recap, an activity is a task to be performed; resources are people or equipment that can be assigned to activities; and facilities are collections of resources. For example, a database is a facility that collects data (and more, as explained in Chapter 5), and a warehouse is a facility that collects inventory items. Finally, data is recorded facts and figures. Data can be simple, like the name of an employee, or structured, like a customer order document.

This definition of *business process* is commonly accepted, but unfortunately dozens of other definitions are used by other authors, industry analysts, and software products. For example, IBM, a key leader in business process management, has a product called WebSphere Business Modeler that uses a different set of terms. It has activities and resources, but it uses the term *repository* for *facility* and the term *business item* for *data*. Other business-modeling software products use other definitions and terms. These differences and inconsistencies can be problematic, especially when two different organizations with two different sets of definitions must work together.

Accordingly, a software-industry standards organization called the **Object Management Group (OMG)** created a standard set of terms and graphical notations for documenting business processes. That standard, called **Business Process Modeling Notation (BPMN)**, is documented at *www.bpmn.org*. A complete description of BPMN is beyond the scope of this text. However, the basic symbols are easy to understand, and they work naturally with our definition of business process. Hence, we will use the BPMN symbols in the illustrations in the chapter. Be aware, however, that the companies you work for may use a different set of terms and symbols. The essence of the ideas you learn here will help you, however, regardless of the tools, symbols, and terms your company uses.

Documenting the As-Is Business Processes at MRV

Figure 7-5 shows a BPMN process diagram of the top-level business process at the river-rafting company. Each of the rectangles with rounded corners represents an activity. The plus sign at the bottom of the *Assemble and Ship Equipment* activity indicates that it contains a documented subprocess (discussed next). The rectangles with the right top corner cut off represent data. The solid arrows document process flow; data often accompanies process flows, but this is not required. The thin-lined circle represents the start of the process, and the heavy-lined circle represents the end. The labels on the top of each activity are resources. The *Trip Scheduler* resource is assigned to the *Register Clients* activity, for example.

Figure 7-6 summarizes the BPMN process symbols that we will use in this text.

We can interpret Figure 7-5 as follows: The river-rafting process begins with the *Trip Scheduler* resource performing the *Register Clients* activity. That process generates *Client Roster* and *Special Requests* data. Those data items flow to a second activity called *Assemble and Ship Equipment* (with a subprocess indicated by the + in the activity symbol). *Assemble and Ship* generates the *Equipment List* and *Roster with Equipment* data as output, and so forth. Notice that the *Final Roster* data, created by *Run Trip*, skips *Restore Equipment* and is sent directly to the *Collect Final Charges* activity.

At Majestic, the first and last processes are performed by someone acting as the Trip Scheduler. The second and fourth processes are performed by someone acting as the Equipment and Logistics Manager, and the *Run Trip* process is managed by a Trip Leader.

Figure 7-5
Top-Level Business Processes for Majestic River Ventures

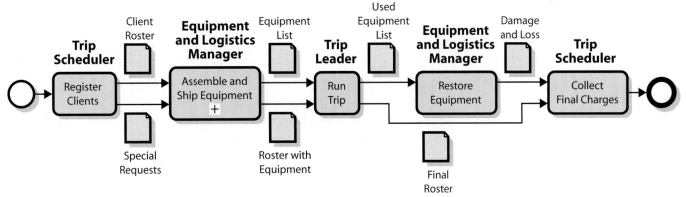

Figure 7-6
Business Process Management
Notation (BPMN Symbols)

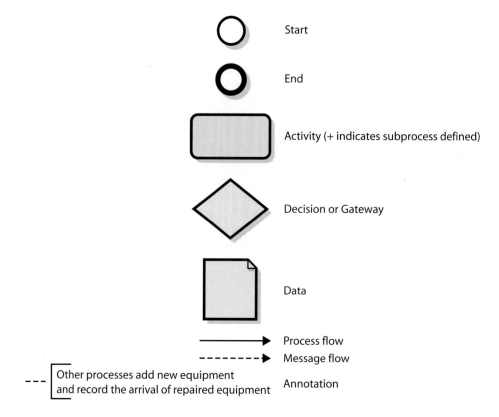

We can show these assignments by depicting the diagram in what is called a **swim-lane layout**, as illustrated in Figure 7-7. Like swim lanes in a swimming pool, each role is shown in its own horizontal rectangle. Swim-lane layout can be used to simplify process diagrams and to draw attention to interactions among components of the diagram.

Figure 7-7
Business Process with
Three Swim Lanes

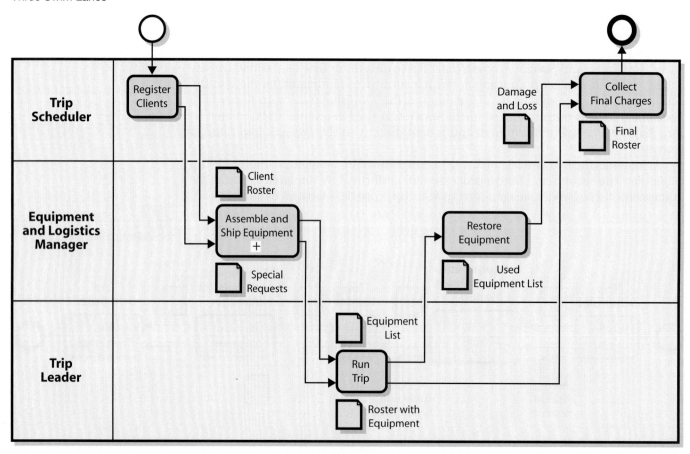

The *Assemble and Ship Equipment* Process

Figure 7-8 shows the subprocess within the *Assemble and Ship Equipment* process. Notice that the inputs to this process (*Client Roster* and *Special Requests*) and the outputs from this process (*Equipment List* and *Roster with Equipment*) are the same as the inputs and outputs for the *Assemble and Ship Equipment* activity in the higher-level diagrams in Figures 7-5 and 7-7. Also, the resources assigned are the same.

This process consists of two parallel flows. Either of the parallel flows can be done before the other, they can be done simultaneously, or some other arrangement can be used (say, do part of one and then do part of another). The diagram does not stipulate any order. The top flow concerns the picking of regular trip equipment from inventory, and the bottom one concerns the picking of special equipment. Notice that if there is a problem with regular equipment (missing an oar, for example), the trip leader is to be contacted. He or she can decide how to deal with the problem. However, if there is a problem with special requests, the trip scheduler is contacted. (He or she may contact the client; we cannot tell that from Figure 7-8, however.) As indicated in Figure 7-6, the dashed-line arrow represents the flow of messages and not of process.

The diagrams shown in Figures 7-5, 7-7, and 7-8 are examples of as-is diagrams. They represent the modelers' best representation of the current processes used by Majestic. If you examine these diagrams, especially that in Figure 7-8, you can begin to see what may have caused the missing-tent problem at the start of the chapter. The diagram indicates that if there is missing special equipment, the logistics manager is to notify the trip scheduler, but take no follow-up action. According to the diagram, the logistics manager makes the notification and then proceeds to *Ship*.

Figure 7-8
Business Process Within the *Assemble and Ship Equipment* Process

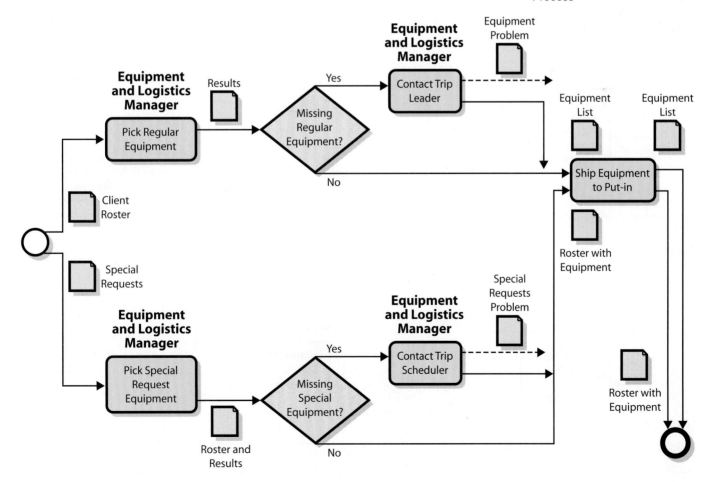

We do not know what the trip scheduler does with the notification. In fact, in this diagram, we do not even know *if* the trip scheduler received the notification. This particular pattern is sometimes called fire-and-forget. That is, the activity sends the message ("fires" it) and then forgets about it. Such a pattern is appropriate in some circumstances, but probably not in this one. You will have a chance to think about this matter in the Using Your Knowledge exercises.

Three Ways of Changing Business Processes

Process designers can increase the performance of a business process in three fundamental ways. First, they can add or remove resources to a given process without changing its structure. MRV, for example, could change personnel to the *Assemble and Ship Equipment* activity. Second, designers can change the *structure* of a process without changing resource allocations. If the change is particularly effective, it can result in greater performance at no additional cost. It does require people to change the way they do things, which can be a difficult transition to make, however. Finally, designers can do both.

Changing a Process by Adding or Removing Resources

Figure 7-9 illustrates a process change by adding resources. Here, a specialist has been added to each of the activities in the process. It is possible that one person would perform all four roles, but in that case the process is essentially unchanged from that in Figure 7-8. Assume instead that Majestic hires someone to perform each of the roles for the activities in Figure 7-9. This change will result in substantially increased cost. Is it worthwhile? According to Porter's model, one should add cost to a value chain (here, the business process) *if the change generates value greater than its cost.*

Figure 7-9
Modified Allocations in the *Assemble and Ship Equipment* Process

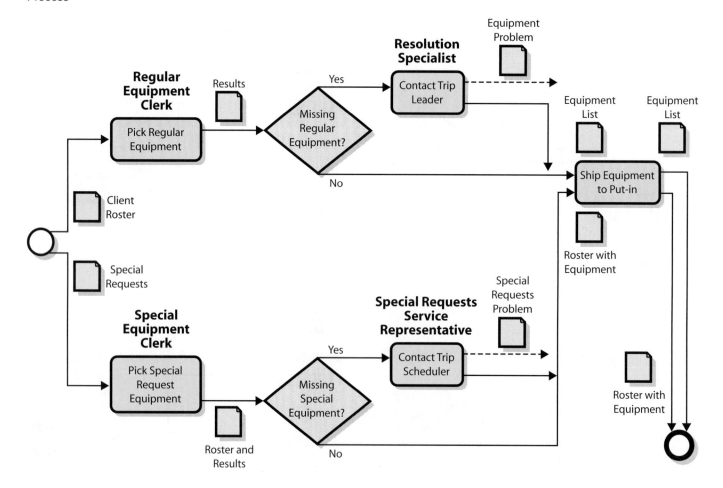

That principle is clear and sensible, but it's a bit like the investment advice to "buy low and sell high." Great, but how do you do it? Some businesses use computer simulations to assess the impact of resource-allocation changes. Other businesses perform other types of financial analysis to determine if the changes are worth the cost.

The resources that are added to a process need not necessarily be humans. Information systems can play a role as well. In Figure 7-9, the contact trip leader or contact trip scheduler activities could be automated. We will explore such possibilities further in Q3.

Changing a Process by Altering Process Structure

A second way of altering a business process is to change its structure. Suppose the equipment and logistics manager at Majestic River Ventures notices that he is wasting time repeating steps when he picks the regular equipment and then picks the special equipment. He goes to an upper floor of the warehouse, finds regular equipment, and then later goes back to that same floor to pick special equipment. Given this inefficiency, process designers could decide to alter the process, as shown in Figure 7-10. Here, the equipment and logistics manager first creates an *integrated* picking list. He organizes the list so as to minimize his travel through the warehouse. This change enables him to pick equipment more quickly and allows him more time to follow up on problem messages that he sends to trip leaders and trip schedulers. In fact, such a change could be one way to eliminate problems like the missing tent. As with resource changes, businesses can investigate the impact of process-structure changes using simulation or other types of analyses.

Also, as stated, a third alternative is a combination of adding (or reducing) resources and changing the process. In fact, the goal of some business process changes is to enable the organization to reduce resources required to obtain the same result. Changing both resources and process structure is obviously more complicated and has greater potential, but will cause the organization more turmoil, and hence will be more difficult to implement.

Figure 7-10
Modified Activities in the
Assemble and Ship Equipment
Process

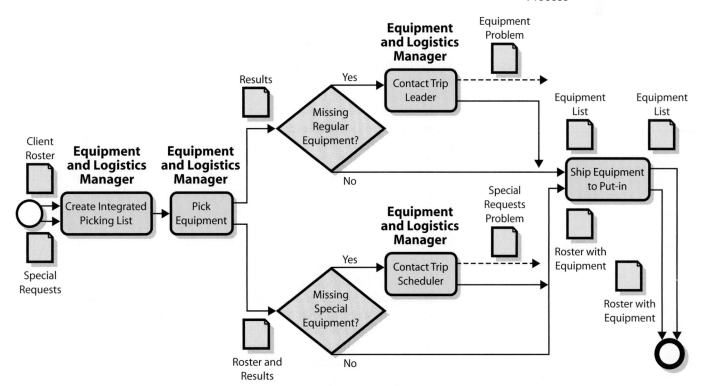

Q3 What Role Do Information Systems Play in Business Processes?

As you can tell, business processes are important to organizations, and you will devote considerable time to such processes in your operations management courses. You might be wondering why we are addressing such processes here, in your MIS class. Today, information systems are playing an increasingly important role in the implementation of business processes. Think again about the tasks that need to be performed just to sell you equipment from REI (Figure 7-2), and you will realize that most of those tasks have an IS component. Back in December 2005, Amazon.com processed over 41 order items per second for 24 hours, an impossible feat without information systems.

What role do information systems play in business processes? They implement process activities. Some of those information systems are entirely manual (they have data, procedures, and people components); some are entirely automated (they have hardware, software, and data components); and some are a mixture, having all five components of an information system—hardware, software, data, procedures, and people. Consider the following two examples.

Alternatives for Implementing the *Register Clients* Activity

Consider the first task in the raft-trip business process, *Register Clients*. It is possible to accomplish this activity entirely with human resources, with a system that is a balance of human and computer resources, or with a system that is totally computer-based. In the first case, the trip scheduler (one or more humans) collects data from clients, determines trip availability, and collects reservation deposits and payments. When it is time to assemble and ship the equipment, the trip scheduler uses a word processing program to prepare documents detailing the client roster and special requests lists.

Another alternative is to use a spreadsheet or database application to record clients and their special requests and prepare the client roster and special requests lists. For this alternative, the trip scheduler manually collects data from clients, determines trip availability, and collects reservation deposits and trip payments. Once the roster is set, the spreadsheet or database application produces the roster and special equipment outputs. Having the automated system create those outputs will save considerable labor and reduce errors.

Finally, it is possible to create an entirely automated *Register Client* system. In this case, clients contact Majestic via the Internet and use a Web site to register for a trip. They enter credit card information for deposits and trip payments on that site and record any special requests. The automated system prepares the client roster and special requests outputs.

In all three alternatives, the *Register Clients* activity is performed by an information system. However, only the last two are computer-based information systems.

Facilitating Linkages Among Activities

Information systems, and database information systems in particular, can play an important role in implementing activities that link other activities. To see why, consider the missing-tent problem. Mr. Butterworth requested and paid for a private tent. His request and payment were processed by the *Register Clients* activity. However, no such tent was available in inventory, and the equipment and logistics manager was supposed to notify the trip scheduler, who was supposed to notify the client. However, this did not happen. It turns out that the tent did exist, but it had been damaged in a prior trip and was sent out for repair. The trip scheduler did not know it was under repair and allocated it to Mr. Butterworth. Notice the linkages about equipment among the *Register Clients, Assemble and Ship Equipment,* and *Restore Equipment* activities.

One solution to this problem is to create a database application to track equipment, its location, and its status. Figure 7-11 shows a new activity, *Process Equipment Database,* which processes updates to the database from *Register Clients, Assemble and Ship Equipment,* and *Restore Equipment* activities. The trip scheduler can use this activity to reserve special equipment and be notified when such equipment is not available. Such an information system implements an activity that provides linkages among several other business process activities. In Figure 7-11, the resource named *Equipment Database Application* is assigned to the *Process Equipment Database* activity. This resource is a computer program running on a server and is entirely automated.

This example shows some of the possibilities for implementing business activities with information systems. As the price performance ratio of computers, storage, and communications continues to plummet, you can expect greater and greater use of information systems in business processes. During your career, you will also see more and more business processes redesigned to take advantage of information systems and cheaper, more powerful computer networks and communications.

Q4 What Are the Most Common Functional Applications Used Today?

As stated in Q1, functional processes are business processes that support a single organizational function. A **functional application** is a computer program that supports or possibly automates the major activities in a functional process. Few organizations develop their own functional applications. Instead, to reduce costs and risks, most license functional application software from a vendor and then adapt. Adaptation is necessary because organizations differ in the way they structure their functional processes; almost never does an off-the-shelf functional application

Figure 7-11
Top-Level Business Processes for Majestic River Ventures

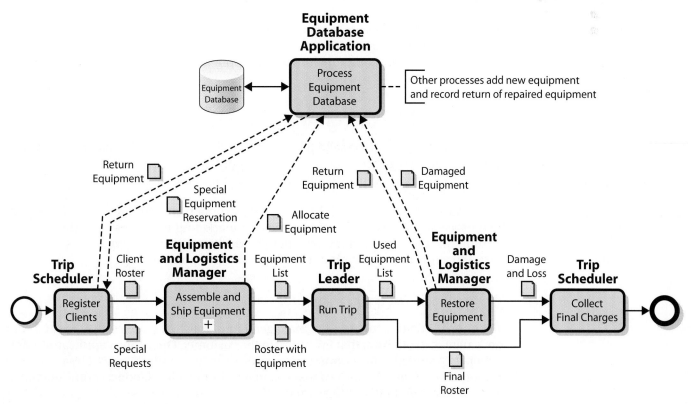

Business Processes	Common Functional Applications
Sales and Marketing	Lead generation Lead tracking Customer management Sales forecasting Product & brand management
Operations	Order entry Order management Finished-goods inventory management
Manufacturing	Inventory (raw materials, goods-in-process), finished goods Manufacturing planning (MRP) Manufacturing scheduling Operations
Customer Service	Order tracking Account tracking Customer support & training
Human Resources	Recruiting Compensation Assessment Development & training HR planning
Accounting	General ledger Financial reporting Cost accounting Accounts receivable Accounts payable Cash management Budgeting Treasury management

Figure 7-12
Common Functional
Applications

provide a perfect fit. A functional information system is an information system that includes a functional application.

Figure 7-12 lists common functional applications. We begin with sales and marketing.

Sales and Marketing Applications

The Ethics Guide on pages 250–251 discusses a company that uses its functional applications to deceive, and the interaction of the applications produces a surprising result.

The primary purpose of the sales process is to find prospects and transform them into customers by selling them something. Sales processes also *manage customers,* which is a euphemism for selling existing customers more products. Other functional sales processes forecast future sales.

In marketing, processes exist to manage products and brands. Companies use such processes to assess the effectiveness of marketing messages, advertising, and promotions and to determine product demand among various market segments. Sales and marketing applications support all of these processes.

Operations Applications

Operations activities concern the management of finished-goods inventory and the movement of goods from that inventory to the customer. **Operations applications** are especially prominent for nonmanufacturers, such as distributors, wholesalers, and retailers. For manufacturing companies, many, if not all, of the operations functions are merged into manufacturing systems.

Figure 7-12 lists the principal operations applications. **Order-entry applications** record customer purchases. Typically, an order-entry application obtains customer contact and shipping data, verifies customer credit, validates payment method, and enters the order into a queue for processing. **Order-management applications** track the order through the fulfillment process, arrange for and schedule shipping, and process exceptions (such as out-of-stock products). Order-management applications inform customers of order status and scheduled delivery dates.

Nonmanufacturing organizations operate **finished-goods inventory applications**. We will discuss inventory applications in the next section.

Manufacturing Applications

The manufacturing applications listed in Figure 7-12 are shown in more detail in Figure 7-13. **Inventory applications** support inventory control and inventory management. In terms of inventory control, inventory applications track goods and materials into, out of, and between inventories. Inventory-management applications use past data to compute stocking levels, reorder levels, and reorder quantities in accordance with inventory policy.

Today, many companies, such as Dell, view inventories as liabilities. In this view, companies seek to keep inventories as small as possible and to eliminate them completely if possible. The ultimate expression of this view is demonstrated in the **just-in-time (JIT) inventory policy**. This policy seeks to have production inputs (both raw materials and work-in-process) delivered to the manufacturing site just as they are needed. By scheduling delivery of inputs in this way, companies are able to reduce inventories to a minimum.

Manufacturing planning applications help businesses allocate inventory and equipment to manufacturing processes. In order to plan materials for manufacturing, it is first necessary to record the components of the manufactured items. A **bill of materials (BOM)** is a list of the materials that comprise a product. This list is more complicated than it might sound, because the materials that comprise a product can be subassemblies that need to be manufactured. Thus, the BOM is a list of materials, and materials within materials, and materials within materials within materials, and so forth. Figure 7-14 shows a BOM for a child's toy wagon.

In addition to the BOM, if the manufacturing application schedules equipment, people, and facilities, then a record of those resources for each manufactured product

Figure 7-13
Functions of Manufacturing Applications

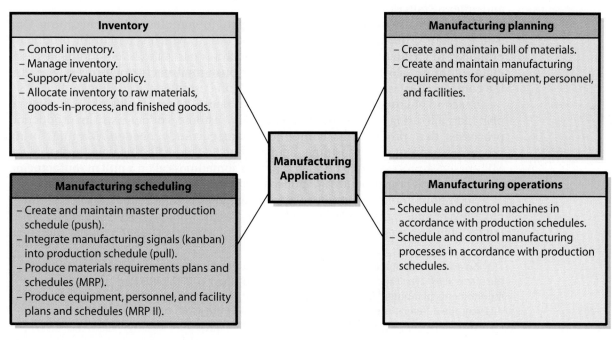

Inventory
- Control inventory.
- Manage inventory.
- Support/evaluate policy.
- Allocate inventory to raw materials, goods-in-process, and finished goods.

Manufacturing planning
- Create and maintain bill of materials.
- Create and maintain manufacturing requirements for equipment, personnel, and facilities.

Manufacturing Applications

Manufacturing scheduling
- Create and maintain master production schedule (push).
- Integrate manufacturing signals (kanban) into production schedule (pull).
- Produce materials requirements plans and schedules (MRP).
- Produce equipment, personnel, and facility plans and schedules (MRP II).

Manufacturing operations
- Schedule and control machines in accordance with production schedules.
- Schedule and control manufacturing processes in accordance with production schedules.

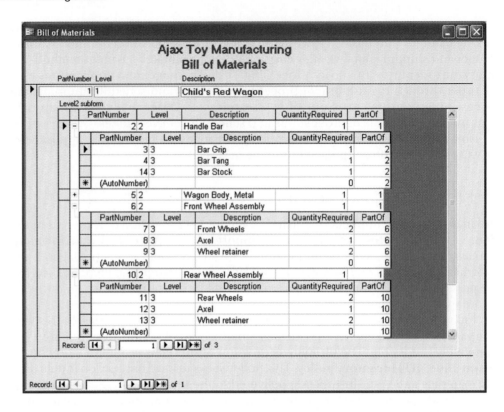

Figure 7-14
Bill of Materials Example

is required as well. The company may augment the BOM to show labor and equipment requirements, or it may create a separate nonmaterial requirements file.

Materials requirements planning (MRP) is an application that plans the need for materials and inventories of materials used in the manufacturing process. MRP does not include the planning of personnel, equipment, or facilities requirements.

Manufacturing resource planning (MRP II) (note the change in the meaning of the M and the R between MRP and MRP II) is a follow-up to MRP that includes the planning of materials, personnel, and machinery. MRP II supports many linkages across the organization, including linkages with sales and marketing via the development of a master production schedule. MRP II also includes the capability to perform what-if analyses on variances in schedules, raw materials availabilities, personnel, and other resources.[1]

Companies use two philosophies with regard to **manufacturing scheduling**. One is to generate a **master production schedule (MPS)**, which is a plan for producing products. To create the MPS, the company analyzes past sales levels and makes estimates of future sales. This process is called a **push manufacturing process**, because the company pushes the products into sales (and customers) according to the MPS.

A second philosophy is not to use a preplanned, forecasted schedule, but rather to plan manufacturing in response to signals from customers or downstream production processes that products or components are currently needed. Manufacturing processes that respond to customer demand must be more flexible than those that are MPS-based. A process based on such signals is sometimes called a **pull manufacturing process**, because the products are pulled through manufacturing by demand.

Operations applications control machinery and production processes. Computer programs operate lathes, mills, and robots, and even entire production lines. In a modern facility, these programs have linkages to manufacturing-scheduling applications.

---

[1]To add even more complication to this subject, some in the operations management field use the terms *MRP Type I* and *MRP Type II* instead of *MRP* and *MRP II. MRP Type I* refers to material requirements planning; *MRP Type II* refers to manufacturing resource planning. When used in this way, the different interpretations of the letters *MRP* are ignored, as if *MRP* were not an acronym. Unfortunately, such sets of confusing terminology cannot be avoided in a growing field.

Customer Service Applications

Customer service applications include order tracking, account tracking, and customer support and training. Customers call customer service to ask questions about order status, to query and report problems with their accounts, and to receive assistance with product use. Today, many organizations are placing as much of the customer service function on Web applications as they can. Many organizations allow customers direct access to order status and delivery information. Also, organizations are increasingly providing product-use support via user-generated content (see Chapter 8) and employee blogs.

Human Resources Applications

Human resources applications support recruitment, compensation, assessment, development and training, and planning. The first-era human resources (HR) applications did little more than compute payroll. Modern HR applications concern all dimensions of HR activity, as listed in Figure 7-12.

Depending on the size and sophistication of the company, recruiting methods may be simple or very complex. In a small company, posting a job may be a simple task requiring one or two approvals. In a larger, more formal organization, posting a new job may involve multiple levels of approval requiring use of tightly controlled and standardized procedures.

Compensation includes payroll for both salaried employees and hourly employees. It may also include pay to consultants and permanent, but nonemployee, workers, such as contractors and consultants. Compensation refers not only to pay, but also to the processing and tracking of vacation, sick leave, and health care and other benefits. Compensation activities also support retirement plans, company stock purchases, stock options and grants, and transferring employee contribution payments to organizations like the United Way and others.

Employee assessment includes the publication of standard job and skill descriptions as well as support for employee performance evaluations. Such support may include applications that allow employees to create self-evaluations and to evaluate peers and subordinates. Employee assessment is used for the basis of compensation increases as well as promotion.

Development and training activities vary widely from firm to firm. Some organizations define career paths formally, with specific jobs, skills, experience, and training requirements. HR applications have features and functions to support the publication of these paths. Some HR applications track training classes, instructors, and students.

Finally, HR applications must support planning functions. These include the creation and publication of organizational standards, job classifications, and compensation ranges for those classifications. Planning also includes determining future requirements for employees by level, experience, skill, and other factors.

Accounting Applications

Typical accounting applications are listed in Figure 7-12. You know what a general ledger is from your accounting classes. Financial reporting applications use the general ledger data to produce financial statement and other reports for management, investors, and federal reporting agencies like the Securities and Exchange Commission (SEC).

Cost-accounting applications determine the marginal cost and relative profitability of products and product families. Budgeting applications allocate and schedule revenues and expenses and compare actual financial results to the plan.

Accounts receivable includes not just recording receivables and the payments against receivables, but also account aging and collections management. Accounts payable applications include features to reconcile payments against purchases and to schedule payments according to the organization's payment policy.

Ethics

GUIDE

Dialing for Dollars

Suppose you are a salesperson, and your company's sales forecasting system predicts that your quarterly sales will be substantially under quota. You call your best customers to increase sales, but no one is willing to buy more.

Your boss says that it has been a bad quarter for all of the salespeople. It's so bad, in fact, that the vice president of sales has authorized a 20 percent discount on new orders. The only stipulation is that customers must take delivery prior to the end of the quarter so that accounting can book the order. "Start dialing for dollars," she says, "and get what you can. Be creative."

Using your customer management system, you identify your top customers and present the discount offer to them. The first customer balks at increasing her inventory, "I just don't think we can sell that much."

"Well," you respond, "how about if we agree to take back any inventory you don't sell next quarter?" (By doing this, you increase your current sales and commission, and you also help your company make its quarterly sales projections. The additional product is likely to come back next quarter, but you think, "Hey, that's then and this is now.")

"OK," she says, "but I want you to stipulate the return option on the purchase order."

You know that you cannot write that on the purchase order because accounting won't book all of the order if you do. So you tell her that you'll send her an email with that stipulation. She increases her order, and accounting books the full amount.

With another customer, you try a second strategy. Instead of offering the discount, you offer the product at full price, but agree to pay a 20-percent credit in the next quarter. That way you can book the full price now. You pitch this offer as follows: "Our marketing department analyzed past sales using our fancy new computer system, and we know that increasing advertising will cause additional sales. So, if you order more product now, next quarter we'll give you 20 percent of the order back to pay for advertising."

In truth, you doubt the customer will spend the money on advertising. Instead, they'll just take the credit and sit on a bigger inventory. That will kill your sales to them next quarter, but you'll solve that problem then.

Even with these additional orders, you're still under quota. In desperation, you decide to sell product to a fictitious company that is "owned" by your brother-in-law. You set up a new account, and when accounting calls your brother-in-law for a credit check, he cooperates with your scheme. You then sell $40,000 of product to the fictitious company and ship the product to your brother-in-law's garage. Accounting books the revenue in the quarter, and you have finally made quota. A week into the next quarter, your brother-in-law returns the merchandise.

Meanwhile, unknown to you, your company's manufacturing system is scheduling production. The program that creates the production schedule reads the sales from your activities (and those of the other salespeople) and finds a sharp increase in product demand. Accordingly, it generates a schedule that calls for substantial production increases and schedules workers for the production runs. The production system, in turn, schedules the material requirements with the inventory application, which increases raw materials purchases to meet the increased production schedule. ■

Discussion Questions

1. Is it ethical for you to write the email agreeing to take the product back? If that email comes to light later, what do you think your boss will say?

2. Is it ethical for you to offer the "advertising" discount? What effect does that discount have on your company's balance sheet?

3. Is it ethical for you to ship to the fictitious company? Is it legal?

4. Describe the impact of your activities on next quarter's inventories.

Cash management is the process of scheduling payments and receivables and planning the use of cash so as to balance the organization's cash needs against cash availability. Other cash management applications concern checking account reconciliation, as well as managing electronic funds transfer throughout the organization. Budgeting applications help plan the need and application of financial resources for some future period. Finally, treasury applications concern the management and investment of the organization's cash and payment of cash dividends.

Q5 What Are the Problems with Functional Information Systems?

Functional systems work. They enable departments to track leads, manage inventory, pay employees, and perform other departmental work. However, as stated in Q1, because they operate in isolation from one another, they create islands of automation or information silos that lead to the problems summarized in Figure 7-15.

First, with functional systems, data is duplicated because each functional application has its own database. If accounting and sales/marketing applications are separated, customer data will be duplicated and may become inconsistent. Changes to customer data made in the sales/marketing application may take days or weeks to reach the accounting application's database. During that period, shipments will reach the customer without delay, but invoices will be sent to the wrong address.

Additionally, when applications are isolated, business processes are disjointed. Suppose a business has a rule that credit orders over $20,000 must be preapproved by

Figure 7-15
Major Problems Created by Isolated Functions System

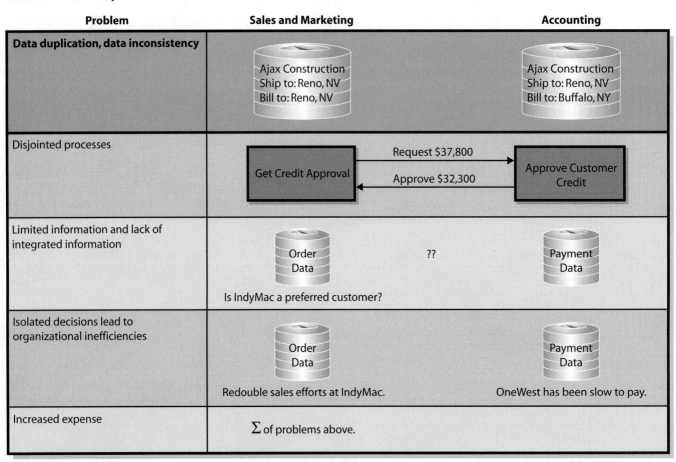

the Accounts Receivable department. From this rule, we can infer that somewhere there is a sales process with an activity called *Get Credit Approval* that needs to interface with an activity called *Approve Customer Credit* in some accounts receivable process. If the supporting applications are separated, it will be difficult for the two activities to reconcile their data and the approval will be slow-to-grant and possibly erroneous.

In the second row of Figure 7-15, Sales and Marketing wants to approve a $20,000 order with Ajax. According to the company's database, Ajax has a current balance of $17,800, so Sales requests a total credit amount of $37,800. The accounting database, however, shows Ajax with a balance of $12,300, because the accounts receivable application has credited Ajax for a return of $5,500. According to Accounting's records, only $32,300 is needed in order to approve the $20,000 order, so that is all they grant. Sales and Marketing doesn't understand what to do with a credit approval of $32,300. Was only $14,700 of the order approved? And why that amount? Both departments want to approve the order. It will take numerous emails and phone calls, however, to sort this out. The interacting business processes are disjointed.

A consequence of such disjointed systems is the lack of integrated enterprise information. For example, suppose Sales and Marketing wants to know if IndyMac is still a preferred customer. Suppose that determining whether this is so requires a comparison of order history and payment history data. However, with isolated functional processes that data will reside in two different databases and, in one of them, IndyMac is known by its new name, OneWest Bank. Data integration will be difficult. Making the determination will require manual processes and days, when it should be readily answered in seconds.

This leads to the fourth consequence of isolated systems: inefficiency. When using isolated functional applications, decisions are made in isolation. As shown in the fourth row of Figure 7-15, Sales and Marketing decided to redouble its sales effort with IndyMac. However, accounting may know that OneWest (its name for IndyMac) has been slow to pay and that there are better prospects for increased sales attention. Without integration, the left hand of the organization doesn't know what the right hand of the organization is doing. Other examples are of sales selling a product that manufacturing can no longer produce, or of customer support giving $1,000 worth of support to a customer whose lifetime sales were $50.

Finally, isolated functional systems can result in increased cost for the organization. Duplicated data, disjointed systems, limited information, and inefficiencies all mean higher costs.

These problems are solved by cross-functional processes, and we consider two of them in the next two questions.

Q6 What Are the Functions and Characteristics of Customer Relationship Management (CRM) Information Systems?

A **customer relationship management (CRM)** is a cross-functional application that tracks all interactions with the customer from prospect through follow-up service and support. Vendors of CRM applications claim that using their products makes the organization *customer-centric.* Though that term reeks of sales hyperbole, it does indicate the nature and intent of CRM systems. Figure 7-16 shows the scope of CRM in the context of the value chain of the bike manufacturer (Figure 3-6, page 69). **CRM applications** integrate all of the primary business activities.

Figure 7-17 shows four phases of the **customer life cycle**: marketing, customer acquisition, relationship management, and loss/churn. Marketing sends messages to the target market to attract customer prospects. When prospects order, they become

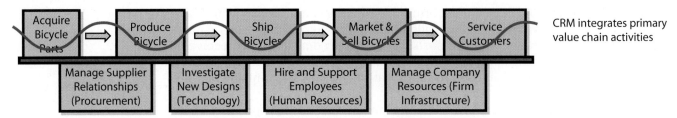

Figure 7-16
Scope of CRM in Value Chain
Activities

customers who need to be supported. Additionally, resell processes increase the value of existing customers. Inevitably, over time the organization loses customers. When this occurs, win-back processes categorize customers according to value and attempt to win back high-value customers.

Figure 7-18 illustrates the major components of a CRM application. Notice that there are components for each stage of the customer life cycle. Some CRM features and functions support solicitation processes, some support lead-tracking processing, and others support relationship management or postsale processes. Examples of these features and functions are shown in Figure 7-18.

CRM applications store data in a single database, as shown in Figure 7-19. Because all customer data reside in one location, CRM processes can be linked to one another. For example, customer-service activities can be linked to customer-purchase records. In this way, both sales and marketing know the status of customer satisfaction, both on an individual customer basis for future sales calls and also collectively for analyzing customers' overall satisfaction. Also, many customer-support applications prioritize customers in order to avoid the problem of giving $1,000 worth of support to a customer with a lifetime value of $50. Finally, customer support has an important linkage to product marketing and development; it knows more than any other group what customers are doing with the product and what problems they are having with it.

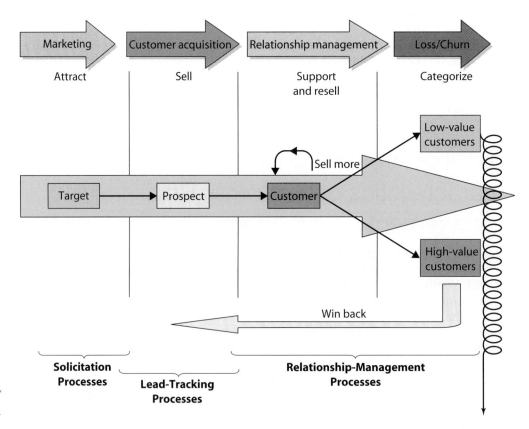

Figure 7-17
The Customer Life Cycle

Source: *The Customer Life Cycle*. Used with permission from Professor Douglas Maclachlan, University of Washington Business School, University of Washington, Seattle, Washington.

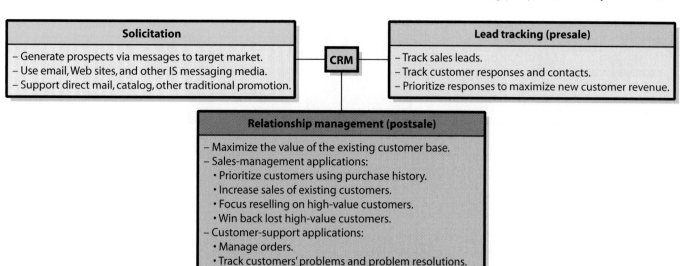

Figure 7-18
CRM Components

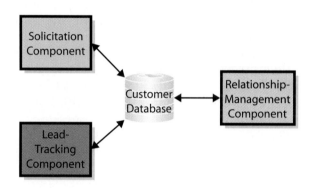

Figure 7-19
CRM Centered on Integrated Customer Database

Q7 What Are the Functions and Characteristics of Enterprise Resource Planning (ERP) Information Systems?

Enterprise resource planning (ERP) applications provide even more integration than CRM. As Figure 7-20 shows, ERP integrates the primary value chain activities with human resources and accounting. ERP systems are truly enterprise-wide. They track customers, process orders, manage inventory, pay employees, and provide general ledger, payable, receivables, and other necessary accounting functions. Thus far, ERP represents the ultimate in cross-functional systems.

The primary ERP users are manufacturing companies. The first and most successful vendor of ERP software is **SAP** (from SAP AG Corp.). According to the company, in the United States in 2008 more than 12 million people used SAP in over 91,000 SAP installations. Worldwide, SAP has over 47,000 different customers. Oracle is a second major ERP vendor. These vendors provide not only software, but also predesigned databases, predefined procedures, and job descriptions for organization-wide process integration.

Before continuing, be aware that some vendors misapply the term *ERP* to their systems. It is a hot topic, and there is no truth-in-ERP-advertising group to ensure that all of the vendors that claim ERP capability have anything remotely close to it. Let the buyer beware.

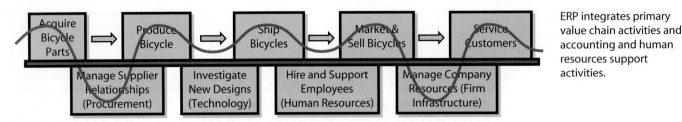

ERP integrates primary value chain activities and accounting and human resources support activities.

Figure 7-20
Scope of ERP in Value Chain Activities

ERP Characteristics

Of the major ERP characteristics listed in Figure 7-21, the first is that ERP takes a cross-functional, process view of the entire organization. With ERP, the entire organization is considered a collection of interrelated activities and cross-functional processes.

Second, true ERP is a formal approach that is based on documented, tested business models. ERP applications include a comprehensive set of inherent processes for all organizational activities. SAP defines this set as the **process blueprint** and documents each process with diagrams that use a set of SAP-standardized symbols. The process diagram in Figure 7-22 is a SAP process diagram.

As stated, ERP applications are based on formally defined procedures, and organizations must adapt their processing to the ERP blueprint. If they do not, the system cannot operate effectively, or even correctly. In some cases, it is possible to adapt ERP software to procedures that are different from the blueprint, but such adaptation is expensive and often problematic.

With ERP systems, organizational data are processed in a centralized database. Such centralization makes it easy for authorized users to obtain needed information from a single source.

Once an organization has implemented an ERP system, it can achieve large benefits. However, as shown in Figure 7-22, the process of moving from separated, functional applications to an ERP system is difficult, fraught with challenge, and can be slow. In particular, changing organizational procedures has proved to be a great

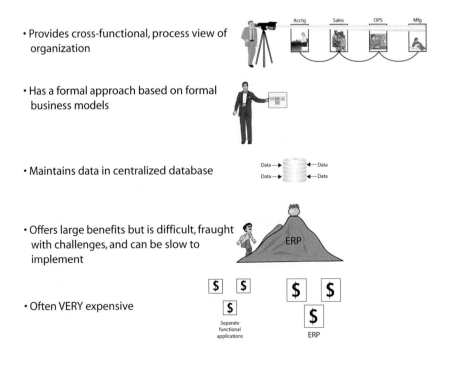

- Provides cross-functional, process view of organization

- Has a formal approach based on formal business models

- Maintains data in centralized database

- Offers large benefits but is difficult, fraught with challenges, and can be slow to implement

- Often VERY expensive

Figure 7-21
Characteristics of ERP

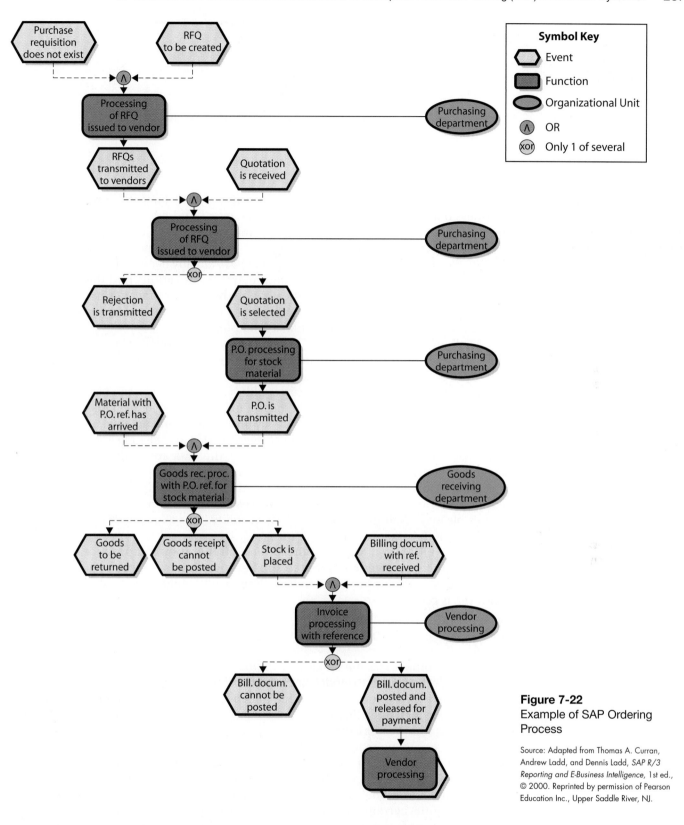

Figure 7-22
Example of SAP Ordering
Process

Source: Adapted from Thomas A. Curran,
Andrew Ladd, and Dennis Ladd, *SAP R/3
Reporting and E-Business Intelligence,* 1st ed.,
© 2000. Reprinted by permission of Pearson
Education Inc., Upper Saddle River, NJ.

challenge for many organizations, and in some cases was even a pitfall that prevented successful ERP implementation. Finally, the switch to an ERP system is very costly—not only because of the need for new hardware and software, but also due to the costs of developing new procedures, training employees, converting data, and other developmental expenses.

- Successful business processes
- Inventory reduction
- Lead-time reduction
- Improved customer service
- Greater, real-time insight into organization
- Higher profitability

Figure 7-23
Potential Benefits of ERP

Benefits of ERP

Despite the clear benefits of inherent processes and ERP, there can be an unintended consequence. See the Guide on pages 264–265 and consider that risk.

Figure 7-23 summarizes the potential benefits of ERP. First, the processes in the business blueprint have been tried and tested over hundreds of organizations. These built-in procedures, which are called **inherent processes**, are effective and often very efficient. Organizations that convert to ERP do not need to reinvent business processes. Rather, they gain the benefit of processes that have already been proved successful.

By taking an organization-wide view, many organizations find they can reduce their inventories, sometimes dramatically. With better planning, it is not necessary to maintain large buffer stocks. Additionally, items remain in inventory for shorter periods of time, sometimes no longer than a few hours or a day.

Another advantage is that ERP helps organizations reduce lead times. Because of the more efficient processes and better information, organizations can respond more quickly to process new orders or changes in existing orders. This means they can deliver goods to customers faster. In some cases, ERP-based companies can receive payments on orders shipped before they pay for the raw materials used in the parts on the order.

As discussed earlier, data inconsistency problems are not an issue because all ERP data are stored in an integrated database. Further, because all data about a customer, order, part, or other entity reside in one place, the data are readily accessible. This means that organizations can provide better information about orders, products, and customer status to their customers. All of this results not only in better, but also less costly, customer service. Integrated databases also make company-wide data readily accessible and result in greater, real-time visibility, thus allowing timely insights into the status of the organization.

Finally, ERP-based organizations often find that they can produce and sell the same products at lower costs due to smaller inventories, reduced lead times, and cheaper customer support. The bottom-line result is higher profitability. The trick, however, is getting there.

How Is an ERP System Implemented?

Figure 7-24 summarizes the major tasks in the implementation of an ERP application. Like BPM, the first task is to model the current business processes. Managers and analysts then compare these processes to the ERP blueprint processes and note the differences. The company then must find ways to eliminate the differences, either by changing the existing business process to match the ERP process or by altering the ERP system.

To appreciate the magnitude of these tasks, consider that the SAP blueprint contains over a thousand process models. Organizations that are adopting ERP must review those models and determine which ones are appropriate to them. Then, they compare the ERP models to the models developed based on their current practices. Inevitably, some current-practice models are incomplete, vague, or inaccurate, so the team must repeat the existing process models. In some cases, it is impossible to reconcile any existing system against the blueprint model. If so, the team must adapt, cope, and define new procedures, often to the confusion of current employees.

Once the differences between as-is processes and the blueprint have been reconciled, the next step is to implement the system. Before implementation starts, however, users must be trained on the new processes, procedures, and use of the ERP system's features and function. Additionally, the company needs to conduct a simulation test of the new system to identify problems. Then, the organization must convert its data,

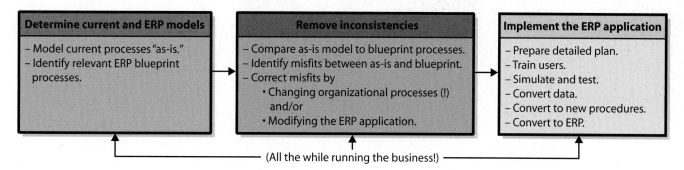

Determine current and ERP models	Remove inconsistencies	Implement the ERP application

– Model current processes "as-is."
– Identify relevant ERP blueprint processes.
	– Compare as-is model to blueprint processes.
	– Identify misfits between as-is and blueprint.
	– Correct misfits by
	  • Changing organizational processes (!) and/or
	  • Modifying the ERP application.
		– Prepare detailed plan.
		– Train users.
		– Simulate and test.
		– Convert data.
		– Convert to new procedures.
		– Convert to ERP.

(All the while running the business!)

Figure 7-24
ERP Implementation

procedures, and personnel to the new ERP system. All of this happens while the business continues to run on the old system.

As you'll learn in Chapter 10, plunging the organization into the new system is an invitation to disaster. Instead, a thorough and well-planned test of the new system is necessary, followed by a careful rollout of the new system in stages. Realize, too, that while the new ERP system is being installed normal business activity continues. Somehow the employees of the organization must continue to run the company while the rollout is underway. It is a difficult and challenging time for any organization that undergoes this process.

Implementing an ERP system is not for the faint of heart. Because so much organizational change is required, all ERP projects must have the full support of the CEO and executive staff. Like all cross-functional processes, ERP crosses departmental boundaries, and no single departmental manager has the authority to force an ERP implementation. Instead, full support for the task must come from the top of the organization. Even with such support there is bound to be concern and second-guessing.

Q8 2020?

The problem with functional systems is that they exist in isolation. Organizations have seen great benefits by moving to integrated applications such as CRM and ERP. However, moving to those applications has been fraught with difficulty, as just described.

To ease the creation of integrated systems, information systems developers studied best-of-practice techniques and from these developed a design philosophy known as *service-oriented architecture (SOA)*. SOA was originally used to design interacting computer programs. More recently, systems designers have applied SOA principles to business process activities, whether those activities are manual, partly automated, or fully automated.

SOA offers great flexibility, ease of use, and adaptability, and we can expect that it will see even greater use by 2020. In fact, by that time, it is likely that all new systems and business processes will be developed using SOA principles. So, what are those principles?

To begin, **service-oriented architecture (SOA)** is a design philosophy in which every activity is modeled as an encapsulated service and exchanges among those services are governed by standards. This definition has three key terms: *service, encapsulation,* and *standards.* Consider each.

First, a **service** is a repeatable task that a business needs to perform. At Majestic, the following are examples of services:

- Check space available on a river trip.
- Enroll client on a river trip.
- Bill client's credit card.

To understand the importance of services, consider the process in Figure 7-25, in which the activities in the circles are job titles, not services, and the result is a mess. To begin, the client requests a private tent and the trip scheduler attempts to compute how many tents there are, how many are needed, and how many are in repair. Given that computation, the trip scheduler responds "Yes" or "No."

Consider some of the problems of this process. First, because the circles are people and not services, we must guess what the trip scheduler is trying to do. Also, if it

SOA represents the latest thinking in business process design, although some professionals treat is as a fad, like the one in the Guide on pages 262–263.

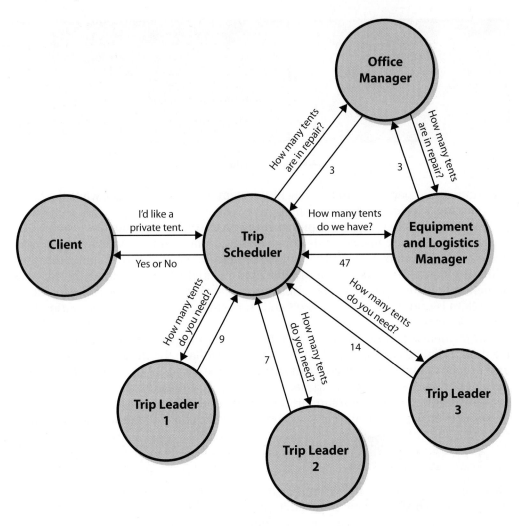

Figure 7-25
Non-SOA Business Process

turns out that Majestic wants to add more resources to answer tent-availability questions, how would it do so? Add another set of symbols for a second trip scheduler? That would be awkward, at best.

Additionally, data about the tent requirements is spread all over the company. In fact, the trip scheduler doesn't know where some of the data is located. He asks the office manager how many tents are out for repair, and the office manager, in turn, asks the equipment and logistics manager. This process is inefficient and error-prone. The design has many other problems as well. What happens when Majestic hires more trip leaders? Or what if one of the trip leaders wants to know if she can borrow a tent for personal use for the weekend? Majestic allows employees to borrow certain equipment, but only if it is not needed. That trip leader will have to duplicate this process to find out if a tent is available.

If Majestic decides to create an information system for this process, what does that information system do? It certainly does not replace any of the blue circles. In fact, to proceed, the designers of the information system must interpret this diagram to infer that there is some computation going on and somehow develop an information system to make that computation. Behind the scenes, or in the creases of this diagram, there is an inventory-management service. But that service is inferred, not modeled. Furthermore, what happens if Majestic changes inventory policy? Suppose it decides to lease tents when necessary. Such a change will have an impact in many places in this diagram and an impact on any information system developed in an attempt to support this process.

Contrast the impact of a change in policy on the SOA business process shown in Figure 7-11 (page 245). Here, each activity (green rectangles with rounded corners) is a service, not a person. If Majestic decides to lease equipment, all that is needed is to add a new *Lease Equipment* service. That activity would use the *Process Equipment Database*

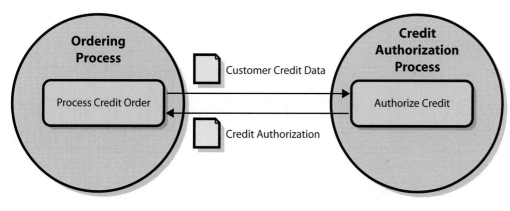

Figure 7-26
Example of Two Independent,
Encapsulated Services

service to indicate the availability of leased equipment. No other service is affected. Also, if a trip leader wants to know if he or she can borrow a tent for the weekend, he or she can get the availability data directly from the *Process Equipment Database* service.

So, now you understand the first key term of the definition of SOA: All activities must be modeled as services (repeatable business tasks).

Now consider *encapsulation,* the second key term in the SOA definition. Figure 7-26 shows the interactions of two services. The *Process Credit Order* service is part of a business process called *Ordering Process. Authorize Credit* is a second service that is part of a different business process called *Credit Authorization Process.* Using SOA principles, each service will be designed to be independent; neither will be aware of how the other does its work and neither will need to know. Instead, these services need only to agree on how they will exchange data and what that exchange means.

Process Credit Order sends customer credit data to the *Authorize Credit* service. It receives back a credit authorization that contains an approval or rejection and other data. The *Credit Authorization Process* could involve flipping a coin, throwing darts, or performing some sophisticated data mining analysis on the customer's data. *Process Credit Order* does not know, nor does it need to know, how that authorization is made.

When the logic for some service is isolated in this way, the logic is said to be **encapsulated** in the service. **Encapsulation** places the logic in one place, which is exceedingly desirable. For one, all other services know to go to that one place for that service. Even more important, if the managers of the credit department decide to change how they make credit authorizations the *Process Credit Order* activity is not affected. As long as the structure and meaning of customer credit data and credit authorization data do not change, *Process Credit Order* is completely isolated from changes in *Authorize Credit* or any other service in the *Credit Authorization Process.*

Because of encapsulation, service implementations can be readily adapted to new requirements, technology, or methodology. In fact, it does not matter who performs the services or where they are performed. Credit authorization could be done by a single company department on a single computer. Later, it could be changed to be performed by a different company, on different computers, in another part of the world. As long as the interface between *Process Credit Order* and *Authorize Credit* does not change, *Authorize Credit* is free to change its implementation.

The third key term in the SOA definition is *standards.* Data, and more generically, messages, are exchanged among services using standardized formats and techniques. In the past, the programmers of the *Process Credit Order* program would meet with the programmers of the *Authorize Credit* program and design a unique, proprietary means for exchanging data via this interface. Such a design is expensive and time-consuming. Consequently, the computer industry developed standard ways for formatting messages, for describing services and standard protocols for managing the exchanges among services. Those standards eliminated the need for proprietary designs and expanded the scope and importance of SOA.

We will not consider the nature of the particular standards in this text. If you wish to learn more, search for the terms *SOA standards, XML, WSDL,* and *REST* on the Web. For now, just understand that by 2020 most organizations and software vendors will design their processes and applications using SOA.

The Flavor-of-the-Month Club

"Oh, come on. I've been here 30 years and I've heard it all. All these management programs. . . . Years ago, we had Zero Defects. Then it was Total Quality Management, and after that, Six Sigma. We've had all the pet theories from every consultant in the Western Hemisphere. No, wait, we had consultants from Asia, too.

"Do you know what flavor we're having now? We're redesigning ourselves to be 'customer-centric.' We are going to integrate our functional systems into a CRM system to transform the entire company to be 'customer-centric.'

"You know how these programs go? First, we have a pronouncement at a 'kick-off meeting' where the CEO tells us what the new flavor is going to be and why it's so important. Then a swarm of consultants and 'change management' experts tell us how they're going to 'empower' us. Then HR adds some new item to our annual review, such as, 'Measures taken to achieve customer-centric company.'

"So, we all figure out some lame thing to do so that we have something to put in that category of our annual review. Then we forget about it because we know the next new flavor of the month will be along soon. Or worse, if they actually force us to use the new system, we comply, but viciously. You know, go out of our way to show that the new system can't work, that it really screws things up.

"You think I sound bitter, but I've seen this so many times before. The consultants and rising stars in our company get together and dream up

one of these programs. Then they present it to the senior managers. That's when they make their first mistake: They think that if they can sell it to management, then it must be a good idea. They treat senior management like the customer. They should have to sell the idea to those of us who actually sell, support, or make things. Senior management is just the banker; the managers should let us decide if it's a good idea.

"If someone really wanted to empower me, she would listen rather than talk. Those of us who do the work have hundreds of ideas of how to do it better. Now it's customer-centric? As if we haven't been trying to do that for years!

"Anyway, after the CEO issues the pronouncements about the new system, he gets busy with other things and forgets about it for a while. Six months might go by, and then we're either told we're not doing enough to become customer-centric (or whatever the flavor is) or the company announces another new flavor.

"In manufacturing they talk about push versus pull. You know, with push style, you make things and push them onto the sales force and the customers. With pull style, you let the customers' demand pull the product out of manufacturing. You build when you have holes in inventory. Well, they should adapt those ideas to what they call 'change management.' I mean, does anybody need to manage real change? Did somebody have a 'Use the cell phone program'? Did some CEO announce, 'This year, we're all going to use the cell phone'? Did the HR department put a line into our annual evaluation form that asked how many times we'd used a cell phone? No, no, no, and no. Customers pulled the cell phone through. We wanted it, so we bought and used cell phones. Same with color printers, Palm Pilots, and wireless networks.

"That's pull. You get a group of workers to form a network, and you get things going among the people who do the work. Then you build on that to obtain true organizational change. Why don't they figure it out?

"Anyway, I've got to run. We've got the kick-off meeting of our new initiative—something called business process management. Now they're going to empower me to manage my own activities, I suppose. Like, after 30 years, I don't know how to do that. Oh, well, I plan to retire soon.

"Oh, wait. Here, take my T-shirt from the knowledge management program 2 years ago. I never wore it. It says, 'Empowering You through Knowledge Management.' That one didn't last long." ■

Discussion Questions

1. Clearly, this person is bitter about new programs and new ideas. What do you think might have been the cause of her antagonism? What seems to be her principal concern?

2. What does she mean by "vicious" compliance? Give an example of an experience you've had that exemplifies such compliance.

3. Consider her point that the proponents of new programs treat senior managers as the customer. What does she mean? To a consultant, is senior management the customer? What do you think she's trying to say?

4. What does she mean when she says, "If someone wants to empower me, she would listen rather than talk"? How does listening to someone empower that person?

5. Her examples of "pull change" all involve the use of new products. To what extent do you think pull works for new management programs?

6. How do you think management could introduce new programs in a way that would cause them to be pulled through the organization? Consider the suggestion she makes, as well as your own ideas.

7. If you managed an employee who had an attitude like this, what could you do to make her more positive about organizational change and new programs and initiatives?

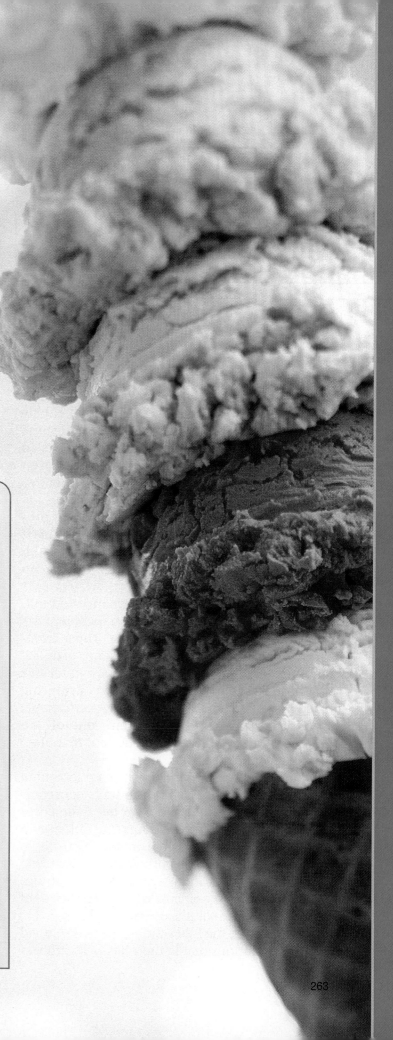

ERP and the Standard, Standard Blueprint

Designing business processes is difficult, time-consuming, and very expensive. Highly trained experts conduct seemingly countless interviews with users and domain experts to determine business requirements. Then, even more experts join those people, and together this team invests thousands of labor hours to design, develop, and implement effective business processes that meet those requirements. All of this is a very high-risk activity, prone to failure. And it all must be done before IS development can even begin.

ERP vendors such as SAP have invested millions of labor hours into the business blueprints that underlie their ERP solutions. Those blueprints consist of hundreds or thousands of different business processes. Examples are processes for hiring employees, processes for acquiring fixed assets, processes for acquiring consumable goods, and processes for custom "one-off" (a unique product with a unique design) manufacturing, to name just a few.

Additionally, ERP vendors have implemented their business processes in hundreds of organizations. In so doing, they have been forced to customize their standard blueprint for use in particular industries. For example, SAP has a distribution-business blueprint that is customized for the auto parts industry, for the electronics industry, and for the aircraft industry. Hundreds of other customized solutions exist as well.

Even better, the ERP vendors have developed software solutions that fit their business-process blueprints. In theory, no software development is required at all if the organization can adapt to the standard blueprint of the ERP vendor.

As described in this chapter, when an organization implements an ERP solution, it first determines any differences that exist between its business processes and the standard blueprint. Then, the organization must remove that difference, which can be done in one of two ways: It changes business processes to fit the standard blueprint. Or, the ERP vendor or a consultant modifies the standard blueprint (and software solution that matches that blueprint) to fit the unique requirements.

In practice, such variations from the standard blueprint are rare. They are difficult and expensive to implement, and they require the using organization to maintain the variations from the standard as new versions of the ERP software are developed. Consequently, most organizations choose to *modify their processes* to meet the blueprint, rather than the other way around. Although such process changes are also difficult to implement, once the organization has converted to the standard blueprint, they need no longer support a "variation."

So, from a standpoint of cost, effort, risk, and avoidance of future problems, there is a huge incentive for organizations to adapt to the standard ERP blueprint.

Initially, SAP was the only true ERP vendor, but other companies have developed and acquired ERP solutions as well. Because of competitive

pressure across the software industry, all of these products are beginning to have the same sets of features and functions. ERP solutions are becoming a commodity.

All of this is fine as far as it goes, but it introduces a nagging question: If, over time, every organization tends to implement the standard ERP blueprint, and if, over time, every software company develops essentially the same ERP features and functions, then won't every business, worldwide, come to look just like every other business, worldwide? How will organizations gain a competitive advantage if they all use the same business processes?

If every auto parts distributor uses the same business processes, based on the same software, are they not all clones of one another? How will one distinguish itself? How will innovation occur? Even if one parts distributor does successfully innovate a business process that gives it a competitive advantage, will the ERP vendors be conduits to transfer that innovation to competitors? Does the use of "commoditized" standard blueprints mean that no company can sustain a competitive advantage? ■

Discussion Questions

1. Explain in your own words why an organization might choose to change its processes to fit the standard blueprint. What advantages accrue by doing so?

2. Explain how competitive pressure among software vendors will cause the ERP solutions to become commodities. What does this mean to the ERP software industry?

3. If two businesses use exactly the same processes and exactly the same software, can they be different in any way at all? Explain why or why not.

4. Explain the following statement: An ERP software vendor can be a conduit to transfer innovation. What are the consequences to the innovating company? To the software company? To the industry? To the economy?

5. In theory, such standardization might be possible, but worldwide, there are so many different business models, cultures, people, values, and competitive pressures, can any two businesses ever be exactly alike?

ACTIVE REVIEW

Use this Active Review to verify that you understand the ideas and concepts that answer the chapter's study questions.

Q1 Why is business process management important to organizations?

Explain why the fact that nothing stays the same gives rise to the need for business process management. Define *BPM*, and name and briefly describe each of the four stages. State how BPM varies in scope. Compare and contrast functional, cross-functional, and interorganizational processes. Summarize the differences and challenges of BPM for each level of business process.

Q2 How do organizations solve business problems?

Define *problem* and explain how that definition relates to the need to document processes. Define *business process,* and name the four components of a business process, according to this chapter. Describe the need for a standard. Define *BPMN.* Explain the meaning of each of the symbols in Figure 7-5. Explain the purpose and role of each of the symbols in Figure 7-6. Define swim-lane layout and explain its advantages in your own words. Explain the meaning of each of the symbols in Figure 7-8, and describe the relationship of this process diagram to that in Figure 7-5. Explain why the fire-and-forget pattern applies to Figure 7-8. Name and illustrate three ways organizations can solve process problems.

Q3 What role do information systems play in business processes?

Explain why business processes are part of an MIS class. Describe the role that information systems play with regard to business processes. Using the five-component model, describe three different types of information system that are used in business processes. Use an example other than trip scheduling. Which of the three types is probably the most common at Majestic River Ventures? Explain how the process in Figure 7-11 facilitates process–activity linkages.

Q4 What are the most common functional applications used today?

Define the terms *functional application* and *functional information system.* Name the five categories of functional application discussed in this chapter. Examine Figure 7-12 and describe the purpose of each of the applications listed.

Q5 What are the problems with functional information systems?

Explain why functional IS cause each of the following five problems: data duplication, disjointed processes, limited information, isolated decisions, and increased expense. Give an example of each.

Q6 What are the functions and characteristics of customer relationship management (CRM) information systems?

What are the functions and characteristics of customer relationship management (CRM) applications? Define *CRM.* Using the Porter value chain model, describe the scope of a CRM application. Describe how a CRM can make an organization customer-centric. Describe each of the four phases in Figure 7-16, and explain how they relate to CRM features and functions. Explain the advantages of having a single CRM database.

Q7 What are the functions and characteristics of enterprise resource planning (ERP) information systems?

Define *ERP.* Using the Porter value chain model, describe the scope of an ERP application. Compare the scope of CRM to that for ERP. Who is SAP? Summarize the characteristics of an ERP application. Define *process blueprint* and *inherent processes.* Summarize the challenges of moving from separated functional applications to ERP. Summarize the benefits of ERP. Describe the process of implementing an ERP solution and explain why it may be difficult and expensive.

Q8 2020?

Define *service-oriented architecture* and state its three key terms. Define *service,* and give three examples not used in this chapter. Describe the problems with a process like that in Figure 7-25, and explain why it does not follow SOA principles. Explain why the process in Figure 7-11 would be easier to change than that in Figure 7-25 if Majestic decides to lease equipment. Define *encapsulation* and explain how that term pertains to Figure 7-26. Describe the advantages of encapsulation. Explain how SOA employs standards. How does SOA relate to 2020?

KEY TERMS AND CONCEPTS

USING YOUR KNOWLEDGE

1. In your own words, explain the characteristic of the business process in Figure 7-8 that most likely caused the missing-tent problem. Describe, in general terms, how you think Majestic's business processes should be changed to prevent such problems.
2. Modify the process shown in Figure 7-8 to conform to the process in Figure 7-11. You will need to cause the *Assemble and Ship Equipment* process to access the *Process Equipment Database* service. You can download PowerPoint diagrams of the processes in this chapter from the book's Web site at *www.pearsonhighered. com/kroenke*.
3. Using your own experience and knowledge, create a process diagram for the *Register Clients* process shown in Figure 7-11. Your process diagram should show the next level of details of *Register Clients* in the same way that the process in Figure 7-8 shows the next level of details of *Assemble and Ship Equipment*.
4. Using your answers to questions 2 and 3, modify the process in Figure 7-8 to work with *Register Clients* so that problems like the missing tent are either not

possible or at least very unlikely. You will have to replace the fire-and-forget interaction in Figure 7-8 with some other type of interaction.
5. Describe potential management challenges when implementing the changes you propose in your answer to question 4. How would you, as a future manager, respond to those challenges?
6. When Neil at FlexTime was asked why he didn't consider an open source program for managing customer interactions, he responded, "Two reasons: One, I didn't want to base our business on software created by a bunch of amateurs. Second, the only programs I could find had too many information silos."

   a. Respond to his comment about amateurs. Do you agree or disagree with him? How would you respond to this comment?
   b. What does he mean by the term *information silo*? Give three examples of processes at FlexTime that would be separate. Explain how information systems could create silos from those processes.

COLLABORATION EXERCISE

Collaborate with a group of students on the following exercise. Recall from Chapter 2 that collaboration is more than cooperation because it involves iteration and feedback. Post a document, a discussion item, a wiki item, or an idea and obtain feedback from your team members. Similarly, read the ideas of others and comment on them. Try to innovate in both the process by which you collaborate and the work product that you create. Avoid face-to-face meetings. Instead, use collaborative software such as Google Docs & Spreadsheets, Microsoft Groove, or Microsoft SharePoint to facilitate your ideas.

The planning office of a particular county government issues building permits, septic system permits, and county road access permits for all building projects in a county in an eastern state. The planning office issues permits to homeowners and builders for the construction of new homes and buildings and for any remodeling projects that involve electrical, gas, plumbing, and other utilities, as well as the conversion of unoccupied spaces such as garages into living or working space. The office also issues permits for new or upgraded septic systems and permits to provide driveway entrances to county roads.

Figure 7-27 shows the permit process that the county used for many years. Contractors and homeowners found this process to be slow and very frustrating. For one, they did not like its sequential nature. Only after a permit had been approved or rejected by engineering review process would they find out that a health or highway review was also needed. Because each of these reviews could take 3 or 4 weeks, applicants requesting permits wanted the review processes to be concurrent rather than serial. Also, both the permit applicants and county personnel were frustrated because they never knew where a particular application was in the permit process. A contractor would call to ask how much longer, and it might take an hour or more just to find which desk the permits were on.

Accordingly, the county changed the permit process to that shown in Figure 7-28. In this second process, the permit

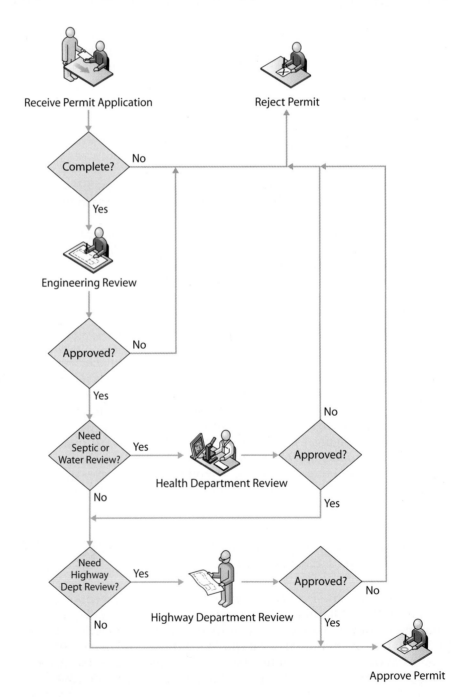

Figure 7-27
Building Permit Process,
Old Version

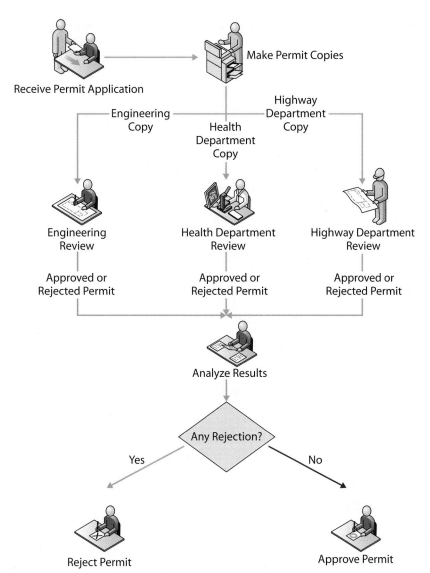

Figure 7-28
Building Permit Process,
Revised Version

office made three copies of the permit and distributed one to each department. The departments reviewed the permits in parallel; a clerk would analyze the results and, if there were no rejections, approve the permit.

Unfortunately, this process had a number of problems, too. For one, some of the permit applications were lengthy; some included as many as 40 to 50 pages of large architectural drawings. The labor and copy expense to the county was considerable.

Second, in some cases departments reviewed documents unnecessarily. If, for example, the highway department rejected an application, then neither the engineering nor health departments needed to continue their reviews. At first, the county responded to this problem by having the clerk who analyzed results cancel the reviews of other departments when he or she received a rejection. However, that policy was exceedingly unpopular with the permit applicants, because once an application was rejected and the problem corrected, the permit had to go back through the other departments. The permit would go to the end of

the line and work its way back into the departments from which it had been pulled. Sometimes this resulted in a delay of 5 or 6 weeks.

Canceling reviews was unpopular with the departments as well, because permit-review work had to be repeated. An application might have been nearly completed when it was cancelled due to a rejection in another department. When the application came through again, the partial work results from the earlier review were lost.

1. Redraw Figure 7-27 so that all activities are services. Use the standard BPMN symbols.
2. Explain the problems in the business process in Figure 7-27.
3. Redraw Figure 7-28 so that all activities are services. Use the standard BPMN symbols.
4. Explain the problems in the business process in Figure 7-28.
5. Develop a process that solves the problems you identified in your answers to questions 2 and 4. Consider the

use of information systems and information technology. Possible technologies to use are email, FTP, and Microsoft SharePoint, but you need not restrict your thinking to these technologies. Document your solution using BPMN symbols; ensure that each activity is a service.

APPLICATION EXERCISES

1. Suppose your manager asks you to create a spreadsheet to compute a production schedule. Your schedule should stipulate a production quantity for seven products that is based on sales projections made by three regional managers at your company's three sales regions.

   a. Create a separate worksheet for each sales region. Use the data in the Word file **Ch07Ex01**, which you can download from the text's Web site. This file contains each manager's monthly sales projections for the past year, actual sales results for those same months, and projections for sales for each month in the coming quarter.

   b. Create a separate worksheet for each manager's data. Import the data from Word into Excel.

   c. On each of the worksheets, use the data from the prior four quarters to compute the discrepancy between the actual sales and the sale projections. This discrepancy can be computed in several ways: You could calculate an overall average, or you could calculate an average per quarter or per month. You could also weight recent discrepancies more heavily than earlier ones. Choose a method that you think is most appropriate. Explain why you chose the method you did.

   d. Modify your worksheets to use the discrepancy factors to compute an adjusted forecast for the coming quarter. Thus, each of your spreadsheets will show the raw forecast and the adjusted forecast for each month in the coming quarter.

   e. Create a fourth worksheet that totals sales projections for all of the regions. Show both the unadjusted forecast and the adjusted forecast for each region and for the company overall. Show month and quarter totals.

   f. Create a bar graph showing total monthly production. Display the unadjusted and adjusted forecasts using different colored bars.

2. Figure 7-14, the sample bill of materials, is a form produced using Microsoft Access. Producing such a form is a bit tricky, so this exercise will guide you through the steps required. You can then apply what you learn to produce a similar report. You can also use Access to experiment on extensions of this form.

   a. Create a table named *PART* with columns *Part Number, Level, Description, QuantityRequired,* and *PartOf. Description* and *Level* should be text, *PartNumber* should be AutoNumber, and *Quantity Required* and *PartOf* should be numeric, long integer. Add the *PART* data shown in Figure 7-14 to your table.

   b. Create a query that has all columns of *PART*. Restrict the view to rows having a value of 1 for *Level*. Name your query *Level1*.

   c. Create two more queries that are restricted to rows having values of 2 or 3 for *Level*. Name your queries *Level2* and *Level3*, respectively.

   d. Create a form that contains *PartNumber, Level,* and *Description* from *Level1*. You can use a wizard for this if you want. Name the form *Bill of Materials*.

   e. Using the subform tool in the Toolbox, create a subform in your form in part d. Set the data on this form to be all of the columns of *Level2*. After you have created the subform, ensure that the Link Child Fields property is set to *PartOf* and that the Link Master Fields property is set to *PartNumber*. Close the *Bill of Materials* form.

   f. Open the subform created in part e and create a subform on it. Set the data on this subform to be all of the columns of *Level3*. After you have created the subform, ensure that the Link Child Fields property is set to *PartOf* and that the Link Master Fields property is set to *PartNumber*. Close the *Bill of Materials* form.

   g. Open the *Bill of Materials* form. It should appear as in Figure 7-14. Open and close the form and add new data. Using this form, add sample BOM data for a product of your own choosing.

   h. Following the process similar to that just described, create a *Bill of Materials Report* that lists the data for all of your products.

   i. (**Optional, challenging extension**) Each part in the BOM in Figure 7-14 can be used in at most one assembly (there is space to show just one *PartOf* value). You can change your design to allow a part to be used in more than one assembly as follows: First, remove *PartOf* from PART. Next, create a second table that has two columns: *AssemblyPartNumber* and *ComponentPart Number*. The first contains a part number of an assembly and the second a part number of a component. Every component of a part will have a row in this table. Extend the views described above to use this second table and to produce a display similar to Figure 7-14.

CASE STUDY 7

Process Cast in Stone

Bill Gates and Microsoft were exceedingly generous in the allocation of stock options to Microsoft employees, especially during Microsoft's first 20 years. Because of that generosity, Microsoft created 4 billionaires and an estimated 12,000 millionaires as Microsoft succeeded and the value of employee stock options soared. Not all of those millionaires stayed in the Seattle/Redmond/Bellevue, Washington, area, but thousands did. These thousands of millionaires were joined by a lesser number who made their millions at Amazon.com and, to a lesser extent, at RealNetworks, Visio (acquired by Microsoft), and Aldus (acquired by Adobe). Today, some Google employees who work at Google's Seattle office are joining these ranks.

The influx of this wealth has had a strong impact on Seattle and the surrounding communities. One result has been the creation of a thriving industry in high-end, very expensive homes. These Microsoft and other millionaires are college educated; many were exposed to fine arts at the university. They created homes that are not just large and situated on exceedingly valuable property, but that also are appointed with the highest-quality components.

Today, if you drive through a small area just south of central Seattle, you will find a half dozen vendors of premium granite, marble, limestone, soapstone, quartzite, and other types of stone slabs within a few blocks of each other. These materials cover counters, bathrooms, and other surfaces in the new and remodeled homes of this millionaire class. The stone is quarried in Brazil, India, Italy, Turkey, and other countries and either cut at its origin or sent to Italy for cutting. Huge cut slabs, 6 feet by 10 feet, arrive at the stone vendors in south Seattle, who stock them in their warehouses. The stone slabs vary not only in material, but also in color, veining pattern, and overall beauty. Choosing these slabs is like selecting fine art. (Visit *www.pentalonline.com* or *www.metamarble.com* to understand the premium quality of these vendors and products.)

Typically, the client (homeowner) hires an architect who either draws plans for the kitchen, bath, or other stone area as part of the overall house design or who hires a specialized kitchen architect who draws those plans. Most of these clients also hire interior decorators who help them select colors, fabrics, furniture, art, and other home furnishings. Because selecting a stone slab is like selecting art, clients usually visit the stone vendors' warehouses personally. They walk through the warehouses, often accompanied by their interior designer, and maybe also their kitchen architect, carrying little boxes into which stone vendor employees place chips of slabs in which the client expresses interest.

Usually, the team selects several stone slabs for consideration, and those are set aside for that client. The name of the client or the decorator is written in indelible ink on the side of the stone to reserve it. When the client or design team makes a final selection, the name is crossed out on the stone slabs they do not purchase. The purchased slabs are set aside for shipping.

During the construction process, the contractor will have selected a stone fabricator, who will cut the stone slab to fit the client's counters. The fabricator will also treat the stone's edges, possibly repolish the stone, and cut holes for sinks and faucets. Fabricators move the slabs from the stone vendor to their workshops, prepare the slab, and eventually install it in the client's home.

Questions

1. Identify the activities that are performed in the process of selecting and installing stone countertops. Ensure that each activity is a service.
2. Identify the resources that apply to these activities.
3. Identify the data that flows among activities.
4. Model the stone selection process using BPMN notation. Use PowerPoint to create your model and construct it in swim-lane format.
5. Suppose that you work for a stone vendor and you realize that there are many slabs of stone that are reserved that ought not to be. (The clients have selected other slabs.) Identify possible causes for this situation and suggest a process remedy.
6. Suppose that you work for a stone vendor and have just learned that seven slabs of rare and expensive stone were installed that the client did not purchase. The slabs that were installed had been selected as a possibility by the client, but the client had intended to purchase a different set of stone slabs. Identify possible causes for this situation. Explain why the interorganizational scope of this process will make problem-resolution difficult. Suggest changes to the process that would prevent this error from occurring again.
7. Explain how a knowledge of business process management could help you become a stone slab client rather than a stone chipper.

8

E-Commerce and Web 2.0

"This is lame, Mr. Butterworth. It really is."

"Look, kid, since we're sharing this tent, let's not be formal. Call me Franklin. What's so bad?"

"There's no girls on this trip. It's so boring."

Butterworth (to himself): "How will I survive 3 days of this?"

"Kid, what's your name?"

"Graham."

"Nice name. Did I hear you're in college?"

"Right."

"How old are you?"

"15."

"Wow. Well, first, since you're in college, you ought to say 'women': 'There's no women on this trip.'"

"Women, girls, whatever, there aren't any."

"What about that woman with Crosby?"

"You mean Ringo? Oh, come on, she's ancient. I mean girls … women … my age."

"Why'd you come?"

"It's a PE credit. Because of my age, they can't put me into basketball or regular

> Is there a way to use computer systems
> or the Internet to create better groups?

sports. I thought it would be better than bowling. Can you believe they give credit for bowling? I don't like putting my fingers in those creepy holes."

"I'm with you there. What are you doing now?"

"What? Oh, playing *Grand Theft Auto*."

"You got earplugs or something? I can hear the game over here."

"I *am* using my earplugs."

"I'm going out to look around. Don't play after 10, OK?"

"You sound like my parents."

Butterworth (to himself): "Three days of this? What a mistake!"

Graham and Butterworth are not realizing their hopes and expectations for their river trip. Of course, longer term, they don't have the problem, Majestic does. MRV differentiates itself on the basis of quality, and creating trips with people having similar perspectives and interests can be an important part of trip quality. Is there a way to use computer systems or the Internet to create better groups? Yes, as you will learn in this chapter. ∎

>> STUDY QUESTIONS

Q1 How do companies use e-commerce?

Q2 What technology is needed for e-commerce?

Q3 How can information systems enhance supply chain performance?

Q4 Why is Web 2.0 important to business?

Q5 How can organizations benefit from social networking?

Q6 How can organizations benefit from Twitter?

Q7 What are the benefits and risks of user-generated content (UGC)?

Q8 2020?

CHAPTER PREVIEW

Chapter 7 surveyed information systems within organizations. This chapter builds on that discussion and describes information systems across and among organizations. Such interorganizational information systems have increased in importance in recent years because of the increased availability of computer networks—the Internet, as well as private and proprietary networks.

This chapter has two major themes: e-commerce and Web 2.0. We begin by discussing how companies use e-commerce and then we survey important e-commerce technologies. We'll conclude that theme by discussing the role of e-commerce in supply chain management. Next, we'll survey Web 2.0, discuss what it means, and describe the capabilities it provides. Then we'll discuss how businesses use social networking, including groups and applications. Twitter has entered e-commerce in a big way, and we'll discuss three primary uses for it in e-commerce. After that, we'll investigate user-generated content and discuss some of the risks it presents. We'll wrap up by pondering how Web 2.0 will impact business and management by 2020.

Q1 How Do Companies Use E-Commerce?

E-commerce is the buying and selling of goods and services over public and private computer networks. Notice that this definition restricts e-commerce to buying and selling transactions. Checking the weather at *http://yahoo.com* is not e-commerce, but buying a weather-service subscription that is paid for and delivered over the Internet is.

Figure 8-1 lists categories of e-commerce companies. The U.S. Census Bureau, which publishes statistics on e-commerce activity, defines **merchant companies** as those that take title to the goods they sell. They buy goods and resell them. It defines **nonmerchant companies** as those that arrange for the purchase and sale of goods without ever owning or taking title to those goods. Regarding services, merchant companies sell services that they provide; nonmerchant companies sell services provided by others. We will consider merchants and nonmerchants separately in the following sections.

E-Commerce Merchant Companies

The three main types of merchant companies are those that sell directly to consumers, those that sell to companies, and those that sell to government. Each uses slightly different information systems in the course of doing business. **B2C**, or **business-to-consumer e-commerce** concerns sales between a supplier and a retail customer (the consumer). A typical information system for B2C provides a Web-based application or **Web storefront** by which customers enter and manage their orders. Amazon.com, REI.com, and LLBean.com are examples of companies that use B2C information systems.[1]

The term **B2B**, or **business-to-business e-commerce** or refers to sales between companies. As Figure 8-2 shows, raw materials suppliers use B2B systems to sell to

Merchant companies	Nonmerchant companies
– Business-to-consumer (B2C) – Business-to-business (B2B) – Business-to-government (B2G)	– Auctions – Clearinghouses – Exchanges

Figure 8-1
E-Commerce Categories

---

[1]Strictly speaking, B2C is not commerce between two organizations. However, because it is commerce between two independently owned entities (the retailer and the consumer), we include it in this chapter.

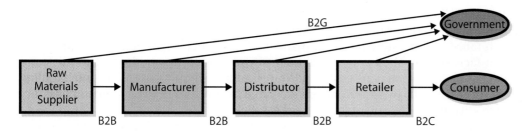

Figure 8-2
Example Use of B2B, B2G, and B2C

manufacturers, manufacturers use B2B systems to sell to distributors, and distributors uses B2B systems to sell to retailers.

B2G, or **business-to-government e-commerce** refers to sales between companies and governmental organizations. In Figure 8-2, the manufacturer that uses an e-commerce site to sell computer hardware to the U.S. Department of State is engaging in B2G commerce. Suppliers, distributors, and retailers sell to the government as well.

B2C applications first captured the attention of mail-order and related businesses. However, companies in all sectors of the economy soon realized the enormous potential of B2B and B2G. The number of companies engaged in B2B and B2G commerce now far exceeds those engaging in B2C commerce.

Furthermore, today's B2B and B2G applications implement just a small portion of their potential capability. Their full utilization is some years away. Although most experts agree that these applications will involve SOA systems that integrate supplier CRM systems with customer purchasing systems, the nature of that integration is being developed. Consequently, you can expect further progress and development in B2B and B2G applications during your career.

Nonmerchant E-Commerce

The most common nonmerchant e-commerce companies are auctions and clearinghouses. E-commerce **auctions** match buyers and sellers by using an e-commerce version of a standard auction. This e-commerce application enables the auction company to offer goods for sale and to support a competitive-bidding process. The best-known auction company is eBay, but many other auction companies exist; many serve particular industries.

Clearinghouses provide goods and services at a stated price and arrange for the delivery of the goods, but they never take title. One division of Amazon.com, for example, operates as a nonmerchant clearinghouse and sells books owned by others. As a clearinghouse, Amazon.com matches the seller and the buyer and then takes payment from the buyer and transfers the payment to the seller, minus a commission. eBay operates in the same manner.

Another type of clearinghouse is an **electronic exchange** that matches buyers and sellers; the business process is similar to that of a stock exchange. Sellers offer goods at a given price through the electronic exchange, and buyers make offers to purchase over the same exchange. Price matches result in transactions from which the exchange takes a commission. Priceline.com is an example of an exchange used by consumers.

How Does E-Commerce Improve Market Efficiency?

The debate continues among business observers as to whether e-commerce is something new or if it is just a technology extension to existing business practice. During the dot-com heyday of 1999–2000, some claimed that e-commerce was ushering in a new era and a "new economy." Although experts differ as to whether a "new economy" was created, all agree that e-commerce does lead to greater market efficiency.

For one, e-commerce leads to **disintermediation**, which is the elimination of middle layers of distributors and suppliers. You can buy a flat-screen LCD HDTV from a typical "bricks-and-mortar" electronics store, or you can use e-commerce to buy it from the manufacturer. If you take the latter route, you eliminate the distributor, the retailer, and possibly more companies. The product is shipped directly from the manufacturer's finished goods inventory to you. You eliminate the distributor's and retailer's inventory carrying costs, and you eliminate shipping overhead and handling activity. Because the distributor and associated inventories have become unnecessary waste, disintermediation increases market efficiency.

E-commerce also improves the flow of price information. As a consumer, you can go to any number of Web sites that offer product price comparisons. You can search for the HDTV you want and sort the results by price and vendor reputation. You can find vendors that avoid your state sales tax or that omit or reduce shipping charges. The improved distribution of information about price and terms enables you to pay the lowest possible cost and serves ultimately to remove inefficient vendors. The market as a whole becomes more efficient.

From the seller's side, e-commerce produces information about **price elasticity** that has not been available before. Price elasticity measures the amount that demand rises or falls with changes in price. Using an auction, a company can learn not just what the top price for an item is, but also the second, third, and other prices from the losing bids. In this way, the company can determine the shape of the price elasticity curve.

Similarly, e-commerce companies can learn price elasticity directly from experiments on customers. For example, in one experiment, Amazon.com created three groups of similar books. It raised the price of one group 10 percent, lowered the price of the second group 10 percent, and left the price of the third group unchanged. Customers provided feedback to these changes by deciding whether to buy books at the offered prices. Amazon.com measured the total revenue (quantity times price) of each group and took the action (raise, lower, or maintain prices) on all books that maximized revenue. Amazon.com repeated the process until it reached the point at which the indicated action was to maintain current prices.

Managing prices by direct interaction with the customer yields better information than managing prices by watching competitors' pricing. By experimenting with customers, companies learn how customers have internalized competitors' pricing, advertising, and messaging. It might be that customers do not know about a competitor's lower prices, in which case there is no need for a price reduction. Or, it may be that the competitor is using a price that, if lowered, would increase demand sufficiently to increase total revenue. Figure 8-3 summarizes the ways e-commerce generates market efficiencies.

What Economic Factors Disfavor E-Commerce?

Although there are tremendous advantages and opportunities for many organizations to engage in e-commerce, the economics of some industries may disfavor e-commerce activity. Companies need to consider the following economic factors:

- Channel conflict
- Price conflict
- Logistics expense
- Customer-service expense

Figure 8-3
E-Commerce Market
Efficiencies

Market Efficiencies
– Disintermediation
– Increased information on price and terms
– Knowledge of price elasticity
• Losing-bidder auction prices
• Price experimentation
• More accurate information obtained directly from customer

Consider the example of the manufacturer selling directly to a government agency shown in Figure 8-2. Before engaging in such e-commerce, the manufacturer must consider the unfavorable economic factors just listed. First, what **channel conflict** will develop? Suppose the manufacturer is a computer maker that is selling directly, B2G, to the State Department. When the manufacturer begins to sell goods B2G that State Department employees used to purchase from a retailer down the street, that retailer will resent the competition and might drop the manufacturer. If the value of the lost sales is greater than the value of the B2G sales, e-commerce is not a good solution, at least not on that basis.

Furthermore, when a business engages in e-commerce it may also cause **price conflict** with its traditional channels. Because of disintermediation, the manufacturer may be able to offer a lower price and still make a profit. However, as soon as the manufacturer offers the lower price, existing channels will object. Even if the manufacturer and the retailer are not competing for the same customers, the retailer still will not want a lower price to be readily known via the Web.

Also, the existing distribution and retailing partners do provide value; they are not just a cost. Without them, the manufacturer will have the increased *logistics expense* of entering and processing orders in small quantities. If the expense of processing a 1-unit order is the same as that for processing a 12-unit order (which it might be), the average logistics expense per item will be much higher for goods sold via e-commerce.

Similarly, *customer-service* expenses are likely to increase for manufacturers that use e-commerce to sell directly to consumers. The manufacturer will be required to provide service to less sophisticated users and on a one-by-one basis. For example, instead of explaining to a single sales professional that the recent shipment of 100 Gizmo 3.0s requires a new bracket, the manufacturer will need to explain that 100 times to less knowledgeable, frustrated customers. Such service requires more training and more expense.

All four economic factors are important for organizations to consider when they contemplate e-commerce sales.

Q2 What Technology Is Needed for E-Commerce?

In Chapter 7, we considered what happens from a business process standpoint when you buy something over the Internet. Here, let's consider the same problem, but this time from the perspective of the technology that is involved in the process of filling your order.

Consider that same REI Web page that you saw in Figure 7-1. You use that page to navigate to the product(s) that you want to buy. When you find something you want, you add it to your shopping cart and keep shopping. At some point you check out by supplying credit card data.

Now, this time consider the technology that is necessary to support the underlying business process. Or, from another perspective, if you want to set up a Web storefront for your company, what facilities do you need?

Three-Tier Architecture

Almost all e-commerce applications use the **three-tier architecture** shown in Figure 8-4. The tiers refer to three different classes of computers. The **user tier** consists of computers that have browsers that request and process Web pages. The **server tier** consists of computers that run Web servers and process application programs. The **database tier** consists of computers that run a DBMS that processes SQL requests to retrieve and store data. Figure 8-4 shows only one computer at the database tier. Some sites have multicomputer database tiers as well.

Three-Tier Architecture

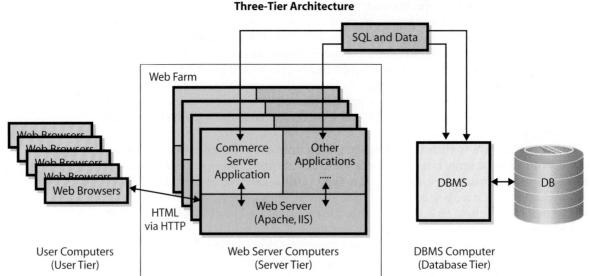

Figure 8-4
Three-Tier Architecture

Communication between the user and server computers is governed by a protocol called **Hypertext Transfer Protocol (HTTP)**. This protocol is a set of rules for transferring documents and data over the Internet. (For more on the HTTP protocol, see the Appendix to Chapter 6, starting on page 202.) A **Web page** is a document, coded in one of the standard page markup languages, that is transmitted using HTTP. The most popular page markup language is the *Hypertext Markup Language (HTML)*, which is described later in this section.

Web servers are programs that run on a server tier computer and that manage HTTP traffic by sending and receiving Web pages to and from clients. A **browser** is a computer program on the client computer that processes Web pages. When you type *http://ibm.com*, your browser issues a request via HTTP for the Web server at the domain name *ibm.com* to send you its default Web page. The two most popular Web server programs are Apache, commonly used on Linux, and IIS (Internet Information Server), a component of Windows Server, Windows Vista, and Windows 7. Common browsers are Microsoft's Internet Explorer and Mozilla's Firefox.

A **commerce server** is an application program that runs on a server tier computer. A commerce server receives requests from users via the Web server, takes some action, and returns a response to the users via the Web server. Typical commerce server functions are to obtain product data from a database, manage the items in a shopping cart, and coordinate the checkout process. In Figure 8-4, the server tier computers are running a Web server program, a commerce server application, and other applications having an unspecified purpose.

To ensure acceptable performance, commercial Web sites usually are supported by several or even many Web server computers in a facility called a **Web farm**. Work is distributed among the computers in a Web farm so as to minimize customer delays. The coordination among multiple Web server computers is a fantastic dance, but, alas, we do not have space to tell that story here. Just imagine the coordination that must occur as you add items to an online order when, to improve performance, different Web server computers receive and process each addition to your order.

Watch the Three Tiers in Action!

To see a three-tier example in action, go to your favorite Web storefront site, place something in a shopping cart, and consider Figure 8-4 as you do so. As stated earlier, when you enter an address into your browser, the browser sends a request for the default page to a server computer at that address. A Web server and possibly a commerce server process your request and send back the default page.

As you click Web pages to find products you want, the commerce server accesses the database to retrieve data about those products. It creates pages according to your selections and sends the results back to your browser via the Web server. Again, different computers on the server tier may process your series of requests and must constantly communicate about your activities. You can follow this process in Figure 8-4.

In Figure 8-5(a), the user has navigated through climbing equipment at REI.com to find a particular item. To produce this page, the commerce server accessed a database to obtain the product picture, price, special terms (a 5 percent discount for buying six or more), product information, and related products.

The user placed six items in her basket, and you can see the response in Figure 8-5(b). Again, trace the action in Figure 8-4 and imagine what occurred to produce the second page. Notice that the discount was applied correctly.

When the customer checks out, the commerce server program will be called to process payment, schedule inventory processing, and arrange for shipping. Most likely the commerce server interfaces with CRM applications for processing the order. Truly this is an amazing capability!

Hypertext Markup Language (HTML)

Hypertext Markup Language (HTML) is the most common language for defining the structure and layout of Web pages. An HTML **tag** is a notation used to define a data element for display or other purposes. The following HTML is a typical heading tag:

```
<h2>Price of Item</h2>
```

Notice that tags are enclosed in < > (called *angle brackets*) and that they occur in pairs. The start of this tag is indicated by <h2>, and the end of the tag is indicated

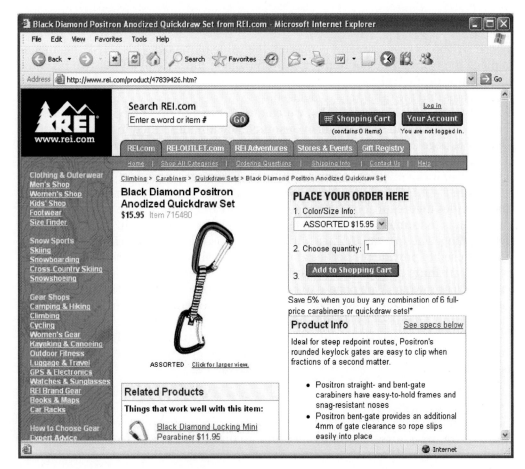

Figure 8-5a
Sample of Commerce Server
Pages: Product Offer Pages

Source: Used with permission of REI and Black Diamond.

Figure 8-5b
Shopping-Cart Page

Source: Used with permission of REI.

by </h2>. The words between the tags are the value of the tag. This HTML tag means to place the words "Price of Item" on a Web page in the style of a level-two heading. The creator of the Web page will define the style (font size, color, and so forth) for h2 headings and the other tags to be used.

Web pages include **hyperlinks**, which are pointers to other Web pages. A hyperlink contains the URL (the Uniform Resource Locator, described in the Appendix to Chapter 6, page 215) of the Web page to find when the user clicks the hyperlink. The URL can reference a page on the server that generated the page containing the hyperlink or it can reference a page on another server.

Figure 8-6(a) shows a sample HTML document. The document has a heading that provides metadata about the page and a body that contains the content. The tag <h1> means to format the indicated text as a level-one heading; <h2> means a level-two heading. The tag <a> defines a hyperlink. This tag has an **attribute**, which is a variable used to provide properties about a tag. Not all tags have attributes, but many do. Each attribute has a standard name. The attribute for a hyperlink is *href*, and its value indicates which Web page is to be displayed when the user clicks the link. Here, the page *www.pearsonhighered.com/kroenke* is to be returned when the user clicks the hyperlink. Figure 8-6(b) shows this page as rendered by Internet Explorer.

By the way, some HTML documents contain program code. That code is sent from the Web server to the user's browser and is processed by the browser on the user's computer.

eXtensible Markup Language (XML)

HTML is the workhorse for Web pages and e-commerce sites. HTML is particularly effective when one of the parties of the e-commerce is human. But what if two computer

```
<html>

<head>
<meta http-equiv="Content-Language" content="en-us">
<title>Using MIS</title>
</head>

<body>

<h1 align="center"><font color="#800080">Using MIS</font></h1>
<p> </p>
<h2><font color="#000080">Example HTML Document</font></h2>

<p> </p>
<p>Click here for textbook web site at Prentice-Hall: 
<a href="http://www.prenhall.com/kroenke">Web Site Link</a></p>

</body>

</html>
```

Figure 8-6a
Sample HTML Document

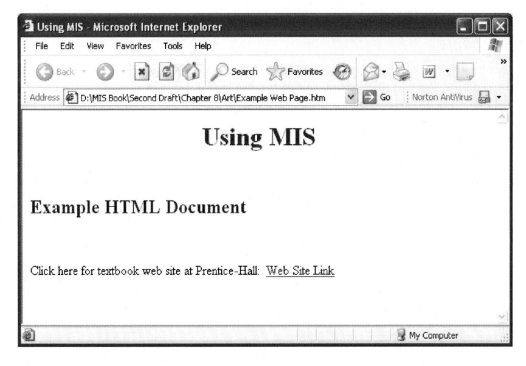

Figure 8-6b
HTML Document in
Figure 8-6a rendered using
Internet Explorer

Source: Microsoft product screenshot reprinted
with permission from Microsoft Corporation.

programs want to exchange data? It turns out that, for this purpose, HTML has major disadvantages that are overcome with a different markup language called XML.

What's Wrong with HTML?

Three problems with HTML are:

- HTML tags have no consistent meaning.
- HTML has a fixed number of tags.
- HTML mixes format, content, and structure.

The first problem is that tags are used inconsistently. For example, in standard use heading tags should be arranged in outline format. The highest-level heading tag should be an h1; within h1, there should be one or more h2 tags; and within the h2 tags there should be h3 tags; and so forth, for as many heading levels as the author of a document wants.

Unfortunately, no feature of HTML forces consistent use. An h2 tag can appear anywhere—above an h1 heading, below an h4 heading, or anyplace else. An h2 tag can represent a level-two heading, but it can also be used just to obtain a particular type of formatting. If I want the words "Prices guaranteed until Jan. 1, 2008" to appear in the formatting of a level-two heading, I can code:

```
<h2>Prices guaranteed until Jan. 1, 2008</h2>
```

This statement is not intended to be a level-two heading, but it will be given the font size, weight, and color that such headings have.

The possibility of tag misuse means that computer programs cannot depend on tags to infer the document's structure. An h2 tag may not be a heading at all. This limitation means that computer programs cannot use HTML tags to reliably exchange documents.

A second problem with HTML is that it defines a fixed set of tags. If two businesses want to define a new tag, say <PriceQuotation>, there is no way in HTML for them to define it. HTML documents are limited to the predefined tags.

The third problem with HTML is that HTML mixes the structure, formatting, and content of a document. Consider the following line of HTML code:

```
<h2 align="center"
font color="#FF00FF">Price of Item</font
/h2>
```

This heading mixes the structure (h2) with the formatting (alignment and color) with the content (Price of Item). Such mixing makes HTML difficult to work with. Ideally, the structure, format, and content should be separate.

How Does XML Fix These Problems?

To overcome the problems in HTML, the computer industry designed a new markup language called the **eXtensible Markup Language (XML)**. XML is the product of a committee that worked under the auspices of the **World Wide Web Consortium (W3C)**, a body that sponsors the development and dissemination of Web standards. By the way, W3C publishes excellent tutorials, and you can find an XML tutorial on its Web site, *http://w3.org*.

XML provides a superior means for computer programs to exchange documents. It solves the problems mentioned for HTML, and it has become a significant standard for computer processing. For example, all Microsoft Office 2007 and 2010 products save their documents in XML format. XML is also the foundation for all of the SOA standards.

The design of XML necessitates that content, structure, and format be separated into different XML documents. Further, document designers can create their own tags and specify the precise arrangement of those tags in metadata. That metadata is usually stored in another document called an XML schema. Formatting the document is done using still other documents that are separate and distinct from the content document. The particulars of XML metadata and formatting are beyond the scope of this text. Perform a search for *DTD, XSD,* and *XSLT* to learn more about these topics. The bottom line is that a computer program can read a content document to find the data to process, it can reference a metadata document to verify that the content is correct and complete, and it can use a formatting document to transform the content into a particular form that it needs.

How Can Suppliers Use XML?

XML has the potential to improve, sometimes drastically, the efficiency of operations among distributors and suppliers. To understand how, consider REI and its relationship to its distributors. Suppose REI wants to transmit counts of inventory items to all of its suppliers. To do so, REI designs an XML document called *ItemCount*. (For now, think of an XML document as a sequence of tags and data, like HTML documents.) Once it has designed the document, REI records the structure of that document in an **XML schema**. As stated, such a schema is just another XML document, but one that records the metadata (structure) of the *ItemCount* document. Call that schema *ItemCount_schema*.

Next, REI prepares inventory count documents according to its design. Before sending those documents to its distributors, REI double-checks that the documents are valid by comparing them to the schema. Fortunately, hundreds of programs are readily available that can validate an XML document against its schema. For example, both Internet Explorer and Mozilla Firefox can validate any XML document. This validation feature means significant cost savings, because human labor is not required to check documents.

Before sending *ItemCount* documents to the distributors, REI shares the *ItemCount_schema* document with them, possibly by publishing it on a Web site that the distributors have permission to access. When a distributor receives an *ItemCount* document from REI, it uses the *ItemCount_schema* to validate the received document. In this way, the distributors ensure that they receive correct and complete documents and that no part of the document has been lost in transmission. Again, this automated process saves labor because it frees the distributors from manually validating the correctness of the documents they receive. This automated validation can mean enormous labor savings.

How Can Industries Use XML?

Now broaden this idea from two businesses to an entire industry. Suppose, for example, that the real estate industry agrees on an XML schema document for property listings. Every real estate company that can produce data in the format of that schema can then exchange listings with every other such real estate company. Given the schema, each company can ensure that it is transmitting and receiving valid documents. Figure 8-7 lists some of the XML document standards that exist as of June 2009.

Given this technology background, we will now consider two ways that e-commerce can be used to improve supply chains.

Standard	Description of Contents
adobe.xml	Adobe schemas
cml.xml	CML: Chemical Markup Language and STMML: A Markup Language for Scientific, Technical, and Medical Publishing
election-4.xml	Election Markup Language (EML) 4.0
epa.xml	Environmental Protection Agency schemas
faml.xml	Financial Analysis Markup Language (FAML)
gpx.xml	GPX: The GPS Exchange Format
jxdd.xml	Justice XML Data Dictionary
msoffice.xml	Microsoft Office schemas
music.xml	MusicXML (http://www.musicxml.org/) interchange language and MIDI (http://www.midi.org/) schemas

Figure 8-7
Selected Industry XML Document Standards

Sources: http://www.altova.com/xml_standards.html; http://www.stylusstudio.com/dtd_standards.html

(Continued)

Standard	Description of Contents
navy.xml	U.S. Navy schemas
nca.xml	National Coffee Association schemas
NewsML.xml	Defines the structure and content of news articles
pmml.xml	Data Mining Group (DMG) Predictive Model Markup Language (PMML)
RIXML.xml	Investment and financial research documents
science.xml	Scientific Schemas: SBML: The Systems Biology Markup Language
uspto.xml	United States Patent and Trade Office schemas
weather.xml	NOAA National Weather Service National Digital Forecast Database (NDFD) Extensible Markup Language Country Codes, Currency Names, ISBN
xfront.xml	Decoding and Units of Measure tables. Courtesy of MITRE (http://www.xfront.com)

Figure 8-7
(Continued)

Q3 How Can Information Systems Enhance Supply Chain Performance?

A **supply chain** is a network of organizations and facilities that transforms raw materials into products delivered to customers. Figure 8-8 shows a generic supply chain. Customers order from retailers, who in turn order from distributors, who in turn order from manufacturers, who in turn order from suppliers. In addition to the organizations shown here, the supply chain also includes transportation companies, warehouses, and inventories and some means for transmitting messages and information among the organizations involved.

Because of disintermediation, not every supply chain has all of these organizations. Dell, for example, sells directly to the customer. Both the distributor and retailer organizations are omitted from its supply chain. In other supply chains, manufacturers sell directly to retailers and omit the distribution level.

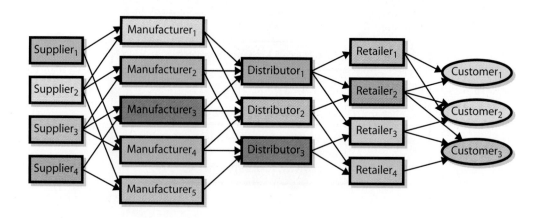

Figure 8-8
Supply Chain Relationships

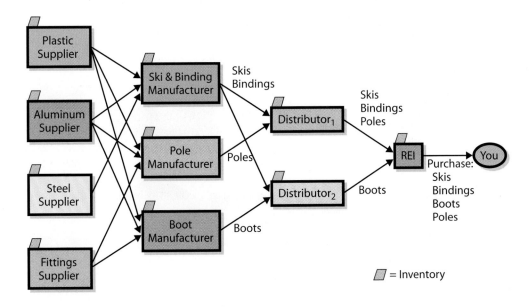

Figure 8-9
Supply Chain Example

The term *chain* is misleading. *Chain* implies that each organization is connected to just one company up the chain (toward the supplier) and down the chain (toward the customer). That is not the case. Instead, at each level an organization can work with many organizations both up and down the supply chain. Thus, a supply chain is a *network*.

To understand the operation of a supply chain, consider Figure 8-9. Suppose you decide to take up cross-country skiing. You go to REI (either by visiting one of its stores or its Web site) and purchase skis, bindings, boots, and poles. To fill your order, REI removes those items from its inventory of goods. Those goods have been purchased, in turn, from distributors. According to Figure 8-9, REI purchases the skis, bindings, and poles from one distributor and boots from a second. The distributors in turn purchase the required items from the manufacturers, which in turn buy raw materials from their suppliers.

The only source of revenue in a supply chain is the customer. In the REI example, you spend your money on the ski equipment. From that point all the way back up the supply chain to the raw material suppliers there is no further injection of cash. The money you spend on the ski equipment is passed back up the supply chain as payments for goods or raw materials. Again, the customer is the only source of revenue.

What Factors Drive Supply Chain Performance?

As shown in Figure 8-10, four factors drive supply chain performance: facilities, inventory, transportation, and information.[2] *Facilities* concern the location, size, and operations methodology of the places where products are fabricated, assembled, or stored. *Inventory* includes all of the materials in the supply chain, including raw materials, in-process work, and finished goods. *Transportation*, the third driver in Figure 8-10, concerns the movement of materials in the supply chain. These three factors are important drivers, but they do not concern IS directly. It is the fourth driver, *information*, that most concerns us.

Information is produced and consumed by e-commerce information systems. When you order from REI.com, REI produces information for you to consider in the form of its online catalog. You consume that information, and respond with information of your own, the items that you wish to order. Throughout your e-commerce transaction, both REI and you are producing and consuming information.

Figure 8-10 considers e-commerce information from a broader perspective. It lists three facets of information: purpose, availability, and means. The *purpose* of the

Interorganizational information systems often require meetings to come to a joint agreement on the process for sharing data. You may be asked to attend such meetings, and, if so, you need to know the proper etiquette for such meetings, as described in the Guide on pages 310–311.

---

[2]Sunil Chopra and Peter Meindl, *Supply Chain Management* (Upper Saddle River, NJ: Prentice Hall, 2004), pp. 51–53.

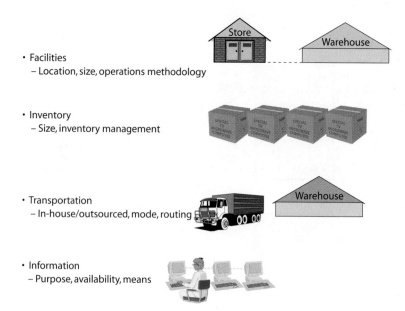

- Facilities
  - Location, size, operations methodology

- Inventory
  - Size, inventory management

- Transportation
  - In-house/outsourced, mode, routing

- Information
  - Purpose, availability, means

Figure 8-10
Drivers of Supply Chain
Performance

information can be transactional, such as the items you wish to order, or it can be informational, such as the items in the online catalog that REI transmits to you. *Availability* refers to the ways in which organizations share their information—that is, which organizations have access to which information and when. REI may want its supplier to be able to access the quantity of items in inventory, but it may not want to share that data with you, the customer. Finally, *means* refers to the methods by which the information is transmitted. E-commerce systems commonly use the three-tier architecture with HTML and XML. Increasingly such systems are using SOA standards as means as well.

To understand the importance of information in the supply chain, consider two ways that information can affect supply chain performance: supply chain profitability and the bullwhip effect.

How Does Supply Chain Profitability Differ from Organizational Profitability?

Each of the organizations in Figures 8-8 and 8-9 is an independent company, with its own goals and objectives. Each has a competitive strategy that may differ from the competitive strategies of the other organizations in the supply chain. Left alone, each organization will maximize its own profit, regardless of the consequences of its actions on the profitability of the others.

Supply chain profitability is the difference between the sum of the revenue generated by the supply chain and the sum of the costs that all organizations in the supply chain incur to obtain that revenue. In general, the maximum profit to the supply chain *will not* occur if each organization in the supply chain maximizes its own profits in isolation. Usually, the profitability of the supply chain increases if one or more of the organizations operates at less than its own maximum profitability.

To see why this is so, consider your purchase of the ski equipment from REI. Assume that you purchase either the complete package of skis, bindings, boots, and poles or you purchase nothing. If you cannot obtain boots, for example, the utility of skis, bindings, and poles is nil. In this situation, an outage of boots causes a loss of revenue not just for the boots, but also for the entire ski package.

According to Figure 8-9, REI buys boots from distributor 2 and the rest of the package from distributor 1. If boots are unavailable, distributor 2 loses the revenue of selling boots, but does not suffer any of the revenue loss from the nonsale of skis, bindings, and poles. Thus, distributor 2 will carry an inventory of boots that is optimized considering only the loss of boot revenue—not considering the loss of revenue for the entire package. In this case, the profitability to the supply chain will increase if distributor 2 carries an inventory of boots larger than is optimal for its business alone.

In theory, the way to solve this problem is to use some form of transfer payment to induce distributor 2 to carry a larger boot inventory. For example, REI could pay distributor 2 a premium for the sale of boots in packages and recover a portion of this premium from distributor 1, who would recover a portion of it from the manufacturers, and so forth, up the supply chain. For higher-priced items or for items with very high volume, there can be an economic benefit for creating an information system to identify such a situation and compute the transfer payments.

What Is the Bullwhip Effect?

The **bullwhip effect** is a phenomenon in which the variability in the size and timing of orders increases at each stage up the supply chain, from customer to supplier (in Figure 8-9, from *You* all the way back to the suppliers). Figure 8-11 depicts the situation. In a famous study,[3] the bullwhip effect was observed in Procter & Gamble's supply chain for diapers.

Except for random variation, diaper demand is constant. Diaper use is not seasonal; the requirement for diapers does not change with fashion or anything else. The number of babies determines diaper demand, and that number is constant or possibly slowly changing.

Retailers do not order from the distributor with the sale of every diaper package. The retailer waits until the diaper inventory falls below a certain level, called the *reorder quantity*. Then the retailer orders a supply of diapers, perhaps ordering a few more than it expects to sell to ensure that it does not have an outage.

The distributor receives the retailer's orders and follows the same process. It waits until its supply falls below the reorder quantity, and then it reorders from the

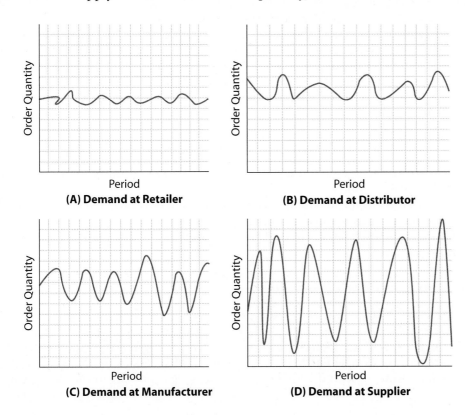

(A) Demand at Retailer

(B) Demand at Distributor

(C) Demand at Manufacturer

(D) Demand at Supplier

Figure 8-11
The Bullwhip Effect

[3]Hau L. Lee, V. Padmanabhan, and S. Whang, "The Bullwhip Effect in Supply Chains," *Sloan Management Review*, Spring 1997, pp. 93–102.

manufacturer, with perhaps an increased amount to prevent outages. The manufacturer, in turn, uses a similar process with the raw-materials suppliers.

Because of the nature of this process, small changes in demand at the retailer are amplified at each stage of the supply chain. As shown in Figure 8-11, those small changes become quite large variations on the supplier end.

The bullwhip effect is a natural dynamic that occurs because of the multistage nature of the supply chain. It is not related to erratic consumer demand, as the study of diapers indicated. You may have seen a similar effect while driving on the freeway. One car slows down, the car just behind it slows down a bit more abruptly, which causes the third card in line to slow down even more abruptly, and so forth, until the 30th car or so is slamming on its brakes.

The large fluctuations of the bullwhip effect force distributors, manufacturers, and suppliers to carry larger inventories than should be necessary to meet the real consumer demand. Thus, the bullwhip effect reduces the overall profitability of the supply chain.

One way to eliminate the bullwhip effect is to give all participants in the supply chain access to consumer-demand information from the retailer. Each organization can thus plan its inventory or manufacturing based on the true demand (the demand from the only party that introduces money into the system) and not on the observed demand from the next organization up the supply chain. Of course, an *interorganizational information system* is necessary to share such data.

Q4 Why Is Web 2.0 Important to Business?

As you saw in the REI example, e-commerce sites duplicate the experience of shopping in a grocery store or other retail shop. The customer moves around the store, places items in a shopping cart, and then checks out. Shopping carts and other e-commerce techniques have been a boon to business, especially B2C commerce, but they do not take advantage of the Web's full potential.

Amazon.com was one of the first to recognize other possibilities when it added the "Customers Who Bought This Book Also Bought" feature to its Web site. With that feature, e-commerce broke new ground. No grocery store could or would have a sign that announced, "Customers who bought this tomato soup, also bought. . . ." That idea was the first step toward what has come to be known as Web 2.0.

What Is Web 2.0?

The term *Web 2.0* originated at a 2001 conference brainstorming session between O'Reilly Publications and MediaLive International.[4]

Although the specific meaning of **Web 2.0** is hard to pin down, it generally refers to a loose grouping of capabilities, technologies, business models, and philosophies. Figure 8-12 compares Web 2.0 to traditional processing. (For some reason, the term *Web 1.0* is not used.)

Software as a (Free) Service

Google, Amazon.com, and eBay exemplify Web 2.0. These companies do not sell software licenses, because software is not their product. Instead, they provide **software as a service (SAAS)**. You can search Google, run Google Docs & Spreadsheets, use Google Earth, process Gmail, and access Google maps—all from a thin-client browser, with the bulk of the processing occurring in the cloud, somewhere on the Internet. Like all Web 2.0 programs, Google releases new versions of

---

[4] *http://oreillynet.com/pub/a/oreilly/tim/news/2005/09/30/what-is-web-20.html.*

Web 2.0 Processing	Traditional Processing
Major winners: Google, Amazon.com, eBay	Major winners: Microsoft, Oracle, SAP
Software as a (free) service	Software as product
Frequent releases of perpetual betas	Infrequent, controlled releases
Business model relies on advertising or other revenue-from-use	Business model relies on sale of software licenses
Viral marketing	Extensive advertising
Product value increases with use and users	Product value fixed
Organic interfaces, mashups encouraged	Controlled, fixed interface
Participation	Publishing
Some rights reserved	All rights reserved

Figure 8-12
B2B in One Section of the Supply Chain

its programs frequently. Instead of software license fees, the Web 2.0 business model relies on advertising or other revenue that results as users employ the software as a service.

Many Web 2.0 programs are perpetually classified as "beta." Traditionally, a **beta program** is a pre-release version of software that is used for testing; it becomes obsolete when the final version is released. In the Web 2.0 world, many programs are always beta. Figure 8-13 shows Gmail as a beta program. I have been using this "beta" program for more than 4 years. Features and functions are constantly changing; none

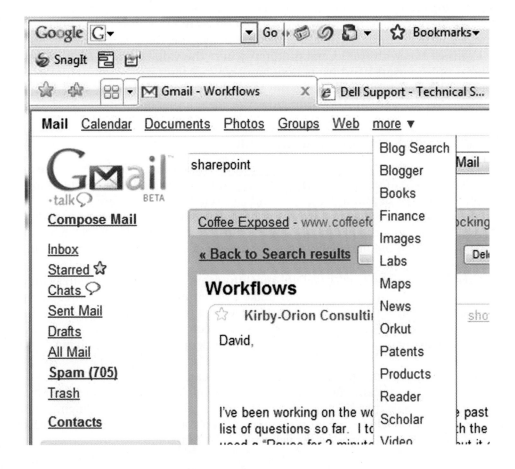

Figure 8-13
Sample Gmail Screen

Source: Gmail™. GOOGLE is a trademark of Google, Inc.

of the functions listed in the *More* menu item existed even 2 years ago. But, because the program remains classified as beta, with no license fee, no user can complain about the changing user interface.

Software as a service clashes with the software model used by traditional software vendors such as Microsoft, Oracle, and SAP. For such companies, software is their product. They release new versions and new products infrequently. For example, 3 years separated the release of Microsoft Office 2007 from 2010. Releases are made in a very controlled fashion, and extensive testing and true beta programs precede every release.

Traditional software vendors depend on software license fees. If many Office users switched to free word processing and spreadsheet applications, the hit on Microsoft revenue would be catastrophic. Because of the importance of software licensing revenue, substantial marketing efforts are made to convert users to new releases.

In the Web 2.0 world, no such marketing is done; new features are released and vendors wait for users to spread the news to one another, one friend sending an ad message to many friends, most of whom send that message in turn to their friends, and so forth, in a process called **viral marketing** (discussed further in Q5 and Q6 later in this chapter). Google has never announced any software in a formal marketing campaign. Users carry the message to one another. In fact, if a product requires advertising to be successful, then it is not a Web 2.0 product.

By the way, traditional software companies do use the term *software as a service*. However, they use it only to mean that they will provide their software products via the cloud rather than having customers install that software on their computers. Software licenses for their products still carry a sometimes hefty license fee. So, perhaps we should say that in the Web 2.0 world software is provided as a *free* service.

Use Increases Value

Another characteristic of Web 2.0 is that the value of the site increases with users and use. Amazon.com gains more value as more users write more reviews. Amazon.com becomes *the* place to go for information about books or other products. Similarly, the more people who buy or sell on eBay, the more eBay gains value as a site.

Contrast this with traditional products where the value is fixed. Millions upon millions of Microsoft Word users may have created templates of potential use to others, but because Microsoft does not serve as a clearinghouse for sharing those templates the value of Word does not grow with the number of Word users.

Organic User Interfaces and Mashups

The traditional software model carefully controls the users' experience. All Office programs share a common user interface; the ribbon (toolbar) in Word is similar to the ribbon in PowerPoint and in Excel. In contrast, Web 2.0 interfaces are organic. Users find their way around eBay and PayPal, and if the user interface changes from day to day, well, that is just the nature of Web 2.0. Further, Web 2.0 encourages **mashups**, which occur when the output from two or more Web sites is combined into a single user experience.

Google's My Maps is an excellent mashup example. Google publishes Google Maps and provides tools for users to make custom modifications to those maps. Thus, users mash the Google map product with their own knowledge. One user demonstrated the growth of gang activity to the local police by mapping new graffiti sites on Google maps. Other users share their experiences or photos of hiking trips or other travel.

In Web 2.0 fashion, Google provides users a means for sharing their mashed-up map over the Internet and then indexes that map for Google search. If you publish a mashup of a Google map with your knowledge of a hiking trip on Mt. Pugh, anyone who performs a Google search for Mt. Pugh will find your map. Again, the more users who create My Maps, the greater the value of the My Maps site.

Participation and Ownership Differences

Mashups lead to another key difference. Traditional sites are about publishing; Web 2.0 is about participation. Users provide reviews, map content, discussion responses, blog entries, and so forth. A final difference, listed in Figure 8-12, concerns *ownership*. Traditional vendors and Web sites lock down all the legal rights they can. For example, Oracle publishes content and demands that others obtain written permission before reusing it. Web 2.0 locks down only some rights. Google publishes maps and says, "Do what you want with them. We'll help you share them."

How Can Businesses Benefit from Web 2.0?

Amazon.com, Google, eBay, and other Web 2.0 companies have pioneered Web 2.0 technology and techniques to their benefit. A good question today, however, is how these techniques might be used by non-Internet companies. How might 3M, Alaska Airlines, Procter & Gamble, or the bicycle shop down the street use Web 2.0?

Advertising

When Oracle runs an ad in the print version of the *Wall Street Journal*, it has no control over who reads that ad, nor does it know much about the people who do (just that they fit the general demographic of *Wall Street Journal* readers). On any particular day, 10,000 qualified buyers for Oracle products might happen to read the ad, or then again, perhaps only 1,000 qualified buyers read it. Neither Oracle nor the *Wall Street Journal* knows the number, but Oracle pays the same amount for the ad, regardless of the number of readers or who they are.

In the Web 2.0 world, advertising is specific to user interests. Someone who searches online for *enterprise database management* is likely an IT person (or a student) who has a strong interest in Oracle and its competing products. Oracle would like to advertise to that person.

Google pioneered Web 2.0 advertising. With its **AdWords** software, vendors agree to pay a certain amount for particular search words. For example, FlexTime (the opening vignette in Chapters 1 through 6) might agree to pay $2 for the word *workout*. When someone Googles that term, Google will display a link to FlexTime's Web site. If the user clicks that link (and *only* if the user clicks that link), Google charges FlexTime's account $2. FlexTime pays nothing if the user does not click. If it chooses, FlexTime can agree to pay only when users in the Indianapolis area click the word.

The amount that a company pays per word can be changed from day to day, and even hour to hour. If FlexTime is about to start a new spinning class, it will pay more for the word *spinning* just before the class starts than it will afterward. The value of a click on *spinning* is low when the start of the next spinning class is a month away.

AdSense is another advertising alternative. Google searches an organization's Web site and inserts ads that match content on that site. When users click those ads, Google pays the organization a fee. Other Web 2.0 vendors offer services similar to AdWords and AdSense.

With Web 2.0, the cost of reaching a particular, qualified person is much smaller than in the traditional advertising model. As a consequence, many companies are switching to the new lower-cost medium, and newspapers and magazines are struggling with a sharp reduction in advertising revenue.

Social Networking

The term *social networking (SN)* refers to connections of people with similar interests. Although sociologists used the term prior to Web 2.0, most people today use it to refer to connections between people that are supported by Web 2.0 technology. Social networking has become so important that we will consider it more deeply in Q5.

Mashups

How can two non-Internet companies mash the content of their products? Suppose you're watching a hit movie and you would like to buy the jewelry, dress, or watch worn by the leading actress. Suppose that Nordstrom's sells all those items. With Web 2.0 technology, the movie's producer and Nordstrom's can mash their content together so that you, watching the movie at home, can click on the watch and be directed to a Nordstrom's e-commerce site that will sell it to you. Or, perhaps Nordstrom's is disintermediated out of the transaction, and you are taken to the e-commerce site of the watch's manufacturer. Such possibilities are on the leading edge of e-commerce today. Many will be developed during your business career.

Who Is in Control?

Before we get too carried away with the potential for Web 2.0, note that not all business information systems benefit from flexibility and organic growth. Any information system that deals with assets, whether financial or material, requires, some level of control. You probably do not want to mash up your credit card transactions on My Map and share that mashup with the world. As CFO, you probably do not want your accounts payable or general ledger system to have an organic user interface; in fact, the Sarbanes-Oxley Act prohibits that possibility.

Q5 How Can Organizations Benefit from Social Networking?

Social networking at work may be problematic ... or not. The Guide on pages 308–309 explores social networking opinions of employees at Pearson Education (publisher of this text).

Social networking (SN) is the interaction of people connected by friendship, interests, business associations, or some other common trait that is supported by Web 2.0 technology. You have undoubtedly used Facebook, MySpace, and Twitter, and you probably have an intuitive understanding of their nature. In this question, we will explore ways that SN adds value to businesses. In Q6, we'll address Twitter in particular.

Fundamental Social Networking Services

In essence, SN supports two fundamental services: **N:M communication** and **social collaboration**. You can use knowledge you've gained from this textbook to understand each. First, recall N:M relationships from Chapter 5. With such relationships, one entity has many connections to another entity, and each connected entity has many other connections. SN facilitates communication among such a network. When you post "Studying Chapter 8 today" on your SN page, that message is communicated to all *N* of your friends and appears on their sites. Meanwhile, each of your friends has *M* friends, all of whom can visit your friends' sites and see your message.

If you have 15 friends and each of them has 10 friends in addition to you (it is unrealistic that they all have exactly 10 such friends, but make this assumption), then with one message post, you have communicated to 150 people. Even more important, however, is that you may not know these 150 people by name but rather you know them by their relationships to your friends. N:M communication makes viral marketing possible, as we discuss in the next section.

The second service is *social collaboration*. Collaboration, by its nature, is social, and so this term may appear redundant. However, appending the word *social* to collaboration emphasizes that the collaboration is done to build and enhance relationships, rather than to solve problems or manage projects, the purpose of the collaboration efforts discussed in Chapter 2.

Like business collaboration, social collaboration is distinguished by feedback and iteration. Relationships grow as you post something on your page and your friends respond, thus providing feedback. You then iterate by responding to their feedback. Over time that conversation enhances the quality and strength of your relationships. (Or, it does not, in which case the social collaboration has enabled you to reduce your interests in someone or some group.)

Viral Marketing with SN

As shown in Figure 8-14, in a traditional business relationship you (the client) have some experience with a business, such as Majestic River Ventures (MRV), and you may express your opinions about that experience to your friends (denoted F1, F2, etc.) by word of mouth. Such communication is unreliable: You are more likely to say something to your friends if the experience was particularly good or bad; but even then, you are likely only to say something to those friends whom you encounter while the experience is still recent.

Social networking communication is considerably more reliable. Suppose MRV establishes a presence on a social network. Majestic might have an SN page for its business, the owner might have a page, or each of the river guides might have a page. The nature of the presence is unimportant here.

When you conduct business with MRV on the social network, something about that business will be broadcast to your N friends, as shown in Figure 8-15. That messaging is automatic; "*Your Name* has just enrolled in the Rogue River trip" will be reliably broadcast to all of your friends. That, in itself, is a powerful marketing tool.

However, SN provides even greater possibilities. As shown in Figure 8-16, you have friends (OK, you have more than five friends, but space is limited), and your friends have friends, and those friends have friends. If something about your message induces F5 (for example) to broadcast something to her friends, and if that message induces F7 to broadcast something to his friends, and so forth, the messaging will be viral.

Figure 8-14
Traditional Marketing at Majestic River Ventures

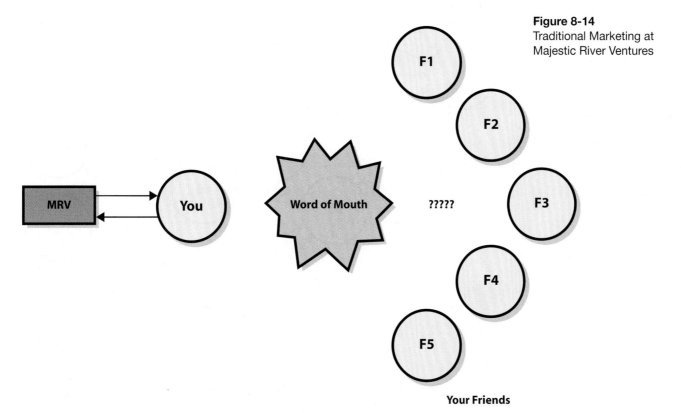

Your Friends

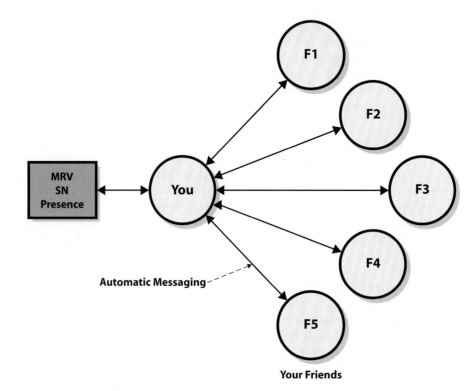

Figure 8-15
Social Network Marketing
at Majestic River Ventures

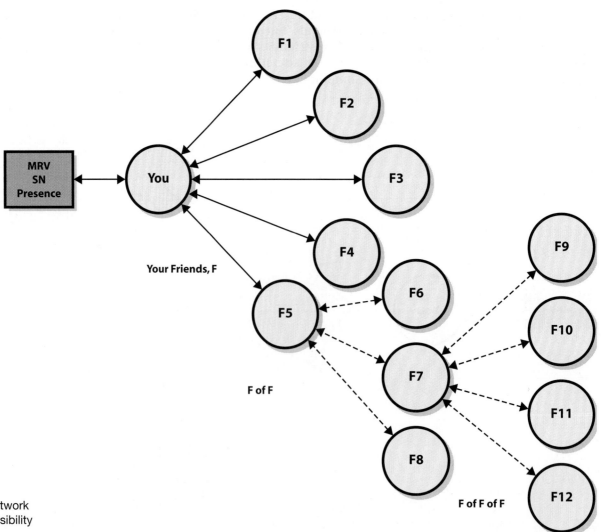

Figure 8-16
Viral Social Network
Marketing Possibility

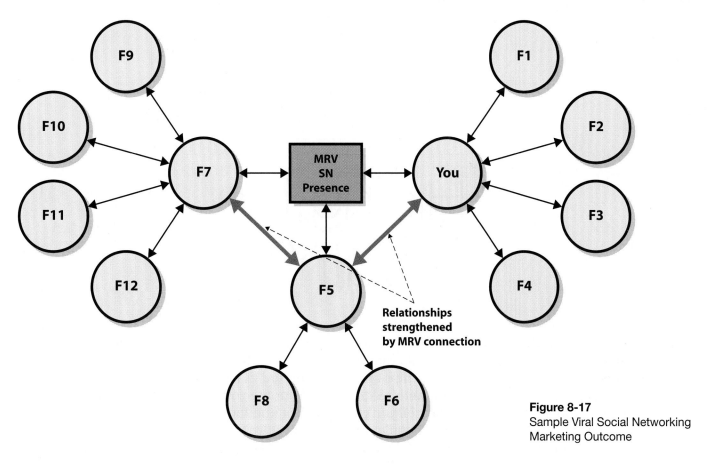

Figure 8-17
Sample Viral Social Networking
Marketing Outcome

Viral marketing will be even more powerful if the message induces your friends (and their friends, etc.) to form a relationship with MRV's SN presence. If you say, "Look at these photos" and the photos are located on an MRV site, then F5 and F7 will form a direct relationship to MRV's presence, as shown in Figure 8-17. This is a win for MRV, especially because the relationships among you, F5, and F7 will be strengthened in the context of Majestic. If Majestic can induce you to say somewhere on your page, "Isn't that a cool picture of F5 on the Rogue? We ought to do that trip again. F7, you should join us!" Majestic has a huge win, because it has made the value you place on your friends part of Majestic's products' benefits! And, by the way, the cost to Majestic of this marketing program is essentially zero. Amazing!

The crux, however, is getting F5 and F7 to form a relationship with Majestic's SN presence. Most commonly, vendors will try to induce current customers to bring their friends. Thus, in our example, Majestic will try to induce you to tell your friends, including F5, to connect with its SN presence by offering you what is termed a **viral hook**. The nature of the viral hook depends on the market and the business. One example would be for MRV to send you a Majestic hat (itself a marketing item) if you induce three friends to form a relationship with it. Determining a proper viral hook is a critical decision when marketing via social networks.

Two common ways that companies form SN relationships with customers are groups and applications. We consider these in the next two sections.

In social networking, people aren't always completely honest. To reflect on ethical issues and social networking, read the Ethics Guide on pages 296–297.

How Can Businesses Utilize Social Networking Groups?

A **social networking group** is an association of SN members related to a particular topic, event, activity, or other collective interest. In addition to members, SN groups have resources such as photos, videos, documents, discussion threads, a wallboard, and features. In some cases, groups have one or more events.

Ethics

Hiding the Truth?

No one is going to publish their ugliest picture on their Facebook page, but how far should you go to create a positive impression? If your hips and legs are not your best features, is it unethical to stand behind your sexy car in your photo? If you've been to one event with someone very popular in your crowd, is it unethical to publish photos that imply you meet as an everyday occurrence? Surely there is no obligation to publish pictures of yourself at boring events with unpopular people just to balance the scale for those photos in which you appear unrealistically attractive and overly popular.

As long as all of this occurs on a Facebook or MySpace account that you use for personal relationships, well, what goes around comes around. But consider social networking in the business arena.

a. Suppose that Majestic starts a group on a social networking site for a particular rafting trip. Graham, the 15-year-old college student who started this chapter, decides to use that group to attract women at his college to join the trip. He posts a picture of a handsome 22-year-old male as a picture of himself, and he writes witty and clever comments on the site photos. He also claims to play the guitar and to be an accomplished masseuse. Are his actions unethical? Suppose someone decided to go on the rafting trip, in part because of Graham's postings, and was

disappointed with the truth about Graham. Would Majestic have any responsibility to refund that person's fees?

b. Suppose you own and manage Majestic. Is it unethical for you to encourage your employees to write positive reviews about MRV? Does your assessment change if you ask your employees to use an email address other than the one they have at MRV?

c. Again, suppose you own and manage Majestic and that you pay your employees a bonus for every client they bring to a rafting trip. Without specifying any particular technique, you encourage your employees to be creative in how they obtain clients. One employee invites his MySpace friends to a party at which he shows photos of prior rafting trips. On the way to the party, one of the friends has an automobile accident and dies. His spouse sues Majestic. Should you be held accountable? Does it matter if you knew about the presentation? Would it matter if you had not encouraged your employees to be creative?

d. Suppose Majestic has a Web site for customer reviews. In spite of your best efforts at camp cleanliness, on one trip (out of dozens) your staff accidentally served contaminated food and everyone became ill with food-poisoning. One of those clients wrote a poor review because of that experience. Is it ethical for you to delete that review from your site?

terminated. You notice that the owner of MRV has no Facebook account, so you create one for her. You've known her for many years and have dozens of photos of her, some of which were taken at parties and are unflattering and revealing. You post those photos along with critical comments that she made about clients or employees. Most of the comments were made when she was tired or frustrated, and they are hurtful, but because of her wit, also humorous. You send friend invitations to people whom she knows, many of whom are the target of her biting and critical remarks. Are your actions unethical? ■

e. Assume you have a professor who has written a popular textbook. You are upset with the grade you received in his class, so you write a scandalously poor review of that professor's book on Amazon.com. Are your actions ethical?

f. Suppose you were at one time employed by Majestic and you were, undeservedly you think, terminated by the company. To get even, you use Facebook to spread rumors to your friends (many of whom are river guides) about the safety of MRV trips. Are your actions unethical? Are they illegal? Do you see any ethical distinctions between this situation and that in item d?

g. Again, suppose that you were at one time employed by Majestic and were undeservedly

Discussion Questions

1. Read the situations in items a through g and answer the questions contained in each.
2. Based on your answers in question 1, formulate ethical principles for creating or using social networks for business purposes.
3. Based on your answers in question 1, formulate ethical principles for creating or using user-generated content for business purposes.
4. Summarize the risks that a business assumes when it uses social networks for business purposes.
5. Summarize the risks that a business assumes when it chooses to sponsor user-generated content.

Three types of groups are possible:

- **Public.**   Anyone can find the group by searching, and anyone can join it.
- **Invitation.**   Anyone can find the group by searching, but members must be invited to join.
- **Private.**   The group cannot be found by searching, and members must be invited to join.

Businesses can use groups to strengthen relationships among customers and to create the possibility of viral marketing. For example, Majestic could create an invitation group or a private group for each river trip. When someone pays a deposit, that person would be invited into the group. Prior to the trip, Majestic could place photos and videos of prior trips on the group site; it could also provide documents, such as equipment lists; advice on common topics, such as river photography; weather forecasts; and so forth. It also could start a discussion list among guides and group members so that guides and clients could get to know each other ahead of time. After the trip, group members could post their own photos, videos, documents, and personal reflections about the trip.

At some point, Majestic might choose to create a public version of the group so that clients can share their experiences with their friends, as shown in Figure 8-18. In this case, the relationship among you and F5 and F7 has been strengthened by your relationship to the trip groups (T1 and T2). You are "alumni" of Majestic, and social networking enables you to broadcast that to your friends while you reminisce with each other. Again, Majestic has co-opted the value of your friendships and made them part of Majestic's products' value.

Notice that social networking groups can be used for more than marketing. In this example, Majestic uses these groups for trip operations as well. Some social networking groups serve a management function. For example, groups of employees at work can use social networking groups to build cohesion with their teammates.

Figure 8-18
Strengthening Ties with Social Networking Groups

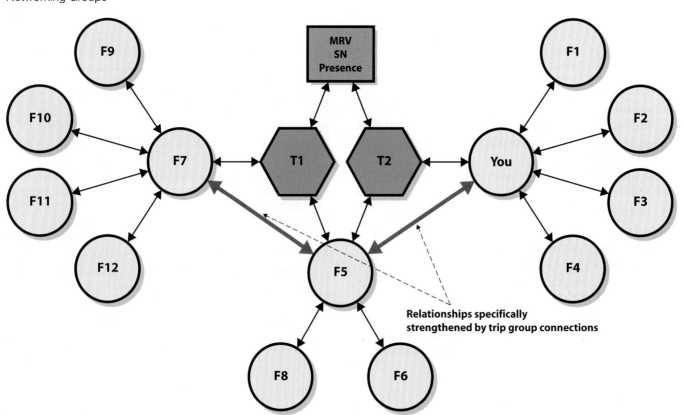

How Can Businesses Utilize Social Networking Applications?

A **social networking application** is a computer program that interacts with and processes information in a social network. For example, consider Survey Hurricane, a Facebook application created by Infinistorm (*www.infinistorm.com*). Users who install the application on their page can survey their friends on topics of interest. The *New York Times* quiz is another application, as are applications for buying and selling items, comparing movies, and so on.

Social networking applications run on servers provided by the application's creator. In SOA terms, the application provider exposes a service that interacts with a service on the SN vendor (Facebook or MySpace, for example). Thus, when you run an application on, say, a Facebook page, Facebook passes your application request, via a service, to the application vendor's server.

The application service calls back to Facebook (or other SN vendor) to create friend requests, find your existing friends, generate email, make requests, poke your friends, or take other actions. In the process, it can collect data about you and your friends for individualized marketing or for data mining (see Chapter 9).

Figure 8-19 shows an application that Majestic created. In this figure, F5, and F7 have installed that application from your page. Suppose this application is called "Let's Go Rafting." (This example is hypothetical; you won't find it on Facebook.) When the three of you install the application, it brings you into a direct relationship with Majestic River Ventures, and depending on the nature of the application, it may strengthen the relationship you have with F5 and F7 in the context of Majestic. If the application is compelling, you, F5, and F7 will encourage your friends to install it, and Majestic will have created a viral marketing program.

Figure 8-19
Strengthening Ties with Social Networking Applications

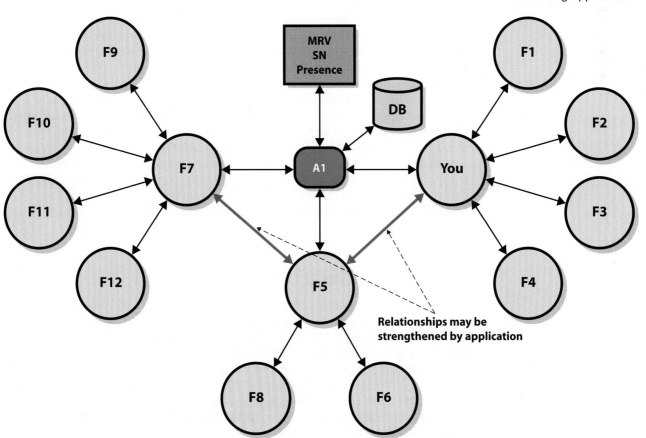

Applications give the application vendor more control over the users' experience than groups do. An application can be developed to require passwords and user accounts. Majestic, for example, could have different versions of the "Let's Go Rafting" application—one for prospects, one for clients enrolled in upcoming trips, and one for veterans of past trips. As stated, applications can also collect data.

The key to success is, of course, to make the application compelling. Facebook publishes considerable documentation and advice to its developers, including advice on application design. Facebook's four principles for a meaningful application are as follows:

- **Social.** *Meaningful applications use information in the social graph.* A **social graph** is a network of relationships; Figure 8-16 shows a portion of the social graph among you and your friends and some of their friends. A survey application uses information from the social graph because it uses the links to your friends to ask the survey questions. If "Let's Go Rafting" asks your friends to label photos of you in rafting situations, it is using the social graph in a compelling way. Both you and your friends will find it far more meaningful than an application that just shows rafting pictures.
- **Useful.** *Meaningful applications address real needs, from entertainment to practical tasks.* In a business setting, no one cares what you had for breakfast or where you put your toothbrush this morning. They might, however, be interested in what cities you'll be visiting on your next business trip. Similarly, if "Let's Go Rafting" is available to clients prior to a trip, a useful feature would be one that enables them to plan ride sharing.
- **Expressive.** *Meaningful applications share a personal perspective on the world.* People participate in SN activities because they want to share something about themselves. An SN application that publishes generic photos, or even personal photos in a generic way, does not allow the user to express his or her individuality. Instead, Majestic would add expressivity to "Let's Go Rafting" if it allowed clients to express how loudly they screamed on a given rapid, how cold the water was when they fell out of the raft, or how the sagebrush campfire filled the air with melancholy fragrance. Such personal reflections induce clients to author more comments and their friends to read them more frequently.
- **Engaging.** *Meaningful applications compel users to come back again, and again, and again.* Engaging applications are dynamic; they give participants a reason to come back. A dynamic application slowly reveals more of its contents, changes its contents, or alters the actions that participants can take. For example, "Let's Go Rafting" could have a "Rapid of the Day" feature in which clients are shown pictures, videos, and commentary about a different rapid, every day. Or, it might have a "River of the Month" feature about the rapids, camps, and sights of a different river each month. In this way, Majestic showcases its river trips while providing engaging content that will bring users back.

SN Applications Versus Web Sites

SN applications share many features and functions with normal Web sites. Majestic can develop a Web site with many photos, even particular group photos. It can also develop a site that has a "River of the Month" or "Rapid of the Day" feature. So why develop an SN application rather than a Web site?

The answer lies with the degree to which the application requires a social graph. Does the application use or benefit from N:M communication? Is there a need for social collaboration? For feedback and iteration? If not, the organization could develop a Web application that would be just as effective, possibly cheaper, and would not run the risks described in Q7.

Q6 How Can Organizations Benefit from Twitter?

Twitter has taken the business world by storm. If you think of Twitter as a place for teenage girls to describe the lipstick they're wearing today, think again. Hundreds of businesses are now using Twitter for legitimate business purposes.

First, in the unlikely case you haven't heard of Twitter, it is a Web 2.0 application that allows users to publish 140 character descriptions of . . . well, anything. Users can follow other Twitter users, and users can, in turn, be followed. Twitter is an example of a category of applications called *microblogs*. A **microblog** is a Web site on which users can publish their opinions, just like a Web blog, but the opinions are restricted to small amounts of text, like Twitter's 140 characters.

You might think that 140 characters is too limiting. However, Twitter has demonstrated the design adage that "structure is liberating." Thousands more people microblog than blog because microblogging is less intimidating. You don't have space to write a well-constructed paragraph; in fact, the character limitation forces you to abbreviate words and grammar. It isn't necessary to spell correctly or to know that sentences need a subject and a verb, either. Microbloggers just have to be (barely) comprehensible to their audience.

Microblog competitors to Twitter are emerging, and it is possible that by the time you read this Twitter will be old news. If so, as you read, replace Twitter with the name of whatever microblog application is currently the rage.

We Are All Publishers Now

Microblogs like Twitter make everyone a publisher. Anyone can join, for free, and immediately publish his or her ideas, worldwide. If you happen to be the world's expert on making pine-bark tea and if you have developed innovative techniques for harvesting pine bark, you have a free, worldwide platform for publishing those techniques.

Before we continue, think about that statement. As recently as 10 years ago, worldwide publishing was expensive and restricted to the very few. The *New York Times*, the *Wall Street Journal*, and a few other newspapers and large television networks were the only worldwide publishing venues in the United States. Publishing was a one-way street. They published and we consumed.

Microblogging enables two-way publishing, worldwide. You publish your ideas on pine-bark harvesting and others can publish you back. Notice that, unlike email, you are both *publishing*, not just communicating to each other. Your interchange, your conversation, is available for others to read, worldwide.

By the way, microblogging would be far less important if it lacked search features. Unfortunately for you, only four other people, worldwide, care about pine-bark harvesting. Were it not for the ability to search microblogs, they and you would never find one another. So, microblogging is important not just because it turns us all into publishers—by itself, that would not be very useful. Equally important is that microblogging enables users with similar interests to find each other.

How Can Businesses Benefit from Microblogging?

As of June 2009, businesses are actively experimenting with microblogging. Three obvious applications have emerged so far:

- Public relations
- Relationship sales
- Market research

We'll examine each of these, in turn, but stay tuned! Newer innovative applications are in the works.

Public Relations

Microblogging enables any employee or business owner to communicate with the world. No longer is it necessary to meet with editors and writers at newspapers and magazines and attempt to influence them to publish something positive about your product or other news. Instead, write it yourself and click Update. The only requirements are having something to say that your customers want to read and using keywords on which your customers are likely to search.

Possible examples are a product manager who's excited about a new use for his product. He can publish the idea and a summary of instructions. If the concept is longer than 140 words, he can include a link to a blog or Web site that has the rest of the description. Or, a customer service representative can publish warnings about possible misuse of a product or provide instructions for a new way of performing product maintenance, again with a link to a Web site, if necessary.

Pete Carroll, coach of the University of Southern California football team, introduced microblogging by football coaches. Coaches can increase fan awareness by blogging with insider details, how the practice went, comments about the recent game, and so forth. Coaches no longer have to depend on sportswriters and sportscasters for team public relations. Furthermore, microblogging means that coaches can control the content that is published.

By the way, these new public relations capabilities are stressing existing institutions. The NCAA has many rules and regulations about how and when coaches can contact potential recruits. How does a coach's microblogging fit into this scheme? The NCAA and others are scrambling to figure it out.

Relationship Sales

Social networking in general and microblogging in particular are all about relationships—forming new relationships and strengthening existing ones. Such relationships can serve as an ideal channel for sales. For example, suppose you are the owner of a plant nursery and you've just received a shipment of 100 hard-to-get plants. If you've formed Twitter relationships with your customers, you can Tweet the arrival of the plants and include a link to a Web site with pictures of how gorgeous these plants can be.

However, experience has shown that pure sales pitches are ineffective when microblogging. People stop following sources that only publish ads and sales pitches. Instead, people look for Tweeters who offer something they value, such as advice, links to resources, and interesting and thought-provoking opinions. So you, as the plant nursery owner, should offer advice and assistance, such as reminders that it's time to prune the roses or fertilize the azaleas. From time to time, you can publish an ad, but, even then, it should be published in a way like that you would use with a friend. Hard come on's won't work; instead, make the pitch in terms of "I thought you might want to know about the arrival of the. . . ." just as you would pass advice on to a friend. You can find many other sales ideas in books such as *Twitter Revolution: How Social Media and Mobile Marketing Is Changing the Way We Do Business and Market Online.*[5]

Market Research

Market research is the third promising business use of microblogging. Want to know what people think of your product? Search Twitter to find out. Windows 7 is an interesting

---

[5] Warren Whitlock and Deborah Micek, *Twitter Revolution: How Social Media and Mobile Marketing Is Changing the Way We Do Business and Market Online* (Las Vegas, NV: Xeno Press, 2008).

example. Windows 7 was pre-released to a limited set of expert users as a beta in the fall of 2008 and to a larger group of experienced users as a release candidate in the spring of 2009. Users of both these releases used Twitter to comment about their experience as well as to ask for help or provide assistance to each other. Meanwhile, Microsoft product managers were searching the Twitter traffic to learn the buzz about the new product. They used knowledge of what users especially liked to craft the launch of the actual product in late 2009. Product developers and technical writers also learned about features that were hard to understand and use.

Of course, such research is only useful if the product has a large following of users who employ Twitter to make comments. As of June 2009, a Twitter search for *Using MIS* (the title of this book), revealed no Tweets. Maybe you can change that?

Q7 What Are the Benefits and Risks of User-Generated Content (UGC)?

Users have been generating content on the Internet since its beginnings. However, with Web 2.0 many companies have found (and are finding) innovative ways of using user-generated content (UGC) for business functions. This section surveys common types of UGC and discusses their business applications.

Types of UGC

Figure 8-20 lists the common types of UGC. You are undoubtedly familiar with most, if not all, of these. Product ratings and surveys have been used for years. Product opinions are also common. Recent research indicates that ratings and opinions of fellow customers are far more trusted than any advertising. Jupiter Research found that social network users are three times more likely to trust their peers' opinions over advertising when making purchase decisions.[6]

Some companies find it advantageous to facilitate customers' storytelling about the use of the company's products. According to Bazaarvoice (*www.bazaarvoice. com*), "Giving visitors a place to share their stories will increase brand involvement, interaction, intimacy and influence. Far beyond just increasing time on site, personal stories engage visitors and writers alike, all increasing overall loyalty to your site—and your brand."[7]

Still other companies sponsor discussion groups for customers to offer advice and assistance to one another. In addition to customer support, those sites provide the company with useful information for product marketing and development. Wikis and blogs are another form of UGC in which customers and partners can offer advice and assistance regarding products.

> • **Ratings and surveys**
> • **Opinions**
> • **Customer stories**
> • **Discussion groups**
> • **Wikis**
> • **Blogs**
> • **Video**

Figure 8-20
Types of User-Generated Content

---

[6]Jupiter Research, "Social Networking Sites: Defining Advertising Opportunities in a Competitive Landscape," March 2007.
[7]Quote from *www.bazaarvoice.com/stories.html* (accessed August 2008).

Video is increasingly used to tell stories, offer product demonstrations, and apply products to specific needs and problems. The amount of UGC video is staggering. According to YouTube, 10 hours of UGC video are uploaded to its site *every minute*. That video is equivalent to 57,000 feature-length movies every week.[8]

UGC Applications

Figure 8-21 lists the most common applications for UGC. In sales, the presence of ratings, reviews, and recommendations increases conversion rates—in some cases doubling the rate of purchase. Interestingly, conversion rates are higher for products with less-than-perfect reviews than for products with no reviews at all.[9]

Furthermore, return rates fall dramatically as the number of product reviews increases.[10]

Crowdsourcing is the process by which organizations involve their users in the design and marketing of their products. For example, as shown in Figure 8-22, the shoe start-up company RYZ (*www.ryzwear.com*) sponsors shoe design contests to help it understand which shoes to create and how to market those designs.

Crowdsourcing combines social networking, viral marketing, and open-source design, saving considerable cost while cultivating customers. With crowdsourcing, the crowd performs classic in-house market research and development and does so in such a way that customers are being set up to buy.

For years, Microsoft has supported its software, database, and other developers on its MSDN Web site (*www.msdn.com*); MSDN stands for "Microsoft Developer Network". Developers post articles, best practices, blogs, code samples, answers to questions, and other resources for developing Microsoft applications.

Yet another UGC business application is product development. Electronic Arts involved game developers worldwide in the development of spore creatures for Spore, its universe-simulation game. Ryz uses UGC to design footwear; if the strategy is successful, it plans to use it to design other clothing items as well.

Application	Example
Sale (ratings, reviews, recommendations, stories)	www.amazon.com
Marketing (crowdsourcing)	www.ryzwear.com
Product support (problem solving, Q&A, advice, applications)	www.msdn.com
Product development (research and development)	www.spore.com www.ryzwear.com
UGC as bait for advertising	www.youtube.com www.funnyordie.com
UGC as part of product	www.finewoodworking.com www.woodenboat.com

Figure 8-21
UGC Applications

[8]N'Gai Croal, "The Internet Is the New Sweatshop," *Newsweek,* July 7–14, 2008, *www.newsweek.com/id/143740* (accessed July 2008).

[9]Bazaarvoice, "Industry Statistics, July 2008," *www.bazaarvoice.com/industryStats.html* (accessed August 2008).

[10]Matt Hawkings, "PETCO.com Significantly Reduces Return Rates," *Marketing Data Analyst,* June 27, 2006, *www.bazaarvoice.com/cs_rr_returns_petco.html* (accessed August 2008).

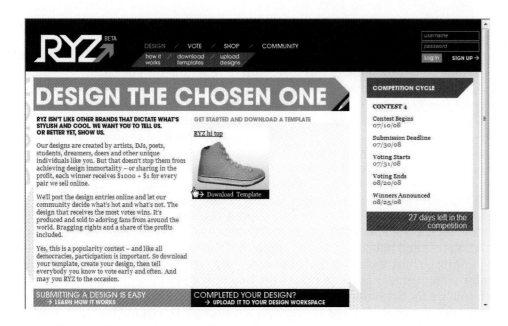

Figure 8-22
Design by Crowdsourcing

YouTube is famous for hosting UGC videos provided as bait for advertising. Finally, some Web sites include UGC as part of the product. The magazines *Fine Woodworking* and *Wooden Boat* both include UGC video as part of their online product offerings.

The use of UGC has been increasing with the growth of e-commerce and Web 2.0. Undoubtedly, many successful applications are yet to be invented. UGC for business will be an exciting field during the early years of your career.

What Are the Risks of Using Social Networking and User-Generated Content?

Before any business plunges full-bore into the world of social networking and UGC, it should be aware of the risks that these tools entail. Some of the major risks are:

- Junk and crackpots
- Inappropriate content
- Unfavorable reviews
- Mutinous movements
- Dependency on the SN vendor

When a business participates in a social network or opens its site to UGC, it opens itself to misguided people who post junk unrelated to the site's purpose. Crackpots may also use the network or UGC site as a way of expressing passionately held views about unrelated topics, such as UFOs, governmental cover-ups, weird conspiracy theories, and so forth. Because of the possibility of such inappropriate content, employees of the hosting business must regularly monitor the site and remove objectionable material immediately. Companies like Bazaarvoice offer services not only to collect and manage ratings and reviews, but also to monitor the site for irrelevant content.

Unfavorable reviews are another risk. Research indicates that customers are sophisticated enough to know that few, if any, products are perfect. Most customers want to know the disadvantages of a product before purchasing so they can determine if those disadvantages are important for their application. However, if every review is bad, if the product is rated 1 star out of 5, then the company is using Web 2.0 technology to publish its problems. In this case, corrective action must be taken.

Mutinous movements are an extension of bad reviews. The campaign Web site *www.my.barackobama.com* had a strong social networking component, and when then-Senator Obama changed his position on immunity for telecoms engaged in national security work, 22,000 members of his site joined a spontaneous group to object. Hundreds of members posted very critical comments of Obama, on his own site! This was an unexpected backlash to a campaign that had enjoyed unprecedented success raising money from small donors via social networking.

Although it is possible for organizations to develop their own social networking capability (as the Obama campaign did), many organizations use social networking vendors such as Facebook, MySpace, and Twitter. Those organizations are vulnerable to the success and policies of those companies. Such SN vendors are new companies with unproven business models; they may not survive. Also, using a social networking vendor for a business purpose makes the business vulnerable to the reliability and performance the SN vendor provides.

The license agreements of SN vendors are strongly biased in favor of the vendor. In some cases, the vendor owns the content that is developed; in other cases, the vendor can remove social networking applications at its discretion. In July 2008, for example, under pressure from Hasbro, the owner of Scrabble, Facebook required the creators of "Scrabulous" to redesign its game into "Wordscraper."[11]

The vulnerability is real, but the choices are limited. As stated, companies can create their own social networking capability, but doing so is expensive and requires highly skilled employees. And, having developed its own capability, no company will have the popularity and mindshare of Facebook, MySpace, or Twitter.

Q8 2020?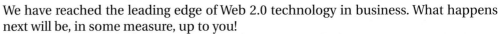

We have reached the leading edge of Web 2.0 technology in business. What happens next will be, in some measure, up to you!

What will you do? We can expect that technology will enable voice and video to be integrated into social networking. Will that become popular? Will you want to speak your Tweets and have a program translate your voice message into text? **Jott.com** already offers a limited version of that service. Or, will you want to Tweet your video? **12Seconds.TV** will allow you to submit, you guessed it, 12 seconds of video. Where will those movements go?

Or, will the future entail capabilities that we cannot fathom. Ten years ago, no one had even imaged YouTube, Facebook, or Twitter. We know that data communications and storage costs will continue to fall, so something new will happen. But what?

Here's a thought to consider: What will social networking do to management? Go through your management textbook and consider how many of the topics presented there can be altered, maybe dramatically, by Twitter . . . or maybe some new microblogging capability that will be built into SharePoint or Google Apps. For example, in the past, 10 to 12 employees were considered the maximum number of people that a single individual could manage. Does microblogging change that? What if the optimal span of control becomes 50? Or 100? Such a change reduces the odds that you'll ever become a manager, but it also means that you'll be much closer to the real decision makers in your organization.

---

[11]Caroline McCarthy, "Why Facebook Left 'Scrabulous' Alone," *CNET News*, August 1, 2008, *http://news.cnet.com/8301-13577_3-10003821-36.html?part=rss&subj=news&tag=2547-1_3-0-5* (accessed August 2008).

Or what will microblogging do to employee evaluation and compensation? Your Tweets (or whatever they're called in SharePoint or Google Apps) will be part of the historical record. Will they be used to gauge your effectiveness, either as an official company Tweeter or as a person who Tweets socially too much? It would be surprising, if not. Again, go through your management text and think about every topic there in the context of social networking.

One last thought to consider: What will happen to language? Will well-constructed paragraphs full of interesting words, all spelled correctly, become a rarity? Will such writing be unique to the few newspapers that will still exist to be read by the 17 people who still choose to read print? R u rdy?

Blending the Personal and the Professional

Many businesses are beginning to use social networking sites like Facebook, MySpace, and Twitter for professional purposes. It began with coworkers sharing their accounts with each other socially, just as they did in college. The first interactions concerned activities such as photos of the company softball team or photos at a cocktail party at a recent sales meeting. However, as stated in the Guide on networking in Chapter 6, every business social function is a *business* function, so even sharing photos and pages with the work softball team began to blur the personal–professional boundary.

The employees of Pearson, the publisher of this textbook, are no exception. When I began work on this chapter, I started a Facebook group called "Experiencing MIS." I then queried Facebook for Pearson employees I guessed might have Facebook accounts and invited them to be "friends." Most accepted, and I asked them to join the Experiencing MIS group.

The first day I checked my account, I found an entry from Anne, one of my new friends, who stated that she had been out too late the prior night. That day she happened to be working on the sales plan for this book, and I realized that I didn't want to know her current condition. So, in the group, I asked whether the blending of the personal and the professional is a good thing, and the following conversation resulted:

Anne: I think that for a lot of reasons it is a good thing . . . within reason. I think that people seeing a personal side of you can humanize you. For example, my "I was out too late last night" post didn't mean that I was not into work early and ready to go (which I was, just with a larger coffee than usual), just that I like to have a good time outside of my work life. Also, with all the time we spend at work, our social lives are intertwined with our work lives.

Also, 9–5 work hours are becoming more and more obsolete. I may be updating my Facebook page at noon on a Friday, but you will surely find me working at least part of my day on Saturday and Sunday.

Bob: I definitely see Anne's point of view. There is the temptation to believe that we are all family. I am too old to believe that, but corporate advancement is always going to be predicated to some degree on your willingness to surrender the personal for the professional and/or allow blur. Technology may give you the illusion that you can safely have it both ways.

I am skeptical of business applications for Facebook. My guess is most folks find them lame in the way that business blogs and Christmas cards from your insurance agent are.

Lisa: I actually think there is a place for Facebook in business. For example, think about how it's connected a team like ours—where everyone is located all over the country—to have a place where we actually get to know each other a little better. It's corny, perhaps, but reading people's status updates on my iPhone gives me a better sense of who they are in "real life," not just on the job. I'd get that if we all sat in the same office every day; given that we don't, it's a pretty decent substitute.

I totally agree with Anne's notion that, in many ways, the personal and the professional already do blur, but I think that's more to do with who we are and

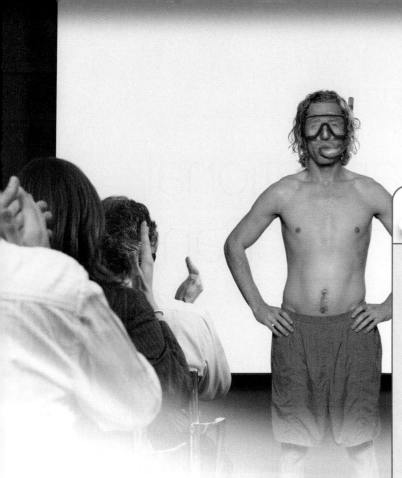

what we do than any specific notion of "corporations." Our work is portable and always on—and judged by results, not hours logged (I think!). In a work universe like that, the lines sort of slowly and inevitably blur . . . PS Anne, I was out too late too. :)

Clearly, I am the curmudgeon here. But, just as I was reflecting on these comments, I received a private email from another person who chose not to be identified:

Other person: A few weeks ago, Pearson started getting really into Facebook. I went from not really using it to getting tons of "friend requests" from coworkers. Then, I got a request from somebody in an executive position at Pearson. I was worried at first—I had heard so many stories of people who had lost their jobs due to social networking, blogging, or other information they posted on the Internet. When I received this request, I must have gone over my profile 10 times to ensure there was nothing that could any way be misconstrued as offensive or illegal. I think many people at the company already know a lot about me, but I . . . I think you would have to be more careful if you're in the introductory months of a new job. ∎

Discussion Questions

1. Do you think Anne's post that she was "Out too late last night" was inappropriate, given that she knew that her professional colleagues were reading her page? Explain.

2. Anne and Lisa contend that Facebook allows employees to get to know each other better in "real life" and not just on the job. Both of these women are very successful business professionals, and they believe such knowledge is important. Do you? Why or why not?

3. Bob is skeptical that Facebook has potential business applications. He thinks social networking sites will become as lame and as uninteresting as business blogs and corporate holiday cards. Do you agree? Why or why not?

4. In the olden days before social networking, instant messaging, email, and "free" long-distance phone calls, social networking was restricted to the people in your department, or maybe those who worked on your floor. You knew the people to whom you revealed personal data, and they were close to you in the organizational hierarchy. You would have had almost no contact with your manager's manager's manager, and what contact you did have would have been in the context of a formal meeting. How do you think management is affected when personal data is readily shared far up and down the organizational hierarchy?

5. Do you think it was appropriate for the senior manager to invite distant subordinates in the organization to be friends? Why did this action put the junior employees in a tight spot? What advantages accrue to the senior manager of having very junior friends? What advantages accrue to the junior professional of having a senior friend?

6. All of the people in this dialog update Facebook using iPhones that they purchased with their own money. Because they are not using a corporate asset, managers at Pearson would be unable to stop these employees from using Facebook, if they wanted to. How does this fact change the power structure within an organization? Consider, for example, what would happen if senior management announced an unpopular change in employee benefits or some other program.

7. As the lawyers say, "You cannot un-ring the bell." Once you've revealed something about yourself, you cannot take it back. Knowing that, what criteria will you use to decide what you will post on a social networking site that is read by your professional colleagues? How do those criteria differ from the criteria you use at school?

Interorganizational Information Exchange

Interorganizational information systems—information systems that connect two or more organizations—require collaborative agreements among independent companies and organizations. Such agreements can be successful only if all parties have a clear idea of the goals, benefits, costs, and risks of working together. The creation of collaborative agreements requires many joint meetings in which the parties make their goals and objectives clear and decide how best to share information and other resources.

During your career, you may be asked to participate is such meetings. You should understand a few basic guidelines before participating.

First, when you meet with employees of another company, realize that you must apply stronger limits on your conversation than when you meet with employees in your own firm. For all you know, the company you are meeting with may become your strongest competitor. In general, you should assume that whatever you say to an employee of another company could be general knowledge in your industry the next day.

Of course, the goal of such meetings is to develop a collaborative relationship, and you cannot accomplish that goal without saying something. The best strategy, however, is to reveal exactly what you must reveal and no more.

Before you meet with another company, you and your team should have a clear and common understanding of the purpose of the meeting. Your team needs to agree beforehand on the topics that are to be addressed and those that are to be avoided. Relationships often develop in stages: Two companies meet, establish one level of understanding, meet again with another level of understanding, and so forth, feeling one another out on the way to some type of relationship.

You may be asked to sign a nondisclosure agreement. Such agreements are contracts that stipulate the responsibilities of each party in protecting the other's proprietary information. Such agreements vary in length; some are a page long and some are 30 pages long. You need to understand the policy of your organization with regard to such agreements before the meeting starts. Sometimes, companies exchange their standard nondisclosure agreements before the meeting so that the respective legal departments can review and approve the agreements ahead of time.

In your remarks, stick to the purpose of the meeting. Avoid conversations about your company or about third parties that do not relate to the meeting topic. You never know the agenda of the other party; you never know what other companies they are meeting; and you never know what other information about your company they may want.

Realize that a meeting isn't over until it's over. The meeting is still underway in the hallway waiting for the elevator. It's still underway at lunch. And it's still underway as you share a cab to the airport. By the way, the only two topics in an elevator should be the weather and the number of the floor you want. Don't embarrass yourself or the employees of the other company by discussing in a public place anything other than the weather.

All of these suggestions may seem paranoid, but even paranoid companies have competitors. There is simply no reason, other than carelessness or stupidity, to discuss topics with another company that do not relate to the matter at hand. Your company will assume enough risk just setting up the interorganizational system. Don't add to that risk by making gratuitous comments about your or any other company. ■

Discussion Questions

1. Suppose you are asked to attend a meeting with your suppliers to discuss the sharing of your sales data. You have no idea as to the specific purpose of the meeting, why you were invited, or what will be expected of you. What should you do?

2. Suppose you flew 1,500 miles for a meeting and at the start of the meeting the other company asks you to sign a nondisclosure statement. You knew nothing about the need to sign such an agreement. What do you do?

3. Some companies have an open, democratic style with lots of collaboration and open discussion. Others are closed and authoritarian, and employees wait to be told what to do. Describe what will happen when employees from two such companies meet. What can be done to improve the situation?

4. Suppose during lunch an employee of another company asks you, "What are you all doing about SOA services?" Assume that this topic has little to do with the purpose of your meeting. You think about it and decide that it doesn't seem too risky to respond, so you say, "Not much." What information have you conveyed by this statement? What is a better way to respond to the question?

5. Suppose you are in a joint meeting and you are asked, "So who else are you working with on this problem?" Describe guidelines you could use in deciding how to answer this question.

6. Explain the statement, "A meeting isn't over until it's over." How might this statement pertain to other meetings—say, a job interview?

ACTIVE REVIEW

Use this Active Review to verify that you understand the ideas and concepts that answer the chapter's study questions.

Q1 How do companies use e-commerce?

Define *e-commerce*, and name and explain categories of e-commerce companies. Explain the terms *B2C, B2B,* and *B2G*. Explain differences between merchant and non-merchant companies. Give examples of each. Discuss how e-commerce improves market efficiency, and describe economic factors that disfavor e-commerce.

Q2 What technology is needed for e-commerce?

Explain the purpose of each of the elements in Figure 8-5. Describe the difference between HTTP and HTML. Trace the online purchase of a basket of goods, using Figure 8-5 as a guide. Explain the purpose of tags and attributes in HTML and XML. Describe different applications for HTML and XML. Explain the three problems of HTML and describe how XML solves them. Summarize the use of XML in supply chains and in specific industries.

Q3 How can information systems enhance supply chain performance?

Define *supply chain* and give an example. Name the four drivers of supply chain performance. Explain the difference between supply chain profitability and organizational profitability. Give an example, other than one in this text, that demonstrates why the two are not maximized in the same way. Explain the bullwhip effect and describe how it can be eliminated.

Q4 Why is Web 2.0 important to business?

How did Amazon.com usher in Web 2.0? Explain the phrase *software as a (free) service* and how it differs from traditional software licensing. Explain the difference in betas between Web 2.0 and traditional software publishing. Describe the difference in business models between Web 2.0 and traditional software companies. Explain the statement, "If a product requires advertising, then it is not Web 2.0." Explain how use increases value in Web 2.0 and define *mashup*. In what way are Web 2.0 interfaces organic? How does rights management differ between Web 2.0 and traditional software? Summarize three major ways that non-Internet companies can use Web 2.0. Explain the difference between Google's AdWords and AdSense.

Q5 How can organizations benefit from social networking?

Define *N:M communication* and *social collaboration*. Explain why the latter term seems redundant but actually isn't. Using your own experience on Facebook or MySpace, explain how these terms characterize social networking. Using Figure 8-17, explain how social networking can become viral. Define *viral hook*. Define *social networking group*, and give an example from your own experience. Name and define three types of SN groups. Explain how Majestic River Ventures might use groups. Describe an SN group that supports operations and management. Use examples other than those in this textbook. Define *social networking application*. Explain the role of services in an SN application. Describe how applications can become viral. Name and explain four characteristics of a meaningful application and give an example of each, other than ones in this book.

Q6 How can organizations benefit from Twitter?

Summarize how Twitter works. Define *microblog*. Explain why the 140-character limit is liberating. Describe how microblogging makes everyone a publisher. Explain how Twitter publishes conversations. Explain the role and importance of being able to search microblogs. Identify and describe three applications for microblogging in business.

Q7 What are the benefits and risks of user-generated content (UGC)?

Give an example of each of the types of UGC in Figure 8-22. Do not use examples in this textbook. Summarize the risks of social networking. Show how those risks apply to Majestic's use of groups, as described in this chapter's opening vignette.

Q8 2020?

Describe how audio and video could be integrated into microblogging. Describe possible implications of social networking for management. Summarize the changes mentioned in this chapter, and add one possible change of your own.

KEY TERMS AND CONCEPTS

USING YOUR KNOWLEDGE

1. Suppose you are a manufacturer of high-end consumer kitchen appliances, and you are about to bring out a new line of mixers that will make an existing model obsolete. Assume you have 500 mixers of that existing model in finished-goods inventory. Describe three different strategies for using an electronic auction for unloading that inventory. Which strategy do you recommend?

2. Visit *www://zillow.com*. Enter the address of someone's home (your parents'?) and obtain an appraisal of it. Check out the appraised values of the neighbors' homes. Do you think this site violates anyone's privacy? Why or why not? Find and describe features that demonstrate that Zillow.com is a Web 2.0 company. Explain why this site might be considered a threat by traditional real estate companies. How might real estate agents use this site to market their services? How might real estate brokers (those who own agencies) use this site to their advantage?

3. Amazon.com makes it exceedingly easy for developers to use its SOA-based Web services. Using these SOA services, Web developers can make portions of the Amazon.com catalog appear to be part of their site. Why do you think Amazon.com does that? What competitive advantage does it receive? Describe another B2C business, in another industry, that might achieve similar benefits by developing an easy-to-use, SOA-based Web service.

4. Suppose that FlexTime creates its own Facebook page. Describe three features that FlexTime could put on that page. Explain how FlexTime could use Facebook groups. Explain the features of a potential Facebook application that FlexTime could develop. Explain how that application would contribute to FlexTime's competitive advantage.

5. Explain how the partners and trainers at FlexTime could use Twitter to further their business goals. Name three different business functions that they could accomplish with Twitter, and explain how those functions contribute to FlexTime's competitive strategy.

6. Suppose that Neil at FlexTime wants to post trainer comments on the FlexTime Facebook page. How could FlexTime use a combination of Twitter and Facebook to accomplish this goal? How effective or important do you think this capability would be to FlexTime's customers?

7. In the MRV case, Butterworth and Graham are ill-matched tent mates. Explain ways that MRV could use the following to create better tent-mate matches:

    a. MRV Facebook page
    b. MRV Facebook group
    c. Twitter
    d. Twitter–Facebook combo (as in question 6)

Which of these options seems the best to you?

COLLABORATION EXERCISE

Collaborate with a group of students on the following exercise. Recall from Chapter 2 that collaboration is more than cooperation because it involves iteration and feedback. Post a document, a discussion item, a wiki item, or an idea and obtain feedback from your team members. Similarly, read the ideas of others and comment on them. Try to innovate in both the process by which you collaborate and the work product that you create. Avoid face-to-face meetings. Instead, use collaborative software such as Google Docs & Spreadsheets, Microsoft Groove, or Microsoft SharePoint to facilitate your ideas.

Clearly, many possibilities exist for the innovative application of Web 2.0 technologies. In this exercise, you will have an opportunity to consider such applications for MRV. One way to proceed is to examine Web 2.0 (including social networking and UGC) in the context of the eight competitive advantage principles in Figure 3-12 (page 77). For example, here is one application of Web 2.0 for each principle:

1. **New product or service.** Use a mashup to combine your company's product with Google Maps.
2. **Enhance product or service.** Use social networking to connect your customers to each other.
3. **Differentiate product or service.** Add a marketplace in which your customers can sell innovative applications of your products to each other.
4. **Lock in customers and buyers.** Provide an information system by which your customers can mash up their product documentation with documentation of components that you sell them. For example, when one of your customer's customers seeks product maintenance instructions, a mashup automatically provides your instructions for the components you supply in your customer's product.
5. **Lock in suppliers.** For a company with part-time contractors, such as FlexTime, use social networking to connect your instructors to their customers, but only in the context of your studio. (But be careful! Many Web 2.0 services that you might develop for your suppliers could benefit your competition as much as yourself.) See also questions Q5 and Q6 (page 292–303).

6. **Raise barriers to entry.** Increase customer loyalty by developing a social network of customers who obtain value from each other via your network.
7. **Establish alliances.** If your organization provides face-to-face services (e.g., FlexTime), organize a consortium of similar companies in different regions to buy AdWords. Your consortium will be better able to compete with national firms that are buying the same words.
8. **Reduce costs.** Reduce sales costs by creating a social network for your sales staff to share knowledge, experience, and sales opportunities. For example, trainers at FlexTime can share their ideas, techniques, and experiences for selling individual personal training sessions to group class attendees.

Questions
a. Explain how MRV could advertise using Google AdWords. In general terms, describe a strategy for changing word bid prices to increase the return on advertising expense.
b. Explain how MRV could earn revenue via Google's AdSense. Do you recommend this source of revenue? Why or why not?
c. Using the Web, investigate Web 2.0 advertising vendors other than Google. Compare the best alternatives you find to Google AdWords and recommend one of the two vendors.
d. Using the elements of competitive advantage described previously:

    (1) Describe four different ways that MRV could use social networking to further implement its competitive strategy.
    (2) Describe four different ways that MRV could use mashups to further implement its competitive strategy.
    (3) Describe four different ways that MRV could use Twitter to further implement its competitive strategy.

e. Select the three best ideas in your answer to part d. Describe criteria for making the selection, and score your ideas based on those criteria.

f. Like most small companies, MRV carefully manages its cash. Explain, at a high level, why you think the ideas in your answer to part e are worth the investment of this critical resource.

g. If you owned MRV, would you implement any of your ideas in part e? Why or why not?

APPLICATION EXERCISES

1. Assume you have been asked to create a spreadsheet to help make a buy-versus-lease decision for the servers on your organization's Web farm. Assume that you are considering the servers for a 5-year period, but you do not know exactly how many servers you will need. Initially, you know you will need 5 servers, but you might need as many as 50, depending on the success of your organization's e-commerce activity.

a. For the buy-alternative calculations, set up your spreadsheet so that you can enter the base price of the server hardware, the price of all software, and a maintenance expense that is some percentage of the hardware price. Assume that the percent you enter covers both hardware and software maintenance. Also assume that each server has a 3-year life, after which it has no value. Assume straight-line depreciation for computers used less than 3 years, and that at the end of the 5 years you can sell the computers you have used for less than 3 years for their depreciated value. Also assume that your organization pays 2 percent interest on capital expenses. Assume the servers cost $5,000 each, and the needed software costs $750. Assume that the maintenance expense varies from 2 to 7 percent.

b. For the lease-alternative calculations, assume that the leasing vendor will lease the same computer hardware as you can purchase. The lease includes all the software you need as well as all maintenance. Set up your spreadsheet so that you can enter various lease costs, which vary according to the number of years of the lease (1, 2, or 3). Assume the cost of a 3-year lease is $285 per machine per month, a 2-year lease is $335 per machine per month, and a 1-year lease is $415 per machine per month. Also, the lessor offers a 5 percent discount if you lease from 20 to 30 computers and a 10 percent discount if you lease from 31 to 50 computers.

c. Using your spreadsheet, compare the costs of buy versus lease under the following situations. (Assume you either buy or lease. You cannot lease some and buy some.) Make assumptions as necessary and state those assumptions.

(1) Your organization requires 20 servers for 5 years.

(2) Your organization requires 20 servers for the first 2 years and 40 servers for the next 3 years.

(3) Your organization requires 20 servers for the first 2 years, 40 servers for the next 2 years, and 50 servers for the last year.

(4) Your organization requires 10 servers the first year, 20 servers the second year, 30 servers the third year, 40 servers the fourth year, and 50 servers the last year.

(5) For the previous case, does the cheaper alternative change if the cost of the servers is $4,000? If it is $8,000?

2. Assume that you have been given the task of compiling evaluations that your company's purchasing agents make of their vendors. Each month, every purchasing agent evaluates all of the vendors that he or she has worked with in the past month on three factors: price, quality, and responsiveness. Assume the ratings are from 1 to 5, with 5 being the best. Because your company has hundreds of vendors and dozens of purchasing agents, you decide to use Access to compile the results.

a. Create a database with three tables: VENDOR (*VendorNumber, Name, Contact*), PURCHASER (*EmpNumber, Name, Email*), and RATING (*EmpNumber, VendorNumber, Month, Year, Price Rating, QualityRating, ResponsivenessRating*). Assume that *VendorNumber* and *EmpNumber* are the keys of VENDOR and PURCHASER, respectively. Decide what you think is the appropriate key for RATING.

b. Create appropriate relationships.

c. Go to this text's companion Web site and import the data in the Excel file **Ch08Ex02**. Note that data for Vendor, Purchaser, and Rating are stored in three separate worksheets.

d. Create a query that shows the names of all vendors and their average scores.

e. Create a query that shows the names of all employees and their average scores. *Hint:* In this and in part f, you will need to use the *Group By* function in your query.

f. Create a parameterized query that you can use to obtain the minimum, maximum, and average ratings on each criterion for a particular vendor. Assume you will enter *VendorName* as the parameter.

g. Using the information created by your queries, what conclusions can you make about vendors or purchasers?

CASE STUDY 8

You, Inc.

Interorganizational information systems enable small businesses to avoid the time and expense of building infrastructure, thus reducing capital requirements and shortening the time to market. In particular, they can help YOU. Consider the following business opportunity:

People often pay more for new items on eBay than they would pay if they shopped for bargains on the Internet. Either they do not like to e-shop, or perhaps they become entangled in the excitement of an auction, lose a bid, and decide to pay the *BuyItNow* price for a similar item in another auction. Whatever the reason, there is often an inefficiency in the flow of price information among eBay users.

Consider that inefficiency as a business opportunity for your own small business. Assume you are willing to invest no more than $500 in a computer, $49 per month for a DSL line, and a few hours of your time each day. How many of the value-chain activities can you outsource using interorganizational information systems?

Begin with market research. Using your Internet connection to the Web, you can investigate auctions, product categories, and related market segments. Doing this work saves hiring market research firms to produce this information for you. You do not need to conduct extensive and expensive market surveys; the information you need is on the Internet. Suppose you notice that there are opportunities on the sale of high-end motorcycle parts. The Baby Boomers are reliving their childhoods and now have considerable disposable income to spend. They cannot stand to lose an auction and will pay to get what they want, right now. You decide to focus on this opportunity.

Using the Internet, you find sources for motorcycle parts. Sourcing is a typical supply-chain activity; and again, by using the Internet, you have avoided hiring someone else to do this work for you. You search for sites that offer the products you want, have free shipping, and (if possible) for which you do not need to pay taxes.

When you find an item offered at a bargain price, you set up an auction for that item on eBay. You have not yet purchased the item; you just know where you can buy it. You set a price and the terms of the auction so that, at whatever price the item sells, you will make some profit (after deducting the cost of the auction). Avoiding the expense of hiring a photo team to take photos, you download pictures of the item from your vendor and copy those photos into your auction. Your only financial exposure if the item does not sell is the cost of the auction.

Suppose the item sells. You then buy it from the vendor you have located, paying for it using PayPal or a credit card, and you request the vendor to ship the item directly to your customer, a process called *drop shipping*. If you pay with a credit card, it is possible you will receive payment from your customer before you pay for the item you sold. Because the item is new, and because you sell only high-quality items, all service and support are handled by the manufacturer.

Review this scenario in terms of Porter's value chain model. You did market research, but you outsourced all of the data-gathering activities to eBay, PriceGrabber, and so on. You set up the auction on eBay, and thus outsourced the sales infrastructure to eBay. You did the product-sourcing yourself, but again, you had considerable help from the Internet. Because you drop-shipped the item to your customer, you outsourced all inventory, operations, and shipping activities to that vendor. If the customer pays you before you pay your credit card, you can even earn interest on the customer's money. You outsourced service and support to the manufacturer.

Consider support activities: Because you avoided building infrastructure, you have only one part-time employee, yourself; you have no payroll or other compensation needs. You might want insurance, but if you sell enough using eBay you can buy life and medical insurance from eBay at attractive terms, so you can outsource those functions as well.

Consider accounting: eBay, PayPal, your credit card company, and the vendor will do most of the work. All you need to do is maintain records to track your income for tax reporting. You can even pay your taxes online if you choose. All of this is possible only because of the prevalence of interorganizational information systems!

Questions

1. Investigate auctions on eBay and, for any category of product in which you have knowledge or interest, compare selling prices to prices of new goods from e-commerce sites. Attempt to find one or more products in which the item sold on eBay costs more than if it had been purchased from a vendor. State the price differential(s). If you find no such products, list the products' eBay prices and vendor prices for five of the products you investigated.

2. Go to *www.ebay.com* and learn how eBay charges for its auctions. You have many options to choose from; select the option(s) that you believe will be best for selling goods using this strategy. Explain why you think that option is the best.

3. Using price comparison sites (such as PriceGrabber, CNET.com, or Froogle), identify three sources for products that you identified in question 1. If you did not find any qualifying products in that question, identify sources for some product in which you have an interest. Seek sources that provide free shipping and to which you do not need to pay taxes.

4. Either by yourself or with a group of classmates, find some product from your answer in question 1 that seems to you to be a good bargain. Set up an auction for that item on eBay, with terms that will enable you to make some profit, even if the product sells at the lowest price.

5. Run the auction. If you make some profit, celebrate, and run it again. If not, state why you did not make a profit and describe what you would do differently to earn some profit.

9

Business Intelligence Systems

"Sue, I'm telling you, Trevor is great. If we don't give him a decent bonus, he'll leave us."

"Well, maybe . . . but what makes you think he's a great guide?"

"He's terrific around the customers. He's personable, nobody can tell a funnier story, his rafting skills are good. Hey, he's just fun to have on the trips."

"Sure. All true. But what does he do for Majestic?"

"What do you mean?"

"What are we trying to do? Form quality relationships with quality customers. Right?"

"Yeah, you say that all the time."

"And why are we doing that? Repeat business. We want our customers to come back, and we want them to tell their friends."

"Well, Trevor does that."

"You think so? Tell me one of Trevor's customers who's come back."

"Well, I can't think of any names. But I'm sure there's a bunch of them."

"You are? Hmpf. Well, I looked through the data and I can't find one."

"That can't be right."

"I think Trevor is fun, I think he's decent on the river, but it's all about Trevor."

"If he finds out other guides got bigger bonuses, he'll leave."

"We may miss his humor and stories, but the business isn't going to miss him. Whatever he does doesn't translate into repeat business. We hand him the customers, and he doesn't develop our relationship with them."

"So, what are you going to do?"

"I want to align guide compensation with our strategy. I want to relate bonuses to repeat customers. Or, maybe give a commission on repeat customers. I was looking at our payroll. This season, we've employed 17 different guides; 14 of those people were here last year, and 11 have been with us 3 years or more."

"Yeah, so what?"

"Well, let's rank those people on the business they've generated. I started to do that, but it's a pain linking all the records together. We should use a computer, I, guess. . . ."

Most companies, Majestic included, are awash in data. Submerged in this data is information that, if found and made available to the right people at the right time, can improve Majestic's decision making. Trevor, the rafting guide, is a good example. ■

>> STUDY QUESTIONS

Q1 Why do organizations need business intelligence?

Q2 What business intelligence systems are available?

Q3 What are typical reporting applications?

Q4 What are typical data-mining applications?

Q5 What is the purpose of data warehouses and data marts?

Q6 What are typical knowledge-management applications?

Q7 How are business intelligence applications delivered?

Q8 2020?

CHAPTER PREVIEW

You can find a free, supplemental study lesson for this chapter at:

www.LearningMIS.com

The information systems described in Chapters 7 and 8 generate enormous amounts of data. Most of these data are used for operational purposes, such as tracking orders, inventories, payables, and so forth. These operational data have a potential windfall: They contain patterns, relationships, clusters, and other information that can facilitate management, especially planning and forecasting. Business intelligence systems produce such information from operational data.

In addition to information in data, an even more important source of information is employees themselves. Employees come to the organization with expertise, and as they gain experience in the organization they add to that expertise. Vast amounts of collective knowledge exist in every organization's employees. How can that knowledge be shared? Knowledge-management applications address this need, and we will conclude this chapter with a description of the purpose, features, and functions of these applications.

This chapter surveys the most common business intelligence and knowledge-management applications, discusses the need and purpose for data warehouses, and explains how business intelligence applications are delivered to users as business intelligence systems. Along the way, you'll learn tools and techniques that MRV can use to identify the guides that contribute the most (and least) to its competitive strategy. We'll wrap-up by discussing some of the potential benefits and risks of mining credit card data.

Q1 Why Do Organizations Need Business Intelligence?

Because data communications and data storage are essentially free, enormous amounts of data are created and stored every day. A study done at the University of California at Berkeley[1] found that a total of 2 exabytes of data were created in 2002. That number has grown exponentially. In 2008, Michael Wesch stated that 70 exabytes of data would be generated in 2009; that is, 12,000 gigabytes per person of data, worldwide. Further, according to Wesch, less than .01 percent of that data will be printed on paper, and 88 percent of it will be new and original.[2]

The terms **petabyte** and **exabyte** are defined in Figure 9-1. As shown there, 70 exabyte is equivalent to 14 times the total number of words ever spoken by humans. That is indeed a lot of data, and it represents only the amount generated in 2008!

Somewhere in all that data is **business intelligence (BI)**—information containing patterns, relationships, and trends. But that information needs to be found and produced. For example, somewhere in the more than 300 million individual demographic records that Acxiom Corporation collects[3] is evidence that someone is going to default on a loan. Or, to bring it closer, somewhere in MRV's megabytes of data is evidence that some guides are much better at generating repeat business than other guides. That information is in the data. The question is: How can Acxiom or MRV get it out?

Businesses use business intelligence systems to process this immense ocean of data; to produce patterns, relationships, and other forms of information; and to deliver that information on a timely basis to users who need it.

---

[1]"How Much Information, 2003," *http://sims.berkeley.edu/research/projects/how-much-info-2003* (accessed July 2009).
[2]*http://umanitoba.ca/ist/production/streaming/podcast_wesch.html* (accessed July 2009).
[3]*http://www.acxiom.com/about_us/Pages/AboutAcxiom.aspxm* (accessed July 2009).

Kilobyte (KB)	*1,000 bytes OR 10^3 bytes* 2 Kilobytes: A typewritten page 100 Kilobytes: A low-resolution photograph
Megabyte (MB)	*1,000,000 bytes OR 10^6 bytes* 1 Megabyte: A small novel OR a 3.5-inch floppy disk 2 Megabytes: A high-resolution photograph 5 Megabytes: The complete works of Shakespeare 10 Megabytes: A minute of high-fidelity sound 100 Megabytes: One meter of shelved books 500 Megabytes: A CD-ROM
Gigabyte (GB)	*1,000,000,000 bytes OR 10^9 bytes* 1 Gigabyte: A pickup truck filled with books 20 Gigabytes: A good collection of the works of Beethoven 100 Gigabytes: A library floor of academic journals
Terabyte (TB)	*1,000,000,000,000 bytes OR 10^{12} bytes* 1 Terabyte: 50,000 trees made into paper and printed 2 Terabytes: An academic research library 10 Terabytes: The print collections of the U.S. Library of Congress 400 Terabytes: National Climactic Data Center (NOAA) database
Petabyte (PB)	*1,000,000,000,000,000 bytes OR 10^{15} bytes* 1 Petabyte: Three years of EOS data (2001) 2 Petabytes: All U.S. academic research libraries 20 Petabytes: Production of hard-disk drives in 1995 200 Petabytes: All printed material
Exabyte (EB)	*1,000,000,000,000,000,000 bytes OR 10^{18} bytes* 2 Exabytes: Total volume of information generated in 1999 5 Exabytes: All words ever spoken by human beings

Figure 9-1
How Big Is an Exabyte?

Source: Used with permission of Peter Lyman and Hal R. Varian, University of California at Berkeley.

Q2 What Business Intelligence Systems Are Available?

A **business intelligence (BI) system** is an information system that employs business intelligence tools to produce and deliver information. The characteristics of a particular BI system depend on the tool in use, so we will begin by categorizing such tools.

Business Intelligence Tools

A **business intelligence (BI) tool** is one or more computer programs that implement a particular BI technique. We can categorize BI tools in three ways: as reporting tools, as data-mining tools, and as knowledge-management tools.

Reporting tools are programs that read data from a variety of sources, process that data, format it into structured reports, and deliver those reports to the users who need them. The processing of the data is simple: Data are sorted and grouped, and simple totals and averages are calculated, as you will see. Reporting tools are used primarily for *assessment*. They are used to address questions like: What has happened in the past? What is the current situation? How does the current situation compare to the past?

Data-mining tools process data using statistical techniques, many of which are sophisticated and mathematically complex. We will explore data mining later in this chapter. For now, it is enough to say that *data mining* involves searching for patterns and relationships among data. In most cases, data-mining tools are used to make *predictions*. For example, we can use one form of analysis to compute the probability that a customer will default on a loan or the probability that a customer is likely to respond positively to a promotion. Another data-mining technique predicts products that tend to be purchased together. In one famous example, a data-mining analysis determined that customers who buy diapers are likely to buy beer.[4] The information prompted store managers to locate beer and diapers near each other in store displays.

Although reporting tools *tend to be* used to assess and data-mining tools *tend to be* used to predict, that distinction is not always true. A better way to distinguish between these two BI tools is that reporting tools use simple operations such as sorting, grouping, and summing, and data-mining tools use sophisticated statistical techniques.

Knowledge-management tools are used to store employee knowledge and to make that knowledge available to employees, customers, vendors, auditors, and others who need it. Knowledge-management tools differ from reporting and data-mining tools because the source of their data is human knowledge, rather than recorded facts and figures. Nonetheless, they are important BI tools.

Tools Versus Applications Versus Systems

It will be easier for you to understand this chapter if you distinguish among three terms. As stated, a *BI tool* is one or more computer programs. BI tools implement the logic of a particular procedure or process. A **business intelligence (BI) application** is the use of a tool on a particular type of data for a particular purpose. A business intelligence (BI) system is an information system having all five components that delivers the results of a BI application to users who need those results.

Consider an example. Later in this chapter, you will learn about a BI tool called *decision-tree analysis.* That BI tool can be used in a BI application to assess the risk of default on an existing loan. A BI system delivers the results of the decision-tree analysis on a particular loan to a banking officer, who then decides whether to buy or sell that loan and for what price.

Given this introduction, we will now illustrate applications of each type of BI tool.

Q3 What Are Typical Reporting Applications?

A **reporting application** is a BI application that inputs data from one or more sources and applies a reporting tool to that data to produce information. The resulting information is subsequently delivered to users by a **reporting system**, which is a BI system that delivers reports to authorized users at appropriate times. This section describes operations commonly used by reporting tools and then illustrates two important reporting applications: RFM analysis and OLAP.

Basic Reporting Operations

Reporting tools produce information from data using five basic operations:

- Sorting
- Grouping
- Calculating
- Filtering
- Formatting

Consider the sales data shown in Figure 9-2. This list of raw data contains little or no information; it is just data. We can create information from this data by *sorting* by

[4]Michael J. A. Berry and Gordon Linoff, *Data Mining Techniques for Marketing, Sales, and Customer Support* (New York: John Wiley, 1997).

CustomerName	CustomerEmail	DateOfSale	Amount
Ashley, Jane	JA@somewhere.com	5/5/2007	$110
Corning,Sandra	KD@somewhereelse.com	7/7/2007	$375
Ching, Kam Hoong	KHC@somewhere.com	5/17/2007	$55
Rikki, Nicole	GC@righthere.com	6/19/2005	$155
Corning,Sandra	SC@somewhereelse.com	2/4/2006	$195
Scott, Rex	RS@somewhere.com	7/15/2007	$56
Corovic,Jose	JC@somewhere.com	11/12/2007	$55
McGovern, Adrian	BL@righthere.com	11/12/2005	$47
Wei, Guang	GW@ourcompany.com	11/28/2006	$385
Dixon,Eleonor	ED@somewhere.com	5/17/2007	$108
Lee,Brandon	BL@somewhereelse.com	5/5/2005	$74
Duong,Linda	LD@righthere.com	5/17/2006	$485
Dixon, James T	JTD@somewhere.com	4/3/2006	$285
La Pierre,Anna	SG@righthere.com	9/22/2007	$120
La Pierre,Anna	WS@somewhere.com	3/14/2007	$48
La Pierre,Anna	TR@righthere.com	9/22/2007	$580
Ryan, Mark	MR@somewhereelse.com	11/3/2007	$42
Rikki, Nicole	MR@righthere.com	3/14/2007	$175
Scott, Bryan	BS@somewhere.com	3/17/2006	$145
Warrem, Jason	JW@ourcompany.com	5/12/2007	$160
La Pierre,Anna	ALP@somewhereelse.com	3/15/2006	$52
Angel, Kathy	KA@righthere.com	9/15/2007	$195
La Pierre,Anna	JQ@somewhere.com	4/12/2007	$44
Casimiro, Amanda	AC@somewhere.com	12/7/2006	$52
McGovern, Adrian	AM@ourcompany.com	3/17/2006	$52
Menstell,Lori Lee	LLM@ourcompany.com	10/18/2007	$72
La Pierre,Anna	DJ@righthere.com	12/7/2006	$175
Nurul,Nicole	NN@somewhere.com	10/12/2007	$84
Menstell,Lori Lee	VB@ourcompany.com	9/24/2007	$120
Pham,Mary	MP@somewhere.com	3/14/2007	$38

Figure 9-2
Raw Sales Data

customer name, as shown in Figure 9-3. In this format, we can see that some customers have ordered more than once, and we can readily find their orders.

This is a step forward, but we can produce even more information by *grouping* the orders, as shown in Figure 9-4. Notice that the reporting tool not only grouped the orders but also *computed* the number of orders for each customer and the total purchase amount per customer.

Suppose we are interested in repeat customers. If so, we can *filter* the groups of orders to select only those customers that have two or more orders. The results of these operations are shown in Figure 9-5. The report in this figure not only has filtered the results, but it also has *formatted* them for easier understanding. Compare Figure 9-5 to 9-2. If your goal is to identify your best customers, the report in Figure 9-5 is far more useful and will save you considerable work.

The five operations just discussed may seem too simple to produce important results, but that is not the case. Reporting tools can produce incredibly interesting and insightful information. We will consider the use of two such tools next.

RFM Analysis

RFM analysis, a technique readily implemented using reporting tools, is used to analyze and rank customers according to their purchasing patterns.[5] RFM considers how *recently* (R) a customer has ordered, how *frequently* (F) a customer ordered, and how much *money* (M) the customer has spent.

---

[5]Arthur Middleton Hughes, "Boosting Response with RFM," *Marketing Tools*, May 1996. See also *http://dbmarketing.com*.

CustomerName ↑	CustomerEmail	DateOfSale	Amount
Adams, James	JA3@somewhere.com	1/15/2007	$145
Angel, Kathy	KA@righthere.com	9/15/2007	$195
Ashley, Jane	JA@somewhere.com	5/5/2007	$110
Austin, James	JA7@somewhere.com	1/15/2006	$55
Bernard, Steven	SB@ourcompany.com	9/17/2007	$78
Casimiro, Amanda	AC@somewhere.com	12/7/2006	$52
Ching, Kam Hoong	KHC@somewhere.com	5/17/2007	$55
Corning,Sandra	KD@somewhereelse.com	7/7/2007	$375
Corning,Sandra	SC@somewhereelse.com	2/4/2006	$195
Corovic,Jose	JC@somewhere.com	11/12/2007	$55
Daniel, James	JD@somewhere.com	1/18/2007	$52
Dixon, James T	JTD@somewhere.com	4/3/2006	$285
Dixon,Eleonor	ED@somewhere.com	5/17/2007	$108
Drew, Richard	RD@righthere.com	10/3/2006	$42
Duong,Linda	LD@righthere.com	5/17/2006	$485
Garrett, James	JG@ourcompany.com	3/14/2007	$38
Jordan, Matthew	MJ@righthere.com	3/14/2006	$645
La Pierre,Anna	DJ@righthere.com	12/7/2006	$175
La Pierre,Anna	SG@righthere.com	9/22/2007	$120
La Pierre,Anna	TR@righthere.com	9/22/2007	$580
La Pierre,Anna	ALP@somewhereelse.com	3/15/2006	$52
La Pierre,Anna	JQ@somewhere.com	4/12/2007	$44
La Pierre,Anna	WS@somewhere.com	3/14/2007	$48
Lee,Brandon	BL@somewhereelse.com	5/5/2005	$74
Lunden,Haley	HL@somewhere.com	11/17/2004	$52
McGovern, Adrian	BL@righthere.com	11/12/2005	$47
McGovern, Adrian	AM@ourcompany.com	3/17/2006	$52
Menstell,Lori Lee	LLM@ourcompany.com	10/18/2007	$72
Menstell,Lori Lee	VB@ourcompany.com	9/24/2007	$120
Nurul,Nicole	NN@somewhere.com	10/12/2007	$84

Figure 9-3
Sales Data Sorted by
Customer Name

CustomerName	NumOrders	TotalPurcha:
Adams, James	1	$145.00
Angel, Kathy	1	$195.00
Ashley, Jane	1	$110.00
Austin, James	1	$55.00
Bernard, Steven	1	$78.00
Casimiro, Amanda	1	$52.00
Ching, Kam Hoong	1	$55.00
Corning,Sandra	2	$570.00
Corovic,Jose	1	$55.00
Daniel, James	1	$52.00
Dixon, James T	1	$285.00
Dixon,Eleonor	1	$108.00
Drew, Richard	1	$42.00
Duong,Linda	1	$485.00
Garrett, James	1	$38.00
Jordan, Matthew	1	$645.00
La Pierre,Anna	6	$1,018.50
Lee,Brandon	1	$74.00
Lunden,Haley	1	$52.00
McGovern, Adrian	2	$99.00
Menstell,Lori Lee	2	$192.00
Nurul,Nicole	1	$84.00
Pham,Mary	1	$38.00
Redmond, Louise	1	$140.00
Rikki, Nicole	2	$330.00
Ryan, Mark	1	$42.00
Scott, Bryan	1	$145.00
Scott, Rex	1	$56.00
UTran,Diem Thi	1	$275.00
Warrem, Jason	1	$160.00

Figure 9-4
Sales Data, Sorted by
Customer Name and Grouped
by Orders and Purchase
Amount

Repeat Customers

NumOrders	CustomerName	TotalPurchases
6	La Pierre,Anna	$1,018.50
2	Corning,Sandra	$570.00
2	Rikki, Nicole	$330.00
2	Menstell,Lori Lee	$192.00
2	McGovern, Adrian	$99.00

Figure 9-5
Sales Data Filtered to Show
Repeat Customers

To produce an RFM score, the RFM reporting tool first sorts customer purchase records by the date of their most recent (R) purchase. In a common form of this analysis, the tool then divides the customers into five groups and gives customers in each group a score of 1 to 5. The 20 percent of the customers having the most recent orders are given an R score of 1, the 20 percent of the customers having the next most recent orders are given an R score of 2, and so forth, down to the last 20 percent, who are given an R score of 5.

The tool then re-sorts the customers on the basis of how frequently they order. The 20 percent of the customers who order most frequently are given an F score of 1, the next 20 percent of most frequently ordering customers are given a score of 2, and so forth, down to the least frequently ordering customers, who are given an F score of 5.

Finally, the tool sorts the customers again according to the amount spent on their orders. The 20 percent who have ordered the most expensive items are given an M score of 1, the next 20 percent are given an M score of 2, and so forth, down to the 20 percent who spend the least, who are given an M score of 5.

Figure 9-6 shows sample RFM results. The first customer, Ajax, has ordered recently and orders frequently. Ajax's M score of 3 indicates, however, that it does not order the most expensive goods. From these scores, the sales team can conclude that Ajax is a good, regular customer, and that they should attempt to up-sell more-expensive goods to Ajax.

The second customer in Figure 9-6 could represent a problem. Bloominghams has not ordered in some time, but when it did order in the past it ordered frequently, and its orders were of the highest monetary value. This data suggests that Bloominghams might have taken its business to another vendor. Someone from the sales team should contact this customer immediately.

No one on the sales team should even think about the third customer, Caruthers. This company has not ordered for some time; it did not order frequently; and, when it did order, it bought the least-expensive items, and not many of them. Let Caruthers go to the competition; the loss will be minimal.

The last customer, Davidson, is right in the middle. Davidson is an OK customer, but probably no one in sales should spend much time with it. Perhaps sales can set up an automated contact system or use the Davidson account as a training exercise for an eager departmental assistant or intern.

Customer	RFM Score		
Ajax	1	1	3
Bloominghams	5	1	1
Caruthers	5	4	5
Davidson	3	3	3

Figure 9-6
Example of RFM Score Data

Online Analytical Processing

Online analytical processing (OLAP), a second type of reporting tool, is more generic than RFM. OLAP provides the ability to sum, count, average, and perform other simple arithmetic operations on groups of data. The remarkable characteristic of OLAP reports is that they are dynamic. The viewer of the report can change the report's format, hence the term *online*.

An OLAP report has measures and dimensions. A **measure** is the data item of interest. It is the item that is to be summed or averaged or otherwise processed in the OLAP report. Total sales, average sales, and average cost are examples of measures. A **dimension** is a characteristic of a measure. Purchase date, customer type, customer location, and sales region are all examples of dimensions.

Figure 9-7 shows a typical OLAP report. Here, the measure is *Net Store Sales*, and the dimensions are *Product Family* and *Store Type*. This report shows how net store sales vary by product family and store type. Stores of type *Supermarket* sold a net of $36,189 worth of nonconsumable goods, for example.

A presentation like that in Figure 9-7 is often called an **OLAP cube**, or sometimes simply a *cube*. The reason for this term is that some software products show these displays using three axes, like a cube in geometry. The origin of the term is unimportant here, however. Just know that an *OLAP cube* and an *OLAP report* are the same thing.

The OLAP report in Figure 9-7 was generated by Microsoft SQL Server Analysis Services and is displayed in an Excel pivot table. The data were taken from a sample instructional database, called Food Mart, that is provided with SQL Server.

It is possible to display OLAP cubes in many ways besides with Excel. Some third-party vendors provide more extensive graphical displays. For more information about such products, check for OLAP vendors and products at the Data Housing Review at *http://dwreview.com/OLAP/index.html*.

As stated earlier, the distinguishing characteristic of an OLAP report is that the user can alter the format of the report. Figure 9-8 shows such an alteration. Here, the user added another dimension, *Store Country* and *Store State*, to the horizontal display. Product-family sales are now broken out by store location. Observe that the sample data only includes stores in the United States, and only in the western states of California, Oregon, and Washington.

With an OLAP report, it is possible to **drill down** into the data. This term means to further divide the data into more detail. In Figure 9-9 (page 328), for example, the user has drilled down into the stores located in California; the OLAP report now shows sales data for the four cities in California that have stores.

Notice another difference between Figures 9-8 and 9-9. The user has not only drilled down, she has also changed the order of the dimensions. Figure 9-8 shows *Product Family* and then store location within *Product Family*. Figure 9-9 shows store location and then *Product Family* within store location.

Both displays are valid and useful, depending on the user's perspective. A product manager might like to see product families first and then store location data. A sales manager might like to see store locations first and then product data.

Figure 9-7
OLAP Product Family
and Store Type

	A	B	C	D	E	F	G
1							
2							
3	Store Sales Net	Store Type ▼					
4	Product Family ▼	Deluxe Supermarket	Gourmet Supermarket	Mid-Size Grocery	Small Grocery	Supermarket	Grand Total
5	Drink	$8,119.05	$2,392.83	$1,409.50	$685.89	$16,751.71	$29,358.98
6	Food	$70,276.11	$20,026.18	$10,392.19	$6,109.72	$138,960.67	$245,764.87
7	Non-Consumable	$18,884.24	$5,064.79	$2,813.73	$1,534.90	$36,189.40	$64,487.05
8	Grand Total	$97,279.40	$27,483.80	$14,615.42	$8,330.51	$191,901.77	$339,610.90

	A	B	C	D	E	F	G	H	I
1									
2									
3	Store Sales Net			Store Type ▼					
4	Product Family ▼	Store ▼	Store State	Deluxe Superma	Gourmet Supermar	Mid-Size Groce	Small Grocery	Supermarket	Grand Total
5	Drink	USA	CA		$2,392.83		$227.38	$5,920.76	$8,540.97
6			OR	$4,438.49				$2,862.45	$7,300.94
7			WA	$3,680.56		$1,409.50	$458.51	$7,968.50	$13,517.07
8		USA Total		$8,119.05	$2,392.83	$1,409.50	$685.89	$16,751.71	$29,358.98
9	Drink Total			$8,119.05	$2,392.83	$1,409.50	$685.89	$16,751.71	$29,358.98
10	Food	USA	CA		$20,026.18		$1,960.53	$47,226.11	$69,212.82
11			OR	$37,778.35				$23,818.87	$61,597.22
12			WA	$32,497.76		$10,392.19	$4,149.19	$67,915.69	$114,954.83
13		USA Total		$70,276.11	$20,026.18	$10,392.19	$6,109.72	$138,960.67	$245,764.87
14	Food Total			$70,276.11	$20,026.18	$10,392.19	$6,109.72	$138,960.67	$245,764.87
15	Non-Consumable	USA	CA		$5,064.79		$474.35	$12,344.49	$17,883.63
16			OR	$10,177.89				$6,428.53	$16,606.41
17			WA	$8,706.36		$2,813.73	$1,060.54	$17,416.38	$29,997.01
18		USA Total		$18,884.24	$5,064.79	$2,813.73	$1,534.90	$36,189.40	$64,487.05
19	Non-Consumable Total			$18,884.24	$5,064.79	$2,813.73	$1,534.90	$36,189.40	$64,487.05
20	Grand Total			$97,279.40	$27,483.80	$14,615.42	$8,330.51	$191,901.77	$339,610.90

Figure 9-8
OLAP Product Family and Store Location by Store Type

OLAP reports provide both perspectives, and the user can switch between them while viewing the report.

Unfortunately, all of this flexibility comes at a cost. If the database is large, doing the necessary calculating, grouping, and sorting for such dynamic displays will require substantial computing power. Although standard commercial DBMS products do have the features and functions required to create OLAP reports, they are not designed for such work. They are designed, instead, to provide rapid response to transaction-processing applications, such as order entry or manufacturing planning.

Accordingly, special-purpose products called **OLAP servers** have been developed to perform OLAP analysis. As shown in Figure 9-10 (page 329), an OLAP server reads data from an operational database, performs preliminary calculations, and stores the results of those calculations in an OLAP database. Several different schemes are used for this storage, but the particulars of those schemes are beyond this discussion. (Search the Web for the terms *MOLAP, ROLAP,* and *HOLAP* if you want to learn more.) Normally, for performance and security reasons the OLAP server and the DBMS run on separate servers.

For a discussion of security issues relating to reporting tools and reporting systems, see the Guide on pages 348–349.

Q4 What Are Typical Data-Mining Applications?

Data mining is the application of statistical techniques to find patterns and relationships among data for classification and prediction. As shown in Figure 9-11 (page 329), data mining resulted from a convergence of disciplines. Data-mining techniques emerged from statistics and mathematics and from artificial intelligence and machine-learning fields in computer science. As a result, data-mining terminology is an odd blend of terms from these different disciplines. Sometimes people use the term *knowledge discovery in databases* (KDD) as a synonym for data mining.

Data-mining techniques take advantage of developments in data management for processing the enormous databases that have emerged in the last 10 years. Of course, these data would not have been generated were it not for fast and cheap computers, and without such computers the new techniques would be impossible to compute.

			Store Type ▼						
Store Sales Net									
Store Country ▼	Store Sta	Store City	Product Family ▼	Deluxe Super	Gourmet Supermar	Mid-Size Groce	Small Grocery	Supermarket	Grand Total
USA	CA	Beverly Hills	Drink		$2,392.83				$2,392.83
			Food		$20,026.18				$20,026.18
			Non-Consumable		$5,064.79				$5,064.79
		Beverly Hills Total			$27,483.80				$27,483.80
		Los Angeles	Drink					$2,870.33	$2,870.33
			Food					$23,598.28	$23,598.28
			Non-Consumable					$6,305.14	$6,305.14
		Los Angeles Total						$32,773.74	$32,773.74
		San Diego	Drink					$3,050.43	$3,050.43
			Food					$23,627.83	$23,627.83
			Non-Consumable					$6,039.34	$6,039.34
		San Diego Total						$32,717.61	$32,717.61
		San Francisco	Drink				$227.38		$227.38
			Food				$1,960.53		$1,960.53
			Non-Consumable				$474.35		$474.35
		San Francisco Total					$2,662.26		$2,662.26
	CA Total				$27,483.80		$2,662.26	$65,491.35	$95,637.41
	OR		Drink	$4,438.49				$2,862.45	$7,300.94
			Food	$37,778.35				$23,818.87	$61,597.22
			Non-Consumable	$10,177.89				$6,428.53	$16,606.41
	OR Total			$52,394.72				$33,109.85	$85,504.57
	WA		Drink	$3,680.56		$1,409.50	$458.51	$7,968.50	$13,517.07
			Food	$32,497.76		$10,392.19	$4,149.19	$67,915.69	$114,954.83
			Non-Consumable	$8,706.36		$2,813.73	$1,060.54	$17,416.38	$29,997.01
	WA Total			$44,884.68		$14,615.42	$5,668.24	$93,300.57	$158,468.91
USA Total				$97,279.40	$27,483.80	$14,615.42	$8,330.51	$191,901.77	$339,610.90
Grand Total				$97,279.40	$27,483.80	$14,615.42	$8,330.51	$191,901.77	$339,610.90

Figure 9-9

OLAP Product Family and Store Location by Store Type, Drilled Down to Show Stores in California

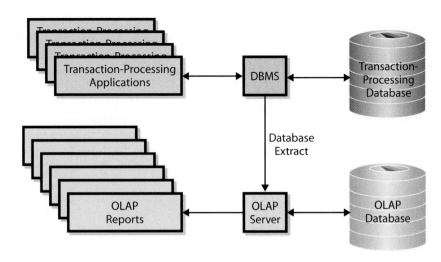

Figure 9-10
Role of OLAP Server
and OLAP Database

Most data-mining techniques are sophisticated, and many are difficult to use well. Such techniques are valuable to organizations, however, and some business professionals, especially those in finance and marketing, have become expert in their use. In fact, today there are many interesting and rewarding careers for business professionals who are knowledgeable about data-mining techniques.

Data-mining techniques fall into two broad categories: unsupervised and supervised. We explain both types in the following sections.

Unsupervised Data Mining

With **unsupervised data mining**, analysts do not create a model or hypothesis before running the analysis. Instead, they apply the data-mining technique to the data and observe the results. With this method, analysts create hypotheses *after the analysis*, in order to explain the patterns found.

One common unsupervised technique is **cluster analysis**. With it, statistical techniques identify groups of entities that have similar characteristics. A common use for cluster analysis is to find groups of similar customers from customer order and demographic data.

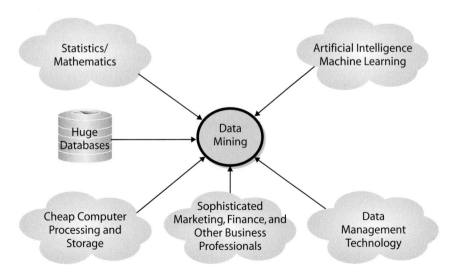

Figure 9-11
Convergence Disciplines
for Data Mining

For example, suppose a cluster analysis finds two very different customer groups: One group has an average age of 33, owns two iPhones, has an expensive home entertainment system, drives a Lexus SUV, and tends to buy expensive children's play equipment. The second group has an average age of 64, owns Arizona vacation property, plays golf, and buys expensive wines. Suppose the analysis also finds that both groups buy designer children's clothing.

These findings are obtained solely by data analysis. There is no prior model about the patterns and relationships that exist. It is up to the analyst to form hypotheses, after the fact, to explain why two such different groups are both buying designer children's clothes.

Supervised Data Mining

With **supervised data mining**, data miners develop a model *prior to the analysis* and apply statistical techniques to data to estimate parameters of the model. For example, suppose marketing experts in a communications company believe that cell phone usage on weekends is determined by the age of the customer and the number of months the customer has had the cell phone account. A data-mining analyst would then run an analysis that estimates the impact of customer and account age.

One such analysis, which measures the impact of a set of variables on another variable, is called a **regression analysis**. A sample result for the cell phone example is:

```
CellphoneWeekendMinutes =
12 + (17.5 * CustomerAge) + (23.7 * NumberMonthsOfAccount)
```

Using this equation, analysts can predict the number of minutes of weekend cell phone use by summing 12, plus 17.5 times the customer's age, plus 23.7 times the number of months of the account.

As you will learn in your statistics classes, considerable skill is required to interpret the quality of such a model. The regression tool will create an equation, such as the one shown. Whether that equation is a good predictor of future cell phone usage depends on statistical factors, such as t values, confidence intervals, and related statistical techniques.

Neural networks are another popular supervised data-mining technique used to predict values and make classifications such as "good prospect" or "poor prospect" customers. The term *neural networks* is deceiving because it connotes a biological process similar to that in animal brains. In fact, although the original *idea* of neural nets may have come from the anatomy and physiology of neurons, a neural network is nothing more than a complicated set of possibly nonlinear equations. Explaining the techniques used for neural networks is beyond the scope of this text. If you want to learn more, search *http://kdnuggets.com* for the term *neural network*.

In the next sections, we will describe and illustrate two typical data-mining tools—market-basket analysis and decision trees—and show applications of those techniques. From this discussion, you can gain a sense of the nature of data mining. These examples should give you, a future manager, a sense of the possibilities of data-mining techniques. You will need additional coursework in statistics, data management, marketing, and finance, however, before you will be able to perform such analyses yourself.

Data mining and other business intelligence systems are useful, but they are not without problems, as discussed in the Guide on pages 350–351.

Market-Basket Analysis

Suppose you run a dive shop, and one day you realize that one of your salespeople is much better than others at up-selling your customers. Any of your sales associates can fill a customer's order, but this one salesperson is especially good at selling customers items *in addition to* those for which they ask. One day, you ask him how he does it.

"It's simple," he says. "I just ask myself what is the next product they would want to buy. If someone buys a dive computer, I don't try to sell her fins. If she's buying a dive computer, she's already a diver and she already has fins. But, these dive computer displays are hard to read. A better mask makes it easier to read the display and get the full benefit from the dive computer."

A **market-basket analysis** is a data-mining technique for determining sales patterns. Such an analysis shows the products that customers tend to buy together. In marketing transactions, the fact that customers who buy product *X* also buy product *Y* creates a **cross-selling** opportunity. That is, "If they're buying *X*, sell them *Y*," or "If they're buying *Y*, sell them *X*."

Figure 9-12 shows hypothetical sales data of 1,000 items at a dive shop. The first row of numbers under each column is the total number of times an item was sold. For example, the 270 in the first row of *Mask* means that 270 of the 1,000 items were masks. The 120 under *Dive Computer* means that 120 of the 1,000 purchased items were dive computers.

We can use the numbers in the first row to estimate the probability that a customer will purchase an item. Because 270 of the 1,000 items were masks, we can estimate the probability that a customer will buy a mask to be 270/1,000, or 0.27.

In market-basket terminology, **support** is the probability that two items will be purchased together. To estimate that probability, we examine sales transactions and count the number of times that two items occurred on the same order. For the data in Figure 9-12, fins and masks appeared together 150 times, and thus the support for fins and a mask is 150/1,000, or 0.15. Similarly, the support for fins and weights is 60/1,000, or 0.06, and the support for fins along with a second pair of fins is 10/1,000, or 0.01.

These data are interesting by themselves, but we can refine the analysis by taking another step and considering additional probabilities. For example, what proportion of the customers who bought a mask also bought fins? Masks were purchased 270 times, and of those individuals who bought masks, 150 also bought fins. Thus, given that a customer bought a mask, we can estimate the probability that he or she will buy fins to be 150/270, or 0.5556. In market-basket terminology, such a conditional probability estimate is called the **confidence**.

Reflect on the meaning of this confidence value. The likelihood of someone walking in the door and buying fins is 280/1,000, or 0.28. But the likelihood of someone buying fins, given that he or she bought a mask, is 0.5556. That is, if someone buys a mask, the likelihood that he or she will also buy fins almost doubles, from 0.28 to 0.5556. Thus, all sales personnel should be trained to try to sell fins to anyone buying a mask.

1,000 Items	Mask	Tank	Fins	Weights	Dive Computer
	270	200	280	130	120
Mask	20	20	150	20	50
Tank	20	80	40	30	30
Fins	150	40	10	60	20
Weights	20	30	60	10	10
Dive computer	50	30	20	10	5
No additional product	10	—	—	—	5

Support = P (A & B)   Example: P (Fins & Mask) = 150/1,000 = .15

Confidence = P (A | B)   Example: P (Fins | Mask) = 150/270 = .5556

Lift = P (A | B)/P (A)   Example: P (Fins | Mask)/P (Fins) = .5556/.28 = 1.98

Note: P(Mask | Fins)/P (Mask) = (150/280)/.27 = 1.98

Figure 9-12
Market-Basket Example

Now consider dive computers and fins. Of the 1,000 items sold, fins were sold 280 times, so the probability that someone walks into the store and buys fins is 0.28. But of the 120 purchases of dive computers, only 20 appeared with fins. So the likelihood of someone buying fins, given he or she bought a dive computer, is 20/120 or 0.1666. Thus, when someone buys a dive computer, the likelihood that she will also buy fins falls from 0.28 to 0.1666.

The ratio of confidence to the base probability of buying an item is called **lift**. Lift shows how much the base probability increases or decreases when other products are purchased. The lift of fins and a mask is the confidence of fins given a mask, divided by the base probability of fins. In Figure 9-12, the lift of fins and a mask is 0.5556/0.28, or 1.98. Thus, the likelihood that people buy fins when they buy a mask almost doubles. Surprisingly, it turns out that the lift of fins and a mask is the same as the lift of a mask and fins. Both are 1.98.

Many organizations are benefiting from market-basket analysis today. You can expect that this technique will become a standard CRM analysis during your career.

Decision Trees

A **decision tree** is a hierarchical arrangement of criteria that predict a classification or a value. Here we will consider decision trees that predict classifications. Decision-tree analyses are an unsupervised data-mining technique: The analyst sets up the computer program and provides the data to analyze, and the decision-tree program produces the tree.

A Decision Tree for Student Performance

The basic idea of a decision tree is to select attributes that are most useful for classifying entities on some criterion. Suppose, for example, that we want to classify students according to the grades they earn in the MIS class. To create a decision tree, we first gather data about grades and attributes of students in past classes.

We then input that data into the decision-tree program. The program analyzes all of the attributes and selects an attribute that creates the most disparate groups. The logic is that the more different the groups, the better the classification will be. For example, if every student who lived off campus earned a grade higher than 3.0, and every student who lived on campus earned a grade lower than 3.0, then the program would use the variable *live-off-campus* or *live-on-campus* to classify students. In this unrealistic example, the program would be a perfect classifier, because each group is pure, with no misclassifications.

More realistically, consider Figure 9-13, which shows a hypothetical decision tree analysis of MIS class grades. Again, assume we are classifying students depending on whether their grade was greater than 3.0 or less than or equal to 3.0.

The decision-tree tool that created this tree examined student characteristics such as students' class (junior or senior), their major, their employment, their age, their club affiliations, and other student characteristics. It then used values of those characteristics to create groups that were as different as possible on the classification grade above or below 3.0.

For the results shown here, the decision-tree program determined that the best first criterion is whether the students are juniors or seniors. In this case, the classification was imperfect, as shown by the fact that neither of the senior nor the junior groups consisted only of students with GPAs above or below 3.0. Still, it did create groups that were less mixed than in the *All Students* group.

Next, the program examined other criteria to further subdivide *Seniors* and *Juniors* so as to create even more pure groups. The program divided the senior group into subgroups: those who are business majors and those who are not. The program's analysis of the junior data, however, determined that the difference between majors is

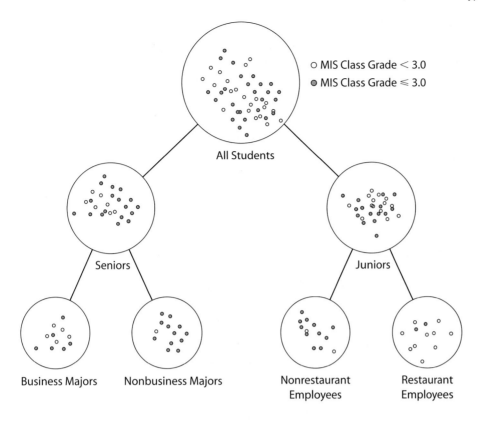

○ MIS Class Grade < 3.0
● MIS Class Grade ≤ 3.0

All Students

Seniors

Juniors

Business Majors

Nonbusiness Majors

Nonrestaurant Employees

Restaurant Employees

Figure 9-13
Grades of Students from Past MIS Class (Hypothetical Data)

not significant. Instead, the best classifier (the one that generated the most different groups) is whether the junior worked in a restaurant.

Examining this data, we see that junior restaurant employees do well in the class, but junior nonrestaurant employees and senior nonbusiness majors do poorly. Performance in the other senior group is mixed. (Remember, these data are hypothetical.)

A decision tree like the one in Figure 9-13 can be transformed into a set of decision rules having the format, **If . . . then . . . .** Decision rules for this example are:

- If student is a junior and works in a restaurant, then predict grade > 3.0.
- If student is a senior and is a nonbusiness major, then predict grade ≤ 3.0.
- If student is a junior and does not work in a restaurant, then predict grade ≤ 3.0.
- If student is a senior and is a business major, then make no prediction.

As stated, decision-tree algorithms create groups that are as pure as possible, or, stated otherwise, as different from each other as possible. The algorithms use several metrics for measuring difference among groups. Further explanation of those techniques is beyond the scope of this text. For now, just understand that maximum difference among groups is used as the criterion for constructing the decision tree.

Let's now apply the decision-tree technique to a business situation.

Many problems arise with classification schemes, especially those that classify people. The Ethics Guide on pages 334–335 examines some of these problems.

A Decision Tree for Loan Evaluation

A common business application of decision trees is to classify loans by likelihood of default. Organizations analyze data from past loans to produce a decision tree that can be converted to loan-decision rules. A financial institution could use such a tree to assess the default risk on a new loan. Sometimes, too, financial institutions sell a group of loans (called a *loan portfolio*) to one another. An institution considering the purchase of a loan portfolio can use the results of a decision-tree program to evaluate the risk of a given portfolio.

Ethics

The Ethics of Classification

Classification is a useful human skill. Imagine walking into your favorite clothing store and seeing all of the clothes piled together on a center table. T-shirts and pants and socks intermingle, with the sizes mixed up. Retail stores organized like this would not survive, nor would distributors or manufacturers who managed their inventories this way. Sorting and classifying are necessary, important, and essential activities. But those activities can also be dangerous.

Serious ethical issues arise when we classify people. What makes someone a good or bad "prospect"? If we're talking about classifying customers in order to prioritize our sales calls, then the ethical issue may not be too serious. What

about classifying applicants for college? As long as there are more applicants than positions, some sort of classification and selection process must be done. But what kind?

Suppose a university collects data on the demographics and the performance of all of its students. The admissions committee then processes these data using a decision tree data-mining program. Assume the analysis is conducted properly and the tool uses statistically valid measures to obtain statistically valid results. Thus, the following resulting tree accurately represents and explains variances found in the data; no human judgment (or prejudice) was involved. ■

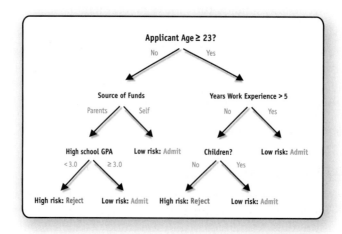

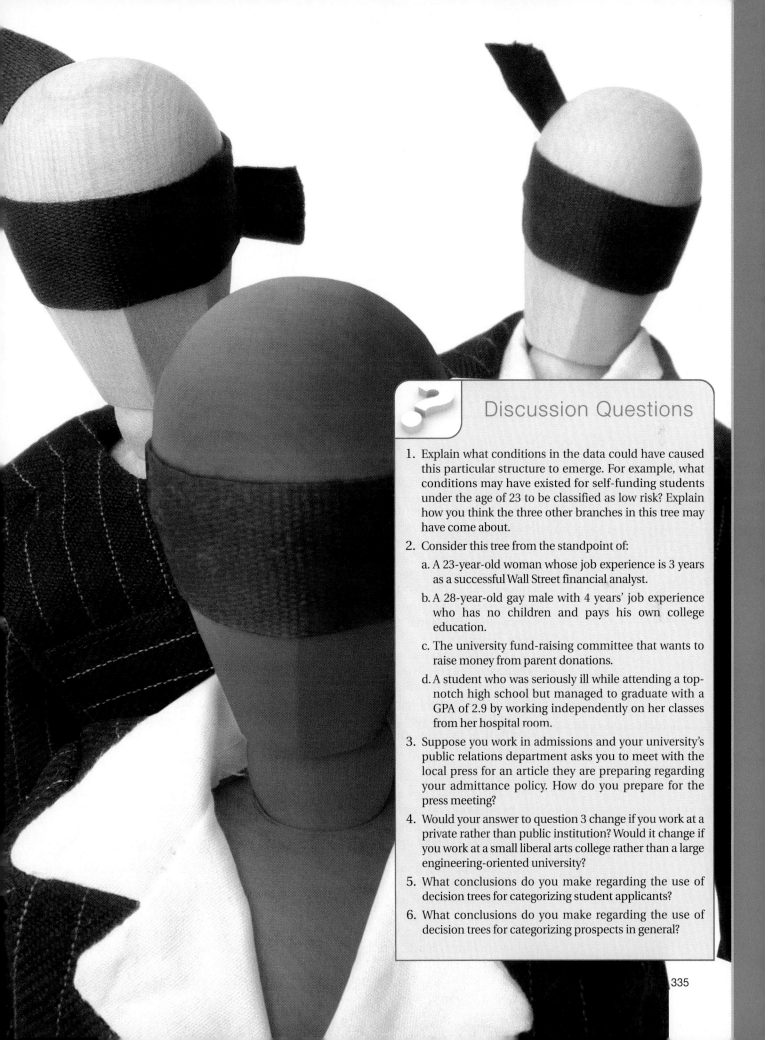

1. Explain what conditions in the data could have caused this particular structure to emerge. For example, what conditions may have existed for self-funding students under the age of 23 to be classified as low risk? Explain how you think the three other branches in this tree may have come about.

2. Consider this tree from the standpoint of:

   a. A 23-year-old woman whose job experience is 3 years as a successful Wall Street financial analyst.

   b. A 28-year-old gay male with 4 years' job experience who has no children and pays his own college education.

   c. The university fund-raising committee that wants to raise money from parent donations.

   d. A student who was seriously ill while attending a top-notch high school but managed to graduate with a GPA of 2.9 by working independently on her classes from her hospital room.

3. Suppose you work in admissions and your university's public relations department asks you to meet with the local press for an article they are preparing regarding your admittance policy. How do you prepare for the press meeting?

4. Would your answer to question 3 change if you work at a private rather than public institution? Would it change if you work at a small liberal arts college rather than a large engineering-oriented university?

5. What conclusions do you make regarding the use of decision trees for categorizing student applicants?

6. What conclusions do you make regarding the use of decision trees for categorizing prospects in general?

335

Figure 9-14
Credit Store Decision Tree

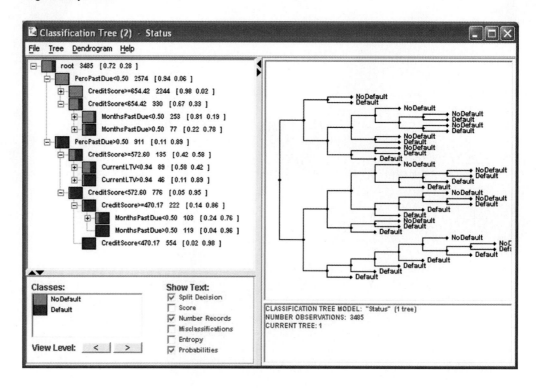

Figure 9-14 shows an example provided by Insightful Corporation, a vendor of business intelligence tools. This example was generated using its Insightful Miner product. This tool examined data from 3,485 loans. Of those loans, 72 percent had no default and 28 percent did default. To perform the analysis, the decision-tree tool examined six different loan characteristics.

In this example, the decision-tree program determined that the percentage of the loan that is past due (*PercPastDue*) is the best first criterion. Reading Figure 9-14, you can see that of the 2,574 loans with a *PercPastDue* value of 0.5 or less (amount past due is less than half the loan amount), 94 percent were not in default. Reading down several lines in this tree, 911 loans had a value of *PercPastDue* greater than 0.5; of those loans, 89 percent were in default.

These two major categories are then further subdivided into three classifications: *CreditScore* is a creditworthiness score obtained from a credit agency; *MonthsPastDue* is the number of months since a payment; and *CurrentLTV* is the current ratio of outstanding balance of the loan to the value of the loan's collateral.

With a decision tree like this, the financial institution can develop decision rules for accepting or rejecting the offer to purchase loans from another financial institution. For example:

- If percent past due is less than 50 percent, then accept the loan.
- If percent past due is greater than 50 percent *and*
  - If *CreditScore* is greater than 572.6 *and*
  - If *CurrentLTV* is less than .94, then accept the loan.
- Otherwise, reject the loan.

Of course, the financial institution will need to combine these risk data with an economic analysis of the value of each loan to determine which loans to take.

Decision trees are easy to understand and, even better, easy to implement using decision rules. They also can work with many types of variables, and they deal well with partial data. Organizations can use decision trees by themselves or combine them with other techniques. In some cases, organizations use decision trees to select variables that are then used by other types of data-mining tools. For example, decision trees can be used to identify good predictor variables for neural networks.

Q5 What Is the Purpose of Data Warehouses and Data Marts?

Whereas basic reports and simple OLAP analyses can be made directly from operational data, more sophisticated reports and nearly all data-mining applications cannot. One problem is that missing values and inconsistencies in the data can adversely affect results. Also, some analyses necessitate merging operational data with data purchased from outside sources. Yet another problem is data format. Operational data is designed to support fast transaction processing and might need to be reformatted to be useful for BI applications.

To address these problems, many organizations choose to extract operational data into facilities called **data warehouses** and **data marts**, both of which prepare, store, and manage data specifically for data mining and other analyses. (We will explain the differences between data warehouses and data marts in a few pages.)

Figure 9-15 shows the components in a data warehouse. Programs read production and other data and extract, clean, and prepare that data for BI processing. The prepared data are stored in a data-warehouse database using a data-warehouse DBMS, which can be different from the organization's operational DBMS. For example, an organization might use Oracle for its operational processing, but use SQL Server for its data warehouse. Other organizations use SQL Server for operational processing, but use DBMSs from statistical package vendors such as SAS or SPSS in the data warehouse.

Data warehouses include data that are purchased from outside sources such as Acxiom Corporation. A typical example is customer credit data. Figure 9-16 (on the next page) lists some of the consumer data that can be purchased from commercial vendors today. An amazing (and from a privacy standpoint, frightening) amount of data is available.

Metadata concerning the data—its source, its format, its assumptions and constraints, and other facts about the data—is kept in a data-warehouse metadata database. The data-warehouse DBMS extracts and provides data to BI tools such as data-mining programs.

Problems with Operational Data

Unfortunately, most operational and purchased data have problems that inhibit their usefulness for business intelligence. Figure 9-17 lists the major problem categories. First, although data that are critical for successful operations must be complete and accurate, data that are only marginally necessary need not be. For example, some

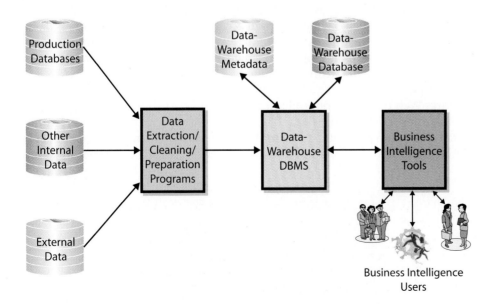

Business Intelligence Users

Figure 9-15
Components of a Data Warehouse

• Name, address, phone	• Magazine subscriptions
• Age	• Hobbies
• Gender	• Catalog orders
• Ethnicity	• Marital status, life stage
• Religion	• Height, weight, hair and
• Income	eye color
• Education	• Spouse name, birth date
• Voter registration	• Children's names and
• Home ownership	birth dates
• Vehicles	

Figure 9-16
Consumer Data Available for
Purchase from Data Vendors

systems gather demographic data in the ordering process. But, because such data are not needed to fill, ship, and bill orders, their quality suffers.

Problematic data are termed **dirty data**. Examples are a value of *B* for customer gender and of *213* for customer age. Other examples are a value of *999–999–9999* for a U.S. phone number, a part color of *gren*, and an email address of *WhyMe@Guess WhoIAM.org*. All of these values can be problematic for data-mining purposes.

Purchased data often contain *missing* elements. Most data vendors state the percentage of missing values for each attribute in the data they sell. An organization buys such data because for some uses, some data are better than no data at all. This is especially true for data items whose values are difficult to obtain, such as *Number of Adults in Household, Household Income, Dwelling Type*, and *Education of Primary Income Earner*. For data-mining applications, though, a few missing or erroneous data points can be worse than no data at all because they bias the analysis.

Inconsistent data, the third problem in Figure 9-17, is particularly common for data that have been gathered over time. When an area code changes, for example, the phone number for a given customer before the change will not match the customer's number after the change. Likewise, part codes can change, as can sales territories. Before such data can be used, they must be recoded for consistency over the period of the study.

Some data inconsistencies occur from the nature of the business activity. Consider a Web-based order-entry system used by customers worldwide. When the Web server records the time of order, which time zone does it use? The server's system clock time is irrelevant to an analysis of customer behavior. Coordinated Universal Time (formerly called Greenwich Mean Time) is also meaningless. Somehow, Web server time must be adjusted to the time zone of the customer.

Another problem is *nonintegrated data*. Suppose, for example, that an organization wants to perform an RFM analysis but wants to consider customer payment behavior as well. The organization wants to add a fourth factor (which we will call *P*) and scale it from 1 to 5 on the basis of how quickly a customer pays. Unfortunately, however, the organization records such payment data in an Oracle financial management database that is separate from the Microsoft CRM database that has the order data. Before the organization can perform the analysis, the data must somehow be integrated.

Data can also have the wrong **granularity**—it can be too fine or too coarse. For the former, suppose we want to analyze the placement of graphics and controls on an order-entry Web page. It is possible to capture the customers' clicking behavior in what is termed **clickstream data**. Those data, however, include everything the customer does at the Web site. In the middle of the order stream are data for clicks on the news, email, instant chat, and a weather check. Although all of that data may be

• Dirty data	• Wrong granularity
• Missing values	– Too fine
• Inconsistent data	– Not fine enough
• Data not integrated	• Too much data
	– Too many attributes
	– Too many data points

Figure 9-17
Problems of Using Transaction
Data for Analysis and Data
Mining

useful for a study of consumer computer behavior, it will be overwhelming if all we want to know is how customers respond to an ad located differently on the screen. To proceed, the data analysts must throw away millions and millions of clicks.

Data can also be too coarse. For example, a file of order totals cannot be used for a market-basket analysis. For market-basket analysis, we need to know which items were purchased with which others. This does not mean the order-total data are useless. They can be adequate for an RFM analysis, for example; they just will not do for a market-basket analysis.

In general, it is better to have too fine a granularity than too coarse. If the granularity is too fine, the data can be made coarser by summing and combining. Only analysts' labor and computer processing are required. If the granularity is too coarse, however, there is no way to separate the data into constituent parts.

The final problem listed in Figure 9-17 is to have *too much data*. As shown in the figure, we can have either too many attributes or too many data points. Think of tables as discussed in Chapter 5. We can have too many columns or too many rows.

Consider the first problem: too many attributes. Suppose we want to know the factors that influence how customers respond to a promotion. If we combine internal customer data with purchased customer data, we will have more than a hundred different attributes to consider. How do we select among them? Because of a phenomenon called the **curse of dimensionality**, the more attributes there are, the easier it is to build a model that fits the sample data but that is worthless as a predictor. There are other good reasons for reducing the number of attributes, and one of the major activities in data mining concerns efficient and effective ways of selecting attributes.

The second way to have too much data is to have too many data points—too many rows of data. Suppose we want to analyze clickstream data on CNN.com. How many clicks does that site receive per month? Millions upon millions! In order to meaningfully analyze such data we need to reduce the amount of data. There is a good solution to this problem: statistical sampling. Organizations should not be reluctant to sample data in such situations.

Data Warehouses Versus Data Marts

So, how is a data warehouse different from a data mart? In a way, you can think of a *data warehouse* as a distributor in a supply chain. The data warehouse takes data from the data manufacturers (operational systems and purchased data), cleans and processes the data, and locates the data on the shelves, so to speak, of the data warehouse. The people who work with a data warehouse are experts at data management, data cleaning, data transformation, and the like. However, they are not usually experts in a given business function.

A *data mart* is a data collection, smaller than the data warehouse, that addresses a particular component or functional area of the business. If the data warehouse is the distributor in a supply chain, then a data mart is like a retail store in a supply chain. Users in the data mart obtain data that pertain to a particular business function from the data warehouse. Such users do not have the data management expertise that data warehouse employees have, but they are knowledgeable analysts for a given business function.

Figure 9-18 illustrates these relationships. The data warehouse takes data from the data producers and distributes the data to three data marts. One data mart is used to analyze clickstream data for the purpose of designing Web pages. A second analyzes store sales data and determines which products tend to be purchased together. This information is used to train salespeople on the best way to up-sell to customers.

The third data mart is used to analyze customer order data for the purpose of reducing labor for item picking from the warehouse. A company like Amazon.com, for example, goes to great lengths to organize its warehouses to reduce picking expenses.

As you can imagine, it is expensive to create, staff, and operate data warehouses and data marts. Only large organizations with deep pockets can afford to operate a system like that shown in Figure 9-18. Smaller organizations operate subsets of this system; they may have just a simple data mart for analyzing promotion data, for example.

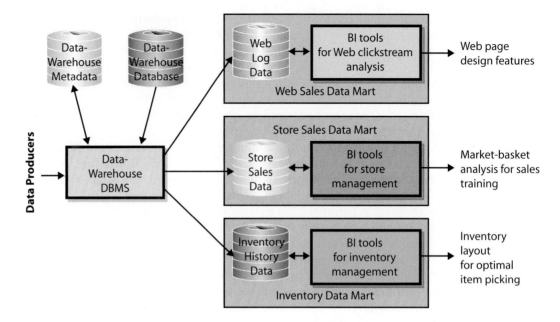

Figure 9-18
Data Mart Examples

Q6 What Are Typical Knowledge-Management Applications?

Knowledge management (KM) is the process of creating value from intellectual capital and sharing that knowledge with employees, managers, suppliers, customers, and others who need it. Whereas reporting and data mining are used to create new information from data, knowledge-management systems concern the sharing of knowledge that is known to exist, either in libraries of documents or in the heads of employees.

KM applications enable employees and others to leverage organizational knowledge to work smarter. Santosus and Surmacz cite the following as the primary benefits of KM:

1. KM fosters innovation by encouraging the free flow of ideas.
2. KM improves customer service by streamlining response time.
3. KM boosts revenues by getting products and services to market faster.
4. KM enhances employee retention rates by recognizing the value of employees' knowledge and rewarding them for it.
5. KM streamlines operations and reduces costs by eliminating redundant or unnecessary processes.[6]

In addition, KM preserves organizational memory by capturing and storing the lessons learned and best practices of key employees.

There are three major categories of knowledge assets: data, documents, and employees. We addressed information derived from data in the reporting and data-mining sections of this chapter. In this section, we will consider KM as it pertains to sharing of document content and employee knowledge.

Sharing Document Content

In Chapter 2, we discussed content management in the context of collaboration systems. The focus on content for KM applications is slightly different. Whereas collaboration systems are concerned with document creation and change management, KM applications are concerned with maximizing content use. In this section, we focus on two key technologies for sharing content: indexing and RSS.

---

[6]Megan Santosus and John Surmacz, "The ABCs of Knowledge Management," *CIO Magazine*, May 23, 2001, *http://cio.com/research/knowledge/edit/kmabcs.html* (accessed July 2005).

Indexing

Indexing is the single most important content function in KM applications. KM users need an easily accessible and robust means of determining whether content they need exists, and, if so, a link to obtain that content. Users need a keyword search that provides quick response and high document relevancy. The higher the relevancy, the more productive users will be.

The largest collection of documents ever assembled exists on the Internet, and the world's best-known indexing engine is operated by Google. When you "Google" a term, you are tapping into the world's largest content-indexing system. Google's limitation is that it can index only publicly accessible documents.

When organizations protect their content by placing it behind firewalls, Google's indexing software cannot find it. If you want to access documents published in, say, *Forbes*, you will have to use an indexing service that has an indexing agreement with *Forbes*. Similarly, organizations must develop their own indexing systems, or license indexing systems from others, in order to make their own protected content available to their employees and other authorized users.

Real Simple Syndication (RSS)

Real Simple Syndication (RSS) is a standard for subscribing to content sources. (Actually, as of 2009 there are *seven* different RSS standards; not all of them mean *real simple syndication*, but we will ignore that issue here. Perform an online search on *RSS standards* to learn more.)

You can think of RSS as an email system for content. With a program called an **RSS reader**, you can subscribe to magazines, blogs, Web sites, and other content sources. The RSS reader will periodically check the sources to which you subscribe to determine whether any content has changed. If so, the RSS reader will place a summary of the change and link to the new content in what is essentially an RSS inbox. You can process your RSS inbox just like your email inbox. You read content changes, delete them in your RSS inbox, and, depending on your reader's features, forward notices of changes to others via email.

Figure 9-19 shows the interface of a typical RSS reader. The left-hand pane shows the RSS sources to which this user is subscribed. Entries are grouped into categories

Figure 9-19
Interface of a Typical RSS Reader

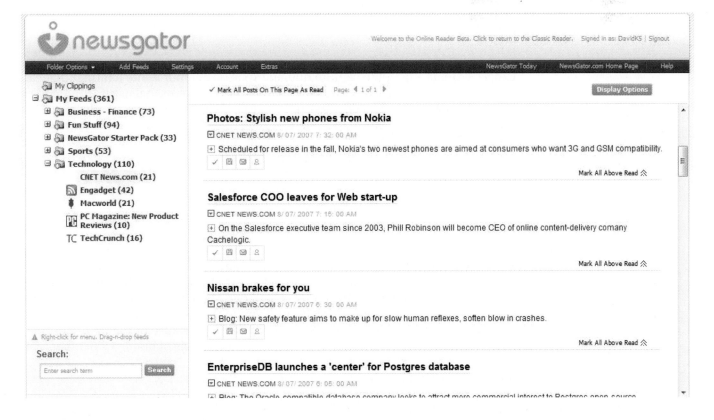

Figure 9-20
Blog Posts of SharePoint Team
Member (Michael Gannotti)

Source: Microsoft Office SharePoint Designer
2007. Reprinted with permission from Microsoft
Corporation.

such as business, technology, and sports. In order to subscribe, the data source must
provide what is termed an **RSS feed**. This simply means that the site posts changes
according to one of the RSS standards.

Today, the employees in many organizations share their knowledge via personal
blogs. Figure 9-20 shows the blog posts of one of the key employees on the Microsoft
SharePoint team. Blogs like this include RSS feeds so that you can subscribe to them
using an RSS reader. You can also configure SharePoint and other content-management
systems to provide an RSS feed on lists or document libraries. Users who subscribe to
those feeds will be notified whenever content changes.

Content-sharing systems are flexible and organic. They are closer to Web 2.0
applications than are applications such as reporting and data mining. In fact, some
people would say that content-sharing systems *are* Web 2.0 applications.

Expert Systems

Expert systems attempt to capture human expertise and put it into a format that can
be used by nonexperts. Expert systems are rule-based systems that use If . . . then rules
similar to those created by decision-tree analysis. However, decision trees' If . . . then
rules are created by mining data. The If . . . then rules in expert systems are created by
interviewing experts in a given business domain and codifying the rules stated by those
experts. Also, decision trees typically have fewer than a dozen rules, whereas expert
systems can have hundreds or thousands of rules.

Problems of Expert Systems

Many expert systems were created in the late 1980s and early 1990s, and a few of them
have been successful. They suffer from three major disadvantages, however. First, they
are difficult and expensive to develop. They require many labor hours from both
experts in the domain under study and designers of expert systems. This expense is
compounded by the high opportunity cost of tying up domain experts. Such experts
are normally some of the most sought-after employees in the organization.

Second, expert systems are difficult to maintain. Because of the nature of rule-
based systems, the introduction of a new rule in the middle of hundreds of others can

have unexpected consequences. A small change can cause very different outcomes. Unfortunately, such side-effects cannot be predicted or eliminated. They are the nature of complex rule-based systems.

Finally, expert systems have been unable to live up to the high expectations set by their name. Initially, proponents of expert systems hoped to be able to duplicate the performance of highly trained experts, such as doctors. It turned out, however, that no expert system has the same diagnostic ability as knowledgeable, skilled, and experienced doctors. Even when expert systems were developed that came close in ability, changes in medical technology required constant changing of the expert system, and the problems caused by unexpected consequences made such changes very expensive.

Today, however, there are successful, less-ambitious expert systems. Typically these systems address more restricted problems than duplicating a doctor's diagnostic ability. We consider one next.

Expert Systems for Pharmacies

The Medical Informatics group at Washington University School of Medicine in St. Louis, Missouri, develops innovative and effective information systems to support decision making in medicine. The group has developed several expert systems that are used as a safety net to screen the decisions of doctors and other medical professionals. These systems help to achieve the hospital's goal of state-of-the-art, error-free care.

Medical researchers developed early expert systems to support, and in some cases to replace, medical decision making. MYCIN was an expert system developed in the early 1970s for the purpose of diagnosing certain infectious diseases. Physicians never routinely used MYCIN, but researchers used its expert system framework as the basis for many other medical systems. For one reason or another, however, none of those systems has seen extensive use.

In contrast, the systems developed at Washington University are routinely used, in real time, every day. One of the systems, DoseChecker, verifies appropriate dosages on prescriptions issued in the hospital. Another application, PharmADE, ensures that patients are not prescribed drugs that have harmful interactions. The pharmacy order-entry system invokes these applications as a prescription is entered. If either system detects a problem with the prescription, it generates an alert like the one shown in Figure 9-21.

A pharmacist screens an alert before sending it to the doctor. If the pharmacist disagrees with the alert, it is discarded. If the pharmacist agrees there is a problem with either the dosage or a harmful drug interaction, she sends the alert to the doctor. The doctor can then alter the prescription or override the alert. If the doctor does not respond, the system will escalate the alert to higher levels until the potential problem is resolved.

Neither DoseChecker nor PharmADE attempts to replace the decision making of medical professionals. Rather, they operate behind the scenes, as a reliable assistant helping to provide error-free care.

Apparently, the systems work. According to the Informatics Web site, "Over a 6-month period at a 1,400 bed teaching hospital, the system [DoseChecker] screened 57,404 orders and detected 3,638 potential dosing errors." Furthermore, since the hospital implemented the system, the number of alerts has fallen by 50 percent, indicating that the prescribing process has been improved because of the feedback provided by the alerts.[7]

---

[7]The Division of Medical Informatics at Washington University School of Medicine for the Department of Pharmacy at Barnes Jewish Hospital. *http://informatics.wustl.edu* (accessed January 2005). Used with permission of Medical Informatics at Washington University School of Medicine and BJC Healthcare.

Pharmacy Clinical Decision Support
Version 2.0

Developed by The Division of Medical Informatics at Washington University School of Medicine
for the Department of Pharmacy at Barnes Jewish Hospital.

Data as of: Mar 10 2000 4:40 AM   **Alert #: 13104**   **Satellite: CHNE**

Patient Name	Registration	Age	Sex	Weight(kg)	Height(in)	IBW(kg)	Location
SAMPLE,PATIENT	9999999	22	F	114	0	0	528

Creatinine Clearance Lab Results (last 3):

Collection Date	Serum Creatinine	Creatinine Clearance
Mar 9 2000 9:55 PM	7.1	14

DoseChecker Recommendations and Thoughts:

Order	Start Date	Drug Name	Route	Dose	Frequency
295	Mar 10 2000 12:00 AM	MEPERIDINE INJ 25MG	IV	25 MG	Q4H
Recommended Dose/Frequency:				**0.0 MG**	**PER DAY**
Comments:	0 <= CrCl < 20. Mependine should not be used for more than 48 hours or at doses > 600 mg per day in patients with renal or CNS disease. Serious consideration should be given to using an alternative analgesic in this patient population.				

Figure 9-21
Alert from Pharmacy Clinical
Decision Support System

Source: The Division of Medicine at Washington University School of Medicine for the Department of Pharmacy at Barnes Jewish Hospital Informatics. *www.wustl.edu.* Used with permission of Medical Informatics at Washington University School of Medicine and BJC Healthcare.

Q7 How Are Business Intelligence Applications Delivered?

By now you should have a good understanding of the potential power and utility of business intelligence applications. However, to make a practical difference the results of the BI analyses need to be delivered to people who can use them. For that, some sort of BI server is needed. Figure 9-22 summarizes the components of a generic business intelligence system. A *data source* is processed by a *BI tool* to produce *application results*. A **business intelligence (BI) application server** delivers those results in a variety of formats to *devices* for consumption by *BI users*.

What Are the Management Functions of a BI Server?

BI servers provide two major functions: management and delivery. The management function maintains metadata about the authorized allocation of BI results to users. The BI server tracks what results are available, what users are authorized to view those results, and the schedule upon which the results are provided to the authorized users. It adjusts allocations as available results change and users come and go.

BI servers vary in complexity and functionality, and their management function varies as well. Some BI servers are simply Web sites from which users can download, or **pull**, BI application results. For example, a BI Web server might post the results of an RFM analysis for salespeople to query to obtain RFM scores for their customers.

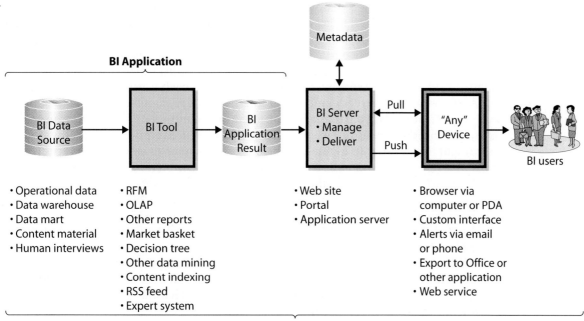

Figure 9-22
Components of a Generic
Business Intelligence System

The management function for such a site would simply be to track authorized users and restrict access to the site to them.

Another option is for the BI server to operate as a portal server, or as part of one. **Portal servers** are like Web servers except that they have a customizable user interface. You have probably used a portal, though you may not have realized it. If you establish an account with iGoogle, for example, you will be given the opportunity to customize the interface to your particular interests. You might, for example, choose to see the weather in certain cities, the values of particular stocks and markets, the results of particular sports events, and so forth. Whenever you sign on to iGoogle, it will present your customized interface. Figure 9-23 shows a sample portal.

Some organizations establish similar portal servers for use by employees within the company. Such portals might provide common data such as local weather, but they would also have links to company news, and, for our purposes, to BI application results such as reports on daily sales, operations, new employees, and so forth. Results of data-mining applications could be presented as well.

To implement such a portal, the organization provides authorized user accounts on the portal server and allows users to place reports, data-mining results, or other BI

Figure 9-23
Sample Portal, Provided
by iGoogle

Source: iGoogle™. iGoogle is a trademark
of Google Inc.

application results on their customized pages. Of course, selections are limited to results that the user is authorized to see. For example, a bank might publish a loan evaluation application based on a decision-tree analysis. Authorized bankers can place that evaluation application on their portal interface and invoke it when necessary. Management functions for BI portals are to track the available BI results, the users and their authorities, and, like all portal servers, the customizations in each user's interface.

A BI application server extends the functionality provided by portals to support user subscriptions to particular BI application results. For example, a user can subscribe to a daily sales report, requesting that it be delivered each morning. Or, the user might request that RFM analyses be delivered whenever a new result is posted on the server. Users can also subscribe to **alerts**, which are messages delivered via email or phone whenever a particular event occurs. A sales manager might want to be alerted, for example, whenever sales in his region exceed $1 million during the week. The BI application server **pushes** the subscribed results to the user.

A **report server** is a special case of a BI application server that serves only reports. BI application servers track results, users, authorizations, page customizations, subscriptions, alerts, and data for any other functionality provided.

As shown in Figure 9-22, all management data needed by any of the BI servers is stored in metadata. The amount and complexity of such data depends, of course, on the functionality of the BI server.

What Are the Delivery Functions of a BI Server?

BI servers use metadata to determine what results to send to which users and, possibly, on which schedule. Today, the expectation is that BI results can be delivered to "any" device. In practice, *any* is interpreted to mean computers, PDAs, phones, other applications such as Microsoft Office, and as an SOA service.

As stated, alerts are simply messages transmitted via email or phone that notify a user that a particular condition has occurred. The condition might be expected, such as the arrival of a new report on the BI server. Or, it might be unexpected, such as an **exception alert** that notifies the user of an exceptional event, such as a dramatic fall in a stock price or exceptionally high sales volume.

A BI system, like all information systems, has hardware, software, data, procedures, and people. So far, we have discussed all of the components except procedures. The particular procedures that BI users follow depends on the nature of the BI system. In general, however, such systems tend to be more flexible than operational systems, such as order entry, CRM, or ERP. BI users tend to be engaged in nonstructured, nonroutine work. In such an environment, procedures are limited to basic operational instructions, such as how to obtain a user account, how to subscribe to a particular BI product, and how to obtain a result. The interpretation of the BI results is not normally prescribed by procedure.

There are, however, a few exceptions. The sales force might develop procedures for using RFM scores. "Always do this for a [2, 1, 1]," or "Never spend time on a [5, 5, 5]" are examples. Similarly, users might have instructions for using the results of market-basket analyses. "If the user orders a widget, attempt to up-sell a widget bracket" is an example.

In most cases, however, the use of a particular BI application result is nonroutine and is determined by the users' unique requirements.

Q8 2020?

Business intelligence systems truly add value. As described in the Guide on page 350, not every system is a success, but simple ones like RFM and OLAP often are, and even complicated and expensive data-mining applications can generate tremendous return if they are applied to appropriate problems and are well-designed and implemented.

For example, suppose you never buy expensive jewelry on your credit card. If you travel to South America and attempt to buy a $5,000 diamond bracelet using that credit card, watch what happens! Especially if you make the attempt on a credit card other than the one for which you paid for the travel. A data-mining application integrated into the credit card agency's purchase-approval process will detect the unusual pattern, on the spot, and require you to personally verify the purchase on the telephone or in some other way before it will accept the charge. Such applications are exceedingly accurate because they are well designed and implemented by some of the world's best data miners.

How will this change by 2020? We know that data storage is free, that CPU processors are becoming nearly so, that the world is generating and storing exponentially more information about customers, and that data-mining techniques are only going to get better. I think it likely that by 2020 some companies will know more about your purchasing psyche than you, your mother, or your analyst.

In fact, credit card companies already know a lot. According to MSN, if you use your card to purchase "secondhand clothing, retread tires, bail bond services, massages, casino gambling, or betting,"[8] you alert the credit card company of potential financial problems and, as a result, it may cancel your card or reduce your credit limit.

This practice raised enough concern that in May 2009 the U.S. Congress passed a credit card reform law that requires the Federal Trade Commission (FTC) to investigate data mining by credit card companies. The FTC is to determine if such practices are discriminatory and report back to Congress in May 2010. (If you're reading this after that date, search online for *credit card data mining* to learn the results of that review.)

Assume that such practices are discriminatory. Should they be stopped? Doesn't every business have the right to determine how much credit it wants to extend? It would seem so.

But, should there be limits? Suppose you stop shopping at Whole Foods (a high-value grocery store chain) and switch to Safeway (a lower-cost grocery store chain). If you pay both with a credit card, the evidence of this switch is obvious in your account record. The credit card company could notify Whole Foods that it lost you as a customer. And, in fact, credit card companies could sell such facts as well as similar data-mining results to the vendors who accept its cards. They could notify Exxon where you buy gas, notify local restaurants where you dine out, and notify airlines when and where you fly with competing airlines. What else might data mining reveal from your credit card purchases? If you take a vacation every year, and you haven't yet taken one, you may be ripe for a personal contact from a travel agency. However, if you just came back from your annual vacation, why bother?

Absent laws to the contrary, by 2020 your credit card data will be fully integrated with personal and family data maintained by the data aggregators (like Acxiom and ChoicePoint). Sophisticated data-mining programs will use cluster analyses, decision tree analyses, regression analyses, and other techniques to accurately predict when you are likely to get married, have a baby (or another baby), buy an auto, buy a house, sell a house, pay college expenses, retire, or die.

Much of this information will be useful for something. But what? You and your classmates will have a chance to develop innovative applications for it during your careers. It should be fascinating!

---

[8]MSN.com, "Can Lifestyle Hurt Your Credit?" *http://articles.moneycentral.msn.com/Banking/FinancialPrivacy/can-your-lifestyle-hurt-your-credit.aspx* (accessed August 2009).

Semantic Security

Semantic Security

GGUIDE

Semantic Security

Security is a very difficult problem—and risks grow larger every year. Not only do we have cheaper, faster computers (remember Moore's Law). We also have more data, more systems for reporting and querying that data, and easier, faster, and broader communication. All of these combine to increase the chances that we inadvertently divulge private or proprietary information.

Physical security is hard enough: How do we know that the person (or program) who signs on as Megan Cho really is Megan Cho? We use passwords, but files of passwords can be stolen. Setting that issue aside, we need to know that Megan Cho's permissions are set appropriately. Suppose Megan works in the HR department, so she has access to personal and private data of other employees. We need to design the reporting system so that Megan can access all of the data she needs to do her job, and no more.

Also, the delivery system must be secure. An application server is an obvious and juicy target for any would-be intruder. Someone can break in and change access permissions. Or, a hacker could pose as someone else to obtain reports. Application servers help the authorized user, resulting in faster access to more information. But, without proper security reporting servers also ease the intrusion task for unauthorized users.

All of these issues relate to physical security. Another dimension to security is equally serious and far more problematic: **semantic security**. Semantic security concerns the unintended release of protected information through the release of a combination of reports or documents that are independently not protected.

Take an example from class. Suppose I assign a group project, and I post a list of groups and the names of students assigned to each group. Later, after the assignments have been completed and graded, I post a list of grades on the Web site. Because of university privacy policy, I cannot post the grades by student name or identifier; so instead, I post the grades for each group. If you want to get the grades for each student, all you have to do is combine the list from Lecture 5 with the list from Lecture 10. You might say that the release of grades in this example does no real harm—after all, it is a list of grades from one assignment.

But go back to Megan Cho in HR. Suppose Megan evaluates the employee compensation program. The COO believes salary offers have been inconsistent over time and that they vary too widely by department. Accordingly, the COO authorizes Megan to receive a report that lists *SalaryOfferAmount* and *OfferDate* and a second report that lists *Department* and *AverageSalary*.

Those reports are relevant to her task and seem innocuous enough. But Megan realizes that she could use the information they contain to determine individual salaries—information she does not have and is not authorized to receive. She proceeds as follows.

Like all employees, Megan has access to the employee directory on the Web portal. Using the directory, she can obtain a list of employees in each department, and using the facilities of her ever-so-helpful report-authoring system she combines that list with the department and average-salary report. Now she has a list of the names of employees in a group and the average salary for that group.

Megan's employer likes to welcome new employees to the company. Accordingly, each week the company publishes an article about new employees who have been hired. The article makes pleasant comments about each person and encourages employees to meet and greet them.

348

Megan, however, has other ideas. Because the report is published on the Web portal, she can obtain an electronic copy of it. It's an Acrobat report, and using Acrobat's handy Search feature, she soon has a list of employees and the week they were hired.

She now examines the report she received for her study, the one that has *SalaryOfferAmount* and the offer date, and she does some interpretation. During the week of July 21, three offers were extended: one for $35,000, one for $53,000, and one for $110,000. She also notices from the "New Employees" report that a director of marketing programs, a product test engineer, and a receptionist were hired that same week. It's unlikely that they paid the receptionist $110,000; that sounds more like the director of marketing programs. So, she now "knows" (infers) that person's salary.

Next, going back to the department report and using the employee directory, she sees that the marketing director is in the marketing programs department. There are just three people in that department, and their average salary is $105,000. Doing the arithmetic, she now knows that the average salary for the other two people is $102,500. If she can find the hire week for one of those other two people, she can find out both the second and third person's salaries.

You get the idea. Megan was given just two reports to do her job. Yet she combined the information in those reports with publicly available information and is able to deduce salaries, for at least some employees. These salaries are much more than she is supposed to know. This is a semantic security problem. ∎

SALARY INFORMATION

Discussion Questions

1. In your own words, explain the difference between access security and semantic security.

2. Why do reporting systems increase the risk of semantic security problems?

3. What can an organization do to protect itself against accidental losses due to semantic security problems?

4. What legal responsibility does an organization have to protect against semantic security problems?

5. Suppose semantic security problems are inevitable. Do you see an opportunity for new products from insurance companies? If so, describe such an insurance product. If not, explain why not.

Data Mining in the Real World

"I'm not really a contrarian about data mining. I believe in it. After all, it's my career. But data mining in the real world is a lot different from the way it's described in textbooks.

"There are many reasons it's different. One is that the data are always dirty, with missing values, values way out of the range of possibility, and time values that make no sense. Here's an example: Somebody sets the server system clock incorrectly and runs the server for a while with the wrong time. When they notice the mistake, they set the clock to the correct time. But all of the transactions that were running during that interval have an ending time before the starting time. When we run the data analysis, and compute elapsed time, the results are negative for those transactions.

"Missing values are a similar problem. Consider the records of just 10 purchases. Suppose that two of the records are missing the customer number and one is missing the year part of transaction date. So you throw out three records, which is 30 percent of the data. You then notice that two more records have dirty data, and so you throw them out, too. Now you've lost half your data.

"Another problem is that you know the least when you start the study. So you work for a few months and learn that if you had another variable; say the customer's Zip code, or age, or something else, you could do a much better analysis. But those other data just aren't available. Or, maybe they are available, but to get the data you have to reprocess millions of transactions, and you don't have the time or budget to do that.

"Overfitting is another problem, a huge one. I can build a model to fit any set of data you have. Give me 100 data points and in a few minutes, I can give you 100 different equations that will predict those 100 data points. With neural networks, you can create a model of any level of complexity you want, except that none of those equations will predict new cases with any accuracy at all. When using neural nets, you have to be very careful not to overfit the data.

"Then, too, data mining is about probabilities, not certainty. Bad luck happens. Say I build a model that predicts the probability that a customer will make a purchase. Using the model on new-customer data, I find three customers who have a .7 probability of buying something. That's a good number, well over a 50–50 chance, but it's still possible that none of them will buy. In fact, the probability that none of them will buy is $.3 \times .3 \times .3$, or .027, which is 2.7 percent.

"Now suppose I give the names of the three customers to a salesperson who calls on them, and sure enough, we have a stream of bad luck and none of them buys. This bad result doesn't mean the model is wrong. But what does the salesperson think? He thinks the model is

worthless and can do better on his own. He tells his manager who tells her associate, who tells the Northeast Region, and sure enough, the model has a bad reputation all across the company.

"Another problem is seasonality. Say all your training data are from the summer. Will your model be valid for the winter? Maybe, but maybe not. You might even know that it won't be valid for predicting winter sales, but if you don't have winter data, what do you do?

"When you start a data-mining project, you never know how it will turn out. I worked on one project for 6 months, and when we finished, I didn't think our model was any good. We had too many problems with data: wrong, dirty, and missing. There was no way we could know ahead of time that it would happen, but it did.

"When the time came to present the results to senior management, what could we do? How could we say we took 6 months of our time and substantial computer resources to create a bad model? We had a model, but I just didn't think it would make accurate predictions. I was a junior member of the team, and it wasn't for me to decide. I kept my mouth shut, but I never felt good about it. Fortunately, the project was cancelled later for other reasons.

"However, I'm only talking about my bad experiences. Some of my projects have been excellent. On many, we found interesting and important patterns and information, and a few times I've created very accurate predictive models. It's not easy, though, and you have to be very careful. Also, lucky!" ■

Discussion Questions

1. Summarize the concerns expressed by this contrarian.
2. Do you think the concerns raised here are sufficient to avoid data-mining projects altogether?
3. If you were a junior member of a data-mining team and you thought that the model that had been developed was ineffective, maybe even wrong, what would you do? If your boss disagrees with your beliefs, would you go higher in the organization? What are the risks of doing so? What else might you do?

ACTIVE REVIEW

Use this Active Review to verify that you understand the ideas and concepts that answer the chapter's study questions.

Q1 Why do organizations need business intelligence?

Identify the economic factors that have caused so much data to be created. Define *petabyte* and *exabyte*. Explain the opportunities that all of this data presents to business.

Q2 What business intelligence systems are available?

Define *business intelligence system* and *business intelligence tool*. Name and describe the use of three categories of BI tools. Define *business intelligence application* and use an example to explain the differences among BI tools, applications, and systems.

Q3 What are typical reporting applications?

Name and describe five basic reporting operations. Explain why the report in Figure 9-5 is more useful than the list in Figure 9-2. Define *RFM analysis* and explain the actions that should be taken with customers who have the following scores: [1, 1, 1,], [5, 1, 1,], [1, 1, 3], and [1, 4, 1]. Explain OLAP and describe its unique characteristics. Explain the roles for measure and dimension in an OLAP cube. Illustrate an OLAP cube with a single measure and five dimensions, two dimensions on one axis and three on another. Show how drill down applies to your example.

Q4 What are typical data-mining applications?

Define *data mining*, and explain how its use typically differs from reporting applications. Explain why data-mining tools are difficult to use well. Describe the differences between unsupervised and supervised data mining. Use an example to illustrate cluster analysis and regression analysis. Define *neural networks*, and explain why the term is a misnomer. Define *support*, *confidence*, and *lift*, and illustrate these terms using the data in Figure 9-12. Describe a good application for market-basket analysis results. Describe the purpose of decision trees and explain how the data in Figure 9-14 is used to evaluate loans for possible purchase.

Q5 What is the purpose of data warehouses and data marts?

Describe the need and functions of data warehouses and data marts. Name and describe the role of data warehouse components. List and explain the problems that can exist in data used for data mining and sophisticated reporting. Use the example of a supply chain to describe the differences between a data warehouse and data mart.

Q6 What are typical knowledge-management applications?

Define *knowledge management,* and describe its primary benefits. Explain how KM document sharing differs from content management. Explain the importance of indexing, and describe when Google indexing is useful and when it is not. Explain the statement, "RSS is like email for content." Define *RSS reader* and *RSS feed,* and explain how they interact. Define *expert system,* and explain why expert systems have a checkered reputation. Describe the purpose of the expert systems in use at the Washington University School of Medicine.

Q7 How are business intelligence applications delivered?

Name the components of a business intelligence system, and briefly describe the nature or purpose of each. Explain the management functions of a BI server, and describe three types of servers defined in this chapter. Explain the difference between push and pull systems. Describe the devices that receive BI results. Summarize the nature of procedures used in BI systems.

Q8 2020?

Summarize the function of the credit card approval application. Explain how you think that application uses data. Describe the factors that favor greater sophistication in business intelligence systems. Explain how credit card companies use purchase patterns to reduce credit limits and revoke cards and how such practices could be discriminatory. Summarize other uses for credit card data. Explain how even more information could be generated if credit card data is combined with personal and family data stored by data aggregators.

KEY TERMS AND CONCEPTS

USING YOUR KNOWLEDGE

1. Reflect on the differences between reporting systems and data-mining systems. What are their similarities and differences? How do their costs differ? What benefits does each offer? How would an organization choose between these two BI tools?

2. Suppose you are a member of the Audubon Society, and the board of the local chapter asks you to help them analyze its member data. The group wants to analyze the demographics of its membership against members' activity, including events attended, classes attended, volunteer activities, and donations. Describe two different reporting applications and one data-mining application that they might develop. Be sure to include a specific description of the goals of each system.

3. Suppose you are the director of student activities at your university. Recently, some students have charged that your department misallocates its resources. They claim the allocation is based on outdated student preferences. Funds are given to activities that few students find attractive, and insufficient funds are allocated to new activities in which students do want to participate. Describe how you could use reporting and/or data-mining systems to assess this claim.

4. Google *RSS reader* and download an RSS product. Set up feeds to your reader to the five most important business sources you know. Add feeds to your reader about technology and about one of your hobbies. Have at least 15 feeds, total. Run your RSS feeder for 3 days, and list the top five most interesting or informative items your reader made available that you would otherwise not have known about. Document your results by naming your reader, listing your sources, and describing the five most interesting items.

5. Suppose you work at Costco or another major, national, big-box store, and you do a market-basket analysis and identify the 25 pairs of items in the store that have the highest lift and the 25 pairs of items that have the lowest lift. What would you do with this knowledge? Costco (or your big-box store) doesn't have salespeople, so up-selling is not an option. What else might you do with information about these items' lift? Consider advertising, pricing, item location in stores, and any other factor that you might adjust. Do you think the lift calculations are valid for all stores in the United States (or other country)? Why or why not? Are the 50 pairs of products with the

highest and lowest lift the best place to focus your attention? What other 50 pairs of products might you want to consider? Explain.

6. Describe the information that MRV needs to identify the guides who are contributing the most to its competitive strategy. Does the production of this information require a reporting, a data mining, or a knowledge-management application? Explain the process that someone at MRV would need to follow to compute the necessary information.

7. In Chapter 5, Neil used data in the FlexTime database to determine that class sizes could not be appreciably increased. Given what you know from this chapter and from the nature of the FlexTime problem (see Chapters 3, 4, and 5), explain why he must have used a reporting application and not a data-mining or knowledge-management application.

8. Suppose FlexTime is considering investing in the IndoRow system described in the Bosu case at the end of Chapter 3. Describe a potential data-mining application that could help FlexTime decide if buying the IndoRow equipment is a good investment.

COLLABORATION EXERCISE

Collaborate with a group of students on the following exercise. Recall from Chapter 2 that collaboration is more than cooperation because it involves iteration and feedback. Post a document, a discussion item, a wiki item, or an idea and obtain feedback from your team members. Similarly, read the ideas of others and comment on them. Try to innovate in both the process by which you collaborate and the work product that you create. Avoid face-to-face meetings. Instead, use collaborative software such as Google Docs & Spreadsheets, Microsoft Groove, or Microsoft SharePoint to facilitate your ideas.

Mary Keeling owns and operates Carbon Creek Gardens, a retailer of trees, garden plants, perennial and annual flowers, and bulbs. "The Gardens," as her customers call it, also sells bags of soil, fertilizer, small garden tools, and garden sculptures. Mary started the business 16 years ago when she bought a section of land that, because of water drainage, was unsuited for residential development. With hard work and perseverance, Mary has created a warm and inviting environment with a unique and carefully selected inventory of plants. The Gardens has become a favorite nursery for serious gardeners in her community.

"The problem," she says, "is that I've grown so large, I've lost track of my customers. The other day, I ran into Tootsie Swan at the grocery store, and I realized I hadn't seen her in ages. I said something like, 'Hi, Tootsie, I haven't seen you for a while,' and that statement unleashed an angry torrent from her. It turns out that she'd been in over a year ago and had wanted to return a plant. One of my part-time employees waited on her and had apparently insulted her, or at least didn't give her the service she wanted. So, she decided not to come back to The Gardens.

"Tootsie was one of my best customers. I'd lost her, and I didn't even know it! That really frustrates me. Is it inevitable that as I get bigger, I lose track of my customers? I don't think so. Somehow, I have to find out when regular customers aren't coming around. Had I known Tootsie had stopped shopping with us, I'd have called her to see what was going on. I need customers like her.

"I've got all sorts of data in my sales database. It seems like the information I need is in there, but how do it get it out?"

In this exercise, you will apply the knowledge of this chapter to Mary Keeling's problem.

1. Mary wants to know when she's lost a customer. One way to help her would be to produce a report, say in PDF format, showing the top 50 customers from the prior year. Mary could print that report or we could place it on a private section of her Web site so that she can download it from wherever she happens to be.

   Periodically—say, once a week—Mary could request a report that shows the top buyers for that week. That report could also be in PDF format, or it could just be produced onscreen. Mary could compare the two reports to determine who is missing. If she wonders whether a customer such as Tootsie has been ordering, she could request a query report on Tootsie's activities.

   Describe the advantages and disadvantages of this solution.

2. Describe the best possible application of an OLAP tool at Carbon Creek. Can it be used to solve the lost-customer

problem? Why or why not? What is the best way, if any, for Mary to use OLAP at The Gardens? If none, explain why.

3. Describe the best possible application of decision-tree analysis at Carbon Creek. Can it be used to solve the lost-customer problem? Why or why not? What is the best way, if any, for Mary to use decision-tree analysis at The Gardens? If none, explain why.

4. Describe the best possible application of RFM analysis at Carbon Creek. Can it be used to solve the lost-customer problem? Why or why not? What is the best way, if any, for Mary to use RFM at The Gardens? If none, explain why.

5. Describe the best possible application of market-basket analysis at Carbon Creek. Can it be used to solve the lost-customer problem? Why or why not? What is the best way, if any, for Mary to use market-basket analysis at The Gardens? If none, explain why.

6. Which of the applications of BI tools in this exercise will provide Mary the best value? If you owned Carbon Creek Gardens and you were going to implement just one of these applications, which would you choose? Why?

APPLICATION EXERCISES

1. OLAP cubes are very similar to Microsoft Excel *pivot tables.* For this exercise, assume that your organization's purchasing agents rate vendors similar to the situation described in Application Exercise 2 in Chapter 8 on page 315.

   a. Open Excel and import the data in the worksheet named *Vendors* from the Excel file **Ch09Ex01**, which you can find on the text's Web site. The spreadsheet will have the following column names: *VendorName, EmployeeName, Date, Year,* and *Rating.*

   b. Under the *Insert* ribbon in Excel, click *Pivot Table.* A wizard will open. Select *Excel* and *Pivot table* in the first screen. Click *Next.*

   c. When asked to provide a data range, drag your mouse over the data you imported so as to select all of the data. Be sure to include the column headings. Excel will fill in the range values in the open dialog box. Place your pivot table in a separate spreadsheet.

   d. Excel will create a field list on the right-hand side of your spreadsheet. Drag and drop the field named *VendorName* onto the words "Drop Row Fields Here." Drag and drop *EmployeeName* on to the words "Drop Column Fields Here." Now drag and drop the field named *Rating* on to the words "Drop Data Items Here." Voilà! You have a pivot table.

   e. To see how the table works, drag and drop more fields on the various sections of your pivot table. For example, drop *Year* on top of *Employee.* Then move *Year* below *Employee.* Now move *Year* below *Vendor.* All of this action is just like an OLAP cube, and, in fact, OLAP cubes are readily displayed in Excel pivot tables. The major difference is that OLAP cubes are usually based on thousands or more rows of data.

2. It is surprisingly easy to create a market-basket report using table data in Access. To do so, however, you will need to enter SQL expressions into the Access query builder. Here, you can just copy SQL statements to type them in. If you take a database class, you will learn how to code SQL statements like those you will use here.

   a. Create an Access database with a table named *Order_Data* having columns *OrderNumber, ItemName,* and *Quantity,* with data types Number (*LongInteger*), Text (50), and Number (*LongInteger*), respectively. Define the key as the composite (*OrderNumber, ItemName*).

   b. Import the data from the Excel file **Ch09Ex02** into the *Order_Data* table.

   c. Now, to perform the market-basket analysis, you will need to enter several SQL statements into Access. To do so, click the queries tab and select *Create Query* in Design view. Click *Close* when the Show Table dialog box appears. Right-click in the gray section above the grid in the *Select Query* window. Select *SQL View.* Enter the following expression exactly as it appears here:

```
SELECT  T1.ItemName as FirstItem,
        T2.ItemName as SecondItem
FROM    Order_Data T1, Order_Data T2
WHERE   T1.OrderNumber =
        T2.OrderNumber
  AND   T1.ItemName <> T2.ItemName;
```

Click the red exclamation point in the toolbar to run the query. Correct any typing mistakes and, once it works, save the query using the name *TwoItemBasket.*

d. Now enter a second SQL statement. Again, click the queries tab and select *Create Query* in Design view. Click *Close* when the Show Table dialog box appears. Right-click in the gray section above the grid in the *Select Query* window. Select *SQL View.* Enter the following expression exactly as it appears here:

```
SELECT    TwoItemBasket.FirstItem,
          TwoItemBasket.SecondItem,
          Count(*) AS SupportCount
FROM      TwoItemBasket
GROUP BY  TwoItemBasket.FirstItem,
          TwoItemBasket.SecondItem;
```

Correct any typing mistakes and, once it works, save the query using the name *SupportCount.*

e. Examine the results of the second query and verify that the two query statements have correctly calculated the number of times that two items have appeared together. Explain further calculations you need to make to compute support.

f. Explain the calculations you need to make to compute lift. Although you can make those calculations using SQL, you need more SQL knowledge to do it, and we will skip that here.

g. Explain, in your own words, what the query in part c seems to be doing. What does the query in part d seem to be doing? Again, you will need to take a database class to learn how to code such expressions, but this exercise should give you a sense of the kinds of calculations that are possible with SQL.

CASE STUDY 9

Business Intelligence for Decision Making at Home Depot

Home Depot is a major retail chain specializing in the sale of construction and home repair and maintenance products. The company has 2,200 retail stores worldwide from which it generated $71 billion in sales in 2008. Home Depot carries more than 40,000 products in its stores and employs more than 300,000 people. Its stores are visited by more than 22 million people each week.

Suppose you are a buyer for the clothes washer and dryer product line at Home Depot. You work with seven different brands and numerous models within each brand. One of your goals is to turn your inventory as many times a year as you can. In order to do so, you want to identify poorly selling models (and even brands) as quickly as you can. This identification is not as easy as you might think, because competition is intense among washer and dryer manufacturers and a new model can quickly capture a substantial portion of another model's market share. Thus, a big seller this year can be a "dog" (a poor seller) next year.

Another problem concerns geography. Some brands are unavailable in some countries. Even within a country some sales trends are national, others pertain to specific regions. In the United States, a strong seller in the Southeast may not sell as well in the Northwest. Thus, a brand can be a big seller in one region, a dog in another, and unavailable in still another.

In answering the following questions, assume you have total sales data for each brand and model, for each store, for each month. Assume also that you know the store's city and state.

Questions

1. Explain how reporting systems could be helpful to you.
2. Show the structure of an OLAP report that you could use to identify poorly selling models. How would you structure the report to identify different sales trends in different regions? Show examples of several different views of your OLAP report.
3. For the OLAP report in question 2, write a description of your requirements for an IT professional. Be as complete and thorough as you can in describing your needs. Use Excel to produce a prototype or mock-up of the reports you'd like to see.
4. Explain how data-mining systems could be helpful to you.

5. How could cluster analysis help you identify poorly selling brands? How could cluster analysis help you determine differences in sales for different geographic regions? Is the unsupervised nature of cluster analysis an advantage or disadvantage for you?

6. How could regression analysis help you determine poorly selling brands?

7. Do you believe there is an application for a KM system for identifying poorly selling brands? Why or why not?

8. Do you believe there is an application for an expert system for identifying poorly selling brands? Why or why not?

PART 3 THE INTERNATIONAL DIMENSION

Global IS and the Value Chain

Q1 How Do Global Information Systems Benefit the Value Chain?

Because of information systems, any or all of the value chain activities in Porter's model can be performed anywhere in the world. An international company can conduct sales and marketing efforts locally, for every market in which it sells. For example, Pearson, the publisher of this textbook, sells in the United States with a U.S. sales force, in France with a French sales force, and in Argentina with an Argentinean sales force. Depending on local laws and customs, those sales offices may be owned by Pearson, or, as in China, they may be locally owned entities with which Pearson contracts for sales and marketing services. Pearson can coordinate all of the sales efforts of these entities using the same CRM (customer relationship management) system. When Pearson executives need to roll up sales totals for a sales projection, they can do so using an integrated, worldwide system.

Manufacturing of a final product is frequently distributed throughout the world. Components of the Boeing 787 are manufactured in Australia, Italy, Japan, Korea, and other countries and delivered to Everett, Washington, for final assembly. Each manufacturing facility has its own inbound logistics, manufacturing, and outbound logistics activity, but those activities are linked together via information systems.

For example, Rolls Royce manufactures an engine and delivers that engine to Boeing via its outbound logistics activity. Boeing receives the engine using its inbound logistics activity. All of this activity is coordinated via shared, interorganizational information systems. Rolls Royce's CRM is connected with Boeing's supply processes, using techniques such as CRM and enterprise resource planning (ERP).

Because of the abundance of low-cost, well-educated, English-speaking professionals in India, many organizations have chosen to outsource their service and support functions to India. Some accounting functions are outsourced to India as well.

World time differences enable global virtual companies to operate 24/7. Boeing engineers in Los Angeles can develop a design for an engine support strut and send that design to Rolls Royce in England at the end of their day. The design will be waiting for Rolls Royce engineers at the start of their day. They review the

design, make needed adjustments, and send it back to Boeing in Los Angeles, where the reviewed, adjusted design arrives at the start of the workday in Los Angeles. The ability to work around the clock by moving work into other time zones has greatly increased productivity.

Q2 What Are the Challenges of International Business Process Management?

Challenges for international business process management depend on whether the process is functional or cross-functional. As you learned in Chapter 7, functional business processes support particular activities within a single department or business activity. Because the systems operate independently, the organization suffers from islands of automation. Sales and marketing data, for example, are not integrated with operations or manufacturing data.

This lack of integration has *advantages*, however, for international organizations and international systems. Because the order-processing functional system in the United States is separate from and independent of the manufacturing systems in Taiwan, it is unnecessary to accommodate language, business, and cultural differences in a single system. U.S. order-processing systems can operate in English and reflect the practices and culture of the United States. Taiwanese manufacturing information systems can operate in Chinese and reflect the business practices and culture of

Taiwan. As long as there is an adequate SOA or other interface between the two systems, they can operate independently, sharing data when necessary.

Cross-functional, integrated systems, such as ERP, solve the problems of data isolation by integrating data into databases that provide a comprehensive and organization-wide view. However, because they are integrated, cross-functional systems do not readily accommodate differences in language, business practices, and cultural norms.

For example, consider the ERP system, SAP. SAP software is developed and licensed by SAP, a German software company. Because SAP addresses a global market, SAP software was localized long ago into English and numerous other foreign languages. Suppose that a multinational company with operations in Spain, Italy, Taiwan, Singapore, and Los Angeles uses SAP. Should this company allow the use of different language versions of SAP? As long as the functionality of the versions is the same, no harm occurs by doing so.

But what if employees enter data in different languages? If this is allowed, much of the value of an integrated database is lost. If you speak English, what good is customer contact data recorded in Spanish, Italian, Chinese, and English? Data isolation entered the ERP system via the back door. For this reason, many companies standardize on English as their "company language."

Inherent processes are even more problematic. Each software product assumes that the software will be used by people filling particular job functions and performing their actions in a certain way. ERP vendors justify this standardization by saying that their procedures are based on industry-wide best practices and that the organization will benefit by following these standard processes. That statement may be true, but some inherent processes may conflict with cultural norms. If they do, it will be very difficult for management to convince the employees to follow those inherent processes. Or at least it will be difficult in some cultures to do so.

Differences in language, culture, norms, and expectations compound the difficulties of international process management. Just creating an accurate as-is model is difficult and expensive; developing alternative international processes and evaluating them can be incredibly challenging. With cultural differences, it can be difficult just to determine what criteria should be used for evaluating the alternatives, let alone performing the evaluation.

Because of these challenges, in the future it is likely that international business processes will be developed more like interorganizational business processes. A high-level process will be defined to document the service responsibilities of each international unit. Then SOA standards will be used to connect those services into an integrated, cross-functional, international system. Because of encapsulation, the only obligation of an international unit will be to deliver its defined service. One service can be delivered using procedures based on autocratic management policies, and another can be delivered using procedures based on collaborative management policies. The differences will not matter to an SOA-based cross-functional system.

Q3 How Does Web 2.0 Affect International Business?

In truth, we do not know, at least not yet, how Web 2.0 affects international business. We do know that Web 2.0 technologies are used internationally: For example, Google AdWords is available in the Japanese and Indian markets, and social networks are popular in any culture with sufficient connectivity. It is possible that Web 2.0 technologies are so culturally biased that they work only in the culture in which they originate. A Facebook social graph of a young college woman in Japan is unlikely to connect in any meaningful way with a similar graph of a male business student in India. Each will have his or her own social network, but they will be domestic, not international.

Similar comments can be made about user-generated content. Teenagers in Chicago are unlikely to be influenced by user-generated tennis shoe designs that are popular in Hanover, Germany. Or are they? Is there a business opportunity for some innovative company to foster user-generated designs in one culture with the express purpose of marketing those designs in another culture? We do not yet know.

We do know, however, that Twitter can be used to disseminate international news. As mentioned in the Part 2 closing, in June 2009 large groups of Iranian citizens protested vote counting in their national election. When the established government closed Iran to foreign correspondents and attempted to control the dissemination of protest news in other ways, the protesters turned to Twitter. They used Twitter to arrange meetings, publish warnings, and to tell the world about the violence they were experiencing. U.S. news bloggers such as Andrew Sullivan at *The Atlantic* picked up the protesters Tweets and broadcast them to the rest of the world via his blog The Daily Dish (*http://andrewsullivan.theatlantic.com).* In a strange turn of events, it was reported that the established government Tweeted news of false meetings so as to lure protesters to a particular place and time and then arrest them.

Opportunities for worldwide use of Web 2.0 will exist for you and your classmates to explore early in your careers. As you use Facebook, MySpace, Twitter, or other microblogs and as you consume or create UGC, think about the international aspects of your activity. Maybe you can be the one to invent the next Twitter, but on an international scale!

Meanwhile, we do know that global information systems have and will continue to have an impact on manufacturing, and we consider international manufacturing in the next two questions.

Q4 How Do Global Information Systems Affect Supply Chain Profitability?

In short, global information systems increase supply chain profitability. Supply chain performance is driven by four factors: facilities, inventories, transportation, and information. Every one of these drivers is positively affected by global information systems. Because of global information systems, facilities can be located anywhere in the world. If Amazon.com finds it economically advantageous to warehouse books in Iceland, it can do so. If Rolls Royce can more cheaply manufacture its engine turbine blades in Poland, it can do so.

Furthermore, information systems reduce inventories and hence save costs. They can be used to reduce or eliminate the *bullwhip effect,* a phenomenon in which the variability in the size and timing of orders increases at each stage of the supply chain. They also support just-in-time (JIT) inventory techniques worldwide. Using information systems, the order of a Dell computer from a user in Bolivia triggers a manufacturing system at Dell,

which, in turn, triggers the order of a component from a warehouse in Taiwan—all automatically.

To underscore this point, consider the inventories that exist at this moment in time, worldwide. Every component in one of those inventories represents a waste of the world's resources. Any product or component sitting on a shelf is not being used and is adding no value to the global economy. In the perfect world, a customer would think, "I want a new computer," and that thought would trigger systems all over the world to produce and assemble necessary components, instantly. Given that we live in a world bound by time and space, instantaneous production is forever unreachable. But the goal of worldwide information systems for supply chain inventory management is to come as close to instantaneous as possible.

Consider transportation, the third driver. When you order a book from Amazon.com, you are presented with multiple shipping options. You can choose the speed and attendant price that is appropriate for your needs. Similar systems for businesses allow them to choose the delivery option that optimizes the value they generate. Further, automated systems enable suppliers and customers to track the shipment's location, 24/7, worldwide.

Finally, global information systems produce comprehensive, accurate, and timely information. As you learned in Chapter 9, information systems produce data at prodigious rates, worldwide. That data facilitates operations as just discussed, but it also produces information for planning, organizing, deciding, and other analyses.

Next time you walk into Wal-Mart, think about the impact global information systems had in producing, ordering, and delivering the thousands of items you see.

Q5 What Is the Economic Impact of Global Manufacturing?

Henry Ford pioneered modern manufacturing methods, and in the process he reduced the price of automobiles to the point that they were no longer the playthings of the very rich but affordable to the general population. In 1914, Ford took the unprecedented step of unilaterally increasing his workers' pay from $2.50 per day for 10 hours' work to $5 per day for 8 hours' work. As a consequence, many of his workers could soon afford to purchase an automobile. By paying his workers more, Ford increased demand.

The increase in demand was not due only to purchases by his workers, of course. Because of what economists call the *accelerator effect*, a dollar spent will contribute two or three dollars of activity to the economy. Ford's workers spent their increased pay not just on autos, but also on goods and services in their local community, which benefited via the accelerator effect. That benefit enabled non–Ford workers to afford an auto, too. Further, because of the positive publicity he achieved with the pay increase, the community was strongly disposed to purchase a Ford automobile.

Consider those events in light of global manufacturing. For example, if Boeing manufactures airplanes entirely in the United States, the U.S. economy will be the sole beneficiary of that economic activity. If an Italian airline chooses to buy a Boeing plane, the transaction will be a cost to the Italian economy. There will be no accelerator effect, and the transaction will have no consequence on Italians' propensity to fly.

However, if Boeing purchases major components for its airplanes from Italian companies, then that purchase will generate an accelerator effect for the Italian economy. By buying in Italy, Boeing contributes to Italy's economy, and ultimately increases Italians' propensity to fly. That foreign-component purchase will, of course, reduce economic activity in the United States, but if it induces Italians to purchase sufficiently more Boeing airplanes, then it is possible that the loss will be compensated by the increase in airplane sales volume. That purchase will also benefit Boeing's image among Italians and increase the likelihood of sales to the Italian government.

The same phenomenon pertains to Dell computers, Cisco routers, and Microsoft software. It also explains why Toyota manufactures cars in the United States.

Q6 Should Information Systems Be Instruments for Exporting Cultural Values?

The question of whether information systems *should be* instruments for exporting cultural values is complex. As discussed under question Q2, it is undeniable that information systems *do* export cultural values. When an organization installs an ERP system, it installs inherent processes. According to ERP vendors, everyone ultimately benefits, because these processes encode each industry's "best practices." But what is deemed a best practice depends heavily on culture. Speed and efficiency might be highly valued in one culture, whereas warm and engaging interpersonal relationships might be highly valued in another. The inherent process, however, will simply encode the cultural values of the designers of the system.

One might say that exporting such cultural values is innocent, and, ultimately, if someone does not like the procedures in place at his or her employer he or she can choose to work elsewhere. But what about values such as freedom of speech? In the spring of 2006, the Chinese government asked MSN to shut down IP support for blog sites that it deemed offensive. The sites, located in China, were criticizing the Chinese government. Had the sites been located in the United States, the First Amendment of the Constitution would have protected the blogs.

The question for MSN was whether it should comply with the Chinese government's request. The values of most—if not all—of the people who constructed the MSN system would support freedom of speech. But the site was operating in China, and as a sovereign government China has the right to enact laws as it sees fit. MSN chose to shut down the sites, and many in the United States criticized that decision. Google experienced similar criticism when, under pressure from China and other countries, it agreed not to allow searching on terms such as *democracy*.

But consider a site that offers online gambling. Gambling is legal in many countries and is considered culturally positive in some. Most European nations allow online gambling. The U.S. federal government, however, outlawed online sports betting, and no state has licensed any form of online games of chance. If a Chinese company were to offer either form of online gambling from a site in the United States, the U.S. government or a state would certainly shut it down.

Is this a double standard? Does the United States want the right to shut down information systems that violate its laws, but disallow other nations from doing the same? Some would say the comparison fails because gambling is a vice and freedom of speech is a basic human right. But, not every nation or culture agrees.

Information systems project human values. The question is, "Whose values?"

ACTIVE REVIEW

Use this Active Review to verify that you understand the ideas and concepts that answer the study questions in the International Dimension.

Q1 How do global information systems benefit the value chain?

Using Porter's model, explain how each primary value chain activity can be performed anywhere in the world. Explain how global, virtual companies operate 24/7. Using the answers to this question, explain three ways that Pearson benefits from global information systems.

Q2 What are the challenges of international business process management?

In your own words, explain why the challenges for international process management depend on whether the process is functional or cross-functional. Explain how lack of integration can have advantages. Discuss the particular challenges of inherent processes. Describe how SOA principles facilitate international business process management.

Q3 How does Web 2.0 affect international business?

Explain the text's response to this study question. Do you agree or disagree with it? Explain the meaning of the following sentence: "It's possible that Web 2.0 technologies are so culturally biased that they work only in the culture in which they originate." Summarize how Twitter was used by Iranian protesters in 2009.

Q4 How do global information systems affect supply chain profitability?

State the short answer to this question. Name the four drivers of supply chain profitability. Discuss how global information systems affect each driver. Explain how inventories represent waste. Summarize the ways that you think global information systems have in filling the shelves at Wal-Mart.

Q5 What is the economic impact of global manufacturing?

Summarize the impact that Henry Ford's act of increasing his workers' pay had on Ford auto sales. Describe how the accelerator effect contributed to the increase in demand. Explain how this same phenomenon pertains to Boeing acquiring major subsystems from manufacturers in Italy or to Toyota building autos in the United States.

Q6 Should information systems be instruments for exporting cultural values?

Describe how information systems export cultural values. Explain how the term *best practice* encodes a cultural bias. State whether you think MSN should have shut down the IP addresses for the blogs in China. Explain the costs and benefits to MSN of its decision. Describe the difference between MSN shutting down the Chinese blog and the United States shutting down an online sports-betting site. If you see no difference, explain why.

The Brose Group supplies windows, doors, seat adjusters, and related products for more than 40 auto brands. Major customers include General Motors, Ford, DaimlerChrysler, BMW, Porsche, Volkswagen, Toyota, and Honda. Founded as an auto and aircraft parts manufacturer in Berlin in 1908, the company today employs more than 13,000 employees in facilities at more than 51 locations in 21 different countries. Revenue for 2008 exceeded 2.8 billion euros. Brose is privately held by the Brose family.

In the 1990s, Brose enjoyed rapid growth but found that existing information systems were unable to support the company's emerging needs. Too many different information systems meant a lack of standardization and hampered communication among suppliers, plants, and customers. Brose decided to standardize operations on SAP R/3, an ERP application licensed by SAP that supports more than a thousand different business processes. Rather than attempt to implement those processes on its own, Brose hired SAP Consulting to lead the project.

The SAP team provided process consulting and implementation support, and it trained end users. According to Christof Lutz, SAP project manager, "Our consultants and the Brose experts worked openly, flexibly, and constructively together. In this atmosphere of trust, we created an implementation module that the customer can use as a basis for the long term."

The Brose/SAP consulting team decided on a pilot approach. The first installation was conducted at a new plant in Curitiba, Brazil. The team constructed the implementation to be used as a prototype for installations at additional plants. Developing the first implementation was no small feat, because it involved information systems for sales and distribution, materials management, production planning, quality management, and financial accounting and control.

Once the initial system was operational at the Curitiba plant, the prototype was rolled out to additional facilities. The second implementation, in Puebla, Mexico, required just 6 months for first operational capability, and the next implementation in Meerane, Germany, was operational in just 19 weeks.

The conversion to the ERP system has contributed to dramatically increased productivity. In 1994, Brose achieved sales of 541 million euros with 2,900 employees, or 186,000 euros per employee. Ten years later, in 2004, Brose attained sales of 2 billion euros with 8,200 employees, or 240,000 euros per employee. Even in 2008, when auto manufacturing began its steep decline, Brose earned $2.8 billion euros with 13,000 employees, or 216,000 euros per employee.

Modern manufacturing seeks to improve productivity by reducing waste, which means eliminating:

- Overproduction that leads to excess inventories
- Unavailable needed parts, which idle workers and facilities
- Wasted motion and processing due to poorly planned materials handling and operations activities

Manufacturing that eliminates these wastes is called *lean manufacturing*.

To accomplish lean manufacturing, SAP has invented a business process it calls *just-in-sequence (JIS)* manufacturing. JIS is an extension of just-in-time (JIT), the pull manufacturing philosophy described in this chapter. JIS extends JIT so that parts not only arrive just in time, but also arrive in just the correct sequence.

For example, the Brose Group factory in Brazil manufactures doors for General Motors. When General Motors starts the construction of a new auto, it sends a signal of the need for doors to the Brose Group. That signal starts the construction of the four doors on four separate production lines in Brazil. Brose schedules the work on each of these lines so as to produce the four doors and their related equipment and deliver them at the correct time and in the correct sequence at General Motors. Thus, if General Motors needs the rear-door frames, then the front-door frames, then the front doors, and finally the rear doors, Brose will schedule manufacturing and delivery accordingly.

To achieve JIS, Brose used SAP R/3 combined with a supplementary SAP module called SAP for Automotive with JIS. Like all ERP software, these applications include inherent (i.e., built-in) processes that the organization does not need to design separately. In this case, those business processes include manufacturing planning methods and procedures for JIS performance.

In 2009, automotive industry analysts estimate that, worldwide, the auto industry has the capacity to produce 90 million autos per year, but that there was demand, in 2008, for only 65 million autos, with expectations that demand will fall further.[1] This fact, coupled with the U.S. government purchasing major shares of both Chrysler and General Motors, means that change is inevitable. Brose is undoubtedly in for some tough years, but views its investment in manufacturing technology and logistics to be key to surviving the automotive crisis:

> With innovative capability, leading edge manufacturing technology and logistics, above all, with its strategic investments and stable ownership structure, we seek to have a long-term partnership with the automakers.[2]

One can only wonder how many automakers will be around, long term, for Brose to partner with.

Sources: Brose, *http://www.brose.net/ww/en/pub/company.htm* (accessed July 2009); *http://sap.com/ industries/automotive/pdf/CS_Brose_Group.pdf*, 2003 (accessed March 2007).

QUESTIONS

1. Reflect on the nature of JIS planning. In general terms, what kinds of data must Brose have in order to provide JIS to its customers? What does Brose need to know? It certainly needs a bill of materials for the items it produces. What other categories of information will Brose need?

2. According to the description on page 366, the SAP system included applications for sales and distribution, materials management, production planning, quality management, and financial accounting and control. Describe, in general terms, features and functions of these applications that are necessary to provide JIS.

---

[1]Choi Jae Kook, Vice Chairman, Hyundai, quoted in *http://www.automonster.ca/?p=906* (accessed July 2009).
[2]*http://www.brose.net/ww/en/pub/company.htm*.

3. The Brose factory in Brazil produces more than doors for General Motors. The factory must coordinate the door orders with orders for other products and orders from other manufacturers. What kinds of IS are necessary to provide such coordinated manufacturing planning?

4. Brazilians speak Portuguese, workers in the United States speak English and Spanish, and personnel at the Brose headquarters speak German. Summarize challenges to Brose and SAP Consulting when implementing a system for users who speak four different languages and live in (at least) four different cultures.

5. Visit *http://sap.com/industries/automotive* and investigate SAP for Automotive with JIS. What features and functions does this product have that standard SAP R/3 does not have? What advantages does SAP obtain by creating and licensing this product? What advantages do SAP's customers obtain from this product? In your response, consider both R/3 customers who are and who are not automotive manufacturers.

6. Brose seeks to provide JIS service to its customers. Does this goal necessitate that Brose suppliers also provide JIS service to Brose? What can Brose do if its suppliers do not provide such service? Is there any reason why Brose would not want them to provide such service? Do you think that before one company in a supply chain can offer JIS, all companies in the supply chain must offer the service?

7. Describe three specific ways that Brose's investment in SAP will help it survive the automotive crisis.

PART 4

Managing Information Systems Resources

FlexTime, the workout studio discussed in Chapters 1 through 6, and MRV, the river-rafting company introduced in Part 3, have much in common. Both are small companies. Both have a small cadre of full-time employees that is supplemented by part-time contractors. Both have a competitive strategy that differentiates on quality of service to customers. Both are known as service leaders in their markets.

They have one crucial difference, however. Neil at FlexTime has considerable knowledge of how best to use and develop information systems. No one at MRV has comparable knowledge and skill. As a result, FlexTime spends its IS budget wisely and has a customer database that enables it to make effective decisions, such as the decision not to consolidate classes (Chapter 5). MRV, however, flounders in its use of information systems and is about to waste considerable money on a poorly conceived attempt to cheaply build an information system, as you will learn in Chapter 10. It is also about to experience a serious data loss, but we are getting ahead of the story.

We will use the MRV example in the three chapters in this part. In Chapter 10, you will learn processes for developing and maintaining new information systems. It is particularly important for you to learn the users' roles in this process, because MIS concerns the *development* and use of IS. Sue at MRV suffers because of a lack of this knowledge. Chapter 11 discusses information systems management and the functions of the IS department, as well as the role of outsourcing. Even though neither FlexTime nor MRV has an IS department *per se*, both need to manage their IS. Finally, Chapter 12 describes the management of information systems security, a topic that grows in importance as organizations store more and more of their data in information systems.

10

Managing Development

"Look, Eddie, I think we've outgrown them. They were fine when all we needed was a simple Web site. Maybe not Picassos with graphics, but they made it work."

"But, Sue, what are we gonna do? Put an ad in our local paper under *P* for programmer? We know nothing about this—at least they knew how to build our Web site."

"Yeah, they did, but every time I tried to talk with them about what I want next, they looked like deer in headlights."

"OK, try it on me. What is it you want?"

"I want to bring our customers closer to us. I want an ongoing relationship with them. We know we're great, but I want them to tell *each other* that we're great. I want two kinds of Web sites, or something like that. One site for the general public—like we have now, but more of our customers' photos and more customer comments. Then I want a second site. Maybe it has a password or something. This site is just for people who've gone on trips with us. It has lots of photos, maybe my blog, or Rueben's blog, a survey about future trips. Anything to keep our customers excited about rafting."

"Reuben???? He can't tell a standing wave from a tree."

"He's smart, Eddie, and articulate. Plus he's still got his newbie enthusiasm, and I want to harness that for our customers."

"You want me to run the ad? How about 'Wanted: Computer programmer. Free food left over from raft trips.' I can put it on Craig's List."

"Eddie, I want someone who can talk with me about what I want, tell me if it makes sense from a technical standpoint, and then give me some idea about costs and how long it will take. Then, maybe that person hires the programmer."

"Sounds expensive."

"Yeah, I know. I'm thinking about hiring Graham."

"Well, he did a good job on the guide performance analysis. But, he has no real experience."

"I know. But he's smart, and it can't be that hard."

Sue meets with Graham later that day. "Graham, you think you could build a web site? Or Two?"

Sue's lament is more common than you might think. She knows what she wants for her business, but she does not know how to proceed. She's about to make a serious mistake in hiring Graham. Without the knowledge of this chapter, she doesn't know what Graham needs to know. And Graham, with little systems development knowledge or experience, is about to start a disaster. Sue, Graham, and you, too, need this chapter! ■

CHAPTER PREVIEW

You can find a free, supplemental study lesson for this chapter at:
www.LearningMIS.com

This chapter considers how people and organizations create information systems. First, we introduce the process of systems development and discuss some of the difficulties and risks involved. Then we describe the systems development life cycle, a standard process used for developing systems. Next we consider systems development project management. We will discuss differences in project scale, trade-offs, and challenges when planning and managing a systems development project. We'll conclude with projections about how systems development will be different in 2020.

You could be Sue. You could have an intuitive understanding of how IS can help you but not know how to proceed. Ultimately, Sue decides to try to build her system on the cheap, and she makes a terrible decision; she hires a student who is smart, but has no knowledge of either systems development processes or project management. Read this chapter to learn what Sue should have known.

Q1 What Is Systems Development?

Systems development, or **systems analysis and design** as it is sometimes called, is the process of creating and maintaining information systems. Notice that this process concerns *information systems*, not just computer programs. Developing an *information system* involves all five components: hardware, software, data, procedures, and people. Developing a *computer program* involves software programs, possibly with some focus on data and databases. Figure 10-1 shows that systems development has a broader scope than computer program development.

Systems Development Is Not Just for Techies

Because systems development addresses all five components, it requires more than just programming or technical expertise. Establishing the system's goals, setting up the project, and determining requirements require business knowledge and management skill. Tasks such as building computer networks and writing computer programs require technical skills, but developing the other components requires nontechnical, human relations skills. Creating data models requires the ability to interview users and understand their view of the business activities. Designing procedures, especially those involving group action, requires business knowledge and an understanding of group dynamics. Developing job descriptions, staffing, and training all require human resource and related expertise.

Thus, do not suppose that systems development is exclusively a technical task undertaken by programmers and hardware specialists. Rather, it requires coordinated teamwork of both specialists and nonspecialists with business knowledge.

Information Systems Are Never Off-the-Shelf

In Chapter 4, you learned three sources for software: off-the-shelf, off-the-shelf with adaptation, and tailor-made. Although all three sources pertain to software, only two

Computer programming concerned
with programs, some data

| Hardware | Software | Data | Procedures | People |

Scope of Systems Development

Figure 10-1
Systems Development
Versus Program Development

of them pertain to information systems. Unlike software, *information systems are never off-the-shelf.* Because information systems involve a company's people and procedures, the company must construct or adapt procedures to fit its business and people, regardless of how it will obtain the computer programs.

As a future business manager, you will have a key role in information systems development. To accomplish the goals of your department, you need to ensure that effective procedures exist for using the information system. You need to ensure that personnel are properly trained and are able to use the IS effectively. If your department does not have appropriate procedures and trained personnel, you must take corrective action. Although you might pass off hardware, program, or data problems to the IT department, you cannot pass off procedural or personnel problems to that department. Such problems are your problems. The single most important criterion for information systems success is ***for users to take ownership of their systems***.

Q2 Why Is Systems Development Difficult and Risky?

Systems development is difficult and risky. Many projects are never finished. Of those that are finished, some are 200 or 300 percent over budget. Still other projects finish within budget and on schedule, but never satisfactorily accomplish their goals. (See Case Study 10 on page 406 for more statistics on development failures.)

You might be amazed to learn that systems development failures can be so dramatic. You might suppose that with the experience of developing thousands of systems over the years by now there would be some methodology for successful systems development. In fact, there *are* systems development methodologies that can result in success, and we will discuss the most common one in this chapter. But, even when competent people follow one of these methodologies, the risk of failure is still high. Hence there is also a need for strong project management, as you will learn.

In the following sections, we will discuss the five major challenges to systems development displayed in Figure 10-2 (on the next page).

The Difficulty of Requirements Determination

First, requirements are difficult to determine. Consider the system that Sue wants at MRV. What particular features does she want on her two different Web sites? She wants it to further MRV's competitive strategy, but how? Strengthen existing relationships? Increase customer referrals? Something else?

These goals lead to specific requirements. Does MRV actually need different Web sites, or would one site work, with password access required for some features? Sue wants some form of user-generated content for customers to rate MRV, but what? Does she want control over those reviews? What other features does she need? Does she want to link Twitter into her site? Does she want MRV to have a companion Facebook page?

In fact, the proposed MRV system is simple. Consider, instead, the development of a new interorganizational system for supply chain management. How does Boeing go about building information systems for the 787 parts supply chain? What features and functions should such a system have? What is to be done if different companies have different ideas about the features required? Companies may disagree about the data they are willing to share. How are those differences to be resolved? Hundreds of hours of labor will be required to determine the requirements.

The questions could go on and on. One of the major purposes of the systems development process is to create an environment in which such questions are both asked and answered.

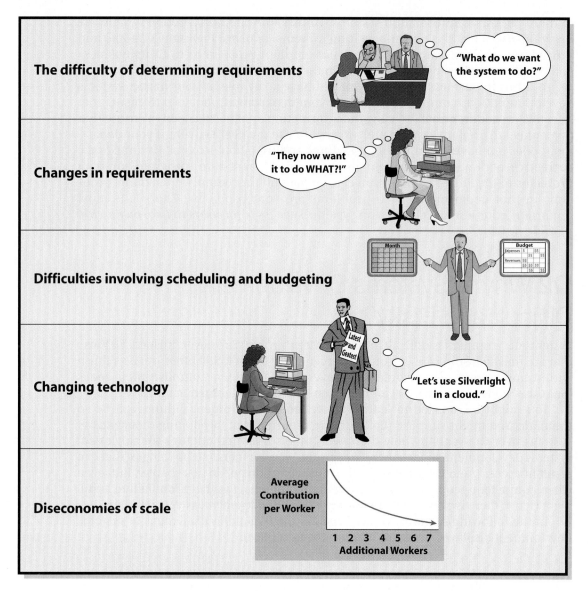

Figure 10-2
Major Challenges
to Systems Development

Changes in Requirements

Even more difficult, systems development aims at a moving target. Requirements change as the system is developed. The bigger the system and the longer the project, the more the requirements change.

When requirements change, what should the development team do? Stop work and rebuild the system in accordance with the new requirements? If they do that, the system will develop in fits and starts and might never be completed. Or, should the team finish the system, knowing that it will be unsatisfactory the day it is implemented and will therefore need immediate maintenance?

Scheduling and Budgeting Difficulties

Other challenges involve scheduling and budgeting. How long will it take to build a system? That question is not easy to answer. Suppose you are developing a new customer database at MRV. How long will it take to create the data model? Even if you know how long it takes to create the data model, Sue and Eddie and others may disagree with your model and with each other's models. How many times will you need to rebuild the data model until everyone agrees?

Again, the MRV system is a simple problem. What if you are building the new database for the supply chain system? How many hours will it take to create the data model, review, and approve it? Consider database applications. How long will it take to build the forms, reports, queries, and application programs? How long will it take to test all of them? What about procedures and people? What procedures need to be developed, and how much time should be set aside to create and document them, develop training programs, and train the personnel?

Further, how much will all of this cost? Labor costs are a direct function of labor hours; if you cannot estimate labor hours, you cannot estimate labor costs. Moreover, if you cannot estimate how much a system costs, then how do you perform a financial analysis to determine if the system generates an appropriate rate of return?

Changing Technology

Yet another challenge is that while the project is underway, technology continues to change. For example, say that while you are developing the MRV system Microsoft releases Silverlight, a new application product and technology for creating dynamic Web sites. You learn that with Silverlight you can give customers a much more interesting and exciting experience, just what Sue wants. Microsoft claims that it will drastically shorten your development time, halve the costs, and result in a better system. That is, it will do those things if it actually works the way Microsoft says it will.

Even if you believe Silverlight is a viable answer, do you want to stop your development to switch to the new technology? Would it be better to finish developing according to the existing plan?

Diseconomies of Scale

Unfortunately, as development teams become larger, the average contribution per worker decreases. This is true because as staff size increases, more meetings and other coordinating activities are required to keep everyone in sync. There are economies of scale up to a point, but beyond a workgroup of, say, 20 employees, diseconomies of scale begin to take over.

A famous adage known as **Brooks' Law** points out a related problem: *Adding more people to a late project makes the project later.*[1] Brooks' Law is true not only because a larger staff requires increased coordination, but also because new people need training. The only people who can train the new employees are the existing team members, who are thus taken off productive tasks. The costs of training new people can overwhelm the benefit of their contribution.

In short, managers of software development projects face a dilemma: They can increase work per employee by keeping the team small, but in doing so they extend the project's timeline. Or, they can reduce the project's timeline by adding staff, but because of diseconomies of scale they will have to add 150 or 200 hours of labor to gain 100 hours of work. And, due to Brooks' Law, once the project is late, both choices are bad.

Furthermore, schedules can be compressed only so far. According to one other popular adage, "Nine women cannot make a baby in 1 month."

Is Systems Development Really So Bleak?

Is systems development really as bleak as the list of challenges makes it sound? Yes and no. All of the challenges just described *do* exist, and they are all significant hurdles that every development project must overcome. As noted previously, once the project is late and over budget, no good choice exists. "I have to pick my regrets," said one beleaguered manager of a late project.

---

[1] Fred Brooks was a successful senior manager at IBM in the 1960s. After retiring from IBM, he wrote a classic book on IT project management called *The Mythical Man-Month.* Published by Addison-Wesley in 1975, the book is pertinent today and should be read by every IT or IS project manager. It's an enjoyable book, too.

The IT industry has over 50 years of experience developing information systems, and over those years methodologies have emerged that successfully deal with these problems. In the next two questions, we will consider the systems development life cycle (SDLC), the standard process used to develop information systems. Other methodologies exist, but they are beyond the scope of this text. For now, if you learn the basic SDLC, you will be well on your way to avoiding the mistakes that Sue made.

Q3 How Do Businesses Use the Systems Development Life Cycle (SDLC) Process?

The **systems development life cycle (SDLC)** is the classical process used to develop information systems. The IT industry developed the SDLC in the "school of hard knocks." Many early projects met with disaster, and companies and systems developers sifted through the ashes of those disasters to determine what went wrong. By the 1970s, most seasoned project managers agreed on the basic tasks that need to be performed to successfully build and maintain information systems. These basic tasks are combined into phases of systems development.

Different authors and organizations package the tasks into different numbers of phases. Some organizations use an eight-phase process, others use a seven-phase process, and still others use a five-phase process. In this text, we will use the following five-phase process:

1. System definition
2. Requirements analysis
3. Component design
4. Implementation
5. System maintenance (fix or enhance)

Figure 10-3 shows how these phases are related. Development begins when a business-planning process identifies a need for a new system. We will address IS planning processes in the next chapter. For now, suppose that management has determined, in some way, that the organization can best accomplish its goals and objectives by constructing a new information system.

Developers in the first SDLC phase, system definition, use management's statement of the system need to define and plan the new system. The resulting project plan is the input to the second phase, requirements analysis. Here, developers identify the particular features and functions of the new system. The output of that phase is a set of approved user requirements, which become the primary input used to design system components. In the fourth phase, developers implement, test, and install the new system.

Over time, users will find errors, mistakes, and problems. They will also think of new features that they need. The need for these changes is input into a system maintenance phase. The maintenance phase starts the process all over again, which is why the process is considered a cycle.

In the following sections, we will consider each phase of the SDLC in more detail.

How Is System Definition Accomplished?

In response to the need for the new system, the organization will assign a few employees, possibly on a part-time basis, to define the new system, to assess its feasibility, and to plan the project. Typically, someone from the IS department leads the initial team, but the members of that initial team are both users and IS professionals.

Define System Goals and Scope

As shown in Figure 10-4, the first step is to define the goals and scope of the new information system. Recall from Chapters 2 and 3 that information systems are developed to facilitate collaboration; to aid in decision making, problem solving, and project

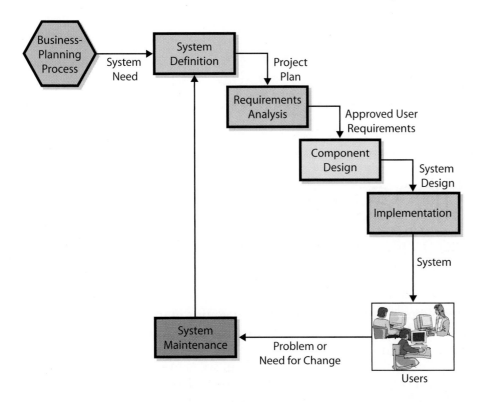

Figure 10-3
Planning the Use of IS/IT

management; and to gain a competitive advantage. At this step, the team defines the goal or purpose of the new system in terms of one or more of these reasons.

Consider MRV's new system of Web sites. What is the purpose of that system? MRV's competitive strategy is to create quality relationships with quality customers and to use those relationships to create new revenue. How does this new system contribute to that strategy? How will it improve the quality of customer relationships? How will it enable MRV to use those relationships to generate revenue?

Another task is to define the project's scope. At MRV, does the new system just foster customer relationships, or does it sell something? Does MRV want to have a commerce server for selling hats and T-shirts or even life jackets and other river gear and equipment?

Assess Feasibility

Once we have defined the project's goals and scope, the next step is to assess feasibility. This step answers the question, "Does this project make sense?" The aim here is to eliminate obviously nonsensible projects before forming a project development team and investing significant labor.

Feasibility has four dimensions: **cost**, **schedule**, **technical**, and **organizational feasibility**. Because IS development projects are difficult to budget and schedule, cost and schedule feasibility can be only an approximate, back-of-the-envelope analysis. The purpose is to eliminate any obviously infeasible ideas as soon as possible.

The cost of a project can be determined in a number of ways. For a discussion of a few of the ethical issues relating to cost estimates, see the Ethics Guide on pages 378–379.

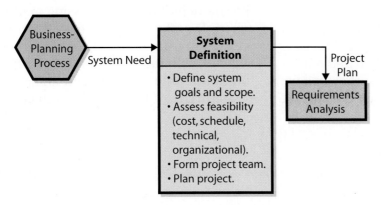

Figure 10-4
SDLC: System Definition Phase

Ethics

Estimation Ethics

A *buy-in* occurs when a company agrees to produce a system or product for less than it knows the project will require. An example for MRV would be if a consultant agreed to build the system for $50,000 when good estimating techniques indicate it will take $75,000. If the contract for the system or product is written for "time and materials," MRV will ultimately pay the $75,000 for the finished system. Or, the customer will cancel the project once the true cost is known. If the contract for the system or product is written for a fixed cost, then the developer will eat the extra costs. The latter strategy is used if the contract opens up other business opportunities that are worth the $25,000 loss.

Buy-ins always involve deceit. Most would agree that buying in on a time-and-materials project, planning to stick the customer with the full cost later, is unethical and wrong. Opinions on buying in on a fixed-priced contract vary. You know you'll take a loss, but why? For a favor down the road? Or some other unethical reason? Some would say that because buying is always deceitful, it should always be avoided. Others say that it is just one of many different business strategies.

What about in-house projects? Do the ethics change if an in-house development team is building a system for use in house? If team members know there is only $50,000 in the budget, should they start the project if they believe that its true cost is $75,000? If they do start, at some point senior management will either have to admit a mistake and cancel the project or find the additional $25,000. Project sponsors can make all sorts of excuses for such a buy-in. For example, "I know the company needs this system. If management doesn't realize it and fund it appropriately, then we'll just force their hand."

These issues become even stickier if team members disagree about how much the project will cost. Suppose one faction of the team believes the project will cost $35,000, another faction estimates $50,000, and a third thinks $65,000. Can the project sponsors justify taking the average? Or, should they describe the range of estimates?

Other buy-ins are more subtle. Suppose you are a project manager of an exciting new project that is possibly a career-maker for you. You are incredibly busy, working 6 days a week and long hours each day. Your team has developed an estimate for $50,000 for the project. A little voice in the back of your mind says that maybe not all costs for every aspect of the project are included in that estimate. You mean to follow up on that thought, but more pressing matters in your schedule take precedence. Soon you find yourself in front of management, presenting the $50,000 estimate. You probably should have found the time to investigate the estimate, but you didn't. Is your behavior unethical?

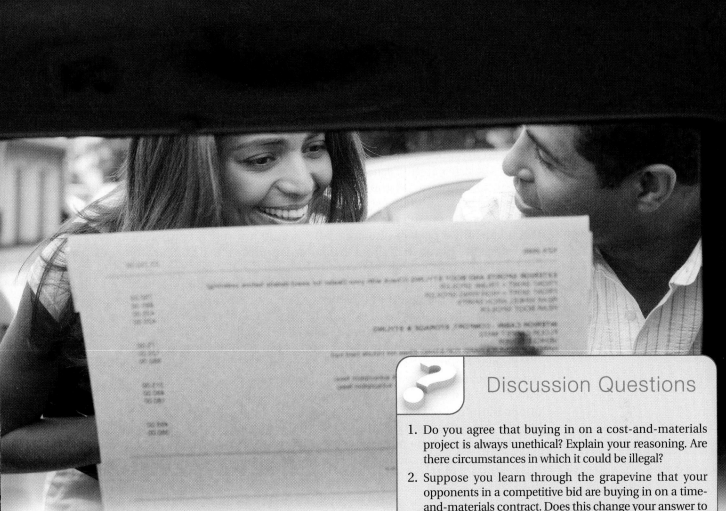

Or, suppose you approach a more senior manager with your dilemma. "I think there may be other costs, but I know that $50,000 is all we've got. What should I do?" Suppose the senior manager says something like, "Well, let's go forward. You don't know of anything else, and we can always find more budget elsewhere if we have to." How do you respond?

You can buy in on schedule as well as cost. If the marketing department says, "We have to have the new product for the trade show," do you agree, even if you know it's highly unlikely? What if marketing says, "If we don't have it by then, we should just cancel the project." Suppose it's not impossible to make that schedule, it's just highly unlikely. How do you respond? ■

Discussion Questions

1. Do you agree that buying in on a cost-and-materials project is always unethical? Explain your reasoning. Are there circumstances in which it could be illegal?

2. Suppose you learn through the grapevine that your opponents in a competitive bid are buying in on a time-and-materials contract. Does this change your answer to question 1?

3. Suppose you are a project manager who is preparing a request for proposal on a cost-and-materials systems development project. What can you do to prevent buy-ins?

4. Under what circumstances do you think buying in on a fixed-price contract is ethical? What are the dangers of this strategy?

5. Explain why in-house development projects are always time-and-materials projects.

6. Given your answer to question 5, is buying in on an in-house project always unethical? Under what circumstances do you think it is ethical? Under what circumstances do you think it is justifiable, even if it is unethical?

7. Suppose you ask a senior manager for advice as described in the guide. Does the manager's response absolve you of guilt? Suppose you ask the manager and then do not follow her guidance. What problems result?

8. Explain how you can buy in on schedule as well as costs.

9. For an in-house project, how do you respond to the marketing manager who says that the project should be cancelled if it will not be ready for the trade show? In your answer, suppose that you disagree with this opinion—suppose you know the system has value regardless of whether it is done by the trade show.

For example, for MRV's Web site, you might investigate how much similar projects have cost in the past. Think about not only development costs, but also the operational costs of hosting the Web site(s) and the cost of employee labor for maintaining the site. It is likely that Sue has some ideas that cost more than the potential benefits they deliver. Or even if those ideas deliver sufficient benefit, the cost may be more than she is willing to spend. In this case, for the project to be cost feasible, she may need to reduce the project's scope.

Like cost feasibility, *schedule feasibility*, is difficult to determine because it is difficult to estimate the time it will take to build the system. However, the team makes the best schedule estimates that it can, possibly adding schedule padding, such as 30 percent, and then decides if it can accept that estimated delivery date. At this stage of the project, the company should not rely on either cost or schedule estimates; the purpose of these estimates is simply to rule out any obviously unacceptable projects.

Technical feasibility refers to whether existing information technology is likely to be able to meet the needs of the new system. At MRV, the new system is most likely well within the capabilities of existing technology. For more advanced systems, this is not always the case. The IRS disaster discussed in Chapter 1 failed, in part, because a rule-based system for examining tax returns was technically infeasible.

Finally, *organizational feasibility* concerns whether the new system fits within the organization's customs, culture, charter, or legal requirements. For example, will MRV incur any legal liability if customers post photos for which they do not have publication rights? If so, the system might be judged to be organizationally infeasible. (In this case, however, MRV can avoid such liability by requiring customers to assert they do have such rights before posting photos—just as Facebook does.) Does MRV have a management policy that prohibits releasing customer data? If so, it may be impossible for them to allow customers to interact with each other on the MRV sites.

Form a Project Team

If the defined project is determined to be feasible, the next step is to form the project team. Normally, the team consists of both IT personnel and user representatives. The project manager and IT personnel can be in-house personnel or outside contractors. We will describe various means of obtaining IT personnel using outside sources and the benefits and risks of outsourcing when we discuss IS management in the next chapter.

Typical personnel on a development team are a manager (or mangers for larger projects), system analysts, programmers, software testers, and users. **Systems analysts** are IS professionals who understand both business and technology. They are active throughout the systems development process and play a key role in moving the project through the systems development process. Systems analysts integrate the work of the programmers, testers, and users. Depending on the nature of the project, the team may also include hardware and communications specialists, database designers and administrators, and other IT specialists.

The team composition changes over time. During requirements definition, the team will be heavy with systems analysts. During design and implementation, it will be heavy with programmers, testers, and database designers. During integrated testing and conversion, the team will be augmented with testers and business users.

User involvement is critical throughout the system development process. Depending on the size and nature of the project, users are assigned to the project either full or part time. Sometimes users are assigned to review and oversight committees that meet periodically, especially at the completion of project phases and other milestones. Users are involved in many different ways. *The important point is for users to have active involvement and to take ownership of the project throughout the entire development process.*

MRV has no IT department, so the development team will consist, at least initially, of Sue and Eddie. As the project progresses, MRV will need to outsource for professional systems developers and programmers (or hire additional IT personnel).

The first major task for the assembled project team is to plan the project. Members of the project team specify tasks to be accomplished, assign personnel, determine task dependencies, and set schedules. We will discuss this further in the second half of this chapter.

What Is the Users' Role in the Requirements Phase?

The primary purpose of the requirements analysis phase is to determine and document the specific features and functions of the new system. For most development projects, this phase requires interviewing dozens of users and documenting potentially hundreds of requirements. Requirements definition is thus expensive. It is also difficult, as you will see.

Determine Requirements

Determining the system's requirements is the most important phase in the systems development process. If the requirements are wrong, the system will be wrong. If the requirements are determined completely and correctly, then design and implementation will be easier and more likely to result in success.

Examples of requirements are the contents of a report or the fields in a data entry form. Requirements include not only what is to be produced, but also how frequently and how fast it is to be produced. Some requirements specify the volume of data to be stored and processed.

If you take a course in systems analysis and design, you will spend weeks on techniques for determining requirements. Here, we will just summarize that process. Typically, systems analysts interview users and record the results in some consistent manner. Good interviewing skills are crucial; users are notorious for being unable to describe what they want and need. Users also tend to focus on the tasks they are performing at the time of the interview. Tasks performed at the end of the quarter or end of the year are forgotten if the interview takes place mid-quarter. Seasoned and experienced systems analysts know how to conduct interviews to bring such requirements to light.

As listed in Figure 10-5, sources of requirements include existing systems as well as the forms, reports, queries, and application features and functions desired in the new system. Security is another important category of requirements.

If the new system involves a new database or substantial changes to an existing database, then the development team will create a data model. As you learned in Chapter 5, that model must reflect the users' perspective on their business and business activities. Thus, the data model is constructed on the basis of user interviews and must be validated by those users.

Sometimes the requirements determination is so focused on the software and data components that other components are forgotten. Experienced project managers ensure consideration of requirements for all five IS components, not just for software and data. Regarding hardware, the team might ask: Are there special needs or restrictions on hardware? Is there an organizational standard governing what kinds of hardware can, or cannot, be used? Must the new system use existing hardware? What requirements are there for communications and network hardware?

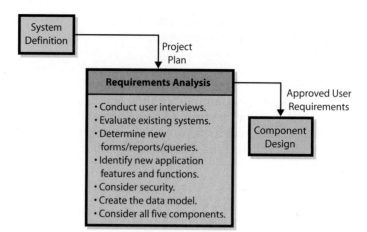

Figure 10-5
SDLC: Requirements
Analysis Phase

Similarly, the team should consider requirements for procedures and personnel: Do accounting controls require procedures that separate duties and authorities? Are there restrictions that some actions can be taken only by certain departments or specific personnel? Are there policy requirements or union rules that restrict activities to certain categories of employees? Will the system need to interface with information systems from other companies and organizations? In short, requirements need to be considered for all of the components of the new information system.

These questions are examples of the kinds of questions that must be asked and answered during requirements analysis.

Obtain User Approval

Once the requirements have been specified, the users must review and approve them before the project continues. The easiest and cheapest time to alter the information system is in the requirements phase. Changing a requirement at this stage is simply a matter of changing a description. Changing a requirement in the implementation phase may require weeks of reworking applications components and the database.

How Are the Five Components Designed?

Each of the five components is designed in this stage. Typically, the team designs each component by developing alternatives, evaluating each of those alternatives against the requirements, and then selecting from among those alternatives. Accurate requirements are critical here; if they are incomplete or wrong, then they will be poor guides for evaluation.

Figure 10-6 shows that design tasks pertain to each of the five IS components.

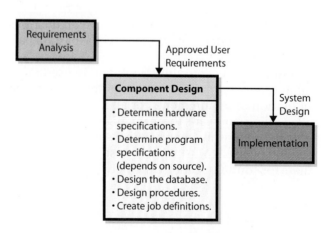

Figure 10-6
SDLC: Component Design
Phase

Hardware Design

For hardware, the team determines specifications for the hardware that they want to acquire. (The team is not designing hardware in the sense of building a CPU or a disk drive.)

For MRV, neither Sue nor Eddie has any idea of the hardware requirements for hosting the new system. They will need to rely on their development contractor. Most likely, MRV will lease time from a Web hosting service. Majestic River Ventures is too small and inexperienced to attempt to acquire and operate hardware itself.

Program Design

Program design depends on the source of the programs. For off-the-shelf software, the team must determine candidate products and evaluate them against the requirements. For off-the-shelf with alteration programs, the team identifies products to be acquired off-the-shelf and then determines the alterations required. For custom-developed programs, the team produces design documentation for writing program code.

Database Design

If developers are constructing a database, then during this phase they convert the data model to a database design using techniques like those described in Chapter 5. If developers are using off-the-shelf programs, then little database design needs to be done; the programs will handle their own database processing.

Procedure Design

For a business information system, the system developers and the organization must also design procedures for both users and operations personnel. Procedures need to be developed for normal, backup, and failure recovery operations, as summarized in Figure 10-7. Usually teams of systems analysts and key users design the procedures.

Design of Job Descriptions

With regard to people, design involves developing job descriptions for both users and operations personnel. Sometimes new information systems require new jobs. If so,

	Users	Operations Personnel
Normal processing	• Procedures for using the system to accomplish business tasks.	• Procedures for starting, stopping, and operating the system.
Backup	• User procedures for backing up data and other resources.	• Operations procedures for backing up data and other resources.
Failure recovery	• Procedures to continue operations when the system fails. • Procedures to convert back to the system after recovery.	• Procedures to identify the source of failure and get it fixed. • Procedures to recover and restart the system.

Figure 10-7
Procedures to Be Designed

the duties and responsibilities for the new jobs need to be defined in accordance with the organization's human resources policies. More often, organizations add new duties and responsibilities to existing jobs. In this case, developers define these new tasks and responsibilities in this phase. Sometimes, the personnel design task is as simple as statements like, "Our admin (currently Jason) will be in charge of making backups." As with procedures, teams of systems analysts and users determine job descriptions and functions.

How Is an Information System Implemented?

Once the design is complete, the next phase in the SDLC is implementation. Tasks in this phase are to build, test, and convert the users to the new system (see Figure 10-8). Developers construct each of the components independently. They obtain, install, and test hardware. They license and install off-the-shelf programs; they write adaptations and custom programs as necessary. They construct a database and fill it with data. They document, review, and test procedures, and they create training programs. Finally, the organization hires and trains needed personnel.

System Testing

Once developers have constructed and tested all of the components, they integrate the individual components and test the system. So far, we have glossed over testing as if there is nothing to it. In fact, software and system testing are difficult, time-consuming, and complex tasks. Developers need to design and develop test plans and record the results of tests. They need to devise a system to assign fixes to people and to verify that fixes are correct and complete.

A **test plan** consists of sequences of actions that users will take when using the new system. Test plans include not only the normal actions that users will take, but also incorrect actions. A comprehensive test plan should cause every line of program code to be executed. The test plan should thus cause every error message to be displayed. Testing, retesting, and re-retesting consume huge amounts of labor. Often, developers can reduce the labor cost of testing by writing programs that invoke system features automatically.

Today, many IT professionals work as testing specialists. Testing, or **product quality assurance (PQA)** as it is often called, is an important career. PQA personnel usually construct the test plan with the advice and assistance of users. PQA test engineers themselves perform testing, and they also supervise user test activity.

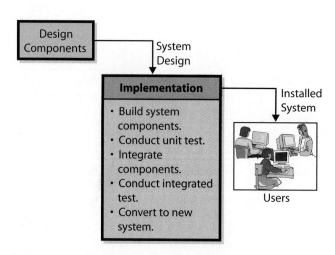

Figure 10-8
SDLC: Implementation Phase

Many PQA professionals are themselves programmers who write automated test programs.

In addition to IT professionals, users should be involved in system testing. Users participate in the development of test plans and test cases. They also can be part of the test team, usually working under the direction of PQA personnel. Users have the final say on whether the system is ready for use. If you are invited to participate as a user tester, take that responsibly seriously. It will become much more difficult to fix problems after you have begun to use the system in production.

Beta testing (in the classic, non-Web 2.0 sense—see pages 289–290) is the process of allowing future system users to try out the new system on their own. Software vendors such as Microsoft often release beta versions of their products for users to try and to test. Such users report problems back to the vendor. Beta testing is the last stage of testing. Normally products in the beta test phase are complete and fully functioning; they typically have few serious errors. Organizations that are developing large new information systems sometimes use a beta-testing process just as software vendors do.

System Conversion

Once the system has passed integrated testing, the organization installs the new system. The term **system conversion** is often used for this activity because it implies the process of *converting* business activity from the old system to the new.

Organizations can implement a system conversion in one of four ways: pilot, phased, parallel, and plunge. IS professionals recommend any of the first three, depending on the circumstances. In most cases, companies should avoid "taking the plunge"!

With **pilot installation**, the organization implements the entire system on a limited portion of the business. An example would be for MRV to use the new system for a selected portion of its customers. The advantage of pilot implementation is that if the system fails, the failure is contained within a limited boundary. This reduces exposure of the business and also protects the new system from developing a negative reputation throughout the organization or with all of its customers.

As the name implies, with **phased installation** the new system is installed in phases across the organization(s). Once a given piece works, then the organization installs and tests another piece of the system, until the entire system has been installed. Some systems are so tightly integrated that they cannot be installed in phased pieces. Such systems must be installed using one of the other techniques.

With **parallel installation**, the new system runs in parallel with the old one until the new system is tested and fully operational. Parallel installation is expensive, because the organization incurs the costs of running both systems. Users must work double time, if you will, to run both systems. Then, considerable work is needed to determine if the results of the new system are consistent with those of the old system.

However, some organizations consider the costs of parallel installation to be a form of insurance. It is the slowest and most expensive style of installation, but it does provide an easy fallback position if the new system fails.

The final style of conversion is **plunge installation** (sometimes called *direct installation*). With it, the organization shuts off the old system and starts the new system. If the new system fails, the organization is in trouble: Nothing can be done until either the new system is fixed or the old system is reinstalled. Because of the risk, organizations should avoid this conversion style if possible. The one exception is if the new system is providing a new capability that will not disrupt the operation of the organization if it fails.

Figure 10-9 summarizes the tasks for each of the five components during the design and implementation phases. Use this figure to test your knowledge of the tasks in each phase.

	Hardware	Software	Data	Procedures	People
Design	Determine hardware specifications.	Select off-the-shelf programs. Design alterations and custom programs as necessary.	Design database and related structures.	Design user and operations procedures.	Develop user and operations job descriptions.
Implementation	Obtain, install, and test hardware.	License and install off-the-shelf programs. Write alterations and custom programs. Test programs.	Create database. Fill with data. Test data.	Document procedures. Create training programs. Review and test procedures.	Hire and train personnel.
	Integrated Test and Conversion				

Unit test each component

Note: Cells shaded tan represent software development.

Figure 10-9
Design and Implementation for the Five Components

What Are the Tasks for System Maintenance?

The last phase of the SDLC is maintenance. In fact, **maintenance** is a misnomer; the work done during this phase is either to *fix* the system so that it works correctly or to *adapt* it to changes in requirements.

Figure 10-10 shows tasks during the maintenance phase. First, there needs to be a means for tracking both failures[2] and requests for enhancements to meet new requirements. For small systems, organizations can track failures and enhancements using word-processing documents. As systems become larger, however, and as the number of failure and enhancement requests increases, many organizations find it

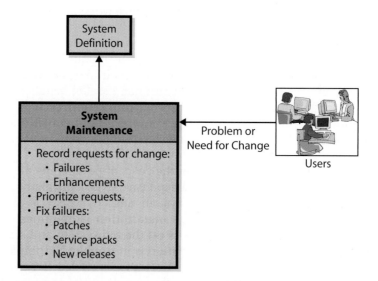

Figure 10-10
SDLC: System
Maintenance Phase

---

[2]A *failure* is a difference between what the system does and what it is supposed to do. Sometimes you will hear the term *bug* used instead of failure. As a future user, call failures *failures*, for that's what they are. Don't have a *bugs list*, have a *failures list*. Don't have an *unresolved bug*, have an *unresolved failure*. A few months of managing an organization that is coping with a serious failure will show you the importance of this difference in terms.

necessary to develop a tracking database. Such a database contains a description of the failure or enhancement. It also records who reported the problem, who will make the fix or enhancement, what the status of that work is, and whether the fix or enhancement has been tested and verified by the originator.

Typically, IS personnel prioritize system problems according to their severity. They fix high-priority items as soon as possible, and they fix low-priority items as time and resources become available.

With regard to the software component, software developers group fixes for high-priority failures into a **patch** that can be applied to all copies of a given product. As described in Chapter 4, software vendors supply patches to fix security and other critical problems. They usually bundle fixes of low-priority problems into larger groups called **service packs**. Users apply service packs in much the same way that they apply patches, except that service packs typically involve fixes to hundreds or thousands of problems.

By the way, you may be surprised to learn this, but all commercial software products are shipped with known failures. Usually vendors test their products and remove the most serious problems, but they seldom, if ever, remove all of the defects they know about. Shipping with defects is an industry practice; Microsoft, Adobe, Oracle, Google, and many others all ship products with known problems.

Because an enhancement is an adaptation to new requirements, developers usually prioritize enhancement requests separate from failures. The decision to make an enhancement includes a business decision that the enhancement will generate an acceptable rate of return. Although minor enhancements are made using service packs, major enhancement requests usually result in a complete new release of a product.

As you read this, keep in mind that although we usually think of failures and enhancements as applying to software, they can apply to the other components as well. There can be hardware or database failures or enhancements. There can also be failures and enhancements in procedures and people, though the latter is usually expressed in more humane terms than failure or enhancement. The underlying idea is the same, however.

As stated earlier, note that the maintenance phase starts another cycle of the SDLC process. The decision to enhance a system is a decision to restart the systems development process. Even a simple failure fix goes through all of the phases of the SDLC; if it is a small fix, a single person may work through those phases in an abbreviated form. But each of those phases is repeated, nonetheless.

What Are the Problems with the SDLC?

Although the industry has experienced notable successes with the SDLC process, there have also been many problems with it, as discussed next.

The SDLC Waterfall

One of the reasons for SDLC problems is due to the **waterfall** nature of the SDLC. Like a series of waterfalls, the process is supposed to operate in a sequence of not-repeated phases. For example, the team completes the requirements phase and goes over the waterfall into the design phase, and on through the process. (Look back to Figure 10-3, page 377.)

Unfortunately, systems development seldom works so smoothly. Often, there is a need to crawl back up the waterfall, if you will, and repeat work in a prior phase. Most commonly, when design work begins and the team evaluates alternatives, they learn that some requirements statements are incomplete or missing. At that point, the team needs to do more requirements work, yet that phase is supposedly finished. On some projects, the team goes back and forth between requirements and design so many times that the project seems to be out of control.

Requirements Documentation Difficulty

Another problem, especially on complicated systems, is the difficulty of documenting requirements in a usable way. I once managed the database portion of a software project at Boeing in which we invested more than 70 labor-years into a requirements statement. The requirements document was 20-some printed volumes that stood 7 feet tall when stacked on top of one another.

When we entered the design phase, no one really knew all the requirements that concerned a particular feature. We would begin to design a feature only to find that we had not considered a requirement buried somewhere in the documentation. In short, the requirements were so unwieldy as to be nearly useless. Additionally, during the requirements analysis interval, the airplane business moved on. By the time we entered the design phase, many requirements were incomplete and some were obsolete. Projects that spend so much time documenting requirements are sometimes said to be in **analysis paralysis**.

Scheduling and Budgeting Difficulties

For a new, large-scale system, schedule and budgeting estimates are so approximate as to become nearly laughable. Management attempts to put a serious face on the need for a schedule and a budget, but when you are developing a large multiyear, multimillion-dollar project, estimates of labor hours and completion dates are approximate and fuzzy. The employees on the project, who are the source for the estimates, know how little they know about how long something will take and how much they guessed. They know that the total budget and timeline is a summation of everyone's similar guesses. Many large projects live in a fantasy world of budgets and timelines.

In truth, the software community has done much work to improve software development forecasting. But for large projects with large SDLC phases, just too much is unknown for any technique to work well. So, development methodologies other than the SDLC have emerged for developing systems through a series of small, manageable chunks. Rapid application development (RAD), object-oriented development (OOD), and extreme programming (XP) are three such methodologies. Discussion of those methodologies is beyond the scope of this text. Search online for any of those three acronyms if you want to learn more.

Q4 How Does Systems Development Vary According to Project Scale?

The SDLC just discussed can be applied to projects of any scale, but the nature, scope, and character of the work performed varies considerably. For example, FlexTime and MRV need to develop small systems. However, consider a major insurance company that wants to create a new system to sell policies over the Internet. That project will involve hundreds of users, potentially worldwide. Although all three companies can use the SDLC, the number of tasks to accomplish and the interaction among those tasks will be much greater for the insurance company than for FlexTime or MRV.

Figure 10-11 summarizes the differences between small and large projects. Small-scale projects have relatively simple requirements. MRV needs to decide the content of each of its two Web sites and how that content is to be accessed and updated. The insurance company needs to determine requirements for selling to existing versus new customers, the type of insurance to be sold, risk and policy premium calculations, the preparation of legal documents, payments and links to accounts receivable, and so forth. Most small-scale projects involve just one or a few business processes. Large-scale projects usually touch and involve many different business processes.

Small-Scale Systems Development	Large-Scale Systems Development
Simple requirements	Complex requirements
Few processes affected	Many processes affected
Little IT expertise	IT personnel with diverse backgrounds
Short development interval	Long development interval
Limited budget	Large budget
Informal/loose	Formal/structured
Inexperienced, often naïve	Experienced, sometimes cynical
Operations support by users	Professional operations support
Security lax	Security important and managed
Backup and recovery lax	Backup and recovery planned and managed

Figure 10-11
Systems Development
Characteristics

Small-scale projects seldom have professional IT support. MRV and FlexTime do not employ professional IT personnel; neither can afford to. Typically, consultants, working on a part-time basis, provide IT support to small projects.

In contrast, large-scale projects always involve IT professionals, and those professionals usually possess many different skills and expertise. A large-scale project will have project managers, systems analysts, network administrators, programmers, database designers, PQA professionals, and trainers and user support personnel.

Small- and large-scale projects also vary in duration. MRV can develop its new Web sites within several months, whereas the insurance company may require a year or more to implement the Web-based policy sales system.

Because of the differences in complexity, personnel, and duration, projects vary in budget as well. Small-scale projects typically have a limited budget; sometimes the budget is unrealistically limited due to the naïveté of business owners or to the company's limited cash. The budget of a large-scale project will be sizable; it must be so to support the personnel and duration of a complex project. Budgeting of large-scale projects is difficult, and sometimes even very large budgets are inadequate. The IRS case in Chapter 1 is a good example.

Small-scale projects tend to be informal and loose. Few users are involved, the progress of the project is easy to review, and a limited budget is involved. Large-scale projects are formal and structured. Tasks are carefully defined, with specific start and finish dates, and specific resource assignments. Task delays are consequential. Budgets are huge and thousands of dollars are easily wasted. Consequently, such projects typically have formal project management.

Small-scale projects usually involve inexperienced personnel who are often naïve. Sue at MRV knows nothing about development processes like the SDLC, and she probably does not even distinguish between a computer program and an information system. Sue, like many mangers of small projects, is a lamb headed for fleecing. Large-scale projects are staffed by personnel with considerable experience and many battle scars. They have seen projects go awry, be delivered late, and have costs well over budgets.

After the system has been installed, small-scale projects are usually operated by the users themselves. Someone at FlexTime will turn on the network equipment, start servers, and initiate the customer management system. Large-scale projects will be supported by professional operations personnel. Such personnel will be trained on formal operations procedures.

Small- and large-scale projects also differ regarding security, backup, and recovery. In a small-scale project, little attention is paid to either. Given their limited IT experience,

User involvement is critical to the systems success, as described in the Guide on pages 400–401.

Estimation can be difficult. The Guide on pages 398–399 discusses some of the problems when estimating projects.

Sue and Eddie won't even consider the possibility of someone stealing MRV's data, nor will they worry about loss of data due to fire or natural disaster. However, the professional IT personnel on a large-scale project will devote considerable time and energy to security, backup, and recovery. IT professionals at the insurance company will consider security threats and develop safeguards against those threats. They will also ensure that the systems are backed up in such a way that they can be recovered in the event of destruction from fire or natural disaster.

In the future, when you are involved in a systems development project, keep these differences in mind. On a small-scale project, the knowledge you gain from this class should help you compensate for the project's limited experience and naïveté. On a large-scale project, this knowledge will help you understand the reason for the project's formal process and enable you to better participate as a team member.

Q5 What Are the Trade-Offs Among Requirements, Schedule, and Cost?

Systems development projects, especially large ones, require the **trade-offs** or balancing of three critical drivers: requirements, cost, and time. To understand this balancing challenge, consider the construction of something relatively simple—say, a piece of jewelry like a necklace or the deck on the side of a house. The more elaborate the necklace or the deck, the more time it will take. The less elaborate, the less time it will take. Further, if we embellish the necklace with diamonds and precious gems, it will cost more. Similarly, if we construct the deck from old crates it will be cheaper than if we construct it of clear-grained, prime Port Orford cedar.

We can summarize this situation as shown in Figure 10-12. We can *trade off* requirements against time and against cost. If we make the necklace simpler, it will take less time. If we eliminate the diamonds and gems, it will be cheaper. The same trade-offs exist in the construction of anything: houses, airplane interiors, buildings, ships, furniture, *and* information systems.

The relationship between time and cost is more complicated. Normally, we can reduce time by increasing cost *only to a point*. For example, we can reduce the time it

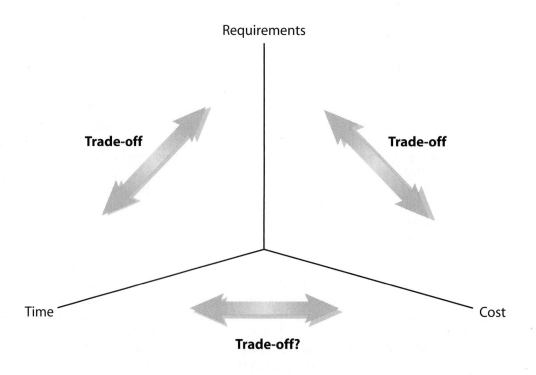

Figure 10-12
Primary Drivers of Systems Development

takes to produce a deck by hiring more laborers. At some point, however, there will be so many laborers working on the deck that they will get in one another's way, and the time to finish the deck will actually increase. As discussed earlier, at some point, adding more people creates **diseconomies of scale**, the situation that occurs when adding more resources creates inefficiencies, such as those that occur when adding more people to a late project (recall Brooks' Law).

In some projects, we can reduce costs by increasing time. If, for example, we are required to pay laborers time-and-a-half for overtime, we can reduce costs by eliminating overtime. If finishing the deck—by, say, Friday—requires overtime, then it may be cheaper to avoid overtime by completing the deck sometime next week. This trade-off is not always true, however. Extending the project interval means that we need to pay labor and overhead for a longer period. Thus, adding more time can also increase cost.

Consider how these trade-offs pertain to information systems. We specify a set of requirements for the new information system, and we schedule labor over a period of time. Suppose the initial schedule indicates the system will be finished in 3 years. If business requirements necessitate the project be finished in 2 years, we must shorten the schedule. We can proceed in two ways: reduce the requirements or add labor. For the former, we eliminate functions and features. For the latter, we hire more staff or contract with other vendors for development services. Deciding which course to take will be difficult and risky.

Furthermore, in most projects, we cannot make these decisions once and for all. We begin with a plan, called the **baseline**. It stipulates the tasks to be accomplished, the labor and other resources assigned to those tasks, and the schedule for completion. However, nothing ever goes according to plan, and the larger the project and the longer the development interval, the more things will violate the plan. Critical people may leave the company; a hurricane may destroy an office; the company may have a bad quarter and freeze hiring just as the project is staffing up; technology will change; competitors may do something that makes the project more (or less) important; or the company may be sold and new management may change requirements and priorities. When these events occur, project managers must reassess the trade-offs between requirements, cost, and time. It is a balancing act undertaken in the presence of continual change and substantial risk and uncertainty.

Q6 What Are the Major Challenges When Planning IS Projects?

The key strategy for large-scale systems development—and, indeed, the key strategy for any project—is to divide and conquer. Break up large tasks into smaller tasks and continue breaking up the tasks until they are small enough to manage, thus enabling you to estimate time and costs. Each task should culminate in one or more results or **deliverables**. Examples of deliverables are documents, designs, prototypes, data models, database designs, working data entry screens, and the like. Without a deliverable, it is impossible to know if the task was accomplished.

Using a Work-Breakdown Structure

Tasks are interrelated, and to prevent them from becoming a confusing morass project teams create a **work-breakdown structure (WBS)**, which is a hierarchy of the tasks required to complete a project. The WBS for a large project is huge; it might entail hundreds or even thousands of tasks. Figure 10-13 shows the WBS for the system definition phase for a typical IS project.

System definition
1.1	Define goals and scope	
	1.1.1	Define goals
	1.1.2	Define system boundaries
	1.1.3	Review results
	1.1.4	Document results
1.2	Assess feasibility	
	1.2.1	Cost
	1.2.2	Schedule
	1.2.3	Technical
	1.2.4	Organizational
	1.2.5	Document feasibility
	1.2.6	Management review and go/no go decision
1.3	Plan project	
	1.3.1	Establish milestones
	1.3.2	Create WBS
		1.3.2.1 Levels 1 and 2
		1.3.2.2 Levels 3+
	1.3.3	Document WBS
		1.3.3.1 Create WBS baseline
		1.3.3.2 Input to Project
	1.3.4	Determine resource requirements
		1.3.4.1 Personnel
		1.3.4.2 Computing
		1.3.4.3 Office space
		1.3.4.4 Travel and Meeting Expense
	1.3.5	Management review
		1.3.5.1 Prepare presentation
		1.3.5.2 Prepare background documents
		1.3.5.3 Give presentation
		1.3.5.4 Incorporate feedback into plan
		1.3.5.5 Approve project
1.4	Form project team	
	1.4.1	Meet with HR
	1.4.2	Meet with IT Director
	1.4.3	Develop job descriptions
	1.4.4	Meet with available personnel
	1.4.5	Hire personnel

Figure 10-13
Example Work-Breakdown
Structure (WBS)

In this diagram, the overall task, *System definition,* is divided into *Define goals and scope, Assess feasibility, Plan project,* and *Form project team.* Each of those tasks is broken into smaller tasks until the work has been divided into small tasks that can be managed and estimated.

Once the project is decomposed into small tasks, the next step is to define task dependencies and to estimate task durations. Regarding dependencies, some tasks must begin at the same time, some tasks must end at the same time, and some tasks cannot start until other tasks have finished. Task dependencies are normally input to planning software such as Microsoft Project. Figure 10-14 shows the WBS as input to Microsoft Project, with task dependencies and durations defined. The display on the right, called a **Gantt chart**, shows tasks, dates, and dependencies.

The user has entered all of the tasks from the WBS and has assigned each task a duration. She has also specified task dependencies, although the means she used are

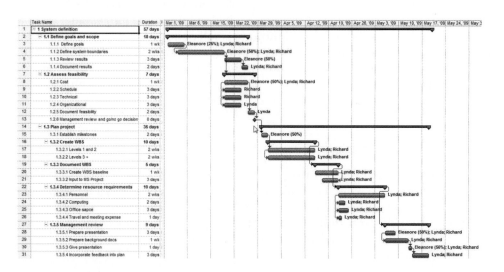

Figure 10-14
Gantt Chart of the WBS
for the Definition Phase
of a Project

beyond our discussion. The two red arrows emerging from task 4, *Define system boundaries,* indicate that neither the *Review results* task nor the *Assess feasibility* task can begin until *Define system boundaries* is completed. Other task dependencies are also shown; you can learn about them in a project management class.

The **critical path** is the sequence of activities that determine the earliest date by which the project can be completed. Reflect for a moment on that statement: The *earliest date* is the date determined by considering the *longest path* through the network of activities. Paying attention to task dependencies, the planner will compress the tasks as much as possible. Those tasks that cannot be further compressed lie on the critical path. Microsoft Project and other project-planning applications can readily identify critical path tasks.

Figure 10-14 shows the tasks on the critical path in red. Consider the first part of the WBS. The project planner specified that task 4 cannot begin until 2 days before task 3 starts. (That's the meaning of the red arrow emerging from task 3.) Neither task 5 nor task 8 can begin until task 4 is completed. Task 8 will take longer than tasks 5 and 6, and so task 8—not tasks 5 or 6—is on the critical path. Thus, the critical path to this point is tasks 3, 4, and 8. You can trace the critical path through the rest of the WBS by following the tasks shown in red, though the entire WBS and critical path are not shown.

Using Microsoft Project or a similar product, it is possible to assign personnel to tasks and to stipulate the percentage of time that each person devotes to a task. Figure 10-15 shows a Gantt chart for which this has been done. The notation means that Eleanore works only 25 percent of the time on task 3; Lynda and Richard work full time. Additionally, one can assign costs to personnel and compute a labor budget for each task and for the overall WBS. One can assign resources to tasks and use Microsoft Project to detect and prevent two tasks from using the same resources. Resource costs can be assigned and summed as well.

Managers can use the critical path to perform critical path analysis. First, note that if a task is on the critical path, and if that task runs late, the project will be late. Hence, tasks on the critical path cannot be allowed to run late if the project is to be delivered on time. Second, tasks not on the critical path can run late to the point at which they would become part of the critical path. Hence, up to a point, resources can be taken from noncritical path tasks to shorten tasks on the critical path. **Critical path analysis** is the process by which project managers compress the schedule by moving resources, typically people, from noncritical path tasks onto critical path tasks.

So far, we have discussed the role of the WBS for planning. It can be used for monitoring as well. The final WBS plan is denoted as the **baseline WBS**. This baseline shows the planned tasks, dependencies, durations, and resource assignments. As the

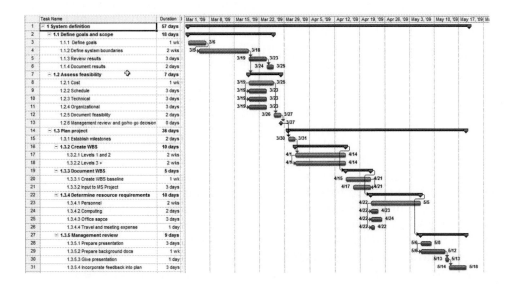

Figure 10-15
Gantt Chart with Resources
Assigned

project proceeds, project managers can input actual dates, labor hours, and resource costs. At any point in time, Microsoft Project can report whether the project is ahead or behind schedule and how the actual project costs compare to baseline costs.

As you can see, the WBS provides invaluable project management information. In fact, it is the single most important management tool for large-scale projects.

But, Reality Always Intercedes

Planning and managing with a WBS sounds logical and straightforward. And it is, in theory at least. But, where do the task durations come from? How long does it take to develop a large data model? How long does it take to adapt that data model to the users' satisfaction? How long does it take to develop a computer program to process orders if that program uses SOA standard services and no one on the team knows how to develop a program according to the SOA standards?

Fred Brooks defined software as "logical poetry." Like poetry, software is not made of wood or metal or plastic; it is pure thought-stuff. Some years ago, when I pressed a seasoned software developer for a schedule, he responded by asking me, "What would Shakespeare have said if someone asked him how long it would take him to write *Hamlet*?" Another common rejoinder is, "What would a fisherman say if you ask him how long will it take to catch three fish? He doesn't know, and neither do I."

No company should know better how to estimate software schedules than Microsoft. It has more experience developing software than any other company; it is loaded with smart, even brilliant developers; it can draw from enormous financial resources; and it has strong incentives to schedule projects accurately. However, Microsoft Vista, was delivered 2 years late. It was supposed to take 3 years, and it took 5. That's a 67 percent schedule overrun from the largest software developer in the world on what is arguably the world's most important computer program. And this is not just one project that ran awry. SQL Server 2005 barely made it into 2005. Office 2007 was late, and so on.

Part of the problem is that errors accumulate. If scheduling a single task is difficult, then scheduling a large-scale project becomes a nightmare. Suppose you have a WBS with thousands of tasks, and any one of those tasks can be 67 percent over schedule. It is impossible to do any credible planning. The term *critical path* loses meaning when there is that much doubt about task duration. In that setting, every task has some chance of being on the critical path.

Organizations take three approaches to this challenge. The first is to avoid the major schedule risks and never develop software in-house. Instead, they license software from vendors. For example, few companies choose to develop their own ERP or CRM software. ERP or CRM systems still have the substantial schedule risks of adapting procedures and training personnel, but those risks are much smaller than the schedule risks of developing complex software and databases.

But what if no suitable software exists? In that case, companies take one of two remaining approaches. They can admit the impossibility of systems development scheduling and plan accordingly. They abandon any confidence in their WBS and decide to invest a certain level of resources into a project, manage it as best they can, and take the schedule that results. Only loose commitments are made regarding the completion date and final system functionality. Project sponsors dislike this approach because they feel they are signing a blank check. But sometimes it is just a matter of admitting the reality that exists: "We don't know, and it's worse to pretend that we do."

The third approach is to attempt to schedule the development project in spite of all the difficulties. Several different estimation techniques can be used. If the project is similar to a past project, the schedule data from that past project can be used for planning. When such similar past projects exist, this technique can produce quality schedule estimates. If there is no such past project, managers can estimate the number of **lines of code** that will need to be written. Then they can use industry or company averages to estimate the time required. Another technique is to estimate the function points in a program, use each function point to determine the number of lines of code, and use that number to estimate schedules. A **function point** is simply a feature or function of the new program. Updating a customer record is an example. For more information on the use of lines of code and function points for software scheduling, visit *http://sunset.usc.edu/csse/research/COCOMOII/cocomo_main.html*. Of course, lines of code and function point techniques estimate schedules only for software components. The schedules for creating databases and the other system components must be estimated using other techniques.

During your career, be aware of the challenges and difficulties of scheduling large-scale information systems development. As a user or manager, do not take schedules as guarantees. Plan for schedule slippage, and if it does *not* occur, be pleasantly surprised.

Q7 What Are the Major Challenges When Managing IS Projects?

The challenges of managing IS development projects arise from four different factors:

1. Coordination
2. Diseconomies of scale
3. Configuration control
4. Unexpected events

IS projects, especially large-scale projects, are usually organized into a variety of development groups that work independently. Coordinating the work of these independent groups can be difficult, particularly if the groups reside in different geographic locations or different countries. An accurate and complete WBS facilitates coordination, but no project ever proceeds exactly in accordance with the WBS. Delays occur, and unknown or unexpected dependencies develop among tasks.

The coordination problem is increased because software is pure thought-stuff. When constructing a new house, electricians install wiring in the walls as they exist; it is impossible to do otherwise. No electrician can install wiring in the wall as designed 6 months ago, before a change. In software, such physical constraints do not exist. It is entirely possible for a team to develop a set of application programs to process a database using an obsolete database design. When the database design was changed, all involved parties should have been notified, but this may not have occurred. Wasted hours, increased cost, and poor morale are the result.

As mentioned in Q2, another problem is diseconomies of scale. The number of possible interactions among team members rises exponentially with the number of team members. Ultimately, no matter how well managed a project is, diseconomies of scale will set in.

As the project proceeds, controlling the configuration of the work product becomes difficult. Consider requirements, for example. The development team produces an initial statement of requirements. Meetings with users produce an adjusted set of requirements. Suppose an event then occurs that necessitates a change to requirements. After deliberation, assume the team decides to ignore a large portion of the requirements changes resulting from the event. At this point, there are four different versions of the requirements. If the changes to requirements are not carefully managed, changes from the four versions will be mixed up, and confusion and disorder will result. No one will know which requirements are the correct, current requirements.

Similar problems occur with designs, program code, database data, and other system components. The term **configuration control** refers to a set of management policies, practices, and tools that developers use to maintain control over the project's resources. Such resources include documents, schedules, designs, program code, test suites, and any other shared resource needed to complete the project. Configuration control is vital; a loss of control over a project's configuration is so expensive and disruptive that it can result in termination for senior project managers.

The last major challenge to large-scale project management is unexpected events. The larger and longer the project, the greater the chance of disruption due to an unanticipated event. Critical people can change companies; even whole teams have been known to pack up and join a competitor. The organization can be acquired, and new management may have different priorities. Because software is thought-stuff, team morale is crucial. I once managed two strong-headed software developers who engaged in a heated argument over the design of a program feature. The argument ended when one threw a chair at the other. The rest of the team divided its loyalties between the two developers, and work came to a standstill as subgroups sneered and argued with one another when they met in hallways or at the coffee pot. How do you schedule that event into your WBS? As a project manager, you never know what strange event is heading your way. Such unanticipated events make project management challenging, but also incredibly fascinating!

Q8 2020?

This is peculiar! In every other chapter, it is easy to imagine change, development of new products, and new trends between now and 2020. But not here. In this chapter, I don't think much will change. I'll bet students in 2020 will still be learning the SDLC. They'll be applying it to different technologies, for different purposes, but, like the scientific method, the process itself will remain the same.

You, however, may be the key to gradual improvements. Or at least the key to avoiding problems like Sue has created at MRV. You and members of your generation are comfortable with technology; there is no mystery to you there, at least not as users. And, you've taken this class and read this chapter. So, maybe, your generation of business professionals will remember to take responsibility for system requirements.

Taking such responsibility is the single most important task you can perform for a development project. Taking responsibility goes beyond participating in requirements meetings and stating your opinion on how things should work. Taking responsibility means understanding that the information system is built for your business function and managing requirements accordingly.

"There are no IT projects," says Kaiser-Permanente CIO Cliff Dodd. Rather, he says, "Some business projects have an IT component."[3] Dodd is right. Information systems exist to help organizations achieve their goals and objectives. Information systems exist to facilitate business processes and to improve decision making. Every information system is simply a part of some larger business project.

When investigating the problems in the IRS modernization program, the IRS Oversight Board stated, "The IRS business units must take direct leadership and ownership of the Modernization program and its projects. In particular this must include defining the scope of each project, preparing realistic and attainable business cases, and controlling scope changes throughout each project's life cycle."[4]

Users cannot be passive recipients of the IT department's services. Instead, users are responsible for ensuring that requirements are complete and accurate. Users must ask only for what they need and must avoid creating requirements that cannot possibly be constructed within the available budget. Because users may not know what is difficult or unrealistic, requirements definition can occur only through an extended conversation among the users and the development team.

Once the requirements are known, the development team will create a project WBS and begin development work. It will staff positions, it will begin the design process,

---

[3]Quoted in Steve Ulfelder, "How to Talk to Business," *www.computerworld.com/managementtopics/management/story/0,10801,109403,00.html*, March 13, 2006 (accessed August 2008).

[4]IRS Oversight Board, "Independent Analysis of IRS Business Systems Modernization Special Report," *www.irsoversightboard.treas.gov* (accessed August 2006).

and, later, it will work on the stated requirements. If users subsequently change their minds about what is needed, considerable rework and waste will occur. **Requirements creep** is the process by which users agree to one set of requirements, then add a bit more ("It won't take too much extra work"), then add a bit more, and so forth. Over time, the requirements creep so much that they describe a completely new project. But the development team is left with the budget and plan of the original project.

Users must take responsibility for managing requirements changes and for avoiding requirements creep. Some requirements change is inevitable; but if changes become extensive, if requirements creep cannot be avoided, start a new project. Don't try to turn a doghouse into a skyscraper. In that course of action, disaster is the only outcome. Complete one small change at a time.

A final part of the users' responsibility for requirements concerns *testing*. You and those who work for you may be asked to help in several different ways. You may be asked to specify testing criteria. If so, you need to help define testable conditions that determine whether a feature or function is complete and operational. Testing may occur in several stages during the project. For example, you may be asked to test design components; evaluating a data model is a good example. Or, you may be asked to provide sample data and sample scenarios for program and systems testing. You may be asked to participate in the testing of beta versions. Because only the users can know if a feature works correctly, testing is part of requirements management.

The Real Estimation Process

"I'm a software developer. I write programs in an object-oriented language called C#. I'm a skilled object-oriented designer, too. I should be—I've been at it 12 years and worked on major projects for several software companies. For the last 4 years, I've been a team leader. I lived through the heyday of the dot-com era and now work in the IT department of a giant pharmaceutical company.

"All of this estimating theory is just that— theory. It's not really the way things work. Sure, I've been on projects in which we tried different estimation techniques. But here's what really happens: You develop an estimate using whatever technique you want. Your estimate goes in with the estimates of all the other team leaders. The project manager sums all those estimates together and produces an overall estimate for the project.

"By the way, in my projects, time has been a much bigger factor than money. At one software company I worked for, you could be 300 percent over your dollar budget and get no more than a slap on the wrist. Be 2 weeks late, however, and you were finished.

"Anyway, the project managers take the project schedule to senior management for approval, and what happens? Senior management thinks they are negotiating. 'Oh, no,' they say, 'that's way too long. You can surely take a month off that schedule. We'll approve the project, but we want it done by February 1 instead of March 1.'

"Now, what's their justification? They think that tight schedules make for efficient work. You know that everyone will work extra hard to meet the tighter timeframe. They know Parkinson's Law—'the time required to perform a task expands to the time available to do it.' So, fearing the possibility of wasting time because of too-lenient schedules, they lop a month off our estimate.

"Estimates are what they are; you can't knock off a month or two without some problem, somewhere. What does happen is that projects get behind, and then management expects us to work longer and longer hours. Like they said in the early years at Microsoft, 'We have flexible working hours. You can work any 65 hours per week you want.'

"Not that our estimation techniques are all that great, either. Most software developers are optimists. They schedule things as if everything will go as planned, and things seldom do. Also, schedulers usually don't allow for vacations, sick days, trips to the dentist, training on new technology, peer reviews, and all the other things we do in addition to writing software.

"So we start with optimistic schedules on our end, then management negotiates a month or two off, and voilà, we have a late project before we've started. After a while, management has been burned by late projects so much that they mentally add the month or even more back onto the official schedule. Then both sides work in a fantasy world, where no one believes the schedule, but everyone pretends they do.

"I like my job. I like software development. Management here is no better or worse than in other places. As long as I have interesting work to do, I'll stay here. But I'm not working myself silly to meet these fantasy deadlines." ∎

Discussion Questions

1. What do you think of this developer's attitude? Do you think he's unduly pessimistic or do you think there's merit to what he says? Explain.

2. What do you think of his idea that management thinks they're negotiating? Should management negotiate schedules? Why or why not?

3. Suppose a project actually requires 12 months to complete. Which do you think is likely to cost more: (a) having an official schedule of 11 months with at least a 1-month overrun or (b) having an official schedule of 13 months and following Parkinson's Law, having the project take 13 months?

4. Suppose you are a business manager and an information system is being developed for your use. You review the scheduling documents and see that little time has been allowed for vacations, sick leave, miscellaneous other work, and so forth. What do you do?

5. Describe the intangible costs of having an organizational belief that schedules are always unreasonable.

6. If this developer worked for you, how would you deal with his attitude about scheduling?

7. Do you think there is something different when scheduling information systems development projects than when scheduling other types of projects? What characteristics might make such projects unique? In what ways are they the same as other projects?

8. What do you think managers should do in light of your answer to question 7?

Dealing with Uncertainty

In the mid-1970s, I worked as a database disaster repairman. As an independent consultant, I was called by organizations that licensed the then-new database management systems but had little idea of what to do with them.

One of my memorable clients had converted the company's billing system from an older-technology system to the new world of database processing. Unfortunately, after they cut off the old system, serious flaws were found in the new one, and from mid-November to mid-January the company was unable to send a bill. Of course, customers who do not receive bills do not pay, and my client had a substantial cash-flow problem. Even worse, some of its customers used a calendar-year tax basis and wanted to pay their bills prior to the end of the year. When those customers called to find the amount they owed, accounts receivable clerks had to say, "Well, we don't know. The data's in our computer, but we can't get it out." That was when the company called me for database disaster repair.

The immediate cause of the problem was that the client used the plunge conversion technique. But looking deeper, how did that organization find itself with a new billing system so full of failures?

In this organization, management had little idea about how to communicate with IT, and the IT personnel had no experience in dealing with senior management. They talked past one another.

Fortunately, this client was, in most other respects, a well-managed company. Senior management only needed to learn to manage their IS projects with the same discipline as they managed other departments. So, once we had patched the billing system together to solve the cash-flow problem, the management team began work to implement policies and procedures to instill the following principles:

- Business users, not IS, would take responsibility for the success of new systems.
- Users would actively work with IS personnel throughout systems development, especially during the requirements phase.
- Users would take an active role in project planning, project management, and project reviews.
- No development phase would be considered complete until the work was reviewed and approved by user representatives and management.
- Users would actively test the new system.
- All future systems would be developed in small increments.

I cannot claim that all future development projects at this company proceeded smoothly after the users began to practice these principles. In fact, many users were slow to take on their new responsibilities; in some cases, the users resented the time they were asked to invest in the new practices. Also, some were uncomfortable in these new roles. They wanted to work in their business specialty and not be asked to participate in IS projects about which they knew little. Still others did not take their responsibilities seriously; they would come to meetings ill prepared, not fully engage in the process, or approve work they did not understand.

However, after that billing disaster, senior management understood what needed to be done. They made these practices a priority, and over time user resistance was mostly overcome. When it was not overcome, it was clear to senior management where the true problem lay.

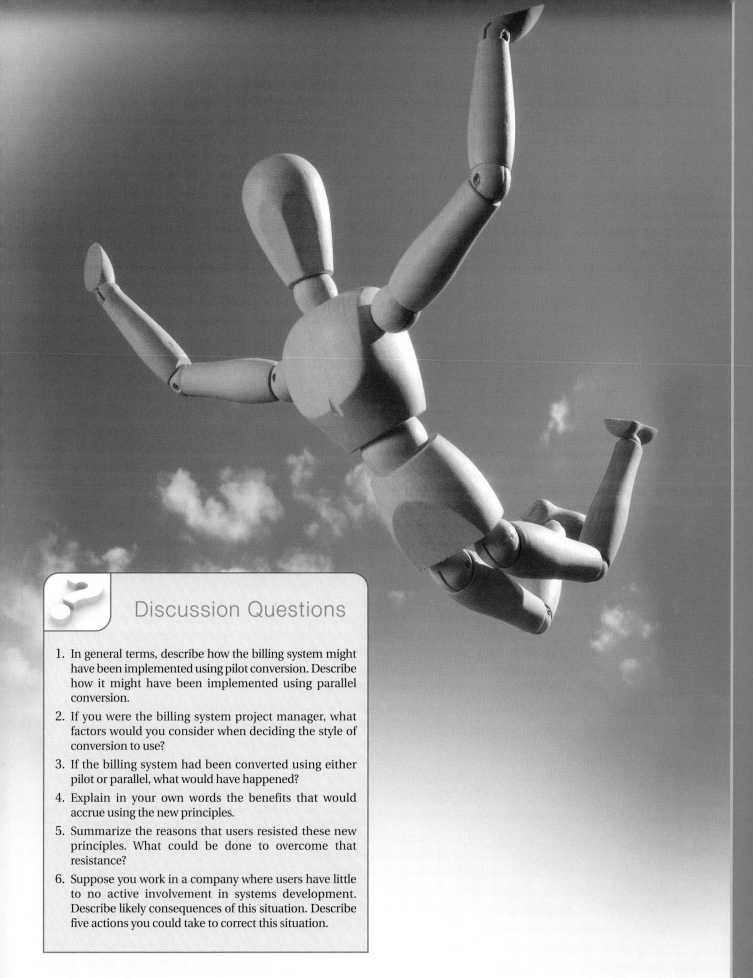

Discussion Questions

1. In general terms, describe how the billing system might have been implemented using pilot conversion. Describe how it might have been implemented using parallel conversion.

2. If you were the billing system project manager, what factors would you consider when deciding the style of conversion to use?

3. If the billing system had been converted using either pilot or parallel, what would have happened?

4. Explain in your own words the benefits that would accrue using the new principles.

5. Summarize the reasons that users resisted these new principles. What could be done to overcome that resistance?

6. Suppose you work in a company where users have little to no active involvement in systems development. Describe likely consequences of this situation. Describe five actions you could take to correct this situation.

ACTIVE REVIEW

Use this Active Review to verify that you understand the ideas and concepts that answer the chapter's study questions.

Q1 What is systems development?

Define *systems development* and explain how it pertains to the five components. Summarize the nature of systems development work and the types of personnel involved. Explain why information systems are never off-the-shelf and what that means for you as a future manager. Explain the term *maintenance* as it pertains to systems development.

Q2 Why is systems development difficult and risky?

Explain the risks of systems development. List five major challenges to systems development and summarize each. State Brooks' Law and explain how it pertains to systems development. Explain why there are four different development methodologies.

Q3 How do businesses use the systems development life cycle (SDLC) process?

Briefly describe the origins of the SDLC. Name the five phases of the SDLC. List the primary tasks in each phase. Explain the role for business users in each phase. Name and explain four dimensions of feasibility. Describe the knowledge needed by systems analysts and summarize their responsibilities. Define *test plan* and *PQA*. Name and describe four types of systems conversion. Explain major tasks in systems maintenance and define *patch* and *service pack*. Summarize the three major problems with the SDLC.

Q4 How does systems development vary according to project scale?

Explain how the SDLC applies differently to small-scale and large-scale projects. Explain each of the differences shown in Figure 10-11.

Q5 What are the trade-offs among requirements, schedule, and cost?

Describe how requirements affect cost and time. Describe the trade-offs that exist between requirements

and time. Explain the trade-offs that exist between time and cost. Describe circumstances in which increasing cost reduces time. Explain circumstances in which increasing cost increases time. Describe circumstance in which time extensions reduce costs.

Q6 What are the major challenges when planning IS projects?

State the key strategy for planning systems development. Explain why each task needs to produce one or more deliverables. Define *work-breakdown structure,* and give an example. In Figure 10-13, explain the numeric notation under task 1.3. Define *Gantt chart,* and describe its contents. Explain how task dependencies influence project work. Define *critical path analysis,* and, using your own words, explain what it means. Define *baseline WBS,* and explain how the baseline can be used to monitor a project.

Name the biggest challenge for large-scale systems development planning. Explain why this is so. Summarize the three approaches that organizations can take to the systems development scheduling challenge. Describe two ways of estimating time to write computer programs. Explain how you can use the knowledge you have about systems development scheduling.

Q7 What are the major challenges when managing IS projects?

Name four factors that create challenges for managing large-scale systems development. Give an example of each factor and explain how it creates management challenges. Define *configuration control.*

Q8 2020?

What is the author's prediction about changes to the SDLC in the next 10 years? Summarize why it might be possible that your generation of businesspeople may have greater success with the SDLC. State and describe the single most important task for users on a large-scale systems development project. Explain why there are no IT projects. Summarize user responsibilities for managing requirements. Define *requirements creep.* Describe the action that should occur if requirements creep cannot be stopped.

KEY TERMS AND CONCEPTS

Analysis paralysis   388
Baseline   391
Baseline WBS   393
Beta testing   385
Brooks' Law   375
Configuration control   395
Cost feasibility   377
Critical path   393
Critical path analysis   393
Deliverables   391
Diseconomy of scale   391
Function point   395
Gantt chart   392

Lines of code   394
Maintenance   386
Organizational feasibility   377
Parallel installation   385
Patch   387
Phased installation   385
Pilot installation   385
Plunge installation   385
Product quality assurance
   (PQA)   384
Requirements creep   397
Schedule feasibility   377
Service packs   387

System conversion   385
Systems analysis and
   design   372
Systems analysts   380
Systems development   372
Systems development life cycle
   (SDLC)   376
Technical feasibility   377
Test plan   384
Trade-offs   390
Waterfall   387
Work-breakdown structure
   (WBS)   391

USING YOUR KNOWLEDGE

1. Reread the Singing Valley Collaboration Exercise at the end of Chapter 3 (page 88). If you have not already answered that question, do so now, but develop just one innovative idea. Consider that idea from the standpoint of a systems development project. Develop a brief plan for this project using the SDLC. List major tasks that need to be performed at each stage.

2. Reread the choir-sheet-music-tracking Collaboration Exercise at the end of Chapter 5 (page 168). Chapter 5 focused on the development of a database for that problem. Now consider that application from the standpoint of a systems development project. Develop a brief plan for this project using the SDLC. Pay particular attention to the systems components other than the database that need to be developed. List major tasks that need to be performed at each stage.

3. Assume that you are the leader of a team that has been assigned this chapter's Collaboration Exercise.

    a. Create a WBS (like that in Figure 10-13) for the tasks that your team will need to complete. Do not do the exercise; do not attempt to perform any of these tasks, just identify tasks that you think will need to be accomplished by the team. Ensure that at least one of your tasks has three levels.

    b. Identify dependencies among the tasks you identified in part a.

    c. Collaboration always involves iteration and feedback. How do you account for those activities in your WBS?

    d. Identify tasks for which you think it will be particularly difficult to specify a duration. Describe characteristics of those tasks that make such specification difficult.

    e. As a team manager, how will you obtain a value for duration for the tasks in part d.

4. Reread Sue and Eddie's conversation at the start of this chapter (page 370). Suppose that Sue knows about the SDLC and has decided to begin a project to complete the tasks in the definition phase, and she has asked you to help her. Specifically, Sue wants you to create a list of questions that MRV needs to answer during the definition phase.

    a. Using Figure 10-5 as a guide, create that list of questions.

    b. Identify the five questions you think will be the most difficult to answer and explain why they will be difficult. Describe the strategy you would recommend that MRV follow to answer those questions.

    c. Assume that a version of the two-Web-site system appears to be feasible. Identify users who you think should be interviewed for requirements. List questions that you would ask each of those users.

    d. Your answers to parts a–c aren't a solution for MRV, but they are much better than the vague ideas Sue has now. Explain the benefit of your answers to MRV.

    e. Summarize the steps that MRV needs to take next.

COLLABORATION EXERCISE

Collaborate with a group of students on the following exercises. Recall from Chapter 2 that collaboration is more than cooperation because it involves iteration and feedback. Post a document, a discussion item, a wiki item, or an idea, and obtain feedback from your team members. Similarly, read the ideas of others and comment on them. Try to innovate in both the process by which you collaborate and the work product that you create. Avoid face-to-face meetings. Instead, use collaborative software such as Google Docs & Spreadsheets, Microsoft Groove, or Microsoft SharePoint to facilitate your ideas.

Wilma Baker, Jerry Barker, and Chris Bickel met in June 2009 at a convention of resort owners and tourism operators. They sat next to each other by chance while waiting for a presentation; after introducing themselves and laughing at the odd sound of their three names, they were surprised to learn that they managed similar businesses. Wilma Baker lives in Santa Fe, New Mexico, and specializes in renting homes and apartments to visitors to Santa Fe. Jerry Barker lives in Whistler Village, British Columbia, and specializes in renting condos to skiers and other visitors to the Whistler/Blackcomb Resort. Chris Bickel lives in Chatham, Massachusetts, and specializes in renting homes and condos to vacationers to Cape Cod.

The three agreed to have lunch after the presentation. During lunch, they shared frustrations about the difficulty of obtaining new customers, especially in the current economic downturn. As the conversation developed, they began to wonder if there was some way to combine forces (i.e., they were seeking a competitive advantage from an alliance). So, they decided to skip one of the next day's presentations and meet to discuss ways to form an alliance. Ideas they wanted to discuss further were sharing customer data, developing a joint reservation service, and exchanging property listings.

As they talked, it became clear they had no interest in merging their businesses; each wanted to stay independent. They also discovered that each was very concerned, paranoid even, about protecting their existing customer base from poaching. Still, the conflict was not as bad as it first seemed. Barker's business was primarily the ski trade, and winter was his busiest season; Bickel's business was mostly Cape Cod vacations, and she was busiest during the summer. Baker's high season was the summer and fall. So, it seemed there was enough difference in their high seasons that they would not necessarily cannibalize their businesses by selling the others' offerings to their own customers.

The question then became how to proceed. Given their desire to protect their own customers, they did not want to develop a common customer database. The best idea seemed to be to share data about properties.

That way they could keep control of their customers but still have an opportunity to sell time at the others' properties.

They discussed several alternatives. Each could develop her or his own property database, and the three could then share those databases over the Internet. Or, they could develop a centralized property database that they would all use. Or, they could find some other way to share property listings.

Because we do not know Baker, Barker, and Bickel's detailed requirements, you cannot develop a plan for a specific system. In general, however, they first need to decide how elaborate an information system they want to construct. Consider the following three alternatives:

a. They could build a simple system centered on email. With it, each company sends property descriptions to the others via email. Each independent company then forwards these descriptions to its own customers, also using email. When a customer makes a reservation for a property, that request is then forwarded back to the property manager via email.

b. They could construct a more complex system using a Web-based, shared database that contains data on all their properties and reservations. Because reservations tracking is a common business task, it is likely that they can license an existing application with this capability.

c. Same as alternative 2, except assume they do not license an existing product, but develop their own database and applications instead.

1. Using Figure 10-4 as a guide, perform the steps required for the systems definition phase for alternative a. You cannot form a project team to complete the project, so, instead, describe the personnel that would need to be on such a team. With regard to planning, specify the tasks that would need to be performed for the requirements, design, and implementation stages.

2. Perform the steps required for the systems definition phase for alternative b. Again, you cannot form a project team to complete the project, so, instead, describe the personnel that would need to be on such a team. With regard to planning, specify the tasks that would need to be performed for the requirements, design, and implementation stages.

3. Perform the steps required for the systems definition phase for alternative c. Assume you use the SDLC. Again, just describe the personnel that would need to be on such a team. With regard to planning, specify the tasks that would need to be performed for the requirements, design, and implementation stages.

4. Given what you know about the BBB alliance and the work you envision in your answers to questions 1, 2, and 3, which alternative do you think makes the most sense? Why? What other information might you need to answer this question? How would you go about finding that information?

5. Clearly, the development of any of these alternatives will be a collaborative effort. Chapter 2 briefly introduced Google Docs & Spreadsheets, Microsoft Groove, and Microsoft SharePoint. Which of these tools would be most appropriate for BBB to use when developing this system? Why? In your answer, use your own experience with these tools, if you have been using them. Explain why the use of one of these tools would be better than email with attachments or FTP.

APPLICATION EXERCISES

1. Suppose you are given the task of keeping track of the number of labor hours invested in meetings for systems development projects. Assume your company uses the traditional SDLC and that each phase requires two types of meetings: *Working meetings* involve users, systems analysts, programmers, and PQA test engineers. *Review meetings* involve all of those people, plus level-1 and level-2 managers of both user departments and the IS department.

   a. Import the data in the Word file **Ch10Ex01** from this text's Web site into a spreadsheet.

   b. Modify your spreadsheet to compute the total labor hours invested in each phase of a project. When a meeting occurs, assume you enter the project phase, the meeting type, the start time, the end time, and the number of each type of personnel attending. Your spreadsheet should calculate the number of labor hours and should add the meeting's hours to the totals for that phase and for the project overall.

   c. Modify your spreadsheet to include the budgeted number (in the source data) of labor hours for each type of employee for each phase. In your spreadsheet, show the difference between the number of hours budgeted and the number actually consumed.

   d. Change your spreadsheet to include the budgeted cost and actual cost of labor. Assume that you enter, once, the average labor cost for each type of employee, as stipulated in the source data.

2. Use Access to develop a failure-tracking database application. Use the data in the Excel file **Ch10Ex02** for this exercise. The data includes columns for the following:

   FailureNumber
   DateReported
   FailureDescription
   ReportedBy (the name of the PQA engineer reporting the failure)
   ReportedBy_email (the email address of the PQA engineer reporting the failure)
   FixedBy (the name of the programmer who is assigned to fix the failure)
   FixedBy_email (the email address of the programmer assigned to fix the failure)
   DateFailureFixed
   FixDescription
   DateFixVerified
   VerifiedBy (the name of the PQA engineer verifying the fix)
   VeifiedBy_email (the email address of the PQA engineer verifying the fix)

   a. The data in the spreadsheet is not normalized. Normalize the data by creating a *Failure* table, a *PQA Engineer* table, and a *Programmer* table. Add other appropriate columns to each table. Create appropriate relationships.

   b. Create one or more forms that can be used to report a failure, to report a failure fix, and to report a failure verification. Create the form(s) so that the user can just pull down the name of a PQA engineer or programmer from the appropriate table to fill in the *ReportedBy*, *FixedBy*, and *VerifiedBy* fields.

   c. Construct a report that shows all failures sorted by reporting PQA engineer and then by *Date Reported*.

   d. Construct a report that shows only fixed and verified failures.

   e. Construct a report that shows only fixed but unverified failures.

CASE STUDY 10 video ▶

Slow Learners, or What?

In 1974, when I was teaching at Colorado State University, we conducted a study of the causes of information systems failures. We interviewed personnel on several dozen projects and collected survey data on another 50 projects. Our analysis of the data revealed that the single most important factor in IS failure was a lack of user involvement. The second major factor was unclear, incomplete, and inconsistent requirements.

At the time, I was a devoted computer programmer and IT techie, and, frankly, I was surprised. I thought that the significant problems would have been technical issues.

I recall one interview in particular. A large sugar producer had attempted to implement a new system for paying sugar beet farmers. The new system was to be implemented at some 20 different sugar beet collection sites, which were located in small farming communities, adjacent to rail yards. One of the benefits of the new system was significant cost savings, and a major share of those savings occurred because the new system eliminated the need for local comptrollers. The new system was expected to eliminate the jobs of 20 or so senior people.

The comptrollers, however, had been paying local farmers for decades; they were popular leaders not just within the company, but in their communities as well. They were well liked, highly respected, important people. A system that caused the elimination of their jobs was, using a term from this chapter, *organizationally infeasible*, to say the least.

Nonetheless, the system was constructed, but an IS professional who was involved told me, "Somehow, that new system just never seemed to work. The data were not entered on a timely basis, or they were in error, or incomplete; sometimes the data were not entered at all. Our operations were falling apart during the key harvesting season, and we finally backed off, rehired the comptrollers, and returned to the old system." Active involvement of system users would have identified this organizational infeasibility long before the system was implemented.

That's ancient history, you say. Maybe, but in 1994 the Standish Group published a now famous study on information systems failures. Entitled "The CHAOS Report," the study indicated that the leading causes of IS failure are, in descending order, (1) lack of user input, (2) incomplete requirements and specifications, and (3) changing requirements and specifications (*http://standishgroup.com*). That study was completed some 20 years after our study.

More recently, in 2004, Professor Joseph Kasser and his students at the University of Maryland analyzed 19 system failures to determine their cause. They then correlated their analysis of the cause with the opinions of the professionals involved in the failures. The correlated results indicate the first-priority cause of system failure was "Poor requirements"; the second-priority cause was "Failure to communicate with the customer" (*http://therightrequirement.com*).

In 2003, the IRS Oversight Board concluded the first cause of the IRS BSM failure (see Case Study 1, page 27) was "inadequate business unit ownership and sponsorship of projects. This resulted in unrealistic business cases and continuous project scope 'creep.'"

For over 35 years, studies have consistently shown that leading causes of system failures are a lack of user involvement and incomplete and changing requirements. Yet, failures from these very failures continue to mount.

Sources: http://standishgroup.com (registration required), www.theright requirement.com (accessed August, 2009).

Questions

1. Using the knowledge you have gained from this chapter, summarize the roles that you think users should take during an information systems development project. What responsibilities do users have? How closely should they work with the IS team? Who is responsible for stating requirements and constraints? Who is responsible for managing requirements?

2. If you ask users why they did not participate in requirements specification, some of the more common responses are the following:

   a. "I wasn't asked."
   b. "I didn't have time."
   c. "They were talking about a system that would be here in 18 months, and I'm just worried about getting the order out the door today."
   d. "I didn't know what they wanted."
   e. "I didn't know what they were talking about."
   f. "I didn't work here when they started the project."
   g. "The whole situation has changed since they were here; that was 18 months ago!"

   Comment on each of these statements. What strategies do they suggest to you as a future user and as a future manager of users?

3. If you ask IS professionals why they did not obtain a complete and accurate list of requirements, common responses are:

   a. "It was nearly impossible to get on the users' calendars. They were always too busy."
   b. "The users wouldn't regularly attend our meetings. As a result, one meeting would be dominated by the

needs of one group, and another meeting would be dominated by the needs of another group."

c. "Users didn't take the requirement process seriously. They wouldn't thoroughly review the requirements statements before review meetings."

d. "Users kept changing. We'd meet with one person one time and another person a second time, and they'd want different things."

e. "We didn't have enough time."

f. "The requirements kept changing."

Comment on each of these statements. What strategies do they suggest to you as a future user and a future manager of users?

4. If it is widely understood that one of the principal causes of IS failures is a lack of user involvement, and if that factor continues to be a problem after 35 years of experience, does this mean that the problem cannot be solved? For example, everyone knows that you can maximize your gains by buying stocks at their annual low price and selling them at their annual high price, but doing so is very difficult. Is it equally true that although everyone knows that users should be involved in requirements specification, and that requirements should be complete, it just can't be done? Why or why not?

11

Information Systems Management

"I can't even print a copy of the clients for this month's trip!"

"Eddie, what do you mean?"

"Sue, someone . . . Graham, I think . . . has been using my computer. They've moved all my files around. I'm gonna kill him when I find him."

"Why was he using your computer?"

"To get the files he needed for the data mining project. Look, Sue, we need a better network. People like Graham need to have controlled access to data over our LAN. Really, we need our own IT person."

"Our own computer department? Eddie, it's not gonna happen. We can't afford the equipment we have, let alone staff."

"Sue, we have data all over the place, here, in the warehouse in Baker, on trip leaders' computers. I even used to have data on this computer!"

"Did you lose your data?"

"Probably not. Someone's just messed up my file system, though. I hope I can make QuickBooks work, Sue."

"Eddie, you're our office manager. You're just going to have to take on the role of

> *" Eddie, I am so ignorant about all this. "*

computer manager, too. Maybe next fall, after the season is over, we can sit down . . . send you to a course or something. Maybe hire a consultant."

"Not Graham, though. He did a fine job on the data mining, but he's in way over his head on the Web site development project. I think even he knows that."

"Yeah, Eddie, you're right. That was too much for him. But, maybe we can roll all this together? Hire a professional to do the new Web sites and also teach you how to manage our computing resources?"

"I doubt one person can do both; those jobs take very different skill sets."

"They do? Eddie, I am so ignorant about all this."

"Sue, we all are. That's what worries me." ∎

>> STUDY QUESTIONS

Q1 What are the functions and organization of the IS department?

Q2 How do organizations plan the use of IS?

Q3 What tasks are necessary for managing computing infrastructure?

Q4 What tasks are necessary for managing enterprise applications?

Q5 What are the advantages and disadvantages of outsourcing?

Q6 What are your user rights and responsibilities?

Q7 2020?

CHAPTER PREVIEW

Information systems are critical to organizational success, and like all critical assets, need to be managed responsibly, in organizations both large and small. In this chapter, we will survey the management of IS and IT resources. We begin by discussing the major functions and the organization of the IS department. Then we will consider each of the major functions in greater detail: planning the use of IT/IS, creating and managing the computing infrastructure, creating and managing enterprise IS, and protecting organizational information assets.

Outsourcing is the process of hiring outside vendors to provide business services and related products. For information systems, outsourcing refers to hiring outside vendors to provide information systems, products, and applications. We will examine the pros and cons of outsourcing and describe some of its risks. Finally, we will conclude this chapter by discussing the relationship of users to the IS department. In this last section, you will learn both your own and the IS department's rights and responsibilities.

The purpose of this chapter is not to teach you how to manage information systems. Such management, in truth, requires many years of experience. Instead, the goal of this chapter is to give you an appreciation for the scale and complexity of the IS management task and to help you become an effective consumer of IS services.

And, if you work for a small company like MRV, you will at least know the elements of IS management and be able to help people like Eddie understand what needs to be done. By the way, FlexTime doesn't have issues like MRV does, primarily because of Neil's knowledge and experience. He's not an IT professional, but he's a smart and effective consumer of IS professional services.

Q1 What Are the Functions and Organization of the IS Department?

The major functions of the information systems department[1] are as follows:

- Plan the use of IS to accomplish organizational goals and strategy.
- Develop, operate, and maintain the organization's computing infrastructure.
- Develop, operate, and maintain enterprise applications.
- Protect information assets.
- Manage outsourcing relationships.

We will consider each of these functions in Q2 through Q5. Before we do that, however, you need to understand how the IS department is organized.

How Is the IS Department Organized?

Figure 11-1 shows typical top-level reporting relationships. As you will learn in your management classes, organizational structure varies depending on the organization's size, culture, competitive environment, industry, and other factors. Larger organizations

---

[1]Often, the department we are calling the *IS department* is known in organizations as the *IT Department*. That name is a misnomer however, because the IT department manages systems as well as technology. If you hear the term *IT department* in industry, don't assume that the scope of that department is limited to technology.

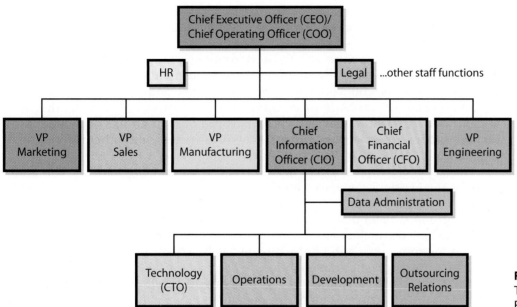

Figure 11-1
Typical Senior-Level Reporting Relationships

with independent divisions will have a group of senior executives like those shown here for each division. Smaller companies may combine some of these departments. Consider the structure in Figure 11-1 as a typical example.

The title of the principal manager of the IS department varies from organization to organization. A common title is **chief information officer**, or **CIO**. Other common titles are *vice president of information services, director of information services*, and, less commonly, *director of computer services.*

In Figure 11-1, the CIO, like other senior executives, reports to the *chief executive officer* (CEO), though sometimes these executives report to the *chief operating officer* (COO), who, in turn, reports to the CEO. In some companies, the CIO reports to the *chief financial officer* (CFO). That reporting arrangement might make sense if the primary information systems support only accounting and finance activities. In organizations such as manufacturers that operate significant nonaccounting information systems, the arrangement shown in Figure 11-1 is more common and effective.

The structure of the IS department also varies among organizations. Figure 11-1 shows a typical IS department with four groups and a data administration staff function.

Most IS departments include a *technology* office that investigates new information systems technologies and determines how the organization can benefit from them. For example, today many organizations are investigating Web 2.0 opportunities and planning how they can use those capabilities to better accomplish their goals and objectives. An individual called the **chief technology officer**, or **CTO**, often heads the technology group. The CTO evaluates new technologies, new ideas, and new capabilities and identifies those that are most relevant to the organization. The CTO's job requires deep knowledge of information technology and the ability to envision and innovate applications in the organization.

The next group in Figure 11-1, *operations*, manages the computing infrastructure, including individual computers, computer centers, networks, and communications media. This group includes system and network administrators. As you will learn, an important function for this group is to monitor the user experience and respond to user problems.

The third group in the IS department in Figure 11-1 is *development*. This group manages the process of creating new information systems as well as maintaining existing information systems. (Recall from Chapter 10 that in the context of information systems *maintenance* means either fixing problems or adapting existing information systems to support new features and functions.)

The size and structure of the development group depends on whether programs are developed in-house. If not, this department will be staffed primarily by systems analysts who work with users, operations, and vendors to acquire and install licensed software and to set up the system components around that software. If the organization develops programs in-house, then this department will include programmers, test engineers, technical writers, and other development personnel.

The last IS department group in Figure 11-1 is *outsourcing relations*. This group exists in organizations that have negotiated outsourcing agreements with other companies to provide equipment, applications, or other services. You will learn more about outsourcing later in this chapter.

Figure 11-1 also includes a *data administration* staff function. The purpose of this group is to protect data and information assets by establishing data standards and data management practices and policies.

There are many variations on the structure of the IS department shown in Figure 11-1. In larger organizations, the operations group may itself consist of several different departments. Sometimes, there is a separate group for data warehousing and data marts.

As you examine Figure 11-1, keep the distinction between IS and IT in mind. *Information systems (IS)* exist to help the organization achieve its goals and objectives. Information systems have the five components we have discussed throughout this text. *Information technology (IT)* is simply technology. It concerns the products, techniques, procedures, and designs of computer-based technology. IT must be placed into the structure of an IS before an organization can use it.

What IS-Related Job Positions Exist?

IS departments provide a wide range of interesting and well-paying jobs. Many students enter the MIS class thinking that the IS departments consist only of programmers and computer technicians. If you reflect on the five components of an information system, you can understand why this cannot be true. The data, procedures, and people components of an information system require professionals with highly developed interpersonal communications skills.

Figure 11-2 summarizes the major job positions in the IS industry. With the exception of computer technician and possibly of PQA test engineer, all of these positions require a 4-year degree. Furthermore, with the exception of programmer and PQA test engineer, all of these positions require business knowledge. In most cases, successful professionals have a degree in business. Note, too, that most positions require good verbal and written communications skills. Business, including information systems, is a social activity.

Many of the positions in Figure 11-2 have a wide salary range. Lower salaries are for professionals with limited experience or for those who work in smaller companies or work on small projects. The larger salaries are for those with deep knowledge and experience who work for large companies on large projects. Do not expect to begin your career at the high end of these ranges. As noted, all salaries are for positions in the United States and are shown in U.S. dollars.

(By the way, for all but the most technical positions, knowledge of a business specialty can add to your marketability. If you have the time, a dual major can be an excellent choice. Popular and successful dual majors are accounting and information systems, marketing and information systems, and management and information systems.)

Title	Responsibilities	Knowledge, Skill, and Characteristics Requirements	2009 U.S. Salary Range (USD)
System analyst	Work with users to determine system requirements, design and develop job descriptions and procedures, help determine system test plans.	Strong interpersonal and communications skills. Knowledge of both business and technology. Adaptable.	$65,000–$150,000
Programmer	Design and write computer programs.	Logical thinking and design skills, knowledge of one or more programming languages.	$50,000–$150,000
PQA test engineer	Develop test plans, design and write automated test scripts, perform testing.	Logical thinking, basic programming, superb organizational skills, eye for detail.	$40,000–$95,000
Technical writer	Write program documentation, help-text, procedures, job descriptions, training materials.	Quick learner, clear writing skills, high verbal communications skills.	$40,000–$95,000
User support representative	Help users solve problems, provide training.	Communications and people skills. Product knowledge. Patience.	$40,000–$65,000
Computer technician	Install software, repair computer equipment and networks.	Associate degree, diagnostic skills.	$30,000–$65,000
Network administrator	Monitor, maintain, fix, and tune computer networks.	Diagnostic skills, in-depth knowledge of communications technologies and products.	$75,000–$200,000+
Consultant	Wide range of activities: programming, testing, database design, communications and networks, project management, security and risk management, strategic planning.	Quick learner, entrepreneurial attitude, communications and people skills. Respond well to pressure. Particular knowledge depends on work.	From $35 per hour for a contract tester to more than $500 per hour for strategic consulting to executive group.
Salesperson	Sell software, network, communications, and consulting services.	Quick learner, knowledge of product, superb professional sales skills.	$65,000–$200,000+
Small-scale project manager	Initiate, plan, manage, monitor, and close down projects.	Management and people skills, technology knowledge. Highly organized.	$75,000–$150,000
Large-scale project manager	Initiate, plan, monitor, and close down complex projects.	Executive and management skills. Deep project management knowledge.	$150,000–$250,000+
Database administrator	Manage and protect database (see Chapter 12).	Diplomatic skills, database technology knowledge.	$75,000–$250,000
Chief technology officer (CTO)	Advise CIO, executive group, and project managers on emerging technologies.	Quick learner, good communication skills, deep knowledge of IT.	$125,000–$300,000+
Chief information officer (CIO)	Manage IT department, communicate with executive staff on IT- and IS-related matters. Member of the executive group.	Superb management skills, deep knowledge of business, and good business judgment. Good communicator. Balanced and unflappable.	$150,000–$500,000+, as well as executive stock, incentives, benefits, and privileges.

Figure 11-2
Job Positions in the Information Systems Industry

Q2 How Do Organizations Plan the Use of IS?

We begin our discussion of IS functions with planning. Figure 11-3 lists the major IS planning functions.

Align Information Systems with Organizational Strategy

The purpose of an information system is to help the organization accomplish its goals and objectives. In order to do so, all information systems must be aligned with the organization's competitive strategy.

Recall the four competitive strategies from Chapter 3: An organization can be a cost leader either across an industry or within an industry segment. Alternatively, an organization can differentiate its products or services either across the industry or within a segment. Whatever the organizational strategy, the CIO and the IS department must constantly be vigilant to align IS with it.

Maintaining alignment between IS direction and organizational strategy is a continuing process. As strategies change, as the organization merges with other organizations, as divisions are sold, IS must evolve along with the organization.

Unfortunately, however, IS infrastructure is not malleable. Changing a network requires time and resources. Integrating disparate information systems applications is even slower and more expensive. This fact often is not appreciated in the executive suite. Without a persuasive CIO, IS can be perceived as a drag on the organization's opportunities.

Communicate IS Issues to the Executive Group

This last observation leads to the second IS planning function in Figure 11-3. The CIO is the representative for IS and IT issues within the executive staff. The CIO provides the IS perspective during discussions of problem solutions, proposals, and new initiatives.

For example, when considering a merger, it is important that the company consider integration of information systems in the merged entities. This consideration needs to be addressed during the evaluation of the merger opportunity. Too often, such issues are not considered until after the deal has been signed. Such delayed consideration is a mistake; the costs of the integration need to be factored into the economics of the purchase. Involving the CIO in high-level discussions is the best way to avoid such problems.

Develop Priorities and Enforce Them Within the IS Department

The next two IS planning functions in Figure 11-3 are related. The CIO must ensure that priorities consistent with the overall organizational strategy are developed and communicated to the IS department. At the same time, the CIO must also ensure that

Figure 11-3
Planning the Use of IS/IT

- Align information systems with organizational strategy; maintain alignment as organization changes.
- Communicate IS/IT issues to executive group.
- Develop/enforce IS priorities within the IS department.
- Sponsor steering committee.

the department evaluates proposals and projects for using new technology in light of those communicated priorities.

Technology is seductive, particularly to IS professionals. The CTO may enthusiastically claim, "With SOA services we can do this and this and this." Although true, the question that the CIO must continually ask is whether those new possibilities are consistent with the organization's strategy and direction.

Thus, the CIO must not only establish and communicate such priorities, but enforce them as well. The department must evaluate every proposal, at the earliest stage possible, as to whether it is consistent with the organization's goals and aligned with its strategy.

Furthermore, no organization can afford to implement every good idea. Even projects that are aligned with the organization's strategy must be prioritized. The objective of everyone in the IS department must be to develop the most appropriate systems possible, given constraints on time and money. Well thought out and clearly communicated priorities are essential.

Sponsor the Steering Committee

The final planning function in Figure 11-3 is to sponsor the steering committee. A **steering committee** is a group of senior managers from the major business functions that works with the CIO to set the IS priorities and decide among major IS projects and alternatives.

The steering committee serves an important communication function between IS and the users. In the steering committee, information systems personnel can discuss potential IS initiatives and directions with the user community. At the same time, the steering committee provides a forum for users to express their needs, frustrations, and other issues they have with the IS department.

Typically, the IS department sets up the steering committee's schedule and agenda and conducts the meetings. The CEO and other members of the executive staff determine the membership of the steering committee.

One other task related to planning the use of IT is to establish the organization's computer-use policy. For more on computer-use issues, read the Ethics Guide on pages 416–417.

Q3 What Tasks Are Necessary for Managing Computing Infrastructure?

Managing the computing infrastructure is the most visible of all of the IS department's functions. In fact, the only interaction most employees have with the IS department is when they receive a computer or when they have problems using it. To many employees, the IS department is the "computer department"; they have little idea of the other important jobs the IS department performs behind that equipment.

This section focuses on the major tasks for this management function. We begin with another alignment issue. This issue, however, does not concern alignment with strategic direction, but rather alignment with infrastructure design.

Align Infrastructure Design with Organizational Structure

The structure of the IS infrastructure must mirror the structure of the organization. A highly controlled and centralized organization needs highly controlled and centralized information systems. A decentralized organization with autonomous operating units requires decentralized information systems that facilitate autonomous activity.

Consider Figure 11-4 (page 418), which shows a distributed check-printing company that grew through a process of acquisition. This company expanded to new

Ethics

GUIDE

Using the Corporate Computer

Suppose you work at a company that has the following computer use policy:

Computers, email, social networking, and the Internet are to be used primarily for official company business. Small amounts of personal email can be exchanged with friends and family, and occasional usage of the Internet is permitted, but such usage should be limited and never interfere with your work.

Suppose you are a manager and you learn that one of your employees has been engaged in the following activities:

1. Playing computer games during work hours
2. Playing computer games on the company computer before and after work hours
3. Responding to emails from an ill parent
4. Watching DVDs during lunch and other breaks
5. Sending emails to plan a party that involves mostly people from work
6. Sending emails to plan a party that involves no one from work
7. Searching the Web for a new car
8. Reading the news on CNN.com
9. Checking the stock market over the Internet
10. Bidding on items for personal use on eBay
11. Selling personal items on eBay
12. Paying personal bills online
13. Paying personal bills online when traveling on company business
14. Buying an airplane ticket for an ill parent over the Internet
15. Changing the content of a personal Facebook page
16. Changing the content of a personal business Web site
17. Buying an airplane ticket for a personal vacation over the Internet
18. Responding to personal Twitter messages ■

Discussion Questions

1. Explain how you would respond to each situation.

2. Suppose someone from the IS department notifies you that one of your employees is spending 3 hours a day writing Twitter messages. How do you respond?

3. For question 2, suppose you ask how the IS department knows about your employee and you are told, "We secretly monitor computer usage." Do you object to such monitoring? Why or why not?

4. Suppose someone from the IS department notifies you that one of your employees is sending many personal emails. When you ask how they know the emails are personal, you are told that IS measures account activity and when suspicious email usage is suspected the IS department reads employees' email. Do you think such reading is legal? Is it ethical? How do you respond?

5. As an employee, if you know that your company occasionally reads employees' email, does that change your behavior? If so, does that justify the company reading your email? Does this situation differ from having someone read your personal postal mail that happens to be delivered to you at work? Why or why not?

6. Write what you think is the best corporate policy for personal computer usage at work. Specifically address Facebook, MySpace, Twitter, and other personal social networking activity.

- Plants acquired by acquisition
- Existing IS legacy from past
- Separate order entry, production, and billing
- Highly distributed organization

Figure 11-4
Distributed Check-Printing Company

Figure 11-5
Problematic Centralized IS

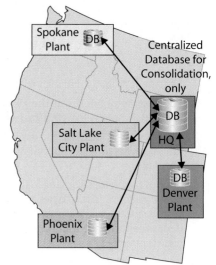

Figure 11-6
Decentralized Order-Management
System

geographic locations by acquiring printers in different cities. As each entity was acquired, the company kept it as an independent operating center. The company held plant managers accountable for the performance of their own facilities, and these managers had considerable operational independence.

Initially, the IS department attempted to develop a centralized order-management system for use by all the plants in the organization. Figure 11-5 shows this situation. The company developed a customer order database at a data center in Denver and required all of the independent plants to process their orders through the centralized order-management system.

Even though all of the printing plants had been producing essentially the same products, there were small but significant differences in the ways that each plant prioritized and processed its orders. However, with the centralized system, the plant managers were unable to implement their own production-scheduling processes. Dissatisfaction with the centralized system was rampant.

At first, the IS department attempted to remedy the problems, but within a few weeks it was clear that the autonomous managers were never going to be satisfied with a centralized system. They wanted control over all aspects of the ordering and manufacturing process.

Accordingly, the IS department abandoned the concept of a single, centralized order-entry system and instead developed a set of distributed order-management systems, as shown in Figure 11-6. Each of these systems was under the control of the local plant manager. The distributed systems did send order and production data to a centralized facility for the production of consolidated reports, but the control of the order entry, scheduling, and manufacturing remained with the local plant managers.

The system in Figure 11-6 was more successful than the centralized system because it was consistent with the organization's underlying management style and philosophy. In fact, the system in Figure 11-5 should never have been developed. At the time it was envisioned, the IS department was buried deep in the accounting department, and it had little visibility to the rest of the company. After this problem developed, the company raised IS in the management hierarchy and instituted a steering committee. Close collaboration between the CIO and the steering committee prohibited the design of any future system that was so greatly misaligned with the organization.

Create, Operate, and Maintain Computing Infrastructure

Three more tasks in managing the computing infrastructure are to:

- Create and maintain infrastructure for end-user computing.
- Create, operate, and maintain networks.
- Create, operate, and maintain data centers, data warehouses, and data marts.

Those are *huge* tasks. They are enormous jobs even for a mid-sized company like that shown in Figure 11-6. Consider just end-user computing. Almost every employee in that company has a computer. Each computer has a set of programs. From time to time, those computers need to be upgraded, and the software that resides on them needs to be upgraded as well. When Microsoft ships a new version of Windows or Office, the IS department immediately has user requests for the new version. (Also, it is likely to receive requests *not* to receive the new version.) How do you install a new version of Windows on 1,000 computers? On 5,000? Keep in mind that you have limited resources and cannot afford to send a trained technician to every user's computer.

Alternatively, suppose the steering committee decides the company needs to invest in a new SOA-based supply chain management application. A different variation of your computer network protocol is required to support the new capability. This requirement means that you have to install a new version of your networking software on every computer, regardless of whether the computer will be involved in Supply Chain Management (SCM). How do you proceed?

Suppose you develop an automated process to upgrade all of the users' computers at night, when they are not in use. Your automated procedure works fine until it encounters a computer that has been modified by its user. She decided, secretly, to use Linux rather than Windows. Because of the difference, your automated upgrade program crashes. The IS department has to send a specialist to Phoenix to find out what went wrong with the install.

We will not address the management of the network and data centers here. The subject is too large and complicated and is not directly related to your future business career. Suffice it to say that when you see a diagram like that in Figure 9-18 (page 340), keep in mind that the IS department has to create, operate, and maintain the computers, software, and personnel in the data warehouse and all of the data marts.

Establish Technology and Product Standards

The failure of the network software upgrade points out the need for technology and product standards. The IS department cannot afford to allow every computer user to have his or her own personal configuration. Doing so not only would mean difficulties for upgrading computers and programs, but it also might mean that some users' computers become incompatible with others. For example, a document created using WordPerfect on a Macintosh might not be readable by a computer that uses Microsoft Word on a Windows machine. For this example, there is a way to import and export such documents, but the IS department has higher priorities for its budget than training users how to do it.

Users' computing needs vary according to the work they do. In response, most IS departments have developed a set of three or four different standard configurations. The most basic configuration might have just email and a Web browser. Another configuration might have Microsoft Office programs as well, and a third might have an extended version of Office, email, and some analysis software. A fourth configuration might be created for software development personnel.

No standard will please all of the users, all of the time. The IS department needs to work with the steering committee and other user groups to ensure the standards are effective for most of the users.

Track Problems and Monitor Resolutions

The IS department provides the computing infrastructure as a service to users. As in any service organization, a system must exist to record user problems and monitor their resolution. This system is no different from other customer service applications we have discussed.

In a well-run IS department, when a user reports a problem the department assigns a tracking number and the problem enters a queue for service. Normally, problems are prioritized on the basis of how critical they are to the user's work. Higher-priority items are serviced first. When the item is placed in the queue, the user is told its priority and given an approximate date for resolution. When the problem is fixed, it is removed from the queue. If the problem is still not resolved, it reenters the queue at a higher priority.

The CIO and the manager of the computer operations group monitor the queue, the average length of time an item remains in the queue, the number of nonresolutions, and so forth. In the future, if you, as a user, encounter such a system, it may seem overly bureaucratic. In fact, it is a sign of good IS management.

Manage Computing Infrastructure Staff

Finally, the IS department also must manage the computing infrastructure staff. The department's employees must be organized, hired, trained, directed, evaluated, and promoted, just as with any other corporate function.

The organization of a typical IS operations department is shown in Figure 11-7. This generic chart has subdepartments for the network, computer center, data warehouse, and user support. In a large organization, these functions might be further divided as well. In particular, a separate department might staff the help-desk function. Sometimes operations groups have specialists for particular applications. There might be, for example, an ERP support group.

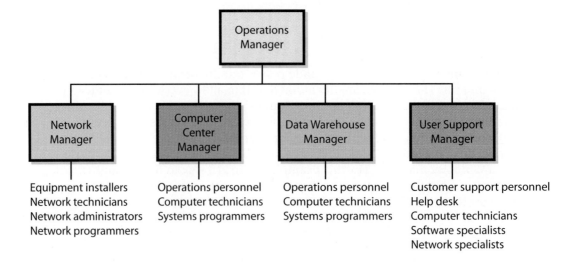

Figure 11-7
Organization of a
Typical IS Operations
Group

Typical job types are shown beneath each subgroup. As you can imagine, each of these specialists needs recurring training. The operations staff must constantly update its knowledge to keep up with upgrades in both hardware and software products. Consider the need for training, coupled with the need for 24/7 operations, coupled with the problems that can occur when a change is first made to, say, the network. Scheduling employees in such an environment is a complex task and a constant problem.

Q4 What Tasks Are Necessary for Managing Enterprise Applications?

In addition to managing the computing infrastructure, the IS department manages enterprise applications as well. The definition of what constitutes an enterprise application varies among organizations. In some organizations, the IS department manages every application, including individual and workgroup applications. In others, individuals and workgroups manage their own applications, with support from the IS department. In the latter case, the term **enterprise applications** is interpreted to mean some functional applications and all cross-functional applications, including CRM, ERP, and SOA-based interorganizational systems.

Develop New Applications

Figure 11-8 lists major application management functions. As shown, the IS department manages the development of new applications. The process of creating a new application begins when the IS department aligns its priorities with the organization's strategy. Using priorities that arise from that alignment, the IS department develops system plans and proposals and submits them to the steering committee (and possibly other executive groups) for approval. Once the company has selected and approved a system for development, it then initiates a development process, as described in Chapter 10.

Maintain (Legacy) Systems

In addition to managing the development of new applications, the IS department has the responsibility for system maintenance. As stated in Chapter 10, *maintenance* means either to fix the system to do what it was supposed to do in the first place or to adapt the system to changed requirements. Either way, the IS department prioritizes maintenance work and implements changes in accordance with those priorities and budget. It might do the maintenance work in-house or outsource it.

Companies need special maintenance activities to support legacy systems. A **legacy information system** is one that has outdated technologies and techniques but is still used, despite its age. Legacy systems arise because organizations cannot afford to replace an IS just because better technology has been developed.

- Manage development of new applications.
- Maintain legacy systems.
- Adapt systems to changing requirements.
- Track user problems and monitor fixes.
- Integrate applications.
- Manage development staff.

Figure 11-8
Managing (Legacy) Enterprise Applications

Usually, legacy system maintenance entails adapting those systems to new tax laws, accounting procedures, or other requirements that must be implemented for the legacy system to be relevant and useful. Although the plan is always to replace legacy systems eventually, the goal is to keep them working until they are replaced.

Developing information systems is a service that is provided to the rest of the enterprise. Accordingly, the IS department must have a means to track user issues and problems, prioritize them, and record their resolution. Although such a tracking and monitoring system is similar to the same function provided for infrastructure management, the department usually uses different systems for these two functions. In fact, for larger organizations each major enterprise application has its own problem-tracking and resolution system. For example, ERP might have one system, e-commerce Web applications a second, and human resources a third.

Integrate Enterprise Applications

The third element in Figure 11-8 concerns enterprise application integration. Some companies develop special-purpose IS, known as **Enterprise Application Integration (EAI)**, that include intermediary layers of software, and possibly intermediary databases, to enable the integration of disparate systems. Because such work requires knowledge of many different systems, including legacy systems, companies usually conduct such work in-house rather than outsource it.

Manage Development Staff

The last management function in Figure 11-8 is to manage the development staff. Figure 11-9 shows the structure of a typical development group. Of course, this structure will be simpler for smaller organizations or for organizations that do little in-house development. In most cases, a computer programmer or developer works both as a software designer as well as a programmer.

Sustaining-application developers work on existing applications. Typically, sustaining developers have fewer years of experience or less knowledge than new-application developers. Figure 11-9 shows sustaining developers and new-application developers as belonging to separate development teams. This arrangement varies considerably depending on the complexity of both sustaining and new development projects.

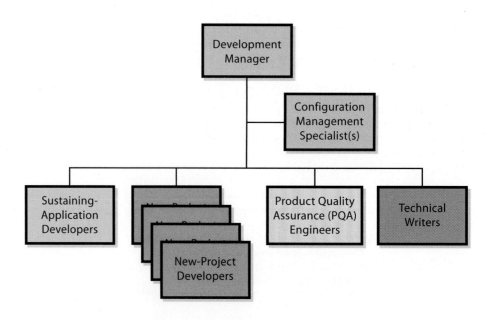

Figure 11-9
Organization of a Typical
IS Development Group

Product quality assurance (PQA) engineers specialize in the testing of software. In many cases, PQA engineers also are programmers who develop automated testing suites. Because applications must be thoroughly tested when they are modified, test automation is a great boon to productivity.

The final group in Figure 11-9 is *technical writers* who develop product installation instructions, help text, and other support documentation.

Administer Data

Data and database administration functions sound similar, but actually are quite different. Typically, the term **data administration** describes a function that pertains to *all* of an organization's data assets. The term **database administration** describes a function that pertains to a *particular* database. A typical larger organization would have one data administrator and several database administrators—say, one for the ERP database, one for the e-commerce database, one for HR database, and possibly others as well.

The terminology *data administrator* and *database administrator* implies that there is a single person for each role. Normally, each data or database administrator has a staff of several employees. The manager of the group is called the *data administrator* or *database administrator*, and the staff members work in the office of data administration or database administration.

We discussed database administration in Chapter 5. Here we will address the organization-wide function of data administration and the four primary responsibilities shown in Figure 11-10.

Define Data Standards

Data standards are definitions, or metadata, for data items shared across the organization. They describe the name, official definition, usage, relationship to other data items, processing restrictions, version, security restrictions, format, and other features of data items that are shared across the organization. Sometimes data standards include the *data owner*, which is a department within the organization that is most concerned with that data item and that controls changes to the definition of that data item.

On the surface, setting data standards may seem like an unnecessary clerical operation. It is not. In fact, the lack of documented and known data standards causes considerable duplication of effort, data inconsistency, wasted labor, and processing errors.

To understand why, consider a data item as simple as *sku_description. SKU* stands for stock-keeping unit, and *sku_description* is a data item for holding the description of each part. But what is it? Without a data standard, one application might include component parts in the description, whereas another might place the component parts in a different data item. Without a standard definition, two different applications will refer to the same item with different names. For example, is a *sku_description* the same as *sku_item_desc?* Assume you are a sustaining developer and you encounter a data item named *sku_desc_2005*. How does that data item relate to the data item *current_sku_description?* Without a data standard, developers will waste considerable time trying to reconcile these differences.

Enterprise-wide function to:
• Define data standards.
• Maintain data dictionary.
• Define data policies.
• Establish disaster-recovery plan.

Figure 11-10
Data Administration
Responsibilities

Maintain the Data Dictionary

To resolve problems like those for the SKU descriptions, almost every organization maintains a data dictionary. A **data dictionary** is a file or database that contains data definitions. It contains an entry for each standard data item. Typically, the entries include the item's name, a description, the standard data format, remarks, and possibly examples, as shown in Figure 11-11.

As noted many times before, information systems evolve as business requirements change. The data administrator must maintain the data dictionary to keep it current. Obsolete entries must be removed, new items inserted, and changes recorded. Without maintenance, the data dictionary, an essential tool, loses its value. Notice, for example, the two versions of *sku_description* in Figure 11-11: How does *sku_description* relate to *current_sku_description*? They appear identical. Should one of them be removed? What if one of them was slightly different from the other? From this example you can see the need for management of the data dictionary.

Define Data Policies

Data administration also is concerned with the creation and dissemination of data policies. Such policies vary in scope. Examples of broad policies are:

- "We will not share identifying customer data with another organization."
- "We will not share nonidentifying customer data with another organization without the approval of the legal department."
- "Employee data are never to be released to anyone other than the employee without the approval of the human resources department."

Narrower data policies pertain to particular data items. An example is: "We will maintain data about past employees for at least 7 years after their last day of work."

Of course, the data administrator does not create the data policies on his own, out of the blue. Instead, the data administrator works with senior executives, the legal department, functional department managers, and others to determine them. Once the company has created data policies, the data administrator then communicates them to appropriate departments and employees. Data policies also are dynamic; they need to be changed as new corporate policies and new systems are developed and as new laws are created.

Plan for Disaster Recovery

Disaster-recovery planning is the creation of systems for recovering data and systems in the event of a catastrophe such as an earthquake, flood, terrorist event, or other

Figure 11-11
Example of Data
Dictionary Fields

Data Item Name	Data Item Description	Standard Data Format	Remarks	Example
sku_description	A description of a stock-keeping unit.	Character; length 1,000	Does not include component parts.	3/16-inch flathead screw, 20 tpi, stainless steel
sku_desc_2005	A description of a stock-keeping unit prior to the parts reorganization in August 2005.	Character; length 500	No longer used. All descriptions should have been converted to the current_sku_description.	
current_sku_description	A description of a stock-keeping unit after the parts reorganization in August 2005.	Character; length 1,000	Does not include component parts.	3/16-inch flathead screw, 20 tpi, stainless steel

Note: Other fields are common. Some data dictionaries record the data owner, aliases for the data item, security requirements, and additional data.

significant processing disruption. We will address this function further in the next chapter when we discuss computer security.

As you can tell from the preceding discussion, managing information systems is a broad and complicated task. Some organizations choose to outsource one or more IS functions. We will consider that alternative in the next section.

Q5 What Are the Advantages and Disadvantages of Outsourcing?

Outsourcing is the process of hiring another organization to perform a service. Outsourcing is done to save costs, to gain expertise, and to free management time.

The father of modern management, Peter Drucker, is reputed to have said, "Your back room is someone else's front room." For instance, in most companies, running the cafeteria is not an essential function for business success; thus, the employee cafeteria is a "back room." Google wants to be the worldwide leader in search and Web 2.0 applications, all supported by ever-increasing ad revenue. It does not want to be known for how well it runs cafeterias. Using Drucker's sentiment, Google is better off hiring another company, one that specializes in food services, to run its cafeterias.

Because food service is some company's "front room," that company will be better able to provide a quality product at a fair price. Hiring that company will also free Google's management from attention on the cafeteria. Food quality, chef scheduling, plastic fork acquisition, waste disposal, and so on, will all be another company's concern. Google can focus on search, Web 2.0, and advertising-revenue growth.

Outsourcing Information Systems

Many companies today have chosen to outsource portions of their information systems activities. Figure 11-12 lists popular reasons for doing so. Consider each major group of reasons.

Management Advantages

First, outsourcing can be an easy way to gain expertise. Suppose, for example, that an organization wants to upgrade its thousands of user computers on a cost-effective basis. To do so, the organization would need to develop expertise in automated software installation, unattended installations, remote support, and other measures that can be used to improve the efficiency of software management. Developing such expertise is expensive, and it is not in the company's strategic direction. Efficient installation of software to thousands of computers is not in the "front room." Consequently, the organization might choose to hire a specialist company to perform this service.

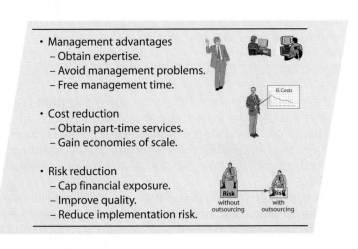

Figure 11-12
Popular Reasons for Outsourcing IS Services

Another reason for outsourcing is to avoid management problems. Suppose Carbon Creek Gardens (Chapter 9 Collaboration Exercise, page 354) decides to share its inventory with its suppliers using SOA services. How will Mary Keeling hire the appropriate staff? She doesn't know if she needs a C++ programmer or an HTML programmer. Even if she could find and hire the right staff, how would she manage them? How would she create a good work environment for a C++ programmer, when she does not know what such a person does? To avoid such management problems, Carbon Creek would hire an outside firm to develop and maintain the Web service.

Similarly, some companies choose to outsource to save management time and attention. Suppose FlexTime decides to sell DVDs, clothing, and books over the Web. Assume Neil is comfortable managing the development of such an application, but he doesn't have time to do so. In this case, outsourcing the e-commerce system will save Neil and others he might hire from development tasks like acquiring the appropriate computers, installing the necessary software, tuning the software for better performance, and possible hiring and managing support staff.

Note, too, that the management time required is not just that of the direct manager of the activity. It is also time from more senior managers who approve the purchase and hiring requisitions for that activity. And, those senior managers, like Neil's partner Kelly, will need to devote the time necessary to understand enough about Web farms to approve or reject the requisitions. Outsourcing saves both direct and indirect management time.

Cost Reduction

Other common reasons for choosing to outsource concern cost reductions. With outsourcing, organizations can obtain part-time services. As Sue says, MRV does not need nor can it afford a full-time network administrator. It does need network administration, but only in small amounts. By outsourcing that function, MRV could obtain network administration in the small amounts needed.

Another benefit of outsourcing is to gain economies of scale. If 25 organizations develop their own payroll applications in-house, then when the tax law changes 25 different groups will have to learn the new law, change their software to meet the law, test the changes, and write the documentation explaining the changes. However, if those same 25 organizations outsource to the same payroll vendor, then that vendor can make all of the adjustments once, and the cost of the change can be amortized over all of them (thus lowering the cost that the vendor must charge).

Risk Reduction

Another reason for outsourcing is to reduce risk. First, outsourcing can cap financial risk. In a typical outsourcing contract, the outsource vendor will agree to provide, say, computer workstations with certain software connected via a particular network. Typically, each new workstation will have a fixed cost, say, $2,500 per station. The company's management team might believe that there is a good chance that they can provide workstations at a lower unit cost, but there is also the chance that they will get in over their heads and have a disaster. If so, the cost per computer could be much higher than $2,500. Outsourcing caps that financial risk and leads to greater budgetary stability.

Second, outsourcing can reduce risk by ensuring a certain level of quality, or avoiding the risk of having substandard quality. A company that specializes in food service knows what to do to provide a certain level of quality. It has the expertise to ensure, for example, that only healthy food is served. So, too, a company that specializes in, say, Web-server hosting, knows what to do to provide a certain level of service for a given workload.

Note that there is no guarantee that outsourcing will provide a certain level of quality or quality better than could be achieved in-house. Google might get lucky and hire only great chefs. The TV station might get lucky and hire the world's best Web farm manager. But, in general, a professional outsourcing firm knows how to avoid giving everyone food poisoning or having 2 days of downtime on the Web servers. And, if that minimum level of quality is not provided, it is easier to hire another vendor than it is to fire and rehire internal staff.

Finally, organizations choose to outsource IS in order to reduce implementation risk. Hiring an outside vendor reduces the risk of picking the wrong hardware or the wrong software, using the wrong network protocol, or implementing tax law changes incorrectly. Outsourcing gathers all of these risks into the risk of choosing the right vendor. Once the company has chosen the vendor, further risk management is up to that vendor.

International Outsourcing

Many firms headquartered in the United States have chosen to outsource overseas. Microsoft and Dell, for example, have outsourced major portions of their customer support activities to companies outside the United States. India is a popular source because it has a large, well-educated, English-speaking population that will work for 20 to 30 percent of the labor cost in the United States. China and other countries are used as well. In fact, with modern telephone technology and Internet-enabled service databases, a single service call can be initiated in the United States, partially processed in India, then Singapore, and finalized by an employee in England. The customer knows only that he has been put on hold for brief periods of time.

International outsourcing is particularly advantageous for customer support and other functions that must be operational 24/7. Amazon.com, for example, operates customer service centers in the United States, India, and Ireland. During the evening hours in the United States, customer service reps in India, where it is daytime, handle the calls. When night falls in India, customer service reps in Ireland handle the early morning calls from the east coast of the United States. In this way, companies can provide 24/7 service without requiring employees to work night shifts.

International IS/IT outsourcing is not without controversy, however. It is one thing to shift a job of making a tennis shoe to Singapore, or even to hire customer support representatives in India. But there was consternation and wringing of hands when IBM stated that it was shifting nearly 5,000 computer-programming jobs to India. Some perceive the moving of such high-tech, high-skill jobs overseas as a threat to U.S. technology leadership. Others say it is just economic factors guiding jobs to places where they are most efficiently performed.

By the way, as you learned in Chapter 1, the key protection for your job is to become someone who excels at nonroutine symbolic analysis. Someone with the ability to find innovative applications of new technology also is unlikely to lose his or her job to overseas workers.

What Are the Outsourcing Alternatives?

Organizations have found hundreds of different ways to outsource information systems and portions of information systems. Figure 11-13 organizes the major categories of alternatives according to information systems components.

Some organizations outsource the acquisition and operation of computer hardware. Electronic Data Systems (EDS) has been successful for more than 20 years as an outsource vendor of hardware infrastructure. Figure 11-13 shows another alternative, outsourcing the computers in a Web farm.

Acquiring licensed software, as discussed in Chapters 4 and 10, is a form of outsourcing. Rather than develop the software in-house, an organization licenses it from another vendor. Such licensing allows the software vendor to amortize the cost of software maintenance over all of the users, thus reducing that cost for all users.

Another outsourcing alternative is to outsource an entire system. PeopleSoft (now owned by Oracle) attained prominence by providing the entire payroll function as an

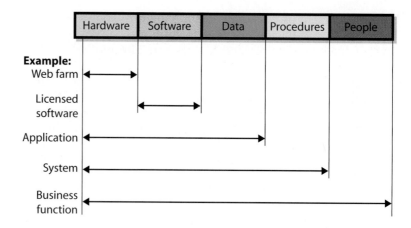

Figure 11-13
IS/IT Outsourcing
Alternatives

outsourced service. In such a solution, as the arrow in Figure 11-13 implies, the vendor provides hardware, software, data, and some procedures. The company need provide only employee and work information; the payroll outsource vendor does the rest.

A Web storefront is another form of application outsourcing. Amazon.com, for example, provides a Web storefront for product vendors and distributors who choose not to develop their own Web presence. In this case, rather than pay a fixed fee for the storefront service, the product vendors and distributors pay Amazon.com a portion of the revenue generated. Such Web-service hosting has become a major profit center for Amazon.com.

Finally, some organizations choose to outsource an entire business function. For years, many companies have outsourced to travel agencies the function of arranging for employee travel. Some of these outsource vendors even operate offices within the company facilities. More recently, companies have been outsourcing even larger and more important functions. In 2005, for example, Marriott International chose Hewitt Associates to handle its human resources needs for the next 7 years. (See Case Study 11, page 440.) Such agreements are much broader than outsourcing IS, but information systems are key components of the applications that are outsourced.

What Are the Risks of Outsourcing?

Not everyone agrees on the desirability of outsourcing. For potential pitfalls, read the example in the Guide on pages 434–435.

With so many advantages and with so many different outsourcing alternatives, you might wonder why any company has any in-house IS/IT functions. In fact, outsourcing presents significant risks, as listed in Figure 11-14.

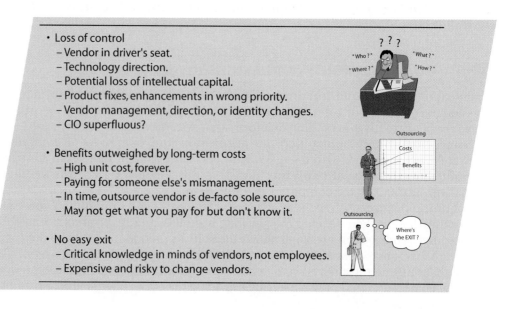

Figure 11-14
Outsourcing Risks

Loss of Control

The first risk of outsourcing is a loss of control. Outsourcing puts the vendor in the driver's seat. Each outsource vendor has methods and procedures for its service. The organization and its employees will have to conform to those procedures. For example, a hardware infrastructure vendor will have standard forms and procedures for requesting a computer, for recording and processing a computer problem, or for providing routine maintenance on computers. Once the vendor is in charge, employees must conform.

When outsourcing the cafeteria, employees have only those food choices that the vendor provides. Similarly, when obtaining computer hardware and services, the employees will need to take what the vendor supports. Employees who want equipment that is not on the vendor's list will be out of luck.

The outsource vendor chooses the technology that it wants to implement. If the vendor, for some reason, is slow to pick up on a significant new technology, then the hiring organization will be slow to attain benefits from that technology. An organization can find itself at a competitive disadvantage because it cannot offer the same IS services as its competitors.

Another concern is a potential loss of intellectual capital. The company may need to reveal proprietary trade secrets, methods, or procedures to the outsource vendor's employees. As part of its normal operations, that vendor may move employees to competing organizations, and the company may lose intellectual capital as that happens. The loss need not be intellectual theft; it could simply be that the vendor's employees learned to work in a new and better way at your company, and then they take that learning to your competitor.

Similarly, all software has failures and problems. Quality vendors track those failures and problems and fix them according to a set of priorities. When a company outsources a system, it no longer has control over prioritizing those fixes. Such control belongs to the vendor. A fix that might be critical to your organization might be of low priority to the outsource vendor.

Other problems are that the outsource vendor may change management, adopt a different strategic direction, or be acquired. When any of those changes occur, priorities may change, and an outsource vendor that was a good choice at one time might be a bad fit after it changes direction. It can be difficult and expensive to change an outsource vendor when this occurs.

The final loss-of-control risk is that the company's CIO can become superfluous. When users need a critical service that is outsourced, the CIO must turn to the vendor for a response. In time, users learn that it is quicker to deal directly with the outsource vendor, and soon the CIO is out of the communication loop. At that point, the vendor has essentially replaced the CIO, who has become a figurehead. However, employees of the outsource vendor work for a different company, with a bias toward their employer. Critical managers will thus not share the same goals and objectives as the rest of the management team. Biased, bad decisions can result.

Benefits Outweighed by Long-Term Costs

The initial benefits of outsourcing can appear huge. A cap on financial exposure, a reduction of management time and attention, and the release of many management and staffing problems are all possible. (Most likely, outsource vendors promise these very benefits.) Outsourcing can appear too good to be true.

In fact, it *can be* too good to be true. For one, although a fixed cost does indeed cap exposure, it also removes the benefits of economies of scale. If the Web storefront takes off, and suddenly the organization needs 200 servers instead of 20, the using organization will pay 200 times the fixed cost of supporting one server. It is likely, however, that because of economies of scale, the costs of supporting 200 servers are far less than 10 times the costs of supporting 20 servers.

Also, the outsource vendor may change its pricing strategy over time. Initially, an organization obtains a competitive bid from several outsource vendors. However, as the winning vendor learns more about the business and as relationships develop between the organization's employees and those of the vendor, it becomes difficult for other firms to compete for subsequent contracts. The vendor becomes the *de facto* sole source and, with little competitive pressure, might increase its prices.

Another problem is that an organization can find itself paying for another organization's mismanagement, with little knowledge that that is the case. If FlexTime outsources the e-commerce site, it is difficult for it to know if the e-commerce vendor is well managed. FlexTime may be paying for poor management; even worse, it may suffer the consequences of poor management, such as lost data. It will be very difficult for FlexTime to learn about such mismanagement.

No Easy Exit

The final category of outsourcing risk concerns ending the agreement. There is no easy exit. For one, the outsource vendor's employees have gained significant knowledge of the company. They know the server requirements in customer support, they know the patterns of usage, and they know the best procedures for downloading operational data into the data warehouse. Consequently, lack of knowledge will make it difficult to bring the outsourced service back in-house.

Also, because the vendor has become so tightly integrated into the business, parting company can be exceedingly risky. Closing down the employee cafeteria for a few weeks while finding another food vendor would be unpopular, but employees would survive. Shutting down the enterprise network for a few weeks would be impossible; the business would not survive. Because of such risk, the company must invest considerable work, duplication of effort, management time, and expense to change to another vendor. In truth, choosing an outsource vendor can be a one-way street.

It may not always be clear whether a company should outsource. The Guide on pages 436–437 considers different scenarios.

Choosing to outsource is a difficult decision. In fact, the correct decision might not be clear, but time and events could force the company to decide.

video

Q6 What Are Your User Rights and Responsibilities?

As a future user of information systems, you have both rights and responsibilities in your relationship with the IS department. The items in Figure 11-15 list what you are entitled to receive and indicate what you are expected to contribute.

Your User Rights

You have a right to have the computing resources you need to perform your work as proficiently as you want. You have a right to the computer hardware and programs that you need. If you process huge files for data-mining applications, you have a right to the huge disks and the fast processor that you need. However, if you merely receive email and consult the corporate Web portal, then your right is for more modest requirements (leaving the more powerful resources for those in the organization who need them).

You have a right to reliable network and Internet services. *Reliable* means that you can process without problems almost all of the time. It means that you never go to work wondering, "Will the network be available today?" Network problems should be a rare occurrence.

You also have a right to a secure computing environment. The organization should protect your computer and its files, and you should not normally even need to think about security. From time to time, the organization might ask you to take particular actions to protect your computer and files, and you should take those actions. But such requests should be rare and related to specific outside threats.

You have a right to:
- Computer hardware and programs that allow you to perform your job proficiently
- Reliable network and Internet connections
- A secure computing environment
- Protection from viruses, worms, and other threats
- Contribute to requirements for new system features and functions
- Reliable systems development and maintenance
- Prompt attention to problems, concerns, and complaints
- Properly prioritized problem fixes and resolutions
- Effective training

You have a responsibility to:
- Learn basic computer skills
- Learn standard techniques and procedures for the applications you use
- Follow security and backup procedures
- Protect your password(s)
- Use computer resources according to your employer's computer use policy
- Make no unauthorized hardware modifications
- Install only authorized programs
- Apply software patches and fixes when directed to do so
- When asked, devote the time required to respond carefully and completely to requests for requirements for new system features and functions
- Avoid reporting trivial problems

Figure 11-15
User Information Systems Rights and Responsibilities

You have a right to participate in requirements meetings for new applications that you will use and for major changes to applications that you currently use. You may choose to delegate this right to others, or your department may delegate that right for you, but if so, you have a right to contribute your thoughts through that delegate.

You have a right to reliable systems development and maintenance. Although schedule slippages of a month or two are common in many development projects, you should not have to endure schedule slippages of 6 months or more. Such slippages are evidence of incompetent systems development.

Additionally, you have a right to receive prompt attention to your problems, concerns, and complaints about information services. You have a right to have a means to report problems, and you have a right to know that your problem has been received and at least registered with the IS department. You have a right to have your problem resolved, consistent with established priorities. This means that an annoying problem that allows you to conduct your work will be prioritized below another's problem that interferes with his ability to do his job.

Finally, you have a right to effective training. It should be training that you can understand and that enables you to use systems to perform your particular job. The organization should provide training in a format and on a schedule that is convenient to you.

Your User Responsibilities

You also have responsibilities toward the IS department and your organization. Specifically, you have a responsibility to learn basic computer skills and to learn the basic techniques and procedures for the applications you use. You should not expect hand-holding for basic operations. Nor should you expect to receive repetitive training and support for the same issue.

You have a responsibility to follow security and backup procedures. This is especially important because actions that you fail to take might cause problems for your fellow employees and your organization as well as for you. In particular, you are responsible for protecting your password(s). In the next chapter, you will learn that this is important not only to protect your computer, but, because of intersystem authentication, it is important to protect your organization's networks and databases as well.

You have a responsibility for using your computer resources in a manner that is consistent with your employer's policy. Many employers allow limited email for critical family matters while at work, but discourage frequent and long casual email. You have a responsibility to know your employer's policy and to follow it.

You also have a responsibility to make no unauthorized hardware modifications to your computer and to install only authorized programs. As described earlier in this chapter, one reason for this policy is that your IS department constructs automated maintenance programs for upgrading your computer. Unauthorized hardware and programs might interfere with these programs. Additionally, the installation of unauthorized hardware or programs can cause you problems that the IS department will have to fix.

You have a responsibility to install computer patches and fixes when asked to do so. This is particularly important for patches that concern security and backup and recovery. When asked for input to requirements for new and adapted systems, you have a responsibility to take the time necessary to provide thoughtful and complete responses. If you do not have that time, you should delegate your input to someone else.

Finally, you have a responsibility to treat information systems professionals professionally. Everyone works for the same company, everyone wants to succeed, and professionalism and courtesy will go a long way on all sides. One form of professional behavior is to learn basic computer skills so that you avoid reporting trivial problems.

Q7 2020?

Two computing movements are likely to increase in size and importance in the next 10 years: cloud computing and green computing.

Cloud Computing

Cloud computing is a form of hardware/software outsourcing in which organizations offer flexible plans for customers to lease hardware and software facilities. Furthermore, the amount of resource leased can increase and decrease dramatically, and customers need to pay only for resources used. Major companies that offer cloud computing products include Amazon.com, Oracle, and Microsoft.

Pearson Education, the publisher of this text, is a primary candidate to use cloud computing for hosting its online student products. Demand for Pearson products varies widely, because some students wait until the end of the term, in December and May, to do the bulk of their coursework. (Imagine that!) Hence, Pearson experiences large demand peaks in those months. With cloud computing, Pearson can negotiate a contract with a vendor like Amazon.com to provide just the computing resources that it needs, when it needs them. Pearson will use much more computing resource in December and May than in other months. Without this option, Pearson must build Web farms to support its largest peak workload, which means that 10 months of the year a good portion of its Web farm will be idle.

Cloud computing allows multiple organizations to utilize the same computing infrastructure. Accounting firms can use the same Amazon.com computers in April that Pearson uses in December and May. Cloud computing is thus a form of CPU-cycle inventory consolidation.

Cloud computing is feasible because cloud vendors harness the power of virtualization. **Virtualization** is the process whereby multiple operating systems share the same computer hardware, usually a server. Thus, with virtualization one server can support, say, two instances of Windows Server, one instance of Linux, and three instances of Windows 7. Because these instances are isolated from each other, it will appear to each company that it has full and exclusive control over the server computer. Hence the term *virtual computer.*

Because of virtualization, it is quite easy for cloud vendors to reconfigure their servers to support changes in workload. If Pearson needs another 100 servers in December, Amazon.com need only add 100 instances of Pearson's server environment to its virtual computers. If, 2 days later, Pearson needs another 100 instances, Amazon.com would allocate another 100. (Keep in mind, this example is only academic. To my knowledge there is no such contract in place.) Behind the scenes, Amazon.com is likely moving these instances around, balancing its workload on the actual computers that run the virtual operating systems. None of that activity is visible to Pearson or to the students using Pearson's sites.

Pearson is a publisher of innovative educational materials. Running a Web farm is not in its "front room." Outsourcing the Web farm, especially one that can be flexibly configured, makes great economic sense, and we can expect that Pearson and similar companies will be running in the cloud by 2020.

Green Computing

Green computing is environmentally conscious computing consisting of three major components: power management, virtualization, and e-waste management. You know, of course, that computers (and related equipment such as printers) use electricity. They also generate heat, which requires air conditioning, which uses more electricity as well as water. Hence, computer use places a burden on electrical resources and the environment.

That burden is light for any single computer or printer. But consider all of the computers and printers in the United States that will be running tonight, with no one in the office. In many organizations, computers, printers, copiers, and other machines run as many hours when the office is vacant as they do when employees are present. Proponents of green computing encourage companies and employees to reduce power and water consumption by turning off devices when not in use. They also encourage employees to consider power consumption when selecting a computer, and to use less energy-hungry devices like laptops rather than desktops.

The green computing movement encourages virtualization because it dramatically reduces server idle time. For example, if Pearson uses computers in the cloud, then any computer that it does not fully utilize is available, via virtualization, to be used by another organization as well. Rather than having two servers at two companies with, say, 30 percent utilization each, virtualization supports the workload with one computer, running at 60 percent utilization. Hence, virtualization reduces power and air conditioning requirements. By the way, companies can practice virtualization without using cloud computing. A company with three different Web servers, supporting three different uses, can use virtualization to support those three uses on a single computer.

Finally, green computing is concerned with **e-trash**, or computers and related devices that are no longer in use. Computers, monitors, printers, and other computing devices contain lead, mercury, cobalt, and other toxic substances. The green computer movement seeks to reduce the creation of such materials by changing the design of computers and related products to remove or limit them. It is also concerned with the recycling of these substances as well as with their proper disposal.

Green computing is new, but it is likely to become a considerable movement by 2020.

Is Outsourcing Fool's Gold?

"People are kidding themselves. It sounds so good—just pay a fixed, known amount to some vendor, and all your problems go away. Everyone has the computers they need, the network never goes down, and you never have to endure another horrible meeting about network protocols, HTTPs, and the latest worm. You're off into information systems nirvana. . . .

"Except it doesn't work that way. You trade one set of problems for another. Consider the outsourcing of computer infrastructure. What's the first thing the outsource vendor does? It hires all of the employees who were doing the work for you. Remember that lazy, incompetent network administrator that the company had—the one who never seemed to get anything done? Well, he's baaaaak, as an employee of your outsource company. Only this time he has an excuse, 'Company policy won't allow me to do it that way.'

"So the outsourcers get their first-level employees by hiring the ones you had. Of course, the outsourcer says it will provide management oversight, and if the employees don't work out, they'll be gone. What you're really outsourcing is middle-level management of the same IT personnel you had. But there's no way of knowing whether the managers they supply are any better than the ones you had.

"Also, you think you had bureaucratic problems before? Every vendor has a set of forms, procedures, committees, reports, and other management 'tools.' They will tell you that you have to do things according to the standard blueprint. They have to say that because if they allowed every company to be different, they'd never be able to gain any leverage themselves, and they'd never be profitable.

"So now you're paying a premium for the services of your former employees, who are now managed by strangers who are paid by the outsource vendor, who evaluates those managers on how well they follow the outsource vendor's profit-generating procedures. How quickly can they turn your operation into a clone of all their other clients? Do you really want to do that?

"Suppose you figure all this out and decide to get out of it. Now what? How do you undo an outsource agreement? All the critical knowledge is in the minds of the outsource vendor's employees, who have no incentive to work for you. In fact, their employment contract probably prohibits it. So now you have to take an existing operation within your own company, hire employees to staff that function, and relearn everything you ought to have learned in the first place.

"Gimme a break. Outsourcing is fool's gold, an expensive leap away from responsibility. It's like saying, 'We can't figure out how to manage an important function in our company, so you do it!' You can't get away from IS problems by hiring someone else to manage them for you. At least you care about *your* bottom line." ∎

Discussion Questions

1. Hiring an organization's existing IS staff is common practice when starting a new outsourcing arrangement. What are the advantages of this practice to the outsource vendor? What are the advantages to the organization?

2. Suppose you work for an outsource vendor. How do you respond to the charge that your managers care only about how they appear to their employer (the outsource vendor), not how they actually perform for the organization?

3. Consider the statement, "We can't figure out how to manage an important function in our company, so you do it!" Do you agree with the sentiment of this statement? If this is true, is it necessarily bad? Why or why not?

4. Explain how it is possible for an outsource vendor to achieve economies of scale that are not possible for the hiring organization. Does this phenomenon justify outsourcing? Why or why not?

5. In what ways is outsourcing IS infrastructure like outsourcing the company cafeteria? In what ways is it different? What general conclusions can you make about infrastructure outsourcing?

What If You Just Don't Know?

What if you have to make a decision and you just don't know which way to go? For complex issues like outsourcing, it can be difficult to know what the right decision is. In many cases, more analysis won't necessarily reduce the uncertainty.

Consider outsourcing as a typical, complex, real-life decision problem. The question is, will outsourcing save your organization money? Will the cap on financial exposure be worth the loss of control? Or, is your organization avoiding managing the IS function because you would just like to have the whole IS mess out of your hair?

Suppose the CIO is adamantly opposed to the outsourcing of computer infrastructure. Why is that? He is obviously biased, because such outsourcing will mean a huge cut in his department and a big loss of control for him. It might even mean he loses his job. But is that all there is to it? Or does he have a point? Are the projected savings real? Or are they the result of a paper analysis that misses many of the intangibles? For that matter, does that analysis miss some of the tangibles?

You could do another study; you could commission an independent consultant to examine this situation and make a recommendation. However, is that avoiding the issue, yet again? Further, what if there is no time? The network is down for 2 days for the third time this quarter, and you've got to act. You've got to do something. But what? Take it to the board of directors? No, they don't know. That's just another way of avoiding a tough decision. You've got to decide.

In some ways, higher education does you a disservice. In school, you're taught that a bit more study, another report, or a little more analysis will help you find a better answer. But many decisions don't work that way. There might not be the time or money for another study or another study might just cloud the issue more. Or maybe it's just not possible to know. What will be the price of Google stock on January 1, 2015? You just don't know. ■

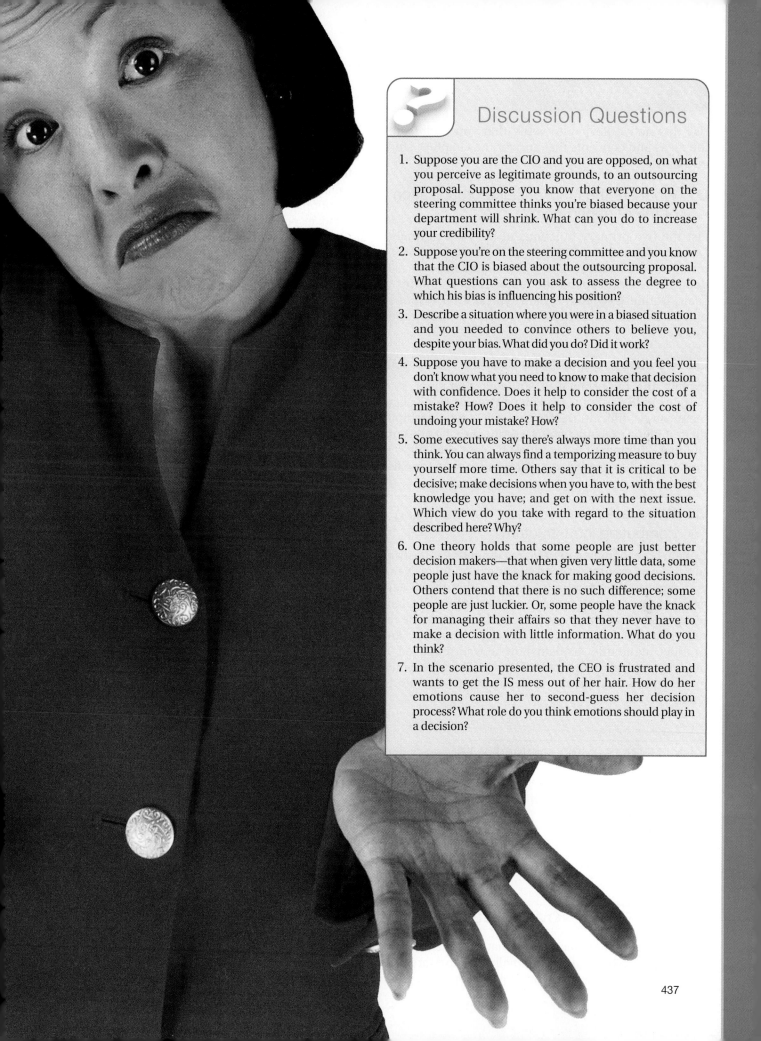

1. Suppose you are the CIO and you are opposed, on what you perceive as legitimate grounds, to an outsourcing proposal. Suppose you know that everyone on the steering committee thinks you're biased because your department will shrink. What can you do to increase your credibility?

2. Suppose you're on the steering committee and you know that the CIO is biased about the outsourcing proposal. What questions can you ask to assess the degree to which his bias is influencing his position?

3. Describe a situation where you were in a biased situation and you needed to convince others to believe you, despite your bias. What did you do? Did it work?

4. Suppose you have to make a decision and you feel you don't know what you need to know to make that decision with confidence. Does it help to consider the cost of a mistake? How? Does it help to consider the cost of undoing your mistake? How?

5. Some executives say there's always more time than you think. You can always find a temporizing measure to buy yourself more time. Others say that it is critical to be decisive; make decisions when you have to, with the best knowledge you have; and get on with the next issue. Which view do you take with regard to the situation described here? Why?

6. One theory holds that some people are just better decision makers—that when given very little data, some people just have the knack for making good decisions. Others contend that there is no such difference; some people are just luckier. Or, some people have the knack for managing their affairs so that they never have to make a decision with little information. What do you think?

7. In the scenario presented, the CEO is frustrated and wants to get the IS mess out of her hair. How do her emotions cause her to second-guess her decision process? What role do you think emotions should play in a decision?

ACTIVE REVIEW

Use this Active Review to verify that you understand the ideas and concepts that answer the chapter's study questions.

Q1 What are the functions and organization of the IS department?

List the five primary functions of the IS department. Define *CIO* and explain the CIO's typical reporting relationships. Name the four groups found in a typical IS department and explain the major responsibilities of each. Define *CTO* and explain typical CTO responsibilities. Explain the purpose of the data administration function.

Q2 How do organizations plan the use of IS?

Explain the importance of strategic alignment as it pertains to IS planning. Explain why maintaining alignment can be difficult. Describe the CIO's relationship to the rest of the executive staff. Describe the CIO's responsibilities with regard to priorities. Explain challenges to this task. Define *steering committee* and explain the CIO's role with regard to it.

Q3 What tasks are necessary for managing computing infrastructure?

Explain how alignment pertains to computing infrastructure. Give an example of good and poor alignment. Name and explain three resource categories that the IS department must create, operate, and maintain. Explain, using examples, why these tasks are huge. Describe the rationale and importance of setting technology and product standards. Explain how a well-managed IS department deals with problem reports. Describe typical job categories within the IS department's operations staff.

Q4 What tasks are necessary for managing enterprise applications?

Define *enterprise application*. Using Figure 11-7 as a guide, summarize the tasks required for managing enterprise applications. Define *legacy information system*. Describe the work responsibilities for each of the types of employee in Figure 11-8. Explain the difference between database administration and data administration. Define *data dictionary* and explain its role and importance. Give an example of a data policy. Explain the term *disaster-recovery planning*.

Q5 What are the advantages and disadvantages of outsourcing?

Define *outsourcing*. Explain how Drucker's statement, "Your back room is someone else's front room" pertains to outsourcing. Summarize the management advantages, cost advantages, and risks of outsourcing. Explain why international outsourcing can be particularly advantageous. Describe skills you can develop that will protect you from having your job outsourced. Summarize the outsourcing risks concerning control, long-term costs, and exit strategy.

Q6 What are your user rights and responsibilities?

Explain in your own words the meaning of each of your user rights as listed in Figure 11-14. Explain in your own words the meaning of each of your user responsibilities in Figure 11-14.

Q7 2020?

Define *cloud computing* and explain its benefits. Describe how cloud computing uses virtualization. Name three major elements of green computing. Explain how virtualization pertains to green computing.

KEY TERMS AND CONCEPTS

Chief information officer (CIO)   411
Chief technology officer (CTO)   411
Cloud computing   432
Data administration   423
Data dictionary   424
Data standards   423
Database administration   423
Enterprise application   421
Enterprise application integration (EAI)   422
e-trash   433
Green computing   433
Legacy information system   421
Outsourcing   425
Steering committee   415
Virtualization   432

USING YOUR KNOWLEDGE

1. According to this chapter, information systems, products, and technology are not malleable; they are difficult to change, alter, or bend. How do you think senior executives other than the CIO view this lack of malleability? For example, how do you think IS appears during a corporate merger?

2. Suppose you represent an investor group that is acquiring hospitals across the nation and integrating them into a unified system. List five potential problems and risks concerning information systems. How do you think IS-related risks compare to other risks in such an acquisition program?

3. What happens to IS when corporate direction changes rapidly? How will IS appear to other departments? What happens to IS when the corporate strategy changes frequently? Do you think such frequent changes are a greater problem to IS than to other business functions? Why or why not?

4. Consider the following statement: "In many ways, choosing an outsource vendor is a one-way street." Explain what this statement means. Do you agree with it? Why or why not?

5. Reread the MRV introductions to Parts 3 and 4, and to Chapters 7 through 11. Using these introductions as background, generate a two- to three-page document for Eddie that summarizes the IS management activities that MRV should practice. As you write the document, keep in mind that MRV is a small company with limited resources that must strike a balance between comprehensive IS management and cost.

COLLABORATION EXERCISE

Collaborate with a group of students on the following exercises. Recall from Chapter 2 that collaboration is more than cooperation because it involves iteration and feedback. Post a document, a discussion item, a wiki item, or an idea and obtain feedback from your team members. Similarly, read the ideas of others and comment on them. Try to innovate in both the process by which you collaborate and the work product that you create. Avoid face-to-face meetings. Instead, use collaborative software such as Google Docs & Spreadsheets, Microsoft Groove, or Microsoft SharePoint to facilitate your ideas.

Is green computing important? Is it a sop to environmentalists to make computing professionals appear virtuous? Or, are there substantial social and planetary benefits to be gained by practicing green computing?

To investigate this question, consider the application of green computing at your campus.

1. Determine the power requirements for typical computing and office equipment. Consider laptop computers, desktop computers, server computers, CRT monitors, LCD monitors, laser and other printers. You may wish to consider other office equipment types, such as copiers, as well.

   Search the Internet for data about power consumption. As you do, be aware that a *watt* is a measure of electrical power. Power companies bill electrical service in terms of watts or kilowatts. It is *watts* that the green computing movement wants to reduce.

2. Estimate the number of each type of device in use on your campus. Use your university's Web site to determine the number of colleges, departments, faculty, staff, and students. Make assumptions about the number of computers, copiers, servers, and other types of equipment used by each.

3. Using the data from questions 1 and 2, compute the total power used by computing devices on your campus.

4. A computer that is in screensaver mode uses the same amount of power as one in regular mode. Computers that are in sleep mode, however, use much less power, something like 6 watts per hour. Observe computer use on your campus and estimate the amount of time that computing devices are in sleep versus screensaver or use mode. Compute the savings in power that result from sleep mode.

5. Computers that are automatically updated by the IS department with software upgrades and patches cannot be allowed to go into sleep mode because if they are sleeping they will not be able to receive the upgrade. Hence, some universities prohibit sleep mode on university computers (sleep mode is never used on servers, by the way). Determine the policy at your university and comment on its appropriateness in terms of green computing.

6. You have no convenient way of knowing the percent of idle time of servers on your campus, and hence cannot compute the savings that might result from virtualization. You also do not know the amount of virtualization that is already being done. For this exercise, assume no servers are currently virtualized and perform a sensitivity analysis for different levels of server utilization as follows: Compute the savings if server utilization is 10, 25, 40, and 60 percent. Assume that 10 percent of a virtual computer's resources must be reserved for the virtual operating system. Thus, for example, only three servers running at 25 percent can be placed on a virtualized server. (Utilization on that server will be three times 25% plus 10%, or 85%). Because only 15 percent remains unused, another server running at 25 percent cannot be accommodated on the virtual server.

7. Determine the number of computers, monitors, and related office equipment that are discarded at your university per year. Your university probably publishes some data about this for the computers that it owns. Make and justify assumptions about the disposal rate of non-university-owned computers.

8. Describe where and how computers and related equipment are disposed of on your campus. A mixture

of disposal techniques is likely used. The university may have an official policy for its computers; students and faculty may have a policy of their own.

9. Using the data and analysis in questions 1 through 8, write a "Green Computing Manifesto" for your university.

Address power use, virtualization, and e-trash in your manifesto. Include recommendations for actions by organizations within the university and by faculty, staff, and students.

APPLICATION EXERCISE

1. Suppose you have just been appointed manager of a help desk with an IS department. You have been there for just a week, and you are amazed to find only limited information to help you manage your employees. In fact, the only data kept concerns the processing of particular issues, called *Tickets*. The following data is kept:

> *Ticket#, Date_Submitted, Date_Opened, Date_Closed, Type (new or repeat), Reporting_ Employee_Name, Reporting_Employee_Division, Technician_Name Problem_System, and Problem_Description*

You can find sample Ticket data in the Excel file **Ch11Ex01** on this text's Web site.

As a manager, you need more information. Among your needs are information that will help you learn who are your best- and worst-performing technicians, how different systems compare in terms of number of problems reported and the time required to fix those

problems, how different divisions compare in terms of problems reported and the time required to fix them, which technicians are the best and worst at solving problems with particular systems, and which technicians are best and worst at solving problems from particular divisions.

a. Use either Access or Excel, or a combination of the two, to produce the information listed above from the data in the Excel file **Ch11Ex01**. In your answer, you may use queries, formulas, reports, forms, graphs, pivot tables, pivot charts, or any other type of Access or Excel display. Choose the best display for the type of information you are producing.

b. Explain how you would use these different types of information to manage your department.

c. Specify any additional information that you would like to have produced from this data to help you manage your department.

d. Use either Access or Excel or a combination to produce the information in part c.

CASE STUDY 11

Marriott International, Inc.

Marriott International, Inc., operates and franchises hotels and lodging facilities throughout the world. Its 2007 revenue was just over $12.9 billion. Marriott groups its business into segments according to lodging facility. Major business segments are full-service lodging, select-service lodging, extended-stay lodging, and timeshare properties. Marriott states that its three top corporate priorities are profitability, preference, and growth.

In the mid-1980s, the airlines developed the concept of *revenue management*, which adjusts prices in accordance with demand. The idea gained prominence in the airline industry, because an unoccupied seat represents revenue that is forever lost. Unlike a part in inventory, an unoccupied seat on today's flight cannot be sold tomorrow. Similarly, in the lodging industry, today's unoccupied hotel room cannot be sold tomorrow. So, for hotels, revenue management translates to raising prices on Monday when a convention is in town and lowering them on Saturday in the dead of winter when few travelers are in sight.

Marriott had developed two different revenue-management systems, one for its premium hotels and a second for its lower-priced properties. It developed both of these systems using pre–Internet technology; systems upgrades required installing updates locally. The local updates were expensive and problematic. Also, the two systems required two separate interfaces for entering prices into the centralized reservation system.

In the late-1990s, Marriott embarked on a project to create a single revenue-management system that could be used by all of its properties. The new system, called One Yield, was custom developed in-house, using a process similar to the SDLC you learned about in Chapter 10. The IT professionals understood the importance of user involvement, and they formed a joint IT–business user team that developed the business case for the new system and jointly managed its development. The team was careful to provide constant communication to the system's future users, and it used prototypes to identify problem areas early. Training is a continuing activity for all Marriott employees, and the company integrated training facilities into the new system.

One Yield recommends prices for each room, given the day, date, current reservation levels, and history. Each hotel property has a revenue manager who can override these recommendations. Either way, the prices are communicated directly to the centralized reservation system. One Yield uses Web-based technology so that when the company makes upgrades to the system, it makes them only at the Web servers, not at the individual hotels. This strategy saves considerable maintenance cost, activity, and frustration.

One Yield computes the theoretical maximum revenue for each property and compares actual results to that maximum. Using One Yield, the company has increased the ratio of actual to theoretical revenue from 83 to 91 percent. That increase of 8 percentage points has translated into a substantial increase in revenues.

Source: Case based on information from *www.cio.com/article/119209/ The_Price_is_Always_Right* (accessed July 2009). Used through the courtesy of *CIO*. Copyright 2005/2007 CXO Media Inc.

Questions

1. How does One Yield contribute to Marriott's objectives?

2. What are the advantages of having one revenue-management system instead of two? Consider both users and the IS department in your answer.

3. At the same time it was developing One Yield in-house, Marriott chose to outsource its human relations information system. Why would it choose to develop one system in-house but outsource the other? Consider the following factors in your answer.

   • Marriott's objectives
   • The nature of the systems
   • The uniqueness of each system to Marriott
   • Marriott's in-house expertise

4. How did outsourcing HR contribute to the success of One Yield?

5. Summarize the reasons why a company would choose to outsource rather than develop a system in-house.

12

Information Security Management

"Sue, I told you Trevor would leave us."

"Yeah, Crosby, you did. So did Eddie."

"He didn't like his tiny bonus—part of *your* new incentive computation—and I heard he's now working for Granite River Rafting."

"He was working for them."

"What do you mean?"

"Jason Taylor over at Granite just called me. He fired him."

"What, so soon? What did he do?"

"Stole our data."

"What are you saying?"

"Apparently, the day Trevor quit us, he was in this office by himself. He got on Eddie's computer and copied all of his data onto a flash drive. Took it with him."

"I heard we lost some data."

"Yeah, we did. He told Jason what he'd done, offered to give Jason all that data, and Jason let him go."

"I called Trevor and told him to give the data back. He says he'll mail it to me."

"How do we know he doesn't make a copy?"

"We don't."

"Jason's a straight-up guy. He'd tell us, but there are people who work these rivers who aren't nearly so honest. What do we do about them?"

"Nothing we can do. I'm wondering if we should tell our customers. Thank heavens we don't store credit card data. He did get all their email addresses, though. I guess I'd better call our lawyer. Not how I wanted to start the day. . . . Let's thank Jason with one of those big Copper River salmon we caught last month. . . . I'll write a note to go with it."

"I'll take care of the salmon, Sue, but I'm sorry to say you're wrong . . . Ringo told me he did get some credit card data . . . "

MRV's security breach occurred for two reasons: a lack of proper IS management,

as you learned in Chapter 11, and a failure to develop effective security program, as you'll learn in this chapter.

Sue has taken some bad hits in Part 4. She tried to develop the new Web sites on the cheap by hiring an inexperienced student to do the work. She knows that she has poor IS management, but was hoping to put off any action on that for a few months. However, now she's learned that she's lost customer data to a disgruntled employee, and she is about to have a series of unpleasant conversations with her customers and a number of expensive meetings with her lawyers. She needed the knowledge that you're learning here! ■

>> STUDY QUESTIONS

Q1 What are the threats to information security?

Q2 What is senior management's security role?

Q3 What technical safeguards are available?

Q4 What data safeguards are available?

Q5 What human safeguards are available?

Q6 How should organizations respond to security incidents?

Q7 What is the extent of computer crime?

Q8 2020?

CHAPTER PREVIEW

This chapter describes the common sources of security threats and explains management's role in addressing them. It also defines the major elements of an organizational security policy. Given that management background, it then presents the most common types of technical, data, and human security safeguards. We then discuss how organizations should respond to security incidents, and, finally, examine common types of computer crime.

The primary focus of this chapter is on management's responsibility for the organization's security policy and for implementing human security safeguards. These are the aspects of security that will most concern you as a future business professional.

As with Chapter 11, we will approach this topic from the standpoint of a major organization that has professional staff. We do so in order for you to learn the tasks that need to be accomplished. Both MRV and FlexTime need security, but they will need to adapt the full-scale security program described here to their smaller requirements and more limited budget.

Q1 What Are the Threats to Information Security?

We begin by describing security threats. We will first summarize the sources of threats and then describe specific problems that arise from each source.

What Are the Sources of Threats?

A **security threat** is a challenge to the integrity of information systems that arises from one of three sources: human error and mistakes, malicious human activity, and natural events and disasters. *Human errors and mistakes* include accidental problems caused by both employees and nonemployees. An example is an employee who misunderstands operating procedures and accidentally deletes customer records. Another example is an employee who, in the course of backing up a database, inadvertently installs an old database on top of the current one. This category also includes poorly written application programs and poorly designed procedures. Finally, human errors and mistakes include physical accidents, such as driving a forklift through the wall of a computer room.

The second source of security problems is *malicious human activity*. This category includes employees and former employees who intentionally destroy data or other system components. It also includes hackers who break into a system and virus and worm writers who infect computer systems. Malicious human activity also includes outside criminals who break into a system to steal for financial gain, and it also includes terrorism.

Natural events and disasters are the third source of security problems. This category includes fires, floods, hurricanes, earthquakes, tsunamis, avalanches, and other acts of nature. Problems in this category include not only the initial loss of capability and service, but also losses stemming from actions to recover from the initial problem.

What Are the Types of Security Problems?

Figure 12-1 summarizes threats by type of problem and source. Five types of security problems are listed: unauthorized data disclosure, incorrect data modification, faulty service, denial of service, and loss of infrastructure. We will consider each type.

		Source		
		Human Error	**Malicious Activity**	**Natural Disasters**
Problem	**Unauthorized data disclosure**	Procedural mistakes	Pretexting Phishing Spoofing Sniffing Computer crime	Disclosure during recovery
	Incorrect data modification	Procedural mistakes Incorrect procedures Ineffective accounting controls System errors	Hacking Computer crime	Incorrect data recovery
	Faulty service	Procedural mistakes Development and installation errors	Computer crime Usurpation	Service improperly restored
	Denial of service	Accidents	DOS attacks	Service interruption
	Loss of infrastructure	Accidents	Theft Terrorist activity	Property loss

Figure 12-1
Security Problems
and Sources

Unauthorized Data Disclosure

Unauthorized data disclosure can occur by human error when someone inadvertently releases data in violation of policy. An example at a university would be a new department administrator who posts student names, numbers, and grades in a public place, when the releasing of names and grades violates state law. Another example is employees who unknowingly or carelessly release proprietary data to competitors or to the media.

The popularity and efficacy of search engines has created another source of inadvertent disclosure. Employees who place restricted data on Web sites that can be reached by search engines might mistakenly publish proprietary or restricted data over the Web.

Of course, proprietary and personal data can also be released maliciously. **Pretexting** occurs when someone deceives by pretending to be someone else. A common scam involves a telephone caller who pretends to be from a credit card company and claims to be checking the validity of credit card numbers: "I'm checking your MasterCard number; it begins 5491. Can you verify the rest of the number?" All MasterCard numbers start with 5491; the caller is attempting to steal a valid number.

Phishing is a similar technique for obtaining unauthorized data that uses pretexting via email. The *phisher* pretends to be a legitimate company and sends an email requesting confidential data, such as account numbers, Social Security numbers, account passwords, and so forth. Phishing compromises legitimate brands and trademarks.

Spoofing is another term for someone pretending to be someone else. If you pretend to be your professor, you are spoofing your professor. **IP spoofing** occurs when an intruder uses another site's IP address as if it were that other site. **Email spoofing** is a synonym for phishing.

Sniffing is a technique for intercepting computer communications. With wired networks, sniffing requires a physical connection to the network. With wireless networks, no such connection is required: **Drive-by sniffers** simply take computers with wireless connections through an area and search for unprotected wireless networks. They can monitor and intercept wireless traffic at will. Even protected wireless networks are vulnerable, as you will learn. Spyware and adware are two other sniffing techniques discussed later in this chapter.

Other forms of computer crime include breaking into networks to steal data such as customer lists, product inventory data, employee data, and other proprietary and confidential data.

Finally, people might inadvertently disclose data during recovery from a natural disaster. During a recovery, everyone is so focused on restoring system capability that they might ignore normal security safeguards. A request like "I need a copy of the customer database backup" will receive far less scrutiny during disaster recovery than at other times.

Incorrect Data Modification

The second problem category in Figure 12-1 is *incorrect data modification*. Examples include incorrectly increasing a customer's discount or incorrectly modifying an employee's salary, earned days of vacation, or annual bonus. Other examples include placing incorrect information, such as incorrect price changes, on the company's Web site or company portal.

Incorrect data modification can occur through human error when employees follow procedures incorrectly or when procedures have been designed incorrectly. For proper internal control on systems that process financial data or that control inventories of assets, such as products and equipment, companies should ensure separation of duties and authorities and have multiple checks and balances in place.

A final type of incorrect data modification caused by human error includes *system errors*. An example is the lost-update problem discussed in Chapter 5 (page 149).

Hacking occurs when a person gains unauthorized access to a computer system. Although some people hack for the sheer joy of doing it, other hackers invade systems for the malicious purpose of stealing or modifying data. Computer criminals invade computer networks to obtain critical data or to manipulate the system for financial gain. Examples are reducing account balances or causing the shipment of goods to unauthorized locations and customers.

Finally, faulty recovery actions after a disaster can result in incorrect data changes. The faulty actions can be unintentional or malicious.

Faulty Service

The third problem category, *faulty service*, includes problems that result because of incorrect system operation. Faulty service could include incorrect data modification, as just described. It also could include systems that work incorrectly by sending the wrong goods to the customer or the ordered goods to the wrong customer, incorrectly billing customers, or sending the wrong information to employees. Humans can inadvertently cause faulty service by making procedural mistakes. System developers can write programs incorrectly or make errors during the installation of hardware, software programs, and data.

Usurpation occurs when unauthorized programs invade a computer system and replace legitimate programs. Such unauthorized programs typically shut down the legitimate system and substitute their own processing. Faulty service can also result from mistakes made during the recovery from natural disasters.

Denial of Service

Human error in following procedures or a lack of procedures can result in **denial of service**. For example, humans can inadvertently shut down a Web server or corporate gateway router by starting a computationally intensive application. An OLAP application that uses the operational DBMS can consume so many DBMS resources that order-entry transactions cannot get through.

Denial-of-service attacks can be launched maliciously. A malicious hacker can flood a Web server, for example, with millions of bogus service requests that so occupy the server that it cannot service legitimate requests. For example, computer worms can infiltrate a network with so much artificial traffic that legitimate traffic cannot get through. Finally, natural disasters may cause systems to fail, resulting in denial of service.

Loss of Infrastructure

Human accidents can cause *loss of infrastructure*. Examples are a bulldozer cutting a conduit of fiber-optic cables and the floor buffer crashing into a rack of Web servers.

Theft and terrorist events also cause loss of infrastructure. A disgruntled, terminated employee can walk off with corporate data servers, routers, or other crucial equipment. Terrorist events also can cause the loss of physical plants and equipment.

Natural disasters present the largest risk for infrastructure loss. A fire, flood, earthquake, or similar event can destroy data centers and all they contain. The devastation of the Indian Ocean tsunami in December 2004 and of Hurricanes Katrina and Rita in the fall of 2005 are potent examples of the risks to infrastructure from natural causes.

You may be wondering why Figure 12-1 does not include viruses, worms, and Trojan horses. The answer is that viruses, worms, and Trojan horses are *techniques* for causing some of the problems in the figure. They can cause a denial-of-service attack, or they can be used to cause malicious, unauthorized data access, or data loss.

What Are the Components of an Organization's Security Program?

All of the problems listed in Figure 12-1 are real and as serious as they sound. Accordingly, organizations must address security in a systematic way. A **security program**[1] has three components: senior-management involvement, safeguards of various kinds, and incident response.

The first component, s*enior-management involvement,* has two critical security functions: First, senior management must establish the security policy. This policy sets the stage for the organization's response to security threats. However, because no security program is perfect, there is always risk. Management's second function, therefore, is to manage risk by balancing the costs and benefits of the security program.

Safeguards are protections against security threats. A good way to view safeguards is in terms of the five components of an information system, as shown in Figure 12-2. Some of the safeguards involve computer hardware and software. Some involve data; others involve procedures and people. In addition to these safeguards, organizations must also consider disaster-recovery safeguards. An effective security program consists of a balance of safeguards of all these types.

Hardware	Software	Data	Procedures	People

Technical Safeguards	**Data Safeguards**	**Human Safeguards**
Identification and authorization	Data rights and responsibilities	Hiring
Encryption	Passwords	Training
Firewalls	Encryption	Education
Malware protection	Backup and recovery	Procedure design
Application design	Physical security	Administration
		Assessment
		Compliance
		Accountability

Effective security requires balanced attention to all five components!

Figure 12-2
Security Safeguards as They Relate to the Five Components

---

[1]Note that the word *program* is used here in the sense of a management program that includes objectives, policies, procedures, directives, and so forth. Do not confuse this term with a computer program.

The final component of a security program consists of the organization's *planned response to security incidents*. Clearly, the time to think about what to do is *not* when the computers are crashing all around the organization. We begin the discussion of the security program with the responsibilities of senior management.

Q2 What Is Senior Management's Security Role?

Management has a crucial role in information systems security. Management sets the security policy, and only management can balance the costs of a security system against the risk of security threats. The National Institute of Standards and Technology (NIST) published an excellent security handbook that addresses management's responsibility. It is available online at *http://csrc.nist.gov/publications/nistpubs/800-12/ handbook.pdf*. We will follow its discussion in this section.

The *NIST Handbook* of Security Elements

Figure 12-3 lists elements of computer security described in the *NIST Handbook*. First, computer security must support the organization's mission. There is no "one size fits all" solution to security problems. Security systems for a diamond mine and security systems for a wheat farm will differ.

According to the second point in Figure 12-3, when you manage a department you have a responsibility for information security in that department, even if no one tells you that you do. Do appropriate safeguards exist? Are your employees properly trained? Will your department know how to respond when the computer system fails? If these issues are not addressed in your department, raise the issue to higher levels of management.

Security can be expensive. Therefore, as shown in the third principle of Figure 12-3, computer security should have an appropriate cost-benefit ratio. Costs can be direct, such as labor costs, and they can be intangible, such as employee or customer frustration. Organizations such as MRV and FlexTime cannot afford to provide the same level of security as Pearson Education or the IRS provide. All the same, they should pay attention to security and manage security risk, as described in the next section.

According to the fourth principle in Figure 12-3, security responsibilities and accountabilities must be explicit. General statements like "everyone in the department must adequately safeguard company assets" are worthless. Instead, managers should assign specific tasks to specific people or specific job functions.

Because information systems integrate the processing of many departments, security problems originating in your department can have far-reaching consequences. If one of your employees neglects procedures and enters product prices

1. Computer security should support the mission of the organization.
2. Computer security is an integral element of sound management.
3. Computer security should be cost-effective.
4. Computer security responsibilities and accountability should be made explicit.
5. System owners have computer security responsibilities outside their own organizations.
6. Computer security requires a comprehensive and integrated approach.
7. Computer security should be periodically reassessed.
8. Computer security is constrained by societal factors.

Figure 12-3
Elements of Computer Security

incorrectly on your Web storefront, the consequences will extend to other departments, other companies, and your customers.

Understanding that computer system owners have security responsibilities outside their own departments and organizations is the fifth principle of computer security.

As the sixth principle in Figure 12-3 implies, there is no magic bullet for security. No single safeguard, such as a firewall, a virus-protection program, or increased employee training, will provide effective security. The problems described in Figure 12-1 require an integrated security program.

Once a security program is in place, the company cannot simply forget about it. As the seventh principle in Figure 12-3 indicates, security is a continuing need, and every company must periodically evaluate its security program.

Finally, social factors put some limits on security programs. Employees resent physical searches when arriving at and departing from work. Customers do not want to have their retinas scanned before they can place an order. Computer security conflicts with personal privacy, and a balance may be hard to achieve.

What Are the Elements of a Security Policy?

As stated, senior management has two overarching security tasks: defining a security policy and managing computer-security risk. Although management may delegate the specific tasks, it maintains the responsibility for the organization's security and must approve and endorse all such work.

A **security policy** has three elements: The first is a general statement of the organization's *security program*. This statement becomes the foundation for more specific security measures throughout the organization. In this statement, management specifies the goals of the security program and the assets to be protected. This statement also designates a department for managing the organization's security program and documents. In general terms, it specifies *how* the organization will ensure enforcement of security programs and policies.

The second security policy element is the *issue-specific policy*. For example, management might formulate a policy on personal use of computers at work and email privacy. The organization has the legal right to limit personal use of its computer systems and to inspect personal email for compliance. Employees have a right to know such policies.

Management sets security policies to ensure compliance with security law, as discussed in the Ethics Guide on pages 450–451.

The third security policy element is the *system-specific policy*, which concerns specific information systems. For example, what customer data from the order-entry system will be sold or shared with other organizations? Or, what policies govern the design and operation of systems that process employee data? Companies should address such policies as part of the standard systems development process.

How Is Risk Managed?

Management's second overarching security task is risk management. **Risk** is the likelihood of an adverse occurrence. Management cannot manage threats directly, but it *can* manage the likelihood that threats will be successful. Thus, management cannot keep hurricanes from happening, but it can limit the security consequences of a hurricane by creating a backup processing facility at a remote location.

Companies can reduce risks, but always at a cost. It is management's responsibility to decide how much to spend, or, stated differently, how much risk to assume.

Unfortunately, risk management takes place in a sea of uncertainty. Uncertainty is different from risk. Risk refers to threats and consequences that we know about. **Uncertainty** refers to the things we do not know that we do not know. For example, an earthquake could devastate a corporate data center on a fault that no one knew about. An employee might have found a way to steal inventory using a hole in the corporate Web site that no expert knew existed. Because of uncertainty, risk management is always approximate.

Ethics

Security Privacy

Some organizations have legal requirements to protect the customer data they collect and store, but the laws may be more limited than you think. The **Gramm-Leach-Bliley (GLB) Act**, passed by Congress in 1999, protects consumer financial data stored by financial institutions, which are defined as banks, securities firms, insurance companies, and organizations that provide financial advice, prepare tax returns, and provide similar financial services.

The **Privacy Act of 1974** provides protections to individuals regarding records maintained by the U.S. government, and the privacy provisions of the **Health Insurance Portability and Accountability Act (HIPAA)** of 1996 gives individuals the right to access health data created by doctors and other health-care providers. HIPAA also sets rules and limits on who can read and receive your health information.

The law is stronger in other countries. In Australia, for example, the Privacy Principles of the Australian Privacy Act of 1988 govern not only government and health-care data, but also records maintained by businesses with revenues in excess of AU$3 million.

To understand the importance of the limitations, consider online retailers that routinely store customer credit card data. Do Dell, Amazon.com, the airlines, and other e-commerce businesses have a legal requirement to protect their customers' credit card data? Apparently not—at least not in the United States. The activities of such organizations are not governed by the GLB, the Privacy Act of 1974, or HIPAA.

Most consumers would say, however, that online retailers have an ethical requirement to protect a customer's credit card and other data,

and most online retailers would agree. Or at least the retailers would agree that they have a strong business reason to protect that data. A substantial loss of credit card data by any large online retailer would have detrimental effects on both sales and brand reputation.

As discussed in Chapter 6, data aggregators like Acxiom Corporation further complicate the risk to individuals because they develop a complete profile of households and individuals. And, as stated in Chapter 6, no federal law prohibits the U.S. government from buying information products from the data accumulators.

But, let's bring the discussion closer to home. What requirements does your university have on the data it maintains about you? State law or university policy may govern those records, but no federal law does. Most universities consider it their responsibility to provide public access to graduation records. Anyone can determine when you graduated, your degree, and your major. (Keep this service in mind when you write your resume.)

Most professors endeavor to publish grades by student number and not by name, and there may be state law that requires that separation. But what about your work? What about the papers you write, the answers you give on exams? What about the emails you send to your professor? The data are not protected by federal law, and they are probably not protected by state law. If your professor chooses to cite your work in research, she will be subject to copyright law, but not privacy law. What you write is no longer your personal data; it belongs to the academic community. You can ask your professor what she intends to do with your coursework, emails, and office conversations, but none of that data is protected by law.

The bottom line: Be careful with your personal data. Large, reputable organizations are likely to endorse ethical privacy policy and to have strong and effective safeguards to effectuate that policy. But individuals and small organizations might not. If in doubt, ask. ■

Discussion Questions

1. As stated in the case, when you order from an online retailer, the data you provide is not protected by U.S. privacy law. Does this fact cause you to reconsider setting up an account with a stored credit card number? What is the advantage of storing the credit card number? Do you think the advantage is worth the risk? Are you more willing to take the risk with some companies than with others? Why or why not?

2. Suppose you are the treasurer of a student club, and you store records of club members' payments in a database. In the past, members have disputed payment amounts; therefore, when you receive a payment, you scan an image of the check or credit card invoice and store the scanned image in a database.

   One day, you are using your computer in a local wireless coffee shop and a malicious student breaks into your computer over the wireless network and steals the club database. You know nothing about this until the next day, when a club member complains that a popular student Web site has published the names, bank names, and bank account numbers for everyone who has given you a check.

   What liability do you have in this matter? Could you be classified as a financial institution because you are taking students' money? (You can find the GLB at *www.ftc.gov/privacy/glbact.*) If so, what liability do you have? If not, do you have any other liability? Does the coffee shop have a liability?

3. Suppose you are asked to fill out a study questionnaire that requires you to enter identifying data as well as answers to personal questions. You hesitate to provide the data, but the top part of the questionnaire states, "All responses will be strictly confidential." So, you fill out the questionnaire.

   Unfortunately, the person who is conducting the study visits the same wireless coffee shop that you visited (in question 2), and the same malicious student breaks in and steals the study results. Your name and all of your responses appear on that same student Web site. Did the person conducting the study violate a law? Does the confidentiality assurance on the form increase that person's requirement to protect your data? Does your answer change if the person conducting the study is (a) a student, (b) a professor of music, or (c) a professor of computer security?

4. In truth, only a very talented and motivated hacker could steal databases from computers using a public wireless network. Such losses, although possible, are unlikely. However, any email you send or files you download can readily be sniffed at a public wireless facility. Knowing this, describe good practice for computer use at public wireless facilities.

5. Considering your answers to the above questions, state three to five general principles to guide your actions as you disseminate and store data.

Risk Assessment

The first step in risk management is to assess what the threats are, how likely they are to occur, and what the consequences are if they do occur. Figure 12-4 lists factors to consider. First, what are the assets that are to be protected? Examples are computer facilities, programs, and sensitive data. Other assets are less obvious. Phishing threatens an organization's customers as well its trademark and brand. Employee privacy is another asset that can be at risk.

Given the list of assets to be protected, the next action is to assess the threats to which they are exposed. The company should consider all of the threats in Figure 12-1; there may be other threats as well.

The third factor in risk assessment is to determine what safeguards, like those in Figure 12-3, are in place. The NIST Handbook expands our definition of **safeguard** to be: any action device, procedure, technique, or other measure that reduces a system's vulnerability to a threat.[2] The Handbook also states that no safeguard is ironclad; there is always a *residual risk* that the safeguard will not protect the assets in all circumstances.

A **vulnerability** is an opening or a weakness in the security system. Some vulnerabilities exist because there are no safeguards or because the existing safeguards are ineffective. Because of residual risk, there is always some residual vulnerability even to assets that are protected by effective safeguards.

Consequences, the fifth factor listed in Figure 12-4, are the damages that occur when an asset is compromised. Consequences can be tangible or intangible. *Tangible* consequences are those whose financial impact can be measured. The costs of *intangible* consequences, such as the loss of customer goodwill due to an outage, cannot be measured. Normally, when analyzing consequences, companies estimate the costs of tangible consequences and simply list intangible consequences.

The final two factors in risk assessment are likelihood and probable loss. *Likelihood* is the probability that a given asset will be compromised by a given threat, despite the safeguards. **Probable loss** is the "bottom line" of risk assessment. To obtain a measure of probable loss, companies multiply likelihood by the cost of the consequences. Probable loss also includes a statement of intangible consequences.

Risk-Management Decisions

Given the probable loss from the risk assessment just described, senior management must decide what to do. In some cases, the decision is easy. Companies can protect some assets by use of inexpensive and easily implemented safeguards. Installing virus-protection software is an example. However, some vulnerability is expensive to eliminate, and management must determine if the costs of the safeguard are worth the benefit of probable loss reduction. Such risk-management decisions are difficult because the true effectiveness of the safeguard is seldom known, and the probable loss is subject to uncertainty.

Uncertainty, however, does not absolve management from security responsibility. Management has a fiduciary responsibility to the organization's owners, and senior managers must make reasonable and prudent decisions in light of available information.

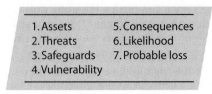

Figure 12-4
Risk Assessment Factors

1. Assets	5. Consequences
2. Threats	6. Likelihood
3. Safeguards	7. Probable loss
4. Vulnerability	

---

[2]*NIST Handbook, http://csrc.nist.gov/publications/nistpubs/800-12/handbook.pdf,* p. 61 (accessed July 2009).

They must consider the factors listed in Figure 12-4 and take cost-effective actions to reduce probable losses, despite the uncertainty.

The next sections discuss safeguards. We begin with technical safeguards, then data safeguards, then human safeguards, and, finally, safeguards against natural disasters.

Q3 What Technical Safeguards Are Available?

 video ▶

Technical safeguards involve the hardware and software components of an information system. Figure 12-5 lists primary technical safeguards. We have discussed all of these in prior chapters. Here we will just supplement those prior discussions.

Identification and Authentication

Every information system today should require users to sign on with a user name and password. The user name *identifies* the user (the process of **identification**), and the password *authenticates* that user (the process of **authentication**).

Passwords

All forms of computer security involve passwords. Review the material on strong passwords and password etiquette in Chapter 1.

Despite repeated warnings to the contrary, users tend to be careless in their use of passwords. For example, you can find yellow sticky notes holding written passwords adorning the computers in many companies. In addition, users tend to be free in sharing their passwords with others. Finally, many users choose ineffective, simple passwords. With such passwords, intrusion systems can very effectively guess passwords. These deficiencies can be reduced or eliminated using smart cards and biometric authentication.

Smart Cards

A **smart card** is a plastic card similar to a credit card. Unlike credit, debit, and ATM cards, which have a magnetic strip, smart cards have a microchip. The microchip, which holds far more data than a magnetic strip, is loaded with identifying data. Users of smart cards are required to enter a **personal identification number (PIN)** to be authenticated.

Biometric Authentication

Biometric authentication uses personal physical characteristics such as fingerprints, facial features, and retinal scans to authenticate users. Biometric authentication

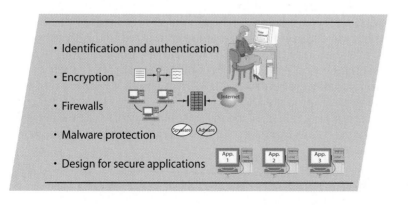

Figure 12-5
Technical Safeguards

provides strong authentication, but the required equipment is expensive. Often, too, users resist biometric identification because they feel it is invasive.

Biometric authentication is in the early stages of adoption. Because of its strength, it likely will see increased usage in the future. It is also likely that legislators will pass laws governing the use, storage, and protection requirements for biometric data.

You can remember authentication methods by understanding they fall into three categories: what you know (password or PIN), what you have (smart card), and what you are (biometric).

Single Sign-on for Multiple Systems

Information systems often require multiple sources of authentication. For example, when you sign on to your personal computer, you need to be authenticated. When you access the LAN in your department, you need to be authenticated again. When you traverse your organization's WAN, you will need to be authenticated to even more networks. Also, if your request requires database data, the DBMS server that manages that database will authenticate you yet again.

It would be annoying to enter a name and password for every one of these resources. You might have to use and remember five or six different passwords just to access the data you need to perform your job. It would be equally undesirable to send your password across all of these networks. The further your password travels, the greater the risk it can be compromised.

Instead, today's operating systems have the capability to authenticate you to networks and other servers. You sign on to your local computer and provide authentication data; from that point on, your operating system authenticates you to another network or server, which can authenticate you to yet another network and server, and so forth.

A system called **Kerberos** authenticates users without sending their passwords across the computer network. Developed by the Massachusetts Institute of Technology (MIT), Kerberos uses a complicated system of "tickets" to enable users to obtain services from networks and other servers. Windows, Linux, Unix, and other operating systems employ Kerberos and thus can authenticate user requests across networks of computers using a mixture of these operating systems.

Despite all that we know about the need for protecting passwords, compliance with password-protection guidelines is still lacking, as the Guide on pages 472–473 demonstrates.

This discussion indicates another reason why you must protect your user name and password. Once you have authenticated yourself on your local system, your operating system will authenticate you to networks and other servers. Someone who obtains your name and password will gain access not only to your computer, but via intersystem authentication, to many other computers and servers as well. The bottom line: Protect your passwords!

Wireless Access

For a wired network, a potential intruder must obtain physical access to the network. For a wireless network, however, no direct connection is needed. Drive-by sniffers can walk or drive around business or residential neighborhoods with a wireless computer and locate dozens, or even hundreds, of wireless networks. The wireless network will broadcast whether it is protected. If it is not, the sniffer can use it to obtain free access to the Internet or to connect to LANs that are connected to the access point.

In 2004, in a short ride through the Back Bay section of Boston, Massachusetts, a security consultant found 2,676 wireless connections, most of which were residential. Of those, almost half were unprotected.[3] Anyone with a wireless device could have connected to those unprotected access points and tapped into the Internet for free or taken more disruptive actions. The need for wireless security is now better known, and more private wireless networks are secure today than they were in 2004. It is still a problem, however.

---

[3]Bruce Mohl, "Tap into Neighbors' Wi-Fi? Why Not, Some Say," *Boston Globe,* July 4, 2004.

It is possible to protect wireless networks. Businesses with sophisticated communications equipment use elaborate techniques—techniques that require the support of highly trained communications specialists. Common protections are the use of VPNs and special security servers.

For the less sophisticated SOHO (small office, home office) market, wireless networks are less secure. The IEEE 802.11 Committee, the group that develops and maintains wireless standards, first developed a wireless security standard called **Wired Equivalent Privacy (WEP)**. Unfortunately, WEP was insufficiently tested before it was deployed, and it has serious flaws. In response, the IEEE 802.11 Committee developed improved wireless security standards called **Wi-Fi Protected Access (WPA)** and **WPA2**. Unfortunately, only newer wireless devices can use these techniques.

Wireless security technology is changing rapidly. By the time you read this, even newer security standards will have been developed. Search the Internet for the term *wireless network security* to learn about the latest standards. In the meantime, on any wireless network you use take the time to enable the highest level of security that you can and be aware that, at present, especially on SOHO networks, wireless networks are not nearly as secure as wired networks.

Encryption

The second technical safeguard in Figure 12-5 is encryption. We described some encryption techniques in Chapter 6 (page 190). To review, senders use a key to encrypt a plaintext message and then send the encrypted message to a recipient, who then uses a key to decrypt the message. Figure 12-6 lists five basic encryption techniques.

Technique	How It Works	Characteristics
Symmetric	Sender and receiver transmit message using the same key.	Fast, but difficult to get the same key to both parties.
Asymmetric	Sender and receiver transmit message using two keys, one public and one private. Message encrypted with one of the keys can be decrypted with the other.	Public key can be openly transmitted, but needs certificate authority (see below). Slower than symmetric.
SSL/TLS	Works between Levels 4 and 5 of the TCP-OSI architecture. Sender uses public/private key to transmit symmetric key, which both parties use for symmetric encryption—for a limited, brief period.	Used by most Internet applications. A useful and workable hybrid of symmetric and asymmetric.
Digital signatures	Sender hashes message, and uses private key to "sign" a message digest, creating digital signature; sender transmits plaintext message and digital signature. Receiver rehashes the plaintext message and decrypts the digital signature with the user's public key. If the message digests match, receiver knows that message has not been altered.	Ingenious technique for ensuring plaintext has not been altered.
Digital certificates	A trusted third party, the certificate authority (CA), supplies the public key and a digital certificate. Receiver decrypts message with public key (from CA), signed with CA's digital signature.	Eliminates spoofing of public keys. Requires browser to have CA's public key.

Figure 12-6
Basic Encryption Techniques

With **symmetric encryption**, both parties use the same key. With **asymmetric encryption**, the parties use two keys, one that is public and one that is private. A message encoded with one of the keys can be decoded with the other key. Asymmetric encryption is slower than symmetric encryption, but it is easier to implement over a network.

Secure Socket Layer (SSL) is a protocol that uses both asymmetric and symmetric encryption. SSL is a protocol layer that works between Level 4 (transport) and Level 5 (application) of the TCP–OSI protocol architecture. With SSL, asymmetric encryption transmits a symmetric key. Both parties then use that key for symmetric encryption for the balance of that session. Because SSL lies between Levels 4 and 5, most Internet applications, including HTTP, FTP, and email programs, can use it.

Netscape originally developed SSL. After a brief skirmish in the marketplace, Microsoft endorsed its use and included it in Internet Explorer and other products. SSL version 1.0 had problems, most of which were removed in version 3.0, which is the version Microsoft endorsed. A later version, with more problems fixed, was renamed **Transport Layer Security (TLS)**.

By either name, SSL or TLS, this is the protocol used whenever you see *https://* in your browser's address bar. As stated in Chapter 6, never send any sensitive data over the Internet unless you see the *s* after *http*.

Using SSL/TLS, the client verifies that it is communicating with the true Web site, and not with a site that is spoofing the true Web site. However, to ease the burden on users, the opposite is not done. Web sites seldom verify the true identity of users. Hence, programs can spoof legitimate users and fool Web sites. Because the consequences affect the Web site and not the client, such spoofing has no direct effect on the consumer. It is a problem that Web site owners must address, however.

Digital Signatures

Because encryption slows processing, most messages are sent over the Internet as plaintext. By default, email is sent as plaintext. This means, by the way, that you ought not to send your Social Security number, credit card numbers, or any other such numbers in email.

Because email is plaintext, it is possible that someone can intercept your email and change the message unbeknownst to you. For example, suppose a purchasing agent sends an email to one of its vendors with the message, "Please deliver shipment 1000 to our Oakdale facility." It is possible for a third party to intercept the email, remove the words "our Oakdale facility," substitute its own address, and send the message on to its destination.

Digital signatures are a technique for ensuring that plaintext messages are received without alteration. Figure 12-7 summarizes their use. The plaintext message is first *hashed*. **Hashing** is a method of mathematically manipulating the message to create a string of bits that characterize the message. The bit string, called the **message digest**, has a specified, fixed length, regardless of the length of the plaintext. According to one popular standard, message digests are 160 bits long.

Hashing is a one-way process. Any message can be hashed to produce a message digest, but the message digest cannot be unhashed to produce the original message.

Hashing techniques are designed so that if someone changes any part of a message, rehashing the changed message will create a different message digest. For example, the email message with the words "our Oakdale facility" and the same message but with the interceptor's address will generate two different message digests.

Authentication programs use message digests to ensure that plaintext messages have not been altered. The idea is to create a message digest for the original message and to send the message and the message digest to the receiver. The receiver hashes the message it received and compares the resulting message digest to the message digest that was sent with the message. If the two message digests are the same, then the receiver knows that the message was not altered. If they are different, then the message was altered.

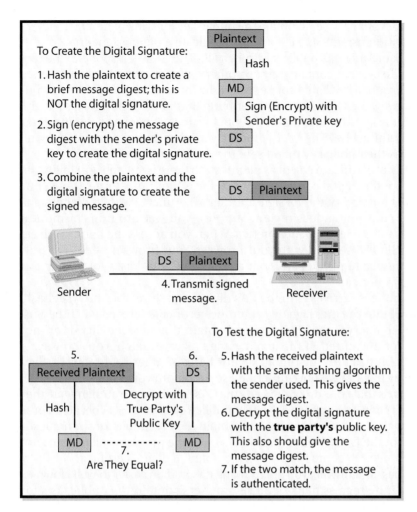

To Create the Digital Signature:

1. Hash the plaintext to create a brief message digest; this is NOT the digital signature.

2. Sign (encrypt) the message digest with the sender's private key to create the digital signature.

3. Combine the plaintext and the digital signature to create the signed message.

Sender

4. Transmit signed message.

Receiver

To Test the Digital Signature:

5. Hash the received plaintext with the same hashing algorithm the sender used. This gives the message digest.

6. Decrypt the digital signature with the **true party's** public key. This also should give the message digest.

7. If the two match, the message is authenticated.

Figure 12-7
Digital Signatures for Message Authentication

Source: R. Panko, *Corporate Computer and Network Security,* © 2004. Reprinted by permission of Pearson Education, Inc., Upper Saddle River, NJ.

For this technique to work, the original message digest must be protected when it is transmitted. Accordingly, as Figure 12-7 shows, the message digest (*MD* in this figure) is encrypted using the sender's private key. The result is called the message's digital signature. Applying one's private key to the message digest is called *signing* the message. As shown in step 4 of Figure 12-7, the system sends the signed message to the receiver.

The receiver hashes the plaintext message that arrived, to produce a message digest for the received message. It then decrypts the digital signature with the sender's public key (called the *true party's* public key, in this figure) and compares the message digest for the received message with the original message digest. If they are the same, then the message was not altered. If the message digests differ, then the receiver knows that someone altered the message somewhere along the line.

Only one problem remains: How does the receiver obtain the true party's public key? The receiver cannot ask the sender for its public key, because the sender could be spoofing. For example, if someone is spoofing Bank of America, the spoofer will send the spoofer's public key while claiming that it is sending the public key for Bank of America. The receiver cannot know the received public key is not the true Bank of America public key. Digital certificates prevent such spoofing.

Digital Certificates

When using public keys, a message recipient must know that it has the true party's public key. As just explained, a program that asks a sender to transmit its public key could be fooled. To solve this problem, trusted, independent third-party companies, called **certificate authorities (CAs)**, supply public keys.

Thus, for your browser to obtain the public key for Bank of America, either to conduct a secure session using SSL/TLS or to authenticate a digital signature, your browser will obtain Bank of America's public key from a CA. The CA will respond to the request with a **digital certificate** that contains, among other data, the name Bank of America and Bank of America's public key. Your browser will verify the name and then use that public key.

By the way, the CA is in no way verifying that Bank of America is a legitimate concern, that it is law abiding, that it has paid its taxes, that its accounting standards are high, or anything else. The CA is simplify verifying that a company known as Bank of America has the public key that it sent to your browser.

The digital certificate is sent as plaintext, so there is still the possibility that an entity can intercept the digital certificate sent by the CA and substitute its own public key. To prevent that possibility, the CA signs the digital certificate with its digital signature.

Before continuing, let's review. Suppose you want to transfer money from one account to another at Bank of America. When you access the bank's Web server, it initiates an SSL/TLS session with your browser. Your browser needs the public key for Bank of America to participate, so it contacts a CA and asks for the digital certificate for Bank of America.

The certificate arrives with the CA's digital signature. Your browser hashes the certificate to obtain the message digest for the certificate it received. It then uses the CA's public key to decrypt the signature and obtain the message digest for the certificate that the CA transmitted. If the two message digests match, your browser can rely on the fact that it has the true public key for Bank of America. Except . . . See if you can find the flaw in what we have described so far before you continue reading.

The flaw is that your browser needs the CA's public key to authenticate the digital certificate. Your browser cannot ask for that public key from the CA because someone could be spoofing the CA. Your browser could obtain the CA's public key by requesting a digital certificate for the first CA from a second CA, but the problem still remains. Your browser would then need to contact a third CA to obtain a digital certificate for the second CA. And so it goes. Meanwhile, you are thinking it would be easier to walk down to the bank.

The infinite regress halts because browsers contain the public keys for the common CAs in their program code. As long as you receive your browser from a reputable source, you can rely on the public keys it uses when authenticating digital certificates from the CAs it uses.

Firewalls

Firewalls are the third technical safeguard listed in Figure 12-5. A firewall is a computing device that prevents unauthorized network access. A firewall can be a special-purpose computer or it can be a program on a general-purpose computer or on a router. We discussed firewalls previously in Chapter 6, starting on page 191.

Malware Protection

The next technical safeguard in our list in Figure 12-5 is malware. The term **malware** has several definitions. Here we will use the broadest one: *Malware* is viruses, worms, Trojan horses, spyware, and adware.

Viruses, Trojan Horses, and Worms

A **virus** is a computer program that replicates itself. Unchecked replication is like computer cancer; ultimately, the virus consumes the computer's recourses. Furthermore, many viruses also take unwanted and harmful actions.

The program code that causes unwanted activity is called the **payload**. The payload can delete programs or data—or even worse, modify data in undetected ways. Imagine the impact of a virus that changed the credit rating of all customers. Some viruses publish data in harmful way—for example, sending out files of credit card data to unauthorized sites.

There are many different virus types. **Trojan horses** are viruses that masquerade as useful programs or files. The name refers to the gigantic mock-up of a horse that was filled with soldiers and moved into Troy during the Trojan War. A typical Trojan horse appears to be a computer game, an MP3 music file, or some other useful innocuous program.

A **worm** is a virus that propagates using the Internet or other computer network. Worms spread faster than other virus types because they are specifically programmed to spread. Unlike nonworm viruses, which must wait for the user to share a file with a second computer, works actively use the network to spread. Sometimes, worms so choke a network that it becomes unusable.

Spyware and Adware

Spyware programs are installed on the user's computer without the user's knowledge or permission. Spyware resides in the background and, unknown to the user, observes the user's actions and keystrokes, monitors computer activity, and reports the user's activities to sponsoring organizations. Some malicious spyware captures keystrokes to obtain user names, passwords, account numbers, and other sensitive information. Other spyware supports marketing analyses, observing what users do, Web sites visited, products examined and purchased, and so forth.

Adware is similar to spyware in that it is installed without the user's permission and that it resides in the background and observes user behavior. Most adware is benign in that it does not perform malicious acts or steal data. It does, however, watch user activity and produce pop-up ads. Adware can also change the user's default window or modify search results and switch the user's search engine. For the most part, it is just annoying, but users should be concerned any time they have unknown programs on their computers that perform unknown functions.

Figure 12-8 lists some of the symptoms of adware and spyware. Sometimes these symptoms develop slowly over time as more and more malware components are installed. Should these symptoms occur on your computer, remove the spyware or adware using antimalware programs.

Malware Safeguards

Fortunately, it is possible to avoid most malware using the following malware safeguards:

1. **Install antivirus and antispyware programs on your computer.**   Your IS department will have a list of recommended (perhaps required) programs for this purpose. If you choose a program for yourself, choose one from a reputable vendor. Check reviews of antimalware software on the Web before purchasing.
2. **Set up your antimalware programs to scan your computer frequently.**   You should scan your computer at least once a week and possibly more. When you detect malware code, use the antimalware software to remove them. If the code cannot be removed, contact your IS department or antimalware vendor.
3. **Update malware definitions.**   **Malware definitions**—patterns that exist in malware code—should be downloaded frequently. Antimalware vendors update these definitions continuously, and you should install these updates as they become available.

- Slow system start up
- Sluggish system performance
- Many pop-up advertisements
- Suspicious browser homepage changes
- Suspicious changes to the taskbar and other system interfaces
- Unusual hard-disk activity

Figure 12-8
Spyware and Adware Symptoms

4. **Open email attachments only from known sources.**   Also, even when opening attachments from known sources, do so with great care. According to professor and security expert Ray Panko, about 90 percent of all viruses are spread by email attachments.[4] This statistic is not surprising, because most organizations are protected by firewalls. With a properly configured firewall, email is the only outside-initiated traffic that can reach user computers.

   Most antimalware programs check email attachments for malware code. However, all users should form the habit of *never* opening an email attachment from an unknown source. Also, if you receive an unexpected email from a known source or an email from a known source that has a suspicious subject, odd spelling, or poor grammar, do not open the attachment without first verifying with the known source that the attachment is legitimate.

5. **Promptly install software updates from legitimate sources.**   Unfortunately, all programs are chock full of security holes; vendors are fixing them as rapidly as they are discovered, but the practice is inexact. Install patches to the operating system and application programs promptly.

6. **Browse only in reputable Internet neighborhoods.**   It is possible for some malware to install itself when you do nothing more than open a Web page. Don't go there!

Bots, BotNets, and Bot Herders

Recently, new terms have been introduced into the computer security vocabulary. A **bot** is a computer program that is surreptitiously installed and that takes actions unknown and uncontrolled by the computer's owner or administrator. The term *bot* is a new catch-all term that refers to any type of virus, worm, Trojan Horse, spyware, adware, or other program not installed and controlled by the computer's owner or manager. Some bots are very dangerous and malicious; some steal credit card data, banking data, and e-mail addresses. Others cause denial-of-service attacks and still others just produce pop-ups and other annoyances.

A **botnet** is a network of bots that is created and managed by the individual or organization that infected the network with the bot program. The individual or organization that controls the botnet is called a **bot herder**. Botnets and bot herders are potentially serious problems not only to commerce, but also to national security. It is believed that a unit of the North Korean Army served as a bot herder for a botnet that caused denial-of-service attacks on Web servers in South Korea and in the United States in July 2009.

The safeguards discussed for malware are the best protection against bots. Stay tuned, however; the end of the bot story has not yet been written.

Malware Is a Serious Problem

America Online (AOL) and the National Cyber Security Alliance conducted a malware study using Internet users in 2004.[5] They asked the users a series of questions and then, with the users' permission, they scanned the users' computers to determine how accurately the users understood malware problems on their own computers. Although this is an old study, its results are still revealing.

Among the users, 6 percent thought they had a virus, but 18 percent actually did. Further, half of those surveyed did not know if they had a virus. Of those computers having viruses, an average of 2.4 viruses were found; the maximum number of viruses found on a single computer was 213!

When asked how often they update their antivirus definitions, 71 percent of the users reported that they had done so within the last week. Actually, only one-third of the users had updated their definitions that recently.

---

[4]Ray Panko, *Corporate Computer and Network Security* (Upper Saddle River, NJ: Prentice Hall, 2004), p. 165.
[5]America Online and National Cyber Security Alliance. *AOL/NCSA Online Safety Study,* October 2004.

The survey found similar results for spyware. The average user computer had 93 spyware components. The maximum number found on a computer was 1,059. Note that only 5 percent of the users had given permission for the spyware to be installed.

Although the problem of malware will never be eradicated, you can reduce its size by following the six safeguards just listed. You should take these actions as a habit, and you should ensure that employees you manage take them as well.

Design Secure Applications

The final technical safeguard in Figure 12-5 concerns the design of applications. As a future IS user, you will not design programs yourself. However, you should ensure that any information system developed for you and your department includes security as one of the application requirements.

Q4 What Data Safeguards Are Available?

Data safeguards are measures used to protect databases and other organizational data. Figure 12-9 summarizes some important data safeguards. First, the organization should specify user data rights and responsibilities. Second, those rights should be enforced by user accounts that are authenticated at least by passwords.

The organization should protect sensitive data by storing it in encrypted form. Such encryption uses one or more keys in ways similar to that described for data communication encryption. One potential problem with stored data, however, is that the key might be lost or that disgruntled or terminated employees might destroy it. Because of this possibility, when data are encrypted, a trusted party should have a copy of the encryption key. This safety procedure is sometimes called **key escrow**.

Another data safeguard is to periodically create backup copies of database contents. The organization should store at least some of these backups off premises, possibly in a remote location. Additionally, IT personnel should periodically practice recovery, to ensure that the backups are valid and that effective recovery procedures exist. Do not assume that just because a backup is made the database is protected.

Physical security is another data safeguard. The computers that run the DBMS and all devices that store database data should reside in locked, controlled-access facilities. If not, they are subject not only to theft, but also to damage. For better security, the organization should keep a log showing who entered the facility, when, and for what purpose.

Physical security was one of the problems that MRV had when it lost its data. The customer data (including credit card data) was stored on Eddie's computer, which was located in an area that was open to easy access. Further, Eddie apparently had no password for his computer, or there was a public account on that computer that enabled Jason to steal the data.

It is unrealistic for a small company like MRV to lock Eddie's computer in a controlled-access facility. It is likely feasible, however, for MRV to lock up a data server in a secure place and allow access to it over their LAN. Then, as long as passwords protect computer access, sensitive data would not be readily accessible. See Q5 on page 462.

- Data rights and responsibilities
- Rights enforced by user accounts authenticated by passwords
- Data encryption
- Backup and recovery procedures
- Physical security

Figure 12-9
Data Safeguards

In some cases, organizations contract with other companies to manage their databases. If so, all of the safeguards in Figure 12-9 should be part of the service contract. Also, the contract should give the owners of the data permission to inspect the premises of the database operator and to interview its personnel on a reasonable schedule.

Q5 What Human Safeguards Are Available?

Human safeguards involve the people and procedure components of information systems. In general, human safeguards result when authorized users follow appropriate procedures for system use and recovery. Restricting access to authorized users requires effective authentication methods and careful user account management. In addition, appropriate security procedures must be designed as part of every information system, and users should be trained on the importance and use of those procedures. In this section, we will consider the development of human safeguards first for employees and then for nonemployee personnel.

Human Safeguards for Employees

Figure 12-10 lists security considerations for employees. The first is the creation of appropriate position definitions.

Position Definitions

It is impossible to have effective human safeguards unless job tasks and responsibilities are clearly defined for each employee position. In general, job descriptions

- Position definition
  - Separate duties and authorities.
  - Determine least privilege.
  - Document position sensitivity.

- Hiring and screening

- Dissemination and enforcement (responsibility, accountability, compliance)

- Termination
  - Friendly

  - Unfriendly

Figure 12-10
Security Policy for
In-House Staff

should provide a separation of duties and authorities. For example, no single individual should be allowed to approve expenses, write checks, and account for the disbursement. Instead, one person should approve expenses, another person pay them, and a third account for the transaction. Similarly, in inventory, no single person should be allowed to authorize an inventory withdrawal, remove the items from inventory, and account for the removal.

Given appropriate job descriptions, users' computer accounts should give users the least possible privilege necessary to perform their jobs. For example, users whose job description does not include modifying data should be given accounts with read-only privilege. Similarly, user accounts should prohibit users from accessing data they do not need. Because of the problem of semantic security (Chapter 9, page 348), access to seemingly innocuous data should be limited if the employee does not need that data for his or her job.

Finally, the security sensitivity should be documented for each position. Some jobs involve highly sensitive data (e.g., employee compensation, salesperson quotas, and proprietary marketing or technical data). Other positions involve no sensitive data. Documenting *position sensitivity* enables security personnel to prioritize their activities in accordance with the possible risk and loss.

Hiring and Screening

Security considerations should be part of the hiring process. Of course, if the position involves no sensitive data and no access to information systems, then screening for information systems security purposes will be minimal. When hiring for high-sensitivity positions, however, extensive interviews, references, and background investigations are appropriate. Note, too, that security screening applies not only to new employees, but also to employees who are promoted into sensitive positions.

Dissemination and Enforcement

Obviously, employees cannot be expected to follow security procedures if they do not know about them. Therefore, employees need to be trained on security policies, procedures, and the responsibilities they will have.

Employee security training begins during new-employee training, with the explanation of general security policies and procedures. That general training must be amplified in accordance with the position's sensitivity and responsibilities. Promoted employees should receive security training that is appropriate to their new positions. The company should not provide user accounts and passwords until employees have completed required security training.

Enforcement consists of three interdependent factors: responsibility, accountability, and compliance. First, the company should clearly define the security *responsibilities* of each position. The design of the security program should be such that employees can be held *accountable* for security violations. Procedures should exist so that when critical data are lost, it is possible to determine how the loss occurred and who is accountable. Finally, the security program should encourage security *compliance*. Employee activities should regularly be monitored for compliance, and management should specify disciplinary action to be taken in light of noncompliance.

Management attitude is crucial: Employee compliance is greater when management demonstrates, both in word and deed, a serious concern for security. If managers write passwords on staff bulletin boards, shout passwords down hallways, or ignore physical security procedures, then employee security attitudes and employee security compliance will suffer. Note, too, that effective security is a continuing management responsibility. Regular reminders about security are essential.

Termination

Companies also must establish security policies and procedures for the termination of employees. Most employee terminations are friendly and occur as the result of promotion, retirement, or when the employee resigns to take another position. Standard human resources policies should ensure that system administrators receive notification in advance of the employee's last day, so that they can remove accounts and passwords. Procedures for recovering keys for encrypted data and any other security assets must be part of the employee's out-processing.

Unfriendly termination is more difficult because employees may be tempted to take malicious or harmful actions. In such a case, system administrators might need to remove user accounts and passwords prior to notifying the employee of her termination. Other actions may be needed to protect the company's information assets. A terminated sales employee, for example, might attempt to take the company's confidential customer and sales-prospect data for future use at another company. The terminating employer should take steps to protect those data prior to the termination. MRV did not take any particular step to protect its data after Jason was fired and the result was a loss of data.

The human resources department should be aware of the importance of giving IS administrators early notification of employee termination. No blanket policy exists; the information systems department must assess each case on an individual basis.

Human Safeguards for Nonemployee Personnel

Business requirements may necessitate opening information systems to nonemployee personnel—temporary personnel, vendors, partner personnel (employees of business partners), and the public. Although temporary personnel can be screened, to reduce costs the screening will be abbreviated from that for employees. In most cases, companies cannot screen either vendor or partner personnel. Of course, public users cannot be screened at all. Similar limitations pertain to security training and compliance testing.

In the case of temporary, vendor, and partner personnel, the contracts that govern the activity should call for security measures appropriate to the sensitivity of the data and the IS resources involved. Companies should require vendors and partners to perform appropriate screening and security training. The contract also should mention specific security responsibilities that are particular to the work to be performed. Companies should provide accounts and passwords with the least privilege and remove those accounts as soon as possible.

The situation differs with public users of Web sites and other openly accessible information systems. It is exceedingly difficult and expensive to hold public users accountable for security violations. In general, the best safeguard from threats from public users is to *harden* the Web site or other facility against attack as much as possible. **Hardening** a site means to take extraordinary measures to reduce a system's vulnerability. Hardened sites use special versions of the operating system, and they lock down or eliminate operating systems features and functions that are not required by the application. Hardening is actually a technical safeguard, but we mention it here as the most important safeguard against public users.

Finally, note that the business relationship with the public, and with some partners, differs from that with temporary personnel and vendors. The public and some partners use the information system to receive a benefit. Consequently, safeguards need to protect such users from internal company security problems. A disgruntled employee who maliciously changes prices on a Web site potentially damages both public users and business partners. As one IT manager put it, "Rather than protecting ourselves from them, we need to protect them from us." This is an extension of the fifth principle in Figure 12-2.

Account Administration

The third human safeguard is account administration. The administration of user accounts, passwords, and help-desk policies and procedures are important components of the security system.

Account Management

Account management concerns the creation of new user accounts, the modification of existing account permissions, and the removal of unneeded accounts. Information system administrators perform all of these tasks, but account users have the responsibility to notify the administrators of the need for these actions. The IS department should create standard procedures for this purpose. As a future user, you can improve your relationship with IS personnel by providing early and timely notification of the need for account changes.

The existence of accounts that are no longer necessary is a serious security threat. IS administrators cannot know when an account should be removed; it is up to users and managers to give such notification.

Password Management

Passwords are the primary means of authentication. They are important not just for access to the user's computer, but also for authentication to other networks and servers to which the user may have access. Because of the importance of passwords, NIST recommends that employees be required to sign statements similar to that shown in Figure 12-11.

When an account is created, users should immediately change the password they are given to a password of their own. In fact, well-constructed systems require the user to change the password on first use.

Additionally, users should change passwords frequently thereafter. Some systems will require a password change every 3 months or perhaps more frequently. Users grumble at the nuisance of making such changes, but frequent password changes reduce not only the risk of password loss, but also the extent of damage if an existing password is compromised.

Some users create two passwords and switch back and forth between those two. This strategy results in poor security, and some password systems do not allow the user to reuse recently used passwords. Again, users may view this policy as a nuisance, but it is important.

Help-Desk Policies

In the past, help desks have been a serious security risk. A user who had forgotten his password would call the help desk and plead for the help-desk representative to tell him his password or to reset the password to something else. "I can't get this report out without it!" was (and is) a common lament.

I hereby acknowledge personal receipt of the system password(s) associated with the user IDs listed below. I understand that I am responsible for protecting the password(s), will comply with all applicable system security standards, and will not divulge my password(s) to any person. I further understand that I must report to the Information Systems Security Officer any problem I encounter in the use of the password(s) or when I have reason to believe that the private nature of my password(s) has been compromised.

Figure 12-11
Sample Account
Acknowledgment Form

Source: National Institute of Standards and Technology, *Introduction to Computer Security: The NIST Handbook*, Publication 800-12, p. 114.

The problem for help-desk representatives is, of course, that they have no way of determining that they are talking with the true user and not someone spoofing a true user. But, they are in a bind: If they do not help in some way, the help desk is perceived to be the "unhelpful desk."

To resolve such problems, many systems give the help-desk representative a means of authenticating the user. Typically, the help-desk information system has answers to questions that only the true user would know, such as the user's birthplace, mother's maiden name, or last four digits of an important account number. Often, too, the method by which the new password can be obtained is sent to the user in an email. Email, as you learned, is sent as plaintext, however, so the new password itself ought not to be emailed. If you ever receive notification that your password was reset when you did not request such a reset, immediately contact IS security. Someone has compromised your account.

All such help-desk measures reduce the strength of the security system, and, if the employee's position is sufficiently sensitive, they might create too large a vulnerability. In such a case, the user may just be out of luck. The account will be deleted, and the user must repeat the account-application process.

Systems Procedures

Figure 12-12 shows a grid of procedure types—normal operation, backup, and recovery. Procedures of each type should exist for each information system. For example, the order-entry system will have procedures of each of these types, as will the Web storefront, the inventory system, and so forth. The definition and use of standardized procedures reduces the likelihood of computer crime and other malicious activity by insiders. It also ensures that the system's security policy is enforced.

Procedures exist for both users and operations personnel. For each type of user, the company should develop procedures for normal, backup, and recovery operations. As a future user, you will be primarily concerned with user procedures. Normal-use procedures should provide safeguards appropriate to the sensitivity of the information system.

Backup procedures concern the creation of backup data to be used in the event of failure. Whereas operations personnel have the responsibility for backing up system databases and other systems data, departmental personnel have the need to back up data on their own computers. Good questions to ponder are, "What would happen if I lost my computer or iPhone tomorrow?" "What would happen if someone dropped my computer during an airport security inspection?" "What would happen if my computer were stolen?" Employees should ensure that they back up critical business data on their computers. The IS department can help in this effort by designing backup procedures and making backup facilities available.

	System Users	**Operations Personnel**
Normal Operation	Use the system to perform job tasks, with security appropriate to sensitivity.	Operate data center equipment, manage networks, run Web servers, and related operational tasks.
Backup	Prepare for loss of system functionality.	Back up Web site resources, databases, administrative data, account and password data, and other data.
Recovery	Accomplish job tasks during failure. Know tasks to do during system recovery.	Recover systems from backed up data. Role of help desk during recovery.

Figure 12-12
Systems Procedures

Finally, systems analysts should develop procedures for system recovery. First, how will the department manage its affairs when a critical system is unavailable? Customers will want to order, and manufacturing will want to remove items from inventory even though a critical information system is unavailable. How will the department respond? Once the system is returned to service, how will records of business activities during the outage be entered into the system? How will service be resumed? The system developers should ask and answer these questions and others like them and develop procedures accordingly.

Security Monitoring

Security monitoring is the last of the human safeguards we will consider. Important monitoring functions are activity log analyses, security testing, and investigating and learning from security incidents.

Many information system programs produce *activity logs*. Firewalls produce logs of their activities, including lists of all dropped packets, infiltration attempts, and unauthorized access attempts from within the firewall. DBMS products produce logs of successful and failed log-ins. Web servers produce voluminous logs of Web activities. The operating systems in personal computers can produce logs of log-ins and firewall activities.

None of these logs add any value to an organization unless someone looks at them. Accordingly, an important security function is to analyze these logs for threat patterns, successful and unsuccessful attacks, and evidence of security vulnerabilities.

Additionally, companies should test their security programs. Both in-house personnel and outside security consultants should conduct such testing.

Another important monitoring function is to investigate security incidents. How did the problem occur? Have safeguards been created to prevent a recurrence of such problems? Does the incident indicate vulnerabilities in other portions of the security system? What else can be learned from the incident?

Security systems reside in a dynamic environment. Organization structures change. Companies are acquired or sold; mergers occur. New systems require new security measures. New technology changes the security landscape, and new threats arise. Security personnel must constantly monitor the situation and determine if the existing security policy and safeguards are adequate. If changes are needed, security personnel need to take appropriate action.

Security, like quality, is an ongoing process. There is no final state that represents a secure system or company. Instead, companies must monitor security on a continuing basis.

Q6 How Should Organizations Respond to Security Incidents?

Every organization needs to be prepared for security incidents. Publicly traded companies are required by the Sarbanes-Oxley Act to do so. Other organizations should do so as a matter of good management. When an incident occurs, whether from an act of nature or from a human threat, time is of the essence. Employees need to know what to do and how to do it. In this section, we will consider backup and recovery sites and incident response plans.

Disaster-Recovery Backup Sites

A computer *disaster* is a substantial loss of computing infrastructure caused by acts of nature, crime, or terrorist activity. As stated several times, the best way to solve a problem is not to have it. The best safeguard against a natural disaster is appropriate

Figure 12-13
Disaster Preparedness Tasks

- Locate infrastructure in safe location.
- Identify mission-critical systems.
- Identify resources needed to run those systems.
- Prepare remote backup facilities.
- Train and rehearse.

location. If possible, place computing centers, Web farms, and other computer facilities in locations not prone to floods, earthquakes, hurricanes, tornados, or avalanches. Even in those locations, place infrastructure in unobtrusive buildings, basements, backrooms, and similar locations well within the physical perimeter of the organization. Also, locate computing infrastructure in fire-resistant buildings designed to house expensive and critical equipment.

However, sometimes business requirements necessitate locating the computing infrastructure in undesirable locations. Also, even at a good location, disasters do occur. Therefore, many businesses prepare backup processing centers in locations geographically removed from the primary processing site.

Figure 12-13 lists major disaster-preparedness tasks. After choosing a safe location for the computing infrastructure, the organization should identify all mission-critical applications. These are applications without which the organization cannot carry on and which, if lost for any period of time, could cause the organization's failure. The next step is to identify all resources necessary to run those systems. Such resources include computers, operating systems, application programs, databases, administrative data, procedure documentation, and trained personnel.

Next, the organization creates backups for the critical resources at the remote processing center. A **hot site** is a utility company that can take over another company's processing with no forewarning. Hot sites are expensive; organizations pay $250,000 or more per month for such services. **Cold sites**, in contrast, provide computers and office space. They are cheaper to lease, but customers install and manage systems themselves. The total cost of a cold side, including all customer labor and other expenses, might not necessarily be less than the cost of a hot site.

Once the organization has backups in place, it must train and rehearse cutover of operations from the primary center to the backup. In the case of a hot site, employees must know how to ensure the handoff occurred without incident, how to run systems while the hot site is active, and how to recover processing when the primary site is again operational. For cold sites, employees must know how to apply backups, how to start systems, and how to run systems from the cold site location. As with all emergency procedures, periodic refresher rehearsals are mandatory.

Backup facilities are expensive; however, the costs of establishing and maintaining that facility are a form of insurance. Senior management must make the decision to prepare such a facility by balancing the risks, benefits, and costs.

Incident-Response Plan

The last component of a security plan that we will consider is incident response. Figure 12-14 lists the major factors. First, every organization should have an

- Have plan in place
- Centralized reporting
- Specific responses
  - Speed
  - Preparation pays
  - Don't make problem worse
- Practice!

Figure 12-14
Factors in Incident Response

incident-response plan as part of the security program. No organization should wait until some asset has been lost or compromised before deciding what to do. The plan should include how employees are to respond to security problems, whom they should contact, the reports they should make, and steps they can take to reduce further loss.

Consider, for example, a virus. An incident-response plan will stipulate what an employee should do when he notices the virus. It should specify whom to contact and what to do. It may stipulate that the employee should turn off his computer and physically disconnect from the network. The plan should also indicate what users with wireless connections should do.

The plan should provide centralized reporting of all security incidents. Such reporting will enable an organization to determine if it is under systematic attack or whether an incident is isolated. Centralized reporting also allows the organization to learn about security threats, take consistent actions in response, and apply specialized expertise to all security problems.

When an incident does occur, speed is of the essence. Viruses and worms can spread very quickly across an organization's networks, and a fast response will help to mitigate the consequences. Because of the need for speed, preparation pays. The incident-response plan should identify critical personnel and their off-hours contact information. These personnel should be trained on where to go and what to do when they get there. Without adequate preparation, there is substantial risk that the actions of well-meaning people will make the problem worse. Also, the rumor mill will be alive with all sorts of nutty ideas about what to do. A cadre of well-informed, trained personnel will serve to dampen such rumors.

Finally, organizations should periodically practice incident response. Without such practice, personnel will be poorly informed on the response plan, and the plan itself might have flaws that become apparent only during a drill.

Q7 What Is the Extent of Computer Crime?

We do not know the full extent of computer crime. Unfortunately, there is no national census of computer crime, and many organizations are reluctant to admit losses due to adverse publicity. We can rely only on surveys taken of sample organizations. One of the oldest and most respected surveys is the one conducted by the Computer Security Institute (CSI; previously known as the FBI/CSI survey).

This survey has been conducted since 1995, and the organizations involved in the survey are balanced among for-profit and nonprofit organizations and government agencies. They are also balanced for size of organization, from small to very large. You can obtain a copy of the most recent survey at *http://gocsi.com* (registration is required).

In the 2009 report, CSI stated that it had no estimate of the total loss to computer crime experienced by its survey respondents. Only 144 of the 522 responding organizations provided information on economic losses to computer crime. Furthermore, some losses are difficult to quantify. For example, what is the cost of a denial-of-service attack on an organization's Web site? If a company's Web site is unavailable for 24 hours, what potential sales, prospects, or employees have been lost? What reputation problem was created for the organization? Some financial loss has occurred, but it is impossible to quantify.

Of those organizations that did report data on financial losses, financial fraud had the highest average incident cost—$463,100—and losses due to bots averaged $345,600.[6] Given the paucity of data and the bias in the survey because responding organizations are security-conscious members of the CSI community, we should follow CSI's lead and simply say that we have no idea of the true cost of computer crime.

---

[6]2008 CSI Computer Crime and Security Survey, p. 16.

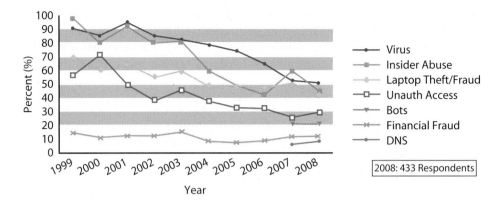

Figure 12-15

Percent of Security Incidents

Source: 2008 CSI Computer Crime and Security Survey, p. 15.

However, the survey does provide data about the percentage of different types of attacks. Figure 12-15 shows the trend in computer crime incidents over the past 10 years. As shown, as a general trend, the number of incidents of all types has been gradually decreasing.

Several trends appear in this figure. For one, the number of virus attacks during this period has steadily decreased, indicating the success of antivirus programs. Financial fraud has remained relatively stable, affecting approximately 12 percent of the respondents over this period.

Laptop theft has declined from around 70 percent in 1999 to 44 percent in 2008. Still, laptop theft does occur, and it is the cause of a considerable portion of the loss of proprietary, customer, and employee data. Every 6 months or so, the press reports another incident in which an organization was exposed to risk when an employee lost his or her laptop.

As a business professional, make it your practice not to carry out of your office on a laptop any data that you do not need. In general, store proprietary data on servers or removable devices that do not travel with you. If you are required to carry proprietary data on your laptop, outside of your office, then guard that data appropriately. Behave as if your laptop is a case containing rare gems; in fact, the data it contains may be worth more than a case of rare gems!

Be careful with your interpretation of Figure 12-15. Note that it shows the *number of incidents,* not the cost of the loss. For the cost of loss data that CSI did receive, financial fraud had the highest average cost, yet it has the lowest frequency in Figure 12-15.

Q8 2020?

Computer security is a field of *cat and mouse.* Computer criminals find a vulnerability to exploit, and they exploit it. Computer security forces discover that vulnerability and create safeguards to thwart it. Computer criminals find a new vulnerability to exploit, computer security forces thwart it, and so it goes. The next challenges are likely to be to iPhones and other mobile devices. Security on those devices will need to be improved as threats emerge that exploit their vulnerabilities. This cat-and-mouse game is likely to continue for at least the next 10 years. I do not believe that any magic bullet will be devised to prevent computer crime, nor do I believe that any particular computer crime will be impossible to thwart. However, the skill level of this cat-and-mouse activity is likely to increase, and substantially so. Because of increased security in operating systems and other software, and because of improved security procedures and employee training, it will become harder and harder for the lone hacker to find some vulnerability to exploit. Not impossible, but vastly more difficult.

The next decade is likely to see the rise of bot herders. These herders may be organized criminals, they may be terrorists, or they may be elements of governments inflicting a new type of cyber warfare on other nations. Given the importance of the Internet to international commerce, banking, finance, and communication, threats from such bot herders are serious. I expect in the next 10 years we will see one or more successful and substantial attacks; we may even see cyber warfare among nations. We can be aware of the risks, be as prepared as we can, and not be surprised and overreact when an attack occurs. Such cat and mouse has been played out in human society for centuries, at least.

Given this prospect, it is not surprising that the number of computer security jobs is projected to increase by 27 percent by 2016.[7] If you are clever, enjoy puzzles and games, and like technology, computer security could be an excellent career choice for you. Given that the CSI survey indicates the largest average loss due to computer crime is financial fraud, another good career choice is auditing, with a specialty in accounting information systems. A dual major in accounting and information systems is particularly desirable.

That's it! You've reached the end of this text. Take a moment to consider how you will use what you learned, as described in the Guide on pages 474–475.

---

[7]iseekcareers, "Computer Security Experts," *http://www.iseek.org/careers/careerDetail?id= 1&oc=100280* (accessed July 2009).

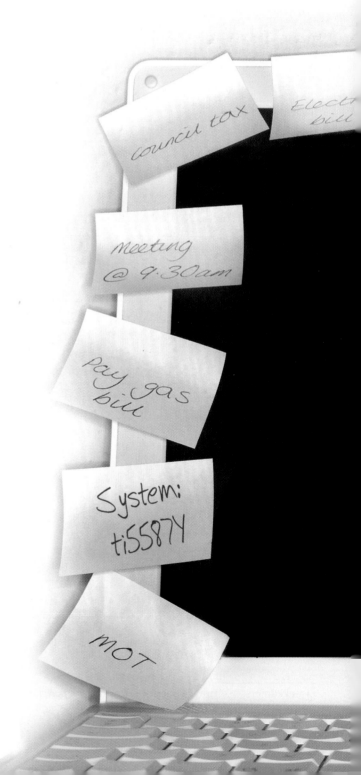

Security Assurance, Hah!

"If I have to go to one more employee meeting about security policy, I'm going to scream. The managers talk about threats, and safeguards, and risk, and uncertainty, and all the things they want us to do to improve security. Has any manager ever watched people work in this department?

"Walk through the cubicles here and watch what is happening. I'll bet half the employees are using the password they were assigned the day they started work. I'll bet they've never changed their password, ever! And for the people who have changed their passwords, I'll bet they've changed them to some simpleton word like 'Sesame' or 'MyDogSpot' or something equally absurd.

"Or, open the top drawer of any of my coworkers' desks and guess what you'll find? A little yellow sticky with entries like OrderEntry: 748QPt#7ml, Compensation: RXL87MB, System: ti5587Y. What do you suppose those entries are? Do you think anyone who worked here on a weekend wouldn't know what to do with them? And the only reason they're in the desk drawers is that Martha (our manager) threw a fit when she saw a yellow sticky like that on Terri's monitor.

"I've mentioned all this to Martha several times, but nothing happens. What we need is a good scare. We need somebody to break into the system using one of those passwords and do some damage. Wait—if you enter a system with a readily available password, is that even breaking in? Or is it more like opening a door with a key you were given? Anyway, we need someone to steal something, delete some files, or erase customer balances. Then maybe the idiotic management here would stop talking about security risk assurance and start talking about real security, here on the ground floor!" ∎

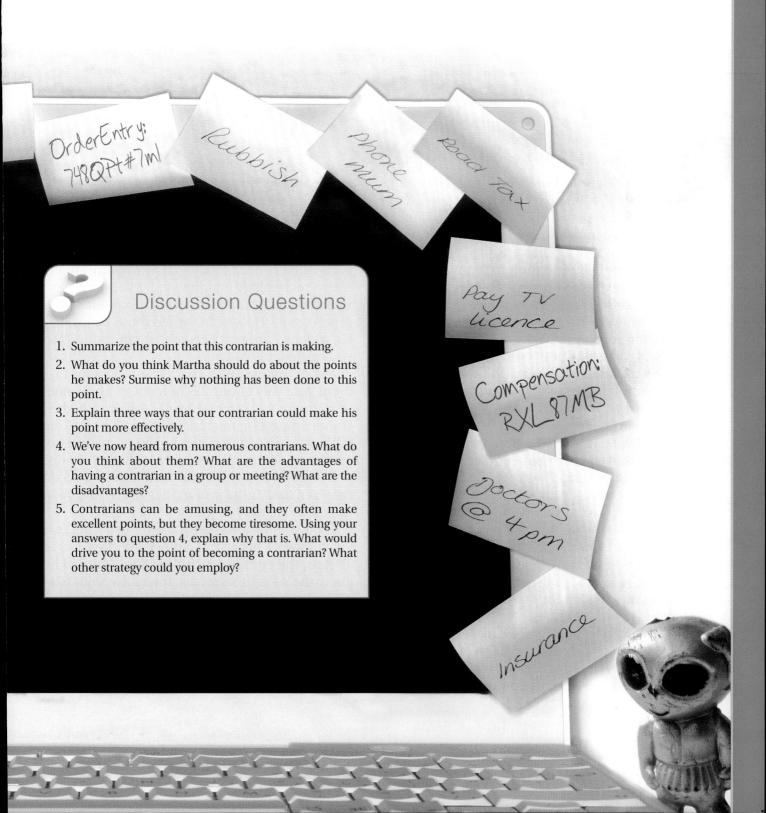

Discussion Questions

1. Summarize the point that this contrarian is making.

2. What do you think Martha should do about the points he makes? Surmise why nothing has been done to this point.

3. Explain three ways that our contrarian could make his point more effectively.

4. We've now heard from numerous contrarians. What do you think about them? What are the advantages of having a contrarian in a group or meeting? What are the disadvantages?

5. Contrarians can be amusing, and they often make excellent points, but they become tiresome. Using your answers to question 4, explain why that is. What would drive you to the point of becoming a contrarian? What other strategy could you employ?

The Final, Final Word

Congratulations! You've made it through the entire book. With this knowledge you are well prepared to be an effective user of information systems. And with work and imagination, you can be much more than that. Many interesting opportunities are available to those who can apply information in innovative ways. Your professor has done what she can do, and the rest, as they say, is up to you.

So what's next? Back in Chapter 1 we claimed that Introduction to MIS is the most important course in the business curriculum today. That claim was based on the availability of nearly free data communications and data storage. By now, you've learned many of the ways that businesses and organizations use these resources and information systems based upon those resources. You've also seen how businesses like FlexTime and MRV use information systems to solve problems and to further their competitive strategies. In some cases, particularly with MRV, they *struggled* to use information systems for those purposes.

How can you use that knowledge? Chapter 1 claimed that future business professionals must be able "to assess, evaluate, and apply emerging information technology to business." Have you learned how to do that? At least, are you better able to do that than you were prior to this class? You probably know the meaning of many more terms than you did when you started this class, and such knowledge is important. But, even more important is the ability to use that knowledge to apply MIS to your business interests.

Chapter 1 also reviewed the work of the RAND Corporation and that of Robert Reich on what professional workers in the twenty-first century need to know. Those sources state that such workers need to know how to innovate the use of technology and how to "collaborate, reason abstractly, think in terms of systems, and experiment." Have you learned those behaviors? Or, at least, are you better at them than when you started this course?

As of August 2009, the national unemployment rate was about 9.5 percent, with projections that it will increase to 10 percent or higher. Under these circumstances, good jobs will be difficult to obtain. You need to apply every asset you have. One of those assets is the knowledge you've gained in this class. Take the time to do the exercises at the end of this guide, and then use those answers in your job interviews!

Look for the job you truly want to do, get that job, and work hard. In the movie *Phillip Glass in 12 Acts,* the composer Phillip Glass claimed he knew the secret to success. It was, he said, "Get up early and work hard all day." That quotation seems obvious and hardly worth stating. Except that it has the ring of truth. And, if you can find a job you truly love, it isn't even hard. Actually, it's fun, most of the time. So, use what you've learned in this class to obtain the job you truly want! ■

Discussion Questions

1. Reflect on what you have learned from this course. Write two paragraphs on how the knowledge you have gained will help you to "assess, evaluate, and apply emerging information technology to business." Shape your writing around the kind of job that you want to obtain upon graduation.

2. Write two paragraphs on how the knowledge and experiences you've had in this class will help you to "collaborate, reason abstractly, think in terms of systems, and experiment." Again, shape your writing around the kind of job you wish to obtain.

3. Using your answer to question 1, extract three or four sentences about yourself that you could use in a job interview.

4. Using your answer to question 2, extract three or four sentences about yourself that you could use in a job interview.

5. Practice using your answers to questions 3 and 4 in a job interview with a classmate, roommate, or friend.

ACTIVE REVIEW

Use this Active Review to verify that you understand the ideas and concepts that answer the chapter's study questions.

Q1 What are the threats to information security?

List five sources of security threats and describe each. List three security problem types and describe each. Give one example of each of the five threats shown in Figure 12-1. Name and describe the three components of an organization's security program. Explain how safeguard types relate to the five components of an information system.

Q2 What is senior management's security role?

Broadly describe senior management's security role. Explain the meaning of each element in Figure 12-3. State three elements of a security policy and explain each. Define *risk* and *uncertainty* and explain the difference between them. Define *safeguard* and *vulnerability* and explain their relationship. Describe two types of consequences. Define *likelihood* and *probable loss* and explain their relationship. Explain computer security risk-management decisions that senior management must make. Explain why uncertainty does not absolve management from security responsibility.

Q3 What technical safeguards are available?

Define *technical safeguard* and explain which of the five components are involved in such safeguards. Explain the use of identification and authentication and describe three types of authentication. List the characteristics of a strong password. Describe the purpose of Kerberos. Explain the security problem posed by wireless networks and describe safeguards that exist for the SOHO market. Describe symmetric and asymmetric encryption and explain how they are used for SSL/TLS. Explain digital signatures and describe how they are used to detect message modification. Define *digital signature* and *hashing*. Explain the role of digital certificates for preventing the spoofing of public keys. Define *certificate authority*, explain its role, and describe the potential infinite regress when using certificate authorities. Explain how that infinite regress is avoided. Name the five types of malware as defined in this text and briefly describe each. Describe the six antimalware techniques presented.

Q4 What data safeguards are available?

Define *data safeguards* and give four examples. Explain each.

Q5 What human safeguards are available?

Name the components involved in human safeguards. Name and describe four human safeguards that pertain to employees. Explain how human safeguards pertain to nonemployee personnel. Summarize account administration safeguards. Describe six types of procedures for system users and system operations personnel. Explain three security monitoring functions.

Q6 How should organizations respond to security incidents?

Explain why organizations need to prepare for security incidents ahead of time. Describe ways of avoiding natural disasters; explain the role for remote processing. Define *hot site* and *cold site* and explain the difference. Explain the importance of an incident-response plan and the need for centralized reporting. Explain why a rapid, but controlled, incident response is needed and why practice is important.

Q7 What is the extent of computer crime?

Explain why we do not know the true extent of computer crime. Characterize the CSI computer crime survey. Name the top four categories of computer crime and give rough percentages of the frequency of each type. As an employee, name the single most important thing you can do to reduce computer crime.

Q8 2020?

Explain how the phrase *cat and mouse* pertains to computer security. What types of security problems are likely to occur in the next 10 years? Summarize computer security job opportunities.

KEY TERMS AND CONCEPTS

Adware 459
Asymmetric encryption 456
Authentication 453
Biometric authentication 453
Bot 460

Bot herder 460
Botnet 460
Certificate authority (CA) 457
Cold sites 468
Denial of service 446

Digital certificate 458
Digital signature 456
Drive-by sniffers 445
Email spoofing 445
Gramm-Leach-Bliley (GLB) Act 450

USING YOUR KNOWLEDGE

1. Search online to find a way to obtain your own credit report. Several sources to check are *http://www.equifax.com, http://www.experion.com,* and *http://www.transunion.com.* Look for a source that provides the report for free.

   a. Review your credit report for obvious errors. However, other checks are appropriate. Search the Web for guidance on how best to review your credit records. Summarize what you learn.

   b. What actions should you take if you find errors in your credit report?

   c. Define identity theft. Search the Web and determine the best course of action if someone thinks he has been the victim of identity theft.

2. Reread the MRV introductions to Parts 3 and 4 and to Chapters 7 through 11 Using those introductions as background, generate a two- to three-page document to Sue that summarizes the security management activities that MRV should practice. Consider each of the threats in Figure 12-1. As you write the document, keep in mind that MRV is a small company with limited resources that must strike a balance between comprehensive security management and cost. Explain what it means for MRV to manage risk. Describe the difference

between not creating a security safeguard because MRV never thought about it and not creating a safeguard because of a risk management decision.

3. Consider the categories of threat in Figure 12-1. Describe the three most serious threats to each of the following businesses:

   a. FlexTime
   b. A neighborhood accounting firm
   c. A dentist's office
   d. A Honda dealership

4. Describe a potential technical safeguard for each of the threats you identified in your answer to question 3.

5. Describe a potential data safeguard for each of the threats you identified in your answer to question 3. If no data safeguard is appropriate to a business, explain why.

6. Describe a potential human safeguard for each of the threats you identified in your answer to question 3.

7. Describe how each of the businesses in question 3 should prepare for security incidents.

8. How likely are the threats you identified in question 3? If you owned these businesses, which of the items you described in questions 3 through 7 would you implement?

COLLABORATION EXERCISE

Collaborate with a group of students on the following exercises. Recall from Chapter 2 that collaboration is more than cooperation because it involves iteration and feedback. Post a document, a discussion item, a wiki item, or an idea and obtain feedback from your team members. Similarly, read the ideas of others and comment on them. Try to innovate in both the process by which you collaborate and the work product that you create. Avoid face-to-face

meetings. Instead, use collaborative software such as Google Docs & Spreadsheets, Microsoft Groove, or Microsoft SharePoint to facilitate your ideas.

Before you read further, realize that the graphics in this exercise are *fake.* They were not produced by a legitimate business, but were generated by a phisher, which is an operation that spoofs legitimate companies in an

Your Order ID: "17152492"
Order Date: "09/07/05"
Product Purchased: "Two First Class Tickets to Cozumel"
Your card type: "CREDIT"
Total Price: "$349.00"

Hello, when you purchased your tickets you provided an incorrect mailing address.

See more details here
Please follow the link and modify your mailing address or cancel your order. If you have questions, feel free to contact us at *account@usefulbill.com*

Figure 12-16
Fake Phishing Email

attempt to illegally capture credit card numbers, email accounts, driver's license numbers, and other data. Some phishers also install bots on users' computers.

Phishing is usually initiated via an email. To understand how, consider the email in Figure 12-16. This bogus email is designed to cause you to click on the "See more details here" link. When you do so, you will be connected to a site that will ask you for personal data, such as credit card numbers, card expiration dates, driver's license number, Social Security number, or other data. In this particular case, you will be taken to a screen that asks for your credit card number (see Figure 12-17).

The Web page in Figure 12-17 is produced by a nonexistent company and is entirely fake, including the link "Inform us about fraud." The only purpose of this site is to illegally capture your card number. It might also install spyware, adware, or other malware to your computer.

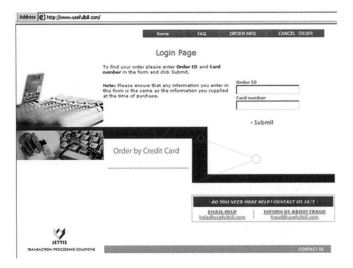

Figure 12-17
Fake Phishing Screen

If you were to get this far, you should immediately close your browser, restart your computer, and go shower and brush your teeth! You should also run antimalware scans on your computer to determine if the phisher has installed program code on your computer. If so, use the antimalware software to remove that code.

How can you defend yourself from such attacks? First, you know that you did not purchase two first-class tickets to Cozumel. (Had you by odd circumstance just purchased airline tickets to Cozumel, you should contact the legitimate vendor's site *directly* to determine if there had been some mix up.) Because you have not purchased such tickets, suspect a phisher.

Second, notice the implausibility of the email. It is exceedingly unlikely that you can buy two first-class tickets to any foreign country for $349. Additionally, note the misspelled word in the last line and the poor grammar ("cortact with us"). All of these facts should alert you to the bogus nature of this email.

Third, do not be misled by legitimate-looking graphics. Phishers are criminals; they do not bother to respect international agreements on legitimate use of trademarks. The phisher might use names and logos of legitimate companies such as Visa, MasterCard, Discover, and American Express on their Web page, and the presence of those names might lull you into thinking this is legitimate. The phisher is *illegally using* those names. In other instances, the phisher will copy the entire look and feel of a legitimate company's Web site.

Phishing is a serious problem. To protect yourself, be wary of unsolicited email, even if the email appears to be from a legitimate business. If you have questions about an email, contact the company directly (*not* using the addresses provided by the phisher!) and ask about the email. And, above all, never give confidential data such as account numbers, Social Security numbers, driver's license numbers, or credit card numbers in response to *any unsolicited email.*

Although it is clear what you should not do in response to phishing, it is less clear what legitimate businesses can do about it. In this exercise you will be asked to determine a policy for organizations to use to protect themselves from phishing attacks.

1. As you can see, phishing is a serious threat to legitimate brands. Go to the FraudWatch site (*http://fraudwatch international.com*) and click " Phishing Alerts." Examine a dozen or more of these alerts and describe five or six techniques that phishers use. The particular attacks on this list depend on when you access it, but, generally, you will find a *who's who* of business organizations on that list. Describe the techniques that you found.
2. Discuss with your group the danger that such attacks present to legitimate brands. Describe monetary and nonmonetary losses that occur from phishing.

3. Describing phishing attacks and attendant losses is the easy part. The hard part is determining what to do about it. Discuss the following issues with your group.

   a. How does an organization know that it has been phished? How will the organization be informed? What damage will have occurred by then?

   b. What should an organization do, once it knows that a phishing attack is underway?

   c. What steps can companies take to forewarn their customers about phishing attacks?

   d. How realistic is it for organizations to sue phishers? What aspects of phishing hamper both legal and law enforcement measures?

   e. Phishing is an industry-wide problem. How can organizations better solve the problem or mitigate its consequences by working together?

   f. What role do organizations like FraudWatch International serve? Can such organizations prevent phishing?

   g. Search the Web to determine if it is possible to buy phishing insurance. Describe any such insurance policies you find.

4. Given the knowledge of this exercise, what do you think organizations can do to protect themselves from phishing attacks? Name and describe the top five actions they should take.

5. Document your conclusions in your answer to part d in a memo to a senior marketing manager. Describe the risks, the potential damage, and possible responses. Recommend an organizational policy regarding phishing attacks.

APPLICATION EXERCISES

1. Develop a spreadsheet model of the cost of a virus attack in an organization that has three types of computers: employee workstations, data servers, and Web servers. Assume that the number of computers affected by the virus depends on the severity of the virus. For the purposes of your model, assume that there are three levels of virus severity: *Low-severity* incidents affect fewer than 30 percent of the user workstations and none of the data or Web servers. *Medium-severity* incidents affect up to 70 percent of the user workstations, up to half of the Web servers, and none of the data servers. *High-severity* incidents can affect all organizational computers.

   Assume 50 percent of the incidents are low severity, 30 percent are medium severity, and 20 percent are high severity.

   Assume employees can remove viruses from workstations themselves, but that specially trained technicians are required to repair the servers. The time to eliminate a virus from an infected computer depends on the computer type. Let the time to remove the virus from each type be an input into your model. Assume that when users eliminate the virus themselves, they are unproductive for twice the time required for the removal. Let the average employee hourly labor cost be an input to your model. Let the average cost of a technician also be an input into your model. Finally, let the total number of user computers, data servers, and Web servers be inputs into your model.

   Run your simulation 10 times. Use the same inputs for each run, but draw a random number (assume a

uniform distribution for all random numbers) to determine the severity type. Then, draw random numbers to determine the percentage of computers of each type affected, using the constraints detailed earlier. For example, if the attack is of medium severity, draw a random number between 0 and 70 to indicate the percentage of infected user workstations and a random number between 0 and 50 to indicate the percentage of infected Web servers.

   For each run, calculate the total of lost employee hours, the total dollar cost of lost employee labor hours, the total hours of technicians to fix the servers, and the total cost of technician labor. Finally, compute the total overall cost. Show the results of each run. Show the average costs and hours for the 10 runs.

2. In the MRV case at the start of this chapter, Jason was able to use Eddie's computer in the middle of the night, when no one was around, because no one remembered to ask Jason to return the key he had been given to the MRV offices. And, MRV is about to discover that Jason kept more than $2,500 worth of equipment that had been checked out to him. All of this could have been prevented if someone had known to ask Jason for keys and equipment at the time he quit. Accordingly, MRV has decided to create an Access database to track assets that have been allocated to individuals who work at MRV.

   Suppose that MRV has asked you to develop an Access database that tracks keys, equipment, and user accounts that have been issued to employees and contractors. Assume your database has four tables: Person, Equipment, Key, and Account. Person has data about employees and contractors, Equipment has data about equipment that has been allocated to individuals in the Person table, Key has data about keys that have been allocated to individuals in Person, and Account has data about accounts that have been created for individuals in Person. (This last table is needed because MRV is about to start a policy that every user of every computer has his or her own account for using that computer. Thus, an account name is an asset, just like a building key or a paddle.)

a. Using your knowledge, experience, and intuition design the Person, Equipment, Key, and Account tables. Name and describe the columns of each table and indicate which columns are the primary key.

b. Specify the maximum cardinality of the relationships between:

   (1) Person and Equipment

   (2) Person and Key

   (3) Person and Account

c. Modify your design in part a to include foreign keys necessary to support the relationships you specified in part b.

d. Create your database in Access and fill it with sample data.

e. Create a form for adding a new Person and equipment assigned to that person.

f. Create a form for allocating a key to an existing Person row.

g. Create a report suitable for use when an employee quits MRV. Your report should include all resources that need to be recovered as well as computer accounts that need to be removed.

h. Create a parameterized query that accepts a person's name and generates the report in part g for that person.

CASE STUDY 12

The ChoicePoint Attack

ChoicePoint, a Georgia-based corporation, is a data aggregator that specializes in risk-management and fraud-prevention data. Traditionally, ChoicePoint provided motor vehicle reports, claims histories, and similar data to the automobile insurance industry; in recent years, it broadened its customer base to include general business and government agencies. Today, it also offers data for volunteer and job-applicant screening and data to assist in the location of missing children. ChoicePoint has over 4,000 employees, and its 2007 revenue was $982 million. It was acquired by Reed Elsevier in 2008.

In the fall of 2004, ChoicePoint was the victim of a fraudulent spoofing attack in which unauthorized individuals posed as legitimate customers and obtained personal data on more than 145,000 individuals. According to the company's Web site:

> These criminals were able to pass our customer authentication due-diligence processes by using stolen identities to create and produce the documents needed to appear legitimate. As small business customers of ChoicePoint, these fraudsters accessed products that contained basic telephone directory-type data (name and address information) as well as a combination of Social Security numbers and/or driver's license numbers and, at times, abbreviated credit reports. They were also able to obtain other public record information including, but not limited to bankruptcies, liens, and judgments; professional licenses; and real property data.

ChoicePoint became aware of the problem in November 2004, when it noticed unusual processing activity on some accounts in Los Angeles. Accordingly, the company contacted the Los Angeles Police Department, which requested that ChoicePoint not reveal the activity until the department could conduct an investigation. In January, the LAPD notified ChoicePoint that it could contact the customers whose data had been compromised.

This crime is an example of a failure of authentication, not a network break-in. ChoicePoint's firewalls and other safeguards were not overcome. Instead, the criminals spoofed legitimate businesses. The infiltrators obtained valid California business licenses, and until their unusual processing activity was detected they appeared to be legitimate users.

In response to this problem, ChoicePoint established a hotline for customers whose data had been compromised. It also purchased a credit report for each victim and paid for a credit-report-monitoring service for one year. In February 2005, attorneys initiated a class-action lawsuit for all 145,000 customers, with an initial loss claim of $75,000 each. At the same time, the U.S. Senate announced that it would conduct an investigation.

Ironically, ChoicePoint exposed itself to a public relations nightmare, considerable expense, a class-action lawsuit, a Senate investigation, and a 20-percent drop in its share price because it contacted the police and cooperated in the attempt to apprehend the criminals. When ChoicePoint noticed the unusual account activity, had it simply shut down data access for the illegitimate businesses, no one would have known. Of course, the 145,000 customers whose identities had been compromised would have unknowingly been subject to identity theft, but it is unlikely that such thefts could have been tracked back to ChoicePoint.

As a data utility, ChoicePoint maintains relationships with many different entities. It obtains its data from both public and private sources. It then sells access to this data to its customers. Much of the data, by the way, can be obtained directly from the data vendor. ChoicePoint adds value by providing a centralized access point for many data needs. In addition to data sources and customers, ChoicePoint maintains relationships with partners such as the vital records departments in major cities. Finally, ChoicePoint also has relationships with the people and organizations on which it maintains data.

Questions

1. ChoicePoint exposed itself to considerable expense, many problems, and a possible loss of brand confidence because it notified the Los Angeles Police Department, cooperated in the investigation, and notified the individuals whose records had been compromised. It could have buried the theft and possibly avoided any responsibility. Comment on the ethical issues and ChoicePoint's response. Did ChoicePoint choose wisely? Consider that question from the viewpoint of customers, law enforcement personnel, investors, and management.

2. Given ChoicePoint's experience, what is the likely action of similar companies whose records are compromised in this way? Given your answer, do you think federal regulation and additional laws are required? What other steps could be taken to ensure that data vendors notify people harmed by data theft?

3. Visit *www.choicepoint.com*. Summarize the products that ChoicePoint provides. What seems to be the central theme of this business?

4. Suppose that ChoicePoint decides to establish a formal security policy on the issue of inappropriate release of personal data. Summarize the issues that ChoicePoint should address in this policy.

Q1 What Characteristics Make International IS Management Challenging?

Size and complexity make international IS management challenging. International information systems are larger and more complex. Projects to develop them are larger and more complicated to manage. International IS departments are bigger and composed of people from many cultures with many different native languages. International organizations have extensive IS and IT assets, and those assets are exposed to more risk and greater uncertainty. Security incidents are more complicated to investigate.

We will consider each of these impacts in more detail in the following questions. The bottom line, however, is that size and complexity make international IS management challenging.

Q2 Why Is International Information Systems Development Difficult?

Before considering this question, realize that the factors that affect international information systems development are more challenging than those that affect international software development. If the *system* is truly international, if many people from many different countries will be using the system, then the development project is exceedingly complicated. For example, consider the effort required for a multinational company like 3M to create an integrated, worldwide CRM. Such a project is massive!

In contrast, creating localized software (one or more programs that are available in different human-language versions) is challenging, but not nearly as daunting. As stated in the International Dimension for Part 2, localizing a program is a matter of designing it to accept program menus, messages, and help text from external files and to translate those files. Of course, different character sets, different sorting orders, different currency symbols, and other complications must be accounted for, but these challenges are surmountable with good software design and development.

Think about the five components of an information system. Running hardware in different countries is not a problem, and localizing software is manageable. Databases pose some problems, namely determining the language, currency, and units of measure used to record data, but these problems are surmountable. A substantial problem arises, however, when we consider procedures.

An international system is used by people who live and work in cultures that are vastly different from one another. The way that customers are treated in Japan differs substantially from the way they are treated in Spain, which differs substantially from the way they are treated in the United States. Therefore, the procedures for using a CRM will be correspondingly different.

Consider the phases of the SDLC. During systems definition, we are supposed to determine the purpose and scope of the system. As you know by now, information systems should facilitate the organization's competitive strategy by supporting business processes. But what if the underlying processes differ? Again, customer support in Japan and customer support in Spain might involve completely different processes and activities.

Even if the purpose and scope can be defined in some unified way, how are requirements to be determined? Again, if the underlying business processes differ, then the specific requirements for the information system will differ. Managing requirements for a system in one culture is difficult, but managing requirements for international systems can be many times more difficult.

The two responses to such challenges are to either define a set of standard business processes or to develop alternative versions of the system that support different processes in different countries. Both responses are problematic. The first response requires conversion of the organization to different work processes, and, as you learned in Chapter 7, such conversion can be exceedingly difficult. People resist change, and they will do so with vehemence if the change violates cultural norms.

The second response is easier to implement, but creates system design challenges. It also means that, in truth, there is not one system, but many.

Despite the problems, both responses are used. For example, SAP, Oracle, and other ERP vendors define standard business processes via the inherent procedures in their software products. Many organizations attempt to enforce those standard procedures. When it becomes organizationally infeasible to do so, organizations develop exceptions to those inherent procedures and develop programs to handle the exceptions. This choice means custom software and high maintenance expenses, as explained in Chapter 4.

Q3 What Are the Challenges of International Project Management?

Managing a global information systems development project is difficult because of the size and complexity of the project. Requirements are complex, many resources are required, and numerous people are involved. Team members speak different languages, live in different cultures, work in different time zones, and seldom meet face-to-face.

Figure 1 summarizes the major challenges. Project integration is more difficult, because international development projects require the complex integration of results from distributed work groups. Also, task dependencies can span teams working in different countries, increasing the difficulty of task management.

Requirements definition for international IS is more difficult for the reasons discussed in Q2. Time management is more difficult because teams in different cultures and countries work at different rates. Some cultures have a 35-hour workweek, and others have a 60-hour workweek. Some cultures expect 6-week vacations, and others expect 2. Some cultures thrive on efficiency of labor, and others thrive on considerate working relationships. There is no standard rate of development for an international project.

In terms of cost, different countries and cultures pay vastly different labor rates. Using critical path analysis, managers may choose to move a task from one team to another. Doing so, however, may substantially increase costs. Thus, management may choose to accept a delay rather than move work to an available (but more expensive) team. The complex trade-offs that exist between time and cost become even more complex for international projects.

Quality and human resources also are more complicated for international projects. Quality standards vary among countries. The IT industry in

Figure 1
Challenges for International IS
Project Management

Management Issue	Challenge
Project integration	Complex integration of results from distributed workgroups. Management of dependencies of tasks from physically and culturally different workgroups.
Requirements	Need to support multiple versions of underlying business processes. Possibly substantial differences in requirements and procedures.
Time	Development pace and workweek vary among cultures and countries.
Cost	Cost of development varies widely among countries. Two members performing the same work in different countries may be paid substantially different rates. Moving work among teams may dramatically change costs.
Quality	Quality standards vary among cultures. Different expectations of quality may result in an inconsistent system.
Human resources	Worker expectations differ. Compensation, rewards, work conditions vary widely.
Communications	Geographic, language, and cultural distance among team members impedes effective communication.
Risk	Development risk is higher. Easy to lose control.
Procurement	Complications of international trade.

some nations, such as India, has invested heavily in development techniques that increase program quality. Other nations, such as the United States, have been less willing to invest in quality. In any case, the integration of programs of varying quality results in an inconsistent system.

Worker expectations vary among cultures and nations. Compensation, rewards, and worker conditions vary, and these differences can lead to misunderstandings, poor morale, and project delays.

Because of these factors, effective team communication is exceedingly important for international projects, but because of language and culture differences and geographic separation such communication is difficult. Effective communication also is more expensive. Consider, for example, just the additional expense of maintaining a team portal in three or four languages.

If you consider all of the factors in Figure 1, it is easy to understand why project risk is high for international IS development projects. So many things can go wrong. Project integration is complex; requirements are difficult to determine; cost, time, and quality are difficult to manage; worker conditions vary widely; and communication is difficult. Finally, project procurement is complicated by the normal challenges of international commerce.

Q4 What Are the Challenges of International IS Management Responsibilities?

Chapter 11 defined the four primary responsibilities of the IS department: plan, operate, develop, and protect information systems and IT infrastructure. Each of these responsibilities becomes more challenging for international IS organizations.

Regarding planning, the principal task is to align IT and IS resources with the organization's competitive strategy. The task does not change character

for international companies; it just becomes more complex and difficult. Multinational organizations and operations are complicated, and the business processes that support their competitive strategies also tend to be complicated. Further, changes in global economic factors can mean dramatic changes in processes and necessitate changes in IS and IT support. Technology adoption can also cause remarkable change. The increasing use of cell phones in developing countries, for example, changes the requirements for local information systems. The rising price of oil will also change international business processes. So, planning tasks for international IS are becoming larger and more complex.

Three factors create challenges for international IS operations. First, conducting operations in different countries, cultures, and languages adds complexity. Go to the Web site of any multinational corporation, say *http://www.3m.com* or *http://lenovo.com,* and you will be asked to click the country in which you reside. When you click, you are likely to be directed to a Web server running in some other country. Those Web servers need to be managed consistently, even though they are operated by people living in different cultures and speaking different languages.

The second operational challenge of international IS is the integration of similar, but different, systems. Consider inventory. A multinational corporation might have dozens of different inventory systems in use throughout the world. To enable the movement of goods, many of these systems need to be coordinated and integrated.

Or, consider customer support that operates from three different support centers in three different countries. Each support center may have its own information system, but the data among those systems will need to be exported or otherwise shared. If not, then a customer who contacts one center will be unknown by the others.

The third complication for operations is outsourcing. Many organizations have chosen to outsource customer support, training, logistics, and other backroom activities. International outsourcing is particularly advantageous for customer support and other functions that must be operational 24/7. Amazon.com, for example, operates customer service centers in the United States, India, and Ireland. Many companies outsource logistics to UPS, because doing so offers comprehensive, worldwide shipping and logistical support. The organization's information systems usually need to be integrated with outsource vendors' information systems, and this may need to be done for different systems, all over the world. The challenges for the development of international information systems were addressed in questions Q1 and Q2.

The fourth IS department responsibility is protecting IS and IT infrastructure. We consider that function in the next question.

Q5 How Does the International Dimension Affect Computer Security Risk Management?

Computer security risk management is more difficult and complicated for international information systems. First, IT assets are subject to more threats. Infrastructure will be located in sites all over the world, and those sites differ in the threats to which they are exposed. Some will be subject to political threats, others to the threat of civil unrest, others to threats from terrorists, and still others will be subject to threats of natural disasters of every conceivable type. Place your data center in Kansas, and it is subject to tornados. Place your data center internationally, and it is potentially subject to typhoons/hurricanes, earthquakes, floods, volcanic eruption, or mudslides. And, do not forget epidemics that might affect the data center employees.

Second, the likelihood of a threat is more difficult to estimate for international systems. What is the likelihood that the death of Fidel Castro will cause civil unrest and threaten your data center in Havana? How does an organization assess that risk? What is the likelihood that a computer programmer in India will insert a Trojan horse into code that she writes on an outsourcing contract?

In addition to risk, international information systems are subject to far greater uncertainty. As discussed in Chapter 12, uncertainty reflects the likelihood that something that "we don't know we don't know" will cause an adverse outcome. Because of the multitude of cultures, religions, nations, beliefs, political views, and crazy people in the world, uncertainty about risks to IS and IT infrastructure is high. Again, if you place your data center in Kansas, you have some idea of the magnitude of the uncertainty to which you are exposed, even if you do not know exactly what it is. Place a server in a country on every continent of the world, and you have no idea of the potential risks to which they are exposed.

Regarding safeguards, technical and data safeguards do not change for international information systems. Because of greater complexity, more safeguards or far more complex ones might be needed, but the technical and data safeguards described in Chapter 12 all work for international systems. Human safeguards are another matter. For example, can an organization depend on the control of separation of duties and authorities in a culture in which graft is an accepted norm? Or, what is the utility of a peer security reference in a culture in which it is considered exceedingly rude to talk about someone when they are not present? Because of these differences, human safeguards need to be chosen and evaluated on a culture-by-culture basis.

In short, risk management for both international IS and IT infrastructure is more complicated, more difficult, and subject to greater uncertainty.

Q6 What Challenges Exist for Investigating Global Computer Crime?

Unfortunately, international computer crime is common. Web sites operated in African countries phish for data in the United States. A scam in the United States steals data from a U.S. corporation and sells that data to an illegal operation in South America. Someone kidnaps a U.S. citizen in a foreign country and sends an email ransom demand to relatives in the United States. The email service provider is located in a Middle Eastern country. In all of these cases, critical evidence is stored in computers located on foreign soil.

With rare exceptions, such as embassies, nations have sovereignty within their borders. A U.S. criminal investigator can obtain evidence only with the consent of the country in which the evidence lies. Most nations have laws, agreements, and treaties for cooperating in criminal investigations, but the formal process for obtaining permission to search is slow and cumbersome. Further, some nations will not cooperate.

For situations in which speed is of the essence, when the data is likely to be moved soon or deleted, the G8 group of nations has developed a 24-hour *point-of-contact system*. This system, which is used by more than 30 nations, requires each country to staff an office that can speed the processing of permission for evidence gathering. For the countries that participate, the system gives international crime investigators a single point of contact.

In some cases, evidence-gathering is facilitated by informal arrangements among individuals in security agencies and organizations. A U.S. investigator may not have permission to search or obtain evidence, but his or her counterpart in another country may be authorized to do so. Informal arrangements are sometimes made, but the law regarding the admissibility of such evidence in court is complicated.

A final consideration is that the U.S. Fourth Amendment can apply in complex ways to searches outside the United States. The law for gathering evidence for computer crimes in the United States is complicated, and it becomes even more so for international investigations. Organizations that suspect they have been the victims of a computer crime, especially international computer crime, should seek legal counsel, first.

ACTIVE REVIEW

Use this Active Review to verify that you understand the ideas and concepts that answer the study questions in the International Dimension.

Q1 What characteristics make international IS management challenging?

State the two characteristics that make international IS management challenging. Explain how those factors pertain to IS development, IS management, and risk management.

Q2 Why is international information systems development difficult?

Explain the difference between international systems development and international software development. Using the five-component framework, explain why international systems development is more difficult. Describe difficulties that arise during the systems definition and requirements phases in the development of an international IS. Describe two responses to these difficulties, and explain why both are problematic. Give an example of how each is used.

Q3 What are the challenges of international project management?

State two words that characterize the difficulty of international project management. Explain how each of the knowledge areas in Figure 1 is more complicated for international projects. Give an example of one complication for each knowledge area.

Q4 What are the challenges of international IS management responsibilities?

State the four responsibilities for IS departments. Explain how each of these responsibilities is more challenging for international IS organizations. Describe three factors that create challenges for international IS operations.

Q5 How does the international dimension affect computer security risk management?

Explain why international IT assets are subject to more threats. Give three examples. Explain why the likelihood of international threats is more difficult to determine. Describe uncertainty, and explain why it is higher for international IT organizations. Explain how technical, data, and human safeguards differ for international IT organizations. Give two examples of problematic international human safeguards.

Q6 What challenges exist for investigating global computer crime?

Give two examples of international computer crime. Explain the constraints U.S. investigators face when gathering evidence in foreign countries. Explain the role of the 24-hour point-of-contact system. Describe how informal arrangements can facilitate evidence-gathering in foreign countries. State the recommended action for organizations that believe they have been the victim of an international computer crime.

The United States Internal Revenue Service (IRS) Business Systems Modernization (BSM) project has been a multiyear attempt to replace the existing tax-processing information systems with systems based on modern technology. Review Case Study 1 (page 27) for a discussion of the underlying need, problems, and suggested problem solutions.

The subsystem that has generated the most controversy and been the cause of the most serious delays is the Customer Account Data Engine (CADE). The heart of CADE is a database of business rules. Unlike most databases that contain facts and figures like *CustomerName, Email, Balance*, and so forth, the CADE database contains business rules, which are statements about how an organization conducts its business. In the context of the IRS, this database contains rules about tax laws and the processing of tax forms. An example of such a rule is:

Rule 10:
    IF the amount on line 7 of Form 1040EZ is greater than zero,
    THEN invoke Rule 15.

With a rule-based approach, the IRS need only develop programs that access the database and follow the rules. No other programs need to be developed.

Rule-based systems differ substantially from traditional application programs. Using traditional technology, the developers interview the users, determine what the business rules are, and then write computer code that operates in accordance with the rules. The disadvantage of such traditional programming is that only technically trained programmers can decipher the rules in the program code. Also, only trained programmers can add, change, or delete rules.

The advantage of rule-based systems such as CADE is that the business rules are stored in the database and can be read, added, changed, or deleted by personnel with business knowledge but little computer training. Hence, in theory, CADE is more adaptable to changing requirements than a system written with traditional programming languages.

Unfortunately, the technical feasibility of using a rule-based system for a problem as large and complex as IRS tax processing is unknown. It appears, at least from public records, that no one ever tried to estimate that feasibility. The result has been a string of schedule delays and cost overruns. The first CADE release, which processes only the simplest individual tax returns (those using IRS Form 1040EZ), was to be completed by January 2002. It was delayed once until August 2003, and then delayed again to September 2004. At that point, a limited version of this first release was demonstrated.

The database for these simple returns has some 1,200 business rules, but no reliable estimate has yet been developed for the number of rules required for the full system. The lack of an estimate is particularly serious because some experts believe the difficulty and complexity of creating rules increases geometrically with the number of rules. Meanwhile, $33 million was invested in 2003, and another $84 million was spent in 2004.

Given the history of problems, the IRS hired the Software Engineering Institute of (SEI) Carnegie Mellon University to conduct an independent audit of the project. SEI verified that no one knows with any certainty how many business rules will eventually be required. Additionally, according to the SEI report:

> We believe that harvesting the business rules, not coding them, will drive the cost and schedule of future CADE releases. By harvesting, we mean capturing, adjudicating, and cataloging the rules. CADE has invested many resources exploring rules engines, but few resources exploring the rules themselves. The IRS needs to understand and document their business rules as well as the rules' complicated interactions. Some of the delays that have already plagued CADE are a direct result of an imperfect understanding of the business rules. This situation will only grow as the number and complexity of the implemented rules increases.

According to the SEI testimony, without reliable estimates of the number of business rules:

> No one knows how long rule harvesting will take, how many people will be required, the background, training and experience of the people required, or how much it will cost. Based on anecdotal information presented to us, we believe the time will be measured in years and cost will be measured in the tens of millions of dollars.
>
> Until sound, supported cost and schedule estimates for rule harvesting are available, future CADE plans and schedules are only tentative and likely subject to delays and missed milestones.

Sources: U.S. House, Committee on Ways and Means, Subcommittee on Oversight, Statement of M. Steven Palmquist, Chief Engineer for Civil and Intelligence Agencies, Acquisition Support Program, Software Engineering Institute, Carnegie Mellon University, Pittsburgh, Pennsylvania, February 12, 2004; and *http://treas.gov/irsob/documents/special_report1203.pdf* (accessed August 2009).

QUESTIONS

1. Ignoring developments that have occurred since this case was written, what statement can be made about the technical feasibility, cost feasibility, and schedule feasibility of this project?

2. Use your imagination to try to understand how this situation came about. The IRS selected a team of contractors to develop the information systems that would support the modernization effort. Those contractors proposed a rule-based system, but apparently no one asked whether such a system would work on a problem this large. How could that come about? Suppose you were a non-IT manager at the IRS. Would you know to ask? Suppose you were a senior manager at one of the contractors. Would you know to ask? If you did ask and your technical people said, "No problem," what would you do?

3. Suppose you are a senior IRS manager. In defense of your management, you say, "We hired reputable contractors who had extensive experience developing large and complicated systems. When they told us that a rule-based approach was the way to go, we agreed. Should we be required to

second-guess the experts?" Comment on that statement. Do you believe it? Do you think it's a justification?

4. Does it seem remarkable that, according to the SEI review, no one has yet considered the time, cost, and difficulty of harvesting the rules? Clearly, the need to allocate time and labor to that problem was visible from the start of the project. How do you think such an oversight occurred? What are the consequences of that oversight?

5. Suppose it turns out that a rule-based system is infeasible for processing more complicated tax returns. What alternatives are available to the IRS? As a taxpayer, which do you recommend?

6. Search online under *IRS CADE problems* and read three or four articles and reports on recent developments. Comment on any recent information that sheds light on your answers to questions 1 through 5. What strategy for solving this problem does the IRS seem to be following? How likely is that strategy to succeed?

Glossary

10/100/1000 Ethernet   A type of Ethernet that conforms to the IEEE 802.3 protocol and allows for transmission at a rate of 10, 100, or 1,000 Mbps (megabits per second).   182

12Seconds.TV   A video status platform Web site where short video clips can be shared with friends and family.   306

32-bit processor   Type of addressing used by PCs, as of 2009. Allows for addressing of up to 4 Gigabytes of main memory.   108

64-bit processor   Type of addressing used by power PCs and new servers, as of 2009. Allows for addressing for practically unlimited main memory.   108

Abstract reasoning   The ability to make and manipulate models.   6

Access   A popular personal and small workgroup DBMS product from Microsoft.   141

Access control list (ACL)   A list that encodes the rules stating which packets are to be allowed through a firewall and which are to be prohibited.   192

Access device   Device, typically a special-purpose computer, that connects network sites. The particular device required depends on the line used and other factors. Sometimes switches and routers are employed, but other types of equipment are needed as well.   187

Access point (AP)   A point in a wireless network that facilitates communication among wireless devices and serves as a point of interconnection between wireless and wired networks. The access point must be able to process messages according to both the 802.3 and 802.11 standards, because it sends and receives wireless traffic using the 802.11 protocol and communicates with wired networks using the 802.3 protocol.   183

Accurate (information)   Information that is based on correct and complete data and that has been processed correctly as expected.   16

Activity   The part of a business process that transforms resources and information of one type into resources and information of another type; can be manual or automated.   71

AdSense   A Web 2.0 product from Google. Google searches an organization's Web site and inserts ads that match content on that site; when users click those ads, Google pays the organization a fee.   291

Adware   Programs installed on the user's computer without the user's knowledge or permission that reside in the background and, unknown to the user, observe the user's actions and keystrokes, modify computer activity, and report the user's activities to sponsoring organizations. Most adware is benign in that it does not perform malicious acts or steal data. It does, however, watch user activity and produce pop-up ads.   459

AdWords   A Web 2.0 advertising product from Google. Vendors agree to pay a certain amount to Google for use of particular search words, which link to the vendor's site.   291

Alert   A form of report, often requested by recipients, that tells them some piece of information, usually time related, such as notification of the time for a meeting.   346

Analog signal   A wavy signal. A modem converts the computer's digital data into analog signals that can be transmitted over dial-up Internet connections.   184

Analysis paralysis   When too much time is spent documenting project requirements.   388

Application software   Programs that perform a business function. Some application programs are general purpose, such as Excel or Word. Other application programs are specific to a business function, such as accounts payable.   114

Architecture   An arrangement of protocol layers in which each layer is given specific tasks to accomplish.   205

As-is model   A model that represents the current situation and processes.   236

Asymmetric digital subscriber lines (ADSL)   DSL lines that have different upload and download speeds.   185

Asymmetric encryption   An encryption method whereby different keys are used to encode and to decode the message; one key encodes the message, and the other key decodes the message. Symmetric encryption is simpler and much faster than asymmetric encryption.   191, 456

Asynchronous communication   Information exchange that occurs when all members of a work team do not meet at the same time, such as those who work different shifts or in different locations.   38

Asynchronous transfer mode (ATM)   A protocol that divides data into uniformly sized cells, eliminates the need for protocol conversion, and can process speeds from 1 to 156 Mbps. ATM can support both voice and data communication.   190

Attribute   (1) A variable that provides properties for an HTML tag. Each attribute has a standard name. For example, the attribute for a hyperlink is *href*, and its value indicates which Web page is to be displayed when the user clicks the link. (2) Characteristics of an entity. Example attributes of *Order* would be *OrderNumber*, *OrderDate*, *SubTotal*, *Tax*, *Total*, and so forth. Example attributes of *Salesperson* would be *SalespersonName*, *Email*, *Phone*, and so forth.   151, 280

Auction   Application that match buyers and sellers by using an e-commerce version of a standard, competitive-bidding auction process.   275

Authentication   The process whereby an information system approves (authenticates) a user by checking the user's password.   453

Baseline   An initial plan that stipulates the tasks to be accomplished, the labor and other resources assigned to those tasks, and the schedule for completion.   391

Baseline WBS   The final work-breakdown structure that shows the planned tasks, dependencies, durations, and resource assignments.   393

Beta program   A prerelease version of software, used for testing. The beta program becomes obsolete when the final version is released.   289

Beta testing   (1) Traditionally, The process of allowing future system users to try out the new system on their own. Used to locate program failures just prior to final program shipment; (2) In the Web-2.0 world, a tactic used by vendors of license-free software to enable the vendor to perpetually change the program, principally its user interface, at its own discretion and on its on time-frame. Such programs are labeled "beta" for many years with no announced schedule for making them "non-beta."   385

Bill of materials (BOM)   A list of the materials that comprise a product.   247

Binary digit   The means by which computers represent data; also called *bits*. A binary digit is either a zero or a one.   105

Biometric authentication   The use of personal physical characteristics, such as fingerprints, facial features, and retinal scans, to authenticate users.   453

Bits   The means by which computers represent data; also called *binary digit*. A bit is either a zero or a one.   105

Bluetooth   A common wireless protocol designed for transmitting data over short distances, replacing cables.   183

Bot   A computer program that is surreptitiously installed and that takes actions unknown and uncontrolled by the computer's owner or administrator.   460

Bot herder   The individual or organization that controls a botnet.   460

Botnet   A network of bots that is created and managed by the individual or organization that infected the network with the bot program.   460

Broadband   Internet communication lines that have speeds in excess of 256 kbps. DSL and cable modems provide broadband access.   186

Brooks' Law   The famous adage that states: *Adding more people to a late project makes the project later*. Brooks' Law is true not only because a larger staff requires increased coordination, but also because new people need to be trained. The only people who can train the new employees are the existing team members, who are thus taken off productive tasks. The costs of training new people can overwhelm the benefit of their contribution.   375

Browser   A program that processes the HTTP protocol; receives, displays, and processes HTML documents; and transmits responses.   278

Bullwhip effect   Phenomenon in which the variability in the size and timing of orders increases at each stage up the supply chain, from customer to supplier.   287

Bus   Means by which the CPU reads instructions and data from main memory and writes data to main memory.   107

Business intelligence (BI)   Information containing patterns, relationships, and trends.   320

Business intelligence (BI) application   Software that uses a tool on a particular type of data for a particular purpose.   322

Business intelligence (BI) application server   A computer program that delivers BI (business intelligence) application results in a variety of formats to various devices for consumption by BI users.   344

Business intelligence (BI) system   An information system, having all five IS components, that provides the right information, to the right user, at the right time.   321

Business intelligence (BI) tool   A computer program that implements a particular BI technique. BI tools include reporting tools, data-mining tools, and knowledge-management tools.   321

Business process   A network of activities, resources, facilities, and information that interact to achieve some business function; sometimes called a *business system*.   71

Business process management (BPM)   A systematic process of modeling, creating, implementing, and assessing business processes.   74, 236

Business process modelling notation (BPMN)   A standard set of terms and graphical notations for documenting business processes.   239

Business-to-business (B2B) e-commerce   Sales between companies.   274

Business-to-consumer (B2C) e-commerce   Sales between a supplier and a retail customer (the consumer).   274

Business-to-government (B2G) e-commerce   Sales between companies and governmental organizations.   275

Byte(s)   (1) A character of data; (2) An 8-bit chunk.   106, 137

Cable modem   A type of modem that provides high-speed data transmission using cable television lines. The cable company installs a fast, high-capacity optical fiber cable to a distribution center in each neighborhood that it serves. At the distribution center, the optical fiber cable connects to regular cable-television cables that run to subscribers' homes or businesses. Cable modems modulate in such a way that their signals do not interfere with TV signals. Like DSL lines, they are always on.   185

Cache   A file on a domain name resolver that stores domain names and IP addresses that have been resolved. Then, when someone else needs to resolve that same domain name, there is no need to go through the entire resolution process. Instead, the resolver can supply the IP address from the local file.   107, 216

Central processing unit (CPU)   The CPU selects instructions, processes them, performs arithmetic and logical comparisons, and stores results of operations in memory.   104

Certificate authority (CA)   Trusted, independent third-party company that supplies public keys for encryption.   457

Channel conflict   In e-commerce, a conflict that may result between a manufacturer that wants to sell products directly to consumers and the retailers in the existing sales channels.   277

Chief information officer (CIO)   The title of the principal manager of the IT department. Other common titles are *vice president of information services, director of information services,* and, less commonly, *director of computer services.*   410

Chief technology officer (CTO)   The head of the technology group. The CTO sorts through new ideas and products to identify those that are most relevant to the organization. The CTO's job requires deep knowledge of information technology and the ability to envision how new IT will affect the organization over time.   411

Clearinghouse   Entity that provides goods and services at a stated price, prices and arranges for the delivery of the goods, but never takes title to the goods.   275

Clickstream data   E-commerce data that describes a customer's clicking behavior. Such data includes everything the customer does at the Web site.   338

Client   A computer that provides word processing, spreadsheets, database access, and usually a network connection.   108

Client hardware   Computers and other communication devices (e.g., iPhones, BlackBerries) that users employ to utilize information systems.   33

Client-server applications   Software applications that require code on both the client computer and the server computer. Email is a common example.   116

Closed source   Source code that is highly protected and only available to trusted employees and carefully vetted contractors.   118

Cloud   The computing network on the Internet.   112

Cloud computing   A form of hardware/software outsourcing in which organizations offer flexible plans for customers to lease hardware and software facilities.   432

Cluster analysis   An unsupervised data-mining technique whereby statistical techniques are used to identify groups of entities that have similar characteristics. A common use for cluster analysis is to find groups of similar customers in data about customer orders and customer demographics.   329

Cold sites   Remote processing centers that provide office space, but no computer equipment, for use by a company that needs to continue operations after a disaster.   468

Collaboration   The situation in which two or more people work together toward a common goal, result, or product; information systems facilitate collaboration.   32

Columns   Also called *fields*, or groups of bytes. A database table has multiple columns that are used to represent the attributes of an entity. Examples are *PartNumber, EmployeeName,* and *SalesDate.*   138

Commerce server   A computer that operates Web-based programs that display products, support online ordering, record and process payments, and interface with inventory-management applications.   278

Communication   A critical factor in collaboration, consisting of two key elements: (1) the abilities of individuals to share information and receive feedback and (2) the availability of effective systems by which to share information.   32

Communications protocol   A means for coordinating activity between two or more communicating computers. Two machines must agree on the protocol to use, and they must follow that protocol as they send messages back and forth. Because there is so much to do, communications tasks are broken up into levels, or layers, of protocols.   204

Competitive strategy   The strategy an organization chooses as the way it will succeed in its industry. According to Porter, there are four fundamental competitive strategies: cost leadership across an industry or within a particular industry segment and product differentiation across an industry or within a particular industry segment.   68

Computer hardware   One of the five fundamental components of an information system.   8

Computer-based information system   An information system that includes a computer.   9

Computers-in-a-product   Computer capabilities embedded within common consumer products.   19

Conference call   A synchronous virtual meeting, in which participants meet at the same time via a voice-communication channel.   38

Confidence   In market-basket terminology, the probability estimate that two items will be purchased together.   331

Configuration control   A set of management policies, practices, and tools that developers use to maintain control over the project's resources.   395

Content management   One of the drivers of collaboration effectiveness, which enables multiple users to contribute to and change documents, schedules, task lists, assignments, and so forth, without one user's work interfering with another's. Content management also enables users to track and report who made what changes, when, and why.   33

Cost   [of a business process] The cost of the inputs to a business process plus the cost of the activities involved in the process.   71

Cost feasibility   Whether an information system can be developed within budget.   380

Critical path   The sequence of activities that determine the earliest date by which the project can be completed.   393

Critical path analysis   A project management planning process by which tasks and resources are re-assigned to tasks so as to reduce the total length of the project's critical path.   393

Cross-functional processes   Processes that involve activities among several, or even many, business departments.   237

Cross-selling   The sale of related products; salespeople try to get customers who buy product *X* to also buy product *Y.*   331

Crowdsourcing The process by which organizations involve their customers in the design and marketing of products.   304

Crow's foot A line on an entity-relationship diagram that indicates a 1:N relationship between two entities.   152

Crow's-foot diagram A type of entity-relationship diagram that uses a crow's foot symbol to designate a 1:N relationship.   153

Curse of dimensionality The more attributes there are, the easier it is to build a data model that fits the sample data but that is worthless as a predictor.   339

Custom-developed software Tailor-made software.   115

Customer life cycle Taken as a whole, the processes of marketing, customer acquisition, relationship management, and loss/churn that must be managed by CRM systems.   253

Customer relationship management (CRM) The set of business processes for attracting, selling, managing, and supporting customers.   253

Customer relationship management (CRM) applications Applications that integrate all of the primary value chain business activities.   253

Data Recorded facts or figures. One of the five fundamental components of an information system.   8

Data administration A staff function that pertains to *all* of an organization's data assets. Typical data administration tasks are setting data standards, developing data policies, and providing for data security.   423

Data aggregators Companies that obtain data from public and private sources and store, integrate, and process it in sophisticated ways.   160

Data channel Means by which the CPU reads instructions and data from main memory and writes data to main memory.   107

Data dictionary A file or database that contains data definitions.   424

Data integrity problem In a database, the situation that exists when data items disagree with one another. An example is two different names for the same customer.   155

Data marts Facilities that prepare, store, and manage data for reporting and data mining for specific business functions.   337

Data mining The application of statistical techniques to find patterns and relationships among data for classification and prediction.   327

Data-mining tools Tools that process data using statistical techniques, many of which are mathematically sophisticated.   321

Data model A logical representation of the data in a database that describes the data and relationships that will be stored in the database. Akin to a blueprint.   150

Data standards Definitions, or metadata, for data items shared across the organization. They describe the name, official definition, usage, relationship to other data items, processing restrictions, version, security code, format, and other features of data items that are shared across the organization.   423

Data warehouses Facilities that prepare, store, and manage data specifically for reporting and data mining.   337

Database A self-describing collection of integrated records.   137

Database administration The management, development, operation, and maintenance of the database so as to achieve the organization's objectives. This staff function requires balancing conflicting goals: protecting the database while maximizing its availability for authorized use. In smaller organizations, this function usually is served by a single person. Larger organizations assign several people to an office of database administration.   145, 423

Database application Forms, reports, queries, and application programs for processing a database. A database can be processed by many different database applications.   146

Database application system Applications, having the standard five components, that make database data more accessible and useful. Users employ a database application that consists of forms, formatted reports, queries, and application programs. Each of these, in turn, calls on the database management system (DBMS) to process the database tables.   141

Database management systems (DBMS) A program for creating, processing, and administering a database. A DBMS is a large and complex program that is licensed like an operating system. Microsoft Access, and Oracle are example DBMS products.   141

Database tier In the three-tier architecture, the tier that runs the DBMS and receives and processes SQL requests to retrieve and store data.   277

DB2 A popular, enterprise-class DBMS product from IBM.   141

Decision tree A hierarchical arrangement of criteria for classifying customers, items, and other business objects.   332

Deliverables The result of each task in a project plan.   391

Denial of service Security problem in which users are not able to access an information system; can be caused by human errors, natural disaster, or malicious activity.   446

Digital certificate A document supplied by a certificate authority (CA) that contains, among other data, an entity's name and public key.   458

Digital divide A divide created between those who have Internet access and those who do not.   81

Digital signature Encrypted message that uses *hashing* to ensure that plaintext messages are received without alteration.   185

Digital subscriber line (DSL) A communications line that operates on the same lines as voice telephones, but do so in such a manner that their signals to not interfere with voice telephone service.   185

Dimension A characteristic of an OLAP measure. Purchase date, customer type, customer location, and sales region are examples of dimensions.   326

Direct installation   See *Plunge installation.*   385

Dirty data   Problematic data. Examples are a value of *B* for customer gender and a value of *213* for customer age. Other examples are a value of *999–999–9999* for a U.S. phone number, a part color of *gren*, and an email address of WhyMe@GuessWhoIAM-Hah-Hah.org. All these values are problematic when data mining.   338

Discussion forum   A form of asynchronous communication in which one group member posts an entry and other group members respond. A better form of group communication than email, because it is more difficult for the discussion to go off track.   39

Diseconomy of scale   A principle that states as development teams become larger, the average contribution per worker decreases.   391

Disintermediation   Elimination of one or more middle layers in the supply chain.   275

Domain name   The registered, human-friendly valid name in the domain name system (DNS). The process of changing a name into its IP address is called *resolving the domain name.*   214

Domain name resolution   The process of converting a domain name into a public IP address.   215

Domain name resolver   Computer that facilitates domain name resolution by storing the correspondence of domain names and IP addresses.   215

Domain name system (DNS)   A system that converts user-friendly names into their IP addresses. Any registered, valid name is called a domain name.   214

Drill down   With an OLAP report, to further divide the data into more detail.   326

Drive-by sniffers   People who take computers with wireless connections through an area and search for unprotected wireless networks in an attempt to gain free Internet access or to gather unauthorized data.   445

DSL (digital subscriber line) modem   A device for converting computer signals to the format needed for DSL transmission.   185

Dual processor   A computer with two CPUs.   105

Dynamic Host Configuration Protocol (DHCP)   A service provided by some communications devices that allocates and de-allocates a pool of IP addresses. A device that hosts the DHCP service is called a *DHCP server.* On request, a DHCP server loans a temporary IP address to a network device such as a computer or printer. When the device disconnects, the IP address becomes available, and the DHCP server will reuse it when needed.   208

E-commerce   The buying and selling of goods and services over public and private computer networks.   274

Electronic exchange   Site that facilitates the matching of buyers and sellers; the business process is similar to that of a stock exchange. Sellers offer goods at a given price through the electronic exchange, and buyers make offers to purchase over the same exchange. Price matches result in transactions from which the exchange takes a commission.   275

Email   A form of asynchronous communication in which participants send comments and attachments electronically. As a form of group communication, it can be disorganized, disconnected, and easy to hide from.   38

Email spoofing   A synonym for *phishing.* A technique for obtaining unauthorized data that uses pretexting via email. The *phisher* pretends to be a legitimate company and sends email requests for confidential data, such as account numbers, Social Security numbers, account passwords, and so forth. Phishers direct traffic to their sites under the guise of a legitimate business.   445

Encapsulated   A circumstance in which the logic for a service is isolated within that service. No service user knows nor needs to know how the service is performed.   261

Encapsulation   An approach that isolates the logic within that service. No service user knows nor needs to know how the service is performed.   261

Encryption   The process of transforming clear text into coded, unintelligible text for secure storage or communication.   190

Encryption algorithms   Algorithms used to transform clear text into coded, unintelligible text for secure storage or communication. Commonly used methods are DES, 3DES, and AES.   190

Enterprise applications   IS applications that span more than one department, such as some functional applications, as well as ERP, EAI, and SCM applications.   000

Enterprise application integration (EAI)   The integration of existing systems by providing layers of software that connect applications and their data together.   421

Enterprise DBMS   A product that processes large organizational and workgroup databases. These products support many users, perhaps thousands, and many different database applications. Such DBMS products support 24/7 operations and can manage databases that span dozens of different magnetic disks with hundreds of gigabytes or more of data. IBM's DB2, Microsoft's SQL Server, and Oracle's Oracle are examples of enterprise DBMS products.   149

Enterprise resource planning (ERP) applications   Applications that integrate the primary value chain activities with human resources and accounting and provide more integration than CRM   255

Entity   In the E-R data model, a representation of some thing that users want to track. Some entities represent a physical object; others represent a logical construct or transaction.   151

Entity-relationship (E-R) data model   Popular technique for creating a data model whereby developers define the things that will be stored and identify the relationships among them.   151

Entity-relationship (E-R) diagrams   A type of diagram used by database designers to document entities and their relationships to each other.   152

Ethernet   Another name for the IEEE 802.3 protocol, Ethernet is a network protocol that operates at Layers 1 and 2 of the TCP/IP–OSI architecture. Ethernet, the world's most popular LAN protocol, is used on WANs as well.   180

e-trash   Computers and related devices that are no longer in use and are disposed. e-trash is a problem because such devices contain toxic materials that are harmful to the environment.   433

EVDO   A WAN wireless protocol standard.   186

Exabyte 10^{18} bytes.   320

Experimentation   A careful and reasoned analysis of an opportunity, envisioning potential products or solutions or applications of technology, and then developing those ideas that seem to have the most promise, consistent with the resources you have.   7

Exception alert   A message that notifies a system user of an out-of-the-ordinary—exceptional—event.   346

Expert system   Knowledge-sharing system that is created by interviewing experts in a given business domain and codifying the rules used by those experts.   341

eXtensible Markup Language (XML)   An important document standard that separates document content, structure, and presentation; eliminates problems in HTML. Used for Web services and many other applications.   282

Face-to-face (F2F) meetings   Meetings that require everyone to be in the same place at the same time.   53

Facilities   Structures used within a business process.   71

Fields   Also called *columns*; groups of bytes in a database table. A database table has multiple columns that are used to represent the attributes of an entity. Examples are *PartNumber*, *EmployeeName*, and *SalesDate*.   138

File   A group of similar rows or records. In a database, sometimes called a *table*.   138

File server   A computer that stores files.   41

File Transfer Protocol (FTP)   A Layer-5 protocol used to copy files from one computer to another. In interorganizational transaction processing, FTP enables users to exchange large files easily.   205

Finished-goods inventory applications   Applications that support inventory control and inventory management of finished goods.   247

Firewall   A computing device located between a firm's internal and external networks that prevents unauthorized access to or from the internal network. A firewall can be a special-purpose computer or it can be a program on a general-purpose computer or on a router.   191

Firmware   Computer software that is installed into devices such as printers, print services, and various types of communication devices. The software is coded just like other software, but it is installed into special, programmable memory of the printer or other device.   115

Five-component framework   The five fundamental components of an information system—computer hardware, software, data, procedures, and people—that are present in every information system, from the simplest to the most complex.   8

Five forces model   Model, proposed by Michael Porter, that assesses industry characteristics and profitability by means of five competitive forces—bargaining power of suppliers, threat of substitution, bargaining power of customers, rivalry among firms, and threat of new entrants.   66

Flow   The movement of resources between or among business activities.   71

Foreign keys   A column or group of columns used to represent relationships. Values of the foreign key match values of the primary key in a different (foreign) table.   140

Form   Data entry forms are used to read, insert, modify, and delete database data.   146

Frame   The container used at Layers 1 and 2 of the TCP/IP–OSI model. A program implementing a Layer-2 protocol packages data into frames.   207

Frame Relay   A protocol that can process traffic in the range of 56 kbps to 40 Mbps by packaging data into frames.   188

FTP   See *File Transfer Protocol*.   41

Function point   A feature of an application program.   395

Functional application   Software that provides features and functions necessary to support a particular business activity (function).   237

Functional process   Processes that involve activities within a single department or function.   237

Gantt chart   A chart that shows tasks, dates, dependencies, and possibly resources.   392

Gigabyte (GB)   1,024MB.   106

GNU   A set of tools for creating and managing open source software. Originally created to develop an open source Unix-like operating system   116

GNU General Public License (GPL) Agreement   One of the standard license agreements for open source software.   117

Google Docs & Spreadsheets   A version-management system for sharing documents and spreadsheet data. Documents are stored on a Google server, from which users can access and simultaneously see and edit the documents.   42

Google's My Maps   Web 2.0 product that provides tools with which users can make custom modifications to maps provided by Google; My Maps is an example of a mashup.   290

Gramm-Leach-Bliley (GLB) Act   Passed by Congress in 1999, this act protects consumer financial data stored by financial institutions, which are defined as banks, securities firms, insurance companies, and organizations that provide financial advice, prepare tax returns, and provide similar financial services.   450

Granularity   The level of detail in data. Customer name and account balance is large-granularity data. Customer name, balance, and the order details and payment history of every customer order is smaller granularity.   338

Green computing   Environmentally conscious computing consisting of three major components: power management, virtualization, and e-waste management.   433

Grid   A network of computers that operates as an integrated whole.   109

Hacking   Occurs when a person gains unauthorized access to a computer system. Although some people hack for the sheer joy of doing it, other hackers invade systems for the malicious purpose of stealing or modifying data.   446

Hardening   A term used to describe server operating systems that have been modified to make it especially difficult for them to infiltrated by mal-ware.   464

Hardware   Electronic components and related gadgetry that input, process, output, store, and communicate data according to instructions encoded in computer programs or software.   104

Hashing   A method of mathematically manipulating an electronic message to create a string of bits that characterize the message.   456

Health Insurance Portability and Accountability Act (HIPAA)   The privacy provisions of this 1996 act give individuals the right to access health data created by doctors and other health-care providers. HIPAA also sets rules and limits on who can read and receive a person's health information.   450

Horizontal-market application   Software that provides capabilities common across all organizations and industries; examples include word processors, graphics programs, spreadsheets, and presentation programs.   114

Hot site   A remote processing center run by a commercial disaster-recovery service that provides equipment a company would need to continue operations after a disaster.   468

HSDPA   A WAN wireless protocol standard.   186

HTTPS   An indication that a Web browser is using the SSL/TLS protocol to ensure secure communications.   191

Hyperlink   A pointer on a Web page to another Web page. A hyperlink contains the URL of the Web page to access when the user clicks the hyperlink. The URL can reference a page on the Web server that generated the page containing the hyperlink, or it can reference a page on another server.   290

Hypertext Markup Language (HTML)   A language that defines the structure and layout of Web page content. An HTML tag is a notation used to define a data element for display or other purposes.   279

Hypertext Transfer Protocol (HTTP)   A Layer-5 protocol used to process Web pages.   205, 278

Identification   The process whereby an information system identifies a user by requiring the user to sign on with a user name and password.   453

Identifier   An attribute (or group of attributes) whose value is associated with one and only one entity instance.   151

IEEE 802.3 protocol   This standard, also called *Ethernet*, is a network protocol that operates at Layers 1 and 2 of the TCP/IP–OSI architecture. Ethernet, the world's most popular LAN protocol, is used on WANs as well.   180

IEEE 802.11 protocol   A wireless communications standard, widely used today, that enables access within a few hundred feet. The most popular version of this standard is *IEEE 802.11g*, which allows wireless transmissions of up to 54 Mbps.   182

IEEE 802.16 protocol   An emerging wireless communications standard, also known as *WiMax*, that enables broadband wireless access for fixed, nomadic, and portable applications. In fixed mode, it enables access across a several-mile or larger region. See also *WiMax*.   201

If . . . then . . .   Format for rules derived from a decision tree (data mining) or by interviewing a human expert (expert systems).   333

Indexing   The most important content function of knowledge-management applications, which uses keyword search to determine whether content exists and provides a link to its location.   341

Information   (1) Knowledge derived from data, where *data* is defined as recorded facts or figures; (2) data presented in a meaningful context; (3) data processed by summing, ordering, averaging, grouping, comparing, or other similar operations; (4) a difference that makes a difference.   12

Information silos   Islands of automation that work in isolation from one another.   237

Information system (IS)   A group of components that interact to produce information.   8

Information technology (IT)   The products, methods, inventions, and standards that are used for the purpose of producing information.   18

Inherent processes   The procedures that must be followed to effectively use licensed software. For example, the processes inherent in MRP systems assume that certain users will take specified actions in a particular order. In most cases, the organization must conform to the processes inherent in the software.   258

Input hardware   Hardware devices that attach to a computer; includes keyboards, mouse, document scanners, and bar-code (Universal Product Code) scanners.   104

Input resources   The resources that a business adds in the course of producing goods or services as part of its value-creating activities.   71

Instruction set   The collection of instructions that a computer can process.   112

Internal firewalls   A firewall that sits inside the organizational network.   191

International Organization for Standardization (ISO)   An international organization that sets worldwide standards. ISO developed a seven-layer protocol architecture called Open Systems Interconnection (OSI). Portions of that protocol architecture are incorporated into the TCP/IP–OSI hybrid protocol architecture.   204

Internet   When spelled with a small *i*, as in *internet*, a private network of networks. When spelled with a capital *I*, as in *Internet*, the public internet known as the Internet.   177

Internet Corporation for Assigned Names and Numbers (ICANN)   The organization responsible for managing the assignment of public IP addresses and domain names for use on the Internet. Each public IP address is unique across all computers on the Internet.   208

Internet Engineering Task Force (IETF)   An organization that specifies standards for use on the Internet. It developed the four-layer scheme called the TCP/IP (Transmission Control Program/Internet Protocol) architecture. TCP/IP is part of the TCP/IP–OSI protocol architecture that is used on the Internet and most internets today.   204

Internet Protocol (IP)   A Layer-3 protocol. As the name implies, IP is used on the Internet, but it is used on many other internets as well. The chief purpose of IP is to route packets across an internet.   207

Internet protocol television (IPTV)   A technology that uses TCP/IP—OSI to transmit television and other video signals.   216

Internet service provider (ISP)   An ISP provides users with Internet access and a legitimate Internet address. It serves as the user's gateway to the Internet, passing communications back and forth between the user and the Internet. ISPs also pay for the Internet, collecting money from their customers and paying access fees and other charges on the users' behalf.   184

Interorganizational process   A business process that crosses organizational boundaries.   238

Inventory applications   Applications that support inventory control and inventory management by using past data to compute stocking levels, reorder levels, and reorder quantities in accordance with inventory policy.   247

IP address   A series of dotted decimals in a format like 192.168.2.28 that identifies a unique device on a network or internet. With the IPv4 standard, IP addresses have 32 bits. With the IPv6 standard, IP addresses have 128 bits. Today, IPv4 is more common, but it will likely be supplanted by IPv6 in the future. With IPv4, the decimal between the dots can never exceed 255.   208

IP spoofing   A type of spoofing whereby an intruder uses another site's IP address as if it were that other site.   445

IPv4   The most commonly used Internet layer protocol.   208

IPv6   An Internet layer protocol created to provide for more IP addresses and other benefits.   208

Islands of automation   The structure that results when functional applications work independently in isolation from one another. Usually problematic because data is duplicated, integration is difficult, and results can be inconsistent.   237

Jott.com   A service that transcribes a user's voice to text.   306

Just-barely-sufficient (information)   Information that meets the purpose for which it is generated, but just barely so.   17

Just-in-time (JIT) inventory policy   A policy that seeks to have production inputs (both raw materials and work-in-process) delivered to the manufacturing site just as they are needed. By scheduling delivery of inputs in this way, companies are able to reduce inventories to a minimum.   247

Kerberos   A system, developed at MIT, that authenticates users without sending their passwords across a computer network. It uses a complicated system of "tickets" to enable users to obtain services from networks and other servers.   454

Key   (1) A column or group of columns that identifies a unique row in a table. (2) A number used to encrypt data. The encryption algorithm applies the key to the original message to produce the coded message. Decoding (decrypting) a message is similar; a key is applied to the coded message to recover the original text.   139, 191

Key escrow   A control procedure whereby a trusted party is given a copy of a key used to encrypt database data.   461

Kilobyte (K)   1,024 bytes.   106

Knowledge management tools   The process of creating value from intellectual capital and sharing that knowledge with employees, managers, suppliers, customers, and others who need it.   340

Knowledge-management (KM) tools   Computer applications used to store employee knowledge and to make that knowledge available to employees, customers, vendors, and others who need it. The source of KM tools is human knowledge, rather than recorded facts and figures.   322

Layered protocols   Different ways of arranging the layers of communication protocols for transmission of data across networks. TCP/IP is one such layered protocol.   204

Legacy information system   An older system that has outdated technologies and techniques but is still used, despite its age.   421

Library   In version-control collaboration systems, a shared directory that allows access to various documents by means of permissions.   44

License   Agreement that stipulates how a program can be used. Most specify the number of computers on which the program can be installed, some specify the number of users that can connect to and use the program remotely. Such agreements also stipulate limitations on the liability of the software vendor for the consequences of errors in the software.   114

Lift   In market-basket terminology, the ratio of confidence to the base probability of buying an item. Lift shows how much the base probability changes when other products are purchased. If the lift is greater than 1, the change is positive; if it is less than 1, the change is negative.   332

Lines of code   The number of lines of text in a computer program.   394

Linkages   Process interactions across value chains. Linkages are important sources of efficiencies and are readily supported by information systems.   71

Linux   A version of Unix that was developed by the open source community. The open source community owns Linux, and there is no fee to use it. Linux is a popular operating system for Web servers.   114

Local area network (LAN)   A network that connects computers that reside in a single geographic location on the premises of the company that operates the LAN. The number of connected computers can range from two to several hundred.   178

Localizing software   The process by which computer programs are modified to use different human languages and character sets.   224

Logical address   Also called an *IP address*, a series of dotted decimals in a format like 192.168.2.28 that identifies a unique device on a network or internet. With the IPv4 standard, IP addresses have 32 bits. IP addresses are called logical addresses because they can be reassigned from one device to another.   208

Lost-update problem   An issue in multiuser database processing in which two or more users try to make changes to the data but the database cannot make all those changes because it was not designed to process changes from multiple users.   149

MAC (media access control address)   Also called a *physical address*. A permanent address given to each network interface card (NIC) at the factory. This address enables the device to access the network via a Level-2 protocol. By agreement among computer manufacturers, MAC addresses are assigned in such a way that no two NIC devices will ever have the same MAC address.   180, 210

Mac OS   An operating system developed by Apple Computer, Inc., for the Macintosh. The current version is Mac OS X. Macintosh computers are used primarily by graphic artists and workers in the arts community. Mac OS was developed for the PowerPC, but as of 2006 will run on Intel processors as well.   113

Machine code   Code that has been compiled from source code and is ready to be processed by a computer.   118

Main memory   A set of cells in which each cell holds a byte of data or instruction; each cell has an address, and the CPU uses the addresses to identify particular data items.   105

Maintenance   In the context of information systems, (1) to fix the system to do what it was supposed to do in the first place or (2) to adapt the system to a change in requirements.   386

Malware   Viruses, worms, Trojan horses, spyware, and adware.   458

Malware definitions   Patterns that exist in malware code. Antimalware vendors update these definitions continuously and incorporate them into their products in order to better fight against malware.   459

Management information system (MIS)   An information system that helps businesses achieve their goals and objectives.   8

Managerial decision   A decision that concerns the allocation and use of resources.   51

Manufacturing planning applications   An application used to plan the needs for materials and inventories of materials used in the manufacturing process. Does not include the planning of personnel, equipment, or facilities.   247

Manufacturing resource planning (MRP II)   A follow-on to MRP that includes the planning of materials, personnel, and machinery. It supports many linkages across the organization, including linkages with sales and marketing via the development of a master production schedule. It also includes the capability to perform what-if analyses on variances in schedules, raw materials availabilities, personnel, and other resources.   248

Manufacturing scheduling   Scheduling methods used to optimize operations and fulfill customer demand.   248

Many-to-many (N:M) relationship   Relationships involving two entity types in which an instance of one type can relate to many instances of the second type, and an instance of the second type can relate to many instances of the first. For example, the relationship between Student and Class is N:M. One student may enroll in many classes, and one class may have many students. Contrast with *one-to-many relationships*.   153

Margin   [of a business process] The difference between the value of outputs in a business process and the cost of the process.   71

Market-basket analysis   A data-mining technique for determining sales patterns. A market-basket analysis shows the products that customers tend to buy together.   331

Mashup   The combining of output from two or more Web sites into a single user experience.   290

Master production schedule (MPS)   A plan for producing products. To create the MPS, the company analyzes past sales levels and makes estimates of future sales. This process is sometimes called a *push manufacturing process*, because the company pushes the products into sales (and customers) according to the MPS.   248

Materials requirements planning (MRP)   An information system that plans the need for materials and inventories of materials used in the manufacturing process. Unlike MRP II, MRP does not include the planning of personnel, equipment, or facilities requirements.   248

Maximum cardinality   The maximum number of entities that can be involved in a relationship. Common examples of maximum cardinality are 1:N, N:M, and 1:1.   153

Measure   The data item of interest on an OLAP report. It is the item that is to be summed, averaged, or otherwise processed in the OLAP cube. Total sales, average sales, and average cost are examples of measures.   326

Megabyte (MB)   1,024KB.   106

Memory swapping   The movement of programs and data into and out of memory. If a computer has insufficient memory for its workload, such swapping will degrade system performance.   107

Merchant companies   In e-commerce, companies that take title to the goods they sell. They buy goods and resell them.   274

Message digest   A bit string of a specific, fixed length that is produced by hashing and used to produce digital signatures.   456

Metadata   Data that describe data.   140

Microblog   A Web site on which users can publish their opinions, just like a Web blog, but the opinions are restricted to small amounts of text. Twitter is a microblogging tool.   301

Microsoft Office Groove   A collaboration product that includes version management and other useful tools. Users can access and edit documents at a workspace; the software automatically propagates changes made by one user to other users' computers.   43

Microsoft SharePoint   A version-control application that includes many collaboration features and functions, including document check-in/checkout, surveys, discussion forums, and workflow.   44

Minimum cardinality   The minimum number of entities that must be involved in a relationship.   153

Modem   Short for *modulator/demodulator,* a modem converts the computer's digital data into signals that can be transmitted over telephone or cable lines.   184

Moore's Law   A law, created by Gordon Moore, stating that the number of transistors per square inch on an integrated chip doubles every 18 months. Moore's prediction has proved generally accurate in the 40 years since it was made. Sometimes this law is stated that the performance of a computer doubles every 18 months. Although not strictly true, this version gives the gist of the idea.   4

MRP I   Another name for *Materials requirements planning (MRP).*   248

MRP II   Another name for *Manufacturing resource planning.*   248

Multiparty text chat   A synchronous virtual meeting in which participants meet at the same time and communicate by typing comments over a communication network.   38

Multi-user processing   When multiple users process the database at the same time.   148

MySQL   A popular open source DBMS product that is license-free for most applications.   141

N:M Communication   Relationships in which one entity has many connections to another entity, and each connected entity has many other connections.   292

Narrowband   Internet communication lines that have transmission speeds of 56 kbps or less. A dial-up modem provides narrowband access.   186

Network   A collection of computers that communicate with one another over transmission lines.   176

Network Address Translation (NAT)   The process of changing public IP addresses into private network IP addresses, and the reverse.   212

Network interface card (NIC)   A hardware component on each device on a network (computer, printer, etc.) that connects the device's circuitry to the communications line. The NIC works together with programs in each device to implement Layers 1 and 2 of the TCP/IP–OSI hybrid protocol.   180

Network of leased lines   A WAN connection alternative. Communication lines are leased from telecommunications companies and connected into a network. The lines connect geographically distant sites.   186

Neural networks   A popular supervised data-mining technique used to predict values and make classifications, such as "good prospect" or "poor prospect."   330

Nonmerchant companies   E-commerce companies that arrange for the purchase and sale of goods without ever owning or taking title to those goods.   274

Nonvolatile (memory)   Memory that preserves data contents even when not powered (e.g., magnetic and optical disks). With such devices, you can turn the computer off and back on, and the contents will be unchanged.   108

Normal forms   A classification of tables according to their characteristics and the kinds of problems they have.   156

Normalization   The process of converting poorly structured tables into two or more well-structured tables.   154

Object Management Group (OMG)   A software-industry standards organization that created a standard set of terms and graphical notations for documenting business processes.   239

Object-relational database   A type of database that stores both OOP objects and relational data. Rarely used in commercial applications.   140

Off-the-shelf software   Software that can be used without having to make any changes.   115

Off-the-shelf with alterations software   Software bought off-the-shelf but altered to fit the organization's specific needs.   115

OLAP   See *Online analytical processing.*   326

OLAP cube   A presentation of an OLAP measure with associated dimensions. The reason for this term is that some products show these displays using three axes, like a cube in geometry. Same as *OLAP report.*   326

OLAP server   Computer server running software that performs OLAP analyses. An OLAP server reads data from an operational database, performs preliminary calculations, and stores the results of those calculations in an OLAP database.   327

Onboard NIC   A built-in network interface card.   180

One-of-a-kind application   Software that is developed for a specific, unique need, usually for a particular company's operations.   115

One-to-many (1:N) relationship   Relationships involving two entity types in which an instance of one type can relate to many instances of the second type, but an instance of the second type can relate to at most one instance of the first. For example, the relationship between *Department* and *Employee* is 1:N. A department may relate to many employees, but an employee relates to at most one department.   153

Online analytical processing (OLAP)   A dynamic type of reporting system that provides the ability to sum, count, average, and perform other simple arithmetic operations on groups of data. Such reports are dynamic because users can change the format of the reports while viewing them.   326

Open source community   A loosely coupled group of programmers who mostly volunteer their time to contribute code to develop and maintain common software. Linux and MySQL are two prominent products developed by such a community.   114

Operating system (OS)   A computer program that controls the computer's resources: It manages the contents of main memory, processes keystrokes and mouse movements, sends signals to the display monitor, reads and writes disk files, and controls the processing of other programs.   107

Operational decisions   Decisions that concern the day-to-day activities of an organization.   51

Optical fiber cable   A type of cable used to connect the computers, printers, switches, and other devices on a LAN. The signals on such cables are light rays, and they are reflected inside the glass core of the optical fiber cable. The core is surrounded by a *cladding* to contain the light signals, and the cladding, in turn, is wrapped with an outer layer to protect it.   180

Oracle   A popular, enterprise-class DBMS product from Oracle Corporation.   141

Order-entry applications   Applications that record customer purchases.   247

Order management applications   Applications that track orders through the fulfillment process, arrange for and schedule shipping, and process exceptions (such as out-of-stock products).   247

Organizational feasibility   Whether an information system fits within an organization's customer, culture, or legal requirements.   380

Output hardware   Hardware that displays the results of the computer's processing. Consists of video displays, printers, audio speakers, overhead projectors, and other special-purpose devices, such as large, flatbed plotters.   105

Output resources   The goods or services that result from a business's value-creating activities.   71

Outsourcing   The process of hiring another organization to perform a service. Outsourcing is done to save costs, to gain expertise, and to free up management time.   425

Packet   A small piece of an electronic message, which has been divided into chunks, which are sent separately and reassembled at their destination.   207

Packet-filtering firewall   A firewall that examines each packet and determines whether to let the packet pass. To make this decision, it examines the source address, the destination addresses, and other data.   192

Parallel installation   A type of system conversion in which the new system runs in parallel with the old one for a while. Parallel installation is expensive because the organization incurs the costs of running both systems.   385

Parallel workflow   A workflow in which activities occur simultaneously.   45

Patch   A group of fixes for high-priority failures that can be applied to existing copies of a particular product. Software vendors supply patches to fix security and other critical problems.   387

Payload   The program codes of a virus that causes unwanted or hurtful actions, such as deleting programs or data, or even worse, modifying data in ways that are undetected by the user.   458

People   As part of the five-component framework, one of the five fundamental components of an information system; includes those who operate and service the computers, those who maintain the data, those who support the networks, and those who use the system.   8

Perimeter firewall   A firewall that sits outside the organizational network. It is the first device that Internet traffic encounters.   191

Permissions   In a version-control system, authorizations to access shared documents stored in various directories. Typical permissions are read-only, read-and-edit, and read-edit-and-delete; some directories have no permission—they are off-limits.   33

Personal DBMS   DBMS products designed for smaller, simpler database applications. Such products are used for personal or small workgroup applications that involve fewer than 100 users, and normally fewer than 15. Today,

Microsoft Access is the only prominent personal DBMS.   149

Personal identification number (PIN)   A form of authentication whereby the user supplies a number that only he or she knows.   453

Petabyte 10^{15} bytes.   320

Phased installation   A type of system conversion in which the new system is installed in pieces across the organization(s). Once a given piece works, then the organization installs and tests another piece of the system, until the entire system has been installed.   385

Phishing   A technique for obtaining unauthorized data that uses pretexting via email. The *phisher* pretends to be a legitimate company and sends an email requesting confidential data, such as account numbers, Social Security numbers, account passwords, and so forth.   445

Physical address   Also called *MAC address*. A permanent address given to each network interface card (NIC) at the factory. This address enables the device to access the network via a Level-2 protocol. By agreement among computer manufacturers, physical addresses are assigned in such a way that no two NIC devices will ever have the same address.   208

Pilot installation   A type of system conversion in which the organization implements the entire system on a limited portion of the business. The advantage of pilot implementation is that if the system fails, the failure is contained within a limited boundary. This reduces exposure of the business and also protects the new system from developing a negative reputation throughout the organization(s).   385

Plunge installation   A type of system conversion in which the organization shuts off the old system and starts the new system. If the new system fails, the organization is in trouble: Nothing can be done until either the new system is fixed or the old system is reinstalled. Because of the risk, organizations should avoid this conversion style if possible. Sometimes called *direct installation*.   385

Point of presence (POP)   The location at which a line connects to a PSDN network. Think of the POP as the phone number that one dials to connect to the PSDN. Once a site has connected to the PSDN POP, the site obtains access to all other sites connected to the PSDN.   188

Portal server   Program similar to a Web server, but with a customizable user interface.   345

Porter's five competitive forces model   See *Five forces model*.   66

Presence   A term meaning that you'll know who is on the system, who is available to the system, and who cannot currently be reached by the system.   193

Pretexting   A technique for gathering unauthorized information in which someone pretends to be someone else. A common scam involves a telephone caller who pretends to be from a credit card company and claims to be checking the validity of credit card numbers. Phishing is also a form of pretexting.   445

Price conflict   In e-commerce, a conflict that may result when manufacturers offer products at prices lower than those available through existing sales channels.   277

Price elasticity   A measure of the sensitivity in demand to changes in price. It is the ratio of the percentage change in quantity divided by the percentage change in price.   276

Primary activities   In Porter's value chain model, the fundamental activities that create value—inbound logistics, operations, outbound logistics, marketing/sales, and service.   69

Privacy Act of 1974   Federal law that provides protections to individuals regarding records maintained by the U.S. government.   450

Private IP address   A type of IP address used within private networks and internets. Private IP addresses are assigned and managed by the company that operates the private network or internet.   208

Probable loss   The "bottom line" of risk assessment; the likelihood of loss multiplied by the cost of the loss consequences (both tangible and intangible).   452

Problem   A *perceived* difference between what is and what out to be.   50

Problem of the last mile   The difficulty involved in getting the capacity of fast optimal-fiber transmission lines from the street in front of buildings into the homes and smaller businesses located in those buildings. Digging up the street and backyard of every residence and small business to install optical fiber is not affordable; it is hoped that WiMax technology will be able to solve the problem of making the network connections of "the last mile."   201

Procedures   Instructions for humans. One of the five fundamental components of an information system.   8

Process blueprint   In an ERP application, a comprehensive set of inherent processes for all organizational activities, each of which is documented with diagrams that use a set of standardized symbols.   256

Product quality assurance (PQA)   The testing of a system. PQA personnel usually construct a test plan with the advice and assistance of users. PQA test engineers perform testing, and they also supervise user-test activity. Many PQA professionals are programmers who write automated test programs.   384

Program   [that implements a protocol] A specific computer product that implements a protocol; for example, Mozilla Firefox and Microsoft Internet Explorer are two such programs.   205

Protocol   A standardized means for coordinating an activity between two or more entities.   177, 204

Protocol architecture   See *Layered protocols.*   204

Public IP address   An IP address used on the Internet. Such IP addresses are assigned to major institutions in blocks by the Internet Corporation for Assigned Names and Numbers (ICANN). Each IP address is unique across all computers on the Internet.   208

Public key/private key   A special version of asymmetric encryption that is popular on the Internet. With this method, each site has a public key for encoding messages and a private key for decoding them.   191

Public switched data network (PSDN)   A WAN connection alternative. A network of computers and leased lines is developed and maintained by a vendor that leases time on the network to other organizations.   188

Pull (results)   Reports that are produced on request by users.   344

Pull manufacturing process   A manufacturing process that initiates production in response to signals from customers or downstream production processes   248

Push (results)   Reports that are published on a scheduled basis to a list of subscribers.   346

Push manufacturing process   A process in which production is initiated based on analysis of past sales and estimates of future sales.   248

Quad processor   A computer with four CPUs.   105

Query   A request for data from a database.   147

RAM   Stands for *random access memory*, which is main memory consisting of cells that hold data or instructions. Each cell has an address that the CPU uses to read or write data. Memory locations can be read or written in any order, hence the term *random access*. RAM memory is almost always volatile.   105

Real Simple Syndication (RSS)   A standard for subscribing to content sources; similar to an email system for content.   341

Record   Also called a *row*, a group of columns in a database table.   138

Reference Model for Open Systems Interconnection (OSI)   A protocol architecture created by ISO that has seven layers. Portions of the OSI model are incorporated into the TCP/IP–OSI hybrid architecture that is used on the Internet and most internets.   204

Regression analysis   A type of supervised data mining that estimates the values of parameters in a linear equation. Used to determine the relative influence of variables on an outcome and also to predict future values of that outcome.   330

Relation   The more formal name for a database table.   140

Relational database   Database that carries its data in the form of tables and that represents relationships using foreign keys.   140

Relationship   An association among entities or entity instances in an E-R model or an association among rows of a table in a relational database.   152

Relevant (information)   Information that is appropriate to both the context and the subject.   17

Replicated database   A database that is stored and processed in two or more locations. Data is duplicated in all of the replications.   226

Report   A presentation of data in a structured or meaningful context.   146

Report server   A special case of a business intelligence (BI) application server that serves only reports.   346

Reporting application   A business intelligence application that produces information from data by applying reporting tools to that data.   322

Reporting system   A business intelligence system that delivers reports to authorized users at appropriate times.   322

Reporting tools   A type of business intelligence tool, these programs read data from a variety of sources, process that data, format the data into structured reports, and deliver those reports to the users who need them.   321

Requirements creep   The process by which users agree to one set of requirements, then add a bit more, then add a bit more, and so forth.   397

RFM analysis   A way of analyzing and ranking customers according to the recency, frequency, and monetary value of their purchases.   323

Risk   The likelihood of an adverse occurrence.   449

Root server   Special computer that is distributed around the world that maintain a list of IP addresses of servers that resolve each type of top-level domain.   215

Router   A special-purpose computer that moves network traffic from one node on a network to another.   187

Routing table   A table of data used by a router to determine where to send a packet that it receives.   211

Row   Also called *record*, a group of columns in a database table.   138

RSS   See *Real Simple Syndication*.   341

RSS feed   A data source that transmits using an RSS standard. The output of an RSS feed is consumed by an RSS reader.   341

RSS reader   A program by which users can subscribe to magazines, blogs, Web sites, and other content sources; the reader will periodically check the sources, and if there has been a change since the last check, it will place a summary of the change and a link to the new content in an inbox.   341

Safeguard   Any action, device, procedure, technique, or other measure that reduces a system's vulnerability to a threat.   452

SAP   The first and most successful vendor of enterprise resource planning software.   255

Schedule feasibility   Whether an information system will be able to be developed on the timetable needed.   380

Secure Socket Layer (SSL)   A protocol that uses both asymmetric and symmetric encryption. SSL is a protocol layer that works between Levels 4 (transport) and 5 (application) of the TCP–OSI protocol architecture. When SSL is in use, the browser address will begin with https://. The most recent version of SSI is called TLS.   191

Security policy   Management's policy for computer security, consisting of a general statement of the organization's security program, issue-specific policy, and system-specific policy.   449

Security program   A systematic plan by which an organization addresses security issues; consists of three components: senior management involvement, safeguards of various kinds, and incident response.   447

Security threat   A challenge to an information system that arises from one of three sources: human error and mistakes, malicious human activity, and natural events and disasters.   444

Segment   The container that a TCP uses to carry messages. The TCP program places identifying data at the front and end of each segment that are akin to the To and From addresses that you would put on a letter for the postal mail.   206

Semantic security   Concerns the unintended release of protected information through the release of a combination of reports or documents that are independently not protected.   348

Sequential workflow   A workflow in which activities occur in sequence.   45

Server(s)   A computer that provides some type of service, such as hosting a database, running a blog, publishing a Web site, or selling goods. Server computers are faster, larger, and more powerful than client computers.   108

Server farm   A large collection of server computers that coordinates the activities of the servers, usually for commercial purposes.   108

Server hardware   Computers that provide communications, database, application, and other computing services to clients; server hardware is selected, operated, and managed by IT professionals.   33

Server tier   In the three-tier architecture, the tier that consists of computers that run Web servers to generate Web pages and other data in response to requests from browsers. Web servers also process application programs.   277

Service   A repeatable task that a business needs to perform.   259

Service pack   A large group of fixes that solve low-priority software problems. Users apply service packs in much the same way that they apply patches, except that service packs typically involve fixes to hundreds or thousands of problems.   387

Service-oriented architecture (SOA)   Processing philosophy that advocates that computing systems use a *standard method* to declare the services they provide and the interface by which those services can be requested and used. Web services are an implementation of SOA.   259

Set-top box   An external device that receives an IPTV (Internet Protocol television) signal and distributes it to multiple television set or home entertainment centers.   216

Shared View   A Microsoft program that enables one person to share his or her desktop with a small group of others using the Internet. Useful for online meetings.   38

SharePoint site   A workflow site, created in Microsoft's collaboration tool SharePoint, that enables team members to define workflows for their group. The software that runs the site will send emails to team members requesting reviews, create task lists defined for the workflow, check documents in, mark tasks as complete, email the next person in the workflow, and email copies of all correspondence to the workflow leader, who can use this capability to ensure that all teammates perform the work they are requested to do.   47

Simple Mail Transfer Protocol (SMTP)   A Layer-5 architecture used to send email. Normally used in conjunction with other Layer-5 protocols (POP3, IMAP) for receiving email.   205

Site license   A license purchased by an organization to equip all the computers on a site with certain software.   114

Skype   A company, owned by Yahoo!, that provides Voice-over-IP (VoIP) phone service.   216

Smart card   A plastic card similar to a credit card that has a microchip. The microchip, which holds much more data than a magnetic strip, is loaded with identifying data. Normally requires a PIN.   453

Sniffing   A technique for intercepting computer communications. With wired networks, sniffing requires a physical connection to the network. With wireless networks, no such connection is required.   445

Social collaboration   Collaboration activity done for the purpose of enhancing relationships.   292

Social graph (SN)   A network of relationships.   300

Social networking   Connections of people with similar interests. Today, social networks typically are supported by Web 2.0 technology.   292

Social networking application   A computer program that interacts with users and processes information in a social network.   299

Social networking group   An association of social network members related to a particular topic, event, activity, or other collective interest.   295

Software   Instructions for computers. One of the five fundamental components of an information system.   8

Software as a (free) service (SAAS)   (1) Business model whereby companies (such as Google, Amazon.com, and eBay) provide license-free services based on their software, rather than providing software as a product (by means of software-usage licenses). Software as a service is an example of Web 2.0. (2) Business model whereby companies (Microsoft, Oracle) provide paid-for services based on their software. Users need not install software on their computer, but rather pay a fee to use software installed on the seller's servers, somewhere in the cloud.   288

Source code   Computer code as written by humans and that is understandable by humans. Source code must be translated into machine code before it can be processed.   118

Special function cards   Cards that can be added to the computer to augment the computer's basic capabilities.   105

Spoofing   When someone pretends to be someone else with the intent of obtaining unauthorized data. If you pretend to be your professor, you are spoofing your professor.   445

Spyware   Programs installed on the user's computer without the user's knowledge or permission that reside in the background and, unknown to the user, observe the user's actions and keystrokes, modify computer activity, and report the user's activities to sponsoring organizations. Malicious spyware captures keystrokes to obtain user names, passwords, account numbers, and other sensitive information. Other spyware is used for marketing analyses, observing what users do, Web sites visited, products examined and purchased, and so forth.   458

SQL Server   A popular enterprise-class DBMS product from Microsoft.   141

Steering committee   A group of senior managers from a company's major business functions that works with the CIO to set the IS priorities and decide among major IS projects and alternatives.   415

Storage hardware   Hardware that saves data and programs. Magnetic disk is by far the most common storage device, although optical disks, such as CDs and DVDs, also are popular.   105

Strategic decision   Decision that concerns broader-scope, organizational issues.   51

Strong password   A password with the following characteristics: seven or more characters; does not contain the user's user name, real name, or company name; does not contain a complete dictionary word, in any language; is different from the user's previous passwords; and contains both upper- and lowercase letters, numbers, and special characters.   22

Structured decision   A type of decision for which there is a formalized and accepted method for making the decision.   51

Structured Query Language (SQL)   An international standard language for processing database data.   144

Sufficient (information)   A characteristic of good information in which information is rich enough to enable the user to accomplish his or her job, but just barely so.   17

Supervised data mining   A form of data mining in which data miners develop a model prior to the analysis and apply statistical techniques to data to estimate values of the parameters of the model.   330

Supply chain   A network of organizations and facilities that transforms raw materials into products delivered to customers.   284

Supply chain profitability   The difference between the sum of the revenue generated by the supply chain and the sum of the costs that all organizations in the supply chain incur to obtain that revenue.   286

Support   In market-basket terminology, the probability that two items will be purchased together.   331

Support activities   In Porter's value chain model, the activities that contribute indirectly to value creation—procurement, technology, human resources, and the firm's infrastructure.   69

Swim-lane layout   A process diagram layout similar to swim lanes in a swimming pool; each role in the process is shown in its own horizontal rectangle, or lane.   240

Switch   A special-purpose computer that receives and transmits data across a network.   177, 207

Switch table   A table of data used by a switch to determine where to send frames that it receives.   211

Switching costs   Business strategy of locking in customers by making it difficult or expensive to change to another product or supplier.   78

Symmetric encryption   An encryption method whereby the same key is used to encode and to decode the message.   191

Symmetrical digital subscriber lines (SDSL)   DSL lines that have the same upload and download speeds.   185

Synchronous communication   Information exchange that occurs when all members of a work team meet at the same time, such as face-to-face meetings or conference calls.   38

System   A group of components that interact to achieve some purpose.   8

System conversion   The process of converting business activity from the old system to the new.   385

Systems analysis and design   The process of creating and maintaining information systems. It is sometimes called *systems development*.   372

Systems analysts   IS professionals who understand both business and technology. They are active throughout the systems development process and play a key role in moving the project from conception to conversion and, ultimately, maintenance. Systems analysts integrate the work of the programmers, testers, and users.   380

Systems development   The process of creating and maintaining information systems. It is sometimes called *systems analysis and design*.   372

Systems development life cycle (SDLC)   The classical process used to develop information systems. These basic tasks of systems development are combined into the following phases: system definition, requirements analysis, component design, implementation, and system maintenance (fix or enhance).   376

Systems thinking   The mental process of making one or more models of the components of a system and connecting the inputs and outputs among those components into a sensible whole, one that explains the phenomenon observed.   7

Table   Also called a *file*, a group of similar rows or records in a database.   138

Tag   In markup languages such as HTML and XML, notation used to define a data element for display or other purposes.   279

TCP/IP–OSI (protocol) architecture   A protocol architecture having five layers that evolved as a hybrid of the TCP/IP and the OSI architecture. This architecture is used on the Internet and on most internets.   204

Team survey   A form of asynchronous communication in which one team member creates a list of questions and other team members respond. Microsoft SharePoint has built-in survey capability.   39

Technical feasibility   Whether existing information technology will be able to meet the needs of a new information system.   380

Technical safeguard   Safeguard that involves the hardware and software components of an information system.   453

Terabyte (TB)   1,024GB.   106

Test plan   Groups of sequences of actions that users will take when using the new system.   384

The Internet   The internet that is publicly used throughout the world.   177

Thick client   A software application that requires programs other than just the browser on a user's computer—that is, that requires code on both client and server computers.   116

Thin client   A software application that requires nothing more than a browser and can be run on only the user's computer.   116

Three-tier architecture   Architecture used by most e-commerce server applications. The tiers refer to three different classes of computers. The user tier consists of users' computers that have browsers that request and process Web pages. The server tier consists of computers that run Web servers and in the process generate Web pages and other data in response to requests from browsers. Web servers also process application programs. The third tier is the database tier, which runs the DBMS that processes the database.   277

Timely (information)   Information that is produced in time for its intended use.   16

Top-level domain (TLD)   The last letters in any domain name. For example, in the domain name *www.icann.org* the top-level domain is *.org*. Similarly, in the domain name *www.ibm.com*, *.com* is the top-level domain. For non–U.S. domain names, the top-level domain is often a two-letter abbreviation for the country in which the service resides.   214

Trade-off   In project management, a choice among scarce resources such as scope, time, cost, quality, risk, people, and other resources. Managers may need to trade off a delay in the project due date to reduce expense and keep critical employees.   390

Transaction processing system (TPS)   An information system that supports operational decision making.   51

Transmission Control Program (TCP)   TCP operates at Layer 4 of the TCP/IP–OSI architecture. TCP is used in two ways: as the name of a Layer-4 *protocol* and as part of the name of the TCP/IP–OSI protocol architecture. The architecture gets its name because it usually includes the TCP protocol. TCP receives messages from Layer-5 protocols (like HTTP) and breaks those messages up into segments that it sends to a Layer-3 protocol (like IP).   206

Transmission Control Program/Internet Protocol (TCP/IP) architecture   A protocol architecture having four layers; forms the basis for the TCP/IP–OSI architecture blend used by the Internet.   204

Transport Layer Security (TLS)   A protocol, using both asymmetric and symmetric encryption, that works between Levels 4 (transport) and 5 (application) of the TCP–OSI protocol architecture. TLS is the new name for a later version of SSL.   191, 456

Trojan horse   Virus that masquerades as a useful program or file. A typical Trojan horse appears to be a computer game, an MP3 music file, or some other useful, innocuous program.   459

Tunnel   A virtual, private pathway over a public or shared network from the VPN client to the VPN server.   189

Twitter   A Web 2.0 application that allows users to publish 140 character descriptions of anything.   301

Uncertainty   Those things we don't know.   449

Unified Modeling Language (UML)   A series of diagramming techniques that facilitates OOP development. UML has dozens of different diagrams for all phases of system development. UML does not require or promote any particular development process.   151

Uniform resource locator (URL)   A document's address on the Web. URLs begin on the right with a top-level domain, and, moving left, include a domain name and then are followed by optional data that locates a document within that domain.   215

Unix   An operating system developed at Bell Labs in the 1970s. It has been the workhorse of the scientific and engineering communities since then.   114

Unshielded twisted pair (UTP) cable   A type of cable used to connect the computers, printers, switches, and other devices on a LAN. A UTP cable has four pairs of twisted wire. A device called an RJ-45 connector is used to connect the UTP cable into NIC devices.   182

Unstructured decision   A type of decision for which there is no agreed-on decision-making method.   52

Unsupervised data mining   A form of data mining whereby the analysts do not create a model or hypothesis before running the analysis. Instead, they apply the data-mining technique to the data and observe the results. With this method, analysts create hypotheses after the analysis to explain the patterns found.   329

User tier   In the three-tier architecture, the tier that consists of computers that have browsers that request and process Web pages.   277

Usurpation   Occurs when unauthorized programs invade a computer system and replace legitimate programs. Such unauthorized programs typically shut down the legitimate system and substitute their own processing.   446

Value   According to Porter, the amount of money that a customer is willing to pay for a resource, product, or service.   69

Value chain   A network of value-creating activities.   69

Version control   Use of software to control access to and configuration of documents, designs, and other electronic versions of products.   44

Version management   Tracking of changes to documents by means of features and functions that accommodate concurrent work. The means by which version management is done depend on the particular version-management system used; three such systems are wikis, Google Docs & Spreadsheets, and Microsoft Groove.   41

Vertical-market application   Software that serves the needs of a specific industry. Examples of such programs are those used by dental offices to schedule appointments and bill patients, those used by auto mechanics to keep track of customer data and customers' automobile repairs, and those used by parts warehouses to track inventory, purchases, and sales.   115

Videoconferencing   Technology that combines a conference call with video cameras.   38

Viral hook   An inducement that causes someone to share an ad, link, file, picture, movie, or other resource with friends and associates over the Internet.   295

Viral marketing   A marketing method used in the Web 2.0 world in which *users* spread news about products and services to one another.   290

Virtual meeting   A meeting in which participants do not meet in the same place and possibly not at the same time.   38

Virtual private network (VPN)   A WAN connection alternative that uses the Internet or a private internet to create the appearance of private point-to-point connections. In the IT world, the term *virtual* means something that appears to exist that does not exist in fact. Here, a VPN uses the public Internet to create the appearance of a private connection.   189

Virtualization   The process by which multiple operating systems share the same computer hardware, usually a server.   432

Virus   A computer program that replicates itself.   54, 458

Voice over IP (VoIP)   A technology that provides telephone communication over the Internet.   43, 216

Volatile (memory)   Data that will be lost when the computer or device is not powered.   108

Vulnerability   An opening or a weakness in a security system. Some vulnerabilities exist because there are no safeguards or because the existing safeguards are ineffective.   452

WAN Wireless   A communications system that provides wireless connectivity to a wide area network.   186

Waterfall   The fiction that one phase of the SDLC can be completed in its entirety and the project can progress, without any backtracking, to the next phase of the SDLC. Projects seldom are that simple; backtracking is normally required.   387

Web 2.0   A loose grouping of capabilities, technologies, business models, and philosophies that characterize new and emerging business uses of the Internet.   288

WebEx   A popular commercial webinar application used in virtual sales presentations.   38

Web farm   A facility that runs multiple Web servers. Work is distributed among the computers in a Web farm so as to maximize throughput.   288

Webinar   A virtual meeting in which attendees view each other on their computer screens.   38

Web page   Document encoded in HTML that is created, transmitted, and consumed using the World Wide Web.   278

Web server   A program that processes the HTTP protocol and transmits Web pages on demand. Web servers also process application programs.   278

Web storefront   In e-commerce, a Web-based application that enables customers to enter and manage their orders.   274

Wide area network (WAN)   A network that connects computers located at different geographic locations.   177

Wi-Fi Protected Access (WPA and WPA2)   An improved wireless security standard developed by the IEEE 802.11 committee to fix the flaws of the Wired Equivalent Privacy (WEP) standard. Only newer wireless hardware uses this technique.   455

Wiki   A knowledge base maintained by its users; processed on Web sites that allow users to add, remove, and edit content.   41

WiMax   An emerging technology based on the IEEE 802.16 standard. WiMax is designed to deliver the "last mile" of wireless broadband access and could ultimately replace cable and DSL for fixed applications and replace cell phones for nomadic and portable applications. See also *IEEE 802.16.* 186

Windows An operating system designed and sold by Microsoft. It is the most widely used operating system. 113

Wired Equivalent Privacy (WEP) A wireless security standard developed by the IEEE 802.11 committee that was insufficiently tested before it was deployed in communications equipment. It has serious flaws. 455

Wireless NIC (WNIC) Devices that enable wireless networks by communicating with wireless access points. Such devices can be cards that slide into the PCMA slot or they can be built-in, onboard devices. WNICs operate according to the 802.11 protocol. 182

Work-breakdown structure (WBS) A hierarchy of the tasks required to complete a project. 391

Workflow A process or procedure by which content is created, edited, used, and disposed. 33

Workflow control Use of software and information systems to monitor the execution of a work team's processes; ensures that actions are taken at appropriate times and prohibits the skipping of steps or tasks. 33

Workspace In Microsoft Goove, an electronic "space" consisting of tools and documents that enable users to collaborate. 43

World Wide Web Consortium (W3C) A body that sponsors the development and dissemination of Web standards. 282

Worm A virus that propagates itself using the Internet or some other computer network. Worm code is written specifically to infect another computer as quickly as possible. 459

Worth-its-cost (information) Information for which there is an appropriate relationship between the cost of the information and its value. 17

WPA2 See Wi-Fi Protected Access. 455

XML schema An XML document that specifies the structure of other XML documents. An XML schema is metadata for other XML documents. For example, a SalesOrder XML schema specifies the structure of SalesOrder documents. 283

Index

Page numbers in **bold** represent definitions; those in *italic* represent figures.

Business intelligence (BI)
    application, **322**
  vs. BI systems and tools, 322
  data mining applications, 327–333,
    336, *329, 331, 333, 336, 338*
    decision trees, 332–333, 336,
     333, 336
    ethics of, 334–335
    market-basket analysis,
     330–332, *331*
    real-world issues, 350–351
    supervised data mining, 330
    unsupervised data mining,
     329–330
  knowledge management
    applications, 340–344, *342, 344*
    expert systems, 342–344, *344*
    sharing document content, 340–342
  reporting applications, 322–325,
    324, 325
    online analytical processing
     (OLAP), 326–327, *326, 327,*
     328, 329
    RFM analysis, 323, 325, *325*
Business intelligence (BI) application
  server, **344**, 344–346, *345*
Business intelligence (BI) system, **321,**
  322, 321–322
  2020 outlook, 346–347
  vs. BI applications and tools, 322
  semantic security, 348–349
Business intelligence (BI) tool, **321,**
  321–322
  vs. BI applications and systems, 322
Business process design, 70
Business process management (BPM),
  74, 236
  challenges of international business
    process management, 359–360
  cross-functional processes, 237–238
  functional processes, 237
  importance of, 234–238, *235, 236, 237*
  interorganizational processes, 238
Business Process Modeling Notation
  (BPMN), **239**
  documenting as-is processes,
    239–242, *239, 240, 241*
  symbols, *240*
Business processes, **71,** *71, 74*
  2020 outlook, 259–261
  blueprints, 264–265
  changing, 242–243, *242, 243*
  competitive advantage via, 77–78
  documenting, 239–242, *239, 240, 241*
  effect of competitive strategy on,
    75–76, *75, 76*
  effect of global economy on, 94
  examples of, *71*
  functional applications, **245,**
    245–249, 252, *246*
    accounting, 249, 252
    customer service, 249

    human resources, 249
    manufacturing, 247–248, *247, 248*
    operations, 246–247
    sales and marketing, 246
  role of information systems, 244–245
  service-oriented architecture (SOA),
    259, 259–261, *260*
  solving business problems, 238–243
    changing processes, 242–243,
     242, 243
    notation standards, 238–239
    process documentation, 239–242,
     239, 240, 241
  value generation, 71, 74–75
Business System Modernization (BSM)
  project (Internal Revenue
  Service), 27–29, 489–491
Business-to-business (B2B)
  e-commerce, *274, 275,* 289
Business-to-consumer (B2C)
  e-commerce, *274, 275*
Business-to-government (B2G)
  e-commerce, 275, *275*
Buy-in, 378–379
Byte, **137**
Bytes, **106**

C

CA (certificate authority), 457–458, **457**
Cable
  optical fiber cables, **180,** *181*
  unshielded twisted pair (UTP) cable,
    180, *180*
Cable modem, **185,** 185–186
Cache, **107, 216**
CADE (Customer Account Data
  Engine), 489–491
Careers
  attaining job security, 5–6
  IS department positions, 412, *413*
  learning nonroutine skills, 6–8, *6*
Case studies
  Aviation Safety Network (ASN)
    (global communication),
    227–229, *227, 228, 229*
  Bosu balance trainer (competitive
    advantage), 90–91, *91*
  business intelligence (Home Depot),
    356–357
  business process management, 271
  causes of IS failure, 406–407
  database benchmarking, 172–173
  Dell Computer, 133–134
  Getty Images, 96–98, *97, 98*
  Internal Revenue Service (IRS)
    Customer Account Data Engine
     (CADE), 489–491
    Business System Modernization
     (BSM) project, 27–29
  international business, SAP
    implementation by Brose
    Group, 366–368, *366, 367*

  interorganizational information
    systems, 316–317
  Managing IS (Marriott International,
    Inc.), 440–441
  Microsoft SharePoint at Intermountain
    Healthcare, 61–63, *62, 63*
  security, ChoicePoint, 481
  SOHO (small office, home office)
    network, 218–221, *218, 219,*
    220, 221
  wireless technology, 201
  YouTube, 97–98
Cash management, **252**
Central processing unit (CPU), **104,**
  104–105
  instruction set, **112**
  speed, 108
Certificate authority (CA), 457–458, **457**
Channel conflict, **277**
The CHAOS Report, 406
Chief information officer (CIO), **410**
Chief technology officer (CTO), **411**
ChoicePoint, 481
Chopra, Sunil, 285
"Churn and burn," 110–111
CIO (chief information officer), **410**
Clearinghouses, **275**
Clickstream data, **338**
Client hardware, **33**
Clients, **108**
  client/server computing, 112
    hardware, 108–109, *109*
    software, 116, *117*
Client-server applications, **116**
Closed source, **118**
Cloud, **112**
Cloud computing, **432,** 432–433
Cluster analysis, **329**
Code (computers), 118–119
Cold site, **468**
Collaboration, 6–7, **32,** 32–33
  2020 outlook, 53
  characteristics of effective
    collaborators, *37*
  security, 54–55
Collaboration information systems
  business uses for, 50–53
    decision making, 51–53, *51, 52, 53*
    problem solving, 50–51
    project management, 50, *50*
  components of, 33–37, *34, 35*
  controlling workflow, 45–47, *45, 46, 47*
  driving factors of, 32–33
  improving team communication
    with, 37–40, *38, 39, 40*
  managing content, 40–45, *41, 42, 43,*
    44, 45
  Microsoft SharePoint, **44,** 44–45, *45*
  security, 54–55
Columns, **137**
  foreign keys, **140**
  keys, **139**